NOTES ON THE GREEK TEXT OF NUMBERS

SOCIETY OF BIBLICAL LITERATURE
SEPTUAGINT AND COGNATE STUDIES SERIES

Series Editor
Bernard A. Taylor

Editorial Advisory Committee

N. Fernández Marcos, Madrid
I. Soisalon - Soininen, Helsinki
E. Tov, Jerusalem

Number 46

NOTES ON THE GREEK TEXT OF NUMBERS

by
John William Wevers

NOTES ON THE GREEK TEXT OF NUMBERS

by

John William Wevers

Scholars Press
Atlanta, Georgia

NOTES ON THE GREEK TEXT OF NUMBERS

by
John William Wevers

Copyright © 1998 by the Society of Biblical Literature

All rights reserved. No part of this work may be reproduced or transmitted in any form or by any means, electronic or mechanical, including photocopying and recording, or by means of any information storage or retrieval system, except as may be expressly permitted by the 1976 Copyright Act or in writing from the publisher. Requests for permission should be addressed in writing to the Rights and Permissions Office, Scholars Press, P.O. Box 15399, Atlanta, GA 30333-0399, USA.

Library of Congress Cataloging-in-Publication Data
Wevers, John William.
    Notes on the Greek text of Numbers / by John William Wevers.
      p. cm. — (Septuagint and cognate studies series ; no. 46)
    Includes bibliographical references and index.
    ISBN 0-7885-0504-1 (cloth : alk. paper)
    1. Bible. O.T. Numbers—Versions—Septuagint. I. Title.
II. Series.
BS1264.G7S478   1998
222'.140486—dc21   98-30968
                             CIP

ISBN 1-58983-158-6 (pbk. : alk. paper)

Printed in the United States of America
on acid-free paper

Table of Contents

Introductory Statement ix
Sigla xxx
Notes 1
Appendix A: Proposed Changes in Num 608
Index of Greek Words and Phrases 610
Index of Hebrew Words and Phrases 629
Index of Grammatical and Textual Items 642
General Index 646

This book is dedicated to Ilmari Soisalon-Soininen, whose work I have long respected, and whose friendship I have cherished for many years.

INTRODUCTORY STATEMENT

I. Character of the Num translation

The Greek translation of Numbers (herein designated as Num) is without a doubt by far the weakest volume in the Greek Pentateuch. What makes work on the book so frustrating is that side by side one can find gross failures to follow ordinary rules of grammar, i.e. of apparent incompetence, as well as acute and even subtle distinctions betraying an active mind engaged in the interpretation of sacred scripture, ready not only to clarify obscure passages, but even to correct what might appear to be factual errors or contradictions within the text.

The only thoroughgoing analysis of the book as a translation of the Hebrew text that I know of is that of Zacharias Frankel published almost a century and a half ago.[1] He believes that this inconsistency is not actually due to ignorance, "sondern es bildet das Zusammenfliessen mehrer Uebersetzungen den eigentlichen Schwerpunkt: die Version des Numeri ging nicht aus einer Hand hervor, sondern es wurden mehre einzelne übersetzte Stellen zusammengetragen, die zu einem Ganzen verbunden, die uns vorliegende Uebersetzung dieses Buches bilden."[2]

This is certainly a possible interpretation. A modern reader is easily disturbed by evidence of such inconsistency of approach. On the other hand, fluctuation between an isolate and a contextual approach may be found in all the books of the Pentateuch, and it is particularly characteristic of many of the later books of the Alexandrian canon. I am quite certain that Frankel's suggestion of Num as a chance amalgam without plan or purpose is an understandable reaction, but that it is wrong, as the following remarks will make clear.

1.0. Admittedly, at times my stated presupposition "that the product of the Alexandrian translators of the Torah was throughout sensible,"[3] is hard put to

---

1. Ueber den Einfluss der palästinischen Exegese auf die alexandrinische Hermeneutik, Leipzig, 1851. The paragraphs dealing with Numbers are Para.30—34 (pp.167—200). He characterizes Num by "es waltet ein blindes Ungefähr, ein sich Ergehenlassen ohne Plan und Ziel; zwar wird ein höheres Moment mitunter erfasst, jedoch bald wieder verlassen. Diese Version gehört zu den verfehltesten der heil. Schrift" (167—168).
2. Idem, p.168.
3. See Note at Gen xiii; see also Note at Exod xv (2.3) and *idem* Deut xii—xiii (2.3) as well.

the test for Num; in a few cases, I have been forced to admit that I was uncertain as to what Num was trying to say.

Thus the translator was careless at 9:10. MT reads "Any individual who might be unclean due to corpse defilement or is on a distant journey או לכם לדרתיכם, may celebrate the Passover." By its ὑμῖν ἢ ἐν ταῖς γενεαῖς ὑμῶν Num has introduced a potential confusion in the context of ἢ ἐν ὁδῷ μακρὰν ὑμῖν ἢ ἐν ταῖς γενεαῖς ὑμῶν. The phrase "in your generations" is hardly coordinate with "or in a road distant for you."

1.2. At 9:22—23 the careless translator omitted two pieces of text due to homoioteleuton. V.22 ends with "when it (i.e. the cloud) would rise they would break camp." Immediately before this it reads "they would not break camp," promoting the omission of בהעלתו יסעו. V.23 then continued with "At the word (פי) of Yahweh they would encamp and at the word (פי) of Yahweh they would break camp." Num only has ὅτι διὰ προστάγματος κυρίου ἀπαροῦσιν. In other words, his eye went from the first פי to the second one, resulting in a somewhat peculiar truncated text.

1.3. At 15:28 reference is made to the priest making atonement for a person who sins without intention before Yahweh (לכפר עליו). This is followed by ונסלח לו, but the granting of pardon is omitted by Num, though hardly intentionally; rather the translator's eye skipped from one prepositional phrase to the next one. Similarly, at 13:34(33) homoioteleuton was the basis for a shorter text. The spies report: "there we saw the Nephilim, Anaqites from the Nephilim." Num simply has "and there we say τοὺς γίγαντας." The shorter text is, however, fully clear.

1.4. The abbreviation of the tabernacle duties of the Gedsonites at 4:26 is partly due to homoioteleuton. Inter alia, they must transport "the hangings of the court (חצר);" this is followed in MT by "and the hangings of the door of the gate of the חצר," which is omitted by Num, presumably because of homoioteleuton. This is defined by "which are on the tent (+ τοῦ μαρτυρίου) ועל המזבח." The second prepositional phrase is also omitted, but the reason for this omission is unclear. The next item was מיתריהם "their tentpins," which was misinterpreted as a noun from the root יתר, thus τὰ περισσά "the extras"; at 3:26 the word was similarly misunderstood as τὰ κατάλοιπα "the things left over," though at v.37 it was correctly rendered by τοὺς κάλους (αὐτῶν)!

2.0. More disturbing are grammatical infelicities, of which the following are merely illustrative.

2.1. Odd, but not necessarily incorrect is 4:42 ἐπεσκέψησαν δὲ καὶ δῆμος υἱῶν Μεραρί. The plural verb has been used to show that δῆμος is collective; a clan does consist of more than one person. Furthermore, the verbal pattern had been used at v.38, and this may have influenced the translator. Incidentally, in v.43, λειτουργεῖν is uniquely modified by a πρός phrase, for which I could not find any parallel.

2.2. Not exactly infelicitous is 6:13, where for יביא אתו "one must bring him," Num reads προσοίσει αὐτός. But "he shall bring (παρά τὰς θύρας)" used absolutely is hardly luminous. The word אתו should have been rendered by an accusative such as αὐτόν, but Num has αὐτός as subject with the transitive verb προσοίσει used absolutely. Hex did change the pronoun to the accusative, and The Others also read this.

2.3. Especially disconcerting are cases where no grammatically fitting antecedent can be found in the context. Thus at 11:10 for the clause "before Moses ἦν πονηρόν," no neuter singular word obtains in the neighbourhood. What was "evil"? V.a reads "and Moses heard them weeping according to their clans, each one at his door." Presumably, what the translator meant was the general reaction of weeping on the part of the people at the appearance of manna.

At 18:15 no actual antecedent obtains for the relative pronoun in πᾶν διανοῖγον μήτραν ἀπὸ πάσης σαρκός, ἃ προσφέρουσιν κυρίῳ (from people to cattle shall be to you). The pronoun obviously refers to πᾶν διανοῖγον, but that is singular. In fact, in the next verse it is correctly referred to in (ἡ λύτρωσις) αὐτοῦ. Similarly, at 23:13 the plural genitive relative pronoun has no antecedent. It reads: "Come with me to yet another place ἐξ ὧν you won't see him (i.e. Israel) from there ...." Once again one has to manufacture some kind of antecedent such as "vantage points, angles," to make sense of Num. And at v.28, an articulated neuter participle is left hanging without a proper context. The reference is found in (ἐπὶ) κορυφὴν τοῦ Φογώρ, τὸ παρατεῖνον εἰς τὴν ἔρημον. Once again one must mentally supply some such word as ὄρος as an apposite for "the crest (which is feminine) of Phogor" in order to make sense out of the Greek.

At 28:6 only carelessness can explain modification of ὁλοκαύτωμα (nominative) by ἡ γενομένη in the nominal structure "the regular holocaust which was created in Mt. Sina (is) for a sweetsmelling savour to the Lord." The only conceivable reason that occurs to me for the feminine gender is that MT's העשיה is feminine, which is of course irrelevant for Greek.

At 22:5 Balak sent elders to Balaam ... Φαθούρα. Presumably, the translator understood this as the name of a city, which would normally be feminine. But it is described as ὅ ἐστιν at the river ..., i.e. a neuter relative pronoun is used to refer to a feminine noun.

At 31:30 an apparent mixup of gender obtains. It concerns the Lord's portion from the Israelites' half of the booty taken from the defeated Midianites, which is to be given to the Levites. From this half (τοῦ ἡμίσους) "you must take ἕνα ἀπὸ τῶν πεντάκοντα," i.e. from people and animals, καὶ δώσεις αὐτά to the Levites. The word ἕνα is masculine singular accusative, but the total is referred to by αὐτά, which is neuter plural accusative. Presumably, the latter refers to τῶν κτηνῶν, and ἕνα, to ἀνθρώπων, i.e. to the first and last items of the booty listed, but it is straining credibility to find such possible antecedents.

2.4. At 15:35 MT uses a contextual free infinitive: רגום him with stones all the assembly. Obviously what is meant is "let all the assembly stone him." Num, however, interpreted the infinitive as an isolate one, i.e. as an imperative, λιθοβολήσατε, which then means that πᾶσα ἡ συναγωγή constitutes the addressee; in other words, it is a vocative! Earlier in the chapter, at v.6, Num attempted to integrate part of v.5 with it by adding ὅταν ποιῆτε αὐτὸν εἰς ὁλοκαύτωμα ἢ εἰς θυσίαν before ποιήσεις θυσίαν σεμιδάλεως .... Not only is the change in number confusing, but the εἰς θυσίαν refers to an animal sacrifice, whereas the second θυσίαν is a meal offering. The result is real confusion.

At v.14 MT ends with "As you do, כן יעשה." Then v.15 continues with הקהל one regulation shall serve for you and the resident alien. Num misunderstood this and added הקהל to v.14 with its οὕτως ποιήσει ἡ συναγωγη κυρίῳ, and v.15 continues with "one regulation shall serve ...." Having failed to understand the syntax of הקהל, the translator added κυρίῳ in order to retain some kind of sense.

At 18:27 the translator must have been inattentive. MT reads "your תרומה (τὰ ἀφαιρέματα ὑμῶν) will be reckoned to you as grain from the threshing floor, and as מלאה from the wine press." But the translator renders מלאה by ἀφαίρεμα, which word occurred not only earlier in the verse, but also in the singular at v.26. He obviously was misled by the context; the rendering is simply a mistake.

Another case of carelessness on the part of the translator obtains at 36:8. MT states that כל בת shall become a wife (תהיה לאשה). The context deals with the five daughters of Zelophehad. But Num has πᾶσα θυγάτηρ ... ἔσονται γυναῖκες, which is obviously impossible! The only way to make sense out of this text is to understand the "every daughter" together with its modifiers as a pendant nominative construction, i.e. "as for every daughter ..., they shall become wives ...," which is awkward, and certainly not what Num had in mind.

2.5. Particularly difficult are anacoloutha in Num. Thus at 26:64 in summarizing the second census on the plains of Moab, MT states that among them there was no one present among those reviewed by Moses and Aaron ... whom they had reviewed of the Israelites in the desert of Sinai (i.e. in the first census). The relative clause reads οὓς ἐπεσκέψαντο τοὺς υἱοὺς Ἰσραὴλ ἐν τῇ ἐρήμῳ Σινά, which is almost impossible to integrate into the syntax of the clause, and one may have to regard it as an anacolouthon.

Two clear cases of anacoloutha occur in ch.35. At v.11 Num reads φυγαδευτήρια ἔσται ὑμῖν φυγεῖν ἐκεῖ τὸν φονευτήν, πᾶς ὁ πατάξας ψυχὴν ἀκουσίως. The sudden change to the nominative interrupts the grammatical structure, probably best rendered by a dash, or possibly by "(I mean) everyone who smites a person without intent." In MT this is simply an apposite.

In v.13 this is even more striking. It reads καὶ αἱ πόλεις ἃς δώσετε, τὰς ἓξ πόλεις shall be cities of refuge for you. The accusative phrase "the six cities" simply does not fit; one expects a nominative, and the accusative is presumably by attraction to ἅς. Again, one can render this by "the cities which you must designate — I refer to the six cities — shall be ...."

2.6. A few more instances of Num show inadequacies or incompetence as a translator. The unfortunate use of σκηνή to translate both משכן and אהל means that problems arise when MT uses them coordinately. At 3:25 the Gershonites are assigned guardianship, משמרת, in the tent of meeting, viz. המשכן והאהל. Num telescopes the two quite wrongly into η σκηνή. This is more serious at 4:25 in which the Gershonites are assigned the duty of transporting inter alia the curtains of המשכן as well as ואת אהל מועד. This becomes τὰς δέρρεις τῆς σκηνῆς καὶ τὴν σκηνὴν τοῦ μαρτυρίου, which is hardly adequate.

In ch.6 the two terms נדר "a vow" and נזר "Naziriteship" occur in similar contexts. The former becomes εὐχή, whereas the latter could be rendered variously by ἁγίασμα, ἅγιος or the root ἁγν-. Unfortunately, Num often fails to distinguish the two, and uses εὐχή for both words.

An odd interpretation occurs at 10:31, where Hobab is being urged to stay with the Israelite camp, because "you know our encampment in the desert" (i.e.

you can advise us of good places to camp), והיית לנו לעינים "and that you might become eyes for us." But Num understands this rather oddly in its rendering of לעינים by (ἐν ἡμῖν) πρεσβύτης. At 16:5 MT reads בקר וידע יהוה "In the morning even Yahweh will make known." Num did not understand this as his ἐπέσκεπται καὶ ἔγνω ὁ θεός makes clear. בקר is taken as a verb, which resulted in quite a different text in Num.

Occasionally, Num may make a technically correct rendering which is rhetorically unfortunate. AT 18:28 MT states "you must give from it את תרומת יהוה לאהרן הכהן," i.e. "Yahweh's portion to Aaron the priest." Num makes this ἀφαίρεμα κυρίῳ Ἀαρὼν τῷ ἱερεῖ, i.e. a dative of possession followed by a dative indicating an indirect object, which is confusing; it would have been better to have read κυριου as ms 72 did. At 23:14 MT has "And he (Balak) built seven altars ויעל a bull and a ram on the altar." Obviously what ויעל intends is "and he offered up," but here he renders it by καὶ ἀναβίβασεν. Of course, העלה can mean "he made to go up," but that is carrying "isolate" translation much too far.

At 31:8 Num begins with a good rendering: "And the kings of Madian they killed together with their wounded ... five kings of Madian, and Balaam ... they killed with a sword σὺν τοῖς τραυματίαις αὐτῶν." The final phrase has no basis in MT, and is a doublet to ἅμα τοῖς τραυματίαις αὐτῶν of v.8. This can not refer to Balaam as the αὐτῶν makes clear; it must refer to the five kings. At first glance, one might consider the phrase a copyist's rather than a translator's error, but it should be noted that what Num says is that they killed *with a sword* Balaam together with the wounded belonging to the Madianite kings. It is, if original text, an unfortunate addition.

At 33:8 the locative במדבר אתם "in the desert of Etham" was completely misunderstood by the translator, who took אתם as a defectively written אותם, i.e. equivalent to αὐτούς, but διὰ τῆς ἐρήμου αυτους would be gibberish. In order to preserve what he thought to be a pronoun, he used αὐτοί, an unnecessary reference to οἱ υἱοὶ Ἰσραήλ of v.5.

And finally, at 35:20 the translator changed the conjunction או to καί. But this is an ill-conceived change. Num has made of the alternative, "either he should shove him or have hurled (some object) on him in ambush (and he dies)," a double condition. What Num says is "(but if on account of enmity) he should shove him and should hurl on him πᾶν σκεῦος from ambush, and he dies." But this is really not well-thought out; it would be quite a feat both to shove the victim as well as to hit him with some object from ambush.

3.0. That Frankel's judgment on the Greek Numbers as cited in the opening paragraphs of this statement is fundamentally wrong is in my judgment clear, as will become obvious from the remainder of this study. Though sections one and two have demonstrated that the translator was guilty of grammatical infelicities, and of thoughtless errors of translation and even of stupid mistakes, the work as a whole shows a mind at work, making judgments at times quite astute in its approach to the task of translating holy writ.

3.1. One characteristic that immediately occurs to the reader of Num is the preference for formulaic patterns. This is immediately obvious from ch.1, which reports on the census of the Israelite tribes, individually reported on for each of the twelve tribes; see vv.20—46. The formula reads κατὰ συγγενείας αὐτῶν, κατὰ δήμους αυτῶν, κατ' οἴκους πατριῶν αὐτῶν, κατὰ ἀριθμὸν ὀνομάτων αὐτῶν, κατὰ κεφαλὴν αὐτῶν, πάντα ἀρσενικὰ ἀπὸ εἰκοσαετοῦς καὶ ἐπάνω, πᾶς ὁ ἐκπορευόμενος ἐν τῇ δυνάμει. Then ἡ ἐπίσκεψις αὐτῶν ἐκ τῆς φυλῆς is followed by the name of the tribe and the total numbers reviewed. In MT the formula might and does vary, but Num rigidly followed the pattern regardless of changes in the parent text.

Ch.2 describes the arrangement of the tribal camps. With the tent of testimony in the middle, there were four τάγματα "divisions," comprising three tribes each, one on each of the four sides of the tent. These are also described in formulaic terms; the structures are τάγμα παρεμβολῆς and σὺν δυμάμει αὐτῶν for each of the four divisions without conjunctions. This was followed by δύναμις αὐτοῦ οἱ ἐπεσκεμμένοι, regardless of MT's reading with pronominal suffixes, i.e. as ופקדיו or ופקדיהם throughout. When Num began with a formulaic pattern, it was rigidly adhered to.

This is particularly true of ch.7 where MT only occasionally deviates slightly from a set pattern. The ch. deals with the offerings presented by the ἄρχων of the various tribes in turn on succesive days for the dedication of the altar. Num however, adhered word for word to the formula. Each leader brought exactly the same offering. The pattern is set by the presentation by Naasson ... the ἄρχων τῆς φυλῆς Ἰούδα on the first day. It reads the text of vv.13—17a, and concludes with τοῦτο τὸ δῶρον Ναασσὼν υἱοῦ Ἀμιναδάβ. This is followed by τῇ ἡμέρᾳ τῇ δευτέρᾳ brought ... the ἄρχων τῆς φυλῆς Ἰσσαχάρ. The text of vv.13—17a is again repeated word for word, and the report ends with "this is the gift of Nathanael son of Sogar." In spite of the fact that MT had no counterpart to τὴν φυλῆς, Num does not deviate from the pattern. And so on for all the twelve tribes.

Ch.33 also follows a set pattern, though extra information does obtain for many cases, which helps to relieve the monotony of the list of stages on Israel's desert journey. What does not change is the formula: "they departed from X, and they encamped in Y," which is used for each of the 42 stages. It should be noted that this pattern is based on the Hebrew pattern ויסעו מן plus place name, followed by ויחנו ב plus place name.

3.2. Occasionally a minipattern obtains which is then reflected in Num over against MT. In 4:41 "(which) ἐπεσκέψατο Μωυσῆς καὶ Ἀαρὼν διὰ φωνῆς κυρίου plus ἐν χειρὶ Μωυσῆ occurs. The plus is absent in MT, but obtains in v.37. In v.44 the phrase κατ' οἴκους πατριῶν αὐτῶν has no counterpart in MT, but its source is clear; it follows the patterns found in vv.2—46.

At 19:19 the verse ends with וטהר בערב "and he will be clean in the evening" which becomes καὶ ἀκάθαρτος ἔσται ἕως ἑσπέρας. The translator followed the set pattern appearing in vv.7,8,10, and comp vv.21 and 22.

4.0. Chh.28—29 describe the regulations for sacrifices for the people, not only for every day, but also for the Sabbath and the various festival or special days. For these both a מנחה as well as a libation are required. MT is, however, often inconsistent with respect to the number of the nouns and of their suffixes. Thus at 29:18 MT has ומנחתם ונסכיהם, but Num has both nouns in the singular. Similarly, at v.11 MT has ומנחתה ונסכיהם, which Num makes consistent by ἡ θυσία αὐτῆς καὶ ἡ σπονδὴ αὐτῆς.

At 4:37 MT begins with a plural אלה פקודי of the clan of the Kohathite, but then details in the singular כל העבד .... Num makes the verse singular throughout: αὕτη ἡ ἐπίσκεψις δήμου Καάθ, πᾶς ὁ λειτουργῶν κ.τ.λ. At 20:8 Yahweh instructs Moses: "take the rod and assemble the assembly, you and Aaron, your brother, and דברתם to the rock before them ..., והוצאת for them water from the rock, והשקית the assembly and their cattle." Num keeps a consistent plural, λαλήσατε ... ἐξοίσετε ... ποτιεῖτε. This not only has an inner consistency, but more importantly makes it consistent with v.12, where the Lord punishes both Moses and Aaron because οὐκ ἐπιστεύσατε ἁγιάσαι με ἐναντίον υἱῶν Ἰσραήλ.

At 21:3 Num makes the account consistent with v.2. In v.2 Israel vowed: "If you should deliver up to me this people as subject (ὑποχείριον), I will anathematize him and his cities." In v.3 MT reads the result: "And he delivered up the Canaanite, ויחרם אתהם ואת עריהם." Num makes this verse consistent with the vow by its καὶ ἀναθεμάτισεν αὐτὸν καὶ τὰς πόλεις αὐτοῦ.

At 23:11 Balak says to Balaam: "to curse my enemies לקחתיך," which Num changes to κέκληκά σε. This is consistent with 22:5,37 (and comp v.20) where reference is made to Balak's sending ... καλέσαι Balaam. This is certainly a smoother text as well. At 24:11 Balak ordered: φεῦγε εἰς τὸν τοπόν σου (מקומך). Then at v.14 Balaam says הנני הולך לעמי, but Num changes the prepositional phrase to εἰς τὸν τόπον μου, which corresponds to Balak's order in v.11.

At 31:27—28 Moses is divinely ordered וחצית the spoils between the soldiers who went out to war in the army and all the assembly, והרמת a tax portion for Yahweh from the soldiers .... Num renders these verbs in the plural. This is in line with v.26 where σὺ καὶ Ἐλεαζὰρ ὁ ἱερεὺς καὶ οἱ ἄρχοντες τῶν πατριῶν τῆς συναγωγῆς are ordered to take up the spoils .... It is also much more sensible. Dividing the spoils taken by an entire army by one person, Moses, is hardly feasible.

At 32:39 MT has inconsistent number. It reads וילכו בני מכיר ... and to Gilead, וילכדה ויורש the Amorite who was in it. Num renders a consistent text by its καὶ ἐπορεύθη υἱὸς Μαχίρ ... καὶ ἔλαβεν αὐτὴν καὶ ἀπώλεσεν the Amorrite the one dwelling in it. And finally, at 36:2 the chieftains of the tribe of the Galaadites say: Yahweh commanded את אדני. The rendering τῷ κυρίῳ ἡμῶν, i.e. with a plural pronoun is consistent with the plural subjects addressing Moses and the chieftains.

5.0. Similar to the trend towards a consistent account is the tendency towards harmonization. The latter is a more deliberate levelling of the text. This may at times be a rather moot point. Thus at 9:10 reference is made to someone being unclean לנפש, which Num renders by ἐπὶ ψυχῇ ἀνθρώπου. The translation is a case of harmonizing with those who are unclean לנפש אדם as in v.6. What is meant in both cases is contact with the corpse of a person.

At 10:36 MT (= v.34) has a nominal clause: "And the cloud (was) over them by day," but Num has after "the cloud" ἐγένετο σκιάζουσα, i.e. it was overshadowing them. This harmonizes with the statements at 9:18 ἐν αἷς, σκιάζει ἡ νεφέλη and 9:22 τῆς νεφέλης σκιαζούσης ἐπ' αὐτῆς, both of which having an equivalent Hebrew text as parent.

5.1. At 16:37(17:2) both את מחתת and ואת האש are resp modified by adjectives. For τὰ πυρεῖα Num added τὰ χαλκᾶ which agrees with v.39 (MT 17:4), מחתות הנחשת, whereas for καὶ τὸ πῦρ Num has characterized it by ἀλλότριον which harmonizes with Lev 10:1 אש זרה, also found at Num 3:4 where the rendering is indefinite, i.e. πῦρ ἀλλότριον. At 26:61 this is also referred to, but it is located ἐν τῇ ἐρήμῳ Σινά. This has no counterpart in MT, but it does harmonize with 3:4, where the phrase occurs in both MT and Num.

5.2. At 27:18 Moses is ordered to take Yesous his successor and ἐπιθήσεις τὰς χεῖράς σου on him. But MT has the singular את ידך. The report of his carrying out this order in MT of v.23 reads "And he placed את ידיו on him." The consistent plural noun is an improvement. At 29:11 Num has καὶ χίμαρον ἐξ αἰγῶν ἕνα περὶ ἁμαρτίας ἐξιλάσασθαι περὶ ὑμῶν. But MT has no equivalent for the last three words, which Num has taken over from v.5 word for word. At v.5, however, MT does have לכפר עליכם at the end of the verse.

5.3. At 31:21 Eleazar is reported as speaking to the men of the army who were going ἐκ τοῦ παρατάξεως τῆς πολέμου, whereas MT refers to the men of the army הבאים למלחמה. This change is a case of harmonization with v.14 where MT has הבאים מצבא המלחמה.

And finally, at 32:11 reference is made to the divine refusal to let the adults who left Egypt experience (יראו) the land which I swore .... But after "Egypt" Num added οἱ ἐπιστάμενοι τὸ κακὸν καὶ τὸ ἀγαθόν. This is based on its text at 14:23 where the children who knew neither good nor evil were excepted. This has no basis in MT either, is in fact a creation of the translator; see comment at 14:23.

6.1. As in the other books of the Pentateuch a number of calques obtain. What I mean is that certain Hebrew words are automatically rendered by certain Greek words; i.e. the Greek word can only be understood as the equivalent of a Hebrew sememe. A few of these occur throughout the translation texts of the Alexandrian canon such as διαθήκη for ברית, or ψυχή for נפש. A few such in Num are προσκυνέω for השתחוה, παραβολή for משל, υἱοί for בני in ch.26, χίμαρον ἐξ αἰγῶν for שעיר עזים, ἀποσκευή for טף, and δύναμις for חיל.

6.2. Also to be considered are certain syntagmemes, such as τίς ἡμᾶς ψωμιεῖ κρέα for מי יאכלנו בשר at 11:4 in which the Greek only makes sense as an imitation of a Hebrew desiderative "O that someone might give us meat." This syntactic calque also occurs at 11:29 in τίς δῴη. Another syntactic calque obtains at 22:15 with προσέθετο ἔτι plus an infinitive, which is readily understood only through the Hebrew עוד ויסף plus infinitive, "and again ...." To a monolingual Greek speaker the χιλίους ἐκ φυλῆς χιλίους ἐκ φυλῆς at 31:4 would be puzzling. It is also a syntactic calque, explicable through אלף למטה אלף למטה, which is a syntagmeme indicating a distributive sense, i.e. "a thousand per clan." The Greek must here be understood as a distributive as well. Incidentally, the term אלף "a thousand" may also mean "a clan."

7.0. A number of instances occur in which the translator misread the parent text. The following are merely illustrative. In Moses' plea for the people at 14:16 he suggests that the nations would say that God was not able to redeem his promises וישחטם "and he slaughtered them (in the desert)." Num has κατέστρωσεν αὐτοὺς (ἐν τῇ ἐρήμῳ) "and he stretched them out." Obviously, Num read וישטחם! And at 22:39 the unknown Moabite place name קרית חצות occurs. Num translated the name by πόλεις ἐπαύλεων. The plural πόλεις is a possible interpretation of קרית, but ἐπαύλεων must have rendered חצרות "unwalled places." Note also 16:15 where Num has ἐπιθύμημα for חמור, obviously having read חמוד.

7.1. The translator was often faced with difficult terms, some of which still baffle translators. Once again the following are but illustrative of Num's way of dealing with such. One such which seems surprising is the term במות "high places" at 22:41. Post-Pentateuch translators regularly use ὑψηλός, but this never occurs in the Pentateuch. It is also rendered by στηλή at 21:28 33:52 and at Lev 26:30. The word במות also occurs twice in Dt. At 32:13 it was translated by τὴν ἰσχύν, and at 33:29 במותימו became ἐπὶ τὸν τράχηλον αὐτῶν. Apparently, the word was not known in the sense of an idolatrous place of worship in Alexandria, i.e. as a high place.

7.2. But of more interest are difficult words such as לשד at 11:8. MT says concerning manna that "its taste was like the לשד of oil." NIV guessed with "something based." NJPS has for לשד השמן "(like) rich cream," whereas NRSV follows Num's ἐγκρίς with "cakes baked." The word is still unknown, and Num simply contextualized. At 14:9 MT speaks of צלם "their shade" as a figure for "their protection," but Num was baffled by this, rendering סר צלם מעליהם by ἀφέστηκεν (γὰρ) ὁ καιρὸς ἀπ' αὐτῶν, "(γὰρ) ὁ καιρός abandoned them," i.e. their moment in history has passed them by."

At 14:34 the difficult את תנואתי occurs. It also obtains at Job 33:10 where it is also unclear. What is clear from the context is that it is something bad, and that it modifies ידעתם. Moderns all guess at the meaning. NJPS has "what it means to thwart me"; NRSV simply reads "my displeasure," and NIV has "have me against you." Num also contextualized with τὸν θυμὸν τῆς ὀργῆς μου. At v.44 the hapax legomenon יעפלו obtains. Again, moderns have guessed from the context, and depended on the parallel at Dt 1:43 תזדו "acted wilfully." Num's guess is also unique, reading διαβιασάμενοι "forcibly, stubbornly."

At 16:1 the tale of Korah's rebellion is introduced in MT by ויקח קרח. Since לקח is a transitive verb, its absolute use is not really sensible. The translator used his common sense and arbitrarily wrote καὶ ἐλάλησεν, as e.g. at 15:1,17; at least Num makes sense.

At 23:14 Balak brought Balaam to שדה צפים "the field of Sophim." The term means "watchers," and Num tried to translate this by εἰς ἀγροῦ σκοπιάν "to a watchtower of the field," a neat attempt to make sense out of "to the field of watchers." At v.22 God is likened to תועפת ראם לו. Unfortunately, the word תועפת is completely unknown; it is something characterizing the wild ox, and moderns have guessed at "horns" or "strength"; Num guessed δόξα, which is probably wrong, but it is not impossible.

7.3. When faced with unintelligible text the translator tried to make some kind of sense. At 32:33 the land of Og is called הארץ לעריה בגבלת ערי הארץ סביב. This looks as though it ought to make sense, but it is difficult to interpret. At least, Num did make sense with τὴν γῆν καὶ τὰς πόλεις σὺν τοῖς ὁρίοις αὐτῆς, πόλεις τῆς γῆς κύκλῳ.

At v.38 the characterization of Baal Maon is מוסבת שם possibly "having been turned about with respect to name" which was not understood by the translator. The relevance of שם escaped him, but he took the participle concretely as περικεκυκλωμένας "having been surrounded" presumably by walls; this would have been a good contextual guess had שם not been present.

8.0. At least, the characterization of Num as an "Ungefähr, ein sich Ergehenlassen ohne Plan und Ziel,"[4] is hardly justified. In fact, the following sections should demonstrate that in spite of a number of lapses, the translator had both plan and purpose. This is immediately clear from attempts at clarification of the Hebrew text and at greater exactness. Already at 1:2 the word order כל זכר לגלגלתם is changed; since this is immediately followed by "from twenty years of

---

4. See footnote no.1 above.

age and upward," the πᾶς ἄρσην is placed at the end of the verse, which is much clearer. At vv.45—46 the summary census reports are doubly introduced in both verses, which Num simplifiies by a single καὶ ἐγένετο πᾶσα ἡ ἐπίσκεψις υἱῶν Ἰσραήλ ....

8.1. A change in number at 4:31a is more accurate than MT's זאת משמרת in Num's ταῦτα τὰ φυλάγματα, since v.b continues with a list of items to be cared for. At 5:3 the antecedent of the relative pronoun is ambiguous. It reads אשר אני שכן בתוכם, but since the gender of מחני is uncertain, either it or the suffix of מחניהם could be referred to. But the uncertainty is removed in Num's ἐν οἷς ἐγὼ καταγίνομαι ἐν αὐτοῖς; the reference must be to αὐτῶν, not to παρεμβολάς, which is feminine. At v.9 a similar confusion is possible. The relative clause reads אשר יקריבו לכהן לו יהיה. Num removes all possible ambiguity by adding κυρίῳ before τῷ ἱερεῖ and omitting לו, thus "which they might bring to the Lord, shall be the priest's."

8.2. Occasionally, an odd Hebrew usage is simplified. At 8:4 the workmanship of the lampstand is described. It consisted of hammered gold עד ירכה עד פרחה. The construction is unusual; one expects either a מן ... עד structure, or a conjunction joining the two. Num is clear; it reads ὁ καυλὸς αὐτῆς καὶ τὰ κρίνα αὐτῆς. What Num says is that both parts of the candlestick were of στερεὰ χρυσῆ, in fact, were στερεὰ ὅλη, the latter representing מקשה הוא.

At 10:8 Num simplifies MT's ambiguous והיו, for which the subject is not clear; presumably the rules concerning trumpet sounding is intended. By changing the number to καὶ ἔσται ὑμῖν νόμιμον αἰώνιον, it can only refer to the sounding of the trumpets.

8.3. At vv.5—6a MT makes what seems to be an incomplete statement. The trumpets sound and the tribes encamped eastward break camp; similarly, this obtains for those encamped southward. Num fills out the account by a third and a fourth σημασίαν for the breaking up camp for those encamped παρὰ θάλασσαν and πρὸς βορρᾶν resp.

8.4. Num sometimes makes a more appropriate statement. At 12:15 MT states that the people did not break camp עד האסף מרים "until Miriam was readmitted (i.e. into the camp)." But the real point of Miriam's not being in the camp was her impure state, i.e. ἕως ἐκαθαρίσθη Μαριάμ.

At 13:20(19) the spies are told by Moses to investigate the "cities הבמחנים אם במבצרים whether in camps or in fortified areas." But a sociological query is not overly important. Invaders are more interested in matters of military relevance; thus εἰ ἐν τειχήρεσιν ἢ ἐν ἀτειχίστοις.

8.5. At 15:4 MT refers to סלת עשרון בלול (with a quarter hin of oil). What is not clear is what בלול modifies. סלת is apparently feminine, and the word must refer to עשרון. Num reads ἀναπεποιημένης which can only modify σεμιδάλεως, which is more logical.

At 19:3,5 singular verbs obtain after "and you shall give it to Eleazar the priest והוציא it outside the camp ושחט it לפניו. Then in v.5 again a singular verb obtains: ושרף the cow לעיניו. At best this is a confusing statement. Num clarifies this by changing the three verbs to the indefinite plural, ridding the text of confusion as to what Eleazar's role in all this is to be. After all, it is Eleazar who is referred to in לפניו and לעיניו!

8.6. In dialogue the use of pronouns can be confusing. Thus at 23:12 ויען ויאמר must refer to Balaam, but Num makes doubly certain who are the speakers and who the addressees, thus here Num reads καὶ εἶπεν Βαλαὰμ πρὸς Βαλάκ. Similarly, in v.15 MT does not name the subject in "And he said to Balak," but Num adds Βαλαάμ after εἶπεν.

8.7. At 25:12 MT speaks of את בריתי שלום. Grammatically שלום must be an appositive, thus "my covenant, even peace." Num's text is simpler: a διαθήκην εἰρήνης. Since it is the Lord who is speaking the suffix is unnecessary, and the genitive probably interprets what the apposite really intends.

At 26:10 במות העדה is ambiguous; it can be taken as "when the assembly died," or "in the death of the assembly." In any event, Num was careful to avoid any notion that the entire assembly of Israel died by adding αὐτοῦ; i.e. it was the assembly of Kore.

The identification of the ancestry of the daughters of Salpaad at 27:1 is inter alia בן מנשה למשפחת מנשה which could be confusing. By coalescing the two phrases into one τοῦ δήμου Μανασσή it is simpler, though not necessarily more accurate. In the next verse, ותעמדנה is made coordinate with προσελθοῦσαι by subordinating it to a participle as well, necessitating the change of לאמר to a finite verb λέγουσιν. This neatly changes the stress quite properly from approaching and appearing on to the actual judicial complaint.

8.8. The text at 30:8: ושמע אישה ביום שמעו והחריש לה is hardly a model of clarity, and Num simplifies and clarifies by rearranging the text as καὶ ἀκούσῃ ὁ ἀνὴρ αὐτῆς καὶ παρασιωπήσῃ αὐτῇ ᾗ ἂν ἡμέρᾳ ἀκούσῃ. This must have been what MT means to say. At 32:23 Moses warns the Roubenites and Gadites to do as they promised; otherwise, דעו חטאתכם אשר תמצא אתכם. What "your sin finding you out" means is made clear in Num, which renders the relative clause by ὅταν ὑμᾶς καταλάβῃ τὰ κακά. And at v.32 these tribes conclude their case by the confidence ואתנו אחזת נחלתנו from Transjordan. Num corrects this by δώσετε τὴν κατάσχεσιν ἡμῖν; the parcelling out of lands is kept in the proper hands. It is not "we will have," but "you will give us the possession."

At 33:37 MT locates Mt.Hor בקצה ארץ אדום which is ambiguous. Does קצה refer to the edge of Edom just inside Edom or just outside it? Num leaves no doubt about it; it is πλησίον γῆς Ἐδώμ.

9. The translator also tends to levelling the text. At 1:54 "the Israelites did according to everything which Yahweh commanded Moses," to which Num added καὶ Ἀαρών. This levels with v.17 where Μωυσῆς καὶ Ἀαρών took those men who had specifically been called.

At 8:13 Moses is ordered to set the Levites "before Aaron and before his sons." But in v.11 Aaron was to set aside the Levites as an ἀπόδομα before the Lord from the Israelites, and so Num added ἔναντι κυρίου καί in front of "before Aaron."

At 22:18 MT has עבדי of Balak, instead of the usual שרי בלק. Since vv.8,13,14,15 referred to οἱ ἄρχοντες, Num substitutes τοῖς ἄρχουσιν Βαλάκ, levelling with the more common designation.

10.1. Closely related to the process of levelling texts are instances of rationalizations on the part of Num. At 4:13 one of the duties of the Kohathites according to MT is "and they must remove the ashes of the altar and spread a purple cloth over it." But the ashes might well be live ashes, and this would be hazardous. Num substitutes for the first clause "and he (i.e. someone?) must place the cover (presumably metallic) over the altar, and they must (then) cover it with a purple cloth."

10.2. The story of Koreh, Dathan and Abiram in ch.16 of MT seems to consist of a weaving together of two narratives, one of Koreh and another of Dathan and Abiram. The assembly of the three was swallowed up alive by the earth, but in vv.16—21 Koreh is told to appear with his 250 men with censers. Then in v.35 we are told that fire came out and devoured the 250 men. Obviously, Num was aware of discrepancies in the account, and tried to rationalize a distinction between the two groups. Thus at v.24 where MT states that the assembly (i.e. of Israel) is ordered "Go up from around למשכן קרח דתן ואבירם, Num shortens to ἀναχωρήσατε κύκλῳ ἀπὸ τῆς συναγωγῆς Κόρε. Then in the next verse both MT and Num read: And Moses ... went to Dathan and Abiram. The assembly is thereupon warned to separate themselves from the tents of those wicked/callous men. V.27 according to MT reads: And they went up from the dwelling of Kore, Dathan and Abiram round about, and Dathan and Abiram went out standing at the door of their tents. But Num tried to rationalize more precisely what happened, and distinguishes once again by omitting the first "Dathan and Abiram" entirely. This hints at two events, with separate denouements.

10.3. MT at 18:28 presents a difficulty in its ממנו, which has no proper antecedent. It reads "so you must raise, even you a תרומת of Yahweh from all your tithes which you shall take from the Israelites, and you must give ממנו Yahweh's תרומה to Aaron the priest." Neither תרומת which is feminine nor מעשרתי which is plural can be referred to by the masculine singular pronoun. Num has rationalized this by its ἀπ' αὐτῶν which refers to the tithes.

At 19:6 the priest must take cedar wood and hyssop and red thread and throw it into the middle of the sacrifice. Num distinguishes between the priest's action and that of the Israelites who bring the δάμαλιν, by putting the second verb into the plural, ἐμβαλοῦσιν.

At 23:6 Balak was standing beside עלתו. But at v.2 Balak offered up μόσχον καὶ κριόν, and Num corrects the text to ἐπὶ τῶν ὁλοκαυτωμάτων αὐτοῦ. Similarly, at 31:6 the חצצרות were בידו. But according to 10:2 there were two trumpets, and they must have been εν ταῖς χερσὶν αὐτῶν (viz. of Phinees and Eleazar).

10.4. At 32:15 עם is translated by συναγωγήν, which only happens here and at Lev 10:3. Moses is addressing the Roubenites and the Gadites. Num is careful to distinguish between συναγωγή and 'Ισραήλ; in fact, at v.4 where עדת ישראל occurs, it is changed to τῶν υἱῶν 'Ισραήλ. Israel can be designated by tribes, army, etc., but never by עדה. Here he avoids "people" in favour of συναγωγή, since a contrast is intended between the people of Israel, of which the Roubenites and Gadites are part, and the assembly of Israel, which is the cultic community from which they are separate. And at 35:5 מדתם is changed to the singular μετρήσεις. This is much more sensible; only one person can be engaged in measuring the four sides, not the people as a whole.

11.1. At times the translator was faced with contradictions to resolve as well as actual corrections of fact to make. One such concerned the age at which

Levites were to begin their tabernacle service. At 4:3 and passim MT set the age of induction at thirty years, but at 8:24 this becomes twenty-five years. Num resolves this by making it consistently twenty-five. At 8:26 MT presents another problem. Concerning the retired Levite it states that "he shall serve his brothers in the tent of testimony by performing guard duty," i.e. he is to serve his active brothers, but according to ch.3 the Levitical clans were all assigned guard duty. So Num resolves the contradiction by changing the clause to read "his brother (i.e. the active Levite) shall serve in the tent ..., but the works he (the retiree) may not perform."

At 33:54 in the course of the assignment of land by lot to the clans, direction for assignments is in the plural התנחלתם and תרבו, but then the orders change to the singular תמעיט. But this cannot be correct, since Moses is being addressed (v.50), and he is to die before the conquest. The translator corrects the narrative by using a consistent plural.

35:4 presents a flat contradiction which has baffled commentators ever since. It concerns the מגרשי of the cities of refuge. Their width, i.e. from the city wall to the outer limit, is given as אלף אמה סביב. But then in v.5 the מגרש on each side is measured, and each one is אלפים באמה. This simply does not make sense, nor did it to the translator who solved this by changing v.4 to δισχιλίους πήχεις κύκλῳ, i.e. 2000 cubits wide throughout, thereby making a consistent account.

11.2. At 5:15 MT states that "the man must bring his wife to the priest והביא את קרבנה on her behalf." Num renders this by καὶ προσοίσει τὸ δῶρον περὶ αὐτῆς, i.e. the suffix is omitted. After all, it was not "her gift," her sacrifice, but simply a gift presented by the husband on her behalf.

At 12:8 Num corrects what the Lord says in defence of Moses his servant ... ותמנת יהוה יביט, i.e. "Yahweh's form he will see." But Moses only saw Yahweh's form in Exod 33:18—23 (and comp 24:17). Never again is there a record of Moses' seeing Yahweh's form, and Num changed the tense of יביט to εἶδεν, thereby referring directly to the Exod event.

11.3. At 14:23 God bluntly states "not shall they experience the land which I swore to their fathers, and all those provoking me shall not see it." The translator has added a fuller statement by inserting between the two clauses "but their children, who are with me here, who have known neither good nor evil, every untried youngster, to them I will give the land." This fuller statement, based on vv.29—35, ensures that the Lord's real intentions are not obscured; a covenant people will remain. Similarly, at v.35 the Lord's oath to destroy כל העדה הרעה הזאת is corrected by omitting כל. After all, both Yesous and Chaleb as well as those under twenty years of age at the time of the Exodus from Egypt were to be spared.

11.4. From ch.1 it was clear that the בית אבות is a smaller unit than "the tribe." But at 17:3(18) the reason for inscribing the name of Aaron on the staff of Levi is given as "because they must assign one staff לראש of their paternal houses." Num's rendering of לראש by κατὰ φυλήν is a more accurate designation. A similar change obtains at 27:11. The context deals with the laws of inheritance. When all others fail, "you must give the inheritance to the relative who is nearest him ממשפחתו. As chapter 36 makes fully clear, the important boundaries that need protection are tribal; land must not on any account leave the tribe, and Num translates by ἐκ τῆς φυλῆς αὐτοῦ.

11.5. At 20:24 Num judged the basis for Aaron's death given in MT as "כי לא יבא into the land" as incomplete. After all, MT continues with "because מריתם against my word at the waters of Meribah." In other words, Moses would also not be allowed to enter Canaan, and so Num changed יבא to εἰσέλθητε as a better statement.

11.6. In response to Israel's idolatry at Baal Peor, Moses is ordered at 25:4 to "take all the leaders of the people and execute (?) them publicly." In the interest of fairness, Num omitted כל; after all, surely not all the leaders had engaged in idolatry.

At 27:12 the Lord commanded Moses to "see the land of Canaan אשר נתתי to the Israelites." But to Num this is premature, and so a more accurate ἣν ἐγὼ δίδωμι "which I am about to give" is used.

At 32:31 MT quotes the response of the Roubenites and Gadites to Moses' direction: אשר דבר יהוה אל עבדיך, thus we will do. It was of course Moses who is here addressed, and Moses who had spoken. Num rather neatly renders this by ὅσα ὁ κύριος λέγει to his servants, so we will do. Since ὁ κύριος never renders יהוה in Num but only אדני, the title can only refer to Moses.

11.7. 33:36 in MT states "And they left Ezion Geber and encamped in the desert of Sin, namely at Kadesh." But this conflicts with 13:27 where the spies returned "to Kadesh in the desert of Paran." Num has corrected the account by adding an extra stage (Stage 33), which reads "And they left the desert of Sin and encamped in the desert of Pharan."

12.0. It should by now be clear that Num was an intelligent translator, who knew what he was doing. He did not mindlessly translate word for word in dull, plodding fashion, but was intent on a sacred task, the rendering of God's word into the language of the people. It might not be amiss at this stage to give a few examples of really intelligent translations.

12.1. Note the use of tenses at 2:17. In כאשר יחנו כן יסעו both verbs are prefix tenses, but what is meant is that they would set out in the same order in which they had encamped. Accordingly Num used a present tense for the first one, παρεμβάλλουσιν, but a future for the second, since this represented a potential, thus ἐξαροῦσιν.

12.2. At 9:7 people who were unclean at the time of the Pascha festival complain: Why נגרע "held back, restrained" so as not to bring Yahweh's sacrifice at his feast in the midst of the Israelites"? Num does not render נגרע literally, but read ὑστερήσωμεν "are we delayed." Num translated in the light of the answer given in vv.10—12, rather than give a word for word rendering. That is translating intelligently.

12.3. At 16:2 the two hundred fifty men who revolted against Moses' authority are called קראי מועד "appointed by the assembly." But Num does not use συναγωγῆς, but rather σύγκλητοι βουλῆς. βουλή is a political term which in Athens referred to a deliberating council, such as the Senate. Only here does βουλή render מועד, and the translator must have understood the term in the sense of a deliberative council with standing in the community, since it could summon leaders.

12.4. At 19:12 the Hithp יתחטא occurs twice. Num, however, with fine insight renders the first one by the middle ἁγνισθήσεται, but the second one by a passive ἀφαγνισθῇ. According to Num he must cleanse himself ... and he will be clean. But if he is not cleansed ... he will not be clean. This shows astute understanding.

12.5. At 25:3 Num interpreted ויצמד "attached himself to, joined up" to Baal Peor, in intelligent fashion. He used ἐτελέσθη, a technical term meaning "was initiated into the cult or into the mysteries." Joining oneself to idol worship for an Alexandrian Jew may well have been understood as partaking in the cult of some mystery religion.

12.6. Occasionally Num betrays a nice sense of style as well. At 27:17 MT records Moses' request to Yahweh for a successor who יצא before them and who יבא before them, and who יוציאם and who יביאם. Num also uses pairs, viz. compounds of ἐλεύσεται for the Qal pair, but of ἄγει for the Hi pair. It is ἐξ- and εἰσ- that contrast for the Hebrew roots יצא and בוא.

12.7. And to give but one more example of good translation: at 32:17 the Roubenites and Gadites promise Moses אנחנו נחלץ חשים "we will arm ourselves hurrying (before the Israelites)." Num changes this to a nominal clause with ἡμεῖς ἐνοπλισάμενοι προφυλακὴ πρότεροι τῶν υἱῶν Ἰσραήλ "we, having armed ourselves, (will be) a vanguard in front of the Israelites."

13. For Dt the notion of a king for Israel was avoided, since only the Lord could be Israel's king, and he regularly avoided using βασιλεύς in such contexts.[5] The notion of king for Israel only occurs rarely in Numbers, but the same impulse is evident. In fact, the notion is present only in the Balaam pericope of chh.23—24.

At 23:21 Israel is spoken of prophetically in glowing terms. The final hemistich reads ותרועת מלך בו "And the acclaim of a king is in it (i.e. Israel)." This was a red flag to Num, and the line is made to read τὰ ἔνδοξα ἀρχόντων ἐν αὐτῷ "the glorious deeds of chieftains are in it."

At 24:7 the second stich in MT reads וירם מאגג מלכו ותנשא מלכתו "And his king shall be higher than Agag, and his kingdom shall be exalted." Num follows the text of Sam with מגוג rather than מאגג. The entire verse is then changed into an eschatological dream: "An ἄνθρωπος (person) will come out from his seed, and lord it over many nations and βασιλεία αὐτοῦ shall be higher than Gog, and ἡ βασιλεία αὐτοῦ shall increase."

And at v.17 the reference to a sceptre in וקם שבט מישראל is avoided; no royal figure is even hinted at in καὶ ἀναστήσεται ἄνθρωπος ἐξ Ἰσραήλ. Not one wielding a שבט, but an individual, a person, shall arise out of Israel.

14. One might expect the person of the great lawgiver, Moses, to be reverenced, and even enhanced. But there is surprisingly little evidence of such in Num. At 12:3 the man Moses is said to be very ענו, more so than anyone who was on the surface of the earth. The term means "humble," but Num renders it by πραΰς, "patient," which is not overly appropriate for the explosive Moses.

At 16:15 MT states that Moses became very angry ויחר למשה מאד. Num pictured Moses in much more sensitive terms: καὶ ἐβαρυθύμησεν Μωυσῆς σφό-

---

5. See J.W.Wevers, The LXX Translator of Deuteronomy, Taylor, IX Congress, 87.

δρα; i.e. he became very heavy of spirit. In other words, Moses became discouraged and downcast at the rebellious complaints which faced him.

But at 20:4 the complaint of the people is voiced: Why did you bring the people ... שם למות to die there; here Num levels with 16:13 where the rebels charge Moses with bringing us להמיתנו in the desert, i.e. ἀποκτεῖναι ἡμᾶς in the desert. This places Moses in a much worse light, viz. that he had brought the people into the desert in order to kill them!

15.1. The translator demonstrates an obvious prejudice against Balaam. The notion that Balaam, a non-Israelite, could be a prophet of Yahweh, disturbed him greatly. This becomes quite evident in the way in which he attempted to avoid recognizing יהוה as the source of Balaam's prophecy, substituting almost throughout ὁ θεός for the usual κύριος. This begins with the first reference to יהוה in the Balaam story at 22:13 where he dismisses the chieftains of Balak saying ὁ θεός/Yahweh has refused to let me go with you. At v.18 Num could hardly avoid recognizing יהוה, since Balaam refers to the word of יהוה אלהי, i.e. κυρίου τοῦ θεοῦ which he cannot oppose. In v.19 Balaam also refers to τί προσθήσει κύριος λαλῆσαι πρός με, but in the story of the talking she-ass, reference to the מלאך יהוה become "angel τοῦ θεοῦ throughout with one exception; in v.34 where Balaam confesses: "I have sinned," κυρίου is used; possibly Num felt that the confession of sin was more fitting for an angel of the Lord to receive.

Through ch.23 all instances of יהוה become "God" in Num except for two. At v.8 both אל and יהוה occur, and Num uses κύριος for the first line of the couplet, and ὁ θεός in the second. And at v.17 Balak asked Balaam τί ἐλάλησεν κύριος, but that was Balak talking, and he wanted some concession from Yahweh, Israel's God. After all, Balak particularly wanted a Yahweh prophet to curse Israel. Though not all instances of יהוה are changed in the narrative, it does seem that there was a strong tendency in Num to avoid the use of κύριος by Balaam as much as possible.

15.2. Num also shows antipathy towards Balaam the diviner. When Balaam refers in 22:18 to the פי of יהוה אלהי Num omits the suffix, thereby neutralizing the reason for Balak's invitation in the first place. What Balak wanted was a Yahweh worshipper to curse the people—that would be effective!

15.3. At 31:16 the word of Balaam was defined by למסר מעל ביהוה. Unfortunately, the meaning of the infinitive is unknown, but Num's rendering τοῦ ἀποστῆσαι καὶ ὑπεριδεῖν τὸ ῥῆμα κυρίου makes Balaam guilty. He had advised the Midianites thus, though there is no evidence in the oracles of chh.23—24 of such apostacy at all. But it does fit in with the prejudice which Num had against the non-Israelite prophet.

16. Instructive for finding prejudice is the account of the ten spies on their return from their survey of Canaan in 13:29—32(28—31). In v.28 MT has them report that the people are עז. Num renders this by θρασύ, i.e. "bold, arrogant"; in other words, it makes a value judgment on the character of the people. In the same verse they report that the cities are בצרות "fortified." Num not only characterizes the walls as ὀχυραί but adds τετειχισμένοι "walled." Then in v.31 MT reads: לא נוכל לעלות אל העם. Num adds a blunt refusal to introduce this: οὐκ ἀναβαίνομεν ὅτι, i.e. their inability is now a ὅτι clause, thereby making it clear that their report is a rebellious one over against the Lord and Moses. Actually, the כי clause of MT "because חזק הוא ממנו" is also exaggerated by the addition of μᾶλλον at the end. Then in v.33(32) "the evil report of the land" (דבת הארץ) is also made worse. It becomes the ἔκστασιν τῆς γῆς "the terror of the land." Num makes the report more tendentious than MT does.

17.1. Of particular interest are cases where the translator intentionally reinterprets what MT says. At 3:10a MT simply says "And Aaron and his sons you must appoint that they may observe their priesthood." This was not detailed enough for Num, which added after "appoint" ἐπὶ τῆς σκηνῆς τοῦ μαρτυρίου, and at the end defining their ἱερατείαν as καὶ πάντα τὰ κατὰ τὸν βωμὸν καὶ τὰ ἔσω τοῦ καταπετάσματος. This defined the work of the priests and clearly marked them, not the Levites, as being in charge of everything in the sanctuary.

17.2. At 8:19b in MT (the Levites are to serve as helpers to the priests, inter alia to make intercession for the Israelites) "that there might not be among the Israelites a נגף when the Israelites approach (בגשת) the sanctuary." Num, however, omits נגף, and thereby changes the point of the clause entirely. V.b in Num reads καὶ οὐκ ἔσται ἐν τοῖς υἱοῖς Ἰσραὴλ προσεγγίζων πρὸς τὰ ἅγια, i.e. no lay Israelite may approach the holy things.

17.3. At 14:3 MT has Israel asking "would not returning to Egypt be good for us"? Num changes this into a strong affirmation νῦν οὖν βέλτιον ἡμῖν ἐστιν ἀποστραφῆναι εἰς Αἴγυπτον. This is a call to action, not a question for debate. A similar change in direction obtains at 15:22. MT speaks of "when תשגו (you should unintentionally err) and fail to do all these commandments," but

Num substitutes διαμάρτητε, i.e. "you fail utterly." This changes inadvertence to utter failure.

17.4. At 20:10 Moses and Aaron ask: המן הסלע הזה shall we bring out water for you? The initial interrogative particle is neutral, but Num renders the question as a μή question, which prejudices the answer; a μή query expects a negative answer; Num renders a judgment, viz. no, we should not bring water out of the rock.

17.5. At 21:1 the inimical king of Arad is called הכנעני "the Canaanite" in MT, but Num avoids the normal rendering of the gentilic in favor of a proper name ὁ Χανανίς and in v.3 (τὸν) Χανανίν. After all, Arad was outside the borders of the Promised Land, which Israel was not yet occupying; in other words, Num felt that ο χαναναιος would here be inappropriate.

17.6. At 30:6,9 and 13 reference is made to ויהוה יסלח לה. The context is that of a vow made by a woman of which her father or her husband is aware, who then negate her vow. MT states that Yahweh will pardon her, since a father's or a husband's authority may overturn such a vow. But according to Num, as a minor she is blameless, and pardon is inappropriate; accordingly, κύριος καθαριεῖ αὐτήν "the Lord will consider her pure." At v.16 the apodosis reads ונשא את עונה "then he (her husband) shall bear her guilt." Num, however, follows the Sam text reading עונו, i.e. his guilt, which is consistent with the renderings for יסלח at vv.6,9,13. Furthermore, עון is rendered by ἁμαρτίαν "mistake, error," probably intentionally chosen to mitigate the notion of עון.

17.7. The word בגד is normally rendered by ἱμάτιον. According to the count of Dos Santos, בגד occurs 181 times, of which 117 are translated by ἱμάτιον (and 10 times by ἱματισμός), and by στολή 41 times, but at 31:20 Num uniquely uses περίβλημα to describe the clothing taken as booty from the Madianites. Probably this was chosen to distinguish between ordinary Israelite ἱμάτια and that of Madian. For ארץ the translator normally used γῆ, but at 32:1 the ארץ of יעזר and that of גלעד become τὴν χώραν Ἰαζήρ and τὴν χώραν Γαλαάδ resp. After all, these regions, though assigned to Israelite tribes, were not part of the γῆ which the Lord was about to give his people, and it seemed appropriate to use the neutral term χώραν instead.

17.8. At 32:12 Caleb the son of Jephunneh is called הקנזי. But the Kenizzites were an Edomite tribe, (see Gen 36:15,42) and that the faithful Caleb should be a non-Israelite was embarrassing. Num substitutes for הקנזי ὁ διακεχωρισμένος "the one who had separated himself" (probably from the majority spy report; see 13:31 and comp 14:24).

18. Num avoids certain anthropomorphisms and anthropopathisms of the Hebrew text. Thus at 11:1 MT says that "the people were complaining ... in the ears (באזני) of Yahweh, and Yahweh heard and his nostril became hot (ויחר אפו) and an אש יהוה (fire of Yahweh) burned ...." Num rendered באזני יהוה by ἔναντι κυρίου thereby avoiding reference to Yahweh's ears; furthermore, the clause ויחר אפו is never rendered literally in Num, but became καὶ ἐθυμώθη ὀργῇ or something similar. The bald directness of "Yahweh's fire" is softened by πῦρ παρὰ κυρίου.

References to פי יהוה are usually understood as φωνῆς κυρίου (eight times), προστάγματος κυρίου (five times), or ῥῆμα κυρίου (four times), but the literal στομα does not occur. In fact, at 20:24 where God, in addressing Moses and Aaron, says מריתם את פי, Num simply takes פי as pars pro toto and renders παρωξύνατέ με. And at 22:34 Balaam addresses Yahweh's angel with אם רע בעיניך "should it be evil in your eyes," but Num avoids a rendering of עיני by εἰ μή σοι ἀρέσκει. Similarly, at 23:27 Balak says אולי יישר בעיני האלהים, and Num renders simply by εἰ ἀρέσει τῷ θεῷ.

19.1. Of particular interest are indications of theological interest on the part of the translator. It was the duty of the Levites to protect the sacred area of the sanctuary, and according to 1:53 they are to encamp immediately around the tent of witness so that קצף, i.e. wrath, presumably divine anger at any possible intrusion of the sacred area might not fall on the Israelites. Num avoids the notion of wrath by its ἁμάρτημα; such intrusion would constitute sin, mistake, error.

19.2. At 3:32 Eliazar is called נשיא נשיאי הלוי, but a literal rendering would be too close to such titles as Lord of lords and king of kings. Num avoids this neatly by ὁ ἄρχων ὁ ἐπὶ τῶν ἀρχόντων τῶν Λευιτῶν "the chieftain who was over the chieftains of the Levites." At 12:5 Yahweh came down ... and stood at the door of the tent ויקרא אהרן ומרים, who had objected to their brother Moses assuming the leadership of the people. But in Num the Lord does not summon them; rather a passive transform is used; the two of them ἐκλήθησαν. The following verse has a real difficulty in the protasis: אם יהיה נביאכם יהוה, which cannot possibly mean what it seems to say: should Yahweh be your prophet. All moderns restate it somehow to make your prophet one of Yahweh. Num does this simply by rendering יהוה by the dative κυρίῳ.

19.3. At the end of ch.6 the section on the Aaronic blessing is recorded. In MT this is followed by "And they (i.e. Aaron and his sons) shall set my name on the Israelites, and I will bless them." Num has placed this statement before the blessing with one difference, adding κύριος after "I." The reordering is strange, since it is preceded by the direct quotation formula λέγοντες. It does place an added emphasis on the placing of the divine name on the people, which is then realized by the pronouncement of the blessing.

19.4. At 14:8 the rendering of חפץ in "If Yahweh is pleased with us" becomes αἱρετίζει. This defines the divine pleasure in terms of choice. To Num the issue is critical; the Lord might reject us, but if he chooses us, he will bring us into this land.

19.5. At 23:19 the opening couplet reads "God is not a man that he should tell lies, nor a human being that he should repent." Num made a number of changes. The notion that God is not a man was toned down by inserting ὡς, thus "God is not like a person (ἄνθρωπος for איש). The active verb ויכזב is changed to a passive infinitive διαρτηθῆναι "that he could be deceived." Furthermore, the notion that God would change his mind, יתנחם, is avoided entirely by using the infinitive ἀπειληθῆναι "that he might be threatened (i.e. be coerced)." Num preserves God's integrity by voiding any possible human characteristic.

19.6. At 25:2 the mind of the translator is also shown. The Moabitesses "summoned the people (i.e. the Israelites) to the sacrifices of אלהיהן and the people יאכל and worshipped לאלהיהן." To the translator "their gods" are idols, and τὰς θυσίας must be τῶν εἰδώλων αὐτῶν, and they did obeissance τοῖς εἰδώλοις αὐτῶν. These are obviously translations. But יאכל has no modifier given in MT, and to avoid the possible misunderstanding that the people ate their idols, Num added a modifier "and the people ἔφαγεν τῶν θυσιῶν αὐτῶν, i.e. they partook of their sacrifices.

19.7. At 32:4 the Roubenites and Gadites are trying to persuade the Israelite leaders to allow them as their inheritance "the land אשר הכה יהוה before the assembly of Israel." The notion of Yahweh smiting the land seemed overly graphic to the translator, and he chose a less colorful ἣν παρέδωκεν κύριος; the Lord had delivered it up before the Israelites.

20.1. The translator lived and did his work in the third century BCE Alexandria, and one might have expected some reflection of this later age in the translation, but there is remarkably little "updating." The designation of the

Transjordan area ἐν τῷ πέραν τοῦ Ἰορδάνου at 35:14 is hardly true to the context, since in both MT and Num ch.35 records a setting which is itself east of the Jordan. It is, however, rectified by being contrasted with ἐν γῇ Χανάαν. Not surprisingly, the three references at 19:14 to an אהל are changed to οἰκία. "Tents" as dwelling places would sound strange in the Jewish quarter of Alexandria, a translation pattern also evident in other volumes of the Pentateuch.

20.2. One instance in which the Alexandrian environment did dictate a particular rendering occurs in ch.25. An example of pagan practice resulting from contacts with the Madianites is given in vv.6—8. According to MT, an Israelite man brought את אחיו את המדינית אל, i.e. introduced his Midianite bride (?) to his family. Incidentally, Num changed this to τὸν ἀδελφὸν αὐτοῦ πρὸς τὴν Μαδιανῖτιν! This was done openly, i.e. "before Moses and all the assembly of the Israelites." Then comes the odd event: the priest Phinehas "stood up from the midst of the assembly, and took a spear in his hand, and he went in after the Israelite man into הקבה, and speared the two of them ... אל קבתה (through her belly)." The result of this action was the staying of the plague. The locative קבה is a hapax legomenon, though *qubba* is well-known in Arabic as the word for "dome," and the word is usually taken to mean a dome structure of some kind here as well. But what could that mean to an Alexandrian urban dweller in the time of the translator? The only domed structure with which he was familiar was the large ovens where pita bread was baked, and so it was εἰς τὴν κάμινον that Phinees did his precipitous deed.

21. From the above statement it should be obvious to the reader that the Greek Numbers may have its weaknesses, but it can hardly be dismissed as a compilation of various attempts at translation. It is a third century BCE product of an Alexandrian translator, not as well-versed in the intricacies of Greek grammar as one might wish, but who tried to interpret the canonical text of the Hebrew book into the language of his contemporaries. He did not slavishly render the Hebrew text into Greek equivalents as some later translators did, but tried to inform his fellow Jews what God had to say to them. That he was not always successful in his work as a translator is obvious. But the modern student of Numbers would be well-advised to study this earliest extant Jewish interpretation or commentary very carefully alongside the Masoretic text.

II. Character of this volume

This is now the fifth and last volume of Notes on a LXX book of the Pentateuch. What had been said of the earlier volumes concerning presuppositions underlying the Notes is equally appropriate for the Notes on the Greek Numbers; furthermore, I have simply taken the introductory remarks of my earlier volumes (more particularly of the Notes on Leviticus) and adapted them to this one.

22.0. The text commented on is not that of Rahlfs (Ra), but that of the Göttingen LXX.[6] The Ra text was not a critical text; it was a student edition, a *Handausgabe*, based mainly on the text of Codex B (Vaticanus) with its obvious errors corrected. A few readings from Codex A as well as occasional *O* (hexaplaric) readings and some *L* (Lucianic or pseudo-Lucianic) readings for certain books constitute a small apparatus. Rahlfs never intended this text to be anything more than an interim text, one that would eventually be replaced by the critical texts of the Göttingen Septuaginta.

It is the volumes of the Göttingen LXX that represent the state of the art; these are based on new collations of all the relevant texts available, including all the extant papyri remains as well as the texts of the sub-versions and of the quotations in the Church Fathers during the first five centuries of our era. What the Göttingen texts provide is as close an approximation to the original LXX as possible, limited only by the inadequacies of the editor.

It is this text which is analyzed. No attempt is made to review scholarly opinions, since it was thought to be much more appropriate to read the LXX text itself than to read about it. The text is far more important than what scholars say about it, and this is equally true of what the author of these Notes has to say.

The professional Greek scholar will probably find my Notes overly elementary and repetitive, but they are not primarily intended for the professional. I have written these Notes to help serious students of the Pentateuch who want to use the LXX text with some confidence, but who are themselves neither specialists in LXX studies nor in Hellenistic Greek. Such students might well need help in understanding the LXX text over against the Hebrew, and it is hoped that such students might find these Notes a useful guide.

---

6. Numeri, SEPTUAGINTA Vetus Testamentum Graecum Auctoritate Academiae Scientiarum Gottingensis edidit John William Wevers. III, 1. Göttingen, 1982.

22.1. The point of departure for these Notes is that of Num, i.e. of the Greek text of Numbers in the Göttingen Septuagint; see the preceding footnote. The problem faced by the translator was how to render the intent of the Hebrew parent text into a Greek form which his synagogal audience and readers would understand. To do this well presupposes an artist who fully understood both the limitations and the possibilities of the two linguistic codes involved, viz. Hebrew and Hellenistic Greek.[7] Stress is intentionally placed on how well the translator carried out his work, thus on how he constructed his Greek text, on how and whether he avoided transfering the characteristics of the source language to the target language. Accordingly the Notes concentrate throughout on the morphological, syntactic and semantic levels of language.

22.2. Since Num is by nature a translation text, a careful comparison at all levels between the presumed parent Hebrew and the resultant Greek texts is basic to the Notes. I have taken the parent text as the consonantal text of MT except where the evidence makes such a parent text unlikely. This consonantal text is an actual text, and throughout an attempt has been made to avoid speculative reconstructions as much as possible, even though at times these might be most attractive.

Other ancient texts which were compared throughout as well were the Samaritan Hebrew (Sam), the Onkelos Targum as representing the Babylonian tradition, and the Pseudo-Jonathan and Neophyti Targums as representing the Jerusalem form of the Targums. Also compared were published Qumran fragments as well as the Peshitta (Syriac) and the Vulgate (Latin) translations. These as a group constitute the ancient witnesses.

22.3. The Notes deal principally with the work of the translator, i.e. they are concerned with how the translator, the original LXX, interpreted the text; they have disregarded how later users of the LXX interpreted the text. To have reviewed how Josephus, Philo and the Church Fathers of the early centuries understood the LXX would simply have duplicated the fine work on Numbers by G.Dorival.[8] Needless to say I have consulted his work at every juncture, and

---

7. For a comparison of these two codes see my Notes on the Greek Text of Exodus, pp.vii—xiv, as well as my "The Use of Versions for Text Criticism: the Septuagint" in La Septuaginta en la Investigacion Contemporanea (V Congreso de la IOSCS), editado por Natalio Fernández Marcos (Madrid, 1894), pp.15—24.
8. Les Nombres: Traduction du texte grec de la Septante, Introduction et Notes par G.Dorival. La Bible d'Alexandrie. 4. Paris, 1994.

have profited immeasurably from this careful piece of work, but my point of departure is quite different from his volume, and the two works are to a great extent in complementary distribution. Dorival has also given a full translation of Deut, whereas I have not done so. I have limited translations to difficult passages, wherever such might facilitate one's understanding of how the translator understood the Hebrew text.[9]

22.4. I have used the term "tradition" throughout to represent the development of the original LXX text, the autographon, from its original form as reconstructed for the critical text up to its form (or forms) in the fifteenth century, when the invention of movable type made possible the production of multiple identical copies of a text, thereby revolutionizing textual development. That tradition in its multiple forms is summarized in the first apparatus of the Göttingen edition(s).

22.4.1. But those for whom the LXX was sacred scripture did not have the original text as it left the hands of the translator, nor did they have the Göttingen text as its approximation. The countless users of the LXX throughout the centuries only had copies, in fact, copies of copies. Such readers had manuscripts which represented later forms of the LXX text. These manuscripts are all eclectic in nature, i.e. they are based on a complicated and often untraceable textual genealogy.

22.4.2. I have not recorded all the evidence for such variant readings in painstaking detail, but rather made generalizations concerning patterns of support, which are explained under 22.4.4—7 below.[10] The interested reader will find details of support in the first apparatus of the Göttingen edition. I have also simplified the evidence and largely disregarded scattered support by concentrating on support by textual families. I have used "textual families" in a quantitative sense, i.e. support by at least half of the members of a textual family as given in 22.4.3. below.

The first apparatus of the Göttingen editions constitutes a digest of this textual history of the LXX. That text underwent a most complicated history of

---

9. The IOSCS is actively engaged in planning and preparing a translation of the Greek O.T. into English.
10. I have explained some of these larger generalizations in my "The Göttingen Pentateuch: Some Post-partem Reflections," in VII Congress of the International Organization for Septuagint and Cognate Studies, edited by Claude Cox (Atlanta, 1991), pp.51—60.

revisions, which is reflected in the texts of the text families. The first apparatus is actually a summary of a living and developing text. What the synagogue, and later the church, used was that living and developing tradition. When the ancient writers quoted and commented on the scriptures, these scriptures were part of that living tradition.

22.4.3. The following table details these families with their members; the numbers follow those of the Rahlfs catalogue.[11]

O = G-58-376-426 Syh
oI = 15-64-381-618
oII = 29-72-82-707
O' = $O + oI$; $O^{\prime}$ = $O + oII$; $O^{\prime\prime}$ = $O + oI + oII$; $oI^{\prime}$ = $oI + oII$

C = 16-77-131-500-529-616-739
cI = 57-73-320-413-528-550-552-761
cII = 46-52-313-414-417-422-551-615
C' = $C + cI$; $C^{\prime}$ = $C + cII$; $C^{\prime\prime}$ = $C + cI + cII$; $cI^{\prime}$ = $cI + cII$

b = 19-108-118-314-537

d = 44-106-107-125-610

f = 53-56-129-246-664

n = 54-75-127-458-767

s = 28-30-85-130-321-343-344-346-730

t = 74-76-84-134-370

x = 71-509-527-619

---

11. A. Rahlfs, Verzeichnis der griechishen Handschriften des Alten Testaments, für das Septuaginta-Unternehmen aufgestellt. MSU 2. Berlin, 1915. The Unternehmen has been keeping the Verzeichnis up-to-date, and Detlef Fraenkel has been assigned the task of preparing a revised edition by the Committee directing the affairs of the Unternehmen.

y = 121-318-392

z = 18-68-120-122-126-128-407-628-630-669

Uncials: A B F K M S V

Papyri: 803 833 933 963

Unclassified Codices = 55 59 319 416 424 624 646 799

Versions = Arab(ic), Arm(enian), Eth(iopic), Co(ptic) which includes Bo(hairic) and Sa(hidic), La (= Vetus Latina), Pal(estinian-syriac), and Syh (= Syrohexaplar)

22.4.4. A variant may be identified as a one, two or three family variant. Thus a *b x z* reading means that the reading is supported by all or a majority of the manuscripts of the *b x* and *z* families; it may also have scattered support from other manuscripts or from the versions, but that is disregarded. When such readings are identified as e.g. a *b* reading, what is meant is that the reading has been judged to be a *b* family reading. But should more than three families support a reading it is simply called a *popular* reading, whereas if the support includes over half of all witnesses, i.e. of manuscripts and versions, it is designated a *majority* reading.

22.4.5. Since the uncial texts, A B F K M S V, and the papyri, constitute on the whole the oldest Greek manuscript witnesses I have often listed them as well, e.g. A F *b f s*. Except for the later F^a and F^b readings, uncial support is only listed if it is unclouded; thus "corrector" readings of uncial manuscripts are usually disregarded.

Occasionally, the + sign is used to signal manuscript support; it is to be understood as meaning "along with scattered support." Thus the designation F+ means that a reading is found in codex F as well as in scattered manuscript(s) not identifiable as constituting a textual family or families.

22.4.6. From the table in 22.4.3. it appears that a large number of manuscripts constitute the Catena text. The edition has subdivided these witnesses into a main group, *C*, and two subordinate groups, *cI* and *cII*. Since most readers will probably not be interested in Catena criticism these have usually all been subsumed under the siglum *C* throughout the Notes.

22.4.7. Frequent reference is also made to a Byzantine text. The term applies to the family readings which characterize the text of the Byzantine lectionaries in the Pentateuch.[12] A Byzantine textual reading means a reading supported by all or at least two of *d n t*.

23.0. Certain information has been almost routinely relegated to footnotes, not because it is unimportant, but rather because it is not central to the Notes.

23.1. The Notes do not detail reasons for choosing the readings of Num in favor of variant readings, except where I now consider the Num reading as secondary. Such arguments concerning the originality of the text are fully discussed in my THGN Chapter 6 (The Critical Text [Num]),[13] and such matters are all referred to in footnotes where the relevant page of THGN is given. The user who is not interested in such matters can simply disregard these references.

23.2. Materials gleaned from the second apparatus of the Göttingen edition are also routinely placed in footnotes. Readings from The Three, Aq, Sym and Theod, are given, usually without comment. In the edition these materials are presented precisely as the manuscripts have the reading, even when they are clearly faultily transmitted. I have seen fit to make judgments on these readings, and to make corrections in the footnotes in order to help the reader to understand them.

The relegation of readings to the footnotes does not constitute a judgment on the value of their evidence; it is solely due to the fact that the Notes deal with the LXX text, whereas the readings of the second apparatus are in essence extra-Septuagintal materials, usually gleaned from the margins of LXX texts, the Church Fathers, of Arm, or of Syh. Such readings have in the long course of LXX tradition history often influenced that tradition, sometimes actively invading it, especially through Origen's hexapla. But their origins are rooted in the Hebrew rather than the LXX tradition, and their interests were revisional. They are thus of importance in understanding the text history rather than the text of LXX, and so should be carefully distinguished from LXX itself.

---

12. See Chapter 11, "The Lectionary Texts" in the author's Text History of the Greek Genesis, MSU XI (Göttingen, 1974), 176—185.
13. Text History of the Greek Numbers, MSU XVI (Göttingen, 1982), 94—135.

24. It should be emphasized that the Notes are not simply another commentary in the usual sense of the term. Rather they examine in detail how the Greek translator interpreted his parent Hebrew text. In other words, Num is essentially an exegetical document, and this exegesis can only be grasped by a close attention to the linguistic mode which Num exploits. In fact, the LXX text is the first document we have in the long history of the exegesis of the Hebrew Bible. What one must look for in particular are fine points of clarification made where the Hebrew is not fully clear, or matters where the Greek text appears to deviate from the apparent meaning of the source text. Whenever Num strays from the obvious intent of the Hebrew, it has been noted, and I have often suggested a possible reason for such deviation.

One should not automatically presuppose a different parent text when differences between the Greek and the Hebrew obtain; rather one should first seek for and pursue other explanations. It is only through such details that a picture of the attitudes, the theological prejudices, as well as of the cultural environment of these Jewish translators can emerge. It is in the confidence that readers will learn to discover something about what these Alexandrian translators thought their Hebrew Torah meant, or ought to mean, that these Notes are presented.

25. As in the case of the earlier volumes no bibliography (except for the Sigla which follows this introductory statement) is included in this volume. It was never the author's intention to present a picture of the state of the art, but rather to provide the serious student some help in his/her comparison of MT and LXX. For readers who must have a detailed bibliography the work of Cécile Dogniez and the earlier Brock, Fritsch, Jellicoe Bibliography may be consulted.[14]

The sigla table which follows contains references to works which I found especially useful in preparing the Notes. Occasional studies not given in the Sigla, but referred to in the Notes are given with full bibliographical details in the footnotes.

26. The reader will note that, as in the case of my Genesis, Leviticus and Deuteronomy Notes, an Appendix A has been added listing suggested changes in the critical text of the Göttingen volume. I trust that the list will not be taken as

---

14. Bibliography of the Septuagint: Bibliographie de la Septante (1970—1993) par Cécile Dogniez, Avec une préface de Pierre-Maurice Bogaert. Leiden, 1995; A Classified Bibliography of the Septuagint, compiled by S.P.Brock, C.T. Fritsch and S.Jellicoe. Leiden, 1973.

evidence that the editor could not make up his mind, but rather as illustrating that the establishment of a critical text is not a case of *ipse dixi*, but a never-ending application of one's critical faculties to the task. Reworking the text from a new point of view has given new insights, and the Appendix simply demonstrates the undeniable fallibility of the editor.

27. It would be remiss of me were I not to acknowledge gratefully the debt I owe to my colleagues in the Department of which I have long been a member, who have sustained me with their friendship and support for more than forty years, and in whose midst I have continued to work in spite of official retirement from the University. I trust that they will not take it amiss if I single out Albert Pietersma whose extensive and detailed knowledge of Hellenistic Greek matters were always readily available to me.

I must also add that I am most grateful to Bernard Taylor, the editor of IOSCS, who once again generously offered to proofread my finished manuscript, and thereby saved me from many embarrassing errors. This is the third time that he has proofread a volume of mine, and I owe him an incalculable debt of gratitude. He is, however, in no way responsible for what I have written; for that I assume full and sole responsibility.

28.0. As in the case of the parallel volumes on Genesis, Exodus, Leviticus and Deuteronomy, which appeared in this series, the author prepared camera ready copy. The software used was Nota Bene 4.5 plus Lingua, and was printed on an HP Laser Jet IV. I owe Paul J. Bodin of Berkeley, CA, formerly of Union Theol. Seminary, NYC, a particular debt of gratitude for his help in overcoming difficulties with the software used; his expertise was freely shared, and I appreciate his friendship and advice at those times when I felt rather desperately in need of it.

Sigla

- AASF = Annales Academiae Scientiarum Fennicae
- AB = Targum Neofiti 1:Numbers, translated with Apparatus and Notes by M. McNamara, and Targum Pseudo-Jonathan: Numbers, translated, with notes by E.G. Clarke. The Aramaic Bible, Volume 4. Collegeville, MN, 1995
- Aejmelaeus = Aejmelaeus, A., Parataxis in the Septuagint: A Study of the Renderings of the Hebrew Coordinate Clauses in the Greek Pentateuch. AASF: Dissertationes Humanarum Litterarum 31. Helsinki, 1982.
- Aq = Aquila
- Aristeas = Aristeas to Philocrates (Letter of Aristeas), edited and translated by M. Hadas. New York, 1973
- Bauer = Arndt, W.P. and Gingrich, F.W., A Greek-English Lexicon of the New Testament and Other Early Christian Literature, transl. and adapt. from W. Bauer, Griechisch-Deutsches Wörterbuch zu den Schriften des Neuen Testaments und der übrigen urchristlichen Literatur, 4te Aufl., 1952. Chicago, 1957; 2nd ed. revised and augmented by F.W.Gingrich and F.W.Danker from the 5te Aufl.
- BDB = Brown, F., Driver, S.R. and Briggs, C.A., A Hebrew and English Lexicon of the Old Testament, with an Appendix containing the Biblical Aramaic. Boston and New York, 1907
- BHS = Biblia Hebraica Stuttgartensia, ed. K.Elliger et W.Rudolph. Stuttgart, 1977; Fasciculus 3: Numeri praeparavit W.Rudolph, 1972
- Bl-Debr = Blass, F., Debrunner, A. u. Rehkopf, Fr., Grammatik des neutestamentlichen Griechisch, 14te völlig neubearb. Aufl. Göttingen, 1975
- Boisacq = Boisacq, E., Dictionaire étymologique de la langue Grecque. Paris, 1938
- Cox, Hex = Cox, Claude E., Hexaplaric Materials Preserved in the Armenian Version, SCS 21, Atlanta, 1986
- idem, VI Congress = Cox, Claude, ed., VI Congress of the International Organization for Septuagint and Cognate Studies: Jerusalem 1986, SBL: Septuagint and Cognate Studies Series 23, Atlanta, 1986
- idem, VII Congress = Cox, Claude, ed., VII Congress of the International Organization for Septuagint and Cognate Studies: Leuven 1989, SBL: Septuagint and Cognate Studies Series 31, Atlanta, 1991
- Crönert = Crönert, W., Memoria Graeca Herculanensis, Lipsiae, 1903

- Dalman = Dalman, G., Aramäisch-neuhebräisches Handwörterbuch zur Targum, Talmud und Midrasch. 3te Aufl. Göttingen, 1938.
- Daniel = Daniel, S., Recherches sur le vocabulaire de culte dans le Septante. Études et Commentaires 61. Paris, 1966
- De Septuuginta = Pietersma A. and Cox, C., edd., De Septuaginta: Studies in honour of John William Wevers on his sixty-fifth birthday. Mississauga, Ont, 1984
- Deut = The text in Deuteronomium, SEPTUAGINTA, Vetus Testamentum Graecum Auctoritate Academiae Scientiarum Gottingensis editit John William Wevers. III,2. Göttingen, 1977
- DJD XII = Discoveries in the Judean Desert XII; Qumran Cave 4 VII: Genesis to Numbers by E.Ulrich and F.M.Cross, + J.R.Davila, N.Jastram, J.E.Sanderson, E.Tov and J.Strugnell. Oxford, 1994
- Dogniéz-Harl = Dogniéz, C. et Harl, M., Le Deutéronome: Traduction du texte grec de la Septante, Introduction et Notes. La Bible d'Alexandrie 5. Paris, 1992
- Dorival = Dorival, G., Les Nombres: Traduction du texte grec de la Septante, Introduction et Notes. La Bible d'Alexandrie 4. Paris, 1994
- Dos Santos = Elmar Camilo Dos Santos, An Expanded Hebrew Index for the Hatch-Redpath Concordance to the Septuagint, Jerusalem, n.d.
- Exod = The text in Exodus, SEPTUAGINTA Vetus Testamentum Graecum Auctoritate Academiae Scientiarum Gottingensis editit John William Wevers. II.1. Göttingen, 1991
- Field = Field, Fr., Origenis Hexaplorum quae supersunt. Oxonii, 1867-1875
- Gen = The text in Genesis, SEPTUAGINTA Vetus Testamentum Graecum Auctoritate Academiae Scientiarum Gottingensis editit John William Wevers. I. Göttingen, 1974
- Greenspoon-Munnich = Greenspoon, L. and Munnich, O., edd., VIII Congress of the International Organization for Septuagint and Cognate Studies: Paris 1992, SBL: Septuagint and Cognate Studies Series 41, Atlanta, 1995
- GK = Gesenius' Hebrew Grammar as edited and enlarged by the late E.Kautzsch. Second English edition revised by A.E.Cowley. Oxford, 1910
- Hesych = Hesychii Alexandrini Lexicon recensuit et emendavit Kurt Latte. Hauniae, 1953, 1966
- Helbing = Helbing, R., Die Kasussyntax der Verba bei den Septuaginta. Göttingen, 1928

- Helbing, Gramm. = Helbing, R., Grammatik der LXX: Laut- und Wortlehre. Göttingen, 1907
- Holladay = Fragments from Hellenistic Jewish Authors. Vol.I: Historians by C.R.Holladay. Texts and Translations no.20. Pseudepigrapha no.10. Chico, CA, 1983
- HR = Hatch, E. & Redpath, H.A., A Concordance to the Septuagint and the other Greek Versions of the O.T. I-II, Suppl. Oxford, 1897-1906
- IOSCS = International Organization for Septuagint and Cognate Studies
- Jastrow = Jastrow, M., Dictionary of the Targumin, the Talmud Babli and Yerushalmi, and the Midrashic Literature. Two volumes. 1943 (reprint)
- Johannessohn, Gebrauch = Johannessohn, M., Der Gebrauch der Präpositionen in der Septuaginta. MSU 3,3. Berlin, 1926
- Josephus = The Jewish Antiquities by Flavius Josephus. Books I-XX. Loeb Classics.
- KB = Koehler, L. and Baumgartner, W., Lexicon in Veteris Testamenti Libros. Leiden, 1953.
- Lampe = Lampe, G.W.H., A Patristic Greek Lexicon, Oxford, 1961
- Later Revisers = οἱ λοιποί or οἱ λ´
- Lee = Lee, J.A.L., A Lexical Study of the Septuagint Version of the Pentateuch. Chico, 1983
- Lev = The text in Leviticus, SEPTUAGINTA Vetus Testamentum Graecum Auctoritate Academiae Scientiarum Gottingensis edidit John William Wevers. II, 2. Göttingen, 1986.
- Levine = Levine, B.A., Numbers 1—20: A translation with Introduction and Commentary. Anchor Bible 4A. New York, 1993
- LS = Liddell, H.G., Scott, R., & Jones, H.S., A Greek-English Lexicon, 9th ed., Oxford, 1940
- Mayser = Mayser, E., Grammatik der griechischen Papyri aus der Ptolemäerzeit. I., Leipzig, 1906. II 1, Berlin, 1926. II 2, 1933/34. II 3, 1934. 2te Aufl. I 1, 1970. I 2, 1938. I 3, 1936
- Milgrom = The JPS Torah Commentary/ Numbers. Commentary by Jacob Milgrom. Philadelphia-New York, 1990
- MSU = Mitteilungen des Septuaginta-Unternehmens
- MT = Masoretic Text as found in BHS
- NIV = New International Version

- NJPS = TANAKH The Holy Scriptures; The New JPS Translation According to the Traditional Hebrew Text
- NRSV = New Revised Standard Version
- Note at Dt = Wevers, J.W., Notes on the Greek Text of Deuteronomy. Atlanta, 1995
- Note at Exod = idem, Notes on the Greek Text of Exodus. Atlanta, 1990
- Note at Gen = idem, Notes on the Greek Text of Genesis. Atlanta, 1993
- Note at Lev = idem, Notes on the Greek Text of Leviticus, Atlanta, 1997
- Num = The text in Numeri, SEPTUAGINTA Vetus Testamentum Graecum Auctoritate Academiae Scientiarum Gottingensis edidit John William Wevers. III.1. Göttingen, 1982
- Pesh = Peshiṭta. The O.T. in Syriac according to the Peshiṭta Version. Part I, fasc 2. Numbers by A.P.Hayman. Leiden, 1991
- Porter = Porter, S.E. Verbal Aspect in the Greek of the New Testament with Reference to Tense and Mood. Studies in Biblial Greek, Vol.I. New York, 1989
- Prijs = Prijs, L., Jüdische Tradition in der Septuaginta. Leiden, 1948
- Ra = Rahlfs, A., Septuaginta, Stuttgart,1935
- Reider-Turner = An Index to Aquila by the late J.Reider, completed and revised by N.Turner. Supplements to VT, Vol.XII, Leiden, 1966
- Sam = Samaritan Pentateuch. Der hebräische Pentateuch der Samaritaner, herausg. von A. von Gall. Giessen, 1918
- SBL = Society of Biblical Literature
- Schl = Schleuser, J.F., Novus Thesaurus philologico-criticus, sive Lexicon in LXX et reliquos interpretes Graecos ac Scriptores Apocryphos V.T. Lipsiae, 1820-1821
- Schwyzer = Schwyzer, E., Griechische Grammatik auf der Grundlage von Karl Brugmanns griechischer Grammatik. Handbuch der Altertumswissenschaft. II.1.Band I:3.Auflage, und Band II:2.Auflage. München, 1959
- SCS = SBL: Septuagint and Cognate Studies Series (Scholars Press)
- Sollamo = Sollamo, R., Renderings of Hebrew Semiprepositions in the Septuagint, AASF: Dissertationes Humanarum Litterarum 19. Helsinki, 1979
- Sollamo, Rep = Sollamo, R., Repetition of the Possessive pronouns in the Septuagint, SCS 40. Atlanta, 1995
- SS = Soisalon-Soininen, I., Studien zur Septuaginta-Syntax, AASF 237. Helsinki, 1987

- SS Inf = idem, Die Infinitive in der Septuaginta. AASF 132, 1. Helsinki, 1965
- Studien = Studien zur Septuaginta — Robert Hanhart zu Ehren Aus Anlass seines 65. Geburtstages. MSU XX. Göttingen, 1990.
- Suidas = (Suda). Suidae Lexicon, Graece & Latine ... Aemilii Porti. Cantabrigiae, 1705
- Suppl.V.T. = Supplements to Vetus Testamentum
- Syh = The Syrohexaplar
- Sym = Symmachus
- Targ = The Targums Pseudo-Jonathan, Neophiti, and Onkelos
- Tar^J = Targum Pseudo-Jonathan of the Pentateuch: Text and Concordance. E.G.Clarke. Hoboken, NJ, 1984
- Tar^O = Targum Onkelos. Sperber, A., The Bible in Aramaic based on Old Manuscripts and Printed Texts. Vol. I. The Pentateuch according to Targum Onkelos. Leiden, 1959
- Tar^P = The Palestinian Targum. A. Díez Macho, Levítico, NEOPHYTI 1: Targum Palestinense ms de la Biblioteca Vaticana. Tomo III. Madrid, 1971
- Taylor, IX Congress = Taylor, B.A. ed., IX Congress of the International Organization for Septuagint and Cognate Studies: Cambridge, 1995. Altanta, 1997
- Thack = Thackeray, H.St.J., A Grammar of the Old Testament in Greek according to the Septuagint: I. Introduction, Orthography and Accidence. Cambridge, 1909
- The Others = οἱ λοιποί or οἱ λ´
- The Three = οἱ γ´
- Theod = Theodotion
- THGD = Wevers, J.W. Text History of the Greek Deuteronomy, MSU 13, Göttingen, 1978
- THGE = idem, Text History of the Greek Exodus, MSU 21, Göttingen, 1992
- THGG = idem, Text History of the Greek Genesis, MSU 11. Göttingen, 1974
- THGL = idem, Text History of the Greek Leviticus, MSU 19. Göttingen, 1986
- THGN = idem, Text History of the Greek Numbers, MSU 16. Göttingen, 1982
- Tov = Tov, E., The Text-Critical Use of the Septuagint in Biblical Research, Jerusalem Biblical Studies 3. Jerusalem, 1981
- Ulrich = Ulrich, E.C., The Septuagint Manuscripts from Qumran: a Reappraisal of Their Value, SCS 33 (Atlanta, 1992), 49—80

- VT = Vetus Testamentum
- Vulg = The Vulgate. Biblia Sacra: Vulgatae Editionis Sixti V Pont. Max. iussu recognita et Clementis VIII auctoritate edita. Romae, 1965
- Walters = Walters, P., The Text of the Septuagint, edited by D.W.Gooding. Cambridge, 1973
- ZürB = Die Zürcher Bibel

NOTES

Heading In the Hebrew the title of the book is the first word: וידבר, but for Num it is Ἀριθμοί, which is occasionally amplified in various ways in some texts, such as by "book four," or "of the Israelites," and even as "ἀριθμοί of the Israelites; a composition of the God-inspired Moses; the fourth book." Most witnesses, however, simply have Ἀριθμοί.

1:1 The location where the Lord spoke to Moses is given as "in the Sina desert," which translates במדבר סיני. One would not expect the proper name to be preceded by an article, though a genitive article, του σινα, as at 9:5 in the majority tradition, would be in order; but the translator took the name adjectivally, i.e. as τῇ ἐρήμῳ τῇ Σινά. Usually the proper noun in the structure "the desert of ..." is not articulated, but Codd A and B as well as most cursive mss attest to the dative article.[1] Since MT does not articulate the name, hex placed the second τῇ under the obelus to indicate that fact. For the regular rendering of מועד in the collocation "tent of testimony" by τοῦ μαρτυρίου, i.e. as though מועד were related to עדות "testimony," see Note at Exod 27:21. The rendering ἡ σκηνὴ τοῦ μαρτυρίου has simply been taken over by later translators from Exod.

The timer is given as "ἐν μιᾷ of the second month[2] of the second year of their going out from the land of Egypt." It is obvious that this verse was not originally separate from the last chapter of Lev, not only from the initial conjunction which coordinates 1:1 with a preceding clause, but also from the fact that αὐτῶν has no referent within the verse, and it must refer to "the Israelites" with which the book of Leviticus ends.

The genitive ἔτους δευτέρου renders the prepositional phrase בשנה השנית, which is more literally reflected in the V 319 recensional variant εν τω ετει τω δευτερω. The use of the genitive is unique for Num for "year," but it is excellent Greek.[3]

1:2 The order שאו את ראש "lift up the head of" is unusual in the context, and the word ראש is usually understood here in the sense of "sum, total," thus

---

1. See THGN 103.
2. Which Tar^J identifies as האייר.
3. See SS 112.

"undertake the census."[4] LXX, however, rendered ראש by ἀρχήν "beginning, origin," i.e. "λάβετε τὴν ἀρχήν of the assembly of Israelites." This is an isolate type of rendering. See also 26:2. At 4:22 the same collocation (though with a singular verb) obtains; it reads λάβε τὴν ἀρχήν; at 4:2, however, the structure is rendered by λάβε τὸ κεφάλαιον, which can be understood as "sum, total."[5] I might suggest some such rendering as "take a head count."[6] τὸ κεφάλαιον also occurs as translation for ראש at 31:26,49. The context here demands that ἀρχήν be understood in a similar fashion. In v.3 the verb ἐπισκέψασθε explicates what λάβετε τὴν ἀρχήν must mean; it can only mean "take up a census," i.e. make a summary count of (...). Actually, ראש is rendered by κεφάλαιον only five times, whereas ἀρχή occurs 61 times (and κεφαλή 299 times!).[7]

The rationale for the plural imperative addressed to Moses becomes clear from v.3 which explains: σὺ καὶ Ἀαρὼν ἐπισκέψασθε αὐτούς.

The norms to be employed for the review are given in four κατά phrases: κατὰ συγγενείας αὐτῶν, κατὰ οἴκους πατριῶν αὐτῶν, κατὰ ἀριθμὸν ἐξ ὀνόματος αὐτῶν, κατὰ κεφαλὴν αὐτῶν.[8]

The first of these is fairly clear; it represents MT's למשפחתם "according to their clans." The word συγγενείας means "kinship," and is regularly used to render משחחה after this chapter. In this chapter it occurs normally for תולדת; cf comment at v.20, where משפחת is translated by δήμους.

The second phrase is also a tribal designation of some kind: "according to their paternal households." In MT the bound noun is singular: לבית אבתם, but either number is sensible. The last two prepositional phrases are both ב phrases in MT, but LXX continues with κατά. MT reads the third one as במספר שמות "according to the number of names." This is no clearer than its translation κατὰ ἀριθμὸν ἐξ ὀνόματος αὐτῶν. Hex has rightly placed the αὐτῶν under the obelus, it having no equivalent in MT. Nor does the preposi-

---

4. This understanding is already in Schl, who translates: "sumite *numerum*, seu *summam*, totius populi Israelis." Similarly, he renders Ps 118:160 ἀρχὴ τῶν λόγων σου ἀλήθεια by "*summa* verborum tuorum veritas."
5. See LS sub κεφάλαιος II.5.b.
6. This is how Tar take it with חשבן "reckoning," hence "count, census."
7. According to the count in Dos Santos.
8. For κατά plus the accusative to express norm, see Johannessohn, Gebrauch 255ff., especially 256–257.

tion ἐξ have a Hebrew counterpart; presumably the translator felt the need to clarify the relation of ἀριθμόν and ὀνόματος, though precisely how he understood this is not clear. Could he possibly have thought in terms of a count by their name? A census list? Incidentally, cod B (along with Byz+ support) has omitted the first three cases of αὐτῶν. This was clearly thought to be a stylistic improvement by which the final αὐτῶν was sufficient for all four κατά phrases.⁹

The last phrase reads κατὰ κεφαλὴν αὐτῶν; just what "according to their head" means is not clear to me. Here "head" renders גלגלת "skulls, crania," which is naturally taken as synecdochic for "heads," which then could be understood as "head by head." It might then be taken as "by their head (count)."

The Greek has also attempted some clarification by a change in word order. In the Hebrew כל זכר "every male" intervened between the third and fourth phrases, and hex has "corrected" this by reordering πᾶς ἄρσην after the fourth phrase. It does fit much better at the beginning of v.3, where Num has it.

1:3 Those who are to be reviewed are males of twenty years of age and over; this is further defined as those eligible for military service, i.e. "every one going out in (or with) the army of Israel." The term δύναμις "power, force" is regularly used to render צבא; after all, Israel's power lay in its army, and translators used δύναμις consistently in the concrete sense of "army, armed force." The Hebrew reads "army in Israel," i.e. בישראל, but Num has no preposition and presumably has "of Israel," in view of the fact that Ἰσραήλ is not articulated.

The rendering of תפקדו by ἐπισκέψασθε should occasion no surprise. The root is rendered in this way 115 times in LXX, with the next most frequent rendering, ἐκδικέω, obtaining only 20 times.¹⁰ I would render it by "review, pass under review." What is clearly meant is to undertake a census count. Unlike Lev the prefix inflection תפקדו is rendered by the aorist imperative, not by the default future tense. These potential recruits are to be reviewed σὺν δυνάμει αὐτῶν "with their host, army."

---

9. See THGN 97.
10. According to Dos Santos.

The final structure identifies those addressed as σὺ καὶ 'Ααρών, to which is added a second ἐπισκέψασθε αὐτούς; this has no counterpart in MT, and hex has placed it under the obelus. This verb is interpreted by a gloss on the margin of two s mss: αριθμησεις "you (singular) must count."

1:4 The verse identifies the assistants to Moses and Aaron for the review or census of Israel's men of military age. Identification as assistants is stated as μεθ' ἔσονται "they shall be with you." LXX divides the text differently from MT, which ends the first clause with למטה, i.e. "each one (איש איש) shall be for a tribe"; what is meant is that each one will represent a tribe.

This is then clarified further in v.b with a nominal clause: "each one is a chieftain (ראש)" on the census committee. The Greek divides by modifying φυλήν by ἑκάστου ἀρχόντων, thus "each according to the tribe of each of the rulers (shall be with you)." The b part then reads: "they shall be according to paternal households," which must refer to ἀρχόντων, i.e. the rulers must be chosen according to paternal households. The Byz text has changed ἀρχόντων to the nominative singular αρχων, which would then mean "each according to the tribe of each one, a ruler." This is probably rooted in a scribal error, based on aural confusion, i.e. /χonton/ becoming /χon/, since *omicron* and *omega* were homophones in Byzantine and Hellenistic Greek. This is not particularly sensible, since ἔσονται 2° is not also changed to εσται.

Of greater interest is the occurrence of איש איש as well as a single איש in the verse. The translator makes no distinction between the two, rendering them by ἕκαστος/ἑκάστου resp. The distributive doubling of איש occurs only five times in the book. At 4:19 it is similarly rendered by a single ἕκαστον. But elsewhere the word is somehow repeated as ἄνδρα κατὰ ἄνδρα (4:49), as ἄνδρος ἄνδρος at 5:12, and as ἄνθρωπος ἄνθρωπος at 9:10.[11] Obviously the translator had no pattern in mind for translating איש איש. Hex added εκαστος so as represent the second איש.[12]

1:5 Vv.5—15 identify these assistants by name, parentage and tribe. These names all recur in chh.2,7 and 10. In each case the tribal name is governed by

---

11. See THGN 114.
12. Theod translated by ἀνὴρ ἀνήρ, whereas Sym attests to ἔστωσαν (for יהיו) ἕκαστοι.

the preposition ל, thus in v.5 לראובן "for Reuben." The translator rendered the preposition in each case by the genitive plural article τῶν, presumably in apposition with ἀνδρῶν in the opening "and these are the names ἀνδρῶν." So what is meant is "of the men of X." I would translate the structure as "of those of X." It should be noted that Byz throughout this section has "corrected" τῶν to τω, thereby representing the Hebrew preposition more accurately. This is undoubtedly a recensional correction. The ἀνδρῶν is then described by a relative clause: οἵτινες παραστήσονται μεθ' ὑμῶν. The compound is well-chosen: "shall stand alongside," representing יעמדו of MT.[13] For the odd transcription of 'Ρουβήν in the versions (and Josephus) see the Note at Gen 29:32.

Rouben's chieftain was Ἐλισοὺρ υἱὸς Σεδιούρ, an adequate Greek equivalent for MT's אליצור בן שדיאור.[14] In the tradition, Elisur becomes εδισουρ in two mss, a reading due to confusion of Λ and Δ. The C tradition has an odd reading ελκουρ. This is palaeographically explicable as a misreading of an uncial text, where the consecution ΙΣ (in early uncial texts the Σ looked like C) was misread as K, i.e. IC as a ligature. The father's name, Σεδιούρ, is also quite stable. The transcription εδιουρ is the result of haplography, since the name is preceded by υἱός, and the b+ ελιουρ is a further development confusing Λ and Δ.

1:6 For "those of Simeon" the chieftain was Σαλαμιὴλ υἱὸς Σουρισαδαί for the Hebrew שלמיאל בן צורישדי. Neither name was well-known, and scribes had some difficulty with the -μιηλ ending of the first name, both -μεηλ and -μαηλ occurring, presumably by dissimulation. The Λ-Δ confusion resulted in *f* mss ending the name with *daleth*, and syncopation produced both σαμιηλ and σαμαηλ. Σουρισαδαί became -σαδδαι or -σαδδε by dittography. The final syllable appeared as -δα, δαμ, -δεμ as well as -μαι or -λαι. Particularly unusual is the reading of one ms as του ρισαβαι, created not only by aphaeresis, but also showing a rare misreading of *delta* as *beta*; furthermore, its articulation is also unique, i.e. Σου- became του.

1:7 For "those of Iouda" the chieftain was Ναασσὼν υἱὸς Ἀμιναδάβ for MT's נחשון בן עמינדב. The doubling of *sigma* is unexpected, and a few wit-

---
13. The Others read the simplex στήσονται.
14. Tar^J introduces each of the twelve chieftains as אמרכול "officer, leader."

nesses do read ναασων. The second *alpha* is an attempt to show the *heth* ending a closed syllable. For this name haplography has created νασσων in a number of mss. The C text has by dissimulation changed -σσ- to -κσ- to read ναακσων. For 'Αμιναδάβ confusion between nasals in cursive script has led to αμιναδαμ. Transposition of consonants resulted in αμιναβαδ in one ms.

1:8 For "those of Issachar" the chieftain was Ναθαναὴλ υἱὸς Σωγάρ for MT's נתנאל בן צוער. For the name 'Ισσαχάρ for יששכר see Note at Gen 30:18. Ναθαναήλ gave little trouble. Parablepsis from one *alpha* to another resulted in ναθαηλ. An inserted *theta* created ναθαθναηλ. Quite unexpected is the reading σαλαμιηλ, which is imported from v.6. Σωγάρ for צוער preserves the early pronounciation of the grapheme ע as a *ghain*; comp the Arabic root ṣġr and the adjective ṣaġir "small, insignificant." By vocalic attraction both σωγωρ and σαγαρ occur as well. Note also σωγχαρ.

1:9 For those of Zaboulon the chieftain was 'Ελιάβ υἱὸς Χαιλών for the Hebrew אליאב בן חלן. The name 'Ελιάβ is quite stable in the tradition; variants obtain only for the final consonant, producing ελιαμ, ελιαθ, ελιαδ and ελιαβδ. His father's name was less stable at the hands of copyists. The C text prefixed the name with an *alpha*, creating αχαιλων, αχελων and αχελλων. The *f* group changed the nasal to form χελωμ, and Λ-Δ confusion created χαιδων.

The remainder of the verse, which is part of v.10 in MT, introduces the first of τῶν υἱῶν 'Ιωσήφ, viz., "for those of Ephraim." Their chieftain was 'Ελισαμὰ υἱὸς 'Εμιούδ for the Hebrew אלישמע בן עמיהוד. The parent text of the C mss misread the -ισ- as -κ-, thus ελκαμα; cf comment on 'Ελισούρ at v.5 above. For 'Εμιούδ the initial vowel became *alpha* in αμιουδ (see also σαμιουδ), and by dittography of the *sigma* of υἱός a popular misspelling occurred as σεμιουδ. Λ-Δ confusion led to εμιουλ, which by a further confusion (i.e. a transposition of consonants) led to ελιουδ.

1:10 For "those of Manasse" the chieftain was Γαμαλιὴλ υἱὸς Φαδασούρ for the Hebrew גמליאל בן פדהצור. Note that Ephraim, the younger son of Joseph, here precedes the elder, for which see Gen 48:17—20. Manasse first occurred at Gen 41:51 where the tradition also created both μαννασση and μανασση; see

Note ad loc. Γαμαλιήλ was misspelled as γαμαιηλ, γαμιηλ, γαμαηλ and γαλαηλ, all by syncopation, the last-named also by vowel change (-αηλ for -ιηλ). His father's name received rough treatment in the tradition; the following list of spellings testify to the strangeness of the name to Greek scribes: φαιδασσουρ, φαδδασουρ, φαλασσουρ, φιδδασουρ, φαλδασσουρ, φωδασουρ, σφαδασουρ and φαδασσουρ.

1:11 For "those of Beniamin" the chieftain was Ἀβιδὰν υἱὸς Γαδεωνί for אבידן בן גדעני. For Βενιαμίν the final nasal does appear in a few mss as *mu*, as it does in Sam consistently. The name Ἀβιδάν ought not to have been troublesome for copyists, but a number of misspellings do obtain; αβιδαμ, αμιδαν, αβδαν and αβιδα all occur. The name was also confused with Aminadab; αμιναδαβ, αμιναδαν and the apocopated αδαβ are all attested. The name γαδεωνί was highly problematic for scribes. Even disregarding all itacistic spellings, a large number of different spellings obtain; the *alpha* was assimilated to the *epsilon*, i.e. as γεδ-; also recurring is the apocopation of the final *iota*. Consonantal confusion led to γαλεωνι, syncopation created γεδωνι, and aphaeresis to αδεωνι.

1:12 For "those of Dan" the chieftain was Ἀχιέζερ υἱὸς Ἀμισαδαί for אחיעזר בן עמישדי. The name Ἀχιέζερ was surprisingly stable in the tradition, it yielding only εχιεζερ, αχεεζερ and αρχιεζερ. Quite otherwise is the case of his father. Scribes doubled the *mu* or the *sigma*; others doubled the final sigma of υἱός to produce σαμ-, or changed the final letter to *nu*, thus -δαν. By aphaeresis of the *alpha*, a μισ- spelling was produced, and by syncopation of the syllable -αδ- αμισαι appears. The *b* text was influenced by the αχι- of Ἀχιέζερ, and produced the blend αχιμσαδε. The reading αβιελδε in one ms is simply bizarre.

1:13 For "those of Aser" the chieftain was Φαγαιὴλ υἱὸς Ἐχράν for the Hebrew פגעיאל בן עכרן. The name Φαγαιήλ was unfamiliar to Greek copyists, and the tradition witnesses to φαγαηλ, φαγεη, φαγαηρ, φεγαιηλ, φαγαλιηλ and φαγελιηλ. The last two spellings reflect the ending of such names in the context as Σαλαμιήλ (v.6) or Γαμαλιήλ (v.10). The name Ἐχράν underwent vocalic change in αχραν, an infixed *theta* in εχθραν, change of nasal in εχραμ, and a suffixed syllable in εχρανειν.

1:14 For "those of Gad" the chieftain was Ἐλισὰφ υἱὸς ῾Ραγουήλ for MT's אליסף בן דעואל; the father's name was read as רעואל, for which see MT at 2:14 and 10:29. The *daleth* and *resh* were and are easily misread. LXX never read the name with *daleth*, but always as ῾Ραγουήλ. In fact, in other books where the name occurs (Genesis and Exodus) it only occurs with *resh*. The Greek tradition throughout the Alexandrian canon attests only to the spelling with *rho*. Which spelling is the earlier cannot be determined.

The name Ἐλισάφ was easily confused with such names as Eliasaph, Elishaphan, or Elishaphat, resulting in ελιασαφ, ελισαφαν, ελισαφατ resp; other misspellings include ελιαφη, ελισαφα, ελισαφαδ and εσαφ. For the *gamma* representing the grapheme ע in ῾Ραγουήλ, see the comment on Σωγάρ at v.8. The name was fully stable in the tradition.

1:15 For "those of Nephthali" the chieftain was Ἀχιρέ υἱὸς Αἰνάν for the Hebrew אחירע בן עינן. The name Νεφθαλί popularly occurs in the tradition with a final *mu*, for which see the Note at Gen 30:8. The name Ἀχιρέ was obviously strange for copyists, who were bothered by the ending -ε, and some omitted it; another changed it to *alpha*, i.e. as αχιρα. The spelling αχειραρ was based on a parent αχειραι, with the copyist misreading an uncial *iota* as a *rho*. Other misspellings include χειραι, αχειρευ, αχειναι, and even αρχιερευς! The name Αἰνάν was fairly stable, and aside from the itacistic εναν and αειναν, the tradition attests only to εvναν and εραν.

1:16 This verse describes these twelve representatives by three different designations: as ἐπίκλητοι τῆς συναγωγῆς, as ἄρχοντες τῶν φυλῶν κατὰ πατριὰς αὐτῶν and as χιλίαρχοι Ἰσραήλ. For the first one "the called ones of the assembly" I would understand the genitive as a subjective one, i.e. that the assembly did the calling. In other words, they were not appointed by Moses, but designated by the συναγωγή.[15] It would not be amiss to render ἐπίκλητοι by "appointees." MT has a double reading for the bound form; the passive

---

15. This is obviously intended by Tar[JN] which inserted "people" before "assembly," i.e. מזוגי עם כנשתא. This is, however, commonly done by Tar[N] before כנשתא, according to AB 7, note 23.

participle of the Kethib is Aramaic, and that of the Qere is Hebrew, but they are semantically the same.

The Hebrew for the second title is נשיאי מטות אבותם "chieftains of the tribes of their fathers." As in v.2 אבותם is rendered by κατὰ πατριῶν αὐτῶν "according to their paternal ancestry." The phrase is actually formulaic; see comment at v.2. I would understand the Hebrew to mean "ancestral tribes," and that LXX correctly rendered the Hebrew.

The third title is the predicate of a nominal clause ראשי אלפי ישראל הם "chieftains of the clans of Israel are they." The word אלפים actually means "thousands," and is often used to designate a clan.[16] LXX renders the bound phrase ראשי אלפי by the compound χιλίαρχοι "chiliarchs," thereby preserving the notion of "thousands."

1:17 Vv.17—19 state that Moses and Aaron carried out the Lord's orders to pass under review, i.e. to count (all men of military age). V.17 introduces this by Moses and Aaron taking the twelve tribal chieftains, i.e. those ἀνακληθέντες ἐξ ὀνόματος, "those called by name" (in vv.5—15). As in MT the verb is singular with a compound subject; only later (v.18) does the verb occur in the plural.[17] LXX has the singular ὀνόματος,[18] whereas MT has the plural שמות. LXX takes the point of view that each one is called up by his name, an equally valid point of view.

1:18 Moses and Aaron brought together[19] all the assembly ἐν μιᾷ τοῦ μηνὸς τοῦ δευτέρου ἔτους. MT has no equivalent for ἔτους, and it is uncertain whether the time intended is "in (day) one of the second month of the year" or "of the month of the second year." Comparison with the timer in v.1 probably shows that if the latter were intended, ετους δευτερου would have been added rather than simply ἔτους. In fact, the addition of ἔτους is odd, and I suspect that it was added under the influence of v.1, though without the adjectival δευτέρου. There is no evidence that hex took note of the word as having no Hebrew equivalent, though one *O* ms, 426, did omit the word.

---

16. According to KB it is used as a synonym of משפחה.
17. See THGN 122.
18. As do the Tar.
19. Instead of συνήγαγον The Others read ἐξεκκλησίασον.

The verb in the next clause in MT is יִתְיַלְדוּ; the Hithp of ילד is a hapax legomenon. It presumably has something to do with one's descent, and probably means "to declare their parentage." LXX chose ἐπηξονοῦσαν, a denominative verb based on the noun ἄξων "axle," used in the plural to designate the wooden tablets of the laws in Athens, since these tablets were on pivots, or axles, so that one could consult them easily. The verb then means "to inscribe or register on tablets."[20] Since the verb is imperfect, it involves a process, i.e. "they were enrolling on tablets ... every male ...." The subject is still Moses and Aaron. In the tradition, Byz reads επεσκεψαντο, and the majority reading is επεσκεπησαν, taken from v.19.[21] But the unusual ἐπηξονοῦσαν, though supported only by B x, must be original.

The enrolment was done in accordance with the instructions of v.2. The first structure in connection with the census was לְמִשְׁפְּחֹתָם, here rendered by κατὰ γενέσεις αὐτῶν, which is simply a synonym for the phrase with συγγενείας in v.2, for which see comment ad loc. The second phrase לְבֵית אֲבֹתָם became κατ' οἴκους πατριῶν αὐτῶν in v.2, but here without an equivalent for בֵית, i.e. κατὰ πατριὰς αὐτῶν "according to their ancestries." No attempt was made in the tradition to supply an οικον to equal the untranslated בֵית. For the third one, see comment at v.2. Since MT simply reads שֵׁמוֹת here and throughout this section, hex has consistently placed the αὐτῶν under the obelus.

The modifier of the verb in MT is מִבֶּן עֶשְׂרִים שָׁנָה וָמַעְלָה "anyone twenty years of age and upwards." LXX made explicit what is only implied in MT that πᾶν ἀρσενικόν was intended. Apparently hex omitted the πᾶν and placed ἀρσενικόν under the obelus.[22] The πᾶν ἀρσενικόν also serves as referent for αὐτῶν 1° 2° 3° and 4°. For κατὰ κεφαλὴν αὐτῶν, see comment at v.2.

1:19 For the first clause[23] אֶת מֹשֶׁה is rendered by τῷ Μωυσῇ. As the addressee for συνέταξεν (or ἐνετείλατο) Μωυσῇ is always articulated with the dative article in LXX.[24]

---

20. See the discussion in Dorival 161—162.
21. The Tar all have the Ethpe of יחס "be enrolled."
22. The Others also omitted πᾶν. Incidentally, so did Syh (along with G-426 as representing hex).
23. The Three have rendered v.a by καθὰ ἐνετείλατο κύριος τῷ (om Sym) Μωυσεῖ.
24. See THGN 108.

The second clause begins in MT with "and he passed in review." LXX has restructured this by a passive plural verb, (καὶ) ἐπεσκέπησαν. Since MT had a verb plus suffix, יִפְקֹד֑ם, hex added αυτοι which does help to identify the subject which is not given, and only common sense dictated that it must refer to αὐτῶν of v.18.

The locative modifying the verb reads as ἐν τῇ ἐρήμῳ τῇ Σινά. In the tradition, the article modifying Σινά is omitted by the oI n+ text, and in the majority of witnesses is changed to the genitive. Usually the proper name modifying ἔρημος is not articulated in Num, but as at v.1, which see, since the dative article is supported by the oldest witnesses, the τῇ is probably original.[25] V.b might then be rendered: "and they were passed under review in the Sina desert."[26]

1:20 Vv.20—46 detail the results of the census for the twelve tribes. The tribe of Levi is dealt with separately in vv.47—53, it not being subject to the census. Vv.20—21 deal with οἱ υἱοὶ 'Ρουβήν, which is the predicate nominative of (καὶ) ἐγένοντο. For the treatment of 'Ρουβήν in the tradition, see comment at v.5. Rouben is characterized as "the first-born of Israel."

What follows in LXX is a pattern which is repeated exactly word for word for each of the eleven which follow, with only the tribal name and the number varying being filled in.

Five κατά phrases follow the tribal name: κατὰ συγγενείας αὐτῶν (for תוֹלְדֹתָם), κατὰ δήμους αὐτῶν (לְמִשְׁפְּחֹתָם), κατ' οἴκους πατριῶν αὐτῶν (לְבֵית אֲבוֹתָם), κατὰ ἀριθμὸν ὀνομάτων αὐτῶν (בְּמִסְפַּר שֵׁמוֹת), and κατὰ κεφαλὴν αὐτῶν (לְגֻלְגְּלֹתָם). In each of the twelve reports these five recur in LXX, but in MT the last one is missing for the last ten; see comment at v.22. For the fourth one, Num adds an αὐτῶν, though MT has no suffix for שֵׁמוֹת, and hex has put the pronoun under the obelus. This same situation obtains throughout the twelve reports.

---

25. See THGN 103.
26. Aq rendered v.b by καὶ ἐπεσκέψαντο αὐτοὺς ἐν ἐρήμῳ Σιναί; Sym translated as ἐπεσκέψατο δὲ αὐτοὺς ἐν τῇ ἐρήμῳ τῇ Σιναί, while Theod has καὶ ἐπεσκέψατο αυτοὺς ἐν τῇ ἐρήμῳ τῇ Σιναί.

תולדתם is rendered by κατὰ συγγενείας αὐτῶν in this chapter, and only twice elsewhere (Exod 6:16,19). It is usually rendered by γενέσεις. The second one, משפחת, is rendered in various ways, but δῆμος is the most common one (112 times). Other frequent renderings are φυλή (42 times), πατριά (26), and συγγένεια (19).[27] For the third, fourth, and fifth κατά phrases, see comments at v.2. What follows in LXX is repeated exactly for each of the twelve tribes: "all males from twenty years (of age) and upwards, everyone who goes out in the army." These are in the nominative case, since they modify ἐγένοντο. That this is a set pattern is proven by their recurrence in the same form for the eleven tribes that follow as well; see comment on τοῖς υἱοῖς at v.22. The Hebrew has both structures in the singular: כל זכר מבן עשרים שנה ומעלה. The Greek, quite correctly, understood כל זָכָר as a collective expression, and thus put the structure in the plural, whereas כל יצא צבא could better be understood as singular.[28]

1:21 Again this verse introduces a pattern which is then repeated for each tribe. Syntactically, the census report is introduced by a caption: ἡ ἐπίσκεψις αὐτῶν, which renders פקדיהם "their review," i.e. their census report. The Hebrew noun is a plural passive Qal participle, "those numbered, or reviewed." Num interprets this by the singular term ἐπίσκεψις "oversight, review," and refers to the result of such a review, hence the rendering "census report." The plural pronoun refers to σὺ καὶ 'Ααρών of v.3; i.e. Moses and Aaron are ordered: ἐπισκέψασθε αὐτούς.[29] The pattern that follows reads: ἐκ τῆς φυλῆς of X, followed by the actual number. In MT the pattern is למטה plus the tribal name and the number. The Greek reads "out of the tribe of Rouben (46 thousand and five hundred)," for the Hebrew "for the tribe of Rouben."

1:22—23 The second report concerns the Simeonites. The initial report had been introduced by καὶ ἐγένοντο οἱ υἱοὶ 'Ρουβὴν πρωτοτόκου 'Ισραήλ. Instead

---

27. According to the count in Dos Santos.
28. Aq rendered the second structure by παντὸς ἐκπορευομένου στρατιάν; Sym has πᾶς ὁ ἐξερχόμενος εἰς στρατιάν, and Theod read: πᾶς ὁ ἐκπορευόμενος δυνάμει.
29. For the text of the verse up to the number Aq reads ἐπεσκεμμένοι αὐτῶν τῆς ῥάβδου 'Ρουβήν. Sym translates as οἱ ἐπεσκεμμένοι αὐτῶν τῆς φυλῆς 'Ρουβήν, and Theod has αἱ ἐπισκέψεις αὐτῶν τῆς φυλῆς 'Ρουβήν.

of this v.22 begins with τοῖς υἱοῖς Συμεών, which pattern is then followed for the rest of the tribes reviewed as well. MT, however, has a variation in the pattern in v.22. It follows the pattern of v.20 in having לגלגלתם after במספר שמות, which is lacking in all the following ten tribes. Unique, however, is the introduction of פקדיו before במספר.[30] Hex has added αι επισκεψεις αυτων under the asterisk to represent it. The plural pronoun is also found in Sam's פקדיהם. For αὐτῶν 4°, see comment at v.20, which also applies here. The number reviewed from the tribe of Simeon was 59,300 men. The *b* text changed the 300 to τετρακοσιοι.

1:24—25(26—27) Vv.24—25 of MT deal with the sons of Gad, but the Greek has moved that account after the Benjamin report, i.e. as vv.36—37. Hex has rearranged the text to equal the order of MT.

LXX deals first with the sons of Iouda. MT's text differs from the usual pattern in that כל זכר is missing, and so hex has placed πάντα ἀρσενικά under the obelus (along with the αὐτῶν κατὰ κεφαλὴν αὐτῶν before it, all of which lacks any correspondence in MT; see comment at v.2 for αὐτῶν 4°, and at v.20 for the κατά clause). The review totalled 74,600 men. It now becomes obvious that Num simply follows the pattern set for Rouben in vv.20—21 rigidly for the census of the twelve tribes, regardless of differences in MT.

In the tradition, the *b* text, presumably tiring of the repetitiveness of the account substitutes for κατά—the end of the verse, καθ ομοιοτητα των πρωτων, and thereupon omits this text for the remainder of the census report, i.e. from vv.26—42. One can sympathize with the parent scribe!

1:26—27(28—29) For Ἰσσαχάρ see comment at v.8. As in v.24 αὐτῶν 4°—ἀρσενικά was placed under the obelus in hex, for which see comment at vv.24—25. Exactly the same obtains for all the remaining tribes. כל זכר obtains only in vv.20,22. The αὐτῶν before it never has an equivalent in MT's שמות, and לגלגלתם occurs only in vv.20,22.[31] For each of the remaining sections i.e. in vv.28,30,32,24,26,28,40,42, hex has placed αὐτῶν 4°—ἀρσενικά under the obelus. The review found 54,400 men of military age in the tribe.

---
30. Kenn 107,152,160,232,234,249,253,260,383,412,543*, 545,595,620 do omit פקדיו, as do Tar^J and Pesh.
31. Tar^J, however, retains לגולגלותיהון for each of the twelve reports.

1:28—29(30—31) For the sons of Zaboulon the review amounted to 57,400 men. In the tradition, cod A changed the 400 to five hundred.

1:30—31(32—33) For the sons of Ioseph, sons of Ephraim, the result of the census came to 40,500 men. As in vv.9—10 the younger brother preceded the older one.

1:32—33(34—35) For the sons of Manasse the review produced a count of 32,200 men. In the tradition, cod B and Byz+ changed διακόσιοι to τριακόσιοι. For Μανασσή and its variant spellings in the tradition, see comment at v.10.

1:34—35(36—37) For the sons of Beniamin the census review found 35,400 men of military age. The Byz text changed τετρακόσιοι to τριακοσιοι, and *cII* read διακοσιοι (from v.33).

1:36—37(24—25) Whether the placement of Gad here, or as in MT immediately after Simeon, for which see ch.2 where the tribe of Gad is to encamp on the south side together with Rouben and Simeon (2:10—16; see also 10:18—21), is to be preferred cannot be determined. In ch.26, Gad's position in MT is also immediately after Simeon, but in LXX it follows that of Zaboulon (vv.24—27). The census count for the tribe of Gad was 45,650.

1:38—39 For the Danites the review produced 62,700 men. Cod F and *b* reduced the count by a hundred, reading εξακοσιοι for ἑπτακόσιοι.

1:40—41 For the sons of Aser, "their review: from the tribe of Aser 41,500." Scattered ms support obtains in the tradition for the spelling ασσηρ, but 'Ασήρ is original.

1:42—43 The last report is "for the sons of Naphthali." Most witnesses add the consonant /m/ at the end of the word; actually, only 21 mss, one Sahidic ms and the Syh lack the consonantal ending. For the popularity of the /-im/ ending see Note at Gen 30:8. The review found 53,400 men of military age in the tribe. In the tradition, a *cII* text has τριακοσιοι instead of τετρακόσιοι.

1:44 MT views the summary statement of the review in the plural: "these are the reviews," whereas LXX takes it as a whole in the singular. Either understanding is sensible. The noun ἐπίσκεψις is modified by a relative clause containing a cognate verb in the singular with the coordinate nouns "Moses and Aaron and the rulers of Israel" as subject. This pattern reflects MT, the number of the verb depending on whether it precedes or follows the compound subject. If the verb precedes, its number is that of the first unit of the subject, here Μωυσῆς; if it follows, it is in the plural. Accordingly, the B Byz+ variant επισκεψαντο must be secondary.[32] The noun ἄρχοντες is then further defined by the apposite structure δώδεκα ἄνδρες.

"Twelve men" is then explained by v.b: "one (i.e. each) man[33] according to one tribe, according to the tribe of their paternal households ἦσαν." This is an expansion of MT, and equals Sam. The text of MT after "one man" reads simply לבית אבתיו היו,[34] but Sam has למטה אחד איש בית אבתם היו. Note how closely LXX resembles this text, even in the plural pronoun αὐτῶν reflecting the suffix of אבתם. The ἦσαν reflects the plural verb היו, it being congruent with the subject ἄνδρες, with v.b constituting the predicate nominative. The Masoretes, however, placed איש (שנים עשר) under the *ethnach*, which Num reflects by the colon after ἄνδρες.

In the tradition, hex placed κατά 1°—φυλήν 2° under the obelus, thereby calling attention to the shorter text of MT. Codd B V+ have omitted αὐτῶν, but this is hardly to be taken seriously.[35]

1:45—46 The final results of the census review. MT totals the twelve reports by two plural constructions: first, ויהיו כל פקודי, and then at the beginning of v.46 reading ויהיו כל הפקדים. LXX does this more economically by making a single structure out of the two verses, more or less on the pattern of the individual reports. It begins with a singular introduction, καὶ ἐγένετο πᾶσα ἡ

---

32. See THGN 121.
33. Tar[N] interprets "one man" by גבר ראש, for which see v.4. This same tendency is reflected in the Byz reading αρχοντες rather than ἄνδρες.
34. Hex has interfered in the text by changing οἴκων to εις οικον so as to reflect MT's לבית.
35. See THGN 97.

ἐπίσκεψις of the Israelites, and ends with the total number of those passed under review.

MT then continues in v.45 with "לבית אבתם of those twenty years (of age) and upwards." LXX does not reflect this as its parent text, since it reads σὺν δυνάμει αὐτῶν ...; LXX is based on the לצבאתם of Sam; see the same word at v.52 of MT, which Num also translates by σὺν δυνάμει αὐτῶν. What LXX states is "and all the review of the Israelites with their army."[36]

The last structure of v.45 in MT reads כל יצא צבא בישראל. LXX treated צבא as an infinitive (as לצבא?), and translated by παρατάξασθαι, thus "everyone going out to be drawn up in order (i.e. ready for battle) in Israel."[37]

V.46 simply gives the summary number as 603,750. Hex has added παντες οι επεσκεμμενοι at the beginning under the asterisk to make up for the ויהיו כל הפקדים of MT which LXX omitted; see comment above.

1:47 Vv.47—53 deal with the Levites, and the Lord's instructions to Moses concerning them. The change of subject from the census account of the tribes to the statement that the Levites were not passed under review is neatly indicated by a contrastive δέ. The descriptive modifier characterizing the Levites as ἐκ τῆς φυλῆς πατριᾶς αὐτῶν occurs here for the first time in the Pentateuch. The combination, φυλῆς πατριᾶς "tribe of (their) paternal ancestry" is limited to Numbers (also at 26:55 32:18 33:54 36:4 and comp τῆς φυλῆς τῆς πατρικῆς at v.7) with the single exception of Est (Add C16), where it also occurs.

The verb is peculiarly appropriate; the double compound (οὐ) συνεπεσκέψησαν means "were passed in review along with." It occurs only in Num (also v.48 2:33 26:62), and it is not surprising that the more popular (ουκ) επεσκεπησαν should occur in B O f x+, but this is secondary.[38] The locative phrase בתוכם is expanded to interpret the suffix by LXX to ἐν μέσῳ υἱῶν Ἰσραήλ, which is a correct interpretation.[39]

---

36. Theod and Aq translate by καὶ ἐγένοντο πάντες οἱ ἐπεσκεμμένοι υἱῶν Ἰσραὴλ εἰς οἶκον πατέρων αὐτῶν, and Sym has ἦσαν δὲ πάντες οἱ ἐπεσκεμμένοι υἱοὶ Ἰσραὴλ κατ' οἶκον πατέρων αὐτῶν.
37. Tar[N] omitted בישראל.
38. See THGN 126.
39. Aq renders the verse by καὶ οἱ Λευῖται εἰς ῥάβδον πατέρων αὐτῶν οὐκ ἐπεσκέπησαν < ἐν μέσῳ αὐτῶν >; Sym renders οἱ δὲ Λευῖται κατὰ τὴν φυλὴν τῶν πατέρων αὐτῶν οὐκ ἐπεσκέπησαν ἐν αὐτοῖς, whereas Theod reads καὶ οἱ Λευῖται εἰς φυλὴν πατέρων αὐτῶν οὐκ ἐπεσκέπησαν ἐν μέσῳ αὐτῶν.

1:49 LXX begins with ὅρα "take note, look." For its use for rendering אַךְ "only, really," see Note at Exod 31:13. The imperative is an attempt to call particular attention to what follows as having an important message, something like "see to it that." That message is "do not also pass in review the Levi tribe." As in v.47, the double compound συνεπισκέπη is used, which I have rendered "also pass in review"; see comment and footnote at v.47.

The parallel injunction says "and τὸν ἀριθμὸν αὐτῶν you shall not take (up) in the midst of the Israelites." Obviously what is meant is Do not include them in the census. MT puts this rather differently: "Do not raise their ראש in the midst of the Israelites." The rendering is unique for the Greek canon, though this is certainly what ראשם תשא means.[40] The same idiom occurs at 1:2 4:22 26:2 where it becomes λάβε(τε) τὴν ἀρχήν, and at 4:2 it becomes λάβε τὸ κεφάλαιον; see also 31:26,49, where ראש is again rendered by τὸ κεφάλαιον; see comment at v.2.

1:50 Moses is ordered: ἐπίστησον the Levites; i.e. "set up the Levites." The Hebrew has הפקד "put in charge." The Hebrew is surprising in view of the recurring Qal of פקד in the sense of "pass in review." The LXX rendering is unique throughout the Greek canon as a translation for the Hi of פקד, but it is contextually a good rendering. Moses must "establish the Levites over the tent of testimony and over all its vessels and over everything that is in it." The usual parent text for the "tent (of testimony)" is אהל, but here it is משכן, which seldom occurs with העדת; in fact, it only occurs twice in v.53, and it is also found at 10:11. Otherwise, it occurs only at Exod 38:21. But the translator has here rendered the phrase by the stereotype rendering for אהל מועד, i.e. as τὴν σκηνὴν τοῦ μαρτυρίου. The phrase ἐν αὐτῇ has as MT counterpart לו in the relative clause, כל אשר לו "everything which belongs to it." The ἐν phrase need not presuppose a parent בו, as is proposed in BHS. Everything that belongs to the tent refers to the furnishings of the tent, all of which are within it; the translator simply used his common sense.

Their instructions are then specified more particularly in the remainder of the verse in three clauses. a) αὐτοὶ ἀροῦσιν the tent and all its vessels. The

---

40. Tar^N makes this ריש סכומתהון "head of their numbers," thus their census. The other Tar both read חשבנהון "their reckoning, their census."

αὐτοί (for המה) serves to single out the Levites in a special way: "it is they (i.e. as over against anyone else) who must carry," i.e. do the carrying of the sacred tent and its contents. b) similarly, αὐτοί (הם) λειτουργήσουσιν ἐν αὐτῇ "it is they who must perform cultic service in it." The verb is the usual one chosen to render שרת "to minister, to serve." In fact, of the 99 instances of שרת in the Hebrew Bible 79 are rendered either by λειτουργέω or its cognate noun λειτουργός. In LXX the verb normally has a religious sense, though in other literatures it also has the wider notion of public service, but the service of the Levites was a purely religious one. c) They "are to encamp around the tent." Note that this is not introduced by an αὐτοί; after all, the tribes according to chapter 2 are also to encamp around the tent, though at some distance from it.

1:51 This verse explicates the first instruction given in v.50. It involves the movement of the tent. "When the tent is to move (ἐξαίρειν), the Levites must dismantle it," and "when the tent is to make camp (i.e. become stationary), they must set (it) up." MT specifies both the object (אתו) and the subject (הלוים) for the second clause as well as for the first clause, and hex has added αυτην οι λευιται for the second clause under the asterisk so as to equal the Hebrew. MT and hex make explicit what is fully implicit in LXX.

The final clause speaks of ὁ ἀλλογενὴς ὁ προσπορευόμενος. What is meant is the non-Levite who approaches, presumably to take part in the dismantling and reassemblage of the sacred tent.[41] This is an unusual description of the non-Levite, but it correctly renders the Hebrew הזר הקרב.[42] The penalty to be imposed on such an approaching stranger is ἀποθανέτω. ἀποθνήσκω, along with θανατόω, are the usual renderings for the Ho of מות, thus "let him be put to death."

1:52 In contrast to the Levites (v.53a), "the Israelites must make camp with their army, each one in his own rank, and each according to his own regiment." For both prepositional phrases modifying ἀνήρ, the genitive pronoun is

---

41. Tar[N] adds למשמשה after "approaches," i.e. "approaches to do service," whereas Tar[J] specifies the punishment by adding after the verb ייי קדם מן מצלהבא באישא.
42. Dorival 111–112 calls attention to the various uses of πορεύεσθαι compounds, particularly to ἐκπορεύεσθαι in ch.1, as well as to εἰσπορεύεσθαι, a phenomenon which has no echo in Hebrew.

reflexive, ἑαυτοῦ. I have rendered these pronouns by "his own." Hex has reordered these to follow the suffixal position of the pronouns in the Hebrew, resp as ταξει αυτου and ηγεμονιαν αυτου. Note that in MT these are both על phrases, but LXX distinguishes more specifically by "ἐν his own rank," and "κατά his own regiment." See ch.2 for a description of the arrangement and position of the tribal camps in detail. The reason for the inclusion of this instruction, which seems extraneous to a section on instructions to Levites, is probably that the Israelites referred to here are themselves actually ὁ ἀλλογενὴς ὁ προσπορευόμενος of v.51. The non-Levites must not encroach on the encampment of the Levites; the latter is ordered in v.53a. For σὺν δυνάμει αὐτῶν, see comment at vv.45—46.

1:53 V.a is introduced idiomatically by a contrastive δέ. According to MT, the Levites are to encamp סביב the tent of meeting; cf c) under v.50 above. For סביב LXX has ἐναντίοι κύκλῳ "over against about (the tent of testimony)." This is a case of harmonization with 2:2 where this also occurs, but where MT has מנגד סביב. I would consider LXX's interpretation to have missed an essential distinction between the two, however. In 2:2 the reference is to the non-Levites, who are to encamp "over against around," i.e. at a distance (ἐναντίοι) on the four sides on the tent (κύκλῳ), but here an adverbial ἐναντίοι is unexpected. What was intended in MT was that the Levites should encamp within an inner circle around the tent, with the Israelites dwelling in the outer circle, i.e. ἐναντίοι κύκλῳ the tent; see 2:2. The ἐναντίοι was placed under the obelus to indicate the lack of an equivalent in MT by hex. The tradition also found it difficult. The C text made it υπεναντιοι, which makes the problem even worse! The Byz text changed it to εναντιον κυριου, but the more difficult ἐναντίοι must be original.

The inclusion of εναντιοι was probably made (i.e. in the sense of "at a distance") to make sense of the next clause: "and there shall be no ἀμάρτημα among the Israelites." But MT has "and there shall be no קצף על עדת בני ישראל, i.e. "no anger shall befall the assembly of the Israelites." The translator clearly is avoiding the notion of divine anger falling on the Israelite assembly in favor of "and there will be no fault among the Israelites";[43] the

---
43. Theod has θυμός instead of ἀμάρτημα, and Sym reads ὀργή (both readings retroverted from Syh). See also Daniel 313.

rendering of קצף in this way is unique in LXX. In both MT and Num, however, the paratactic clause is to be understood as constituting the reason for the encampment of the Israelites outside the Levites' camp. The rendering ἁμάρτημα is an obvious case of avoidance of an anthropopathism on the part of the translator.[44] Hex has noted the lack of an equivalent for על עדת, and has added under the asterisk επι την συναγωγην before ἐν υἱοῖς ᾿Ισραήλ, without, however, changing the ἐν phrase to των υιων ισραηλ, which would result in a puzzling text for any reader of the hex text.

V.b explicates the b) charge of v.50. MT simply states ושמרו הלוים את משמרת of the tent of testimony, but Num, probably in view of the הם/αὐτοί of v.50, has added αὐτοί after οἱ Λευῖται, i.e. "the Levites themselves." The unnecessary pronoun has been placed under the obelus by hex to show that it is a gloss added by the translator.

1:54 The Israelites carried out the Lord's orders. The norm for their action was "according to everything ὅσα the Lord commanded." The majority B F M V text has α instead of ὅσα, but only the latter can be original. Num always uses ὅσα when its antecedent is πᾶς, except at 19:16 πᾶς ὅς and 19:22 παντὸς οὗ. It is obviously an easy mistake to make when it modifies πάντα which ends in *alpha*.[45]

MT has as modifier of צוה the single את משה, but LXX has τῷ Μωυσῇ καὶ ᾿Ααρών. Actually, according to v.1 the Lord spoke to Moses. In v.17, however, it was Moses and Aaron who take the tribal leaders, and carry out the orders which the Lord had given to Moses. Hex has placed καὶ ᾿Ααρών under the obelus to indicate its absence from MT. It has been suggested[46] that the addition may well have been a case of rationalization, since in v.2 what the Lord says to Moses is initiated by the plural imperative λάβετε.

---

44. See the discussion in Dorival 156—157 on the elimination or attentuation of certain anthropomorphisms/-pathisms.
45. See THGN 99.
46. By Dorival ad loc.

Chapter 2

2:2 The verse begins with a nominative structure ἄνθρωπος ἐχόμενος αὐτοῦ κατὰ τάγμα, which structure must modify οἱ υἱοὶ Ἰσραήλ 1°. MT has איש על דגלו "each one according to his standard." LXX's interpretative gloss ἐχόμενος has no basis in MT, and is a case of harmonization with the pattern occurring throughout the chapter (οἱ παρεμβάλλοντες) ἐχόμενοι (see vv.5,7,12,14,20,22 and 27,29); see comment at v.5. It is intended to show the positioning of members of the army as being adjacent to each other. Such harmonization in which patterns were followed was already seen in ch.1, and is typical of this translator. I would take ἄνθρωπος in the Hebrew sense of "each one," thus "each one in adjacent position according to his division." Though ἐχόμενος usually takes a genitive modifier, it sometimes appears without (as in vv.5,7,10), and here the αὐτοῦ which follows probably modifies τάγμα in view of the Hebrew דגלו. In fact, the majority A F M text transposes αὐτοῦ to follow τάγμα, which may constitute a hex rearrangement in origin. דגל is usually rendered by τάγμα in the book (12 out of 14 occurrences), but at v.17 and 1:53 the word is rendered by the synonym ἡγεμονία "regiment." The term דגל actually means "a standard, a banner," and the rendering τάγμα interprets the word as referring to those who are united or act under such a single standard, hence "a division" in the army.

The verb for the first clause is a third person aorist imperative: "let the Israelites encamp." It is modified by two κατά phrases, κατὰ σημέας[1] "according to sign (i.e. of or on the tribal banner)," and κατ' οἴκους πατριῶν αὐτῶν, for which see comment at 1:2. That the former also modifies the verb, rather than ἄνθρωπος, as αὐτοῦ κατὰ τάγμα does, is clear from MT in which the noun is plural אתת "signs."

The second clause begins with ἐναντίοι for מנגד and is in turn followed by "around the tent of testimony." What is probably meant by the consecution ἐναντίοι κύκλῳ "over against (or facing?) around (the tent)" is that, the division(s) will be arrayed at a distance from the inner circle occupied by the Levites, but with the tabernacle as the focal point for both the Levites and the army corps, i.e. facing inwards. This is clear from the parent text מנגד "over against."[2] Since

---
1. For σημέα, see LS sub σημεία IV.
2. Instead of ἐναντίοι Aq reads ἀπὸ κατέναντι, and Sym has μακρόθεν, whereas Theod renders by ἐξ ἐναντίας.

ἐναντίοι is masculine plural in form, the translator perforce repeated the subject οἱ υἱοὶ 'Ισραήλ, which hex placed under the obelus, since MT did not repeat it. Note that the יחנו for the second clause is rendered by the future: "the Israelites must encamp." This is a common consecution. If the first clause is imperatival, the next one usually has a future verb, which can imply commands as well.³

2:3 MT characterizes Judah as "those encamping קדמה מזרחה." The word קדמה means "eastward," and מזרחה also means "eastward" (literally "towards the sunrise"). But קדם also means "in front of, before," and the translator rendered the two words by πρῶτοι κατ' ἀνατολάς, i.e. "(those encamping) first towards the east," which is a possible interpretation, though it occurs only here in LXX. The word קדם is most often rendered by ἀνατολή (20 times), but ἀρχή also occurs (nine times), as does ἀρχαῖος (14 times).⁴ Possibly the translator thought in terms of v.9's πρῶτοι ἐξαροῦσιν, which, however, renders ראשנה.

In the tradition, B x+ read κατα νοτον instead of πρῶτοι. This is an old reading already present in the text as a doublet in Origen's day, since hex read it as a doublet after πρῶτοι and marked it with an obelus. But it should be noted that in Exod (10:13 14:21) νότον rendered קדים; see Note at Exod 10:13. Its history is uncertain, but I suspect it was added in prehexaplaric times by a bilingual scribe; it seems to reflect a misreading of MT's קדמה.

The first ones encamping were the τάγμα παρεμβολῆς of Iouda σὺν δυνάμει αὐτῶν. These structures are pattern structures recurring for every tribe leading the encampments on each of the four sides; see vv.10,18,25. In the tradition, the C+ text has pluralized τάγμα. Since the four divisions (see also vv.10,18, 25), each consisted of three tribes, the variant text betrays an understanding of each tribe being a τάγμα; the plural is obviously secondary. For the σύν phrase see comment at 1:45—46.

The second phrase identifies the leader (ἄρχων) of the Ioudaites. For Ναασσὼν υἱὸς 'Αμιναδάβ, see comments at 1:7.

2:4 MT begins with a conjunction, i.e. with ויצאו. Throughout the chapter this occurs 12 times, and the Greek always disregards the *waw*; it reads δυνάμει

---
3. See Porter 419—420.
4. According to Dos Santos. Tar^N with its קדמיין agrees with the interpretation of LXX, where Tar^JO read ק(י)דמונא with MT.

αὐτοῦ. In each case (also at vv.6,8,11,13,15,19,21,23,26,28,30) this is followed by οἱ ἐπεσκεμμένοι for MT's ופקדיהם or ופקדיו; i.e., LXX uses an apposite participle, rather than a coordinate noun, and in each case the suffix is disregarded. In every case hex has added either αυτων or αυτου to agree with MT's text, though no asterisks are extant for the added pronouns.

The pattern rigidly observed throughout the chapter is δύναμις αὐτοῦ used as a nominative absolute, thus "as for its (i.e. of the particular tribe concerned) army, those passed under review were XXX" (i.e. the number passed under review)—in this verse XXX is 74,600, for which see 1:25.

2:5 The subject of the first nominal clause is (καὶ) οἱ παρεμβάλλοντες ἐχόμενοι "those camping in adjacent position (i.e. next door)." This renders the structure והחנים עליו "and those camping alongside it." The participle is a present participle, which is sensible, since it is semantically a process, a continuous action. The predicate is φυλὴ Ἰσσαχάρ, i.e. מטה יששכר.[5] For the leader of the Issacharites Ναθαναὴλ υἱὸς Σωγάρ, as well as for Ἰσσαχάρ, see comments at 1:8. In the tradition, most witnesses follow A B F M in reading φυλης, but the genitive can hardly be taken seriously as original text. It is rather due to the influence of the ἐχόμενοι preceding it which usually takes a genitive modifier, but this is syntactically quite wrong in the present context. The same variant recurs at vv.7,12,14,20,22,27 and 29, and is always secondary.[6]

The pattern of this verse is reproduced exactly at vv.7 and 20, whereas at vv.12,14,22,27 and 29 an αὐτοῦ follows ἐχόμενοι as well.

2:6 For the structure of this verse, see v.4. For the number in the army, 54,400, see the comment at 1:27. MT's text differs in reading ופקדיו instead of the ופקדיהם at v.4, but Num does not deviate from its pattern established at v.4. The reading in cod A ηριθμημενοι for ἐπεσκεμμένοι recurs throughout the chapter, and is a secondary attempt at clarification.[7]

2:7 The third tribe in the triad facing the tabernacle eastward is the tribe of Zaboulon. For the leader of the Zaboulonites, Ἐλιὰβ υἱὸς Χαιλών, see com-

---

5. All Three retain the καὶ οἱ παρεμβάλλοντες of LXX, but for ἐχόμενοι φυλή Aq substitutes ἐπ' αὐτῷ ῥάβδος; Sym has παρ' αὐτὸν φυλή, and Theod, ἐπ' αὐτῷ φυλή.
6. See THGN 98.
7. See U.Quast in Studien 238—248 for a detailed analysis of this variant.

ments at 1:9. For the variant φυλης, see comment at v.5. MT has a shorter text, lacking an equivalent for καὶ οἱ ἐπεσκεμμένοι ἐχόμενοι; accordingly, hex has placed these words under the obelus.

2:8 Those who passed under review were 57,400, for which number see comment at 1:29. For the b reading ηριθμημενοι for ἐπεσκεμμένοι, see comment at v.6.

2:9 The total number for the encampment of Iouda is given as 186,400 σὺν δυνάμει αὐτῶν. Since the παρεμβολή of Iouda consists of the tribes of Iouda, Issachar and Zaboulon, the αὐτῶν must refer to the three φυλαί. One would have expected δυνάμει to have been put in the plural as in MT's לצבאתם, but the singular is used throughout, i.e. the single army belongs to the three tribes. For the A b+ reading ηριθμημενοι for the participle ἐπεσκεμμένοι, see comment at v.6. It might be noted that the recensors did not change Num's participle.[8] In the tradition, an A b s+ text has substituted the more technical term for breaking up camp αναζευξουσιν for ἐξαροῦσιν.

Hex has changed the format of the compound number to equal the Hebrew parent more precisely, by adding χιλιαδες after ἑκατόν, and a και before ὀγδοήκοντα, both under the asterisk. The purpose underlying such "corrections" is certainly not to improve the Greek text, but rather to show the Hebrew text.

2:10 Vv.10—16 describe the camp of Rouben in almost exactly the same pattern as that used for the camp of Iouda in Num, though more differences obtain in the Hebrew. V.10, however, begins with τάγμα παρεμβολῆς 'Ρουβὴν πρὸς λίβα, and then continues the pattern of v.3 with σὺν δυνάμει. This corresponds to MT.[9] For the popular variant plural, ταγματα, see the comment at v.3.

The remainder of the verse up to the name of the leader is formulaic.[10] For the leader of the Roubenites, Ἐλισοὺρ υἱὸς Σεδιούρ, see comments at 1:5.

---

8. At least, ἐπεσκεμμένοι is attested by The Others.
9. Instead of πρὸς λίβα Aq reads νότον δέ; Theod and Sym have κατὰ νότον. The reading of Syh attributing λίβα to The Others is clearly a mistake, and it should be omitted or changed in the second apparatus; what Syh actually says is: The Others *tymn'* which means "south," followed by ΛΙΒΑ ΝΟΤΟΝ. The Greek words both mean "south" as well.
10. But for the pattern Aq reads εἰς στρατιὰς αὐτῶν καὶ ἐπηρμένος τῶν υἱῶν; Sym has κατὰ στρατιὰς αὐτῶν σὺν τῷ ἄρχοντι τῶν υἱῶν, whereas Theod revised LXX slightly with εἰς τὰς δυνάμεις αὐτῶν καὶ ἄρχων τῶν υἱῶν.

In the tradition, the F M oI² C s+ text has νοτον instead of λίβα, as did The Three from whom this reading was undoubtedly derived.

2:11 Hex has added αυτου after ἐπεσκεμμένοι to equal MT's פקדיו. For the A b+ variant ηριθμημενοι, see comment and footnote at v.6. The number of those that passed under review was 46,500, for which see 1:21.

2:12—13 The tribe next to the Roubenites was that of Simeon. The pattern differs from that used in vv.5—6 in the addition of αὐτοῦ after ἐχόμενος.[11] For the leader of the Simeonite tribe, Σαλαμιὴλ υἱὸς Σουρισαδαί, see comment at 1:6. For οι ηριθμημενοι as the variant A b+ text, see comment at v.6. The total count for the Simeonites was 59,300 men; see 1:23. For the popular A F M V reading φυλης instead of φυλή, see comment at v.5.

Since MT's text read ופקדיהם, hex added the pronoun αυτων after ἐπεσκεμμένοι, though some O witnesses have αυτου, which equals Sam's ופקדיו, but the hex text was probably the plural pronoun.

2:14—15 Num follows the pattern of v.12 exactly for the tribe of Gad, though MT has a shorter text. Instead of the usual והחנים עליו מטה it simply has ומטה. Hex has taken note of this by placing οἱ παρεμβάλλοντες ἐχόμενοι αὐτοῦ under the obelus. That the Numbers translator is much more formulaic in his rendering than Lev in which a love of variation in translation was characteristic was evidenced already in ch.1.

For the reading ηριθμημενοι in A+, and the b text's πας ο αριθμος αυτου, see comment at v.6. Hex has added αυτων after ἐπεσκεμμένοι to represent the suffix of פקדיהם of MT. For the leader of the Gadites, Ἐλισὰφ υἱὸς Ῥαγουήλ, see comment at 1:14. Those who were reviewed from the Gadites amounted to 45,650 men, for which see 1:37.[12]

2:16 For the popular A text's ηριθμημενοι, see comment at v.6. The total number for those passed under review for the camp of Rouben was 151,450. The number 151,000 is given without conjunctions in Num, but in the tradition και̃ς are

---

11. See THGN 98.
12. Tar^J omitted "and fifty."

inserted by hex to produce εκατον και πεντηκοντα και μια χιλιαδες which equals MT. The Byz text has changed παρεμβολῆς to φυλης, which is a thoughtless error. Each of the four camps consist of three tribes; here it is the camp on the south side that is designated as 'Ρουβήν; see also v.10.

The Greek also follows the pattern of v.9 in lacking a conjunction to introduce δεύτεροι ἐξαροῦσιν over against MT which has ושנים יסעו,[13] though hex has corrected Num by adding και before δεύτεροι to equal MT. For εξαρουσιν A b s^{mg}+ read αναζευξουσιν, as at v.9, which see.[14]

2:17 MT begins with ונסע, which the Masoretes vocalized as Qal, but the translator with his ἀρθήσεται understood as Ni, which the consonantal text also allows, thus "and the tent of testimony shall be moved and the camp of the Levites in the middle of the camps." LXX has simplified MT by making the subject coordinate; in MT מחנה is in apposition to אהל, which is odd. For μέσον, ms 426 which may represent hex, reads εν μεσω for בתוך. The Byz text is also recensional with its εις μεσον.

What is meant by this clause is clarified by v.b: ὡς καὶ παρεμβάλλουσιν οὕτως καὶ ἐξαροῦσιν. In MT both verbs are prefix inflections, but LXX distinguishes the two by rendering יחנה by a present tense, and only the second verb, יסעו, by a future. This is an intelligent differentiation. "As they are encamping, so they must break camp."[15] Both parts of v.b add an emphatic καί, thus ὡς καί ... οὕτως καί. I would render this by "just as ... so also." It should be noted, however, that the majority A F M text omits the καί after ὡς, but only three scattered mss plus La and Eth omit the second καί.

The subject of the οὕτως clause is individualized by ἕκαστος ἐχόμενος καθ' ἡγεμονίαν "each one next (to each other) by regiment." This is a free, but not inaccurate, rendering of MT's איש על ידו לדגליהם. For ἡγεμονίαν as rendering for דגל see comment at v.2. The more usual rendering τάγμα(τα) is a popular A M variant text in the tradition. Also popular is the majority A F M text, viz. the hex addition of αυτων to represent the suffix. LXX interprets על ידו by ἐχόμενος

---

13. Only Sam and Tar^O of the old witnesses support MT. Tar^{JN} Pesh and Vulg are all asyndetic.
14. See in particular Quast in Studien 250—251.
15. Only Theod retains the ἐξαροῦσιν of LXX; Aq and Sym render the verb by ἀπαροῦσιν.

in view of the pattern set for the 12 tribes who are arranged in adjacent positions. What על ידו means here is probably "(each) in his place, position."[16]

2:18—19 The pattern is exactly that of vv.10—11, except for the preposition παρά instead of πρός. Since the word for "westward" is ימה, i.e. "seaward," the translator might well have preferred παρά "near, alongside (the sea)." The reference is of course to the Mediterranean, which was the western boundary of the Promised land. MT has a different word order in that ימה follows לצבאתם, and hex has transposed παρὰ θάλασσαν after "with their army" to equal the order of MT.

For the leader of the Ephraimites, 'Ελισαμὰ υἱὸς 'Εμιούδ, see comment at 1:9b. For the rationale of the Byz+ reading ταγματα, see comment at v.3. For ηριθμημενοι of b+, see comment at v.6. Hex has also added αυτων after ἐπεσκεμμένοι to represent the suffix of פקדיהם. The total number of those reviewed for the tribe was 40,500, for which see 1:31.

2:20—21 The pattern of v.5 is used for v.20, i.e. ἐχόμενοι is used absolutely for the tribe of Manasse. For the leader of the tribe, Γαμαλιὴλ υἱὸς Φαδασούρ, see comments at 1:10.[17] The Hebrew for v.20 is again shorter than usual, in that it has no counterpart for οἱ παρεμβάλλοντες, which hex, accordingly, placed under the obelus. Presumably, the ועליו with which the verse begins simply means "alongside it," i.e. alongside the tribe of Ephraim. Hex did supply the pronoun αυτου to represent the suffix of עליו. Similarly, hex added αυτων after ἐπεσκεμμένοι to equal MT. The total number of those reviewed was 32,200, for which see 1:33. Why the Byz text should have changed διακόσιοι (for מאתים) to τριακοσιοι is puzzling.

2:22—23 Here the pattern of v.12 with its ἐχόμενοι αὐτοῦ is followed. MT, however, begins as v.14 without an equivalent for the introductory οἱ παρεμβάλλοντες ἐχόμενοι αὐτοῦ, which hex has therefore placed under the obelus. For the leader of the Beniaminites, 'Αβιδὰν υἱὸς Γαδεωνί, see comments at 1:11. For

---
16. Aq reflects the Hebrew text in typical isolate fashion by his ἀνὴρ ἐπὶ χεῖρα αὐτοῦ εἰς τάγματα αὐτῶν. Sym has ἕκαστος ἀνὰ χεῖρα τοῦ ἰδίου κατὰ τάγματα αὐτῶν, whereas Theod reads ἀνὴρ ἐπὶ χεῖρα αὐτοῦ εἰς τάγμα αὐτῶν. Note how Aq is probably based on Theod, only correcting τάγμα to the plural.
17. For Φαδασούρ, see also THGN 120.

the variant text of b+ ηριθμημενοι instead of ἐπεσκεμμένοι, see comment at v.6. Hex has added an αυτων to provide an equivalent for the suffix of פקדיהם in MT. Those who passed under review amounted to 35,400, for which see 1:35; once again, τριακοσιοι was read by a Byz x+ text for τετρακόσιοι; cf comment at vv.20—21.

2:24 The total number of those passed under review for the camp of Ephraim is 108,100. Within the tradition, the Byz text has changed 100 to διακοσιοι. In this verse the variant A text reading ηριθμημενοι is popular, being supported by ol C b s+. For this reading, see footnote at v.6.

The hex text has added και before τρίτοι so as to equal the ושלשים of MT. An A b s^mg+ text has substituted αναζευξουσιν for ἐξαροῦσιν. The verb ἀναζεύγνυμι is a more technical term used for breaking up a camp;[18] see comments at vv.9,16.

2:25—26 The last division is that of Dan on the north side of the tent. For its leader, 'Αχιέζερ υἱὸς 'Αμισαδαί, see comment at 1:12.[19] For the variant plural ταγματα in f+, see comment at v.3 The A b+ text has ηριθμημενοι instead of ἐπεσκεμμένοι, for which see comment at v.6. The hex text has added αυτων to represent the suffix of MT's פקדיהם. The number of those who were passed under review was 62,700; cf 1:39. The b text has substituted εξακοσιοι for ἑπτακόσιοι, but only the latter can be original.

2:27—28 The account of the next tribe, Aser, follows the pattern set by v.12, in which ἐχόμενοι is followed by αὐτοῦ. The V z+ tradition has changed αὐτοῦ to αυτων, but MT has עליו. For the leader of the tribe of Aser, Φαγαιὴλ υἱὸς 'Εχράν, as well as for the tribal name 'Ασήρ, see comments at 1:13. For ἐπεσκεμμένοι the b+ text read ηριθμημενοι, for which see comment at v.6. The hex text has added αυτων to represent the pronominal suffix in MT. The census report for the tribe was 41,500, for which see 1:41. Instead of πεντακόσιοι the F z+ text wrongly reads επτακοσιοι.

---

18. See LS 2 sub voce for the absolute use of this verb. See also Quast in Studien 250—251.
19. The spelling 'Αειέζερ attributed to Aq on the margin of ms 344 is obviously a transcription error. Aq could only have read 'Αχιέζερ as Theod and Sym.

2:29—30 As in the case of the preceding tribe, the account for the tribe of Nephthali follows the pattern set by v.12. As in the cases of Gad (v.14) and Beniamin (v.22), MT has a shorter text, beginning with וּמַטֵּה. Accordingly, hex has placed οἱ παρεμβάλλοντες ἐχόμενοι αὐτοῦ under the obelus to indicate its lack of an equivalent in MT. For the leader of the Nephthalites, Ἀχιρὲ υἱὸς Αἰνάν, as well as for the treatment of Νεφθαλί in the tradition, see comments at 1:15. For αὐτοῦ in v.30 a z text wrongly reads αυτων. For ἐπεσκεμμένοι the b+ text reads ηριθμημενοι, for which see v.6; the hex text has added αυτων to represent the pronominal suffix of פקדיהם in MT. The number of the census count for the tribe was 53,400, for which see 1:43.

2:31 The summary statement for the fourth division. For ἐπεσκεμμένοι the A C b s+ text read αριθμηθεντες, while oI+ preferred the usual variant form ηριθμημενοι; for the variants, see comment at v.6. The number given as the total of those passed under review for the camp of Dan is given as "100 and 57,000 and 600" in Num. MT's counterpart reads "hundred thousand and seven and fifty thousand and six hundred." Hex has, accordingly, added χιλιαδες after ἑκατόν, and changed "57,000" to "seven and fifty thousand," so as to equal MT exactly. An A M oI C s+ reading has reordered LXX to read "seven and fifty and a hundred thousand (and 600)," whereas the b text has wrongly changed 600 to πεντακοσιοι, and C reads πεντακοσιοι μαλλον δε εξακοσιοι! The compound number is followed by σὺν δυνάμει αὐτῶν as in the summary statements for the first three divisions (vv.9,16 and 24), but MT lacks an equivalent. In consequence, hex has placed it under the obelus, thereby promoting the likelihood of the longer text being original; it is also typical of this translator to follow the dominant patterns set up for the chapter.[20]

On the other hand, Num departs from the pattern by reading κατὰ τάγμα αὐτῶν at the end of the verse, i.e. after ἔσχατοι ἐξαροῦσιν. This is of course derived from MT's לדגליהם. The noun is changed by the majority M V text to the plural ταγματα equalling the plural noun of MT, and this may be a hex correction, it being supported *inter alia* by cod G, the oldest member of the O text.

---

20. See THGN 131.

2:32 A summary statement on the review. MT views the reviews as the summary of four such, i.e. reads "אלה פקודי" of the Israelites" and כל פקודי המחנת, which Num interprets by singulars, i.e. αὕτη ἡ ἐπίσκεψις ... πᾶσα ἡ ἐπίσκεψις τῶν παρεμβολῶν. Either is defensible, and no recensional attempt obtains to change to the futures. As might be expected, the variants ουτος ο αριθμος (in b s^{mg}+) and πας ο αριθμος (s^{mg}) do obtain; for these, comp the comment and footnote at v.6. For κατ' οἴκους πατριῶν αὐτῶν, see comment at 1:2. לצבאתם when applied to individual tribes was rendered by σὺν δυνάμει αὐτῶν, for which see comment 1:3, but here the term is applied to the Israelites in general, and so it is correctly rendered by a plural noun in σὺν ταῖς δυνάμεσιν αὐτῶν. The grand total of Israelite men passed under review was 603,550. πεντακόσιοι πεντήκοντα represents וחמשים וחמש מאות, and the majority text has added και before both words; this is likely to be a recensional correction, probably hex in origin.

2:33 This verse contrasts with v.32, which the translator neatly shows by a contrastive δέ: "but the Levites (were not passed under review)." The verb rendering the Hebrew Hithp התפקדו was an excellent choice; συνεπεσκέπησαν "were passed under review together (with them)" is exactly right in the context. The reading ηριθμηθησαν is substituted for the verb in s^{mg}, for which see comment (and footnote) at v.6. The verb is modified by ἐν αὐτοῖς, which refers to the τῶν υἱῶν 'Ισραήλ of v.32. Actually, MT reads בתוך בני ישראל, and in the tradition b s^{mg} z substitute εν τοις υιοις ισραηλ, which was undoubtedly mediated through one of The Three. Oddly enough, at 1:47, which is a parallel statement, exactly the reverse occurred. Num has ἐν τοῖς υἱοῖς 'Ισραήλ, but MT read בתוכם. It is also fully possible that the b s^{mg} z variant text was actually ex par rather than mediated recensionally. Most witnesses omit ἐν, but the earliest witness, Cod B, as well as F V (and many others), witness to the preposition, and it must be original. The simple dative in cod A would be an unusual rendering for בתוכם.

2:34 According to Num. "the Israelites did πάντα ὅσα συνέταξεν the Lord to Moses." Since MT has "ככל that Yahweh commanded Moses," hex has added κατα before πάντα.[21] A popular A V text substituted ενετειλατο for συνέταξεν; this presumably was influenced by v.33 where צוה was rendered by ἐνετείλατο.

---

21. The Others also read κατὰ πάντα.

The two verbs are synonyms. ἐντέλλομαι is by far the more popular rendering of צוה, occurring 345 times in LXX, while συντάσσω is used only 81 times,[22] though it is almost impossible to distinguish the two semantically.

The failure to render the preposition in ככל resulted in a different syntactic cut for LXX. The Masoretes made the cut before ככל, i.e. ישראל was accented with an *ethnach*. So MT understood v.b as reading "according to everything which ..., so they encamped ... and so they broke camp ...." But LXX could not make that comparison, and v.b begins with the first οὕτως, i.e. "so they encamped according to τάγμα αὐτῶν." As at v.31 לדגליהם is translated by a singular τάγμα, and as at v.31 a popular F V text has changed it to the plural ταγματα, which may well be a recensional (probably hex) change.

The verse ends in MT with איש למשפחתיו על בית אבתיו. The Greek has interpreted this by plural pronouns, αὐτῶν, whereas one would have expected αυτου in view of the headword איש. But this has probably been occasioned by the arbitrary insertion of ἐχόμενοι after ἕκαστος: "each one, adjacent ones according to their clans, according to their paternal households." For both nouns, see comment at v.2. The term ἐχόμενοι has no basis in MT, and must be original. No Greek witness lacks it or changes it, and hex has placed it under the obelus to indicate its lack of equivalent in MT. The word is of course ex par, since it occurs regularly throughout the chapter.

---

22. According to the count of Dos Santos.

Chapter 3

3:1 Vv.1—13 detail what the Lord said to Moses about Aaronids and Levites at Mount Sinai. It begins (vv.2—4) with the Aaronids. In the tradition, the C text has added τεσσαρες after γενέσεις. This refers to the four sons of Aaron. Obviously, the Catena glossator understood γενέσεις as referring specifically to the first generation. It may be noted that תלדת is no longer being rendered by (κατὰ) συγγενείας as in ch.1, but by the more usual (23 times) word γενέσεις.[1]

3:2 The names of the Aaronids are given. The first one is designated as πρωτότοκος, and is named Ναδάβ, whereas MT has נדב הבכור.[2] Oddly enough, only two f mss articulate πρωτότοκος, but only the unarticulated noun can be considered as original. The second one is named Ἀβιούδ, though MT has אביהוא. The Greek always transcribes this name as Ἀβιούδ, as though the Hebrew had אביהוד, as at 1Chr 8:3. I have no explanation for this phenomenon; see Note at Exod 6:23. The hex text has changed the name to αβιου to equal MT.

3:3 This verse appears as a doublet to v.2, both beginning with "(and) these are the names of the Aaronids," the only difference being the presence of the "and" at the beginning of v.2.[3] Here, instead of their names being given, their status is described; they are: the anointed priests οὓς ἐτελείωσαν τὰς χεῖρας αὐτῶν ἱερατεύειν "whom they ordained to serve as priests."[4] For the idiom τελειόω τὰς χεῖρας, see Note at Exod 29:9; "to validate the hands" is a technical idiom for "to ordain to office," in the same sense as the Hebrew מלא ידם in MT. In MT, however, the verb is singular, which reflects the description in Lev 8, in which Moses performed the rites of ordination for both Aaron and his sons. But the Greek changes the verb to the plural, though the hex text has revised this to the

---

1. The count is that of Dos Santos.
2. For variations on spelling of the sons' names, see Notes at Exod 6:23.
3. Num follows the ואלה of Sam Tar^JN; Kenn 84,95*,107*,150,157,199,225 also read the conjunction.
4. Both Tar^JO simply read לשמשא, whereas Tar^N adds בכהנתה רבתה.

singular to agree with MT.⁵ The plural is difficult to interpret. I would take the plural here as an indefinite "they," as in "they say," meaning "it has been said."⁶

3:4 The reference to the death of Nadab and Abioud is to Lev 10:1—3. The pseudo genitive absolute gives the reason for their premature death. προσφερόντων αὐτῶν renders the Hebrew pattern ב plus bound infinitive plus pronominal suffix, "when they offered *(strange fire* before the Lord)." ἔναντι κυρίου locates the offering in the sanctuary,⁷ presumably on the incense altar;⁸ for "strange fire," see Note at Lev 10:1.

In the second clause, the neuter plural is taken in the Classical sense of a collective, and has a singular predicate in ἦν (αὐτοῖς), in spite of the Hebrew היו.

V.b follows MT in having a singular verb with the compound predicate following. In the tradition, the majority F M text reads the plural, but the oldest witnesses, codd A B G, all witness to the original singular. The singular is fully legitimate, since when a compound subject follows the verb, the number of the verb is often attracted to that of the nearer subject. When the verb follows, only a plural verb may be used. The verb is modified in MT by על פני "before," i.e. in the presence of. This is rendered in the Greek by μετά plus the genitive.⁹ According to Num, serving as priests על פני Aaron their father, meant that they too served as priests, which is a reasonable conclusion; after all, על פני is sometimes intended in the sense of "besides."

3:6 Highly unusual is the rendering of λάβε for הקרב; in fact, this equation occurs elsewhere only at Ezek 43:22, according to HR. The Hi of קרב usually refers to the bringing of sacrifice, and it should occasion no surprise that προσφέρω should occur 91 times for הקריב, and προσάγω, 72 times, whereas

---

5. 4QNumᵇ also reads the plural.
6. I find the explanation of the plural in Dorival 84—85 as referring to the Lord and Moses unconvincing. Ordination is a ritual, and is hardly to be understood as performed by deity and man in concert.
7. Tarᴶ omits this locative along with the next one "in the desert of Sinai," and substitutes מן תפיין "from the hearth" as modifier of "strange fire."
8. According to Levine ad loc, citing Exod 30:9.
9. Levine follows NJPS in rendering על פני by "in (during) the lifetime of," comparing Gen 11:28, where LXX renders על פני by ἐνώπιον. Rashi also interprets על פני here by בחייו.

ἐγγίζω, which would have been appropriate here, obtains only ten times.[10] That Moses shold be ordered to "take" the tribe of Levi (and station it before Aaron) is a neutral and colorless rendering, but it is obvious that the rendering of the same verb at v.4, προσφερόντων, would have been inadequate here.[11]

In the tradition, a popular A F M text has repeated the article την before Λευί in "the tribe of Levi," but this would be unusual in Num. Nor does MT promote this interpretation.

MT has אתו as modifier of "you must station"; the reference is to מטה. Num makes this plural, αὐτούς, since "tribe" is composed of people; the Greek thinks in terms of the members of the tribe.

I would understand the last clause, καὶ λειτουργήσουσιν αὐτῷ, as indicating the purpose of the "taking" and "stationing" of the tribe before Aaron. This relation is signalled by the change to a third plural future verb. Moses is to set the tribe before Aaron, "so that they may serve him." The use of λειτουργέω is usual for שרת. Out of 99 cases of שרת in MT, only 20 are not rendered by λειτουργέω or its cognate noun λειτουργός.[12] The verb is commonly used to refer to public service, though in the LXX it often refers specifically to cultic service.[13] The Levites are to assist as helpers for Aaron, who accordingly, is their superior.

3:7 The relation between Aaron and the Levites is then clarified in vv.7—10. The Greek renders the cognate expression of MT in isolate fashion, i.e. also as cognate. Thus φυλάξουσιν τὰς φυλακὰς αὐτοῦ translates שמרו את משמרתו. What LXX means is "they must perform guard duties for him." Note that the Greek uses a plural noun to render משמרת. That it is a matter of guard duties is clear from its coordinate "and the guard duties for the Israelites ἔναντι the tent of testimony." MT has כל העדה "all the community," which Num identifies as τῶν υἱῶν Ἰσραήλ.[14] The addition of παντων to define "the Israelites" by O is likely a hex attempt at compromise. העדה is understood as equal to "the Israelites," but

---

10. According to Dos Santos.
11. Dorival suggests that "de cette manière, la LXX exclut tout rapprochement entre Nadab et Abioud d'une part, et Moïse d'autre part," which is an interesting possibility.
12. Acording to the count in Dos Santos.
13. Bauer s.v. defines the verb as "*perform a public service, serve in a (public) office*, in our lit. exclusively of religious and ritual services both in a wider and a more restricted sense." Note also that Schl defines the adjectival λειτουργικός by "*ministerio*, speciatim sacro."
14. Tar^J interprets with כל עם כנישתא.

כל had no equivalent, and hex supplied a translation. From 1:50 it is clear that the Levites "must camp around the tent," and from ch.2 that the twelve tribes in turn are to camp around the Levites. That the performance of guard duties is, however, more broadly conceived than mere protection against illegitimate intrusion is clear from the explicative infinitival construction which ends the verse, ἐργάζεσθαι τὰ ἔργα τὴν σκηνῆς "to work the works of the tent," i.e. so as to perform the various duties pertaining to the tent. Num interprets the noun עבדת as a plural noun, which the consonantal text allows. What is meant is the various duties connected with the sacred tent. In MT "the tent" is המשכן, whereas "the tent (of witness) is אהל, but LXX does not distinguish between the two.[15]

3:8 This verse is similar to v.7, but differs in that here it is πάντα τὰ σκεύη of the tent of testimony which needs protective care.[16] The main difference between the two verses is in the first משמרת; in v.7 it refers to Aaron, but in v.8 it concerns all the vessels of the sacred tent.

In both verses, however, the verse ended with לעבד את עבדת המשכן. The translator understood its intent differently here, by rendering it by a κατά phrase, i.e. "according to all the works of the tent." In v.7 Num took the infinitival structure as explicative; it defined what was meant by φυλάξουσιν τὰς φυλακὰς τῶν υἱῶν Ἰσραήλ, but here it becomes the norm or standard for the Israelites' guard duties. The πάντα has no basis in MT; it is an interpretive gloss. Why the translator, who usually follows set patterns, should render this quite differently here may be due to the reference to the furnishings, the σκεύη of the tent, that promoted the change.

---

15. For καί 2° — fin Aq has καὶ τὴν φυλακὴν πάσης τῆς συναγωγῆς εἰς πρόσωπον σκέπης συνταγῆς τοῦ δουλεύειν τὴν δουλείαν τῆς σκηνῆς. Sym translates καὶ τὴν φυλακὴν πάσης τῆς συναγωγῆς κατὰ πρόσωπον τῆς σκηνῆς τῆς συνταγῆς λατρεύειν τὴν λατρείαν τῆς σκηνῆς, whereas Theod has καὶ τὴν φυλακὴν πάσης τῆς συναγωγῆς κατὰ πρόσωπον τῆς σκηνῆς τοῦ μαρτυρίου τοῦ δουλεύειν τὴν δουλείαν τὴν σκηνῆς. For a discussion of Aq and Sym and their rendering of עבד עבדת, see Daniel 113—114.
16. Milgrom makes the interesting, though disputable, distinction that v.7 refers to the guard duty "when the camp was at rest," whereas v.8, to their duty when the camp was "in transit." But this involves rather fancy footwork in the translation of καὶ τὰς φυλακὰς τῶν υἱῶν Ἰσραήλ. He renders this as a parenthetical "—a duty on behalf of the Israelites—," but in v.7 the parallel structure as "and for the whole community." In both cases a coordinate ומשמרת is involved.

3:9 Moses is to "give (i.e. assign) the Levites to Aaron and his sons the priests." MT lacks "the priests"; the addition serves to ensure the distinction betwen Levites and priests. What is meant is that the Levites are to serve in a subordinate rank to the Aaronids. Hex has rightly placed τοῖς ἱερεῦσιν under the obelus.

V.b states that נתונם נתונם המה לו מאת בני ישראל, "they are specifically given to him (i.e. to Aaron) from the Israelites." The repeated participle probably is intended as an intensification, i.e. as his very own.[17] The Greek followed Sam with its μοί (i.e. reading לי, not לו). The Sam reading harmonizes with the parallel passage at 8:16 which reads לי/μοί.[18]

Num was troubled by the repeated participle, and interpreted it by δόμα δεδομένοι "as a gift (they are) given (to me)," which is a good attempt at finding a semantic equivalent to the Hebrew in acceptable Greek. This translation preserves the cognates of the passage: δώσεις, δόμα δεδομένοι. Clearly these must be understood as reflecting a single semantic core, that of "gift"; the Levites are understood, not as equals to the Aaronids, but as subordinates who owe allegiance and service to the Aaronids; they have been given as δόμα to the priests.

In the tradition, the majority A F M text has identified Ἀαρών as τω αδελφω σου; this unnecessary gloss has no basis in MT, and is secondary. Hex was puzzled by μοί, since Origen only found לו in his Hebrew text, and so μοί was placed under the obelus, but he did not then also add an αυτω under the asterisk, but transposed εἰσιν, which has no basis in MT, before οὗτος. The change of μοί to μου is palaeographically inspired; in some cursive texts the οι and ου are easily confused.

3:10 The higher status of the Aaronids is made even clearer in LXX which has interpreted הפקד by καταστήσεις ἐπὶ τῆς σκηνῆς τοῦ μαρτυρίου. Obviously, the verb does not mean "pass under review, add," but "appoint."[19] By using καθίστημι some type of modifier is needed; one must appoint someone either as something or over something; hence the gloss "over the tent of testimony," which hex has accordingly put under the obelus. The translator thereby makes it obvious

---

17. See GK 123e.
18. See the discussion in Dorival 113.
19. Rashi makes this clear by לשון פקידות ואינו לשון מנין. Tar^Jo render by the Pa תמני "appoint."

that the Aaronids, not the Levites, are in charge over the tabernacle, even though the Levites must take care of πάντα τὰ σκεύη of the tent (v.8).

This then means that the Aaronids must take care of or guard (φυλάξουσιν) their ἱερατείαν, i.e. their כהנה "their priesthood." What is meant by ἱερατείαν is defined by καὶ πάντα τὰ κατὰ τὸν βωμὸν καὶ τὰ ἔσω τοῦ καταπετάσματος. This has no corresponding text in MT, and is accordingly placed under the obelus in hex. It is, however, Biblically based on 18:7, where the כהנה is defined as לכל דבר המזבח ולמבית לפרכת, which Num translated by κατὰ πάντα τρόπον τοῦ θυσιαστηρίου καὶ τὸ ἔνδοθεν τοῦ καταπετάσματος. Unique, however, is the rendering here of τὸν βωμόν for המזבח, since this is otherwise used only for non-Israelite altars; in fact, at 18:7 it is translated by τοῦ θυσιαστηρίου. That the tradition was troubled by the use of τὸν βωμόν for the altars in the tabernacle is clear from various attempts to substitute or add a reference to του θυσιαστηριου (possibly direct influence of 18:7?) in F V Byz *b z*+.[20]

The second priestly duty concerns τὰ ἔσω τοῦ καταπετάσματος, i.e. matters which concern the adytum. In the tradition, B *x*+ have omitted the τά. That this is a secondary omission I have fully argued elsewhere.[21]

The final clause, i.e. v.b, is exactly the same in 1:51 in MT, but LXX has ἁπτόμενος rather than προσπορευόμενος, for which see comment at v.38. MT has the subject of יומת given as הזר הקרב.[22]

3:12 Vv.12—13 constitute the Lord's explanation for the separate character of the Levites; comp the more detailed parallel passage in 8:16—19. V.12 begins with a preposed nominative pronoun (καὶ) ἐγώ, which might be rendered "And as for me," i.e. it serves as a discourse marker. This becomes clear from ἰδοὺ εἴληφα, with the clause marker ἰδού/הנה introducing a first person singular verb. The Lord says "See I have taken the Levites from the midst of the Israelites."[23] The ἀντί structure explains the divine action: the Levites are the substitute for "every firstborn, opening the womb, from the Israelites." This is defined by λύτρα αὐτῶν ἔσονται, which has no equivalent in MT, but is based on the פדויהם יהיו of

---

20. For another interpretation of the amplifications by Num for this verse, see Daniel 25—26.
21. In THGN 106.
22. Sym, as well as Aq, read ὁ δὲ ἀλλότριος ὃς ἐὰν προσέλθῃ ἀποθανέτω. I would take this text to have originated with Sym.
23. Tar[N] has אתפרשת "I have separated, set apart."

Sam. For the notion of Levites as redemption for the Israelite firstborn, see v.46. Hex placed it under the obelus to show its absence from MT.

V.b then gives the logical conclusion: "And the Levites shall be ἐμοί," a dative of possession reflecting the לי of MT.[24]

3:13 That every firstborn belonged to the Lord was well-known; cf Exod 34:19—20, as well as 22:29b. This the Lord had rationalized by the sparing of the firstborn at the time of the tenth plague in Egypt, when all the firstborn of the Egyptians were killed; see Exod 11:4 12:29. At that time, ἡγίασα ἐμοί πᾶν πρωτότοκον ἐν Ἰσραήλ.[25] For the consecration of the firstborn, see Exod 13:1.

3:15 The passing under review of the Levites is to be done κατ' οἴκους πατριῶν αὐτῶν, for which see comment at 1:2, and κατὰ δήμους αὐτῶν, for which see comment at 1:20. The third prepositional phrase, κατὰ συγγενείας αὐτῶν, has no equivalent in MT, and hex has quite rightly placed it under the obelus. Its omission in B x+ is, however, not a case of recensional activity, but a case of parablepsis due to homoioteleuton, i.e. the recurrent αὐτῶν is responsible for the error. The phrase occurred at 1:2, but for למשפחתם, which is more commonly rendered as here by κατὰ δήμους αὐτῶν. It is then an apparent doublet, but original to Num.

Every male over one month of age is to be reviewed, i.e. counted, registered, in contrast to that of the twelve tribes in ch.1. But the purpose of the review was different in ch.1; there it concerned males of military age; the Levites, however, were excluded from conscription into the army. The reason for the registration of the Levites is not given.

Moses is ordered: "you must pass them under review." Num follows MT in a consistent singular verb throughout the verse. In the tradition, a majority B M V text has the plural ἐπισκεψασθε, which cannot be correct.[26] Presumably, it was created because the registry was carried out in Num by Moses and Aaron according to v.16, but see comment ad loc.[27] Also in the tradition is the reading

---
24. Tar^N has לשמי "for my name" instead of לי, both here and three times in v.13.
25. Both Tar^JO read קדמי instead of ἐμοί; Tar^N has לשמי.
26. See THGN 121.
27. Difficult to understand is the attribution of the plural ἐπισκέψασθε to The Others on the margin of ms 344.

αριθμησον/αριθμημησονται in a popular A text. Since the αριθμε— root occurs throughout the Num tradition, it must be an early interpretive revision indeed.[28]

3:16 MT, consistent with the divine order of v.15, has Moses alone responsible for the registry of the Levites, but Num has added καὶ 'Ααρών to the subject of ἐπεσκέψατο, which hex has placed under the obelus to indicate its absence in MT. The translator obviously felt that the registration of the Levites was a matter which was of particular concern to the priest Aaron, and his inclusion throughout this verse was clearly intentional. As in v.15 a majority B M text reads the verb as επεσκεψαντο.[29] This would be due to the compound subject of Num, but congruence of number between compound subject and predicate in Num is dependent on word order. If the predicate follows the subject, congruence is the rule, but if not, number congruence is normally only with the nearer element of the subject; in other words, the singular is here original. Also as in v.15, a popular A text avoided the root ἐπισκέπτομαι in favor of ἀριθμέω and reads ηριθμησεν, for which see comment and footnote at v.15.

V.b in MT is כאשר צוה, with the verb perforce vocalized as Pu, i.e. "as he was ordered," with Moses as subject. The translator has changed this to ὃν τρόπον συνέταξεν αὐτοῖς κύριος. This not only identifies the Lord as subject, but also identifies Moses and Aaron as the ones receiving the order, which is consistent with v.a.[30]

3:17 The sons of Levi are listed by their names: Γεδσών, Καὰθ καὶ Μεραρί. For the misreading of *resh* as *daleth*, thereby producing Γεδσών for גרשון, see Note at Exod 6:16. From that point on, the Greek Pentateuch always read Γεδσών. The hex text corrected the spelling to γηρσων so as to correspond to MT.[31] The names appear in the tradition as γεδεων in many mss through confusion of the uncials Σ—E; others read γεθσων by assimilation to the voiceless *sigma*; also attested are γεσων and γεδισων. In MT, the second name קהת is preceded by a conjunction, but Num follows Sam's pattern of ab+c rather than the a+b+c of MT. Spelling errors for μεραρί included μαραρι, αμεραρι, μαρι and μερανη.

---

28. U.Quast calls it such in Studien 231—248. See also my "An Early Revision of the Septuagint of Numbers," in Eretz—Israel 16 (the H.M.Orlinsky volume), 236*—238*.
29. See THGN 121.
30. Comp Sam which reads צוהו "he ordered him."
31. The Three all read Γηρσών as well.

3:18 The names of the sons of Γεδσών are given according to their clans (δήμους).³² For the spelling of Γεδσών, see comment at v.17. Hex has corrected its spelling to γηρσων. These sons are Λοβενί and Σεμεί. Both names, aside from itacisms, are rather stable in the tradition. For the former, λουβενι occurs in *x*; λοβονι is due either to an E/O confusion in the uncial tradition, or to vowel assimilation to the first *omicron*; the *nu* is doubled in an *n* reading, and *beta* becomes *mu* by cursive confusion of β and μ in a *z* reading. The only misreading of significance for the second clan name is a *z* reading σεμεσει (through dittography with E/Σ confusion).

3:19 The sons of Kaath according to clans are given in two pairs. The first pair is Ἀμράμ and Ἰσαάρ. Ἀμράμ is misspelled in a variety of ways; see Note at Exod 6:18 for an explanation of the various misreadings: αμβραν, αβραν, αμβρααμ, αβρααμ, αβραμ and αμβραμ; the spelling γαμβραμ in ms V is not based on a Hebrew pronunciation of the ע grapheme, but is simply a thoughtless mistake. The second name is also variously realized in the tradition: ισσαρ, ισαρ, ιεσααρ, ιεσσααρ, ισαχαρ, ισσαχαρ, ιεσαχαρ, ιεσσαχαρ and the popular ισσααρ. Since the Hebrew יצהר is parent text, only a transcription with a single *sigma* and a double *alpha* can be taken as original.³³

The second pair is stable in the tradition as far as the spelling is concerned, only χευρων for *d* occurring; since both *upsilon* and *beta* were homophonic, both being pronounced as /v/ in Byzantine Greek, it is readily explicable. For the last name only ουζιηλ differs from Num. The pair is, however, introduced by και in Byz+, but the two pair pattern is dominant and original.

3:20 "The sons of Merari according to their clans are Μοολί καὶ Μουσί," representing מחלי and מושי resp. Misspellings of Μοολί are abundant at Exod 6:19, which see, but are far fewer here. Aside from itacisms, only μοολλει and μολι occur in Greek witnesses. ומושי "and Moushi" was transliterated as Ὀμουσί at Exod 6:19, but here it became καὶ Μουσί. Unfortunately, the Exod spelling strongly influenced the tradition here as well; Exod actually had καὶ Ὀμουσί, and most spellings in the tradition begin with a vowel; in fact, the only non-itacistic

---

32. The Others read Γηρσών.
33. See the discussion in THGN 115—116.

misspelling beginning with *mu* is a *b* reading μοουσι! For the dominant spellings in the tradition, see Note at Exod 6:19.

V.b is a subscription to vv.16—19, identifying these as the clans of הלוי. Num interprets this quite correctly as τῶν Λευίτων. For κατ' οἴκους πατριῶν αὐτῶν, see comment at 1:2.

3:21 Vv.21—26 give details concerning the clans of Gedson.[34] V.21 is introduced by a dative of possession, τῷ Γεδσών, i.e. "to Gedson belonged ...." For the two clans, see v.18 and comments ad loc.

V.b identifies these as being "the clans τοῦ Γεδσών." But MT has the articulated gentilic הגרשני "of the Gershonite." For Γεδσών, see comment at v.17.

3:22 The first clause is a pendant construction, which introduces the second clause. The clause reads "ἡ ἐπίσκεψις αὐτῶν according to the number of every male from a month old and upwards," the pronoun's referent being to the clan of Λοβενί and the clan of Σεμεί. For variations on the spellings of these names, see comments at v.18.

The second clause gives the results of the review as 7000 and 500.[35] In the tradition, the *b* text changed the genitive παντὸς ἀρσενικοῦ to the accusative, παν αρσενικον. For the popular A reading ο αριθμος αυτων in the second clause, see footnote at v.15. Also in the tradition, *b* read διακοσιοι instead of πεντακόσιοι, which is probably merely a careless mistake.

3:23 The verse begins with καὶ οὗτοι, followed by the subject οἱ υἱοὶ Γεδσών. MT begins with משפחת הגרשני.[36] Obviously, καὶ οὗτοι has no equivalent in MT, and hex has placed these words under the obelus. Hex, however, also changed υιοι to οι δημοι to represent the משפחת; comp v.29, where οἱ δῆμοι τῶν υἱῶν obtains. The text of Num is admittedly peculiar. Since οὗτοι is followed by υἱοί, which is itself not a rendering of משפחת, as Origen realized as evidenced by his change of

---
34. The Others read Γηρσών, as does hex.
35. The Three all substantiate the number, but differ in their rendering of פקדיהם. Aq has ἐπεσκεμμένοι αὐτῶν; Sym reads οἱ ἐπεσκεμμένοι αὐτῶν, and Theod changes Num to the plural αἱ ἐπισκέψεις αὐτῶν.
36. Theod and Aq read συγγένειαι τοῦ Γηρσοννεί, whereas Sym has ὁ δῆμοι ὁ Γηρσοννίτης.

υἱοί to οι δημοι, it is possible that οὗτοι was an early dittography of a misread υἱοί. If so, it is an error made before the time of Origen, since hex has καὶ οὗτοι under the obelus. Actually the majority A B F M text omitted οὗτοι, and it is fully possible that the original text read και (οι) υιοι, with the addition of ουτοι as a prehexaplaric insertion, but one hesitates to suggest this in view of the hex evidence.[37]

The location of their camp is given in two locative phrases, ὀπίσω τῆς σκηνῆς and παρὰ θάλασσαν. In MT the verb is placed between the two phrases. LXX, however, has παρεμβαλοῦσιν at the end. The majority A F M V text has reordered the text to equal that of MT, which is a recensional correction, probably hex in origin. At v.29 the direction is indicated by a κατά phrase, and the popular A F V text also reads κατα here instead of παρά. Which is original is uncertain, but it is prudent to follow the oldest extant witness, cod B, with παρά.

3:24 The chieftain of the בית אב for the Gershonites was Ἐλισὰφ υἱὸς Λαήλ. The term בית אב refers to the larger unit, the Gershonites; Num makes this clear by its οἴκου πατριᾶς τοῦ δήμου "the patriarchal house of the clan (τοῦ Γεδσών)." For τοῦ Γεδσών as rendering for the Hebrew gentilic, see v.23 and comment at v.21. Hex has put τοῦ δήμου under the obelus, since it has no isolate correspondence in MT, but the translator used the longer unit found at vv.30,35 because the larger δῆμος was intended; comp vv.30,35 for this larger unit. It should be noted that Origen was apparently troubled by this, since τοῦ δήμου was transposed after τοῦ Γεδσών. The name Γεδσών was also corrected to γηρσων by hex. For various other spellings, see comment at v.17.

Ἐλισάφ represents אליסף, but only one ms, 426, corrects to ελιασαφ. Other spellings include ελισαβ, ελισαφαν, ελισαφαθ, ελεισαφατ and ελισαφα.

The name Λαήλ for לאל, is only supported by two hex witnesses, 426 and Syh, whereas all but two other mss support *delta* instead of the initial λαμβδα; the two exceptions are αηλ and φαηλ. It is true that if δαηλ were original, the reading λαηλ would be a hex correction, but an original δαηλ is hard to imagine. A palaeographic confusion between ר and ל is hardly possible, whereas the confusion betwen Λ and Δ is common among copyists. So in spite of its weak support I believe that Λαήλ must be original.[38]

---

37. See THGN 131.
38. The Others also read Λαήλ.

3:25 Vv.25—26 describe the φυλακή of the Gedsonites in the tent of testimony. The term φυλακή renders משמרת, and is a cover term referring to all the elements of the sacred tent entrusted for safekeeping, possibly best rendered by "charge" or "custody." The area of their charge was the tent of testimony complex, for which MT has the usual equivalent, but followed by המשכן והאהל, i.e. "the tabernacle (by which the sacred compound was intended) and the tent" (by which the tent in the middle of the compound was designated). Num does not distinguish between the two, since it uses the same word, σκηνή, for both Hebrew words.³⁹ Hex has added και η σκεπη after σκηνή under the asterisk in order to represent MT more adequately. Syntactically I would take v.a as the subject, with v.b and v.26 constituting the predicate. The critical text has separated the two by a colon, which is admittedly an unusual punctuation, but how else can one designate the difference between v.a and v.b?

V.b then continues by listing the various elements that constitute the charge of the Gedsonites along with ἡ σκηνή, viz. with מכסהו and the מסך of the door of the tent of meeting. The Greek renders the first of these by τὸ κάλυμμα to which hex added αυτης to equal the suffix. In the Exod tabernacle account the מכסה refers to the overal covering of the tent, i.e. the covering (κατακάλυμμα) of the skin dyed red, and the covering (ἐπικάλυμμα) for the blue skin; see Note at Exod 26:14. The more difficult term is מסך, also a kind of covering (from the root סכך), a type of screen placed either at the gate of the courtyard or at the entrance of the tent as here (first appearing at Exod 26:36, where it is rendered by the hapax legomenon ἐπίσπαστρον; see Note ad loc). Its translation by κατακάλυμμα occurs at v.31 and 4:25 as well. At 4:25 the word is also modified by "τῆς θύρας of the tent of testimony," and the rendering by "screen" would be adequate. Though the two terms κάλυμμα and κατακάλυμμα are semantically hardly distinguishable, the translator does not mix the two, i.e. the former is never used for מסך, nor the latter for מכסה.⁴⁰

3:26 This verse continues with more elements of the sacred tent, which are under the charge of the Gedsonites. The first item is קלעי החצר "the hangings of the court." This is rendered adequately by τὰ ἱστία τῆς αὐλῆς, for which see Note at

---
39. The Tar distinguish the two as משכן and משכנה.
40. See THGN 127.

Exod 27:9. The second one is ואת מסך פתח החצר אשר על המשכן ועל המזבח סביב. This is translated by καὶ τὸ καταπέτασμα τῆς πύλης τῆς αὐλῆς τῆς οὔσης ἐπὶ τῆς σκηνῆς "and the curtain of the gate of the court which is by the tent." The rendering καταπέτασμα is common for מסך.[41] Obviously LXX has omitted the second prepositional phrase, and hex has added και επι του θυσιαστηριου κυκλω under the asterisk to make up for it. On the other hand, MT has no equivalent for the expansion οὔσης, and the participle has been placed under the obelus by hex.[42]

The verse ends with: "את מיתריו for all its service." In its place LXX has "καὶ τὰ κατάλοιπα πάντων τῶν ἔργων αὐτοῦ. The term מיתר has been understood, not as "cord," i.e. the cords of the tabernacle, but in the sense of יתר "remainder, rest." The translator was misled by understanding the prepositional phrase as applying to כל עבדתו rather than to the משכן "the tabernacle," and contextualized freely to produce "and the remaining elements of all its works." The suffix was perforce not rendered.[43]

3:27 Vv.27—32 deal with the clans of Kaath. V.27 follows the pattern set out in v.21 exactly; in fact, it differs from MT in not recognizing the initial conjunction, i.e. it is asyndetic as v.21. From v.19 it was clear that there were four subclans for Kaath, which are here repeated as clan names, i.e. as gentilics.[44] The first one, 'Αμράν, becomes העמרמי, i.e. ὁ 'Αμραμίς. In MT the gentilic is the free element of the bound phrase משפחת העמרמי, but the Greek realized the phrase as δῆμος ὁ 'Αμραμίς. This pattern of an unarticulated δῆμος followed by an articulated gentilic is used consistently, both in this and the following section (vv.33—37). Syntactically, the articulated gentilic is an apposite to δῆμοι in each case. The clan name suffered badly in the tradition, with most witnesses adding a *beta* after the initial αμ, or changing αμ- to αβ-. Also witnessed is the doubling of the second *alpha*, as well as the change of the second *mu* to a *nu*.

The second δῆμος is ὁ 'Ισααρίς. For the spelling of the tribal name see the discussion at v.18. Actually, no extant witness has the correct spelling, though

---

41. According to Dos Santos it occurs eight times, i.e. more than any other rendering.
42. The article alone is sufficient for rendering אשר.
43. See SS 100.
44. Neither Tar[JO] render the clans by a gentilic, but Tar[N] does do so; in fact, it also reads in each case "sons of" before the gentilic name.

four mss have the itacistic variant ισααρεις. The majority variant has omitted the initial *iota*, i.e. σααρεις, but this cannot be original.⁴⁵

The last two clans, ὁ Χεβρωνίς and ὁ Οζιηλίς, were both quite stable in the tradition, and hardly need comment.

The verse ends with "these are (the) clans of הקהתי. MT continues using the gentilic form, which the translator rejected; he rendered the gentilic simply by the clan name τοῦ Κααθ, as was done in the pattern set out in v.21.

3:28 This verse differs considerably from its parallel v.22 in that neither instance of ἡ ἐπίσκεψις αὐτῶν obtains. The shorter text reproduces MT correctly, but it does create a grammatical problem in that the clausal structure is not clear. Obviously, it is not an SP structure. It is introduced by an exact translation of במספר כל זכר word for word, i.e. κατὰ ἀριθμὸν πᾶν ἀρσενικόν, which along with "from a month old and upward" constitutes the theme introducing the head count. Note also that the simpler ἀριθμὸν παντὸς ἀρσενικοῦ of v.22 is avoided in favor of a more difficult accusative "according to number, even every male." The 8000 and 600 are characterized as φυλάσσοντες τὰς φυλακὰς τῶν ἁγίων, preserving the cognate structure of MT's שמרי משמרת הקדש "those entrusted with the charges of the sanctuary."⁴⁶ The translator treated the cognate noun as plural, which the consonantal text allows. The rendering of הקדש by the plural is used erratically in Num; thus at v.38 the singular occurs in precisely the same context.⁴⁷ One might render the Num text by "those entrusted with the care for the sanctuary."

In the tradition, the ἑξακόσιοι is changed to τριακοσιοι in Byz+, but MT has שש מאות.

3:29 The location of the Kaathite clans was to be ἐκ πλαγίων τῆς σκηνῆς κατὰ λίβα " from the side of the tent towards the south." ἐκ πλαγίων renders על ירך "on the side." The plural πλάγια with a preposition can be used in an adverbial sense.⁴⁸ κατὰ λίβα translates תימנה adequately.⁴⁹ In the tradition, the popular A

---

45. As is argued in THGN 115—116.
46. Levine freely but cleverly renders this by "the maintenance personnel for the shrine"; NJPS more conservatively translates "attending to the duties of the sanctuary."
47. See THGN 112 for more examples.
48. See LS sub πλάγιος I.4.
49. The Others render by κατὰ νότον.

F M text reads κατα νοτον, which is a synonym, and can also be used to render תימן. In fact, it occurs nine times as such, whereas λίψ is used 11 times.[50]

3:30 The chieftain is identified as בית אב למשפחת הקהתי "of the ancestral house for the clans of the Kahathite." This became οἴκου πατριῶν τῶν δήμων τοῦ Καάθ. In the parallel v.24, the word משפחת was absent, so that the preposition governed "the Gershonite." There the translator had added τοῦ δήμου for clarification. see comment ad loc. The presence of למשפחת signalled not only its translation "of the clans," but also the plural πατριῶν. As in v.27 הקהתי is interpreted as τοῦ Καάθ; see comment ad loc. In the tradition, τῶν δήμων is changed to the singular, either with or without the article in C n s+, but there were four clans, and the plural is to be preferred; the singular may well be due to the influence of v.24..

The chieftain's name was Ἐλισαφὰν υἱὸς Ὀζιήλ. The father's name is stable in the tradition, but not Ἐλισαφάν. In fact, the following variant spellings are attested: ελισσαφαν, ελσαφαν, ελισαφ, ελισαφα, ελισαφατ and ελιφαν, but the text of Num is never in doubt.

3:31 The charge of the Kaathites (ἡ φυλακὴ αὐτῶν) consists of seven items individually joined by καί throughout. They were to care for a) the ark; see Exod 25:9—21; b) the table, for which see Exod 25:22—29; c) the lampstand; see Exod 25:30—39; d) the altars, i.e. the altar of burnt offering, Exod 27:1—8, and the altar of incense, Exod 30:1—10; e) τὰ σκεύη τοῦ ἁγίου, which were mentioned as τὰ σκεύη of the tent of testimony in v.8. These vessels are described in a ὅσα clause, ὅσα λειτουργοῦσιν ἐν αὐτοῖς,[51] with the present tense rendering the prefix inflection ישרתו idiomatically; the cultic service is a process, a regular practice. f) the κατακάλυμμα or "screen," for which see comment at v.25, and finally g) πάντα τὰ ἔργα αὐτῶν; comp vv.7—8. The αὐτῶν is plural, and finds its referent in the sum of a) to g). The plural suffix follows the Sam text עבדתם, whereas MT (followed by the Tar) has a singular suffix עבדתו, in which the suffix probably refers to הקדש.

---
50. Acording to the count of Dos Santos.
51. For λειτουργέω ἐν, see SS 120.

3:32 MT begins with (הלוי) ונשיא נשיאי, "the head chieftain of the Levites." But Num avoids a word for word rendering ο αρχων των αρχοντων as too reminiscent of such titles as Lord of Lords, king of kings,[52] and by inserting ὁ ἐπί,[53] i.e. "the chieftain who was over the chieftains" makes it innocuous.[54] A popular B reading omits the ὁ before ἐπί, but this is secondary; it is a haplograph based on the similarity in uncial script of O and E.[55] This head chieftain was Ἐλεάζερ υἱὸς Ἀαρών τοῦ ἱερέως, first mentioned in Exod 6:23, which see. The articulation of υἱός by B V Byz+ is stylistic in nature, but is secondary. Nowhere in the chapter is the nominative singular υἱός ever articulated.

This head man is described as καθεσταμένος φυλάσσειν τὰς φυλακὰς τῶν ἁγίων. The rendering καθεσταμένος is peculiarly apt in the context for MT's פקדת. Eleazar is the one "set down," i.e. "appointed, commissioned" for taking care of the charges τῶν ἁγίων. The plural does not mean "of the holy objects," but represents הקדש "the sanctuary," exactly as at v.28; see comment ad loc.

3:33 Vv.33—38 concern the clans of Merari. The pattern followed in v.33 follows that of v.27 exactly, except for the absence of του before Μεραρί 2°. For Μοολί and Μουσί, see comments at v.20.[56] For the pattern δῆμος ὁ, see comment at v.27. For Μεραρί, see comment at v.17.

3:34 Num omits the initial conjunction. In contrast to v.28, the κατά phrase modifies an initial ἡ ἐπίσκεψις αὐτῶν/ופקדיהם. For κατὰ ἀριθμὸν πᾶν ἀρσενικόν, see v.28 and comments ad loc. The number for the Merari clan according to MT was "6000 and 200," but LXX has "6000 καὶ πεντήκοντα." The reason for the difference is not known. Hex tried to fix up the number by adding και διακοσιοι before καὶ πεντήκοντα which was then put under the obelus.[57] The Byz+ text substituted διακοσιοι for πεντήκοντα, thereby equalling MT. The z+

---

52. An uneasiness shared by Tar. All render the נשיאי by על רברבי, but the נשיא became אמרכ(ו)ל(א) in Tar^JO, and רבה in Tar^N.
53. See THGN 105—106.
54. Sym had no such fears as his ὁ δὲ ἄρχων τῶν ἀρχόντων (retroverted from Syh) shows.
55. See THGN 106.
56. Theod and Aq have ὁ τοῦ Μουσί instead of ὁ Μουσί. Sym read <ὁ> Μουσίτης.
57. The Others witness to the amplified text καὶ διακόσιοι καὶ πεντήκοντα according to 344^mg, but the correctness of this is dubious.

text has added καὶ τριακόσιοι rather than the καὶ διακόσιοι of hex, of which text it is undoubtedly a corruption.

3:35 The first clause follows the pattern of v.30, except for the singular τοῦ δήμου instead of τῶν δήμων; see comment at v.30, and also at v.24, where τοῦ δήμου occurs as well. The name of the chieftain for Merari was Σουριὴλ υἱὸς Ἀβιχάιλ. Variants on Σουριήλ are minor; by dittography of the *iota* of Μεραρί, ισουριηλ is produced; by vowel assimilation, σουρουηλ occurs, and the cursive confusion of *upsilon* and *beta* resulted in σοβιηλ in one ms. Ἀβιχάιλ suffered greatly. The majority text αβιχαια reflects the Λ—Α confusion; cf related spellings, with some also confusing μ/β; also found are αβιχαι (Byz); αμιχαια, and σαβιχαια (by dittography of sigma of υἱός); see also αβιχαιου and αβιμεηλ. For ἐκ πλαγίων, see comment at v.29. The Merarites were to place their camp πρὸς βορρᾶν. The locative "to the north" reflects צפנה; comp the renderings of ימה (v.23) by παρὰ θάλασσαν, and of תימנה (v.29) by κατὰ λίβα, each with a different preposition, but all meaning the same.

3:36 The verse begins in MT with ופקדת משמרת, which seems like a doublet, as does its translation ἡ ἐπίσκεψις ἡ φυλακή.[58] In the parallel passages (vv.25,31) only the second one occurs. One might render the doublet by "the oversight (even) the charge (of the Merarites)." The items entrusted to them are listed in vv.36,37, six in v.36 and four in v.37. The first one is τὰς κεφαλίδας of the tent (המשכן), for which see Exod 40:16; it is an unusual rendering for קרשי, which really means "pillars," and is usually rendered by στύλους, but this is reserved for the עמודי of the tabernacle as the third item, and for the עמודי of the court as the first item in v.37. See Note at Exod 40:16(18).[59] The next items are its μοχλούς (for בריחיו) and its στύλους, and its βάσεις (אדניו) "bases." The last two are וכל כליו וכל עבדתו "and all its vessels and all its service." The suffixes refer to המשכן. The Greek, however, has καὶ πάντα τὰ σκεύη αὐτῶν καὶ τὰ ἔργα αὐτῶν. The pronouns are put in the plural, and refer to the κεφαλίδας, μοχλούς, στύλους and βάσεις. Furthermore, the כל modifying עבדתו is omitted,

---

58. Sym has ἡ ἐπίσκεψις τῆς φυλακῆς (retroverted from Syh). This more accurately reflects the bound phrase of MT.
59. The Others read σανίδες (retroverted from Syh).

3:37 Pillars and bases were already mentioned in v.36, but here they refer to the courtyard, not to the tent itself. The third item under the care of the Merari clans is τοὺς πασσάλους "the tentpins." MT has a pronominal suffix, יתדתם, and the majority A F M text supports the recensional plus of αυτων (hex?).

The last item is מיתריהם "their cords." The word also occurred at v.26 where it was misread. The word was known to the translator, however, since here it is correctly rendered by τοὺς κάλους αὐτῶν "their cords"; cf also 4:32. In the tradition, an A b y text reads κλαδους, an obvious misreading of ΚΑΛ- as ΚΛΑΔ-; it is, however, not completely senseless. It usually means "branch, twig," but apparently the meaning "plank" is attested as well.[60]

3:38 MT begins rather verbosely with "And those encamping before the Tabernacle (המשכן) eastward (קדמה) before the tent of meeting eastward (מזרחה)." LXX has shortened and simplified the doublet locatives by its "(and those encamping) in front of the tent of testimony from the east (i.e. on the east side)." Hex tried to correct the text by adding between σκηνῆς and τοῦ μαρτυρίου the words απο ανατολων κατεναντι της σκηνης, which does equal MT. It is not certain whether Num actually read a shorter text or simply compressed it.[61] Num incorrectly reads ἀπ' ἀνατολῆς. ἀνατολή is used to represent מזרח 72 times in the Greek Bible.[62] Only three times, 3Reg 7:13(25) Jer 38(31):40 and 2Esd 13:29, is the singular employed, but whenever it is governed by a preposition it is always in the plural. Furthermore, ἀπ' ἀνατολῆς is supported only by B and n. Hex, i.e. O, has corrected to κατ ανατολας, and all other witnesses read απο (or απ) ανατολων. The critical text should be changed to ἀπὸ ἀνατολῶν.

The east or front side was to be occupied by Moses and Aaron and the Aaronids, who "φυλάσσοντες τὰς φυλακὰς τοῦ ἁγίου εἰς τὰς φυλακὰς of the Israelites." The translator has taken משמרת either as a collective or a plural noun, which is sensible. They are entrusted with the charges of the sanctuary overall,

---

60. See LS sub voce, 2 where a third century papyrus is cited as having this sense.
61. Since Tar^J reads ודישרן קדם משכן זימנא מדינחא, i.e. the same text as Num, it seems likely that homoioteleuton, i.e. לפני ... לפני, was the occasion for parablepsis on the part of both.
62. According to the count of Dos Santos.

and that "for the responsibilities ("the charges") of the Israelites." What is meant is that on behalf of the people Moses, Aaron and the Aaronids are the ones who have the overall responsibility for the care of the sanctuary. This responsibility is solely theirs. The final clause makes that clear: "and the foreigner who touches (it) shall die." The term ἀλλογενής refers to the non-Israelite. The term is often used for the זר "the stranger." The participle interprets הקרב "the one encroaching" even more intensely, viz. as ὁ ἁπτόμενος.[63] The holiness of the sanctuary is of such noumenous character that even touching it was fatal to the laity; see also v.10.

3:39 "All the review ... (which Moses and Aaron undertook)" refers to the total count of the Levites according to divine instruction; see vv.1,2. The total register of the Levites according to their clans at the Lord's behest (διὰ φωνῆς κυρίου implies a particular command) ... amounted to two and twenty thousand. The sum total of 22,000 accords neither with that of the Greek (22,150) nor with that of MT (22,300). Num has simply taken over MT. One scribe did some homework. The corrector of ms 46 added after χιλιάδες the words και ρν, i.e. "and 150," which would then come out to 22,150. And an Old Latin ms has added CCC, which would then equal the correct addition for MT, 22,300. For the reading πας ο αριθμος, see the footnote reference at 2:6.

3:40 "The Lord said to Moses λέγων." MT has no לאמר to correspond to the direct speech signal, and hex has placed it under the obelus. Moses is told to pass under review every Israelite firstborn male, using the same criterion as that for the Levitical census, i.e. "from one month old and upward." Of some interest is the reading of the Qumran ms 803, which uniquely substituted αριθμησον for ἐπίσκεψαι. In view of the age of this text special consideration should be given to its reading. U.Quast has discussed this usage carefully, and has rightly concluded on the basis of the character of the scribal activity of this early text that it is not original LXX, but a secondary attempt at a more exact representation of the

---

63. Aq is more exact with his καὶ ὁ ἀλλότριος ὁ προσερχόμενος θανατωθήσεται, whereas Theod changes LXX only for the participle: προσπορευόμενος, and Sym reads ὁ δὲ ἀλλότριος ὁ προσεγγίζων θανατωθήσεται.

Hebrew text.[64]
The second clause reads καὶ λάβε τὸν ἀριθμὸν αὐτῶν ἐξ ὀνόματος. MT has no suffix with מספר to represent αὐτῶν, but it was apparently present in 803, and its omission in B n z+ does not represent original text.[65] The αὐτῶν was transposed after ὀνόματος to correspond to MT's שמתם,[66] and it is uncertain whether the translator intended the pronoun to modify ἀριθμόν or ὀνόματος; either is possible.

3:41 God is still speaking to Moses: "and you must take the Levites for me."[67] The reference continues to be to the firstborn; i.e. τοὺς Λευίτας is metonymic for "the firstborn of the Levites." These are to be ἐμοί. Their devotion to the tabernacle service is to serve as surrogate for the firstborn of the Israelites. The self-identification formula ἐγὼ κύριος serves to position the ἐμοί, which it follows in the text, as the significant center of the verse.[68] The redemption of the firstborn was a motif in the story of the Exodus departure from Egypt—an interesting reflection on the paschal event.

The firstborn of the cattle of the Levites are also to serve as redemption of the firstborn among the cattle of the Israelites. The verse is paralleled at v.45.

3:42 Num does not render the אתו modifier of צוה. The majority A F M text has added an αυτω afer κύριος, which equals MT exactly. V Byz+ have added the pronoun before κύριος. The addition is probably recensional.

---

64. In Studien 248—290. Specifically, he says about this reading "kann es sich um eine genauere Wiedergabe des hebräischen Textes handeln, sofern פקד also inhaltlich gleichbedeutend mit ושא את מספר am Ende des Verses aufgefasst wurde"(p.250). One should not overlook E.Ulrich's plea (in SCS 33, 70—72) to take the reading of 803 as original LXX. What Ulrich has failed to do, however, is to discover how the root פקד is rendered throughout the book by the translator. It is rendered consistently by the verb ἐπισκέπτομαι and its cognates, not by the root αριθμε—. It is a dubious methodological practice to consider the matter of text in isolation from the general practice of the translator.

Ulrich 70—72 has tried to make a case for the originality of ἀριθμησον. Throughout the book Num has used ἐπισκέπτομαι to render פקד, and never does he use either the verb ἀριθμέω or its cognate noun to render this root. It can not, in spite of the appropriateness of the variant text, be taken seriously as Num.
65. As argued in THGN 98.
66. See SS 100.
67. Tar^N interprets the verb by תפרש "you shall separate, set apart."
68. Tar^N defeats this by its אמר הי "says Yahweh."

3:43 Num is inconsistent in its treatment of congruence with neuter plural subjects. Here it has the plural ἐγένοντο,[69] though the majority F text changed it to the singular. The more Classical singular marked the pseudoClassicalism of the later centuries of the Hellenistic/Byzantine scribal practice.[70] The singular verb of MT, ויהי כל בכור זכר, was possibly occasioned by the grammatically singular בכור, though with כל it is always plural in intent; see v.45. That בכור is fully understood as a collective is abundantly clear from v.46. For κατὰ ἀριθμὸν ἐξ ὀνόματος, see comment at 1:2. Hex "corrected" ὀνόματος to ονοματων to correspond to the שמות of MT.

3:45 An imperatival restatement of v.41. Moses is to take the Levites as substitutes for all the firstborn of the Israelites, and the cattle of the Levites as substitute "for their cattle." Presumably ἀντὶ τῶν κτηνῶν αὐτῶν is metonymic for "instead of all the firstborn among the cattle of the Israelites" of v.41. And instead of (καὶ λήμψῃ τοὺς Λευίτας) ἐμοὶ ἐγὼ κύριος of v.41 the fuller statement of v.b obtains as "and the Levites shall be mine: I am the Lord."

3:46 Not only must the initial καὶ τὰ λύτρα τριῶν καὶ ἐβδομήκοντα καὶ διακοσίων be taken as a nominative pendant, but the remainder of the verse is also syntactically peculiar, since οἱ πλεονάζοντες is masculine. An attempt to simplify the syntax was made by the popular Byz C s+ text by changing the nominative to the genitive των πλεοναζοντων, but this is not original. The entire verse is a pendant nominative structure intended to introduce vv.47—48.

The Hebrew is also peculiar, since the numbers of the compound are all articulated as is the העדפים which follows. I would take the Hebrew to mean "And as for the redemption cost, even the 273 which exceeds."[71] The masculine οἱ πλεονάζοντες is best understood as a further pendant, but referring to the number 273, i.e. 273 Israelites. The prepositional phrases modifying the participle neatly state precisely what is meant: "those exceeding παρά the Levites ἀπό

---

69. Following the ויהיו of Sam rather than the ויהי of MT.
70. See SS 197—198.
71. The explanation of GK 117m of את as introducing "a noun with more or less emphasis" is not overly helpful nor is it convincing. Does this mean some thing is to be understood before the את such as "and now dealing with"? To me, the את simply introduces a long pendant structure.

the firstborn of the Israelites," i.e. the excess beyond the Levites from the Israelite firstborn.[72] There were 273 more Israelite firstborn than Levite firstborn.

3:47 This verse and the following reflect on what is to be done with respect to the 273 Israelite firstborn that exceed the number of Levites. Moses is told to collect חמשת חמשת שקלים. The repetition of חמשת is not really translatable. It probably means "five shekels each." LXX responsibly does not repeat πέντε; i.e. it says "five shekels per head," fully realizing that לגלגלת is to be understood as synecdochic for "per person." Hex has, as might be expected, added a second πεντε under the asterisk, though what πεντε πεντε was to mean to the reader is not clear, except that it reflects MT.[73]

The official measure Moses must use is בשקל הקדש "according to the shekel of the sanctuary."[74] LXX renders שקל, not by σίκλος as in v.a, but by δίδραχμον, as at Exod 30:13.[75] The גרה was one twentieth of a shekel, and the translator renders this by ὀβολούς, which creates an anomaly, because there were six oboli in the drachm. For the problem of the didrachm equalling twenty oboli, see Note at Exod 30:13.[76] The term δίδραχμα was not current to Byzantine copyists, and in the tradition the -χμ- spelling often appears as -γμ- and even as -γχμ-; see the Note at Exod 30:13.

3:48 The moneys collected are to be given to Aaron and the Aaronids as λύτρα τῶν πλεοναζόντων ἐν αὐτοῖς. The λύτρα is a second accusative "you must give the money as ransom cost." The antecedent for αὐτοῖς is the τῶν υἱῶν Ἰσραήλ of v.49. For the meaning of τῶν πλεοναζόντων, see the discussion at v.46.

3:49 So Moses carried out what he was told to do; he took the money, i.e. the ransom price of those in excess (i.e. the 273) for the ἐκλύτρωσιν of the Levites. The use of ἐκλύτρωσιν differs from τὰ λύτρα, as does MT which has הפדיום for the latter, but the more usual פדויי for the former! The term ἐκλύτρωσιν is a

---

72. SS 168 calls the ἀπό partitive.
73. Aq and Sym read στατῆρες instead of σίκλους.
74. See SS 129.
75. For λήμψη 2°—fin Aq has λήψη εἴκοσι ὀβολῶν τὸν στατῆρα; Sym reads λήψη εἴκοσι νομισμάτων ὁ στατήρ, and Theod renders by λήψη εἴκοσι ὀβολοὶ ὁ σίκλος.
76. See also the full discussion in Dorival concerning the various equivalences attested from Elephantine to Eusebius.

hapax legomenon, and must be understood as modified by a subjective genitive; the sense with the εἰς is then "for those redeemed by the Levites." Thus πλεοναζόντων plus εἰς means "those who exceed the number redeemed by the Levite firstborn." I would suggest that the comma following the participle is misleading, and that it should be removed from the critical text. What is clear is that Num means that the moneys are paid by the 273 who exceed the Levite census for the benefit of their redemption.

3:50 Since it is the Israelite firstborn who exceed the 22,000 Levites by 273, Moses took the money from them, viz. 1365 shekels. Num reads χιλίους τριακοσίους ἑξήκοντα πέντε σίκλους, whereas MT has "five and sixty and three hundred and a thousand." MT has no equivalent for σίκλους, and hex has placed it under the obelus, and has also reordered the compound with a καὶ joining each number to equal MT exactly. The hex form of the compound became the popular reading for most mss, including the uncials, A and F. The standard employed was once again (see v.47) בשקל הקדש, but this time Num rendered by κατὰ τὸν σίκλον τὸν ἅγιον; see comment at v.47. Obviously, the translator thought that δίδραχμον and σίκλον were the same.

3:51 Moses carried out the Lord's orders. The כסף הפדים "the ransom money" is translated by τὰ λύτρα τῶν πλεοναζόντων in Num "the ransom price for those in excess;" what is meant is the ransom moneys for the 273 Israelite firstborn who exceeded the 22,000 Levites in number. Hex tried to clarify this in two ways. Since כסף had no equivalent in Num, Origen added το αργυριον before τὰ λύτρα. And because τῶν πλεοναζόντων had no equivalent in MT, it was placed under the obelus. Why Num should have rendered this in this way is not obvious; possibly the reference to the 273 extra firstborn seemed a better concluding statement, since τὰ λύτρα by itself appeared incomplete. For διὰ φωνῆς κυρίου, which also occurred at vv.16,39, see comment at v.39.

V.b is formulaic, with variations on the "as" throughout. The formula occurs with συνέταξεν 17 times in the book. A popular F V text reads ενετειλατο;[77] see comment at 2:34.

---

77. Instead of συνέταξεν, The Others have ἐνετείλατο.

Chapter 4

4:2 Num translates נשא את ראש by λάβε τὸ κεφάλαιον (of the Kaathites), rightly understanding the isolate free infinitive נשא as imperatival in force. The use of κεφάλαιον is a clever one in that ראש "head" is reflected by the etymological use of κεφαλή "head," in κεφάλαιον which here must mean "sum total, summation";[1] cf also 31:26,49.[2] What is meant by "take a sum total" is to take them as a group apart from the other Levites, since they are to be assigned particular duties in the tabernacle. This is clear from the modifier "out of the midst of the Levites." For κατὰ δήμους αὐτῶν see comment at 1:20, and for κατ' οἴκους πατριῶν, see comment at 1:2.

4:3 MT makes the years of service for the Levitical clans begin at thirty years of age, and end at fifty throughout this chapter, but at 8:24—25 it begins five years earlier, i.e. from 25 years to 50 years as the period of service. Num has made the text consistently 25 to 50. The translator has rid the text of an inconsistency, i.e. has harmonized the text throughout with the starting age at 25.[3] The inconsistency of the Hebrew has troubled commentators, e.g. Rashi.[4]

The structure "up to fifty years" is introduced by a conjunction in MT, i.e. ועד, but Num simply uses ἕως. In the tradition, a popular B F M V 833 text has added καί before ἕως. But the translator never translates the *waw* of ועד any place, except at 14:11 where two ἕως clauses occur coordinately and the second one requires a καί. Since ἕως occurs 51 times in Num, and Num never makes a distinction between עד and ועד except once where coordination must be expressed, it is clear that ἕως must be original text.[5]

---

1. See LS sub voce II.5.b.
2. See Dorival 57 where ראש as ἀρχή and as κεφάλαιον are contrasted.
3. Dorival 115 disagrees with this reasoning, since it would be much simpler to have changed the single occurrence at 8:24 to 30, rather than to change the seven cases in ch.4 to 25 (also vv.23,30,35,39,43 and 47); Rather, he says, "il faut songer à un modèle hébreu différent du TM." This is always a possibility, but it is rather unlikely.
4. On 8:24 he comments: מבן כ"ה בא ללמד, i.e. "how is this to be explained?" הא כיצר הלכות עבודה ולומד חמש שנים ובן שלשים עובד. So the actual service in the Tabernacle begins at 30; the preceding five years the Kaathite spends in learning how to perform the service.
5. See THGN 100.

This κεφάλαιον is to consist of "everyone coming in λειτουργεῖν to perform all the works (services) in the tent of testimony." MT has לצבא modifying בא here as well as at vv.23,30,35,39 and 43. At v.23 לצבא is followed by a cognate צבא as well. Num throughout the chapter renders by (ὁ εἰσπορευόμενος) λειτουργεῖν, though the Masoretes vocalized לצבא throughout as a noun (except at v.23 where it was perforce an infinitive followed by a cognate noun), i.e. "everyone entering for service." The translator took the structure as a marked bound infinitive (and disregarded the cognate צבא at v.23 entirely, which once again illustrates Num' preference for patterns of translation). The equation is unique to this chapter. The noun צבא usually has a military flavor, i.e. as "host, army," thus "entering the army," presumably the army of the Lord, thus an assigned service in the sanctuary. Since Num interpreted the form as an infinitive, it must be understood as purposive, i.e. "(entering) in order to do public (or cultic) service," and it is in turn modified by an explicative infinitive explaining the public service: ποιῆσαι πάντα τὰ ἔργα "to perform all the services." MT simply has עבודה, and hex has put πάντα under the obelus. ἔργα is followed by a locative phrase "ἐν τῇ σκηνῇ of testimony," which a V f s^mg z+ text improved stylistically by της σκηνης, thereby making it modify ἔργα. The locative renders word for word the באהל מועד of MT. Incidentally, hex has also added υιου under the asterisk before πεντήκοντα, since MT shows age by בן plus a number. A person who is fifty years old is a בן חמשים שנה. The υιου is a pure Hebraism.

4:4 Over against MT, Num begins the verse asyndetically. It designates the tasks (ἔργα) assigned to the Kaathites in the tent of testimony. These are called ἅγιον τῶν ἁγίων. The phrase is simplified by Byz, which has changed ἅγιον to αγια, i.e. the tasks assigned are very holy. A parallel case might well be that of Exod 30:29 where ἅγια τῶν ἁγίων refers to the various pieces of furniture which the tent contains as well. Since the tasks assigned are particularized in the following verses as dealing precisely with these furnishings, the likely referent is to the tasks. In other words, ἅγιον is best understood as a collective referring to ἔργα.[6] The same collocation, ἅγιον τῶν ἁγίων, occurs elsewhere in the Pentateuch at Exod 30:10,36 and 40:9, resp referring to the rite of atonement, the use of the compound of spices for the incense altar, and the altar of burnt offering, and at

---

6. Tar^N has בבית קודשיה instead of קדש הקדשים, which, since it follows "in the tent of witness," apparently specifies the adytum, which is odd indeed.

Lev 2:3, to the Lord's sacrifices, and at 27:28 (but without τῶν) to πᾶν ἀνάθεμα. More often the plural ἅγια occurs; in fact, at v.19 τὰ ἅγια τῶν ἁγίων refers precisely to the furnishings of the tent which the Kaathites are to transport; cf comment ad loc. In Lev the structure ἅγια ἁγίων occurs eight times (6:17,25,31,36 10:12,17 14:13 and 24:9) referring throughout to one of the sacrifices, except for the last reference which concerns the loaves placed before (the Lord) on the table in the sanctuary. I would suggest that here one should translate: "very holy are they" (i.e. τὰ ἔργα).[7]

In the tradition, an A F M V majority text has added εκ μεσου υιων λευι κατα δημους αυτων κατ οικους πατριων αυτων. This has no basis in MT, but is an obvious import from v.2, and is not original Num text.

4:5 "Aaron and his sons must enter (the tent) whenever the camp might break up (i.e. be about to move)." The verb is singular, as in MT, since the coordinate subject which follows the verb has Ἀαρών as the nearer subject. The majority A F M V text has changed it to the plural εισελευσονται. Only the priests may touch the very holy things, and vv.5—14 describe how the priests are to cover with cloths all the items which the Kaathites are to convey, so that they may carry these objects without touching them, which would be fatal (v.15).

Their first task is to take down τὸ καταπέτασμα τὸ συσκιάζον, for which see Note at Exod 26:31. The curtain was that one which hid the adytum from popular (even priestly) view. It is described as "the one that overshadows," a unique reading for מסך "the screen," more usually rendered either by καταπέτασμα (eight times), or by (κατα)κάλυμμα (seven times). But καταπέτασμα is the usual rendering for פרכת (25 out of 26 times; the exception is κατακάλυμμα).[8] Since the Hebrew פרכת המסך could be construed as a near doublet expression, the translator makes good sense by using a descriptive participle.[9] For the use of the participle, see also Note at Exod 25:19, where this participle is used as well (for סככים).

---

7. Dorival renders in isolate fashion: "chose sainte entre les saintes." See his detailed discussion ad loc (219—220); see also THGN 112.
8. According to Dos Santos.
9. Theod retained τὸ συσκιάζον for המסך, whereas Sym rendered by τὸ τῆς σκέπης, and Aq, by τοῦ παρατανυσμοῦ, thereby retaining the etymological notion of מסך as something stretching out.

What the Aaronids do with the dismantled overshadowing curtain is to "cover the ark of the testimony with it." The Hebrew refers to the ארן העדת, which is so called because the עדות were put into the ark; see Note at Exod 25:15 where τὰ μαρτύρια refers to the Ten Words, after which the ark became known as the "ark τοῦ μαρτυρίου" (also 7:89 Exod 16:21 26:33,34 30:26 35:11 40:3,19 Lev 16:2). Because of the genitive τοῦ μαρτυρίου here, the tradition easily changed κιβωτόν to σκηνην in the A V 833 C'+ text, which is due to the frequent occurrence of "the tent of testimony," but here this would be bizarre.

4:6 The priests are then to place a second covering over it, called a κατακάλυμμα δέρμα ὑακίνθινον. That the כסוי was a covering is undoubtedly correct, since the root כסה is well-known.[10] The covering was made of blue leather. The term ὑακίνθινον is always used to render תחש; it first occurs at Exod 25:5; see Note ad loc. The word is unknown, though it is often rendered by "dolphin skin," a meaning derived from Akkadian, but dolphins in a desert context is highly unlikely.[11]

Furthermore, they are to cast a third "cloth ὅλον ὑακίνθινον επ' αὐτήν on top." What the translator meant by this, in distinction from the second blue-dyed leather was a cloth (or garment, ἱμάτιον) completely blue, since a cloth in contrast to leather would be blue through and through. The ἐπ' αὐτήν has no equivalent in MT, but depends on the עליו of Sam.[12] Hex has placed the phrase under the obelus.

Finally, "they must thrust the poles through." The ark was provided with rings; see Exod 25:12—13, and the verb διεμβάλλω is well-chosen. MT has בדיו, and hex has added αυτης to represent the suffix. But the omission of suffixes is common in Num.[13] The term בד when it refers to staves is commonly rendered throughout the LXX by ἀναφορεύς (18 times) or by διωστήρ (five times),[14] but never by ἀρτήρ; in fact, ἀρτήρ is never used in the Greek O.T.[15]

---

10. See THGN 127.
11. H.Tadmor in the Hebrew Encylopaedia is quoted by Milgrom (see Note 7, p.301) as understanding the word as a "yellow-orange dye." But the evidence of the Alexandrian should not be left out of consideration. It should be noted that Tar with their סםגונא also consider the word to be a color word; it means "bright red, vermillion."
12. Also supported by Tar[JN].
13. See SS 99.
14. According to the count of Dos Santos.
15. For a statement explaining the secondary nature of αρτερας/-ος for ἀναφορεῖς see my article in Eretz-Israel 236*—238*.

4:7 For τὴν τράπεζαν τὴν προκειμένην see Note at Exod 38:9, the only other case of "the table which is set before" (i.e. before the Lord), where it has no counterpart in MT. It is probably metonymic for the table of the bread which is set before.[16] The phrase לחם (ה)פנים occurs in Exod at 25:30(29), where it is uniquely rendered by ἄρτους ἐνωπίους, at 35:13(15) where it is not translated, but hex has added τους του προσωπου, and at 39:36(18), where it becomes τοὺς ἄρτους τοὺς προκειμένους, which may have influenced the translator here.

Over this table they (i.e. the priests) must throw ἐπ' αὐτήν a cloth (ἱμάτιον) ὁλοπόρφυρον. MT does not have this superfluous prepositional phrase, and hex has placed it under the obelus. The adjective "completely purple" represents תכלת "violet."[17] The rendering is unique, since תכלת is usually rendered by ὑακίνθινος, e.g. Exod 28:27(31), where ὅλον υακίνθινον (for כליל תכלת) occurs. Since ms 803 reads νακινθινον E.Ulrich believes that another Hebrew parent text must have existed,[18] but when an early bilingual scribe has the usual equivalent, one may well question whether unconscious influence on the Hebrew text, which he would know thoroughly, may not have impelled an automatic correction. It is of course always possible that, as Ulrich suggests, the parent text read ארגמן as at v.13, particularly since the word ארגמן is always rendered by the root πορπυρ—.

MT continues with a new clause, ונתנו עליו, but Num simply continues with καί followed by a list of vessels. Hex has added δωσουσιν επ αυτης after καί 2° under the asterisk to equal MT. This had already been corrected by the scribe copying 803, but there is no evidence that any other preOrigenian text had it. It must be borne in mind that the early copyists were Jewish scribes, who knew their Hebrew Torah thoroughly. For the four items to be placed on the table, τρύβλια, θυΐσκας, κυάθους and σπονδεῖα and for their Hebrew parents see Notes at Exod 25:28(29). The last item has a modifying clause, ἐν οἷς σπένδει, which has as its Hebrew equivalent הנסך (קשות) "the jugs for libation," an adequate rendering. It might be noted that in the parallel Exod passage MT has אשר יסך בהם, which may well have influenced the translator here. In fact, 803 and the Byz text actually add εν αυτοις, which is even more reminiscent of Exod.

---

16. So Levine ad loc.
17. See SS 64.
18. In SCS 33, 73—74.

The last clause states that "οἱ ἄρτοι οἱ διὰ παντός shall be on it." The Hebrew לחם התמיד occurs only twice in the Hebrew Bible. At Exod 25:29(30) it becomes ἄρτους ἐνωπίους, but here "perpetual loaves" is used. What is meant is "the loaves which are to be always present."

4:8 In MT the priests must throw עליהם the scarlet cloth, i.e. over the various vessels listed in v.7, but Num has ἐπ' αὐτήν, i.e. over the table. Since the vessels are on the table, I suppose that it comes to the same result. The Hebrew equivalent for κόκκινον is תולעת שני. For the meaning of שני see Note at Exod 25:4. Here the translator has disregarded שני entirely, and hex has added διάφορον under the asterisk to make up for it; this is, however, based on a mistranslation of שני, as though it were related to the verb שנה "to change."

For ὑακινθίνῳ as rendering for תחש see comment at v.6. For the last clause see the parallel clause at v.6, from which it differs only in the sensible addition of δι' αὐτῆς. As at v.6, a recensional plus of αυτης after ἀναφορεῖς to represent the suffix of בדיו is provided in the tradition; it actually received majority support, including that of the uncials A F M.[19] As at v.6, ms 803 reads αρτηρας instead of ἀναφορεῖς.[20]

4:9 The priests are then to take a blue cloth and cover the λυχνίαν τὴν φωτίζουσιν, which renders מנרת המאור, for which see Note at Exod 35:16(14). For λυχνίαν, λαβίδας and ἐπαρυστρίδας,[21] see Notes at Exod 38:17. The last item is "all τὰ ἀγγεῖα τοῦ ἐλαίου with which they perform the service."[22] MT has a suffix in שמנה, and the majority A F M text has added αυτης to represent it. This is probably recensional in origin (hex?). Actually, MT has two prepositional phrases modifying the verb ישרתה, viz. לה בהם. Accordingly, hex has added αυτη before ἐν αὐτοῖς to represent the לה.

4:10 Then they must thrust it (i.e. the lampstand) and all its vessels (those listed in v.9) into a blue leather κάλυμμα. The term κάλυμμα is regularly used to ren-

---

19. But see SS 99.
20. Which E.Ulrich in SCS 33, 72—73 says may be original LXX, but see THGN 127, and particularly f.n. at v.6 above.
21. For τὰς ἐπαρυστρίδας The Others read τὰ πυρεῖα (retroverted from Syh).
22. For ὅσοις as original text see THGN 99.

der מכסה by the Num translator,²³ rather than its synonym κατακάλυμμα which he reserves for מסך.²⁴ For the rendering of תחש by ὑακίνθινον, see comment at v.6.

The second clause in MT reads ונתנו על המוט. The term מוט refers to a kind of carrying frame.²⁵ LXX translates by the usual rendering for בדים, ἀναφορέων "poles, staves," probably being influenced by the story in 13:23(24) where two men carried a βότρυν σταφυλῆς במוט, translated by ἐπ' ἀναφορεῦσιν.²⁶ LXX also added an accusative pronoun, αὐτήν, after the verb ad sensum, which hex placed under an obelus.

4:11 Then they must ἐπικαλύψουσιν the golden altar with a blue cloth, and καλύψουσιν it with a blue leather covering.²⁷ The adjective ὑακίθινον occurs twice, once for תכלת, which is usual, but also for תחש, for which see comment at v.6.²⁸ The compound verb represents יפרשו "they must spread over," and the simplex renders כסו "they must cover."²⁹

The last clause is paralleled in vv.6 and 8, but here Num translated בדיו by τοὺς ἀναφορεῖς αὐτοῦ; comp comments at vv.6,8.

4:12 All the service vessels (τὰ σκεύη τὰ λειτουργικά) are to be treated as was the golden altar, i.e. covered with two coverings, a blue cloth and a blue leather covering. The phrase ἐν αὐτοῖς simply represents an ἐν expressing means,³⁰ with αὐτοῖς referring to τὰ σκεύη. The translator has varied the renderings somewhat, however. When MT changes the verb, so does Num. In v.11 the priests יפרשו a blue garment, which becomes ἐπικαλύψουσιν. but here it becomes ἐμβαλοῦσιν/נתנו. In v.11 they שמו its staves/διεμβαλοῦσιν; here נתנו על המוט becomes καὶ ἐπιθήσουσιν ἐπὶ ἀναφορεῖς. For the rendering of המוט see comment at v.10.

---

23. See THGN 127.
24. See THGN 127.
25. So Milgrom, citing Gray (see philological note, p.37).
26. For the difference between מוט and ἀναφορέων see Dorival 119—120.
27. Using a dative of instrument, SS 121.
28. Tar all distinguish between ת(י)כלת and נא(ו)ססג.
29. See Dorival 120.
30. See SS 120.

4:13 V.a in MT reads ודשנו את המזבח "and they must rid the altar of its ashes," but Num has a different text: καὶ τὸν καλυπτῆρα ἐπιθήσει ἐπὶ τὸ θυσιαστήριον "And the cover he shall place upon the altar"; see Note at Exod 27:3. The statement is fully sensible. Before the altar can be covered with a cloth covering, either the ashes must be removed, as MT has it, or a cover for the altar, which would enclose the altar and its ashes, would be necessary. The interpretation of the priestly duties is well thought out. Since sacrifices are regularly burned on the altar, simply removing the ashes would not make it prudent to place a fine cloth over it; the cloth would burn. But to put an altar cover, presumably of metal, would make v.b a viable next step: "and they must cover it over with a cloth entirely purple."

Somewhat puzzling is the use of the singular verb ἐπιθήσει, since the subject is not expressed. If it is the addressee of v.2, it would presumably be Moses (or Aaron; see v.1), and one wonders who the interpreter had in mind. This also troubled the tradition, and a popular variant text read the plural επιθησουσιν. Could the odd singular be the interpreter's way of signalizing that this differed from the parent text, a kind of code to warn the wary reader of this fact?

The verb in v.b in MT is ופרשו, and as at v.11, it is rendered by καὶ ἐπικαλύψουσιν "they shall cover over"; cf also vv.7,8 where the same Hebrew verb obtains.[31] The Byz text has changed the verb to κατακαλυψουσιν, but the ἐπ' αὐτό modifier makes Num the more likely original text. The O text has also changed the verb, but to ἐπιθησουσιν, which is unexpected; I suspect that this was an error, due to the influence of v.a, where ἐπιθήσει occurred, and was popularly changed to the plural form.

4:14 MT reads "and they must put on it all כליו," but Num simply has τὰ σκεύη. The majority A F M V text added αυτου, which is probably recensional in origin (hex?). Num commonly neglects the suffix, especially when its reference is contextually obvious. For the ὅσοις clause, see comment at v.9. Here hex has added επ αυτο before ἐν αὐτοῖς to represent the (בהם) עליו of MT.[32] Num has καί before τὰ πυρεῖα and before τὰς κρεάγρας, but BHS has no equivalents. For the second καί, however, BHS is in the minority, since many mss read the conjunc-

---

31. Aq renders by καὶ ἐκπετάσουσιν; Sym, by καὶ ἐκτενοῦσιν, and Theod, by καὶ περιβαλοῦσιν, and he also substitutes ἐπ' αὐτοῦ for ἐπ' αὐτό.
32. See THGN 132—133.

tion, as do Sam and all the other ancient witnesses. For the vessels, πυρεῖα, κρεάγρας and φιάλας, see Notes at Exod 27:3. Since מזרקת is usuallly rendered by φιάλας, it would appear that the third and fourth items, ואת היעים ואת המזרקת, have been transposed by Num. In other words, καὶ τὸν καλυπτῆρα, for which see comment at v.13, is substituted for והיעים "and the shovels" which was omitted.³³ It is of course not a translation, but in view of v.13's inclusion of "the cover" for the altar, it was added here, whereas "and the shovels" was omitted.

For κάλυμμα δερμάτινον ὑακίνθινον see comment at v.11. For καὶ διεμβαλοῦσιν τοὺς ἀναφορεῖς αὐτοῦ, see comment at v.11 as well. The remainder of the verse (καί 9°—fin) is based on Sam, which reads ולקחו בגד ארגמן וכסו את הכיור ואת כנו ונתנו אתם אל מכסה עור תחש ונתנו על המוט; since it is absent from MT, probably due to homoioteleuton, i.e. בדיו to בדיו, hex has placed this under the obelus. Num translates the Sam text literally, and the only point of interest worthy of comment is the use of the compound συγκαλύψουσιν for כסו. The compound is well chosen, since the covering of all the vessels of v.a is paralleled with v.b; in both cases it involves κάλυμμα δερμάτινον ὑακίνθινον. For the ἀναφορεῖς at the end representing המוט of Sam, see comment at v.10.

4:15 Unusual is the use of the plural verb when preceding the subject, Ἀαρὼν καὶ οἱ υἱοὶ αὐτοῦ. Normally it would follow the singular of MT, וכלה, by attraction to the number of the nearer subject, but the plural was probably used because the context had been plural throughout the description of the activity of the priests.³⁴ MT used a marked complementary infinitive לכסות to modify כלה. Num changed the construction by using a participle καλύπτοντες, which correctly interprets the Hebrew. Num used τὰ ἅγια to render the coordinate modifiers את הקדש and הקדש (כלי), i.e. rendered the bound phrase "the vessels

---

33. Ulrich in SCS 33,74 states that καλυπτῆρα is simply an error. In reflecting on the reading τα σπ[ονδεια] uniquely witnessed by 803 he states: "The issue whether the error was made by the OG translator and was later corrected in 4QLXXNum toward the correct Hebrew, or whether the correct OG is faithfully represented by 4QLXXNum and became distorted ...." I do not understand this comment, since σπονδεια does not reflect "the correct Hebrew" any more than Num does. I suspect that the lacuna should read σπ[οδεια], i.e. a form of the adjectival σπόδιος "ash-colored, in which case Ulrich's statement would make better sense; comp τὴν σποδιάν at Lev 4:12.
34. See THGN 121—122.

of the sanctuary" by the adjectival phrase τὰ σκεύη τὰ ἅγια.³⁵ The difference between τὰ ἅγια and πάντα τὰ σκεύη τὰ ἅγια is in their reference. The first τὰ ἅγια refers to the sacred furniture, the altar, lampstand, etc., whereas "all the sacred vessels" are the objects used in the cult the dishes, censers, forks, etc.

What the priests must do is propaedeutic for the work of the Kaathites. This becomes evident in what occurs afterwards. When the Kaathites enter to carry out the transport "they may not touch τῶν ἁγίων lest they should die." The "lest" clause correctly interprets what the paratactic ומתו intends. MT reads "and not may they touch the holy things and die." The priests had to wrap everything at least doubly before the Levitical porters could safely do their work. The interpretation of הקדש by the plural τῶν ἁγίων is correct; it can hardly refer to the sanctuary, but must intend its contents, the furniture and the vessels all carefully wrapped.

V.b is a kind of subscription: "these (i.e. the holy things) the Kaathites must carry in the tent of testimony." Num has changed the nominal clause, אלה משא בני קהת "these constitute the task (i.e. the transport duties) of the Kaathites" into a verbal one: ταῦτα ἀροῦσιν οἱ υἱοὶ Καάθ.

4:16 Four elements of the cult need special assignment. "The overseer is Eleazar the son of Aaron the priest." This differs from MT, which begins the verse with ופקדת אלעזר "And the oversight by Eliezer, i.e. the responsibility of Eliezer ... is the oil ...."³⁶ Num by interpreting פקדת as an actor noun, i.e. as though it were פקיד, changes an ordinary nominal clause with פקדת אלעזר as subject, and the list of elements as predicate, to a lead statement as to who is in charge, followed by a list, best expressed by a colon plus the list: "the oil for the light, and the incense compound, and the daily sacrifice, and the anointing oil, (the oversight of the entire tent and whatever is in it in the sanctuary, with all the works)." The first item translates שמן המאור, which also occurred at Exod 35:14, where LXX did not translate it; it was, however, rendered in Num by Theod; see Note at Exod 35:16. The second item also occurred at Exod 31:11; see Note at Exod 30:7. For the daily sacrifice, see Lev 6:12—13, and for its ritual, vv.14—18. Here, however, it is uniquely rendered by καθ' ἡμέραν, which Daniel describes

---

35. See THGN 112.
36. Theod and Sym render more accurately by ἡ ἐπισκοπὴ Ἐλεάζαρ υἱοῦ (retroverted from Syh).

as "pour plus clarté."[37] And for the anointing oil, see Exod 30:23—25 and the Notes ad loc.

In MT v.b is a new definition of "the oversight," a further elaboration of Eliezar's duties; syntactically, it is in apposition to v.a. This is not how Num interpreted it, since ופקדת had been interpreted as agentive, but here פקדת is correctly rendered by ἡ ἐπισκοπή. It is then a fuller statement on the list. I would suggest something like "(in fact,) the oversight of the entire tent and whatever is in it ...." The ἐν αὐτῇ is then oddly explicated by ἐν τῷ ἁγίῳ ἐν πᾶσιν τοῖς ἔργοις "in the sanctuary in all the works," i.e. the works pertaining to the sanctuary. One might have expected an αυτου after ἔργοις, and hex has actually added such under the asterisk to reflect the fact that the last word in MT does have a suffix, but the word is כליו "its vessels." It is difficult to understand "in all the works" as a translation of ובכל כליו. It seems to me clear that the translator abandoned MT in favor of saying that Eleazar was actually responsible for the tent of testimony as a whole and everything connected with it, i.e. בקדש ובכליו "in the sacred furniture and in its vessels"; see comment at v.15—but this is not what MT says. It should be noted that the conjunction is also omitted, which I suspect is part of the same reinterpretation by Num of what Eleazar's charge was. In the tradition, the majority A F M V text has added a και to introduce "in all the works," which is either a recensional change or simply an attempt to clarify a difficult text. Somehow, an "and" uniting the two ἐν phrases seems easier, though if my interpretation of what Num was trying to say is correct, it is secondary.

4:18 The choice of ὀλεθρεύσητε as original LXX might well be questioned by some, since this is the only case in the OT where the simplex rather than the compound with εξ— translates the Hi of כרת: the most common rendering is ἐξολεθρεύω (43 times; the next most frequent equivalent is nine each for ἀπόλλυμι and ἐξαίρω).[38] The compound verb which usually renders הכרית, occurs here, but only in cod A. The simplex is far rarer; in fact, it occurs only twice elsewhere in the Pentateuch, both times for תשחית; cf HR). A change from the simplex to the compound is much more easily visualized than the reverse, and the reading of A must be secondary.

---

37. P.267, Note 41.
38. According to Dos Santos.

Its modification is quite unusual: τῆς φυλῆς τὸν δῆμον τὸν Κααθ. The Hebrew has שבט משפחת הקהתי, which is also odd. The Masoretes vocalized משפחת as plural, and since הקהתי must modify שבט the structure would mean "the Qohathite tribe of clans," or more idiomatically "the Qohathite tribal clans." Possibly τῆς φυλῆς could be taken as a partitive,[39] though this is an odd way of representing MT, but if one fails to understand משפחת as plural, it becomes difficult to make good sense of שבט. It is also difficult to see how the translator could understand משפחת הקהתי as an adjectival phrase, τὸν δῆμον τὸν Κααθ. I would render Num by "the Kaath clan of the tribe (from the midst of the Levites)."

4:19 Num follows Sam by beginning asyndetically over against MT with τοῦτο ποιήσατε αὐτοῖς.[40] The τοῦτο is not realized until v.b "let Aaron and his sons enter ...." The antecedent of αὐτοῖς must be τῶν Λευιτῶν as does the Hebrew בהם, though in sense what is meant is τὴν δῆμον/משפחת from the midst of the Levites. The subject of "they may live and not die" is again the Kaath clan. The genitive absolute which follows is a pseudo construction, since the αὐτῶν has the same reference as αὐτοῖς, and the reference is also the subject of the verbs.

V.b states what τοῦτο is that you must do for them: "Let Aaron and his sons enter and appoint αὐτοὺς ἕκαστον κατὰ τὴν ἀναφορὰν αὐτοῦ. ἕκαστον renders איש איש and hex has added ενα before ἕκαστον.[41] In the tradition, B V y+ read προσπορευεσθωσαν, but this is by attraction to the προσπορευομένων earlier in the verse.[42] The αὐτούς must refer to the Kaathites whom Aaron and the Aaronids are to assign each according to his transport duty." The ἀναφοράν refers to the carrying task. MT has a doublet expression על עבדתו and ואל משאו "according to his task and to his transport duty," but the Num single reference is adequate. Hex has inserted after ἕκαστον the phrase επι την δουλειαν αυτου under the asterisk so as to render על עבדתו, though failing to render the waw introducing the next phrase.[43]

---

39. As Dorival ad loc suggests; he translates "une partie de la tríbu—le dème de Kaath."
40. Kenn 18,84,173,181 also read זאת.
41. See THGN 114.
42. See THGN 126. That προσπορεύομαι is not original is certain, since it occurs uniquely for בוא at 2Par 13:9, whereas εἰσπορεύομαι is used 125 times in LXX (according to HR).
43. Daniel 79 quite rightly calls ἀναφοράν a hendiadys.

4:20 No subject is given for εἰσέλθωσιν. thereby following MT exactly, but common sense makes it obvious that the Kaathites are meant. What is to be avoided is going into the sanctuary "to see ἐξάπινα τὰ ἅγια and die." For ἐξάπινα, see Note at Lev 21:4. I would translate "(to see) the holy things unawares." The term, as its parent כבלע, means "suddenly, unexpectedly," i.e. "like the automatic swallowing (of spittle)." Instead of τὰ ἅγια most witnesses have the singular, but the plural makes better sense, even though MT has the singular הקדש. Actually, Num is quite inconsistent in the rendering of קדש, varying between singular and plural without apparent reason.[44] Since cod B, the oldest extant witness, has the plural, it is probably original. The Byz text has added των αγιων, making it refer to the adytum. This was certainly not the intent of MT, and is an import from v.19 where τὰ ἅγια τῶν ἁγίων obtains as rendering of את קדש הקדשים.

Num renders MT's ומתו literally by καὶ ἀποθανοῦνται "and they would die." One would expect a "lest" construction, since it refers to potential death resulting from seeing holy objects. The Byz text has succumbed to simplification by its και ου μη αποθανωσιν, but the more difficult text of Num (and MT) is original.

4:22 Vv.22—28 deal with the Gedsonites. For Γεδσών transcribing גרשון, see 3:17 and the Note at Exod 6:16. Hex has corrected the spelling to γηρσων.[45] At v.2 נשא את ראש was translated by λάβε τὸ κεφάλαιον; see comment at v.2, but here את ראש is rendered by τὴν ἀρχήν as at 1:2; see the discussion at 1:2 with its suggestion that this can only be understood calquelike in the sense of "sum, total." The καὶ τούτους renders גם הם, which contextually must mean "also these," since the order had also been given for the Kaathites (v.2). For κατ᾽ οἴκους πατριῶν αὐτῶν see comment at 1:2, and for κατὰ δήμους αὐτῶν, comment at 1:20.

4:23 For Num πεντεκαιεικοσαετοὺς instead of בן שלשים שנה see the detailed discussion at v.3. Num uses an imperative ἐπίσκεψαι for תפקד, but this is an acceptable equivalent. As at v.3, Num defines those counted by a nominative structure. MT has לצבא לעשות in modification at v.3, but at vv.35,39 read לעבדה instead

---
44. See THGN 112.
45. The Others also read Γηρσών.

of לעשות. Here the pattern of vv.35,39 is used, but repeating צבא, as well as עבדה. The translator, however, disregarded the extra צבא entirely, which hex made up for by adding λειτουργιαν under the asterisk after λειτουργεῖν. In all three cases, however, Num joined two infinitives, λειτουργεῖν καὶ ποιεῖν τὰ ἔργα, in spite of MT's lack of a conjunction throughout. Only here is the καί brought into question, since B x+ omit it, but in view of the parallels at vv.35,39 it must be original.[46]

To see the translator at work, it is instructive to compare the nominal structure of Num here with that of v.3. Over against v.3, Num here reads καὶ ποιεῖν rather than ποιῆσαι, and omits πάντα before τὰ ἔργα. In other words, Num at v.3 was a greater influence here than the MT of v.23.

A popular B V reading has added αυτου after ἔργα, but Num is careful throughout this chapter about the contrast between עבדתם (vv.31,33) and עבדה (vv.23,35,39,47) as to the presence or absence of a genitive pronoun. The B V reading must be secondary.[47]

4:24 This verse introduces the service expected of the clan of Γεδσών, defined as λειτουργεῖν καὶ αἴρειν. Unusual is the rendering of the verb עבד by λειτουργέω; in fact, it occurs here for the first time in LXX, though it obtains ten times in the book. Outside of Num, it occurs only twice, at Deut 18:5 and 2Par 35:2. The cognate noun, however, commonly renders עבדה (36 times, 17 of which are found in Num). It is almost as common as ἔργον which occurs for עבדה 38 times.[48] MT defines the clan by the gentilic הגרשני, but Num simply by τοῦ Γεδσών.[49] MT has defined the service by לעבד ולמשא, i.e. by a marked infinitive and a prepositional phrase. משא also occurred at v.15, where Num used a verb, ἀροῦσιν, but here an infinitive. This is a matter of style, i.e. of coordinate infinitives, "to serve and to transport."

4:25 MT begins with a plural verb ונשאו; this refers to the plural noun משפחת, which Num had rendered by a singular τοῦ δήμου, and so perforce used a singular verb (καὶ) ἀρεῖ. The Gedsonites' duties are the transport of the tent itself, its two

---

46. See THGN 100.
47. See THGN 133.
48. The count is that of Dos Santos.
49. As at v.22 The Others read Γηρσών.

coverings and the screen covering of the tent door. Since המשכן and the אהל (of meeting) are both rendered by σκηνή, the text of Num creates some confusion. For a discussion of this, see comment at 3:25. Similarly, for the use of κάλυμμα (twice) for מכסה and κατακάλυμμα for מסך, see comments at 3:25. These are quite confused in the tradition, but the translator is consistent in his choice.[50] For the two cases of κάλυμμα of the tent of testimony, especially the blue one on top of the first one, see the discussion at 3:25 as well. There is textual uncertainty as to the originality of ἐπ' αὐτῆς for עליו, with support for the genitive αὐτῆς somewhat weak (B F V C'⟩ s 319), a popular A M tradition reading αυτην, and the majority text witnessing to the dative. Since all three are possible in the context, the genitive was chosen because it is supported by the oldest witness, Cod B.

The last item in the verse is (καὶ) τὸ κατακάλυμμα of the door of the tent of testimony. Though the simplex form is supported inter alia by the oldest Greek witness, it is secondary; the reading is due to homoioteleuton, with the scribal eye spanning from κα(τα) to κά(λυμμα).[51]

4:26 Num has considerably shortened the first part of this verse. MT begins with "and the hangings of the courtyard," which is adequately rendered, and then continues with ואת מסך פתח שער החצר, which was overlooked because of homoioteleuton. Then (אשר על המשכן ועל המזבח סביב) is rendered by ὅσα ἐπὶ τῆς σκηνῆς τοῦ μαρτυρίου.[52] Hex has made a number of changes in order to approximate MT. After αὐλῆς, only partly (wrongly) under the asterisk, και το επισπαστρον της θυρας της πυλης της αυλης was added from Theod. Hex also placed τοῦ μαρτυρίου under the obelus, as unsupported by MT, and then added και επι του θυσιαστηριου κυκλω under the asterisk to equal the omitted ועל המזבח סביב.

---

50. See THGN 127.
51. Aq translated the item by καὶ τὸ παρατάνυσμα ἀνοίγματος σκέπης συνταγῆς; Sym made it καὶ τὸ καταπέτασμα τῆς θύρας τῆς σκηνῆς τῆς συνταγῆς, whereas Theod has καὶ τὸ ἐπίσπαστρον τῆς θύρας τῆς σκηνῆς τοῦ μαρτυρίου.
52. Aq translates καὶ τοὺς ἱστοὺς τῆς αὐλῆς καὶ τὸ παρατάνυσμα ἀνοίγματος πύλης τῆς αὐλῆς ὅσα <ἐπὶ τῆς σκηνῆς>; Sym translates καὶ τὰ ἱστία τῆς σκηνῆς καὶ τὰ παραπέτασμα τῆς θύρας τῆς πύλης τῆς αὐλῆς τὸ ἐπὶ τῆς σκηνῆς, and Theod has καὶ τὰ ἱστία τῆς αὐλῆς καὶ τὸ ἐπίσπαστρον τῆς θύρας τῆς πύλης τῆς αὐλῆς ἥ ἐστιν ἐπὶ τῆς σκηνῆς.

Furthermore, hex has added αυτων after περισσά as well as after λειτουργικά to represent the suffixes of מיתריהם and עבדתם resp, and a παντα before ὅσα 2° in view of MT's כל אשר.[53] מיתריהם "their tentpins" or "ropes" was misunderstood as at 3:26 where the noun was rendered by τὰ κατάλοιπα. The translator etymologized from the root √יתר, and made it τὰ περισσά "the remainders."

4:27 The preposing of κατὰ στόμα Ἀαρὼν καὶ υἱῶν αὐτοῦ follows MT, and places the emphasis properly on the fact that the duties of the Gedsonites are controlled by the priests. Their service (λειτουργία) is defined as κατὰ τὰς λειτουργίας αὐτῶν καὶ κατὰ πάντα τὰ ἀρτὰ δι' αὐτῶν; for λειτουργία as rendering for עבדה, see comment at v.24. This differs from MT, first of all, in omitting כל at the beginning, which hex "corrects" by adding πᾶσα before ἡ λειτουργία under the asterisk. Furthermore, MT has the two prepositional phrases transposed as well.

The term משאם "their porterage" occurs twice, and is translated by ἀρτά, a neuter plural adjective based on αἴρω. It is a rare form, in fact, only occurring here in the Greek OT, and it led to popular variants, both εργα and εργαλεια, but Num correctly renders משא in the sense of "that which is to be carried."[54]

V.b has the verb in the singular, ἐπισκέψῃ, referring to Μωυσήν of v.21. MT has the plural פקדתם; presumably the reference is to the priests, since they are to oversee them in the observance of all their porterage. The Byz text has "corrected" the verb to the plural, probably as a recensional correction. The word for observance is משמרת. But Num, possibly under the influence of v.32's בשמת תפקד has ἐπισκέψῃ αὐτοὺς ἐξ ὀνομάτων "you must pass them under review by name." But the word משמרת is easily misread; a small *resh* can readily be mistaken for a *waw*, i.e. as משמות. Presumably, the reverse misreading is equally possible. MT continues with את כל משאם, which LXX translates by a second accusative πάντα τὰ ἀρτὰ ὑπ' αὐτῶν. Since the verb is used throughout the book in this sense, it creates both here and in v.22 an odd usage with a double accusative. Possibly contextually the verb has the sense of "overseeing" in the sense of

---

53. See THGN 100, which also comments on the omission of the καὶ ὅσα by B *b* x+ as secondary.
54. For ἀρτά 2° Aq reads ἄρμα, and Sym, ἄρσιν. LS does not record the adjective at all; Schl translates *portatus, gustatus*.

"assigning," thus "you must assign them personally with all the matters to be carried by them."

4:28 A summary statement on the service of the Gedsonites.[55] MT reads משפחת בני הגרשני, but Num omits משפחת.[56] Hex has added τοῦ δήμου before τῶν υἱῶν so as to equal MT.

V.b places their ἡ φυλακή as the responsibility of "Ithamar son of Aaron the priest." The structure is a nominal clause; the subject is ἡ φυλακή, and ἐν χειρὶ Ἰθαμάρ .... is the predicate. What is meant is "their guard" is ἐν χειρί, i.e. the watchful eye of Ithamar is to be over the service of the Gedsonites; it was Ithamar who had charge over their work. It might be noted that υἱοῦ is unarticulated in Num, which is supported by only five cursive mss, all others having τοῦ υιου. But whenever υἱός refers to membership in a clan (88 times in the book), it is never articulated, and the addition of an article in almost all witnesses must be adjudged secondary.[57]

4:29 Vv.29—33 deal with the Merarites. V.a is a nominative pendant, which is then brought into the main clause by means of αὐτούς, both in vv.29 and 30. For κατὰ δήμους αὐτῶν, see comment at 1:20, and for κατ' οἴκους αὐτῶν, comment at 1:2. The verb enjoining a passing under review, in both vv.29 and 30, is plural over against the singular of MT. This change is a case of harmonization with the statement of v.34 that Moses and Aaron and the rulers of Israel were responsible for the review.[58]

4:30 For the harmonization of Num throughout as to the age at which the review of Levites begins, i.e. 25 years of age rather than the "thirty" of MT, see discussion at v.3. Since age is normally expressed in Hebrew by "son of (fifty years)," hex has added υιον under the asterisk before πεντηκονταετοῦς, though not before πεντεκαιεικοσαετοῦς!

Num has shortened לצבא לעבד את עבדת to λειτουργεῖν τὰ ἔργα, which hex expanded by prefixing the structure with εἰς τὴν δυναμιν. LXX also understood

---

55. The Others read Γηρσών instead of Γεδσών as did hex.
56. Kenn 84,132 also omits the word, and the shorter text is probably textual in origin. Note that both words, עבדת משפחת, end with *taw*.
57. See THGN 105—106.
58. See THGN 122.

עבדת as plural, which the consonantal text allows, though the Masoretes vocalized the word as singular.

4:31 Since there is a list of items in v.b, the translator changed the introductory וזאת משמרת משאם לכל עבדתם "and this is the charge of their porterage for all their work" into the plural: "and these are the charges (φυλάγματα) of the objects carried by them according to all their works," i.e. all the nominals are in the plural. Note that the word משאם "their porterage" has been rendered by a passive participle τῶν αἰρομένων, modified by a ὑπό phrase of personal agent. This is a good example of how the translator does not translate unthinkingly in isolate fashion word for word, but shows a fine appreciation of the context; comp the use of ἀρτά for משא in v.27 as well.

V.b, along with v.32, list those objects which are entrusted to the Merarites for transport. The four items are correctly rendered. For κεφάλιδας and στύλους, see Exod 40:16; for μοχλούς, Exod 26:26, and for βάσεις, Exod 26:19.

The tradition has expanded the list at the end of the verse considerably; in fact, almost all witnesses have added some form of και το κατακαλυμμα και αι βασεις αυτων και οι στυλοι αυτων και το κατακαλυμμα της θυρας της σκηνης. This was a pre-Origenian expansion, as the hex placement of this expansion under the obelus shows.[59]

4:32 A further list of items coordinate with those in v.31. The first four items are an exact copy of 3:37, except for the addition of αὐτῶν after πασσάλους; cf comments ad loc. As in the case of v.31, the tradition added items which had no basis in MT. Instead of καὶ τὰς βάσεις αὐτῶν almost all witnesses (in fact, all but six mss) read και τους στυλους του καταπετασματος της πυλης της αυλης και τας βασεις αυτων. As in the case of v.31, the addition was pre-Origenian, as its placement under the obelus proves.[60] Note that the obelus wrongly includes και τας βασεις αυτων, which does have an equivalent in MT. MT continued with two coordinate prepositional phrases: לכל כליהם ולכל עבדתם, which Num rendered as two further coordinate items: "and all their vessels and all their services."

---

59. See THGN 133—134 for a fuller discussion of this widely supported expansion, and a demonstration of its secondary character.
60. See THGN 133—134.

V.b is an elaboration of v.27b, for which it in turn apparently served as model. At least, its שמות may well have impelled the ἐξ ὀνομάτων at v.27, which see. Num has disregarded the initial conjunction, but instead of the single modifier of the verb משאם משמרת כלי את, has inserted αὐτοὺς καὶ πάντα before τὰ σκεύη τῆς φυλακῆς τῶν αἰρομένων ὑπ' αὐτῶν. The three words have been dutifully put under the obelus by hex. The αὐτούς may have well been taken from v.27; see comment ad loc, whereas the πάντα is probably based on a dittograph of כל before כליו. For τῶν αἰρομένων ὑπ' αὐτῶν, see comment at v.31.

4:33 The verse is paralleled by v.28. For αὕτη ἡ λειτουργία, see v.28. Over against v.28, Num does include δήμου for משמרת. In the tradition, δήμου is articulated by hex, which is puzzling, since משמרת is a bound form, and therefore without an article. That the του is a hex plus seems clear from the asterisk in cod G, but this must represent some error of transmission. In Syh the word δήμου is followed by a metobelus, and I suspect that the ms which Origen used lacked δήμου as in the parallel v.28, which see. Origen then added του δημου with an asterisk, and followed it with a metobelus. Otherwise, I am baffled by the asterisked plus of του.

4:34 Vv.34—49 detail a second review of the Levites. Vv.34—37 deal with the Kaathites, who were passed under review by Moses and Aaron and the rulers of 'Ισραήλ. As throughout chh.3 and 4, Num renders the gentilic הקהתי by Καάθ; in fact, only at 26:57 does the gentilic Κααθί occur in Num. MT has העדה "the community." That the community is to be identified as Israel is not incorrect, but why Num should avoid rendering העדה is not evident. Elsewhere in the same context (16:2 31:13 32:2), it becomes (τῆς) συναγωγῆς. possibly v.46 influenced the translator.

For the two prepositional phrases, see references at v.29. Num follows Sam in lacking a conjunction between the two phrases.[61]

4:35 For πεντεκαιεικοσαετοῦς for בן שלשים שנה, see comment at v.3. As at v.30, hex has added υιου under the asterisk before πεντηκονταετοῦς to equal the בן of MT. הבא is modified by לצבא לעבדה "to the army for work." Num renders

---

61. But Kenn 1,80,150,185 also read לבית.

the first word by an infinitive λειτουργεῖν and לעבדה by a coordinate καὶ ποιεῖν τὰ ἔργα. In the tradition, B f x+ omit τὰ ἔργα, but עבדה באהל מועד is always rendered by τὰ ἔργα ἐν τῇ σκηνῇ τοῦ μαρτυρίου throughout the chapter, e.g. vv.23,39, where the structure is also introduced by λειτουργεῖν καὶ ποιεῖν.[62] What Num did was to provide a doublet translation for לצבא, understood as a marked infinitive, i.e. λειτουργεῖν καὶ ποιεῖν.

4:36 Their review κατὰ δήμους αὐτῶν, for which see comment at 1:20, amounted to 2750. The "700" was not stable in the tradition. B x+ read διακοσιοι, whereas A z+ have τριακοσιοι, whereas a b reading is πεντακοσιοι. But the total in Num equals that of MT. For the variant reading ο αριθμος in b+ see comment at v.37.

4:37 For the recensional character of the b s^mg+ reading ουτος ο αριθμος instead of αὕτη ἡ ἐπίσκεψις, see the discussion and footnote at 2:6. MT has the plural nominal clause: "These are the reviews of the clans of the Qohathite," but Num has the singular throughout. For Καάθ, see comment at v.34. Since MT continues with an apposite in the singular, כל העבד "everyone working," which is singular, Num is more consistent with its singular. The καθά clause translates an אשר clause as though it were כאשר, but for the rest it is an exact word-for-word translation.

4:38—39 Vv.38—41 deal with the Gedsonites.[63] In MT vv.38—39 constitute a pendant structure to the ויהיו פקדיהם of v.40: "As for those passed under review ... in the tent of testimony." LXX has simplified this considerably by rendering ופקודי of v.38 as a passive verb, καὶ ἐπεσκέπησαν, thereby making vv.38—39 a verbal clause: "And the Gedsonites were passed under review ...." For κατά to the end of v.38, see comments at v.34. For v.39, see comments on v.35, with which it is identical, both in MT and in Num.

4:40 For the variant reading of b+, ο αριθμος for ἡ ἐπίσκεψις, see the references in the footnote at 2:6. As in v.36, the opening clause is changed to the singular in Num; see comment at v.36. For κατά—αὐτῶν 2°, see comments at v.34. The

---

62. See THGN 133.
63. Instead of Γεδσών The Others read Γηρσών, as did hex.

review consisted of 2630 Gedsonites, i.e. of men from 25 years of age up to fifty.

4:41 This verse parallels v.37, which see, differing only in having υἱῶν Γεδσών instead of Καάθ. MT, however, lacks an equivalent for ἐν χειρὶ Μωυσῆ, which hex has placed under the obelus.[64] Once again Num shows its tendency to harmonize, and follow translation patterns.

4:42 Vv.42—45 concern the Merarites. For the syntax of vv.42—43, see the comment on vv.38—39. Num has, however, an odd incongruence as the result of the attempt to follow the pattern of v.38. Again, the same plural aorist passive verb is employed, but the subject is not υιοι μεραρι as one might expect, but δῆμος υἱῶν Μεραρί, which should then have a singular predicate. In fact, the Byz text has "corrected" the pattern by changing δῆμος to δημοι. The translator, however, understood δῆμος as a collective, and so used a plural verb. Also unusual is the rendering of the initial *waw* by a postpositive δὲ καί "but also"; this represents the translator introducing the last of the three review summaries, an example of the translator's awareness of Greek style. For κατά—fin, see comments at v.34.

4:43 V.43 differs from vv.35,39 in the rendering of לעבדה באהל מועד, which becomes πρὸς τὰ ἔργα τῆς σκηνῆς τοῦ μαρτυρίου. Rather unexpected is the isolate rendering of לעבדה by πρὸς τὰ ἔργα. The plural noun also occurred at vv.35,39, but the use of πρός in modification of λειτουργεῖν is unique in LXX as far as I know. Apparently, it is not unknown elsewhere; in fact, it is attested in Aristotle.[65] Over against vv.35,39, v.43 has no doublet rendering for לעבדה, but simply has λειτουργεῖν. Probably the differences are merely variations in the pattern to avoid monotony. Admittedly, Num tends to repetition, but slight variations which do not affect the intent of a passage do occur at times. It should also be noted that hex has added και under the asterisk before ἕως so as to represent the conjunction in ועד.

---

64. Kenn 80 also add ביד משה. BHS is mistaken in stating that Tar^J also has the phrase. All the Tar agree with MT.
65. According to LS sub λειτουργέω II.

4:44 MT begins as at v.36 with ויהו פקדיהם, but Num uses the passive ἐγενήθη instead of the middle ἐγένετο; there is no difference in intent. In fact, a popular A F text substitutes εγενετο. In the tradition, the b s^mg+ text reads ο αριθμος for ἡ ἐπίσκεψις, for which see comment and f.n. at 3:15. Num differs from MT which has no equivalent for κατ' οἴκους πατριῶν αὐτῶν, but the Greek follows the pattern set throughout the chapter (see vv.2,29,34,38,40,42,46), i.e. Num harmonizes its text. Hex has placed the phrase under the obelus to show the absence of an equivalent in MT. The count is 3200 Merarites.

4:45 This verse follows the pattern of v.41 precisely, except for lacking πᾶς ὁ λειτουργῶν ἐν τῇ σκηνῇ τοῦ μαρτυρίου. See comments at v.41. It might be noted, however, that here MT does have an equivalent for ἐν χειρὶ Μωυσῆ, which is probably its source at v.41.

4:46 The syntactic pattern of vv.46—47 is similar to that occurring in vv.38—39 and vv.42—43. The structure πάντες οἱ ἐπεσκεμμένοι "all those who were passed under review" is modified by a relative clause, in which those who did the reviewing are identified. The relative pronoun οὕς is then further identified by τοὺς Λευίτας, i.e. those passed under review were the Levites. The structure is throughout rhetorically loose. The two prepositional phrases must modify the verb of the relative clause, which verb is singular by attraction to the nearest element of the compound subject, "Moses and Aaron and the chieftains of Israel." For the prepositional phrases, see comments at v.34. Num follows Sam in lacking a conjunction joining the two phrases.

In the tradition, the majority A F V M text adds υιοι before Ἰσραήλ, but this is ex par. The phrase υἱοὶ Ἰσραήλ is very common, but here MT has נשיאי ישראל without an intervening בני. The popular variant is secondary. It might also be noted that cod B is not overly trustworthy in its text of the two prepositional phrases. It has added a και between the two, which happens to equal MT, but is in B an error palaeographically inspired; it comes before κατ' and is a dittograph. The codex also has omitted both instances of αὐτῶν; the shorter text is demonstrably secondary.[66]

---

66. See THGN 97 for its demonstration.

4:47 V.a follows the usual pattern, for which see the discussion at v.3. As at v.43, hex has added και before ἕως under the asterisk to represent ועד of MT fully. The usual pattern modifying "everyone who enters" is considerably amplified in this summary statement to πρὸς τὸ ἔργον τῶν ἔργων καὶ τὰ ἔργα τὰ αἰρόμενα. MT has an even longer text for the first element; it has לעבד עבדת עבדה; i.e. Num omits the infinitive, substituting the preposition πρός modifying the participle εἰσπορευόμενος for it. Furthermore, it has ἔργον modified by the plural τῶν ἔργων, by which the translator used the singular to define the class, i.e. "the task," and the plural to designate the various tasks assigned. One might then render the sense by "the task of performing services." The second unit is singular in MT, ועבדת משא "the work of carrying," but the sense is understood by Num as collective. What LXX says is "and the tasks that consisted of being carried." I would translate: "and the porterage services." In the tradition, a Byz $S^{mg}+$ text has αγιων for ἔργων; this would make sense, but it is secondary, the result of palaeographic confusion.

4:48 In the tradition, the popular A F text omitted the initial καί, but Num equals MT; comp vv.36,40,44. As in v.46, the participle פקדי is rendered literally by a Greek participle, rather than by the usual noun ἐπίσκεψις (see vv.36,37, 40,41,44,45 as well as throughout chh.1 and 3). Here, however, the participle is aorist, ἐπισκεπέντες, rather than the perfect which is actually read by the majority A M text under the influence of v.47. Since MT reads פקדיהם, hex has added αυτων to represent the suffix.[67] The Byz y+ text has added παντες, which is a gloss added from v.47 where it belongs.

The total review is correctly stated as consisting of 8580 men, but in the tradition, f reads 8880, and instead of the 80, cod A has πεντηκοντα, and one ms has εβδομηκοντα.

4:49 The preposed διὰ φωνῆς κυρίου places the stress on the divine origin of the passing under review, as in MT. Odd is the use of a singular verb, פקד/ἐπεσκέψατο, since no subject is given, but the support of both MT and Num mitigates against BHS's note: "prp pl." Presumably the subject is indefinite as in "on dit," or in "man sagt," which would then probably best be rendered by a

---

67. But see SS 100.

passive transform in which αὐτούς would become the subject. Scribes were troubled by the grammatical difficulty, and a *b* text changed ἐν χειρὶ Μωυσῆ to μωυσης, whereas the *n* tradition added μωυσης και ααρων as subject, but the more difficult reading is to be preferred as original text.

The verb is modified by ἄνδρα κατὰ ἄνδρα, a unique rendering for the distributive איש איש in the Greek OT; in fact, the Greek structure occurs only here. In the tradition, the *f* text omits the first ἄνδρα.[68] The popular B F V elided form κατ ανδρα is secondary, a case of haplography. Aside from elision of the final vowel of a preposition with pronouns or with ἀνατολάς/-τῶν, Num regularly avoided elision entirely.[69]

One might have expected that עבדתו would have been translated by a singular genitive pronoun, but the translator understood איש איש as referring to "each one of them," i.e. individually, thus ἐπὶ τῶν ἔργων αὐτῶν with the pronoun referring to αὐτούς. The rendering by the plural noun furthered the use of αὐτῶν as well. The coordinate prepositional phrase modifier, ועל משאו "and according to his porterage," is freely rendered by a preposition plus a relative clause, καὶ ἐπὶ ὧν αἴρουσιν αὐτοί,[70] with the αὐτοί explicating the ἄνδρα κατὰ ἄνδρα.

V.b has a relative clause as a predicate for פקדיו as subject. As usual, Num rendered פקדיו by a verb, here by the passive ἐπεσκέπησαν. Accordingly, the relative pronoun is rendered by ὃν τρόπον, which is sensible, and need not presuppose the כאשר of Sam. Why *O* Syh, the usual supporters of hex, should have added αυτοι after the verb is not clear; it could hardly be hex in origin. The *b* text substituted ενετειλατο for συνέταξεν, but the two are synonyms; for their use in LXX, see discussion at 2:34.

---

68. See THGN 114.
69. See THGN 97.
70. But see SS 100; The plural αὐτοί, however, does recognize the suffix; cf αὐτῶν.

Chapter 5

5:2 Vv.1—4 deal with people who are unclean. Such people are of three kinds: λεπρόν "leper," γονορρυῆ "spermatorrheic," and the ἀκάθαρτον ἐπὶ ψυχῇ "one who is unclean through a corpse." For λεπρός see Note at Lev 13:44; λεπρός is one who is afflicted with λέπρα, for which see Note at Lev 13:2. For γονορρυής, see Note at Lev 15:4. The Greek ψυχή is a calque for נפש, and its meaning must be sought in the Hebrew; נפש means "person, self," but occasionally can refer to a dead person as here; cf Lev 19:28 21:1 22:4, and for נפש מת, 21:11 (ψυχῇ τετελευτηκυίᾳ).[1]

What the Israelites are ordered by divine direction to do is ἐξαποστειλάτωσαν everyone of these three out of the camp, i.e. "let them send away, banish" all such. Num continues the imperative of πρόσταξον, but in third person plural, since MT has ישלחו.

5:3 Num continues with an imperative, ἐξαποστείλατε, for the prefix inflection, תשלחו, and the order applies to both male and female; you must send them "outside the camp." The ἀπό ... ἕως pattern is a merism; i.e. it includes any and everyone. MT then repeats תשלחום, which the translator omitted as unnecessarily repetitious, but hex added εξαποστειλατε αυτους under the asterisk so as to equal MT.

V.b gives the reason for this order, though formally it is in the form of parataxis of the Hebrew ולא יטמאו. That this is the purpose of the sending away of all these impure ones is only clear from the context; it reads "and they shall not defile," but what is meant is that the impure ones are banished outside their camps in order to retain the purity of those camps.

The verse closes with a relative clause which in MT is ambiguous as to its reference. מחניהם is modified by אשר אני שכן בתוכם. Since the gender of מחנה is uncertain, the antecedent could be either the מחני or the הם of מחניהם, some arguing for the one, others for the other.[2] In Num the antecedent of οἷς can only

---
1. See BDB s.v.4.c.(5), and see also LS s.v.II "departed spirit, ghost." Tar^J actually has נפש דמית.
2. NJPS reads "the camp of those in whose midst I dwell," whereas Levine renders "their encampment, where I maintain a residence in their midst."

be αὐτῶν, not περεμβολάς which is feminine. The reason for the exclusion is now clear. The camp is the place where God himself dwells among his people, and nothing unclean can abide in that presence.

5:4 The Israelites carried out the orders of expulsion in accordance with the Lord's instructions to Moses. The two parts of the verse are repetitive, and Num translates word for word.

5:6 Vv.5—8 concern πλημμέλεια "trespass, guilt," and what must be done about it. In the command to Moses to speak to the Israelites Num follows Sam in adding the direct speech indicator λέγων; this has no equivalent in MT, and hex has accordingly placed it under the obelus.

What is then given is the protasis of a condition, for which v.7 is the apodosis. "As for any man or woman, ὅστις ἂν ποιήσῃ ἀπὸ τῶν ἁμαρτιῶν τῶν ἀνθρωπίνων." The indefinite relative pronoun is used to render כי, a particle introducing a protasis. The ἀπό is partitive, i.e. means "one of."[3] Unusual is the rendering of חטאת האדם, a bound phrase in which I would understand the free element to be objective in character, i.e. "sins over against some person or individual." Bound phrases are sometimes rendered by adjectival phrases as here,[4] in which the free member is descriptive in character. Num has taken it in this sense, τῶν ἁμαρτιῶν τῶν ἀνθρωπίνων "human sins," which is unusual. Presumably, what Num intends is to characterize these as sins rooted in humanity, faults committed by inadvertence. This is also clear from the coordinate clause which follows: καὶ παριδὼν παρίδῃ "and should actually disregard, overlook," for which see Note at Lev 6:2. MT has למעל מעל ביהוה, which denotes a violation over against the Lord, a kind of betrayal, possibly one of sacrilege.[5] Hex has added εν κυριω after παρίδῃ under the asterisk. The omission of ביהוה substantially changes the nature of the offence; it is no longer sacrilege, but simply once again stresses the inadvertence of what has been done.

The third condition is καὶ πλημμελήσῃ ἡ ψυχὴ ἐκείνη "and that person has committed a trespass." The verb "commit a trespass" in this context must entail

---

3. See SS 162.
4. See SS 66.
5. NRSV and NJPS translate: "breaking faith with the LORD," and NIV reads: "and so is unfaithful to the LORD." Levine has: "committing an act of betrayal against YHWH."

something concrete over against someone, i.e. some damage or injury has been created.⁶

5:7 Num has the first clause in the singular: "and he must publicly state (i.e. confess openly) the sin which he committed"; The subject is the ψυχή of v.6. For ἐξαγορεύσει as an excellent rendering for the Hithp of ידה, see Note at Lev 5:4. MT has this in the plural, and only changes to the singular in the next clause.⁷ MT makes the rule a general one, whereas Num is still referring to "that person." MT has חטאתם, "their sins," but Num has disregarded the suffix.⁸ Hex has added an αυτων under the asterisk to equal the suffix.

That πλημμέλειαν involves more than simply a sense of guilt, but has resulted in some kind of injury or damage to someone is clear from the next clause, καὶ ἀποδώσει τὴν πλημμέλειαν τὸ κεφάλαιον; the πλημμέλεια is something which can be and must be, repaid. In MT τὴν πλημμέλειαν is אשמו, and hex has added αυτου under the asterisk to represent the suffix. This restitution is put in economic terms; it amounts to בראשו, rendered by τὸ κεφάλαιον "the capital amount," to which hex has again added αυτου under the asterisk. To the capital amount he must add its fifth.

Num also uses ἀποδώσει in the last clause, though the Hebrew has changed verbs from השיב to נתן; the reuse of the verb lays stress on the notion that the "giving" is a "restitution," a repaying of what ἐπλημμέλησεν αὐτῷ.

5:8 But suppose the one offended had no "redeemer." For the meaning of ὁ ἀγχιστεύων, see the discussion in the Note at Lev 25:25.⁹ The redeemer would act as a surrogate, i.e. ὥστε ἀποδοῦναι αὐτῷ τὸ πλημμέλημα πρὸς αὐτόν. MT has no equivalent for the αὐτῷ, and hex has placed it under the obelus. Since both αὐτῷ and πρὸς αὐτόν modify ἀποδοῦναι, it would seem tautologous. Possibly the αὐτῷ might be rendered "for him," i.e. on his behalf.

The apodosis states that in such a case τὸ πλημμέλημα τὸ ἀποδιδόμενον κυρίῳ τῷ ἱερεῖ ἔσται, i.e. the liability which was due to be returned to the Lord must belong to the priest. The situation described is akin to the estate of someone

---

6. Dorival renders by "cause a préjudice," which is probably what is intended.
7. Theod and Aq attest to the plural verb ἐξαγορεύσωσιν.
8. See SS 99.
9. For a discussion of the term ἀγχιστεύων see Dorival 167. He defines the term as «celui qui agit en tant que proche [parent],» i.e. the nearest relative.

who dies intestate going to the state, but here to the priest. In MT this is a nominal clause, and hex has placed ἔσται under the obelus to indicate the absence of the verb in the Hebrew. The verb does serve a function in making this the rule rather than simply a statement of fact. I would suggest that the ἔσται correctly interprets the intent of MT.[10]

The πλήν structure gives an additional proviso, the sacrificial ram of atonement "through which one must make atonement ἐν αὐτῷ concerning him." The "him" refers to the offender, The ἐν αὐτῷ "with it" designates the instrument.[11] The term ἱλασμοῦ occurs elsewhere for כפרים only at Lev 25:9, which see. For ἐξιλάσεται, see the Note at Lev 1:4 for a fuller discussion.

5:9 The term תרומה "dedicatory gift"[12] is often translated by ἀπαρχή as here (40 times in OT), and is probably not far different in meaning from the more literal ἀφαίρεμα, which is often used as well. For an explanation of ἀπαρχή rendering תרומה see Note at Lev 22:12. It is appropriate that the offering which is taken up, lifted up, should be removed first as a gift (a firstfruit) before the remainder was used for secular use. The particular ἀπαρχή intended here is "κατὰ τὰ ἁγιαζόμενα among the Israelites," i.e. "of the sanctified offerings."[13] In the tradition, the majority A F M V text has και instead of κατά, but the לכל קדשי cannot possibly mean "in addition to all the sanctified (offerings)," since πᾶσα ἀπαρχή is itself a sanctified offering. The και is simply a copyist error. These sanctified offerings refer to such edibles as grains, fruits or meat, which could be offered as dedicatory gifts to the Lord. This is made clear in Num by the inclusion of κυρίῳ in the relative clause ὅσα ἂν προσφέρωσιν. This is an explanatory gloss obviating the possible misunderstanding of יקריבו followed by לכהן in the sense of offering to the priest. The hex text has placed κυρίῳ under the obelus as having no correspondent in MT. The gloss is clearly based on a correct interpretation of יקריבו. I would render: "which they might bring for the Lord to the priest, to him (i.e. to the priest) it shall be."

It might be noted that a popular B tradition articulates κυρίῳ. Usually, the dative κυρίῳ is unarticulated in the oldest witnesses; in fact, of the 72 cases of

---

10. Tar^J also makes this a verbal clause with its יתן.
11. See SS 121.
12. Levine translates it by "levied donation."
13. For the rendering of κατά as a periphrasis of a genitive see Bauer s.v. II.7.c.

κυρίῳ in the book, B supports the article in only three instances. In view of the normal practice of Num, the unarticulated noun is to be preferred here as well.[14]

5:10 The verse is difficult, since the pronouns are ambiguous. The opening clause reads καὶ ἑκάστου τὰ ἡγιασμένα αὐτοῦ ἔσται. In view of v.9 where Num has clarified an abstruse statement by the gloss κυρίῳ, the referent of ἑκάστου must be the one who brings the offering, whereas that of αὐτοῦ could then be the priest. Note that the subject is neuter plural, and so can be taken as congruent with the singular ἔσται.[15] What the clause means is "the sanctified offerings of each (i.e. worshiper) shall belong to him (i.e. the officiating priest)." On the other hand, it can also be understood as "his sanctified offerings will be his own," i.e. belong to himself, making v.b contrastive. MT is usually understood in this way, but the Hebrew text is also ambiguous.[16] Which interpretation is correct remains uncertain, though my personal preference is for the first one.

The second clause is even more unclear. It reads καὶ ἀνὴρ ὃς ἂν δῷ τῷ ἱερεῖ αὐτῷ ἔσται. The entire clause was omitted by F z+, but this was due to homoioteleuton, i.e. the scribe skipped from ἔσται 1° to ἔσται 2°. The text which Origen used for the hexapla must have lacked the clause as well, since hex has the entire clause under the asterisk.[17] Furthermore, the clause in MT is asyndetic, and cod B has actually omitted the καί, but this is hardly original LXX. The word immediately preceding איש is יהי, and the parent text read ואיש with Sam; this is a case of dittography/haplography.

The clause can best be understood by taking δῷ in the sense of the ὅσα clause in v.9, i.e. as explicative of προσφέρωσιν. Thus "anyone (ἀνήρ) who brings a gift (δῷ) to the priest, it (i.e. the gift) will belong to him (i.e. the priest). The verse is largely tautological; it says the obvious, but it is clothed in a plethora of ambiguous referents.[18]

5:12 The remainder of the chapter deals with the case of a woman suspected of adultery. The condition is portrayed in vv.12—14. The initial איש איש כי is translated by the genitive ἀνδρὸς ἀνδρὸς ἐάν. The genitives are used in apposition to

---
14. See THGN 104.
15. See SS 197.
16. Tar^JO both interpret את קדשיו as "מעשר of his holy things," but Tar^N equals MT.
17. See THGN 101.
18. See the extensive explanation of this verse in Dorival.

αὐτοῦ (of which they are the referent), an odd usage indeed. More common would be a nominative pendant preceding the ἐάν particle.

MT has two clauses: תשטה אשתו and מעלה בו מעל. The first one means "should his wife stray, err," which Num renders by παραβῇ ἡ γυνή αὐτοῦ "should his wife commit transgression," which is adequate, though not quite what MT says. The second clause uses the verb מעל, which is elsewhere always used of violation against God, and signifies some act of betrayal. Here then it means a breaking faith with the husband. Num interprets the verb by παρίδῃ as at v.6, i.e. disregard, neglect; see Notes at Lev 5:15 6:2. But then rather than using the cognate παριδών as at v.6 he uses ὑπεριδοῦσα. This introduces an interesting interpretation which makes sense in the context. The second compound means "look down on, despise," thus the wife neglects her husband despising him. This clearly removes מעל out of its usual sacral realm into that of relations between husband and wife.[19]

5:13 For κοίτην σπέρματος meaning "an emission of semen," see Note at Lev 15:16. The term κοίτη is a calque for the Hebrew שכבה. Thus what is meant is "some man should have sexual intercourse with her." Furthermore, "she kept it unknown to her husband, and hid (it)—but she had been defiled, and there was no witness present, nor had she been taken by force (i.e. raped)." MT uses a number of passive constructions: ונעלם "and it was concealed," נסתרה "it was undetected," נטמאה "she was defiled," and נתפשה "she was taken," but Num renders the first two actively, thus λάθῃ "she concealed (it from her husband)," and κρύψῃ "she hid (it but was defiled)." For Num it was not accidental that her husband was kept in the dark about her extra-marital activities, and she kept these matters secret. It might be noted that twice the pronoun αὐτή is used as the stated subject with the verb ᾖ plus a participle.[20]

5:14 The final condition to be met is the jealous suspicion of the husband, either founded or unfounded. The verse begins with "and there should come upon him (αὐτῷ) a spirit of jealousy." In MT, the verb is עבר; the spirit of jealousy passes over him. In both parts of the verse עליו is rendered by αὐτῷ, which is sufficient in view of the compound verb ἐπέλθῃ. In both cases scattered support added επ

---

19. The Tar are also aware of this, and use the root שקר "deal falsely."
20. See SS 83.

before the αὐτῷ, which would equal MT, but this was not recensional; rather it was an ad sensum gloss in modification of the επ- compound verb. The referent of the pronoun must be τοῦ ἀνδρὸς αὐτῆς of v.13, and the Byz text makes this certain by its variant τω ανδρι αυτης for αὐτῷ 1°, though not for αὐτῷ 2°. The result of this attack is that ζηλώσῃ τὴν γυναῖκα αὐτοῦ "and he should be jealous of his wife, and she (αὐτὴ δέ) has defiled herself."

V.b is an exact repetition of v.a except for the final clause, which is the unfounded alternative for the situation: "and she had *not* been defiled (μὴ ᾖ μεμιαμμένη)."

5:15 The man must bring his wife to the priest, and present the offering (δῶρον, the usual translation for קרבן[21]) on her behalf. In both clauses MT has הביא, but Num rightly uses ἄξει for the first one, since he is to bring his wife, but in the second case it is an offering which is brought, and προσοίσει is contextually appropriate. MT has for "the offering" קרבנה "her offering," and hex has supplied an αυτης under the asterisk to represent the pronominal suffix. The translator may have omitted the suffix intentionally, since it is the husband who is bringing the sacrifice, not the wife, and an αυτης might confuse the situation. Hex has tried to clarify this by adding a το after the αυτης as well, i.e. has nominalized περὶ αὐτῆς as "her (sacrifice) namely, the one on her behalf."

The sacrifice brought was unique in that it was to consist of the tenth of an ephah of barley flour rather than of σεμίδαλις, but barley was "the ordinary food of the poorer classes."[22] For the οἰφί as a dry measure, see the Note and footnote at Lev 5:11. That this was indeed a poor man's offering is clear from the fact that the δῶρον was to be a bare sacrifice, i.e. without oil or frankincense, which also characterized the sin offering of those too poor to present the normal offering according to Lev 5:11, which see.

The reason given is, however, different: "for it is a sacrifice of jealousy, a sacrifice of remembrance recalling sin." This should not be confused with the sacrifice called τὸ μνημόσυνον. This is clear from the Hebrew which for "the memorial sacrifice" uses אזכרה, for which see Lev 2:9,16, and for the sacrifice of remembrance has זכרון. The phrase recurs in v.18. In MT the word for "jealousy" is plural, probably since a sacrifice of jealousy is meant to refer to a

---

21. See THGN 113.
22. Gray ad loc, p.50.

sacrifice occasioned by acts or feelings of jealousy. The Greek singular is not incorrect; the Hebrew plural can also be understood as an abstract noun. The notion that the sacrifice is one of remembrance recalling sin, prepares one for the ordeal to follow; the sacrifice is to be part of the ritual which will recall whether ἁμαρτία occurred. ἁμαρτίαν, however, renders עון, which implies more than simple error or a mistake; it involves iniquity, and guilt.

5:16 Theoretically the use of αὐτήν could be ambiguous; the text reads "and the priest shall bring αὐτήν forward, and set αὐτήν before the Lord." The pronoun could refer either to θυσία or to γυνή, but the context makes it clear that it is the woman. Actually, the Byz text allows for no misunderstnading, by changing αὐτήν 2° to την γυναικα. The verb στήσει renders העמד, "cause to stand," since ἵστημι can also be transitive; he is to set her before the Lord.

5:17 The priest must then take מים קדשים; just what "holy water" means is not clear.[23] LXX does not actually translate קדשים, but rather explains it by its ὕδωρ καθαρὸν ζῶν "pure, living water." Neither adjective translates קדשים; a proper translation would be ὕδωρ ἅγιον, as Dorival shows.[24] That the translator hardly thought of the water in the laver of the temple as the source of the "holy water" is shown by the description "pure, living water," since living water designates running water over against still-standing or stagnant water. Nor would an Alexandrian translator make reference to a temple, as the Tar might; see footnote above. Origen had a problem with this text; on the basis of a one-for-one correspondence, LXX had two adjectives for one Hebrew word, and so hex has placed ζῶν under the obelus. The water in any event had to be placed in a ceramic container.

The priest is then to take "τῆς γῆς τῆς οὔσης on the floor of τῆς σκηνῆς τοῦ μαρτυρίου, and cast (it) into the water." The τῆς γῆς is a fine example of a partitive genitive; it can hardly mean all the dirt, but only "some of the dirt (which was on the floor)."[25] Since MT read מן העפר, hex added απο before τῆς γῆς, though it is unnecessary for the sense.

---

23. The Targums present a divided picture. Tar⁰ has מי כיור, which is amplified by Tar^J by מיין קדישין מן כיורא בנטלא, "holy water from the laver in a small container," whereas Tar^N simply has מיין דכין "pure water."
24. See his discussion at pp.120—122.
25. See SS 162.

MT simply read "the floor of המשכן." Since σκηνή is used as the LXX translation for either משכן or אהל, the translator opted for the notion that the tent that was intended was the tent of meeting, and so defined "the tent" by τοῦ μαρτυρίου. Hex correctly placed this under the asterisk to indicate that it had no equivalent in MT.

MT's paratactic construction יקח (הכהן) ונתן is translated idiomatically by an attributive participle plus an inflected verb: καὶ λαβὼν ὁ ἱερεὺς ἐμβαλεῖ. The verb "shall throw into" is contextually quite correct for ונתן "and he shall place."

5:18 As in v.16 "the priest must set the woman before the Lord," presumably before the altar. Then "he must ἀποκαλύψει the head of the woman, and place in her hands the sacrifice of remembrance, the sacrifice of jealousy." The verb in MT is פרע, which could mean either to unloose (i.e. the hair) or to uncover (i.e. remove the veil).[26] Num understood the verb in the second sense.[27]

The placing of the sacrifice in her hands is necessary; though it was brought by the husband, it is she who must present it; it was, after all, περὶ αὐτῆς (v.15). The two descriptions of sacrifice were transposed in v.15; there a sacrifice of jealousy came first, and only secondarily is it called a sacrifice of remembrance recalling sin. Here it is the character of remembrance that is the important notion, and signals the purpose of the ordeal to come. Both genitives are here articulated, though in MT the second one, קנאת, remains unarticulated.

V.b contrasts with v.a. In the hands (plural) of the woman is the sacrifice, but (δέ) in the hand (singular) of the priest must be τὸ ὕδωρ τοῦ ἐλεγμοῦ τοῦ ἐπικαταρωμένου τούτου. MT reads מי המרים המאררים "the waters of bitterness which evoke a curse." Incidentally, the Hebrew with its alliterative sonant sounds much like a magical potion. Just what is meant by the "waters of bitterness" is not known. Num has τοῦ ἐλεγμοῦ "(waters of) reproof, conviction." Could he have understood המרים as the Hi participle of ירה "to instruct"? Since drinking the water was somehow to reveal the truth or falsehood of the charge, it could be reasoned that the potion led to the truth.[28] The water is then some kind of test, one which brings about a curse, i.e. this ἐλεγμός has had a curse placed upon it,

---

26. NJPS understood it as "to bare," whereas NIV translated by "loosen," and NRSV, by "dishevel."
27. For a full discussion of this double sense, see Dorival 125—126.
28. Theod and Aq understood the word as τῶν πικρῶν (retroverted from Syh).

whereby this curse will become effective if the one drinking the water is guilty; the curse will automatically be transferred to a guilty party. Since MT has no equivalent for the τούτου, hex has placed it under the obelus. The pronoun is an importation from v.19's האלה. I would take τούτου as modifying ἐλεγμοῦ.

5:19 The priestly adjuration. The two εἰ μή conditionals are asyndetically presented, though MT has coordinated them. Hex has added και before the second εἰ under the asterisk to equal MT. The idiom ὑπὸ τὸν ἄνδρα τὸν σεαυτῆς means "under your own husband's jurisdiction." Note how the same Hebrew text, תחת אישך, is differently rendered in v.20.

The Ni imperative הנקי "be rendered innocent" is translated by an adjective ἀθῴα plus the imperative ἴσθι. How being innocent from the ordeal is realized is clear from the effects of the ordeal when guilty in vv.21—25; see comments ad loc. For "the water τοῦ ἐλεγμοῦ τοῦ ἐπικαταρωμένου τούτου, see discussion at v.18. Here τούτου has a parent text, האלה.

5:20 The contrastive δέ indicates an alternative: should the wife be guilty of adultery. For תחת אישך Num simply has ὑπ' ἀνδρὸς οὖσα "being under a husband's jurisdiction," i.e. as a married woman. In contrast to v.19 the suffix is not rendered, since it is now quite unnecessary.[29] In MT the next clause is "and have defiled yourself," which Num renders by a correlative clause, ἢ μεμίανσαι, which is sensible.[30] A V s^mg+ text has changed ἢ to και, undoubtedly under the influence of one of The Three. The O Byz text has added a συ before μεμίανσαι, thereby making a more precise parallel to the first protasis with its εἰ δὲ σύ. But it is a secondary, stylistic gloss.

The last clause describes the adulterous action in plain terms: "and someone has put his semen (κοιτήν) into you, other than your husband." The πλήν structure is a case of aposiopesis, a delayed modifier of τις; it is, however, a case of imitating the Hebrew. The use of ἐν in the sense of "into" (as though it were εἰς) is good Hellenistic usage.[31]

---

29. See SS 99.
30. Aq and Sym have καὶ ὅτι μεμίανσαι; Theod translated as καὶ ἐμάνθης.
31. See SS 136.

5:21 The adjuration now becomes more specific than at v.19a; what is new is the prepositional phrase modifying ὁρκιεῖ, which reads ἐν τοῖς ὅρκοις τῆς ἀρᾶς ταύτης "by the oath of this curse."[32] The word ὅρκοις is plural, since the oath consists of words, possibly then "the words of the oath of this curse." MT reads בשבעת האלה, and it is possible to read שבעת as a plural word. Num has added ταύτης to stress that the actual curse follows, though this has no equivalent in MT, and hex has placed it under the obelus; but see v.22 where τοῦτο does have a correspondent in MT, though not in modification of האלה, but of המאררים.

The actual imprecation is in unusual form. The Hebrew says: יתן יהוה אותך לאלה ולשבעה; what is meant is "may Yahweh activate for you the curse and the oath." This must be what Num is also trying to say, though its syntax is peculiar. δῴη is modified not only by σε, but also by ἐν ἀρᾷ καὶ ἐνόρκιον; presumably: "may the Lord effect you with a curse and (as) an imprecation." MT has two ל phrases: לאלה ולשבעה. The change in structure to an accusative is possibly intended to address the locative which follows: "in the midst of your people." In other words, the imprecation may then be used by contemporaries: may he do to me as was sworn by the guilty woman.[33]

This ἐνόρκιον is clarified by v.b: "when the Lord makes (δοῦναι) your thigh fallen and your belly inflamed." The fallen thigh probably refers to the fallen uterus, which would mean that further conception would become improbable. The second condition is also not fully clear. MT has בטנך צבה, but precisely what צבה means is not known. It is unique to this section, and by contrast to the נזרעה זרע "she may retain seed" of v.28, possibly involuntary abortion is intended. Num, however, speaks of inflammation of the κοιλίαν, although in the passive the verb may also mean "distended,"[34] but in view of the active πρῆσαι in v.22, this would not seem to be its intent here.[35]

5:22 The curse continues from v.21: "and this curse-producing water shall enter your belly to inflame your stomach and make your thigh to sag." This in part repeats v.21b, which see. It might be noted that the demonstrative adjective τοῦτο has an equivalent in MT's האלה over against vv.18,19; the τούτου in those verses

---

32. Which Tar^J interprets as בקיום קינומתא.
33. Rashi comments on שבעה בך: שיהיו הכל נשבעין בך.
34. See LS sub πίμπρημι II.
35. The Tar all use the passive participle of נפך "swollen."

is probably a matter of harmonization with this verse. The participle in τὸ ὕδωρ τὸ ἐπικαταρώμενον τοῦτο renders the water effective by making the drinker cursed, as the effects demonstrate; see comments at v.19. For πρῆσαι and διαπεσεῖν, see the comments on πεπρησμένην and διαπεπτωκότα at v.21. Num has obviously read the final grapheme of ירך twice, producing μηρόν σου, and hex has correctly placed σου under the obelus, since it has no equivalent in MT.[36]

The woman must then affirm the curse by saying γένοιτο γένοιτο. The optative "may it be (so)" translates אמן. It is doubtful that the repetition of γένοιτο/אמן has any particular significance beyond that of greater emphasis. The repeated γένοιτο is elsewhere limited to the end of Books 1,2,3 and 4 of the Psalter (41:14 71:19 89:53 105:48).[37]

5:23 The priest must then "write these curses in a book;" whether βιβλίον/ספר actually intended anything more than that these curses be written down is doubtful. I would suggest that what is meant is "put these curses into written form." Then he must "wipe (them) off into the water of the curse-producing reproach"; obviously the wiping off words is to be taken as a symbolic gesture. For τὸ ὕδωρ τοῦ ἐλεγμοῦ τοῦ ἐπικαταρωμένου, see the comment at v.18.[38] MT simply has מי המרים, and Num has added the articulated particle ex par, which hex has rightly placed under the obelus. Hex has also rearranged ὁ ἱερεύς to follow the modifier τὰς ἀρὰς ταύτας to equal the Hebrew word order. Underlying the rite of transference of the written curse into the water to be drunk is a belief in sympathetic magic.

5:24 V.24 explains how the rite becomes effective. "The priest must make the woman drink the water of the curse-producing reproach," according to v.a, whereas v.b refers to the "curse-producing water of reproach." This change of expression simply follows the Hebrew, though it is doubtful that the difference is occasioned by anything more than the wish to avoid a repetitious structure within the same verse. For the use of τοῦ ἐλεγμοῦ, see comment at v.18. It is clear from the double use of both ἐλεγμός and the participle ἐπικαταρώμενον, that the former is meant to render מרים, and the latter, מאררים.

---

36. Tar[N] also attests to a suffix with ירכיך.
37. Sym adopts the text of Num, but Aq translates as πεπιστωμένως πεπιστωμένως.
38. Instead of τοῦ ἐλεγμοῦ The Others read τοῦ πικροῦ.

5:25 This verse is the continuation of v.18, where the priest had set the woman before the Lord, uncovered her head, and put into her hands the sacrifice of remembrance, the sacrifice of jealousy. Here the priest is to "take from the hand of the woman the sacrifice of jealousy." For the "sacrifice of jealousy," see the discussion at v.15.

The second clause states that "ἐπιθήσει the sacrifice before the Lord." MT has והניף,[39] and it is uncertain what is meant by הניף and its cognate noun תנופה. Certainly the Alexandrians were not fully clear on what distinguished it from other sacrifices. The verb is discussed in some detail along with its translations in Lev at Lev 7:20(30); see Note ad loc. The rendering ἐπιθήσει is probably taken from Lev.

The third clause has the priest presenting αὐτήν πρός the altar. The antecedent of αὐτήν is θυσίαν (not γυναῖκος), and the preposition πρός is original in spite of the majority A F M 963 reading επι. That πρός is correct is clear from a) the verb προσοίσει which prefers πρός; b) the support of the old uncial B, and c) the Hebrew אל. The επι is an instance of rationalization; sacrifices are made "on" the altar—but the verb does mean "bring to."

5:26 For the first clause, see Lev 2:2 and the Notes ad loc. For the second clause, MT has והקטיר. The Hi of קטר occurs only three times in the book, of which two are translated by ἀναφέρω (also at 18:17). Num has added αὐτό as an ad sensum gloss modifying the verb. In Lev the verb is translated in blocks by different verbs: see Note at Lev 2:16. Only then does the priest make the woman drink the water. This had already been said at v.24, but here the time of drinking is specified as following on the presentation of the sacrifice of jealousy, for which see the comment at v.15. For τὸ μνημόσυνον/אזכרתה, see the Note at Lev 2:2.

5:27 MT begins with והשקה את המים, which the translator overlooked because of homoioteleuton, the word המים also coming at the end of v.26. Hex has added a translation, και ποτιει αυτην το υδωρ, under the asterisk at the beginning. Most witnesses add μεν after ἐάν, which certainly makes good sense since the next verse begins (and contrasts with its ἐὰν δέ. But the oldest uncials, B S and 963, all lack it. Nor is it necessary, since the δέ of v.28 represents the initial *waw*.

---

39. Tar[N] takes over the verb as וינף, but Tar[JO] both have וירים.

The condition is a summary of the conditions presupposing the woman to be guilty, viz. ᾗ μεμιαμμένη καὶ λήθη λάθῃ τὸν ἄνδρα αὐτῆς, for which see v.13 and comments ad loc. In v.12 מעל מעלה was translated by παριδὼν ὑπεριδοῦσα, whereas λάθῃ in v.13 translated נעלם; here λάθῃ is modified by a cognate dative noun, and MT has תמעל מעל. In this verse, the text is merely a summation, with no attempt at conveying all the details of vv.12–13.

The ordeal is again recapitulated as the apodosis: "the curse-producing water of reproach (v.24) must go into her, and it shall inflame the belly (v.22), and her thigh shall sag (v.22)." MT has "her belly," to which hex has added αυτης under the asterisk after κοιλίαν.⁴⁰ The end result will be that ἔσται ἡ γυνὴ εἰς ἀρὰν ἐν τῷ λαῷ αὐτῆς. The Greek has taken over the Hebrew idiom of היתה ל in the sense of "become" as a syntactic stereotype.

5:28 The alternative: should the woman not be defiled and be pure, what then? She will be both innocent and produce seed (i.e. be capable of producing seed). In the tradition, the Byz text has changed the aorist μιανθῇ to the perfect passive μεμιανται; this seems to be an exegetical attempt to show that the woman had been and still was undefiled, but this is not the point at issue; it is rather a suspected case of adultery, and the aorist as default tense is the correct form.

The apodosis, the onset of which is marked by the future ἔσται, is introduced by a καί, which is common throughout the Greek Pentateuch, since this imitates Hebrew usage. Its omission in b n+ is simply a matter of improving the Greek style. The z text's change of ἐκσπερματιεῖ to the Hellenistic εκσπερματισει is secondary; Num throughout prefers the Attic future inflection.

5:29 Vv.29–31 constitute a summary recapitulation. It begins with "this is the rule about jealousy (νόμος τῆς ζηλοτυπίας).⁴¹ The genitive is objective; the instruction governs cases of jealousy. The case is one ᾧ ἂν παραβῇ ἡ γυνὴ ὑπ' ἀνδρὸς οὖσα καὶ μιανθῇ "in which a married woman might transgress and be defiled." For ὑπ' ἀνδρὸς οὖσα, see comment at v.20. Note that the summation presupposes a guilty wife throughout!

---

40. See SS 99.
41. Since תורה is here only a single law, Tarᴶ specifies this by אחויית, "an instruction (of the Torah)," and Tarᴺ, by גזרת "a decree (of the Torah)."

5:30 From the husband's point of view, "should a spirit of jealousy come on him, and he would be jealous (i.e. suspicious) of his wife." For this condition, see comments at v.14.

The apodosis reads: "and he shall set his wife before the Lord, and the priest shall carry out for her all this instruction (νόμον)." The first clause differs from the detailed instructions which precede this statement. In v.15 the man must bring her to the priest, and it is the priest (v.16) who must set her before the Lord; see comments ad loc. MT reads את האשה, i.e. without a pronominal suffix, but Num still recognizes the woman as τὴν γυναῖκα αὐτοῦ; hex has placed the αὐτοῦ under the obelus. The structure πάντα τὸν νόμον τοῦτον means the entire ritual of the ordeal including its sacrifice as detailed in vv.16—28.

5:31 The judgment is limited to the case of the wife being guilty, i.e. nothing is said in case the outcome of the ritual should clear the woman. The judgment is in two parts. a) "the man shall be innocent ἀπὸ ἁμαρτίας." This represents the Hebrew מעון, which is not quite the same. Being declared free of sin is not the same as "free from wrongdoing," or "from guilt," hence "from punishment." b) "That woman shall bear her ἁμαρτίαν." Here again, MT has עונה "her wrongdoing, punishment." Num uses ἁμαρτία 57 times; 10 times it represents עון, twice it is a free paraphrase, once it stands for אשם, and 43 times it renders חטאת or חטא;[42] though the root חטא is the dominant parent text for ἁμαρτία, as it is in Lev (and Deut), עון occurs sufficiently often to admit of no exegetical conclusions on the use of ἁμαρτία here.

---

42. According to HR.

Chapter 6

6:2 Vv.1—21 deal with the phenomenon of the Nazirite. Becoming a Nazirite was a voluntary dedication of one's person, either man or woman, to a restricted life of sanctity devoted to the Lord. The presupposition is that someone might μεγάλως εὔξηται εὐχὴν ἀφαγνισάσασθαι ἀγνείαν κυρίῳ. MT has יפלא לנדר נדר נזיר להזיר ליהוה. The root פלא usually means "to be special, extraordinary." What MT probably means it "(who) vows a special vow as a Nazirite to set himself apart for Yahweh."[1] The rendering of יפלא by μεγάλως is unique and unexpected. The translator has taken the notion of פלא in extended fashion in connection with vows in the same sense as in 15:3,8 where לפלא נדר occurs, and which Num translated by μεγαλῦναι εὐχήν "to make a large (i.e. important) vow." Why the translator used the adverb here is not clear. What is clear is that he was trying to apply the notion in the sense of something extraordinary to the verb εὔξηται. It presents the agent as involved in a fully responsible fashion in the exercise of the vow; it is an action fully thought out, and it would not be amiss to understand the adverb paraphrastically as "exceptionally," possibly "in the full awareness of what he is doing."[2]

The vow being made is ἀφαγνίσασθαι ἀγνείαν "to consecrate himself as one of purity (to the Lord)." MT has נזיר להזיר. Not only are the words transposed, but the noun is also not the same as ἀγνεία. A נזיר is an individual who has devoted himself to an ascetic life, whereas ἀγνεία is an abstract noun meaning "purity, chastity." The notion of ἀγνεία is largely a negative one; it involves a life of abstinence as the next verses make fully clear. Furthermore, the notion of consecration engendered by the infinitive is basically one of self-restriction. This is not an incorrect understanding of להזיר.[3]

---

1. For a careful review of the distinction between the related concepts of נדר and נזר, see Levine 218—219, and of נזיר, pp.229—244. It should be said that Num does not distinguish the two at all carefully.
2. Dorival 131—132 believes that the vow of the Nazirites is *le grand voeu*, quite distinct from other vows, and he suggests that "Le modèle hébreu de le LXX était sûrement différent du TM au verset 2." I find this to be somewhat of an overstatement.
3. Levine translates "to place restrictions on himself."

6:3 MT begins with "from wine and intoxicant he must abstain," to which Num added ἀπὸ οἴνου, thereby making the initial ἀπὸ οἴνου καὶ σίκερα modify the ἁγνείαν of v.2; this does point up the negative aspect of "purity"; it involves a life of abstinence. Hex has placed the second ἀπὸ οἴνου under the obelus, since it does not reflect MT. Its omission in Byz+ may well be recensionally inspired, though good sense might well have dictated its absence. The indeclinable σίκερα is a borrowed word reflecting the Aramaic שכרא, and is best rendered by "intoxicant."[4] The Nazirite may not drink any ὄξος "vinegar" of either wine or intoxicant, i.e. of wines improperly made, and therefore sour.[5] Num translates חמץ by καὶ ὄξος, i.e. adds a conjunction over against MT. The b+ text omits the καί, but whether this was due to MT influence cannot be determined.

V.b consists of two clauses, the first of which reads ὅσα κατεργάζεται ἐκ σταφυλῆς οὐ πίεται "whatever is made from the grape, he may not drink." MT refers to וכל משרת ענבים, which probably means "and any grape juice."[6] The second clause forbids consumption of food from the grape, either fresh (πρόσφατον) or dried, i.e. raisins (σταφίδα). The terms are obviously collective.

6:4 MT speaks of all the days of נזרו "his Nazirite status," but Num speaks of τῆς εὐχῆς αὐτοῦ, i.e. as though MT had read נדרו. But Num tends to make little distinction between the two roots, and often renders the root נזר as though it were נדר.

As long as his vow lasts, he may not eat from anything which derives from a vine. The ἀπό is a good example of a partitive preposition.[7] This is defined as extending οἶνον ἀπὸ στεμφύλων ἕως γιγάρτου. The two Hebrew terms, חרצנים and זג, are hapax legomena, neither of which is certain. The ἀπό ... ἕως structure is a merism, and the usual rendering for the Hebrew text is "from pits to skin," i.e. the entire grape. These are reversed by Num: "from must to pit."

6:5 Num speaks of τῆς εὐχῆς τοῦ ἁγνισμοῦ "the vow of purification" instead of "his Nazirite vow" of MT. The A F M V majority text has followed hex in adding αυτου; it is placed under the asterisk in hex. During this time "no razor ἐπελεύσεται on his head"; the verb in MT is יעבר, and Num fully understood it.

---

4. Aq and Sym translate שכר by μεθύσματος.
5. Tar distinguish the two kinds of vinegar as of "new wine" vs of "old wine."
6. Aq and Sym read πᾶσαν ἀπόβρεξιν σταφυλῆς "all the moisture from the grape."
7. See SS 162.

The Nazirite must remain ἅγιος until the times which he had vowed to the Lord are completed.[8] To remain ἅγιος means to remain in a sacred state, i.e. the conditions of being a Nazirite continue to apply, viz., no grape product may he use and no razor may come on his head. Again, the translator has failed to distinguish between הזיר and נדר, rendering יזיר by εὔχηται.

This sacral state is described as τρέφων κόμην τρίχα κεφαλῆς, which renders גדל פרע שער ראשו "letting the hair of his head to grow loose (i.e. unattended)."[9] The two words κόμη and θρίξ both mean "hair," but τρέφων κόμην means "growing loose." Hex has added αυτου after κεφαλῆς under the asterisk to represent the suffix of ראשו.

6:6 MT speaks of the time of הזירו "of his being restricted as a Nazirite," while Num simply has τῆς εὐχῆς "of the vow." Hex has added αυτου under the asterisk to represent the suffix. As usual, ליהוה becomes κυρίῳ in Num, but somewhat unusual is hex's prefixing it with the article τω under the asterisk to represent the preposition. Origen added the dative article before κυρίῳ only occasionally, which fact is puzzling.; why should there be no consistency in this matter?

The restriction placed upon the Nazirite here is ἐπὶ πάσῃ ψυχῇ τετελευτηκυίᾳ οὐκ εἰσελεύσεται. MT lacks an equivalent for πάσῃ, and hex has placed the word under the obelus. That ψυχῇ does not mean "soul" is clear from its modification by τετελευτηκυίᾳ. The word means "person, individual." What is forbidden is entering any place in which there is a corpse.

6:7 "For father and for mother and for brother and for sister, he may not defile himself when they die." MT has a third masculine singular suffix for each of the four relatives, but Num omits the suffixes, since the reference is obvious; in such cases Greek style does not usually add αυτου. But in each case, hex has added αυτου under the asterisk so as to equal MT exactly. The αὐτῶν of the genitive absolute structure must refer to αὐτοῖς, i.e. the four relatives mentioned at the beginning.

The reason for the prohibition is given in the ὅτι clause; it is because "the vow of his God is on his head." MT's text is somewhat different: נזר אלהיו על

---

8. Rashi understands קדש to refer to the hair rather than to the Nazirite: קדש יהיה השער שלו. This is not how Num understood it; ἅγιος must refer to the person.
9. Instead of τρέφων, Aq has μεγεθύνων, and Sym renders by αὔξων.

ראשו. The word נזר must refer to the uncut hair which is consecrated to his God, i.e. it is that which has been devoted. This is only clear from the על ראשו.[10] Num has kept the figure of the נזר by the rendering εὐχή, but since "the vow of his God (is) on his head" seems to make little sense, has added ἐπ' αὐτῷ to modify "vow of his God." This then means that the vow of his God which is on him (i.e. the consecrated uncut hair) is on his head.

6:8 What had been said in v.5 is now stated quite bluntly: "all the time of his vow he must be sacred (i.e. consecrated) to the Lord." What ἅγιος means is being in a sacral state in which all defilement must be avoided. The majority F M 963 text has added τω before κυρίῳ, which must have been introduced by hex; cf comment at v.6.

6:9 Vv.9—12 detail what the Nazirite must undergo, should he accidentally come in contact with a dead person. The condition described in MT is "should someone ימות מת near him בפתע פתאם." Num does not render the cognate מת, but simply has ἀποθάνῃ. The addition of the participle is simply used as an indeterminate subject, as Num with its τις ἀποθάνῃ understood.[11] The majority A F M V text has added θανατω in front of the verb. This is an early error based on the Hebrew, but not likely original, since both B and 963 support the shorter text. It must be said, however, that the "correction" is also probably not hex, since Origen would have placed θανατω after the verb. The gloss is based on a misunderstanding of מת as a free infinitive instead of as a participle.

Num has tried to differentiate between בפתע and פתאם; the two are more or less synonymous, and might be translated by "very suddenly." Num has placed ἐξάπινα "suddenly" before ἐπ' αὐτῷ, though the majority A F V text has transposed the two to equal MT.[12] Then the translator used παραχρῆμα "on the spot" to translate the second word; thus "should someone die suddenly near him on the spot." The critical text would be improved by moving the comma after αὐτῷ to follow παραχρῆμα. This is a purely editorial matter, since the autographa would have had no punctuation.

---

10. In fact, NJPS actually has נזר by "hair set apart." NIV translates "symbol of his separation," whereas NRSV interprets as "their consecration (to God!)," which is plainly wrong.
11. See GK 144e.
12. See SS 127—128.

In MT the apodosis is introduced by a conjunction, a practice common to MT; Num improves the text by omitting it. The apodosis states that μιανθήσεται ἡ κεφαλὴ εὐχῆς αὐτοῦ "the head of his vow shall be defiled." The "head" must be metonymic for the uncut hair which was consecrated (by his vow) to the Lord; see v.7. Furthermore, v.b states what must be done about it. It is introduced by καί, since it is coordinate to the μιανθήσεται clause. He must shave his head in the day in which he would be cleansed. This is further clarified as being on the seventh day. In MT it reads "on the seventh day יגלחנו (he must shave it)." Num reads the passive ξυρηθήσεται, which is adequate by itself, but hex has woodenly added αυτην under the asterisk in order to render the suffix, which is hardly an aid to clarity!

6:10 On the eighth day he must bring two turtledoves or two young doves to the priest. This is identical to the sacrifice to be brought by the indigent in the case of an inadvertent sin; see Notes at Lev 5:7, and see also v.11 below. These are to be brought to τὰς θύρας of the tent of testimony. Why Num should use the plural for פתח is not known. In Lev the choice of number was completely arbitrary, and so it appears to be in Num as well. In the tradition, the majority A M text reads νεοσσούς instead of νοσσούς, but Pentateuch translators avoided the Attic spelling.[13]

6:11 That one should be used as a sin offering (περὶ ἁμαρτίας) and one for a burnt offering (εἰς ὁλοκαύτωμα) is also attested at Lev 5:7 (and passim), for which see Note at Lev 5:7. For ἐξιλάσεται see Note at Lev 1:4. Its subject, ὁ ἱερεύς, has no counterpart in MT, and hex has placed it under the obelus. The atonement is to be made περὶ ὧν ἥμαρτεν περὶ τῆς ψυχῆς. The ὧν is plural, since the reference is indefinite; how often or with how many corpses he erred through contact is not said. τῆς ψυχῆς refers to the dead person; see comment at v.6. The ἁμαρτία that needs atonement is the contact with a corpse.

What is required is ἁγιάσει τὴν κεφαλὴν αὐτοῦ in that (same) day. For the use of κεφαλήν as metonymic for the hair and its sanctification, see the comments at vv.7,9. Contact with a corpse has undone the Nazirite vow, and he must start again; he must reconsecrate his hair. The phrase ביום ההוא is rendered by ἐν

---

13. See Walters 79—80.

ἐκείνῃ τῇ ἡμέρᾳ. Hex has transposed ἐκείνη after the noun to agree with the word order of MT.

6:12 Num disregarded the initial conjunction, and hex has added καί under the asterisk to equal it. MT simply has והזיר ליהוה "and he shall renew his Nazirite commitment," whereas Num ties the opening clause to the ἐν ἐκείνῃ ἡμέρᾳ at the end of v.11: ᾗ ἁγιάσθη κυρίῳ "(the days of the vow) in which he must be sanctified to the Lord for the time of the vow." The accusative τὰς ἡμέρας (τῆς εὐχῆς) shows extent of time, i.e. "the days of the vow." The hex text "corrected" the verb to διαφυλάξει as a more appropriate verb in the context: "in which he would carefully observe the days of his vow," hex also having added αυτου under the asterisk to represent the suffix of נזרו. I suspect that the translator felt that והזיר was out of place here. After all, that he should יזיר the days of his נזר had been said before, and so he reasoned that this statement must interpret the "in that day" at the end of v.11. What he overlooked was the need to renew his Nazirite pledge, since that had been nullified by inadvertence. It could hardly be wrong to state that the individual had to be placed in a holy state for the days of his Nazirite commitment. Hex had also articulated κυρίῳ under the asterisk (in cod G wrongly including not only the τω, but also the preceding word διαφυλάξει).

He must then bring a yearling lamb for a trespass offering. This was an offering for an inadvertent sin, i.e. ἁμάρτῃ ἀκουσίως ἀπὸ τῶν ἁγίων κυρίου (Lev 5:15). For the πλημμέλειαν and its required sacrifice, see Notes at Lev 5:15—16.

V.b in MT states that "the former days יפלו, because נזהר had become unclean." Num interprets יפלו by ἄλογοι ἔσονται. What this means is that "they will not be counted," i.e. reckoned as valid for the time of his vow.[14] Furthermore, instead of simply translating נזרו as "his εὐχή," Num interprets this once again as referring metonymically to the hair as defiled by his κεφαλὴ εὐχὴν αὐτοῦ, for which see references in v.11. Oddly, hex apparently did not place κεφαλή under the obelus, even though it has no equivalent in MT.

6:13 Vv.13—21 deal with the ritual to be observed once the period of the vow has been completed. It begins with the common introductory καὶ οὗτος ὁ νόμος

---

14. See Lee 50.

"And this is the regulation." This is defined as being "on which day he would complete the days of his vow προσοίσει αὐτὸς παρά the doors of the tent of testimony." MT reads יביא אתו "one shall bring him," i.e. he shall be brought. Num has translated this by taking προσοίσει, normally a transitive verb requiring an accusative modifier, as an intransitive, but reflecting אתו by a nominative, thus "he himself must apply to." Hex has "corrected" the αὐτός by reading αυτον.[15] This is a good example of how carefully the translator regarded his parent text. That the parent had an אתו is shown by αὐτός;[16] since no subject is given for יביא, he has supplied it with αὐτός, thereby forcing an understanding that the Hi of בוא was read, but making προσφέρω intransitive (or possibly reflexive?) I would suggest that one translate: "he shall bring (himself) to the doors of the tent of testimony,"[17] thereby showing that it was προσοίσει, in its reflecting יביא that was used, though in an unusual sense. For the plural τὰς θύρας, see comment at v.10.

6:14 Three sacrifices are to be presented on the occasion. The offerings are called a δῶρον "a gift." This, as its Hebrew counterpart, קרבן, is a cover term for sacrifices in general.[18] The first one is the burnt offering,[19] which is described in detail in Lev ch.1. It is to consist of a yearling male lamb. All sacrifices must also be unblemished (ἄμωμον). The second sacrifice is a female yearling lamb which is to be offered εἰς ἁμαρτίαν "for sin." The Hebrew term is חטאת, which can mean either "sin" or "sin offering." In Lev לחטאת in the sense of "for a sin offering" is never rendered by an εἰς construction, but always by (τὸ) περὶ (τῆς) ἁμαρτίας.[20] Num does not follow the pattern of Lev, since here εἰς ἁμαρτίαν must mean "for a sin-offering." Num has also reordered the Hebrew modifiers אחת בת שנתה תמימה as ἐνιαυσίαν ἄμωμον μίαν; hex has transposed these to equal MT: μιαν ενιαυσιαν αμωμον. For details of the sin offering ritual, see Lev

---

15. As do The Others.
16. Cf especially Prijs 57, who suggests that אתו can be understood not only as a reflexive pronoun, i.e. that "wie gewöhnlich, nota accusativi, sondern Verstärkung des Nominativs ist." See also the references given in his Footnote 1.
17. Cf especially Tar^J: ימטי ית גרמיה "he brings himself."
18. The terms are collective; see THGN 113.
19. For the choice of the minority reading ὁλοκαύτωσιν rather than ολοκαυτωμα, see THGN 112.
20. See THGL 78.

ch.4. The third sacrifice is a single unblemished ram "for deliverance." Sacrifices for deliverance, the שלמים, are discussed in detail at Lev ch.3.

6:15 Further elements of the δῶρον (v.14) are "a basket of unleavened cakes of fine flour, loaves made up with oil and unleavened wafers anointed with oil, both their sacrifice and their libation." ἄρτους "loaves of bread" is the usual rendering in LXX for חלות "small cakes"; these are described as בלולת with oil "mixed with oil." בלולה is rendered in LXX either by φυρᾶν "mixed" or with ἀναποιεῖν "made up."[21]

The last two read καὶ θυσίαν αὐτῶν καὶ σπονδὴν αὐτῶν "both their sacrifice and their libation." In MT מנחתם is probably to be understood as a collective noun, since the coordinate נסכיהם is plural. Num made both singular, possibly as collectives? In any event, they constitute part of the δῶρον of v.14, and must therefore be accusatives, not nominatives as B 963 n x read. In spite of the support of the two oldest extant Greek witnesses, the nominative cannot be correct.[22]

6:16 The verb προσοίσει is used here without an accusative modifier in imitation of MT; it is unnecessary in view of the context; what is to be presented are the offerings listed in vv.14—15. In contrast to the εἰς ἁμαρτίαν of v.14, here the חטאת can only be understood as the sin offering, and Num realized this with its τὸ περὶ ἁμαρτίας, a structure created by the Lev translator.[23] The עלה is rendered by ὁλοκαύτωμα over against ὁλοκαύτωσιν at v.14. The two are synonyms, and are semantically indistinguishable.[24] In any event, the plural τα ολοκαυτωματα of b cannot be original. Whenever עלה obtains, Num always uses the singular.[25]

6:17 The ram is to be offered as "a sacrifice for deliverance to the Lord along with (ἐπί with the dative) the basket of unleavened cakes." The V O C s+ text articulated κυρίῳ; this is almost certainly a hex revision, since the dative divine name was never articulated in Num, but hex does on occasion add τω to designate the preposition of ליהוה.[26]

---

21. See SS 123—124.
22. See THGN 109.
23. See THGL 78.
24. See THGN 112.
25. See THGN 111.
26. See THGN 104—105.

As in v.15 Num has taken both θυσίαν and σπονδήν as singular. Here, unlike in v.15, MT has both pronominal suffixes in the singular, and Num follows MT.

6:18 The ηὐγμένος (perfect middle participle of εὔχομαι) "the one who has pledged himself" must "shave τὴν κεφαλὴν τῆς εὐχῆς αὐτοῦ at the doors of the tent of testimony."[27] The augmented diphthong of Attic Greek is retained in the Pentateuch for the perfect middle participle of εὔχομαι as well as for its aorist indicative, though in the tradition, this is lost in many witnesses; ευγμενος did become popular in Hellenistic Greek, but the Attic form is original. For τὰς θύρας, see comment at v.10. Actually, though פתח is always singular in MT when governing the tent, the plural accusative occurs five times, the singular also occurs five times, and the singular genitive τῆς θύρας occurs six times in the book. Num is just as arbitrary as Lev as far as the number of "door(s)" of the tent is concerned. For "the head of his vow," i.e. the consecrated hair, see comment at v.9.

MT then states: "and he shall take the hair of the head of his נזר and put (it) on the fire." Num abbreviates to καὶ ἐπιθήσει τὰς τρίχας ἐπὶ τὸ πῦρ. In the context this states all the essentials. That he must first "take" the hair before putting it on the fire is obvious; furthermore, the hair had already been defined in v.1 as being the head of his vow. Origen was uncertain how to correct this text. He left ἐπιθήσει as filling the יקח slot; then under the asterisk after τρίχας he added της κεφαλης ευχης αυτου και θησει. At least, each slot is then filled, but it leaves ἐπιθήσει as representing יקח, which it does not and cannot do.

In the tradition, the A F M V majority text read επι instead of ὑπό. This is, however, a quite inferior reading. The first is not *upon*, but *under* the sacrifice for deliverance, as in MT's תחת.[28]

6:19 The priest is then to take three things: a) from the ram the shoulder which was boiled, and b) one unleavened loaf from the basket, and c) one unleavened wafer. The shoulder, according to Deut 18:3, was part of the priestly meat allotment from the sacrifice of deliverance.[29] For b) MT has the modifiers for ἄρτον

---

27. Aq renders הנזיר by ὁ ἀφωρισμένος, while Sym has Ναζιραῖος.
28. The Tar add דודא, i.e. "the pot" containing the sacrifice.
29. For Near Eastern parallels, see Milgrom ad loc.

ordered as ἕνα ἄζυμον, whereas MT reads מצה אחת. The popular A V reading transposing the two equals MT, but that it was created by hex is likely, but uncertain. For ἄρτον as the usual rendering for חלה, see comment at v.15.

He must then place (these) on the hands of the one who undertook the vow (see comment at v.18). MT has על כפי הנזיר "on the palms of the Nazirite."[30] The subject of ἐπιθήσει must be the priest, i.e. the subject of the coordinate clause, and the Byz text made this explicit by adding ο ιερευς.

This was to be done subsequent to the removal of the consecrated hair, i.e. μετὰ τὸ ξυρήσεσθαι αὐτὸν τὴν εὐχὴν αὐτοῦ. The referent in the pronouns is obviously τοῦ ηὐγμένου. The εὐχήν represents נזרו, which in v.18 had been the ראש נזרו. It is hardly surprising that the A F M V 963 majority text changed εὐχήν to κεφαλην as the modifier of "shave."

6:20 MT has והניף plus תנופה, which Num renders by καὶ προσοίσει ἐπίθεμα. For הניף תנופה, see Note at Lev 7:20(30), where the various Greek renderings in Lev are also shown. But the Hi of נוף is never rendered elsewhere in Num by προσφέρω. At 5:25 the verb was rendered by ἐπιθήσει; at 8:11, by ἀφοριεῖ; at 8:13,15, by ἀποδώσεις, and at 8:21, by ἀπέδωκεν.

The cognate noun is rendered at 8:11,16,21 by ἀπόδομα. As in the case of the Lev translator, Num was uncertain of the type of sacrificial ritual involved. Nonetheless προσφέρω is unique.

On the other hand, the verb has two accusative modifiers, and this is the first mention of this sacrifice in the book. It should also be noted that תנופה is here twice rendered by ἐπίθεμα, as well as at 18:11,18; it also occurs regularly (six times) in Lev. The first time that it occurs Num simply has the offering brought before the Lord. It is always possible that Num's parent text read something like הקריב, but there is no evidence whatsoever to support a different text. The notion of הקריב תנופה does not occur elsewhere, nor would one expect it. I suspect that this is simply a matter of rationalization on the part of the translator. That one might bring (or present) a deposit just fits well here.

---

30. Field attributes the following readings to two mss cited by Montfaucon (B.de Montfaucon, Origenis Hexaplorum quae supersunt, multis partibus auctiora quam a F.Nobilio et J.Drusio edita fuerint. 1713); I have been unable to identify these mss, and verify the readings. The readings are: Aq ἐπὶ τοὺς ταρσοὺς τοῦ ἀφωρισμένου and Sym ἐπὶ τὰς παλάμας τοῦ Ναζηραίου. Comp readings in footnote at v.18.

This ἐπίθεμα must be considered ἅγιον for the priest. Num may reflect the Sam text which has an extra יהיה after קדש, though it also retains הוא after קדש, whereas Num substitutes ἔσται for הוא. The notion of ἅγιον should not be taken in any other sense but that of "set apart," i.e. solely for the use of the priest. As someone or something which is holy to the Lord is completely set apart for exclusive service or use, so too is the offering, along with (ἐπί plus the genitive) the breast of the offering (ἐπιθέματος) and the shoulder of the ἀφαιρέματος, both traditionally being portions assigned to the priest(s). The shoulder (βραχίονος) is regularly used in Lev for שוק "thigh"; see Note at Exod 29:22. The term ἀφαιρέματος is the sacrifice that has been raised; see Note at Exod 29:27. This is then a sacrifice that has been removed from ordinary use, thus a dedication gift; see Note at Lev 7:4(14). The two sacrifices, תנופה and תרומה, are not always carefully kept distinct; comp Lev 7:4 and 20 for the contrast between ἀφαίρεμα (תרומה) and ἐπίθεμα (תנופה).

6:21 The opening clause repeats the formulaic "this is the regulation of ..." of v.13, which see. So the formula creates an envelope pattern, serving both as superscription and as subscription to this section, which describes the details of the end of the Nazirite commitment. The rhetoric of this verse is even looser than that of MT which probably means something like: "whoever might vow his sacrifice (קרבנו) to Yahweh according to his Nazirite obligation (נזרו)—besides what he can afford; according to his vow which he might vow, so must he do alongside (על) the regulation of his Nazirite commitment (נזרו).

Num has unfortunately omitted כן יעשה "so must he do," which makes it difficult to make good sense of the Greek. Hex has duly added ουτως ποιησει after "he might vow." Num also omitted "his" in both cases of נזרו, and hex has in each case added αυτου under the asterisk. On the other hand, Num has added κυρίῳ after the first εὔχηται; this was apparently omitted by hex on the evidence of O, though it is possible that the shorter text is actually original. The longer text is, however, probably to be taken as original text in view of the support by the oldest texts, including A B 963. Num may then be understood provisionally as saying "who may have vowed to the Lord, (viz.,) his sacrifice (δῶρον) to the Lord for his vow, besides whatever he could (also) afford, according to the force (or power, δύναμιν) of his vow which he may have vowed in accordance with the rule of purity." I am not quite clear what κατὰ δυναμὶν τῆς εὐχῆς αὐτοῦ of Num intends; it seems to give a standard for the payment of the vows. He cannot escape the δυναμίν of his vow. The stress must then fall on the χωρίς; he must fulfill what he promised quite "apart from what he could afford," thus it must be according to the force of his vow. His ability to pay is then not a limitation on the need to fulfill the terms of his vow. To make this clearer, I would suggest that a comma should be placed after αὐτοῦ 2° in the critical text.

6:23 Vv.22—27 deal with the Aaronic benediction. Moses is directed to speak to Aaron and his sons. What is intended is the dictation of the form in which the priestly blessing is to be recited.

Unusual is the use of אמור להם, where one might have expected the direct quotation formula לאמר. What is given seems to be a syntactic blend of ואמרת להם and לאמר. It is, however, a fully valid syntagm. The contextual free infinitive simply takes on the usage of the context, i.e. that of תברכו, thus "you must speak ... you must say (to them)." Num simplifies this by using the direct speech formula λέγοντες (αὐτοῖς).

6:24(27) Hex has transposed this verse to the end of the chapter where MT also has it. The verse constitutes an official interpretation of the benediction. There are two parts to the interpretation. The first clause states that "they (i.e. Aaron and his sons) must place my name on the Israelites." In some way, the pronouncing of the blessing places the divine name in an effective manner on the people (σε, i.e. the congregation of Israel). Precisely what "placing the divine name" on the people meant has been disputed.[31] I would take this to be related to the next clause: "and I, the Lord, will bless them." By placing, i.e. by pronouncing, the divine name over the Israelite community, the actual blessing is not that of Aaron anymore; it has become ἐγὼ κύριος who will actually bless them. This becomes particularly clear from the fact that Num has added κύριος after ἐγώ, whereas MT simply has אני.

By placing the interpretation of the benediction before the actual blessing, the Alexandrian has changed it to the forefront rather than as a conclusion or af-

---

31. Tar^{JO} interpret שמי as the ברכת שמי, whereas Tar^N simply says שמי ית ממרי. Instructive is the comment of Rashi: יברכום בשם המפורש "they shall bless them by means of the actual divine name (i.e. the tetragrammaton)."

terthought as in MT.³² The preposing of this verse effectively places the divine name on the Israelites, and ensures that the blessing will be effective. It does this through the recitation of ἐγὼ κύριος εὐλογήσω αὐτούς. Furthermore, it means that the actual name involved in "κύριος" is the tetragrammaton. It is Israel's God as revealed at Sinai who will effect the covenantal blessing on his people. Num is the only early witness to the preposing of the interpretation.³³

6:25(24) Throughout the benedictions Num correctly used aorist optatives, since the verbs in MT are intended to be short forms as well; note יאר (not יאיר) in v.25 and ישם (not ישים) in v.26. For the first blessing: "may the Lord bless you," the clearest interpretation of what "blessing" means is given in the catalogue of blessings to be conferred "if you obey the Lord your God" in Deut 28:3—14. This is seconded by καὶ φυλάξαι σε, the blessing of protection, i.e. from all harm.³⁴ Incidentally, our two oldest extant witnesses, B and 963, both omit the final σε, a clear case of haplography. The word follows φυλάξαι, and in Byzantine times the two words would be realized as /pilakse se/. The second /se/ was omitted by mistake.

6:26(25) The next benediction is ἐπιφάναι κύριος τὸ πρόσωπον αὐτοῦ ἐπὶ σέ "may the Lord show his face to you." The verb ἐπιφαίνω plus τὸ πρόσωπον when said of deity means "to reveal himself (to mankind)." That the preposition modifying the verb is not πρός but ἐπί is due to the compound verb ἐπιφαίνω. That the Lord should reveal himself to the people favorably is meant is even more clearly stated in MT by the verb יאר "may he illumine (his face)." The self-revelation of the Lord to the congregation is particularly distinctive of Israel's God. Furthermore, καὶ ἐλεήσαι σε "and may he be merciful to you." The verb is most

---

32. Interesting is what Tar have done with the actual blessing. Tar^NO have not translated it, but reproduced it in Hebrew, thereby perpetuating the early notion that the benediction should be given only in Hebrew. Tar^J also gives each clause in Hebrew, but then adds in each case an Aaramaic interpretation, e.g. for the first one it has יברכינך ייי בכל עיסקך.
33. Dorival not only calls this reordering surprising, but "il apparaît ainsi comme mal placé." I would suggest that "badly placed" in Dorival is inappropriate. To my mind there is purpose underlying the transposition.
34. Tar^J gives a list of evil spirits from which protection is sought: מן לילי ומזייעי ובני טיהררי ובני צפרירי ומזיקי וטלני "from the Liliths and terrible demons and midday demons and morning demons and destructive spirits and night devils."

often used to translate חנן "to be generous, gracious" (44 times), but also for רחם "to take pity" (29 times).³⁵ Here the verb stresses the notion of mercy, grace, a notion which eventually developed into that of charity; note the sense of "almsgiving" for ἐλεημοσύνη. What is meant is that the Lord would not deal with Israel according to its sins, but in mercy, i.e. kindly.

6:27(26) That the Lord should raise his face towards the congregation means "to favor the congregation," thus "be attentive towards," or negatively put, not to disregard. The Lord will listen with favor to the people. And finally, δῴη σοι εἰρήνην. The notion of εἰρήνη is not a negative one, i.e. lack of strife, of warfare, but one of well-being. It is a stereotype rendering of שלום. In fact, out of 222 cases of שלום translated into Greek, 182 become εἰρήνη. 12 times the adjective εἰρηικός is used, twice the verb εἰρηνεύω occurs, and the remaining 26 are a scattered lot of equivalences.³⁶ Since the root שלם involves the idea of completeness, wholeness, שלום, and thereby εἰρήνη, it relates to the well-being or wholeness of the community, thus the full life and health of the group. "Peace" then is the blessing of completeness, of communal well-being.

---

35. The statistics are from Dos Santos.
36. According to Dos Santos.

Chapter 7

7:1 Ch.7 is an administrative account outlining the gifts given for the tabernacle cult by the twelve tribal leaders. V.1 sets the time for the account. It presupposes the final chapter of Exodus, i.e. the completion of the tabernacle, the installation of its furniture as well as the cloud of the glory of the Lord filling the tent.[1] This is what the opening clause refers to: "And it happened at the time when (ᾗ ἡμέρᾳ) Moses ...." The relative clause encompasses the rest of the verse. Μωυσῆς is the subject throughout, and vv.2—3 are the "then" clauses. Thus "when Moses finished ... and anointed and ..., then the rulers of Israel ...." For the anointing and sanctifying of the tent, see Lev 8:10.

I would translate v.1 by "and it happened when Moses had finished setting up the tent and had anointed it and sanctified it and all its vessels, and the altar and all its vessels and had anointed them and sanctified them, ..." The pronoun αὐτά refers in both cases to "all its vessels" (i.e. of the altar). Unusual is the marking of the complementary infinitive with ὥστε. In fact, this occurs only three times in the book (also at 5:8 8:11).[2]

7:2 The verb προσήνεγκαν is normally a transitive verb (as is יקריבו), but here it is used absolutely, thus "made a presentation offering." The chieftains of Israel are called δώδεκα ἄρχοντες οἴκων πατριῶν αὐτῶν.[3] For οἴκων πατριῶν αὐτῶν, see comment at 1:2. MT does not mention the number, so hex placed δώδεκα under the obelus. They are also characterized by two nominal clauses: "these (are) chieftains of tribes" and "these (are) the ones who had been in charge of the review," a reference to the census review of chapter 1. MT, however, has על הפקדים, i.e. a plural passive participle "those reviewed," which Num changed to ἐπὶ τῆς ἐπισκοπῆς. The same rendering occurs at 14:29 26:18(22) 47(43).

7:3 The chieftains brought their τὸ δῶρον. The majority A F M V text attests to the plural τα δωρα, but in spite of its strong support, it is a secondary adaptation

---

1. Tar^J adds "the first of the month Nisan" after "day," which is based on Exod 40:2.
2. See THGN 134.
3. Tar^J also calls them הינון דמתמנן במצרים אמרכולין.

to the plural verb; comp also vv.10,11. The singular, like its Hebrew counterpart, קרבן, is retained throughout the chapter.[4] The gifts brought were six λαμπηνικάς wagons and twelve cattle, a wagon from two chieftains, and an ox from each one. The term λαμπανικάς is actually a hapax legomenon. Apparently, it is an adjective formed from λαμπήνη "a covered chariot."[5] MT has the noun [6]צב which only occurs once elsewhere (at Isa 66:20, where it is rendered by <ἐν> λαμπήναις).[7]

The last clause states "and they brought (them) before the tent (i.e. המשכן)." Num has not translated אותם, and hex has supplied an αυτα under the asterisk. The verb is προσήγαγον, which has been accepted as Num on the basis of its support by B 963. The A F M V majority text reads προσήνεγκαν, the verb read by Num in v.2 as translation for יקריבו, which is also read here. The two verbs are synonyms. In v.a Num used the simplex ἤνεγκαν for יביא; thus a succession of three different verbs in Greek obtain: προσήνεγκαν, ἤνεγκαν, and then for variation(?) προσήγαγον, but in MT they are יקריבו, יביאו and יקריבו.

7:5 Moses is then told by the Lord to take (them) from them (i.e. from the chieftains). The imperative λάβε is used absolutely, as is the Hebrew קח; the purpose of taking is described as καὶ ἔσονται πρὸς τὰ ἔργα τὰ λειτουργικά of the tent of testimony. I would understand the καὶ ἔσονται, since it is coordinate with the imperative λάβε, as imperatival in sense, i.e. "and let them be." The translator has then rewritten the purposive infinitive of MT as a prepositional phrase. As for the לעבד את עבדת "to work the work of," he misunderstood the infinitival marker ל as a preposition, thus translating by "for the service works." The "works" refer specifically to the transport duties of the Levites.

Moses is to give these vehicles and draft animals to the Levites in accordance with their several services, as had been detailed in ch.4. Num describes this as being "to each one according to τὴν αὐτοῦ λειτουργίαν." Hex has reordered this as την λειτουργιαν αυτου to equal the Hebrew order.

---

4. See THGN 113.
5. Aq translates by κατασκεπαστάς, and Sym, by ὑπουργίας.
6. Tar[JO] both agree that it means "covered," but Tar[J] adds ומטקען "and equipped." Tar[N] translates by מזווגן "yoked."
7. For a detailed discussion of the word, see Dorival ad loc.

7:6 Instead of the paratactic clauses of MT, the Greek reduces "ויקח ... ויתן" to καὶ λαβὼν ... ἔδωκεν, which reduction is a normal Greek syntactic pattern.

7:7—8 The assignment of wagons and cattle to the Levite clans. Two wagons and four cattle he (i.e. Moses) gave to the Gedsonites in accordance with their (assigned) services. For the transport assignments of the Gedsonites, see 4:24— 28. And the Merarites received double that amount, four wagons and eight cattle in accordance with their (assigned) services. Their transport duties are described in 4:29—33.

The concluding structure is a διά phrase modifying ἔδωκεν 1° and 2°, i.e. Moses gave to ... τοῖς υἱοῖς Γεδσών ... τοῖς υἱοῖς Μεραρί ... through (or by) Ithamar. Its meaning is clear from 4:28,33 ἐν χειρὶ Ἰθαμάρ. The porterage assignment for the two clans was in the charge of Ithamar, son of Aaron the priest. The use of διά plus a genitive for ביד is unusual,[8] but is not incorrect.[9]

7:9 In contrast to the other Levitical clans, the Kaathites received no transport means, i.e. no wagons nor cattle. The reason given is that "they have τὰ λειτουργήματα τοῦ ἁγίου. This translates the Hebrew "the service of the sanctuary is upon them." Hebrew has no verb "to have" as the Greek does, but here ἔχουσιν is a fine interpretation of the predicate עלהם.[10] Presumably, by τὰ λειτουργήματα is meant the furniture and its service objects (i.e. of the sanctuary). This is clear from 4:4—15, in which the porterage duties of the Kaathites are described; cf comments ad loc. What is clear is those their porterage duties are quite distinct from that of the other two clans who received wagons and cattle for transport services. The Kaathites, being entrusted with the transport of the ark, the table, the lampstand, the golden altar, along with all their vessels, must carry these on the shoulders.[11] MT has the singular כתף, but the plural is also legitimate. One, i.e. each one, carries things on the shoulder, but the Kaathites carry things on shoulders. It depends on one's point of view.

---

8. For other examples of this equation, see Johannessohn, Gebrauch 238.
9. For διά see Bauer s.v. III.2.a.
10. For the use of this verb in the LXX, see "Der Gebrauch des verbs ἔχειν in der Septuaginta," in SS 181—188.
11. Tar^N specifies what they carry by its ארונה ית טענין הוון "they carry the ark."

7:10 Num has two προσήνεγκαν clauses, but in the first one the verb is used absolutely as at v.2; cf comment ad loc. In MT the two יקריבו verbs are modified by את phrases, and one would have expected both cases of προσήνεγκαν to be rendered transitively, i.e. with accusative modifiers, but this obtains only for the second one, where τὸ δῶρον αὐτοῦ modifies the verb. It should be noted that only Eth supports a singular noun; all Greek witnesses read (τὰ δῶρα). But as noted at v.3 קרבן throughout the chapter is rendered by the singular τὸ δῶρον (18 times), and never by the plural. The plural here, as well as in v.11, has become dominant in the tradition by attraction to the plural referent, οἱ ἄρχοντες, but the singular is original.[12]

In the first clause, את חנכת המזבח "the dedication offering for the altar" modifies the verb, but Num has changed this to an εἰς phrase, εἰς τὸν ἐγκαινισμὸν τοῦ θυσιαστηρίου "for the inauguration of the altar." The term ἐγκαινισμόν is a creation of Num, as is the cognate ἐγκαίνισις of v.88; both refer to the inauguration of the altar in the tabernacle.[13] The interpretation is fully logical. A dedication only happens at the beginning; it is indeed an inauguration.

The chieftains presented their offering in the day ᾗ ἔχρισεν αὐτό," i.e. in which he (presumably Moses; cf v.1) anointed it (i.e. the altar)." But MT reads המשח אתו. The verb is Ni, and the structure is a passive transform of "he anointed it"; see ימשח אתו of v.1; it can only be intended in the sense of "when it was anointed." Num simplified the construction by making the verb active.

According to the last clause of the verse, these chieftains brought their gift before the altar, i.e. the altar of burnt offering in the courtyard. In the tradition, the V b t+ text has identified ἄρχοντες 1° by an unnecessary gloss ισραηλ, as "the chieftains of Israel," though it is difficult to conceive of any other chieftains in the context.

7:11 This verse serves to rationalize the order of events for vv.12—83, in which are detailed the individual τὸ δῶρον which the chieftains of the twelve tribes were to bring on successive days. This was by divine direction. The order concerns נשיא אחד ליום נשיא אחד ליום. The repetition of "one chieftain per day" is a recognized way in which Hebrew expresses the distributive sense.[14] Num has

---
12. See THGN 113.
13. For the word חנכה and its translation by the root ἐγκαιν—, see Dorival 126—127.
14. See GK 123d.

rendered this word for word into Greek, which is an obvious syntactic calque; it can only be explained through the Hebrew. I doubt that a monolingual Greek speaker would understand it.

In any event, "they (i.e. the twelve chieftains) must bring their gift for the inauguration of the altar, one chieftain per day."[15] For the singular τὸ δῶρον as original text, see the discussion and footnote at v.10.

7:12 Vv.12—17 describe the gift of Naasson, son of Aminadab, chieftain of the tribe of Iouda. MT lacks the word "chieftain," though in the case of the next eleven it is always present. Hex has, accordingly, placed ἄρχων under the obelus to indicate its absence from MT. For Ναασσὼν υἱὸς 'Αμιναδάβ, see comments at 1:7. The timer, τῇ ἡμέρῃ τῇ πρώτῃ, is placed between the articulated participle ὁ προσφέρων and its accusative modifier, τὸ δῶρον αὐτοῦ, in imitation of MT.

7:13 Vv.13—17a tabulate "his gift"; this tabulation is repeated word for word for each of the twelve chieftains, even when the Hebrew text varies slightly. Comments made in this verse may be considered applicable for the next eleven gifts as well. Over against MT Num has a verb προσήνεγκεν to introduce the tabulation. Hex has placed it under an obelus.

The gift of Naasson comprises the following: a) "one silver bowl, its weight 130." No unit of weight is given, though for the next item the weights are given as σίκλων, which is a calque for the Hebrew שקל. The term משקל is translated throughout the chapter by ὁλκή, a word which Classically meant "drawing, dragging," but in Hellenistic Greek means "a weight."[16] b) "one silver flat bowl, 70 shekels according to the sacred shekel." The norm "sacred shekel" was intended to guard against debased weights. See Note at Exod 30:13 on the "sacred didrachma." The rendering τὸν σίκλον τὸν ἅγιον is a possible rendering for the consonantal text, which the Masoretes vocalized as a bound structure, i.e. as the shekel of the sanctuary."[17]

It is also stipulated that both containers are πλήρη σεμιδάλεως ἀναπεποιημένης ἐν ἐλαίῳ for a sacrifice. MT has "full of fine flour בלולה with oil for a מנחה. The word בלולה is translated throughout this chapter by "made up," as

---
15. Both Tar^JN gloss חנוכת with רבותה, i.e. "a dedication by anointment."
16. See Lee 62—63.
17. See SS 129.

well as elsewhere in the book. In Lev it was more commonly rendered by πεφυραμένη, "mixed." The מנחה was the grain or meal sacrifice, regularly rendered by θυσία; this is fully presented in Lev chapter 2, which see.[18]

7:14 c) "one censer, ten (shekels) of gold, full of incense."[19] MT has כף "palm" (i.e. of the hand), but since it is full of incense, the word probably refers to the shape of the censer, i.e. a censer shaped like a palm.

7:15—16 d) "one ox from the cattle, one ram, one year-old lamb for the burnt offering," and e) "one kid from the flock for a sin offering." The חטאת, when it refers to the sin offering, is rendered by περὶ ἁμαρτίας. The "sin offering" is always in the genitive (though not necessarily governed by a preposition). In the other cases, the noun refers to "sin." For the burnt offering and the sin offering, see Lev chapters 1 and 4 resp.

7:17 f) "for the sacrifice for deliverance two heifers, five rams, five he-goats, five year-old lambs." For this sacrifice for deliverance in detail, see Lev chapter 3. The section concludes with "τοῦτο τὸ δῶρον of Naasson, son of Aminadab."

7:18—23 "On the second day προσήνεγκεν Nathanael, the son of Sogar, chieftain of the tribe of Issachar." MT lacks an equivalent for "of the tribe," and hex has placed τῆς φυλῆς under the obelus. V.19 begins with הקרב, but Num has καὶ προσήνεγκεν. The initial καί of v.22 also has no equivalent in MT, but it follows Sam. This pattern becomes the typical opening for the next ten chieftains as well, except for the verb which occurs only in this section. For the proper names and their variant realization in the tradition, see comments at 1:8.

7:24—29 "On the third day, the chieftain of the Zaboulonites, Eliab, son of Chailon." For these names, see comments at 1:9a. V.28 lacks an equivalent for the opening καί in MT, and follows Sam which does have the conjunction. Exactly the same thing is true for vv.34,40,46,52,58,64,70,76 and 82.

---

18. See SS 123—124.
19. For χρυσοῦς/זהב as a designation for a weight, i.e. shekels, see Lee 64—65.

7:30—35 "On the fourth day, the chieftain of the Roubenites, Elisour, son of Sediour." For these names, see comments at 1:5. For v.34, see comment at v.28.

7:36—41 "On the fifth day, the chieftain of the Simeonites, Salamiel, son of Sourisadai." For these names, see comments at 1:6. For v.40, see comment at v.28.

7:42—47 "On the sixth day, the chieftain of the Gadites, Elisaph, son of Ragouel." For these names, see comments at 1:14. For v.46, see comment at v.28.

7:48—53 "On the seventh day, the chieftain of the Ephraimites, Elisama, son of Emioud." For the names, see comments at 1:9b. For v.52, see comment at v.28.

7:54—59 "On the eighth day, the chieftain of the Manassites, Gamaliel, son of Phadasour." For the names, see comments at 1:10.[20] For v.58, see comment at v.28.

7:60—65 "On the ninth day, the chieftain of the Beniaminites, Abidan, son of Gadeoni." For the names, see comments at 1:11. For v.64, see comment at v.28.

7:66—71 "On the tenth day, the chieftain of the Danites, Achiezer, son of Amisadai." For these names, see comments at 1:12. For v.70, see comment at v.28.

7:72—77 "On the eleventh day, the chieftain of the Aserites, Phagaiel, son of Echran." For these names, see comments at 1:13. For v.76, see comment at v.28.

7:78—83 "On the twelfth day, the chieftain of the Naphthalites, Achire, son of Ainan." For these names, see comments at 1:15. For v.82, see comment at v.28.

7:84 Vv.84—88 constitute a summary statement, in which the twelve presentations of the tribal chieftains are summarized. For ἐγκαινισμός "inauguration" as

---

20. See also THGN 120 for Φαδασούρ.

an interpretation of חנכת, see comment at v.10. For ἔχρισεν αὐτό in the relative clause as a simplification for the Ni המשח אתו, see discussion at v.10. MT reads "from the נשיאי ישראל," whereas Num inserts τῶν υἱῶν, i.e. "from the chieftains of the Israelites." Hex has placed τῶν υἱῶν under the obelus.[21]

7:85 The first item reads τριάκοντα καὶ ἑκατὸν σίκλων τὸ τρύβλιον τὸ ἕν. MT lacks an equivalent for σίκλων, and adds כסף at the end. Hex has placed σίκλων under the obelus to indicate its absence in MT.[22] Hex has also added αργυριου under the asterisk after ἕν to represent MT's כסף.

Similarly for the next item, σίκλων is placed under the obelus by hex, since again it has no correspondent in MT. In the last element dealing with "all the silver of the vessels," the weight is also described in terms of σίκλοι, which is also placed under the obelus in hex, since MT does not have a שקל.[23] The standard employed is, however, given as בשקל הקדש. This occurred regularly throughout the chapter, and was rendered by κατὰ τὸν σίκλον τὸν ἅγιον, for which see comment at v.13.[24] Here, however, it becomes ἐν τῷ σίκλῳ τῶν ἁγίων "according to the shekel of holy things," or "of the sanctuary." The majority A F M V text read τω σικλω instead of τῶν σίκλων, under the influence of the adjectival variant, which occurs in the chapter in Num twelve times. The oldest witnesses, B and 963, both support Num, which is probably original. It is much easier to explain τω σικλω as a variant text, than the Num text as secondary.[25]

7:86 Num is considerably shorter than MT. It reads: "gold censers twelve, full of incense. All the gold of the censers, 120 χρυσοῖ." MT lacks an equivalent for the last word, and hex has placed it under the obelus. MT, however, has between the two clauses עשרה עשרה הכף בשקל הקדש. Hex has supplied equivalent text under the asterisk: δεκα δεκα η θυισκη εν τω σικλω τω αγιω, i.e. "each censer ten (i.e. shekels) according to the sacred shekel." It is possible that this was omitted as overly obvious; on the other hand, it seems odd that the translator should have been bothered by the inclusion of the obvious in view of the repetitiousness

---
21. Tar^N agrees with Num in its רברבני דבני ישראל.
22. The Tar all add סלעון.
23. But Tar^JN both include ס.(י)לעון.
24. See also SS 129.
25. See especially THGN 126—127.

throughout this chapter. I suspect that the omission may well have been textually based, though admittedly there is no extant Hebrew text that omits it.

7:87 In each case, Num has placed the number of the sacrificial animals at the end, which is the more common pattern. But MT is inconsistent; it has שנים עשר פרים, whereas Num has μόσχοι δώδεκα. Hex has transposed these words to equal the word order of MT.

Instead of ומנחתם "and their meal offering," Num has αἱ θυσίαι αὐτῶν καὶ αἱ σπονδαὶ αὐτῶν. There are two differences between the two texts: the conjunction of MT is lacking in Num. MT usually has a conjunction when this pair of nominals (either singular or plural) occurs, but only twice (6:15 29:6) did Num begin with καί. That the και variant in B* Byz f+ is secondary seems clear.[26] That the και is palaeographically inspired is clear from its context; it occurs between (δώδε)κα and αἱ.

The second difference is the absence in MT of an equivalent for καὶ αἱ σπονδαὶ αὐτῶν. The pair occurs frequently in the book (18 times), and the translator has harmonized with the common collocation. Interestingly enough, there is no direct evidence that hex took notice of this addition, although one O ms did omit it. Ms 58 does on occasion omit materials under the obelus, and thus evidences post-hexaplaric activity on the part of its scribe. In other words, this may indicate secondary evidence for hex activity.

7:88 MT begins with וכל, but Num begins asyndetically. In the tradition, Byz has added και, which is probably recensional in character. In the list of sacrificial animals Num used the preferred order throughout, i.e. animals followed by number. This differs from MT for the first one, δαμάλεις εἴκοσι τέσσαρες for MT's "twenty and four bullocks." Hex, as expected, has transposed δαμάλεις after the number to agree with MT. For the fourth one, Num has "lambs sixty," followed by ἐνιαύσιαι ἄμωμοι. MT has בני שנה after כבשים; accordingly, hex has transposed ἑξήκοντα after ἐνιαύσιαι, but placed ἄμωμοι under the obelus, since MT does not have an equivalent

V.b is the subscription to the chapter. In MT this reads: "This is the dedication offering for the altar אחרי המשח אתו." חנכת is rendered by ἐγκαίνισις,

---

26. See THGN 100.

which is a synonym of ἐγκαινισμός that had been used at vv.10,11,84; see comment at v.10. Here ἐγκαινισμός is supported by only one ms, 767, and it is clear that the translator was choosing a synonym, probably for variety's sake. Most witnesses support Num, with only B 426 509 reading ἐγκαίνωσις, but Num is original.[27] For the rendering המשח אתו by (μετὰ) τὸ χρῖσαι αὐτόν, see comment on the ᾗ clause at v.10.

But Num has a longer text. It has two μετά structures: μετὰ τὸ πληρῶσαι τὰς χεῖρας αὐτοῦ καὶ μετὰ τὸ χρῖσαι αὐτόν "after (he) had filled his hands and after (he) had anointed him." The reference is to Aaron's being anointed and ordained; see Exod 28:37 where God commands Moses καὶ χρίσεις αὐτοὺς (i.e. Aaron and his sons) καὶ ἐμπλήσεις αὐτῶν τὰς χεῖρας; see Note ad loc. Comp also 29:9 where "you shall fill the hand" becomes τελειώσεις τὰς χεῖρας; see Note ad loc as well; see also 29:29. Num has in this subscription brought the anointing of the priest into the context of his ordination. The translator has interpreted אתו, not as a reference to the altar, but rather to Aaron. That the anointing of Aaron was tied to the sanctification of the altar is clear from Exod 40:9,11; note that this took place in "day one (of the first month)" according to 40:2.[28] Hex has, of course, placed the first μετά clause plus the following καί under the obelus, since MT does not attest to it. What Num has done is to bring the inauguration of the altar, on the basis of the Exod 40 account, into the context of Aaron's place in the cult of the altar, by taking אתו as reference to Aaron; thereby, he legitimizes the context by referring to the ordination of the high priest.

7:89 Num begins asyndetically over against MT: "when Moses entered the tent of testimony to speak to him." The pronoun has no obvious antecedent; at first blush, one might think αὐτῷ refers to Aaron in view of the αὐτόν of v.88. This is indeed a possible understanding. This would mean that Moses entered the tent to speak to his brother, the high priest, whom he had anointed and ordained. In any event, the verse is only loosely connected to the chapter, to which it is the subscription, since the apodosis refers to his hearing "the voice of the Lord which was speaking to him." This, however, is not what MT says; it has את הקול "the

---

27. See THGN 127.
28. As Dorival ad loc points out.

voice." Hex has placed κυρίου under the obelus; I have no doubt that Num was correct in identifying "the voice" as the voice of the Lord.[29]

That he heard the voice of the Lord λαλοῦντος πρὸς αὐτόν, makes the final clause of MT "and he spoke to him" tautological. The translator tried to mitigate this redundancy by making the verb imperfect: καὶ ἐλάλει πρὸς αὐτόν "and he was speaking to him." If Levine is correct in his understanding of the Hithp particple as stressing continuity, Num may be reflecting this notion. Though the Hebrew participle is rendered by a Greek present participle, the imperfect does contrast with the default aorist by promoting the notion of process, i.e. of continuity.

---

29. Levine understands the מדבר which the Masoretes vocalized as a Hithp participle of דבר, as meaning "continuously speaking." This would then contrast with the וידבר אליו which ends the verse.

Chapter 8

8:2 According to Exod 38:13,17 (comp 25:30—39), Moses made the lamps and the lampstand; it was, however, his brother Aaron who was entrusted with their care. That בהעלתך does not mean "when you are lighting (the lamps),"[1] but rather "when you are setting up,"[2] was understood by Num which has ὅταν ἐπιτιθῇς. If properly placed, then "ἐκ μέρους κατὰ πρόσωπον τῆς λυχνίας the seven lamps will shine." What is meant is that the lamps will give light on the side in front of the lampstand. The Byz text made sure that ἐκ μέρους would be correctly understood by inserting του ενος, i.e. "from the one side"; this reading is based on v.3. The translator used the present subjunctive, since the setting up of the lights was a regular (daily) affair; a popular reading read the aorist by syncopation of the middle syllable, but this is an inferior reading.

8:3 Num has added τοῦ ἐνός before μέρους, i.e. "(from) the one side." This is probably a case of harmonization with Exod 25:37,[3] where Moses is ordered: ἐπιθήσεις τοὺς λύχνους καὶ φανοῦσιν ἐκ τοῦ ἐνὸς προσώπου. In carrying out the divine orders, Aaron העלה "set up" the lamps, but Num interpreted this action as ἐξῆψεν "he hung up, suspended" the lamps; here, however, the verb chosen is probably based on Exod 30:8, where the suspension of the lamps led to θυμιάσει ἐπ' αὐτοῦ; thus having suspended the lamps which involved lighting them, he would burn incense on it (i.e. the altar). The translator may well be engaged here in a *double entendre*, since העלה does have a double sense; see comment at v.2.[4]

8:4 The term κατασκευή is well-chosen to represent מעשה; it is a descriptive term for "construction," or "structure." What is meant by the opening nominal clause is that this is how one must make the lampstand. MT uses the technical term מקשה to describe the gold, i.e. "hammered (gold)," but Num, probably on the basis of Exod 38:14, renders by στερεὰ χρυσῇ "solid gold"; see Note at

---
1. As Tar^JO: באדלקותך. Rashi rationalizes this interpretation by noting that שלהב עולה. Tar^N reads בסדרותך "when you arrange."
2. For the notion of "lighting," see Note at Exod 25:37.
3. As Dorival ad loc suggests.
4. See also Dorival 85.

38:14. This in turn was more fully stated in MT by עד ירכה עד פרחה מקשה הוא. What is probably meant is "it was hammered from its base to its petal," (word for word: "up to its base, up to its petal), though I can find no other case of עד ... עד ... in the sense of "from ... to." Num also found this strange, and simplified the clause as an explication of στερεὰ χρυσῆ, i.e. "its stem and its corolla, all solid." For καυλός and κρίνα (literally "lilies"), see Notes at Exod 25:30. By omitting the prepositions entirely, Num made good sense; even the substitution of ὅλη for הוא serves to make a clearer picture; the entire lampstand was of solid gold. Origen made no attempt to correct the text by a rendering for the two cases of עד, or by recognizing the word הוא.

This all was in accord with the εἶδος "form, shape," thus pattern. For the pattern which the Lord showed Moses, see τὸν τύπον τὸν δεδειγμένον (σοι) ἐν τῷ ὄρει at Exod 25:40.[5]

8:6 Vv.5—26 deal with the Levites, their consecration and their tabernacle service. Those rites connected with their ἁγνισμός are described in vv.6—19. Moses is told to take the Levites from among the Israelites and ἀφαγνιεῖς them. This renders טהרת, and thus involves ritual purification or cleansing; comp the use of the middle ἀφαγνίσασθαι referring to the vow to set oneself apart as a Nazirite at 6:2. The future verb as a coordinate with an imperative must be understood as an imperatival as well.[6] The verb περιρρανεῖς is future, and it renders a singular imperative הזה.

8:7 The opening statement in MT reads "and thus must you do to them so as to cleanse them." Num renders this neatly by "and thus must you effect for them their cleansing," i.e. Num treats לטהרם as a nominal rather than as an infinitive.

This cleansing consists of three rites. a) you must besprinkle them with water of cleansing, ὕδωρ ἁγνισμοῦ. The Hebrew term is מי חטאת. The term is probably used metaphorically as "the water for the removal of sin," thus "water of purification or cleansing." At 19:9 Num reads ὕδωρ ῥαντισμοῦ ἁγνισμά ἐστιν, which translates MT's למי נדה חטאת הוא "water of lustration; it is a sin offering," whereas Num has "water of sprinkling, it is a cleansing." The terms

---
5. Tar[JN] make Bezalel the subject of עבד; this accords with Exod 31:2—9; see especially v.8.
6. See Porter 419—420.

ἁγνισμά and ἁγνισμός are synonyms; in fact, at v.17 החטאת is rendered by τοῦ ἁγνισμοῦ. To the translator, the water of sprinkling is characterized as a cleansing, whereas in our verse sprinkling is to be done with the water of cleansing. That the two are closely related in Num seems obvious. In both cases, impurity is removed by sprinkling of water. What this means for the Levites is that the water for the removal of חטאת removes what is impure; it transforms, as in the case of menstrual impurity, to a clean or pure status.[7] In the tradition, the V Byz text reads the compound αφαγνισμον, which is never attested anywhere in LXX. The compound is probably somewhat more technical than the simplex in its use, though there is no great difference between the two.

b) "A razor must pass over all their body." MT has a transitive verb in the plural with תער as a modifier, but the plural העבירו must be understood as having an indefinite plural subject, as in the English "they say." c) "They must wash their garments."

Oddly enough, Num has three different subjects for the three verbs, a second singular, a third singular, referring to ξυρόν, and a third plural, referring to the Levites. There is a progressive involvement of the Levites in the ritual, from a passive one in which they are the objects of sprinkling, to a neutral one in which a razor is to pass over their body, and finally to their own washing of their clothes. Only after these three rites are completed, καθαροὶ ἔσονται.

8:8 MT distinguishes the two animals by פר בן בקר "a bull of the herd" and פר שני בן בקר "a second bull of the herd." Num probably understood שני as ἐνιαύσιον, i.e. as though it were reading בן שנה, and modified the first μόσχον as μόσχον ἕνα. Hex placed ἕνα under the obelus, since it has no correspondent in MT. Hex also "corrected" the rendering for מנחתו τούτου θυσίαν by transposing the two words. Presumably, the first bullock was intended for a burnt offering, since the second is said to be περὶ ἁμαρτίας "a sin offering." Why Num should designate the first sacrifice as ἕνα over against MT, but fail to designate the next sacrifice as δεύτερον so as to render the שני of MT is peculiar. Hex did nothing to make up for this lack as far as the extant tradition is concerned.

The first sacrifice is accompanied by a meal offering; it is called τούτου θυσίαν; the genitive pronoun specifies that it is in particular the meal offering for

---
7. See Dorival 124—125.

the μόσχον ἕνα. This θυσίαν is σεμίδαλιν made up with oil. In the tradition, the B z+ text read σεμιδαλεως, but this is an ex par variant reading. Only the accusative can make sense here; it is the fine flour which is mixed with oil, not the sacrifice.[8] The ἐν of "with oil" is instrumental.[9]

8:9 The two verbs, הקרבת of the first clause and הקהלת of the second, are rendered by two compounds of ἄγω, i.e. προσάξεις "bring forward" and συνάξεις "bring together" resp. The result is the presence of the Levites and of all the assembly of the Israelites before the tent of testimony.

8:10 V.a repeats v.9a, except that "before the tent of testimony" here becomes ἔναντι κυρίου. Though often the two are synonyms in intent, the phrase "before the Lord" is used intentionally, since it is in the presence of Israel's God that the ceremony of the imposition of hands on the Levites must take place. It should be noted that in v.9 all the Israelites are assembled, but the "all" is not repeated for the laying on of hands; it would stretch one's imagination to have all the Israelites imposing their hands on the Levites. But even having some Israelites do so, would be quite a feat, since according to 4:48 the review of the Levites who were eligible for performing Levitical tasks, i.e were between 25 and 50 years of age, numbered 8,580.

8:11 MT begins with והניף, which is modified by the cognate noun תנופה. This also occurs at vv.13,15,21, where ἀποδίδωμι ἀπόδομα (omitted at v.15) is used. Here it is rendered by ἀφοριεῖ ... ἀπόδομα "set aside, separate as a presentation." For the meaning of הניף תנופה and its translation in Lev, see Note at Lev 7:20. In Lev the structure refers to a particular kind of offering, but here it is used metaphorically. The noun ἀπόδομα never renders תנופה in Lev, though δόμα is used twice. The verb ἀφορίζω occurs twice as well for the verb in Lev (10:15 14:12), but not with δόμα. It is clear that Num distances itself intentionally from this Lev usage. Since here הניף occurs for the first time in the book, it is appropriate to use ἀφορίζω, thereby assuring the reader that the Levites are to be separated from the other tribes as an ἀπόδομα ἔναντι κυρίου.

---

8. See THGN 109.
9. See SS 123.

The noun actually means "restitution,"[10] and I would translate the word by "restitution offering"; see comment at v.13.

The second clause has the awkward structure ἔσονται ὥστε plus infinitive in imitation of MT's היו לעבד. The unusual ὥστε—it occurs only three times in the book in similar contexts (also at 5:8 7:1[11])—serves to emphasize the purpose of setting aside "the Levites as a restitution offering before the Lord from the Israelites," viz. "so that they may perform the Lord's services." Num interprets the singular עבדת correctly as a collective, i.e. as τὰ ἔργα (κυρίου). In the tradition, the Byz text has added της σκηνης, an exegetical gloss defining the works of the Lord as being of the Lord's tabernacle.

8:12 The subject change to οἱ Λευῖται is signalized by the δέ construction. They are to place τὰς χεῖρας ἐπὶ τὰς κεφαλὰς τῶν μόσχων. Hex has added αυτων under the asterisk after χεῖρας to represent the suffix of MT's ידיהם.[12] Num also uses the plural τὰς κεφαλάς, since the two bullocks being sacrificed each have a head. MT uses the singular with equal validity, i.e. no bullock had more than one head.

MT begins v.b with ועשה; the Masoretes vocalized עשה as an imperative, which is odd indeed, since the only one addressed is Moses. Num took it as a third masculine singular verb by its καὶ ποιήσει, which the consonantal text also allows; this must then refer to Ἀαρών of v.12. A popular text changed the verb to ποιησεις, which in view of v.5, would be directed to Moses. But it was the high priest who was to perform the sacrifices of the two animals, "the one as a sin offering, and the other for a burnt offering to the Lord," thereby effecting atonement for the Levites, and certainly not Moses. For the meaning of ἐξιλάσασθαι, see Note at Lev 1:4.

8:13 MT orders Moses: "you shall set the Levites before Aaron and before his sons." This could be interpreted as inconsistent with v.11 where Aaron was to set apart the Levites ἀπόδομα ἔναντι κυρίου. Surely the Levites should be made to stand "before the Lord" as well as before Aaron and the Aaronids. Num has

---

10. Dorival translates the first clause by "et Aaron mettra à part les Lévites à titre de restitution, devant Seigneur, de la part des fils d'Israel."
11. See THGN 134.
12. See SS 99.

inserted κυρίου καὶ ἔναντι before Ἀαρών, which hex has in turn placed under the obelus, since MT does not witness to these words. The translator wanted to be certain that Israel's God was not neglected in the ceremony.

The second clause is an abbreviated version of v.11. MT's והנפת אתם תנופה ליהוה is translated by καὶ ἀποδώσεις αὐτοὺς ἀπόδομα ἔναντι κυρίου. In v.11, the verb had been translated by ἀφοριεῖ, but here the Hebrew cognate structure is retained in translation. If, as in v.11, ἀπόδομα should be translated by "restitution offering," then the cognate structure must mean "you must restore them as a restitution offering before the Lord." This would mean that their ἁγνισμός involved a return, a repayment, which in turn suggests that the Israelites from whom the ἀπόδομα came belonged to the Lord; they were all his people, but now the Israelites are to give or designate the Levites as a special restitution, specifically to engage in tabernacle activities; comp v.14, which also favors this interpretation.

8:14 The special status of the Levites is stressed by the two parts of the verse. V.a states "and διαστελεῖς the Levites from the midst of the Israelites." The Hebrew verb is הבדלת, the same verb which was used in the creation account of Gen (1:4b), in which God made a division between light and darkness, though Gen translated by a different verb, διεχώρισεν. Here, the verb also makes the distinction; you must "set apart" the Levites from the others. Num articulates υἱῶν here, but no particular pattern as to the articulation of υἱῶν Ἰσραήλ obtains in the book.[13] The article is omitted by a popular A B text, but it is attested in the oldest extant Greek witness, 963. In such cases it seemed prudent to follow the oldest witness.

V.b is shorter in Num than in MT, which repeats הלוים as subject, i.e. "and the Levites shall be mine." Hex has added οἱ λευιται at the end of the clause so as to equal MT. No possible confusion obtains from the omission; the subject of ἔσονται can only be the Levites. The statement here must have a special significance, since after all the Israelites as a whole were also claimed by God as his people. But the Levites belong to the Lord in a special way; they have been given back, restored to their God for special service.

---

13. See THGN 105.

8:15 This becomes clear from v.a: "and after these (things) the Levites shall go in to perform the services of the tent of testimony." MT has a shorter text for the infinitival structure, reading לעבד את אהל מועד "to serve the tent of meeting." Num has followed Sam, which reads עבדת before אהל.[14] Num renders the word correctly as a collective, τὰ ἔργα.

V.b is difficult to reconcile with its context, since it repeats "and you must cleanse them (see v.7) and ἀποδώσεις them before the Lord (see v.13). It does seem out of place, but this is due to the parent text. Modern English versions have voided the contradiction by making v.b propaedeutic to v.a, e.g. "once you have cleansed them and presented them as an elevation offering" (NRSV), but this is not what the text says. Num has made one change, however. The word for תנופה has been omitted, and hex has added (ἀπο)δομα to make up for it. It is possible that the omission was intentional, i.e. calling attention to the fact that this verse is different from v.13; there restoring the Levites as a restitution offering was clearly prior to their entering the tent. But now they have entered, and in performing the services of the tent, you may thereby cleanse and restore them before the Lord. MT also has no correspondent to the final ἔναντι κυρίου, which hex has therefore placed under the obelus.

8:16 Vv.16—19 are an elaboration of 3:9, where Moses is told to assign the Levites to Aaron and the Aaronids. There they were characterized as δόμα δεδομένοι οὗτοί μοί εἰσιν ἀπὸ τῶν υἱῶν Ἰσαρήλ. In fact, נתנים נתנים המה is a copy of 3:9; see the discussion ad loc on the meaning of the clause. Here the translator has used the compound root: ἀπόδομα ἀποδεδομένοι (οὗτοί μοί εἰσιν ἐκ μέσου υἱῶν Ἰσραήλ). The translator cleverly used the compound which recurs in vv.13,21; in view of v.b there is a repayment to the Lord involved; the Levites constitute an ἀπόδομα "restitution offering." The Lord says: "I have taken them (i.e. the Levites) for myself in place of those opening every womb, of the first born of all from the Israelites." Sam has simplified this by its תחת כל בכור פטר רחם בבני ישראל "instead of every first born opening the womb among the Israelites," but Num retains the odd syntax of MT, except for understanding the singulars פטרת and בכור כל as collectives, i.e. rendering them by plurals.

Origen was apparently puzzled as to what to do about οὗτοί μοί εἰσιν, since MT has only two words: המה לי. Is οὗτοί or εἰσιν the equivalent for המה?

---

14. As do Kenn 6,199 as well as Tar[J].

According to Syh, he placed οὗτοί under the obelus, and to make clear that it was an extra word, transposed it after μοί.

8:17 The basis for the substitution made in v.16 is given in a ὅτι clause; it is "because mine is every firstborn among the Israelites ἀπὸ ἀνθρώπου ἕως κτήνους." MT reads באדם ובבהמה "among man and among cattle," whereas Num renders this as though it were an מן ... עד structure. Exactly the same translation pattern occurs, however, at 18:15 31:11,26.[15]

V.b begins with a timer: "ביום הכתי every firstborn in the land of Egypt," which modifies the core clause הקדשתי אתם לי. Num renders this by a relative clause: "in which day I smote every firstborn in Egypt land." The phrase ἐν γῇ Αἰγύπτῳ also occurs at 14:2 33:4 for בארץ מצרים, but at 3:13 this is rendered by ἐν γῇ Αἰγύπτου. The bound phrase "land of Egypt" also occurs at 1:1 9:1 15:4 33:1,38, but the genitive Αἰγύπτου is used. It should be noted, however, that in each of these five cases it modifies γῆς, not γῇ. In any event, MT is adequately rendered. What is being said is that the Lord had sanctified the Levites at the time of the last plague, i.e. when he killed all the firstborn among the Egyptians. In other words, the sanctification of the Levites is rooted in the Exodus motif.

8:18—19 V.18 simply repeats in summary fashion: "and I took the Levites instead of every firstborn among the Israelites," but then in v.19 goes on to say "καὶ ἀπέδωκα the Levites ἀπόδομα δεδομένους to Aaron and his sons." Here the cognate structure is interpreted as δεδομένους, reflecting the נתנים of MT. What Num says is "and I returned the Levites as restitution offering as a given to Aaron." The Levites were returned as a restitution offering to the Lord; see vv.11,13 and 16; now the Lord returns them as a given to Aaron, i.e. reassigns them to the charge of Aaron and the Aaronids. MT, however, simply has ואתנה נתנים "I gave (the Levites) as assignees (to Aaron and the Aaronids)." Formally, Num has an extra word, and hex has placed ἀπόδομα under the obelus. The participle is, however, a simplex form, modifying not ἀπόδομα, but τοὺς Λευίτας, thus "I restored the Levites assigned to Aaron and his sons from the midst of the Israelites as a restitution offering"

The assignment is described in two coordinate infinitival structures. a) "To perform the services of the Israelites in the tent of testimony." Num has rightly

---

15. As Dorival points out.

understood עבדת as a collective (it never renders the word by εργον), and interprets it by τὰ ἔργα (τῶν υἰῶν Ἰσραήλ). What the Levites are to do is that which the Israelites cannot do for themselves, since they are forbidden entrance to the tabernacle area. b) To make atonement for the Israelites." For the notion of atonement, see Note at Lev 1:4. As in the case of v.a the Levites labor on behalf of the people.

V.b is paratactically expressed, but, as the future ἔσται implies, describes the result of actions a) and b). As stated above, the Israelites need cultic personnel to act on their behalf. For them to approach the sacral area would have been dangerous, in fact even fatal. The result of the Levites' actions on their account is that there will be no one among the Israelites, i.e. in distinction from the tribe of Levi, who will approach the holy things, thereby risking the danger of encroachment. This differs from MT which states: and there shall not be among the Israelites נגף בגשת בני ישראל אל הקדש i.e. "a plague when the Israelites come near the sanctuary." Note that Num has omitted both נגף and the repeated בני ישראל. The latter omission would not by itself change the sense, though hex does add των υιων ισραηλ to equal MT. Similarly, hex has added θραυσις under the asterisk before προσεγγίζων to represent the absent נגף. But why should Num have omitted נגף? It has been suggested[16] that reference to a plague was omitted to distinguish what is actually a general observation from the specific event of ἡ θραῦσις breaking out among the Israelites (at 16:47—50) on the occasion of their murmuring against Moses and Aaron because of the destruction of Kore and his company, when ὥρμησαν ἐπὶ τὴν σκηνὴν τοῦ μαρτυρίου. The translator may well have felt this notion of a plague to be a case of overkill,[17] unnecessary here since approaching τὰ ἅγια on the part of laymen was avoided through the work of the Levites. On the other hand, what Num has effectively done by its substitution of προσεγγίζων for נגף בגשת בני ישראל is to deny an approach on the part of the Israelites to the sanctuary and its contents. After all, MT took for granted that Israelites could and would approach the sanctuary, but because the Levites now were to perform all the non-priestly functions within the tabernacle, any need for an individual Israelite approaching the tent was voided. Any danger attached to touching the sacred could now be avoided by limiting the approach to Aaronids and Levites.

---

16. By Dorival.
17. Tar^{JO} render נגף by מותא, but Tar^N, by רגוז "disturbance."

It might also be noted that Num seems to have made no distinction in number in rendering the word הקדש,[18] at times using τὸ ἅγιον and at times the plural as in this verse; here, however, the plural has been preferred, since the emphasis is not so much on the Levites being in the sanctuary as on the Levites' labors in the sanctuary in handling the holy objects of the cult.

8:20 Vv.20—22 simply state that the divine orders in connection with the Levites were carried out. The three subjects, Moses, Aaron and all the assembly of the Israelites, all did as ordered. The norm was "καθά the Lord commanded Moses concerning the Levites." MT has ככל אשר, and so hex corrected καθά by reading κατα παντα α.[19] That the translator interpreted intelligently, and not in a wooden word-for-word fashion is clear from his rendering of the two cases of ללוים. For the first one he used τοῖς Λευίταις, but for the second one, περὶ τῶν Λευίτων.

8:21 Num uses the simplex ἡγνίσαντο to render the Hithp יתחטאו, but the compound ἀφαγνίσασθαι to translate לטהר.[20] The distinction was not particularly meaningful to Num, however, except that the simplex was never used for טהר. But התחטא was rendered by the simplex, not only here but also at 19:12 31:19,23, whereas it was rendered by the compound verb at 19:12,13,20 and 31:20.[21] The two verbs are synonyms; both mean "to cleanse." In this verse, the active is not used. In the first clause, the middle obtains, whereas the infinitive is probably best taken as a passive with αὐτούς as its subject, i.e. "(made atonement) that they might be cleansed." This has been "corrected" by the Byz text to reflect the transitive לטהר of MT to αφαγνισαι.

The second clause reads "and they washed the garments." Since MT has בגדיהם, the majority A F M V text added αυτων, which must be a recensional addition, probably hex in origin;[22] the shorter text is idiomatic Greek, since it is unnecessary to state that the garments were "theirs." They would hardly have washed someone else's, or each other's garments. In the tradition, the B M Byz+ text read επλυναντο, which can hardly be original. The verb must be transitive;

---

18. See THGN 112.
19. Theod and Aq also read κατὰ πάντα <ἄ>.
20. The Tar distinguish the two by using a passive form of דכא to render יתחטאו, but an active one for לטהר.
21. According to HR.
22. See SS 99.

in fact, the variant text is particularly misleading, since it would probably be understood as passive.[23]

For the third clause and its rendering of וינף תנופה, see comment at v.13 as well as at v.11. For ἐξιλάσατο see Note at Lev 1:4.

8:22 After these matters of cleansing were accomplished the Levites entered לעבד את עבדתם in the tent. Num has λειτουργεῖν τὴν λειτουργίαν αὐτῶν, which renders MT literally, but at both vv.15 and 19 ἐργάζεσθαι τὰ ἔργα had been used. But the translator did not want to use τὰ ἔργα, since he wished to use a singular concept. But τὸ ἔργον is never used in Num to render עבדת, and so he used λειτουργία, which is almost exclusively used to render עבדה (17 times in Num). This cognate structure also means "to perform service," and differs from the עבד structure only in its use of the singular noun. In the tradition, the majority A F M text read the Hellenistic first aorist inflection εισηλθοσαν instead of the Classical εἰσῆλθον of Num, but Num never uses the Hellenistic inflections for ἔρχομαι or its compounds, and εἰσῆλθον must be original.[24] They perform their service ἔναντι Aaron and ἔναντι his sons. What is meant by "before" is "in their presence," since they were under the supervision of the priests; comp v.13 in MT. Num, however, included the Lord; see comment ad loc.

V.b concludes the section. "καθά the Lord had commanded Moses concerning the Levites, so they (i.e. the Israelites) did to them (the Levites)." It might be noted that B+ read καθως instead of καθά, but Num never uses καθως, either for כאשר as here, or for אשר. Only καθά is original.[25]

8:24 Vv.23—26 constitute a prescription dealing with the age limits for Levitical service. The superscription reads τοῦτό ἐστιν τὸ περὶ τῶν Λευίτων "this is that which pertains to the Levites."[26] The age at which the service is to begin is at 25 years of age. This is consistently maintained in Num, whereas in MT in ch.4 (see comment at 4:3) the starting age is 30 years. Here, however, MT also reads 25. What he enters, according to MT, is לצבא צבא בעבדת of the tent of meeting. The term צבא is commonly used as a military term, as "army, host," but in Num it

---

23. See THGN 126.
24. See THGN 123.
25. See THGN 127.
26. See SS 59 and 183.

means "work force."[27] What is meant then is "to share in the work force for the service (of the tent)." Num abbreviates considerably by its ενεργείν "to work in."[28] Instead of ἐνεργεῖν, the V Byz text has substituted λειτουργειν. A more substantial change is witnessed by the A M V majority text, which has λειτουργειν λειτουργιαν εν εργοις. This may well be hex in origin. It is hardly original text, as is clear from the rendering of בעבדת אהל by εν εργοις εν τη σκηνη, but must be recensional. In other words, the change of ἐνεργεῖν to εν εργοις is not an error, but a correction, which was not extended to changing ἐν τῇ σκηνῇ to a genitive (της) σκηνης.

The main verb, εἰσελεύσεται, represents יבוא literally. Almost all Greek witnesses read the plural, which is a simplification, since the reference to Levites is plural in the previous clause, περὶ τῶν Λευίτων. The next verse also uses singular verbs, however, as does MT. Obviously, the two verses must be consistent, and only the singular is appropriate.[29]

8:25 Retirement from Levitical service is mandatory at the age of fifty. This is stated as ἀποστήσεται ἀπὸ τῆς λειτουργίας "shall stand away from service," i.e. "withdraw from."[30] This represents MT's ישוב מצבא העבדה. This hardly satisfied Origen, and hex added της δυναμεως after ἀπό to represent צבא. But as explained in a comment at v.24, the Hebrew means "the work force," and λειτουργία is adequate.

This is clear from the following clause: καὶ οὐκ ἐργᾶται ἔτι "and he will not work any more." Since MT reads יעבד, it seems strange that the Origenian text, represented inter alia by O, should read the plural εργωνται.[31] This is probably due to the fact that O consistently read the plural in vv.24—25: εισελευσονται, αποστησονται, εργωνται. Of Greek witnesses, only O and two z witnesses use the plural throughout these verses.

---

27. See Levine ad loc for this insight.
28. Aq follows the more usual understanding by his τοῦ στρατεύεσθαι στρατείαν δουλείας. Sym renders more freely, but intelligently, with παρίστασθαι παράστασιν εἰς λατρείαν.
29. See THGN 122—123.
30. See Lee 35—36.
31. Theod and Aq rendered the clause by καὶ οὐ δουλεύσει ἔτι, but Sym, by καὶ οὐκ ἐργάσεται οὐκέτι.

8:26 The text of MT creates a problem, since it begins with: ושרת את אחיו in the tent of meeting לשמר משמרת, which means "and he (i.e. the Levite) shall serve his brothers (i.e. those still active) by standing on guard." This certainly seem to contradict ch.3 where the Levitical clans are assigned their משמרת in turn; see v.25 for that of the Gershonites, v.31 for that of the Qohathites, and v.36 for that of the Merarites. These instances of φυλακή/משמרת were the tasks assigned to the various Levitical clans.

Num was aware of the problem, and changed the clause to mean "and his brother shall serve in the tent of testimony by doing guard duties, but he may not perform services (ἔργα)." His brother refers to the active Levite, which then contrasts (δέ) with his own status. Note that the subject of ἐργᾶται is the αὐτοῦ of ὁ ἀδελφὸς αὐτοῦ. This is an obvious case of rationalizing the text, i.e. of removing the contradiction in the MT text.[32]

V.b makes a clear reference to the φυλακιᾶς of the Levitical clans of ch.3. Whatever MT of v.a means, the לשמר משמרת must refer to those clanal duties. MT remains puzzling, but Num is clear. Only the active Levite, and not the retirees, may ἐργᾶατι the ἔργα of the tabernacle.

---

32. One of the more popular attempts at resolving the problem is to take את as the preposition meaning "with." Thus Tar^JO have עם אחוהי, though Tar^N has ית אחוי. Aq also reads σὺν ἀδελφοῖς, and Theod has μετὰ τῶν ἀδελφῶν, but Sym translates τοῖς ἀδελφοῖς. Modern versions void the problem by redefinition. E.g., NIV's translation is representative; it translates "they may assist their brothers in performing their duties at the Tent of Meeting, but they themselves must not do the work." NJPS and NRSV render in similar fashion. I find it difficult to justify this as a rendering of MT.

Chapter 9

9:1 Vv.1—14 deal with the Paschal festival celebrated in the desert of Sina. A number of mss, mainly from the *n* group, correct Σινά to σιναι so as to conform to the סני of MT. The *n* group usually corrects to σιναι in the Pentateuch, probably under the influence of one of the Revisers. The genitive structure ἐξελθόντων αὐτῶν ἐκ γῆς Αἰγύπτου must be understood as referring to ἐν τῷ ἔτει τῷ δευτέρῳ, not to the verb ἐλάλησεν. The time of their leaving Egypt was a year earlier, but the second year is of their going out of the land of Egypt. The comma after δευτέρῳ in the critical text should be deleted; its presence leaves the impression that the genitive participle which follows is unrelated to the phrase "in the second year."

The pronoun αὐτῶν must refer to οἱ υἱοὶ Ἰσραήλ of v.2. It cannot refer to the preceding αὐτῶν ending 8:26, since that refers to the Levites. The first paschal celebrations, described in Exod 12—13, occurred as they were on the point of their leaving Egypt. What is now described took place in the second year of that great event. In the tradition, ἐξελθόντων becomes εκπορευομενων in *b n* s^{mg}+; this is a synonym, but is secondary. The reference to the Exodus is usually ἐξέρχομαι rather than ἐκπορεύομαι.

9:2 MT begins the direct speech by ויעשו. LXX, possibly because of the initial conjunction, has εἶπον before καὶ ποιείτωσαν, an unusual expression; what is probably meant is "give orders that they should observe." εἶπον must be taken as an imperative; hex has placed it under the obelus as having no correspondent in MT.[1] It is quite possible that in view of לאמר preceding ויעשו, that the translator read the אמר of לאמר twice, thereby creating the tautological "saying: say" of Num. But I doubt that the Hebrew text actually read such peculiar Hebrew. What the Israelites are to observe is τὸ πάσχα. Num reflects a transcription of the Aramaic פסחא, rather than of the Hebrew הפסח.[2] Unique is the rendering of במועדו. מועד occurs regularly throughout the Pentateuch in the phrase אהל מועד

---

1. Dorival states: "il faut plutôt songer à un modèle different," but this is not necessarily so.
2. Which Sym seems to reflect by his φασεκ.

"tent of meeting," which is always mistranslated as σκηνὴ τοῦ μαρτυρίου "tent of testimony" in the Greek; see the discussion in the Note at Exod 27:21. The term is also used to designate "set festivals," as at Exod 13:10, where, however, it is uniquely translated by κατὰ καιροὺς ὡρῶν; see Note ad loc. The verb first occurs in the creation account of Gen 1:14 as למועדים, rendered by εἰς καιρούς. Here it is rendered uniquely by καθ' ὥραν αὐτοῦ, but comp Exod 13:10, which probably influenced the translator here. It is best rendered by "at its specific time." In the tradition, καθ' ὥραν becomes κατα καιρον in V b+, but this is due to the influence of v.7, where the מעדו is rendered by κατὰ καιρὸν αὐτοῦ.

9:3 The festival is to be held "on the fourteenth day τοῦ μηνὸς τοῦ πρώτου at eventide." What is referred to is the beginning of the feast at which time the paschal lamb was to be slain; see Exod 12:6. MT refers to the month as בחדש הזה, which is correctly understood to be the "first month" as in v.1. The term "at eventide" refers to the twilight period immediately following sunset, i.e. "vespers." The Hebrew designates this by בין הערבים "between the settings (of the sun)," which is correctly rendered by πρὸς ἑσπέραν, a rendering already found in Exod 12:6, and comp 16:12 where the phrase is articulated by τό. The latter also occurs in Num at v.11 and 28:4,8; at v.5 Num omits the phrase. The Hebrew phrase occurs only in the Pentateuch, though at Exod 29:39,41 it becomes τὸ δειλινόν, and at 30:8, ὀψέ, and at Lev 23:5 it is uniquely rendered in Hebraic fashion by ἀνὰ μέσον τῶν ἑσπερινῶν.

Why Num should here change תעשו to the singular ποιήσεις is not immediately clear, but that it was intentional is obvious, since it is repeated at the end of the verse. In v.a the singular is only supported sparsely (by B M V ol f x z), most witnesses attesting to the plural, though the Byz text renders it by the third person plural under the influence of v.2. In v.b, however, the second person plural is a hex correction,[3] with Byz again reading a third person plural verb. The translator's point of view is simply that the celebration is incumbent on each individual Israelite. This becomes especially clear in vv.6—14, and more particularly in vv.10—14, which probably facilitated the use of the singular here.

The verb in v.a is modified as in v.2 by במועדו, which is here rendered by κατὰ καιρούς. Both in v.7 and v.13 where the same prepositional phrase recurs

---

3. The Others, presumably The Three, all read the plural ποιήσετε in v.b.

in MT, Num translates more literally by κατὰ (τὸν) καιρὸν αὐτοῦ. In the tradition, this reading also obtains in a popular A M text. In fact, the αυτου is read by the A F M V majority text, but is probably of hex origin. The plural noun used without a genitive pronoun occurs only for the first occasion, i.e. as a general rule, "according to appropriate, set times." When it recurs in vv.7 and 13, it becomes specific.[4]

The final clause orders the Israelite to celebrate it (ποιήσεις αὐτό) according to its rule (νόμον) and according to its constitution (σύγκρισιν). This is, at best, a free interpretation of MT which reads "according to all its statutes (חקתיו) and according to its judgments (משפטיו). In MT the reference is to all the rules and regulations concerning the keeping of the Paschal festival. The use of νόμον is sensible; it was used as a cover term throughout Lev for a set of cultic regulations, and this is its sense here as well. As such, it did not need to translate the כל modifying חקתיו, though hex has added παντα under the asterisk to correspond to it. The second noun, σύγκρισιν, is only used elsewhere in the OT in ch.29 (at vv.6,11,18,21,24,27,30,33 and 37). The term refers to the customary practice, the usual constitution (of the festival). Hex has rendered the כל of MT here as well by πασαν under the asterisk.

9:4 Num renders the Hebrew literally, i.e. ἐλάλησεν ... ποιῆσαι τὸ πάσχα. One might well render ἐλάλησεν by "told," thus "told the Israelites to observe (or carry out) the Paschal festival."

9:5 MT begins with ויעשו את הפסח "and they performed the Paschal feast," which is omitted by Num, and Hex has added και εποιησαν το πασχα under the asterisk at the beginning of the verse. MT then continues with בראשון "in the first," i.e. in the first month. Num has understood this quite differently, i.e. as "in the beginning" or "as at the beginning," with its ἐναρχομένου. The genitive participle is used here without an expressed subject. The subject is contextually to be understood as being the celebration of the Pascha. Theoretically, a genitive noun does occur, τοῦ μηνός, but this modifies ἡμέρα, and could not possibly be the subject; months do not begin on the fourteenth day! The genitive participle actually refers to the complementary infinitival structure ποιῆσαι τὸ πάσχα, and

---

4. Dorival states: "Sans doute les traductions ont-ils voulu áviter une expression usée pour mieux marquer la solemnité de l'ordre de notre verset."

what is meant is "(the celebration) beginning on the fourteenth day of the month."

This is followed in MT by the temporal expression: בֵּין הָעַרְבַּיִם, for which see comment at v.3. Num has also omitted this phrase, and hex has added ανα μεσον των εσπερινων under the asterisk to equal it; see the discussion at v.3. The locative structure which follows reads ἐν τῇ ἐρήμῳ Σινά. Most witnesses in the tradition follow Cod B in articulating the proper noun, but this would be uncharacteristic of Num;[5] comp v.1.

The verse concludes by saying that the Israelites were obedient in carrying out the Lord's orders: "καθά the Lord commanded Moses, so the Israelites did." MT reads ככל אשר, and hex has the more exact κατα παντα α.

9:6 MT begins with ויהי האנשים, but Num follows Sam's plural ויהיו with its καὶ παρεγένοντο.[6] The use of παραγίνομαι to render היה is unusual; in fact, according to HR, it occurs elsewhere in OT only at 1Reg 20:24. Num was probably trying to avoid using ἦσαν, since this is used to render היו in the relative clause which follows immediately, thus "there came some men who were ...." Contextually, that they came and spoke makes excellent sense; in fact, this is more appropriate than "they were ... and spoke." These men were unclean ἐπὶ ψυχῇ ἀνθρώπου, i.e. "through (contact with) a human corpse." For ψυχῇ in the sense of "corpse," see comment at 5:2. ἐπί is here used correctly with the dative in a causal sense, i.e. "because of a ψυχῇ ἀνθρώπου."[7]

Because of their cultic uncleanness they were unable to observe the Paschal festival on that day, "and so on that day they approached Moses and Aaron," literally "and they approached before Moses and Aaron." In accordance with normal Hebrew usage MT repeats לפני before Aaron as well as before Moses, and hex dutifully added εναντιον under the asterisk before Ἀαρών to reproduce the Hebrew word for word. Num had omitted it as unnecessary before a coordinate noun.

The phrase ביום ההוא occurs twice. The first time it is translated by ἐν τῇ ἡμέρᾳ ἐκείνῃ, but in the second for the sake of variety the equally valid ἐν ἐκείνῃ τῇ ἡμέρᾳ obtains. Hex, however, had to correct the word order, and placed

---

5. See THGN 103.
6. As do all the Tar as well as Kenn 1c,192*,158mg,233mg,242,390*,471mg,639*.
7. See LS sub ἐπί B.III.

ἐκείνῃ at the end to represent MT more precisely. "That day" refers to the fourteenth day of the month, the day on which the festival was to begin.

9:7 Num reproduces MT exactly by its "and those men said πρὸς αὐτόν"; though they had approached Moses and Aaron, it was only Moses to whom they presented their problem. Not unexpected is the majority change in the tradition of αὐτόν to αυτους; in fact, the B reading of αὐτόν is supported by only three other mss. That the singular is correct is clear from v.8 where only Moses replies.[8] A popular reading has the Classical second aorist inflection ειπον instead of εἶπαν, but Num always uses the Hellenistic form for this verb.

According to MT, what they asked Moses was: "Why should we be restrained so as not to present את קרבן יהוה at its set time in the midst of the Israelites?" Num does not ask why, but rather μὴ οὖν ὑστερήσωμεν προσενέγκαι the δῶρον of the Lord ...," which I would translate by "should we actually be delayed in presenting the Lord's sacrifice at its appropriate time in the midst of the Israelites?" This also calls into question the rationale for the restraint, or rather as Num has it, any delay. The choice of ὑστερήσωμεν demonstrates that the translator does not simply translate in word-for-word fashion, but does his work in the context of the entire section; in other words, he is aware of the Lord's answer, viz. a month's postponement of the feast; see vv.10—12.

In the tradition, the A F M majority text has introduced the infinitive προσενέγκαι with ωστε, but this is secondary.[9] Num only uses ὥστε three times to introduce an infinitive; cf comment at 7:1.

9:8 In MT Moses replies: "עמדו and אשמעה what Yahweh would command you." Num reproduces the imperative as στῆτε, but adds an adverbial αὐτοῦ, i.e. "stand here." The αὐτοῦ probably is added to show that the inquirers are to remain where they are, presumably at the door of the sanctuary. Hex has placed αὐτοῦ under the obelus, since MT does not have an adverb here.

The long form of the first person verb often expresses hortation, thus "let me hear." The translator, however, does not use the hortatory subjunctive, but simply a future indicative. Actually, the long form does not necessarily express hortation, and often cannot be distinguished from the simple future. In Num

---

8. See THGN 113.
9. See THGN 134.

Moses merely expresses intention: "but I will hear what the Lord will order concerning you." The prepositional phrase in MT is לכם, i.e. expressing the indirect object of יצוה, which Num renders by περὶ ὑμῶν "concerning you."

9:10 What the Lord says is a general injunction, i.e. "speak to the Israelites," not just "to you." This confirms the intuition that περὶ ὑμῶν correctly renders לכם in v.9. The repetition ἄνθρωπος ἄνθρωπος to mean "any person" simply reproduces MT's איש איש; it is a Hebraism.[10] For ἐπὶ ψυχῇ ἀνθρώπου, see comment at v.6. The Hebrew, however, has no equivalent here for ἀνθρώπου, and hex has placed it under the obelus. Its occurrence in Num is a case of harmonization with v.6.

The other possible reason for being unable to celebrate the Paschal festival at its set time is ἢ ἐν ὁδῷ μακρὰν ὑμῖν ἢ ἐν ταῖς γενεαῖς ὑμῶν "or on a way at a distance (i.e. on a distant journey), for you or among your generations." What is meant by this awkward syntax is that the ἄνθρωπος ἄνθρωπος might pertain "to you or your household." This is clearer in MT with its לכם או לדרתיכם. Why Num added ἐν before ταῖς γενεαῖς is not clear; at first blush it seems to coordinate with ἐν ὁδῷ, which would be senseless, though I suspect that it was influenced by ἐν ὁδῷ; i.e. the translator nodded at this juncture. The word μακράν is an adverbial, and in the tradition, the O+ text changed it to the adjectival μακρα, but the adverbial accusative must be original; comp v.13.[11]

The last clause is clearly the apodosis, as the future indicative ποιήσει demands. I would translate: "he must also observe the Pascha to the Lord." I doubt that this was intended by MT, where ועשה may well introduce a further condition, i.e. "and he (i.e. anyone) would keep the Paschal festival to the Lord." The text, however, could be interpreted as Num did.

9:11 The second Paschal celebration is to be delayed exactly one month, i.e. on the fourteenth day of the second month. The rendering of בין הערבים has been nominalized by articulation, thus as τὸ πρὸς ἑσπέραν, though at v.3 the structure appears without τό. In the tradition, the majority A F text has omitted the article under the influence of v.3, but this is secondary. For ἀζύμων and πικρίδων, see Note at Exod 12:8, where, however, the text reads ἄζυμα ἐπὶ πικρίδων.

---

10. See THGN 114.
11. See THGN 109.

9:12 For the first two clauses, see Notes at Exod 12:10. Unique for the book is the rendering of עד בקר by εἰς τὸ πρωί, since עד is usually rendered by ἕως; in fact, at Exod 12:10 the more literal ἕως πρωί is used. Actually, εἰς τὸ πρωί occurs only ten times in the entire Pentateuch (also four times in Exod 16, twice in Exod 34, Lev 7:15 22:30 and Dt 16:4); otherwise עד in the context of בקר is always rendered by ἕως.

The last clause refers to τὸν νόμον τοῦ πάσχα, a reference to Exod 12:43—49. MT has "all the law of the Pesach," and hex has prefixed παντα to the structure under the asterisk.

9:13 The protasis is syntactically a pendant nominative, since the subject "καὶ ἄνθρωπος ὃς ἂν καθαρὸς ᾖ ...." is restated as ἡ ψυχὴ ἐκείνη in the apodosis; thus "and as for the man who ..., that person shall be destroyed from his people." The pendant differs from MT only in lacking an article; MT has האיש. The conditions are three in number: καθαρὸς ᾖ "he is clean," and he is not ἐν ὁδῷ μακράν, for which see comment at v.10, but he delays celebrating the Paschal festival. In the tradition, the adverbial accusative μακράν becomes an adjectival μακρα in a B V O+ variant text, but this is a simplification of the text, and clearly secondary.[12] MT lacks an equivalent, and Num has harmonized with the μακράν of v.10. Hex has correctly placed the word under the obelus.[13]

MT introduces the apodosis with a conjunction, but Num does not. The n+ text has introduced a και, which could be, but is not necessarily, recensional. The apodotic καί appears with such frequency in the book that it is quite possible to understand the variant gloss as ex par in origin. The apodosis simply reads "that person shall be utterly destroyed from his people."

The reason for this being a capital offence is given in a ὅτι clause: "the sacrifice (τὸ δῶρον) to the Lord he did not bring at its set time." MT has קרבן יהוה, and an A F popular text, which could well be hex in origin, reads δωρον κυριου. The genitive reflects MT more exactly.

The final clause restates the apodosis in theological rather than in juridical terms: "that man shall bear his guilt." The word ἁμαρτίαν/חטא not only means "sin," but also the results of sin, i.e. the guilt associated with sin.

---

12. See THGN 109, as well as comment at v.10.
13. Tar^N also reads ובארח רחיקה with Num.

9:14 The most plausible understanding of the protasis in MT is that it covers two clauses: "and if a sojourner should sojourn with you and would celebrate the Pesach," but Num did not interpret it this way. Only the first clause contains a verb in the subjunctive; the second clause reads καὶ ποιήσει τὸ πασχα κυρίῳ. In other words, this is the apodosis. Any "resident alien who resides with you in your land must celebrate the Pascha festival to the Lord."[14] It should be noted that an F M V text with a great deal of support among scattered mss read ποιηση instead of ποιήσει. This would be closer to MT's intent as suggested above, but this is a coincidence. It is an itacistic spelling as the scattered nature of its support shows. Num has added ἐν τῇ γῇ ὑμῶν after προσήλυτος over against MT, and hex has placed the phrase under the obelus. The phrase may reflect Lev 19:33 where it appears in a similar context.[15]

For νόμον as rendering for חקת, see comment at v.3. The translation of כמשפטו by κατὰ τὴν σύνταξιν αὐτοῦ "according to its regulation" is used here for the first time, and recurs at 15:24. It is based on συντάσσω "to order, command," and is a possible understanding of משפט in the verse in the sense of that which has been ordered, thus "regulation, arrangement, ordinance." In accordance with the νόμον and the σύνταξιν of the festival, οὕτως ποιήσει αὐτό, but MT read כן יעשה, thus MT has no equivalent for the pronoun, which is an ad sensum gloss, and hex has placed it under the obelus. Incidentally, cod B along with some n x mss omitted οὕτως, but this cannot be taken seriously, since Num never fails to render כן.[16]

The verse concludes with the general statement: "one rule there shall be for you and the resident alien and the native born of the land."[17]

9:15 Vv.15—23 describe how the Lord led the people in the wilderness by means of the fiery cloud. V.15 recalls Exod 40:28—32, which conclude the Book. It

---

14. Field cites the text of Num for the first clause as supported by Aq; he quotes De Montfaucon as "sic unus codex." I have not found this codex, and I am sceptical about this as an Aq reading. That Aq who regularly uses either παροικέω or προσηλυτεύω to render גור should uniquely adopt προσέλθῃ here is out of character. I would have expected some cognate rendering such as προσηλυτεύσῃ προσήλυτος. Nor is πρὸς ὑμᾶς an expected rendering for אתכם.
15. Dorival suggests a possible harmonization with the Lev passage; this would be an interesting case, since harmonization in Num is usually internal to the book.
16. See THGN 131.
17. For a discussion of אזרח, here rendered by αὐτόχθονι, see Levine ad loc.

continues the narrative of Exod 40, by its opening καὶ τῇ ἡμέρᾳ ᾗ ἐστάθη ἡ σκηνή. In MT the verb is active: וביום הקים את המשכן "and on the day of setting up the tent," and Num correctly rendered this by a passive, a tradition continuing until the present.[18] On that occasion "the cloud covered the tent, the house of the testimony." The translator usually followed the pattern of his predecessor, Exod, in translating both משכן "tabernacle" and אהל (מועד) "tent" by the same word, σκηνή. But here MT reads את המשכן לאהל מועד, which created a difficulty. The translator solved the problem in ingenious fashion. Since the אהל מועד was the home of the עדות, i.e. τὰ μαρτύρια, especially The Ten Words which were housed in the ark within the אהל מועד, one might speak of the tent (tabernacle) as the home of the testimony. For this mistranslation one might consult the Notes at Exod 27:21 and 25:15.[19] For the Exod translator facing the same problem and his various solutions, see Notes at Exod 26:7—13 and 35:10; see also 40:17,26. In the tradition, the V Byz+ text introduced it by και, i.e. "tent and house of the testimony." This is obviously a mistaken interpretation.

In v.b the cloud over the tent at eventide was ὡς εἶδος πυρός until morning. The prepositional phrase בערב was translated by the idiomatic adverbial τὸ ἑσπέρας; comp בין הערבים and its rendering πρὸς ἑσπέραν; see discussion at v.3. The two can hardly be differentiated lexically; they mean "at eventide." The subject of ἦν must be ἡ νεφέλη;[20] apparently only in the daytime, i.e. when the sun shone, did the cloud look like a cloud. The divine presence, often revealed in fire, only appeared when the sun was no longer competing; it then had the appearance of fire, which continued ἕως πρωί.[21]

9:16 The imperfect ἐγίνετο is used intentionally to render יהיה. Since it narrates what was happening διὰ παντός, only the imperfect was fitting. The variant ἐγένετο of C′ x+ is clearly a copyist's mistake. This is then carried on into the explication: "The cloud ἐκάλυπτεν it (i.e. the tent) ἡμέρας, and the appearance of fire, τὴν νύκτα." The imperfect shows a process; it was covering. MT does not have an equivalent for ἡμέρας, and hex has therefore placed it under the obelus. The gloss is a correct interpretation; it contrasts with τὴν νύκτα. The two

---

18. Note the renderings of NRSV, NJPS and NIV which read "on the day the tabernacle was set up."
19. See also Tov 246.
20. Tar^J calls it ענן יקרא here as well as in v.16.
21. Tar^N describes the fire as אכלה אשא "(fire) eating fire," i.e. an inextinguishable fire.

timers are, however, in different cases. The genitive is used to denote the period of time within which something happens, thus the cloud covered the tent within the time of daylight. τὴν νύκτα is accusative, and more specifically indicates how long something lasted; the appearance of fire is stretched out during the time of darkness.

9:17 The initial ולפי "and according to," i.e. "as," is correctly rendered temporally by καὶ ἡνίκα "and whenever." The פי is bound to העלת, a Ni bound infinitive, which is then translated by (ἡνίκα) ἀνέβη. In the Pentateuch, this verb translates the Ni of עלה only with reference to the cloud (also at v.21 10:11 Exod 40:30,31). In fact, ἀναβαίνω translates the Ni of עלה elsewhere in OT only at 2Reg 2:27 for נעלה העם as ἀνέβη ὁ λαός, and at Ezek 36:3 where תעלו is vocalized as Ni by the Masoretes, but is interpreted as a Qal in LXX. Throughout the accounts of the cloud "being lifted up" from over the tent, LXX consistently uses ἀνέβη. In the tradition, the Byz+ text uses the imperfect ανεβαινεν, which must be secondary.

The ἡνίκα clause has its counterpart introduced by (καὶ) μετὰ ταῦτα, which simply imitates MT's ואחרי כן; the sense is that immediately after the cloud lifted up, "the Israelites broke camp (ἀπῆραν)." In MT, the prefix stem inflection is used, i.e. "the Israelites would be breaking camp (יסעו). This continues in v.b; "and in the place where the cloud ישכן, there the Israelites יחנו." Thus where the cloud would settle down, there ... they would encamp. Num, however, makes the verbs aorist, ἔστη "stood" and παρενέβαλον "encamped." So Num describes this as narrative action which took place, while MT stresses this as general practice. The majority A F M V text read the Classical second aorist απηρον, but Num uses only the Hellenistic form. Though this is its first occurrence, it reappears a further 44 times in the book, and always as ἀπῆραν.

9:18 The first two clauses reverse those of MT. MT reads: "according to Yahweh's command (פי), the Israelites would break camp (יסעו), and according to Yahweh's command, they would emcamp (יחנו)." It is to be noted that the hex text did not transpose the two verbs; after all, the slots were filled, and that was what interested Origen. Num translates על פי by διὰ προστάγματος "by the order of," and also renders the verbs by future verbs. These futures are omnitemporal in character, i.e. describe customary verbal action.²²

V.b begins with an accusative of duration of time, thus πάσας τὰς ἡμέρας ἐν αἷς "all the days in which" means "as long as." In MT the relative clause reads "which ישכן the cloud over the משכן." In v.17 ישכן was translated by ἔστη "remained," but here Num uses the present tense verb σκιάζει "overshadow," which is more picturesque than MT. The reason for this choice may be an interpretative impulse to stress the protective nature of the divine presence. This is reflected in the cherubim "spreading their wings upwards συσκιάζοντες with their wings over the propitiatory (Exod 25:19)," and the Lord promised two verses later in v.21: γνωσθήσομαί σοι ἐκεῖθεν. Furthermore, according to Lev 16:2 he says ἐν γὰρ νεφέλῃ ὀφθήσομαι ἐπὶ τοῦ ἱλαστηρίου. And in v.13 "the ἀτμίς of the incense must cover the propitiatory." The cloud denotes the presence of deity, a deity who reveals himself.²³ The use of the present tense is also intentional, since it is durative. I would render: "as long as the cloud is overshadowing the tent." The apodosis is then in the future: "the Israelites would be encamping." MT does not identify the subject, and hex has placed οἱ υἱοὶ Ἰσραήλ under the obelus.

9:19 Num translates האריך ... ימים "lengthen days" in clever fashion by ἐφέλκεται ... ἡμέρας (πλείους) "drag out many days," i.e. delay for many days. What is meant is "when the cloud stayed over the tent many days."²⁴

The apodosis simply states that the Israelites were obedient. The cognate structure φυλάξονται τὴν φυλακὴν (τοῦ θεοῦ) "they would be guarding God's watch," i.e. obeying God's orders (and not break camp)." The divine φυλακή is defined as "not breaking camp." Num defines the φυλακή as being τοῦ θεοῦ, whereas MT reads משמרת יהוה. Since the section as a whole only uses יהוה to designate Israel's deity, a unique האלהים would certainly be secondary. But it is difficult to understand why the translator substituted τοῦ θεοῦ for יהוה here. This is especially incomprehensible when in v.23 τὴν φυλακὴν κυρίου obtains. Here it

---

22. See Porter 423—424.
23. Dorival 60, 147—148 also suggests a kind of word play, since משכן is rendered by σκηνή, whereas the cloud σκιάζει, thus the assonance of /ski-/ also propelling the choice of this verb. Dorival, however, also feels that the protective aspect of "overshadowing" was the major factor in the choice of this verb.
24. Sym translates ובהאריך by καὶ ὅποτε ἐχρόνιζεν.

seems to contrast with v.20, where the impetus for making camp was διὰ φωνῆς κυρίου, and for breaking camp, διὰ προστάγματος κυρίου.

9:20 MT begins with ויש אשר יהיה "and it happened that (the cloud) would be (over the tent)." Num renders this freely by "and it would be (ἔσται) whenever the cloud would cover (σκεπάσῃ)." For Num the position of the cloud over the tent constituted a protection; see comment at v.18 on σκιάζει. The structure ימים מספר is difficult, and is usually interpreted as "days (governed by) number," thus a specific number of days, rather than an unspecified ימים רבים, possibly then "a few days."[25] The translator rendered this by placing "number" in the dative case, ἡμέρας ἀριθμῷ "days in number," so probably "a number of days" is intended.

V.b repeats על פי יהוה as in v.18 where it was translated by διὰ προστάγματος κυρίου, but here the translator varied the translations, i.e. the first instance as διὰ φωνῆς κυρίου and the second one as at v.18; see comment ad loc. No lexical difference was intended; the change simply avoided the monotony of constant repetition. In both cases future tenses were used, correctly rendering MT's יחנו and יסעו resp. The latter was rendered by its popular counterpart, ἀπαροῦσιν. ἀπαίρω occurs 81 times as rendering for the Qal of נסע. A popular A M text reads εξαρουσιν. The two compounds are synonyms, but ἐξαίρω is used only 37 times for נסע in LXX.[26]

9:21 Vv.21—22 give rather confused statements as to what happened. In general terms, it is clear that the lifting of the cloud signalled breaking camp, whereas the cloud staying in position signalled remaining encamped.

For v.21 MT is somewhat clearer than Num. The punctuation in Num is somewhat misleading. I would suggest placing a colon after both cases of ἀπαροῦσιν. This breaks the verse into two parts. a) "when the cloud would continue (γένηται) from eventide until morning, and the cloud would rise in the morning (τὸ πρωί), then (καί) they would break camp." Thus during the night the cloud would naturally stay in position. An M b n s^mg text added a clarifying εαν before ἀναβῇ 1°, thereby ensuring that the clause would be understood as part of the protasis. The apodosis, ἀπαροῦσιν 1°, is introduced by καί. As usual the apodosis is signalled by the use of the future tense.

---

25. Tar^J interprets by adding הינון שבעתי יומי שבעתא "i.e. seven days of the week."
26. According to Dos Santos.

V.b presents another possibility: "ἡμέρας ἢ νυκτός and the cloud would rise, they would break camp." The genitive nouns indicate the time during which something takes place. The majority F V text also added an εαν before the ἀναβῇ of v.b to clarify its conditional status, though the contrast of ἀναβῇ as a subjunctive and ἀπαροῦσιν as a future should have been sufficient. Num does not use an apodotic καί here, though MT does read ונסעו. MT begins with the correlative conjunction, and hex has added η before ἡμέρας under the asterisk. In the tradition, the B x+ text has omitted καὶ ἀνέβη ἡ νεφέλη ἀπαροῦσιν (22) ἡμέρας ἤ. This would continue "day or night" with μηνός, which would make for awkward Greek. The original scribe's eye skipped from νυκτός to μηνός;[27] it was a simple scribal mistake.[28]

9:22 V.22 is a further explication of how the Israelites were dependent on the movement of the cloud. MT begins with או ימים או חדש או ימים. The Masoretes have vocalized the first ימים as a dual, and the second one as a plural, thus "Either two days or a month or days (i.e. an indefinite number of days).[29] Num has ἡμέρας ἢ μηνὸς ἡμέρας, which in my opinion is senseless. Hex has added η at the beginning under the asterisk to represent או 1°. I would suggest that an η, which is witnessed by three mss, V 58-72, has also fallen out before the second ἡμέρας by haplography, and that it should be added in the critical text. Admittedly, this still lacks full lucidity, and I would take the genitive structure that follows as describing the second ἡμέρας, i.e. "a day when the cloud overshadowing it abounds." What is meant by "abounds" is that a day multiplies, becomes abundant, and probably a year is intended by it. For such times, regardless of how long the period might be, "the Israelites would encamp and not break camp."

Num has omitted the prepositional phrase על המשכן which follows הענן. This phrase is, however, useful, since it names an antecedent for עליו, which the Greek's ἐπ' αὐτῆς must find in the context; it is of course "the tent." Hex has added επι της σκηνης under the asterisk after νεφέλης to equal MT. Num has also overlooked ובהעלתו יסעו due to the יסעו which precedes it, i.e. because of

---

27. See THGN 131.
28. Sym translates v.21 according to Syh by wʾyt ʾmty dhwyʾ hwt ʿnnʾ mn rmšʾ ʿdmʾ lṣprʾ mtʿlyʾ hwt. dyn mnnʾ ʿṣprʾ mšqlyn hww. ʾw ʾymmʾ wllyʾ kd mtʿlyʾ hwt ʿnnʾ mšqlyn hww.
29. Tar^J interprets the second ימים as שתא שלמתא "a complete year."

homoioteleuton. Hex has added εν τω αναχθηναι αυτην εξηραν under the asterisk to make up for the omission.³⁰

9:23 MT makes a full statement of Israel's conduct in v.a: "At the command of Yahweh they would encamp, and at the command of Yahweh they would break camp." Num has only the second statement, having omitted the first because of homoioteleuton, i.e. the repetition of על פי. The omitted clause has been added under the asterisk by hex as οτι δια προσταγματος κυριου παρεμβαλουσιν και. For διὰ προστάγματος as rendering for על פי, see comment at v.18.

V.b concludes the section by stating that the Israelites did as demanded through Moses. For the interpretation of the cognate φυλακήν ... ἐφυλάξαντο, see comment at v.19. The verb is quite properly an aorist inflection; the Israelites obeyed the Lord's orders διὰ προστάγματος κυρίου ἐν χειρὶ Μωυσῆ, i.e. "by order of the Lord by means of Moses." What is meant is "on account of the Lord's order communicated by (ἐν χειρί) Moses."

---

30. Syh has again recorded the text of Sym: 'w ywmt'. 'w 'wyrḥ'. 'w zbn'. kd mštwḥr' hwt 'nn' 'l mškn' lmqwyw lh. šryn hww bny' dysr'yl. wl' mšqlyn hww.

Chapter 10

10:2 Vv.1—10 describe the trumpets and their use. Moses is ordered to make two silver trumpets σεαυτῷ; there is no particular significance in the reflexive dative pronoun after an imperative. It certainly does not mean "make for your personal use," but as in the case of לך, it fills out a singular imperative; there is little if any distinction between עשה and עשה לך. The two silver trumpets are to be made ἐλατάς, i.e. of hammered (silver).

V.b describes their use: they serve you for calling the assembly and for breaking up the camps. In MT "calling" and "breaking up" are abstract nouns. The translator has changed these into complementary infinitives complementing ἔσονται. The syntactical structures are quite different, but the renderings are fully adequate. How these are to be done is then described in vv.3—8. For the παρεμβολάς, see ch.2.

10:3 The verb σαλπίζω is used ten times throughout this section. Here it occurs in the future as σαλπιεῖς. The translator uses only the Attic future (nine times), and never the Hellenistic inflection. Here cod B z+ read σαλπισεις, but this must be secondary.[1] The translator does use σαλπίσωσιν in v.4, but that is an aorist subjunctive form.[2] MT has the verb in third person plural, ותקעו, but Num continues with the second person singular of v.2. Obviously, the Greek does not mean that Moses is personally to sound the trumpets, since v.8 assigns this task to the Aaronids. The second singular has the same intent as ποίησον and ποιήσεις in v.1, where the orders to Moses really mean "see to it that the trumpets are made." This is fully clear from the plural αὐταῖς; no one could possibly understand this to mean that Moses was required personally to blow on two trumpets! The verb σαλπιεῖς is modified by an instrumental ἐν, thus "you must sound with them," i.e. blow the trumpets.[3]

At the blowing of the trumpets, "then (καί) all the assembly will be brought together." The verb is singular in grammatical agreement with the subject

---
1. See THGN 124.
2. For the Attic future of —ιζω verbs, see Schwyzer I 785, and for Hellenistic forms, see Mayser I 2,128.
3. See SS 119,121.

συναγωγή, but MT views the עדה as a collective, and uses the plural verb נועדו. MT also adds אליך after the verb over against Num, and hex has added πρὸς σε under the asterisk to represent it.

10:4 The protasis contrasts with v.3's καὶ σαλπιεῖς ἐν αὐταῖς in that ἐν μιᾷ σαλπίσωσιν. The subject of the verb is the indefinite "they," thus "but (note the contrastive δέ) if they blow on one," i.e. sound one trumpet. As in the case of the second singular verb in v.3, so the third plural verb must not be taken literally; naturally only one individual could blow ἐν μιᾷ. The apodosis is indicated by the change to the future tense; it is asyndetic over against MT's ונועדו אליך, exactly as in v.3. Num, however, employs a different verb, προσελεύσονται, and also translates the prepositional phrase by πρὸς σέ. In MT the subject is given as הנשיאים, rendered in Num by πάντες οἱ ἄρχοντες, thus "all the chieftains will come to you." Since MT has no correspondent to πάντες, hex placed it under the obelus. These "chieftains" are then further defined in MT by ראשי אלפי ישראל, a structure which also occurs at 1:16; see comments ad loc. There Num translates ראשי אלפי by χιλίαρχοι, but here Num appears to have overlooked אלפי, since it renders by the simplex ἀρχηγοί.[4] Hex has added χιλιάδων under the asterisk to represent the absent אלפי. In the tradition, a V *ol* C⁽ⁿ⁾ s+ text substituted χιλιαρχοι for ἀρχηγοί.

10:5 Vv.5—6 speak of sounding a σημασίαν.[5] Just what sounding a "signal" means is uncertain, but it translates תרועה, which is usually understood either as a (loud) alarm or a shout of joy. Here it must be some kind of alarm sounded on the trumpet, but what kind is not known.[6] Num translates by σημασίαν, but how this contrasts with the absolute use of σαλπίζω I do not know. The difference was obvious to the Israelites, since they responded in a different way to the two.

V.5 refers to the first sounding of a signal. The response to this signal called on "the camps who were encamped towards the east" to break camp. "Towards the east" at 2:3 was a prepositional phrase, κατ' ἀνατολάς, which is the more usual expression in Greek. But here the accusative is used by itself, as is

---
4. Theod and Sym also read χιλίαρχοι here, whereas Aq has ἄρχηγοι χιλιάδων.
5. Aq translated תרועה by ἀλαλαγμόν "a shouting."
6. Thus NJPS renders the word by "short blasts," whereas Levine translates by "long blasts!" On the other hand, NRSV translates by "alarm," and NIV, by "(trumpet) blast."

λίβα in v.6. In both cases the Hebrew has nouns with the directional *he* at the end, i.e. "towards the east ... south." For these camps, see 2:3—9.

10:6 Both MT and Num continue after v.5 with the order "and you shall sound a second signal (for תרועה), and the camps which are encamped to the south must break camp."[7] Num then proceeds in the same fashion with a third signal for those παρὰ θάλασσαν, and for a fourth signal for those πρὸς βορρᾶν. MT has only the second signal ordered. Hex has taken note of this, and placed και 3°— βορρᾶν all under the obelus to show that it had no basis in MT.

Num follows the same order as that of ch.2, where the encampments on the east side are followed successively by those on the south side (vv.10—16), the west side (vv.18—24), and the north side (vv.25—31). In ch.2 they are also described as πρῶτοι ἐξαροῦσιν, then δεύτεροι ..., then τρίτοι ..., and for the north side ἔσχατοι ἐξαροῦσιν. The close relation of our section with ch.2 is clear. Num has "completed" the cycle to include all four parts of the encampment on the basis of ch.2. The translator must have felt that the breaking up of the camp could hardly be limited to half the camp, i.e. to the two camps given in MT. Undoubtedly the amplification by Num is not incorrect—it just does not obtain in MT; it is the creation of Num.

The final clause reads "with a signal they must sound ἐν τῇ ἐξάρσει αὐτῶν." The noun occurs only twice in LXX (also in Jer 12:17), but only here for מסעי(הם). It is an abstract noun based on ἐξαίρω, thus "removal." What is meant is "when they are to break camp."

10:7 At v.3 the cognate structure נועדו העדה was translated by a cognate structure as well: συναχθήσεται ἡ συναγωγή. Here another cognate structure obtains in Num, συναγάγητε τὴν συναγωγήν, but it represents a different cognate collocation of MT: הקהיל את הקהל. It is odd that the translator should have used exactly the same cognates in both places. By doing so, he calls attention to the fact that it is exactly the same group and action in both places. What is new is calling attention to the difference in the trumpet call; for assembling the assembly (or in MT to convoke the convocation), σαλπιεῖτε "you must sound (the trumpet)," but not σημασίᾳ "with a signal." In MT both parts are verbal, i.e.

---

7. Instead of λίβα The Others read νότον.

תתקעו, but לא תריעו. One might render this by "you must sound (the trumpet), but may not signal."

10:8 It is now made clear who were to perform on the trumpets; not Moses (see v.3), but the Aaronid priests, must sound the trumpets. The dative ταῖς σάλπιγξιν is instrumental.[8] It might be noted that a popular V Byz text has added εν before the dative nominal; since this represents the MT ב phrase, this may well be recensional in origin. MT then states והיו לכם לחקת עולם. What is not clear is what היו refers to; the only plural referents are החצרת and "the Aaronid priests," and neither is overly appropriate. Moderns tend to follow Num which changed to the singular: "ἔσται ὑμῖν νόμιμον αἰώνιον for your generations," thus "it will be for you a lasting prescription for your descendants." What is probably meant by the singular verb is that the sounding of the trumpets "shall be." The plural of MT may be defended as referring to "these matters," i.e. the rules about the trumpets and their blasts. The term νόμιμον is a stipulation, a prescription, rather than a νόμος which often occurs in legal matters as "a set of regulations"; note the common οὗτος ὁ νόμος concerning ...."[9]

10:9 The unique תבאו מלחמה is normalized by Num as ἐξέλθητε εἰς πόλεμον. This does not mean that the parent text read למלחמה; omitting the preposition would be impossible Greek.[10] MT then uses a cognate expression in the singular: הצר הצרר (על). Num not only changes to the plural, understanding the Hebrew rightly as a collective, but also fails to translate by a cognate expression. The translation reads (πρὸς) τοὺς ὑπεναντίους τοὺς ἀνθεστηκότας "the enemies who have opposed (i.e. stood against)," a fully adequate rendering.[11]

The apodosis consists of three clauses, and in imitation of MT is introduced by an apodotic καί. The first clause states καὶ σημανεῖτε ταῖς σάλπιγξιν "then you shall signal with trumpets (i.e. with trumpet blasts)." The verb translating הרעתם is consistent with the rendering σημασίαν for תרועה in vv.5 and 6; see comment ad loc. Since MT has בחצצרות, the prefixing of εν before ταῖς in the Byz text may well be recensional; see comment at v.8.

---

8. See SS 121.
9. Dorival 171 makes the interesting distinction: "il semble en effet que le *nómimon* un point particulier du *nómos* divin."
10. Theod and Sym retain the ἐξέλθητε of Num, but Aq has the more literal εἰσέλθητε.
11. Tar[N] has a doublet rendering: על סנאה דעמיק לכון and על בעלי דבביכון.

The second clause reads "καὶ ἀναμνησθήσεσθε before the Lord." The passive verb correctly reflects the Ni verb נזכרתם, "and you shall be brought to remembrance before the Lord." MT, however, has "before Yahweh your God," and hex has added θεοῦ ὑμῶν under the asterisk after κυρίου. The last clause constitutes the divine promise "and you shall be saved from your enemies." It might be observed that here MT also uses the plural word for "enemies," i.e. abandons the collective used in the protasis. The second and third clauses actually depend on the execution of the first one.

10:10 Num interprets וביום not incorrectly by a plural ἐν ταῖς ἡμέραις, since coordinate with "time of your rejoicing" are both "and in your feasts and in your new moons." Furthermore, "your rejoicing" certainly is spread over more than one day. The ἑορταῖς renders (מועדי(כם "your fixed feasts," i.e. the annual festivals, which contrast with the monthly ראשי חדשיכם. The Hebrew uses a bound phrase to represent new moons: "the beginnings of your months," which Num simplifies by νουμηνίαις. In the tradition, the V O b n+ text has the late uncontracted spelling νεομηνιαις, but the Attic form is original.[12] For such occasions, on which both burnt offerings and sacrifices for deliverance are offered, you must sound trumpets over them. Fortunately, Num disregards the conjunction of ותקעתם, which apparently Num found as disturbing as I did. No attempt was made by hex to represent it either. I would translate the conjunction as meaning "also."

Their purpose is to serve as "a reminder before your God." MT is slightly different, reading והיו לכם לזכרון "so that they will be for you a reminder"; היה plus ל often means "to become," but Num simply has ἔσται ἀνάμνησις. The subject of ἔσται is not stated, and must be an indefinite "it." MT is much clearer with its plural היו, which refers to the trumpet (blasts). The verse and the section end with the self-identification formula "I am the Lord your God."[13]

10:11 Vv.11—28 describe the ordered departure of the Israelites from Mt. Sinai, and reflect in this departure the encampment regiments of the tribes around the tabernacle in ch.2, as well as the duties of the Levites in ch.4. The date is given

---

12. See Walters 113—114.
13 . I am puzzled by the rendering of NJPS which disregards the conjunctive accent on יהוה, and translates "I, the LORD, am your God."

as the second year (of the Exodus), the second month, on the twentieth day of the month; the signal for the departure is divinely given: ἀνέβη ἡ νεφέλη from the tent of testimony; cf comments at 9:17.

10:12 MT begins with a cognate structure ויסעו למסעיהם "And they set out on their marches," but Num found this difficult, and probably under the influence of σὺν τῇ ἀπαρτίᾳ αὐτῶν at Exod 40:30, changed it to σὺν ἀπαρτίαις αὐτῶν "with their household goods." See Note at Exod 40:30—31. Num simply made good sense. Since as usual he used ἐξῆραν for יסעו, a literal rendering of למסעיהם would have been senseless.[14] The phrase "ἐν τῇ ἐρήμῳ of Sina" is odd, since what is spoken of is a departure; this is clear from MT which has ממדבר "from the desert," and the ἐν phrase must then mean that ἐξῆραν with ἐν signifies "they set out in (the desert)," and eventually arrived in another one; the Byz text which reads εκ της ερημου has "corrected" the text to equal MT more precisely.

It should be noted that the proper nouns modifying ἐρήμῳ 1° and 2° are both articulated, though a B V O d x text did omit the article before Σινά. A few d mss also omit the other article, but the articles must be original for both.[15] For Φαράν and its location, see Bible Dictionaries. The verse states that the desert journey started at Sina, and ended ("the cloud stood") in the desert of Pharan.

10:13—14 MT begins with "and they moved בראשנה ('at first') through the voice (i.e. at the command) of the Lord by the hand of Moses." Num was bothered by the prepositional phrase; just what could "at the first" mean? In v.14 it also occurs and must refer to those who moved first, i.e. began the march, and so Num simply used πρῶτοι in both places. Here, however, it could even be understood nominally, i.e. as "the first ones" moved, though I would prefer to understand the word adverbially.

V.14 identifies the first division to break camp. For τάγμα as "regiment" or "division," see comments at 2:2 and 1:45—46. For σὺν δυνάμει αὐτῶν as a recurring pattern for לצבאתם, recurring in vv.18,22 and 25, see comment at 2:3. For the one "over the army," Ναασσὼν υἱὸς Ἀμιναδάβ, see comments at 1:7.

---

14. The Three did use a plural cognate noun, ἐν ταῖς ἐξάρσεσι αὐτῶν (retroverted from Syh). Presumably, it meant במסעיהם, nothing more nor less.
15. See THGN 103.

V.14 begins in MT with ויסע דגל, but Num continues with the plural verb, reading καὶ ἐξῆραν τάγμα, presumably understanding τάγμα as an accusative; see also vv.18,22,25. In all cases, the sense demands a plural understanding, whether aorist or future. The text of Num correctly understood what MT must have intended.

10:15 For the one over the army of the tribe of the Issacharites, Ναθαναὴλ υἱὸς Σωγάρ, see comments at 1:8.

10:16 And for the one over the army of the tribe of the Zaboulonites, Ἐλιὰβ υἱὸς Χαιλών, see comments at 1:9.

10:17 In MT the first clause has a Ho verb הורד with המשכן as subject, i.e. "And the tabernacle was brought down." This was changed by Num into an active construction, with οἱ υἱοὶ Γεδσὼν καὶ οἱ υἱοὶ Μεραρί of the second clause serving as subject, thus "And the Gedsonites and the Merarites took down the tent, and carrying the tent, moved on." For a detailed statement on the role of the Gedsonites and the Merarites, see 4:21—33. As elsewhere, Γεδσών occurs for גרשון.[16]

10:18 Vv.18—21 detail the position of the next regiment, that of the camp of Rouben; see 2:10—16. The pattern of v.18 is similar to that of the first regiment at v.14; see comments at vv.13—14. For the one over their army, Ἐλισοὺρ υἱὸς Σεδιούρ, see comments at 1:5.

10:19 For the one "over the army of the tribe of the Simeonites, Σαλαμιὴλ υἱὸς Σουρισαδαί, see comments at 1:6.

10:20 For the army chieftain of the Gadites, Ἐλισὰφ ὁ τοῦ Ῥαγουὴλ, see comments at 1:14.

10:21 V.a is straightforward: "The Kaathites carrying the sacred objects (i.e. the furniture of the tent) would move on,"[17] but with v.b common sense dictates that

---

16. The Others all read Γηρσών.
17. Instead of τὰ ἅγια The Others have τὸ ἁγιαστήριον (retroverted from Syh).

the subject must change; it must be the other Levites, the Gedsonites and the Merarites, who, according to v.17, had gone on ahead carrying the tent. They must be the ones who would be erecting (στήσουσιν) it *before* (ἕως ἄν) they (i.e. the Kaathites) arrived. This all makes sense; the two clans carrying the tent had followed the first regiment, and were thus able to have the tent set up before the Kaathites who followed the second regiment, that of Rouben, carrying the furnishings of the tent, arrived.[18]

10:22 The third regiment is that of Ephraim; see 2:18—24. MT has בני אפרים, and hex has added υιων before 'Εφράιμ to equal the Hebrew. The verb has also changed to the third person plural future, ἐξαροῦσιν, though MT maintains the singular, both here and at v.25. Num has changed from the grammatical singular of its parallel vv.14 and 18, to the collective notion; see also v.25.

For the leader of the army, Ἐλισαμὰ υἱὸς Ἐμιούδ, see comments at 1:9b.

10:23 For the chieftain of the army of the tribe of the Manassites, Γαμαλιὴλ ὁ τοῦ Φαδασούρ, see comments at 1:10.[19]

10:24 For the leader of the army of the tribe of the Beniaminites, Ἀβιδὰν ὁ τοῦ Γαδεωνί, see comments at 1:11.

10:25 For ἐξαροῦσιν, see comment at v.22. Last of all the camps (ἔσχατοι), the regiment of the camp of the Danites moved; see 2:25—31. The word ἔσχατοι is taken from 2:31 where it renders לאחרנה. Here MT has מאסף plus ל, thus "gathering up for (all the camps)," i.e. serving as rear-guard. Num does not translate MT, but interprets it in accordance with the ch.2 account. Of course, the rear-guard is at the tail-end of those on the march. For the leader of their army, Ἀχιέζερ ὁ τοῦ Ἀμισαδαί, see comments at 1:12.

10:26 For the one "over the army of the tribe of Aser," Φαγαιὴλ υἱὸς Ἐχράν, see comments at 1:13.

---

18. The Tar were aware of the problem too, and tried to solve it by changing הקימו to the participle מקימין.
19. See THGN 120 for a defence of the spelling Φαδασούρ.

10:27 And for the chief of the army of the Naphthalites, Ἀχιρὲ υἱὸς Αἰνάν, see comments at 1:15.

10:28 Num concludes with "These are the hosts of the Israelites, and they moved with their army." MT identifies them as the מסעי of the Israelites. The rendering by στρατιαί is unique in OT; it was probably used by Num to describe the armies in the field, the hosts of Israel on the move, and the translator tried to reproduce what was intended. At v.12 Num had rendered the word by ἀπαρτίαις, and in ch.33, three times by σταθμός. Obviously, the Hebrew word gave trouble to this translator, as it did to others.

MT has divided the verse differently: לצבאתם ויסעו. What MT says is "These were the troop movements according to their hosts, and they set out." Num has reinterpreted this essentially by transposing the two words, i.e. v.b reads "and they set out with their army," and hex has transferred καὶ ἐξῆραν to the end, thereby equalling MT.

10:29 The name Ὠβάβ occurs only three times in OT (also in Jdg 1:16 4:11) as γαμβρός of Moses. Like MT's חתן, the exact relation intended by such a designation is not fully certain; it means a relative by marriage on the wife's side, either as father-in-law or as brother-in-law. It is also problematic, since the father-in-law of Moses is elsewhere given another name. At Exod 2:18 the father of Moses' future wife is called Ῥαγουήλ; comp v.21 and ch.18. But at Exod 3:1 the father-in-law is called Ἰοθόρ the priest of Madian. It is, however, uncertain that father-in-law was meant. Since here Hobab is called the son of Ragouel, it is probable that Hobab is a brother-in-law of Moses. For the name Ῥαγουήλ, see Note at Exod 2:18. Furthermore, "son of Ragouel" is followed by τῷ Μαδιανίτῃ τῷ γαμβρῷ Μωυσῆ. Probably "the Madianite" refers to Ragouel, but does τῷ γαμβρῷ Μωυσῆ refer to Hobab or to Ragouel? This is also uncertain. To make matters even more confusing, the name Ῥαγουήλ also occurs for a Gadite at v.20; see also 1:14 2:14 7:42,47, but this Ragouel is not to be confused with Moses' relative by marriage here and at Exod 2:18. The relationship would be clarified, if instead of γαμβρῷ, πενθερω would obtain,[20] but only in the A tradition at Jdg 1:16 does πενθεροῦ obtain, whereas the B tradition reads γαμβροῦ; I

---

20. As it does in two mss.

am not clear which of the two is original LXX. Nonetheless, if I were forced to translate, I would choose: "to Hobab, son of Ragouel the Madianite, the brother-in-law of Moses." This seems to agree with Exod 2:18, and it creates less confusion than "father-in-law."[21] In the tradition, the article before γαμβρῷ is omitted by the majority A F M text; the article is retained in Num, chiefly due to the support of the oldest witness, cod B. Its originality is, however, quite uncertain.

The name Ὠβάβ has been severely dealt with in the tradition, with the popular F M V tradition adding an *iota* at the beginning. The transcription ιωβαβ originated in an uncial parent text in which the dative article was written out as ΤΩΙ. The *iota* of ιωβαβ is thus the result of dittography in an uncial script.[22]

What Moses said to his brother-in-law is "ἐξαίρομεν ἡμεῖς to the place ...." The inclusion of the pronoun is otiose in Num, but in MT a pronoun is necessary. It reads נסעים אנחנו, a nominal construction in which the pronoun is the subject, and the participle is the predicate, a pattern commonly rendered in the Pentateuch by pronoun plus a present tense inflection.

The bait which Moses holds out to Hobab is "εὖ σε ποιήσομεν because the Lord spoke καλά concerning Israel." MT has הטבנו לך "we will do you well." Hex has transposed σε ποιήσομεν to equal the order of MT.

In the concluding ὅτι clause, καλά, as an accusative modifier of ἐλάλησεν, is the neuter plural of καλός, and renders טוב, which is more commonly translated by the adjective ἀγαθός (367 times vs 103 times as καλός).[23] But καλά "fine things" is also adequate.

10:30 The subject of εἶπεν is Hobab, and the reference in αὐτόν is Moses. In MT the reply is in two clauses: "I will not go," and "but to my country and to my birthplace I will go." Num does not repeat the verb πορεύσομαι for the second phrase, reading "but to my land and to τὴν γενεάν μου, i.e. "to my generation," which is a possible interpretation.[24] Hex has added πορευσομαι under the asterisk to represent the untranslated אלך of MT.

---

21. See also the discussion in Dorival 101–102.
22. See THGN 120.
23. According to the count of Dos Santos.
24. Rashi makes the interesting comment: משפחתי בשביל אם נכסי בשביל אם "whether it be on account of my property (or) it be on account of my kindred."

10:31 As usual, Num disregarded the particle of entreaty נא, saying "Do not leave us." Ms 426, a hex ms, has added δη after μή, which represents the נא. The reason for Moses' plea is given as οὗ εἵνεκεν ἦσθα μεθ' ἡμῶν ἐν τῇ ἐρήμῳ, "because of the fact that you were with us in the desert." What is meant is that Hobab was a native of the desert. MT is much clearer with its כי על כן ידעת חנתנו instead of ἦσθα, i.e. "because of the fact that you know our encampment." What this means is that Hobab understands where one might conveniently camp in the desert. The Greek offhand seems to be quite inadequate as a rendering of MT. Both ידעת and חנתנו are common words, but the translator paraphrases; that Hobab is fully acquainted with the desert, and knows how to survive in it is more to the point as a reason for asking him to stay than that "he knows our encampment."[25] Hex has tried to fix up the text by adding εν τη παρεμβολη under the asterisk after ἦσθα, and placing μεθ' ἡμῶν under the obelus; what hex presupposes is that MT had μεθ' ἡμῶν instead of חנתנו, but this is inadequate. ἦσθα does not equal ידעת, and חנתנו has a first plural suffix. It would have been more accurate to have placed only μεθ' under the obelus.

MT ends with the clause והיית לנו לעינים "and you would be for us eyes (i.e. a guide)." Num interprets this by καὶ ἔσῃ ἐν ἡμῖν πρεσβύτης "and you would be an elder among us." Presumably an elder is someone who has insight (i.e. can serve as eyes, for seeing); in other words, Hobab's rank would be that of an elder, and he would serve as an adviser.[26] On the other hand, what MT says may well have influenced the rendering of the preceding clause, whereas following this with an offer of eldership as a rank of honor is probably intended to serve as an enticement to Hobab to stay.[27]

10:32 Moses promises Hobab a share in the good fortunes which the Lord would bestow on Israel. The plural τὰ ἀγαθὰ ἐκεῖνα correctly interprets MT's singular הטוב ההוא as a collective. טוב is here rendered by ἀγαθά, the rendering more popular than the καλά of v.29; see comment ad loc. Hex has "corrected" the σε

---

25. The Tar all had difficulty with this text as well. Tar[O] speaks of your knowing גבורן דאתעבדינן לנא, whereas Tar[N] refers to the נסיא דעבד הי עמן. Tar[J] is farthest removed from MT, interpreting the clause as "having taught legal procedure (עיסק דינא) when we were encamped in the desert."
26. See the discussion at Dorival 102.
27. Tar[O] interprets the clause by חזיתא בעיניך, and Tar[N] makes of it ותיהוי לן לסהדותה, and Tar[J] flatters Hobab with והוית חביב עלן כבבת עיננא.

ποιήσομεν in the light of MT's הטבנו לך by changing σε to σοι, and then transposing the two words.

10:33 The plural verb ἐξῆραν has no stated subject, but it must be the Israelites. The "we" of vv.29—32 refers to the Israelites, and now *they* begin their departure from Mt. Sina, here uniquely called ὄρους κυρίου; elsewhere in the Pentateuch the collocation "mountain τοῦ θεοῦ" occurs only three times (Exod 4:27 18:5 19:3), but "mountain of the Lord" does not obtain anywhere else. For the structure ὁδὸν τριῶν ἡμερῶν, see Exod 3:18 5:3.

The second clause brings the ark of the Lord's covenant into prominence. That this was particularly significant is clear from the verb προπορεύετο, uniquely chosen as a substitute for נסע. It fits well with προτέρα αὐτῶν which modifies it. The ark "was going ahead before them;" note the proper use of the imperfect indicating the process of leadership. The imperfect correctly renders the participle נסע "moving." The verb is modified by a purposive infinitive "κατασκέψασθαι (for them a resting place)." The ark leads "in order to search out a resting place." That the ark is described as τῆς διαθήκης κυρίου calls attention to the contents of the ark, the "tablets of the covenant," even "the stone tablets, πλάκας διαθήκης which the Lord διέθετο to us," Dt 9:9; comp also vv.11,15. The ark symbolizes the divine presence; one is reminded of its role in battle, see e.g. 1Reg 4:4—8. Nothing is said of the cloud which at 9:15—17 determined the starting and stopping of the tribal movements of the Israelites in the desert; here it is the ark's leadership which determines the location of the first ἀνάπαυσιν. Only v.36 calls attention once again to the cloud.

In the tradition, the majority A F M V text omits the articulation of διαθηκής. It has been retained in Num based on the oldest extant witness, cod B, but its originality is uncertain.

10:34(35) By moving vv.34—35 immediately after v.33, the translator has connected these verses with the statement about the ark's role and position in the desert journey. Note that the movement of the ark differs from v.33. There, it was going before them, i.e. leading the way. Now that statement is no longer necessary, and what "took place (ויהי) ἐν τῷ ἐξαίρειν τὴν κιβωτόν is that Moses said"; what Moses said is timed precisely as the time when the ark moved; ἐξαίρω is the usual translation for נסע, especially when it refers to the beginning of a stage of travel in Israel's desert trek.

In the tradition, hex has moved vv.34—35 to the end of the chapter to conform to the order of MT. Part of the *O* tradition, along with *z*+ support, has a translation of v.36 in both places. Origen obviously intended a transposition.

The usual rendering of the root קום is ἀνίστημι (320 times, plus 45 times for הקים); ἐξεγείρω renders קום only three times (though 14 times for הקים).²⁸ The choice of the passive aorist imperative of ἐξεγείρω is particularly appropriate. What it means is "awake, rouse yourself." The Lord is called to attention.²⁹

The couplet that follows is in parallelism: "May your enemies be scattered about; may all those who hate you flee." MT presents both hemistichs syndetically, and the tradition does add καί, though not through known recensional activity. With that exception stated, the first stich is translated exactly, whereas the second one differs somewhat from MT. MT has no equivalent for πάντες, and hex has placed it under the obelus. Furthermore, MT has a modifier מפניך at the end of the line; hex has accordingly added απο προσωπου σου under the asterisk to represent the modifier. Its omission in Num is puzzling; the modifier affirms the basis for the flight of God's enemies, and one would expect Num to have rendered it. Its parent text may well have lacked it, since poetically the shorter text would have three bicola lines. In other words, the omission was probably textually based.

10:35(36) The prepositional phrase ἐν τῇ καταπαύσει contrasts with the ἐν τῷ ἐξαίρειν τὴν κιβωτόν of v.34. The reference to the "stopping" or "comng to rest" must be to the ark here as well. יאמר "he would say" is, however, rendered by the aorist εἶπεν, probably because of its use in v.34.

What Moses said when the ark came to rest, is again addressed to the Lord: ἐπίστρεφε κύριε "return, o Lord." Note the use of the present infinitive. The remainder of the line is fairly straightforward in Num: χιλιάδας μυριάδας ἐν τῷ Ἰσραήλ "to the thousands, even myriads in Israel." The verb could, however, also be understood as transitive, in which case it would mean "bring back the thousands, the myriads in Israel"; but ἐπιστρέφω is more commonly intransitive, and this is probably what the translator intended.

---

28. The count is that of Dos Santos.
29. Tar^N translates literally, but softens the imperative addressed to deity considerably by its משה מצלי אמר קום בבעו; Both Tar^JO have אתגלי "reveal yourself."

Precisely what MT means is unclear as the different renderings of the line in modern English translations illustrate. NRSV has "Return, O LORD of the ten thousand thousands of Israel." NJPS translates "Return, O LORD, You who are Israel's myriads of thousands," while NIV has "Return, O LORD, to the countless thousands of Israel."[30] MT has, as these translations show, the numbers in reverse order: אלפי רבבות "myriads, thousands of," and hex has transposed χιλιάδας μυριάδας to equal the word order of MT. In the tradition, the C' s Byz text has simplified the text, and secured the intransitive sense of ἐπίστρεφε by inserting καί between the two nouns and introducing the coordinate pair by εἰς, thus "(return, o Lord) to the thousands and the myriads," but this is clearly secondary. The more difficult text of Num is to be preferred.

10:36(34) Hex has placed this verse before v.34, thereby equaling the verse order of MT; see the comment at v.34. MT has, however, marked the end of each of the two verses of the Song, vv.34—35 (vv.35—36 in the Hebrew), with the letter *nu* reversed, presumably suggesting that their position is questionable. MT states: "And the cloud of Yahweh (was) over them by day when they were moving from camp."

Num has not only supplied the verb ἐγένετο to connect the subject and predicate of the nominal clause, but also added the participle σκιάζουσα to inform what the purpose of the divine cloud was; it was overshadowing them by day. This is an excellent example of harmonization with 9:18,22 on the part of the translator. Hex has quite rightly placed ἐγένετο σκιάζουσα under the obelus; they have no counterpart in MT. On the other hand, Num failed to render יהוה, and hex has added κυριου after νεφέλη to make up for the omission.

---

30. To which I might add the rendering of Levine: "Bring back, O YHWH, The myriads of Israel's militias!" For a summary of the renderings of Tar, see Dorival ad loc.

Chapter 11

11:1 Vv.1—3 relate an incident of murmuring at Empurismos. MT begins with ויהי העם כמתאננים רע "And the people were like those who were complaining evilly." The use of the preposition כ with a participle is unusual, but the meaning is clear. רע is used adverbially, and might best be rendered by "bitterly." Num has disregarded the preposition entirely in its ἦν ... γογγύζων; this verbal figure is a progresive past tense, and means "were murmuring." Hex has corrected the failure to render the preposition by adding ὡς under the asterisk before the participle. The verb אנן occurs only twice in the Hebrew Bible (also at Lam 3:39), and in both cases the verb γογγύζω is used. The latter along with the compound διαγογγύζω is the usual rendering for the Ni or Hi of לון. Num also changed the anthropomorphic באזני יהוה "in the ears of Yahweh" to a neutral ἔναντι κυρίου.

The immediate divine reaction was καὶ ἐθυμώθη ὀργῇ "and he was provoked to anger," a common idiom which avoids the crassness of MT's ויחר אפו "and his nostril became hot," a metaphor for "he became angry." Origen felt that, quantitatively reckoned, the suffix of אפו had been omitted, and so hex added αυτου after ὀργῇ. All of this ended with "a fire was kindled among them from the Lord." Again, the Hebrew's bald directness "and Yahweh's fire burned among them," was tempered by referring to "a fire παρὰ κυρίου." Hex placed παρά under the obelus, as being unrepresented in MT.

This manifested itself according to the last clause as: καὶ κατέφαγεν μέρος τι τῆς παρεμβολῆς, i.e. and it devoured a portion of the camp." MT is more specific in locating "a portion" as בקצה "on the border, edge, outskirts (of the camp)."

11:2 Levine suggests that the verb צעק plus אל may mean "to express a formal grievance brought to the attention of a king or other person in authority," and so translates "raised their grievance."[1] It is doubtful that Num with its ἐκέκραξεν had such a specialized meaning in mind; the word simply means "cried out." The

---
1. P.320.

Classical form εκραξεν occurs in *ol C'f+*, but the unusual inflection with -κεκρ- is common throughout LXX.

The second clause states that "Moses ηὔξατο to the Lord." The verb εὔχομαι is used commonly for translating נדר "to make a vow" (28 times), but for התפלל it occurs only eight times, three instances occurring in Num. This dominance of the notion "vow" or "promise" is even clearer with the noun εὐχή; it is used 50 times to render נדר, but only four times for תפלה (once in Job, twice in Prov, and once here).² Actually it is προσεύχομαι which is the common rendering for התפלל (69 times).³ Here, however, the simplex is used in the sense of προσεύχομαι, i.e. "to pray." The result of Moses' prayer was that the fire ἐκόπασεν "abated."

11:3 MT begins with ויקרא, which is then modified by שם המקום ההוא; the subject must be Moses. Num has translated the verb by ἐκλήθη with τὸ ὄνομα (τοῦ τόπου ἐκείνου) as subject. An indefinite subject is more commonly shown by an indefinite plural, though the singular is quite possible; e.g. one might note "They say" vs "On dit." The rendering of Num is not incorrect, seeing that the subject of ויקרא is not actually stated. The name given to the place was תבערה, which Num translated by Ἐμπυρισμός "A Burning." The folk folk etymology attributes the name to the narrative of vv.1—2, and uses the cognate verb בערה, but Num used a different verb, ἐξεκαύθη. The plural αὐτοῖς refers to λαός, which is ad sensum a plural concept. The place תבערה is completely unknown.⁴ For παρὰ κυρίου, see comment at v.1.

11:4 Vv.4—34 describe the people's rebellion at Μνήματα τῆς ἐπιθυμίας, and its result. The insurrection was stirred up by ὁ ἐπίμικτος ὁ ἐν αὐτοῖς. MT reads האספסף אשר בקרבו, with the suffix referring to העם of v.1.⁵ The word אספסף is a hapax legomenon, usually thought to refer to "the rabble" or "riffraff" who were in their midst. This understanding is probably based on the ערב רב "large mixture" which accompanied Israel when they left Egypt; see Exod 12:38.⁶ By

---

2. According to HR.
3. Acording to Dos Santos.
4. Tar^JO call it דל(י)קתא, but Tar^N has בית יקידתא.
5. Aq translates האספסף by συνειλεγμένοι, but Theod by ὁ ἐπισυστρέφων.
6. For a detailed discussion of this term, see Dorival ad loc; he renders ἐπίμικτος by "la foule mêlée."

this interpretation, the responsibility for the revolt is put on the shoulders of the hangers-on, rather than on the Israelites themselves. There is a certain irony in this reliance on the Exod passage, since the same passage lists not only the "large mixture" as travelling with the exiting Israelites, but also πρόβατα καὶ βόες καὶ κτήνη πολλὰ σφόδρα.

In any event, they (the mixed group) were "stirred with a strong desire." The cognate ἐπιθύμησαν ἐπιθυμίαν renders the Hebrew התאוו האוה, "craved a craving." The root אוה is normally rendered by ἐπιθυμέω. In the tradition, a popular B text (including Byz x+) reads επιθυμησεν to agree with the singular ἐπίμικτος, but the plural, understanding the term as a collective, is original. MT continues with וישבו ויבכו גם בני ישראל "and again (for the verb שוב) there wept even the Israelites." The translator understood וישבו as representing the root ישב, and translated it by "and sitting down, there wept even (or also) the Israelites." This is a fully possible rendering of the consonantal text. The verb ἔκλαιον is imperfect, since the weeping is an ongoing process.

The Israelites' complaint in Num is a Hebraism. τίς ἡμᾶς ψωμιεῖ κρέα is not a question asking "who will feed us meat," but translates the Hebrew מי יאכלנו בשר, an idiom meaning "if only we had meat to eat." The interrogative מי is used to express desire.[7] This is particularly idiomatic with יתן; thus מי יתן means "o that we had." Only a Hebrew speaker would comprehend what the Israelites' question with τίς meant. Hex transposed ἡμεῖς ψωμιεῖ to equal the יאכלנו of MT more precisely.

11:5 The Byz text has made this verse, which is asyndetic in Num, a γαρ clause; this is a stylistic gloss. The feminine דגה is normally a collective, and the Greek τοὺς ἰχθύας is correct. The next item remembered is את הקשאים, which Num introduces with a conjunction, καὶ τοὺς σικύους "and the cucumbers." Since the Hebrew word means "cucumbers" rather than "gourds," the early A B F *f n y*+ reading σικυας "gourds" must be secondary.[8] The word for "garlic" is σκόρδα, the contracted form of σκόροδα (plural of σκόροδον). The uncontracted form is supported popularly by almost 40 cursive mss, but by no old uncial (though cod M does read κοροδα), and the contracted form is probably original.

---

7. See GK 151a, note 3.
8. See THGN 127–128.

11:6 The opening clause reflects a word-for-word rendering of the Hebrew, which says "and now our נפש is dried up." LXX uses a contrastive δέ, however, since it contrasts with the euphoric memories of Egyptian varieties. It naturally uses ψυχή, since that is a calque for נפש, and the understanding of Num depends on what נפש means; the usual meaning of ψυχή as "person" hardly fits here. That נפש does not mean "person, self, soul" is clear.[9] I suspect that what נפש means here is "throat."[10]

MT follows with אין כל, and divides the verse at this point; thus "there is nothing at all." Num makes this part of v.b by its οὐδέν, which is then modified by πλὴν εἰς τὸ μάννα, and the structure as a whole is the predicate of ὀφθαλμοὶ ἡμῶν. Since there is no verb, v.b must mean something like "our eyes (observe) nothing at all except (towards) the manna." The word μάννα represents the Aramaic form of the Hebrew מן; see Note at Dt 8:3. In Exod it is always the Hebrew form that is used, i.e. μάν; see Note at Exod 16:31.

11:7 The manna is described in two clauses. It is, first of all, said to be ὡσεὶ σπέρμα κορίου ἐστίν; for "coriander seed," see Note at Exod 16:31, where μάννα is said to be λευκόν "white" as coriander seed; in fact, that is the text which the *b* text cites here with its ην ως σπερμα κοριου λευκον. Furthermore, "its appearance (was) the appearance of ice crystal"; in other words, manna looked like pellets of ice. The rendering κρυστάλλου is unexpected (as an interpretation of בדלח "bdellium") The Hebrew occurs only here and at Gen 2:12 where it is rendered by ἄνθραξ. The fact is that the Hebrew word is not fully understood, but is usually thought to be some kind of resinous substance, but this is not certain. The word κρύσταλλος means "ice," so the picture that Num has of manna was of small translucent pellets.[11] Since the preposition כ is repeated with עין, hex has added ως before εἶδος 2° under the asterisk to represent it.

11:8 MT begins syndetically, starting with שטו, but Num translates this by καὶ διεπορεύετο. The singular agrees grammatically with its subject העם, whereas MT uses the plural ad sensum; Num however, changes to the plural with the next

---

9. NJPS translates by "gullets"; NRSV has "strength," and NIV reads "appetite." Dorival's "notre âme" can hardly be correct; it simply reflects the isolate meaning of ψυχή.
10. As rendered by Levine; see his comment ad loc.
11. The Others read βδελλίου.

clause. Throughout v.a with its six verbs, the translator used the imperfect, since what is being depicted is the people's customary actions. Thus the people would go around and would collect and would grind, etc. The third verb, ἤληθον, is modified by αὐτό, which is an ad sensum gloss unrepresented in MT, but necessary for good sense in the Greek; hex has, however, placed the pronoun under the obelus.

The fourth verb, ἔτριβον, is correctly introduced by ἤ, which equals the אז of MT. It is supported by V b and one other ms, all other Greek witnesses having changed it to καί. But καί cannot be correct. No one would both grind on a millstone and pound on the mortar. The variant was created under the influence of the oft-recurring καί in the context.[12] The term עגות "cakes" occurs seven times in the Bible, and is always translated by ἐγκρυφίας.

V.b reads "and its flavor was like the taste, even a cake made with oil." The usual meaning of ἡδονή is "pleasure," but apparently it can mean "flavor, taste" as well.[13] The translation ἐγκρίς "cake" is a pure guess on the part of Num. The word לשד is completely unknown.[14] The free element of a bound phrase is at times rendered by a prepositional phrase, as ἐξ ἐλαίου shows.[15] The rendering of Num is probably contextual, taking its sense from ἐγκρυφίας.[16]

11:9 ὅταν κατέβη ἡ δρόσος correctly interprets the ב plus bound infinitive plus noun, ברדת הטל. The Byz text tried to improve on the default aorist by substituting the imperfect, since the falling of dew is a process, but the default tense is quite adequate. The verb of the apodosis, κατέβαινεν, is correctly in the imperfect, and undoubtedly provoked the variant Byz text.

---

12. See THGN 128.
13. See LS sub voce II.
14. As is clear from modern renderings. The bound structure לשד השמן is rendered by NRSV as "cakes baked with oil," which may well be based on Num; NIV's "something made with olive oil" is an honest admission of ignorance, and NJPS makes it "rich cream." Milgrom states that לשד, like Akkadian *lishdu*, means "cream," i.e. the upper layer of the first pressing of olives. Tar⁰ has דליש במשחתא, which contrasts with Tarᴶ's ביזא די מסרבלא בשומנא, whereas Tarᴺ reads ששיין בדבש.
15. See SS 63.
16. Aq renders v.b by καὶ ἦν τὸ γεῦμα αὐτοῦ ὡς γεῦμα τοῦ πεφυραμένου ἐν ἐλαιῷ (retroverted from Syh); Sym translated it by ἦν δὲ τὸ γεῦμα αὐτοῦ τῇ σκευασίᾳ ὡς γεῦμα μαστοῦ εἰς λίπος.

11:10 MT states that Moses heard את העם weeping; Num substitutes the pronoun αὐτῶν; the pronoun is genitive, modifying ἤκουσεν. For δήμους rendering משפחת, see comment at 1:20. Apparently, hex did not restore an equivalent for "the people"; after all, αὐτῶν did fill the slot for "the people"! The following word, ἕκαστον, is in apposition with δήμους, as the accusative inflection demands. The locative phrase modifying ἕκαστον is "at his door," which abbreviates the Hebrew's לפתח אהלו. Hex has corrected the Greek by adding της σκηνης under the asterisk after θύρας to represent the untranslated אהל.

For ἐθυμώθη ὀργῇ, see comment at v.1. The final clause admits of more than one interpretation. It reads "and before Moses it was πονηρόν." The neuter serves as a noun from the adjective πονηρός. There is no neuter term in the context which might serve as its referent, so one must infer it from the genral context. Does the noun refer to the people's reaction, i.e. to κλαιόντων αὐτῶν, or to the immediately preceding clause, i.e. to the divine wrath? In view of v.11, the latter was probably intended.

11:11 Vv.11—15 describe Moses' reaction to the anger of the Lord in an extended apologia to the Lord. Obviously, Moses is speaking in self-defence, as though he were responsible for the divine anger. He asks two questions: a) "why did you maltreat your servant?" Since πονηρόν/רע described Moses' state in v.10, one might have expected πονηρεύομαι to be used to translate the Hi of the cognate verb רעע (20 times in LXX), instead of κακόω (19 times),[17] but the translator chose to differentiate, hence my translation "maltreat." Num uses θεράποντα, the favorite rendering for עבד in Exod, here; in Num it only occurs four times (also at 12:7,8 32:31) out of a possible 11 times, but it is used only of God's servant.

b) "Διὰ τί have I not found favor before you by placing (ἐπιθεῖναι) τὴν ὁρμήν of this people on me"? For the first question Num used ἵνα τί. The change to διὰ τί has no lexical significance whatsoever; it also means Why? MT has למה in both cases. The infinitive is an explicative infinitive, i.e. it explains what not finding divine favor consisted of. The Hebrew underlying τὴν ὁρμήν is את משא "the burden." Its translation by ὁρμή occurs in the OT only here and in v.17, and interprets the burden of (all) this people as an "onslaught," as something over-

---

17. The count is that of Dos Santos.

whelming.[18] What the translator is conveying is a sense of desperation on Moses' part; the burden is an inordinate one. One gets the sense of the passage by paraphrasing the infinitival construction as "by (your) placing the overwhelming load of this people on my shoulders." Num has failed to render כל in "all this people," and hex has added παντος under the asterisk before τοῦ λαοῦ.

11:12 The opening negative particle μή is here used in a question expecting a "no" answer. The idiom λαμβάνω (or συλλαμβάνω) ἐν γαστρί is the most common rendering in OT for הרה, thus "to conceive." The repeated use of ἐγώ plus inflected verb imitates MT, and places the stress on the pronoun. One can get the flavor of its intent by the paraphrase: "was it actually I who conceived ... or was it I who bore." The accusative modifier of ἔλαβον is τὸν πάντα λαὸν τοῦτον. A popular B V reading has transposed τὸν πάντα, which was probably due to the more common order reflected in παντὶ τῷ λαῷ τούτῳ of v.13, but it is secondary. The order of Num reflects MT's את כל העם הזה, with τόν equalling the preposition את.[19]

The ὅτι clause describes the condition giving rise to Moses' querulous question. Its verb λέγεις is in the present tense, since it defines the contemporary problem: "that you say (or are saying)." λάβε reflects שא "take up." The verb also occurred in v.a with ἐν γαστρί as modifier, thus "to conceive"; in the imperative it is modified by εἰς τὸν κόλπον σου. The verb נשא occurs twice in v.b: it is rendered by λάβε "take (into your bosom)," and then in the ὡσεί clause which follows, by αἴρω: ὡσεὶ ἄραι "as (a nurse) carries (the suckling)." λάβε is modified by αὐτούς, though MT reads שאהו. A popular B variant text reads αυτον, which may well be a hex "correction," but it is not original. The reference is to λαόν, which consists of individuals. Throughout the verse MT retains the grammatical reference to העם in the singular; see also ילדתיהו and לאבתיו, but Num consistently uses plural pronouns. Oddly, only the one plural pronoun was changed by the recensor.[20] It would have seemed odd in Greek to make the final pronoun singular, i.e. "his fathers."

---

18. Instead of τὴν ὁρμήν, Aq has τὸ ἅρμα, and Sym reads τὸ βάρος, while Theod retained the Num text.
19. See THGN 103.
20. See THGN 113.

The phrase εἰς τὴν γῆν with its relative clause modifier is a delayed modifier of λάβε, thus "take (them) ... into the land which you swore to their fathers."

11:13 Moses continues with his complaint: "whence (is there) to me meat to give to all this people"? The closing ἵνα clause illustrates how the translator rendered the *waw* plus the long form of the first person verb נאכלה correctly; it is a typical way of expressing intention or purpose in Hebrew.[21]

11:14 One might have expected a present tense rather than the default future here, since Moses is speaking of his inability to carry (φέρειν) this people, but Num has δυνήσομαι "I shall (not) be able to carry," i.e. from now on I shall be unable, though the prefix inflection verb אוכל simply means "I am (un)able." The future tense is an overly mechanical rendering of the Hebrew.[22] The infinitive לשאת is correctly understood as "to carry," though it is more commonly rendered by αἴρω (180 times) or λαμβάνω (161 times). φέρω is used in LXX for נשא only 26 times. Other renderings for the verb (mainly in the Qal, but including other stems as well) used more than a dozen times are ἀναλαμβάνω (36), ἐπαίρω (32), and ἀναβλέπω (23).[23] Num also uses the φέρω rendering at v.17. MT has as modifier את כל העם הזה, but Num fails to render כל, and hex has added παντα under the asterisk before τὸν λαόν to represent it.

The reason for the complaint is given in a ὅτι clause. The comparative βαρύτερόν μοί correctly interprets the Hebrew כבד ממני in the elative sense, thus "too heavy for me."[24] Num has, however, added ἐστιν τὸ ῥῆμα τοῦτο. Only the ἐστιν was placed under the obelus in Syh; since Syh also transposed the verb with μοι, the metobelus perforce was placed after ἐστιν as well. I presume that Syh's parent Greek text placed ἐστιν—τοῦτο under the obelus; only such a parent could explain the Syh witness in which τὸ ῥῆμα τοῦτο was not placed under the obelus, though it has no equivalent in MT. A few witnesses did omit this collocation, but the shorter text is probably not recensional.

---

21. See GK 108d.
22. The Others have kept the future verb as well.
23. The count is that of Dos Santos.
24. See SS 149.

11:15 Num renders the opening conjunction by a contrastive δέ. The protasis uses σύ plus a present tense, the usual rendering for a nominal clause with pronominal subject and a participial predicate. The context suggests that the present tense intends incipient action, i.e. "if thus you are going to do to me."

The apodosis requests death in MT, as the נא particle suggests, but this is given as an imperative plus a cognate free infinitive: הרג (נא) הרגני which is difficult to translate. Thus NRSV renders the infinitive by "at once"; NJPS, by "rather," and NIV, by "right now." I would render it by the emphatic "Do kill me." Num has tried to reflect the Hebrew by rendering the infinitive by a noncognate synonym in the form of a dative noun. Its translation read ἀπόκτεινόν με ἀναιρέσει, which might be translated: "kill me with destruction." The noun means "removal," and often refers to the removal of the dead. The implication is then that Num was as troubled by the intent of the infinitive as modern translators were, but kept somewhat closer to the parent text.[25] Num as usual also omitted נא, thereby omitting any softening of the imperative by a "please, I pray you"; he could have added δή, but chose not to do so.

A further εἰ clause does place Moses in a somewhat more submissive light: "if I have found ἔλεος παρὰ σοί." MT reads "if I have found חן בעינך." The word חן "grace, favor" is usually rendered by χάρις (66 times),[26] but here ἔλεος "compasssion, pity" is used, though in the tradition, the F O+ text changed ἔλεος to χαριν, whereas the f n+ text has a doublet "grace and compassion." The Byz text has also changed ἔλεος to ελεον, but in LXX the neuter, rather than the Classical masculine inflection, dominates.[27] The equivalence ἔλεος for חן occurs only three times in OT (also at Gen 19:19 Jdg 1:24); see Note at Gen 19:19. Moses pleads for divine compassion "in order that I might not experience my misfortune." In MT this is introduced syndetically, but Num's interpretation is quite correct. What Moses desires is an end to his wretched state, his κάκωσιν. Num translated ברעתי by μου τὴν κάκωσιν. In the tradition, the majority A F M text has transposed μου to the end. Since this more exactly equals MT, the variant text could be recensional, possibly hex.

---

25. Dorival suggests that ἀναίρεσις may denote violent death, and translates the clause by "tue-moi de male mort."
26. Acording to the count of Dos Santos.
27. See Thack 158.

11:16 With v.16 the Lord's response both to the people's insurrection and to Moses' complaint begins, and then continues throughout the rest of the chapter. Moses is ordered: "collect μοι seventy men[28] from the elders of Israel."[29] That they are to be brought together "to me," i.e. to the Lord, is meant in a literal fashion; Moses is to bring them to the tent of testimony, where God would meet with Moses and the elders; see v.17.

This is followed by a relative clause modifying ἄνδρας. These men are to be ones that Moses can vouch for personally that they are "elders of the people and their γραμματεῖς." Num has amplified MT's ידעת "(whom) you know (that they are ...)," and reads αὐτὸς σὺ οἶδας. Hex has placed αὐτὸς σύ under the obelus, since it has no basis in MT. The gloss is interesting in the stress that it places on Moses in person. I would translate the clause as "whom you personally know that they are ...." What is meant is that Moses is personally to choose his cabinet of advisers. The majority A F M V text has transposed αὐτὸς σύ to συ αυτος. I can see no reason for preferring one order to the other, except that the oldest witness supports Num. Note in particular that they are not only elders of the people, but are also "their scribes." The Hebrew has שטריו; Num understands λαοῦ as a collective and so uses a plural genitive pronoun. γραμματεῖς is the most common rendering of שטרים (17 times out of 26); see Note at Exod 5:6 for a more complete statement on what is meant by such "scribes," and also on its rendering in the Hexateuch.[30]

Moses is then to bring them πρός the tent of meeting, not εις as the majority A F M variant text would have it. He brings them to the tent, not into it, as εις might easily lead a reader to understand. MT uses לקחת "you shall take (them)." This verb is usually rendered by λαμβάνω (801 times), whereas Num has ἄξεις; the verb ἄγω is used to translate לקח only eight times in LXX, but it is fitting here.[31]

In the final clause the subject changes to the third person plural; it is the seventy men who will stand at attention there with Moses. στήσονται translates התיצבו "they shall take their place, station themselves." The Hithp of יצב is almost always rendered either by the simplex ἵστημι or one of its compounds. I have contextualized the verb by rendering it by "will stand at attention."

---

28. Tar^J describes them as גוברין זכאין.
29. The ἀπό is partitive; see SS 168.
30. Tar^J makes them סרכוי במצרים.
31. The count is that of Dos Santos.

11:17 Since Moses and the seventy men are at the tent of testimony, it is appropriate that the Lord should use this as the place of revelation, hence: "and I will come down and speak ἐκεῖ μετὰ σοῦ."[32] MT has עמך שם, and hex has transposed ἐκεῖ after the prepositional phrase to equal the Hebrew order. The Num order harmonizes with v.16.

The divine appointment of the seventy men to serve as relief for Moses in the performance of his various duties is detailed in the Lord's removal ἀπὸ τοῦ πνεύματος τοῦ ἐπὶ σοί and ἐπιθήσω ἐπ' αὐτούς.[33] The term πνεύματος and its Hebrew counterpart רוח are not defined as such,[34] but are apparently some form of divine empowerment enabling the recipient both to govern and to make judgments. The taking away of an element and bestowing it on others may be compared to the taking from another element, fire, and giving it to another. This simply means sharing in rather than an actual removal of pneumatic powers.

The result of this empowerment is that they (the seventy men) will assist in carrying Moses' ὁρμήν of the people; for ὁρμήν as rendering of משא, see the discussion at v.11. MT has a cognate structure here: נשאו ... במשא, but the translator retained the translation of משא which he had made at v.11, and used a double compound verb, συναντιλήμψονται, which is particularly apt, since it means "to share in helping to carry." In turn, this sharing of the load means: καὶ οὐκ οἴσεις αὐτοὺς σὺ μόνος "and you will not carry them alone." One might have expected Num to use αυτην; after all, it is the ὁρμήν that is carried, but Moses' complaint (vv.13—15) had been one of being unable to carry the people. The reference in αὐτούς is not stated; it is obviously not the same as for the pronoun in ἐπ' αὐτούς (i.e. the seventy); common sense dictates that it must refer to λαοῦ of the preceding clause. "To carry the people" is metonymic for "to carry the burdens inherent in leading the people," for which see v.14. MT has no modifier named for תשא, and hex has placed αὐτους 2° under the obelus. It might also be noted that the root נשא occurs twice in the verse, but is translated by different Greek verbs, contextually suitable, נשאו, by συναντιλήμψονται and תשא, by οἴσεις.

---

32. The Tar all interpret "I will come down" by אתגלי(תי).
33. The ἀπό is clearly a partitive one; see SS 162.
34. Though Tar^N does interpret as רוח קדשה.

11:18 Moses is told to order the people "ἁγνίσασθε for tomorrow." The verb occurs in the book only here to render התקדשו, it being used four times uniquely in the book for התחטאו. ἁγνίζω is used particularly in the sense of making oneself cultically clean, cleansing through washing after some obvious defilement such as contact with a corpse. The use of this verb to translate the Hithp of קדש is particularly frequent in Par I and II.[35] Here it simply means "prepare yourselves for what the Lord is going to do"; the same kind of preparation was called for preparatory to the Lord's appearance to the people at Mt. Sina at Exod 19:10: ἅγνισον αὐτοὺς σήμερον καὶ αὔριον; see Notes ad loc. Here, however, the use is ironic; though the Lord is going to reveal himself in the narrative, it is hardly in the sense of Exod 19. The gift of meat is not intended as a gift of grace, but rather one of divine impatience with the complaining people, and of wrath because of their ingratitude. Nonetheless, the preparation for meeting the Lord must involve an assurance that one is cultically clean, i.e. of ἁγνισμος.

A ὅτι clause gives the reason for the Lord's intention to give the complaining Israelites meat to eat. For the τίς interrogative clause, see the discussion at v.4. Hex has corrected its word order by transposing ἡμᾶς ψωμιεῖ to equal יאכלנו of MT more exactly. This outcry is followed by its own ὅτι clause: "for καλόν for us is it in Egypt." The choice of καλόν rather than ἀγαθόν should not be overlooked. What the people were recalling with bitter nostalgia was the fine condition of life in Egypt. Hex has omitted ἐστιν, since there is no linking verb in the Hebrew.

The verse ends in MT with the promise "and the Lord will give to you בשר ואכלתם." Num has amplified this somewhat by its κρέα φαγεῖν καὶ φάγεσθε κρέα. Hex has placed φαγεῖν under the obelus to show that it was a gloss, and has omitted the last word as well, since MT simply has "and you shall eat."

11:19 Num renders MT word-for-word, except for its rendering of ימים by δύο. Hex "corrected" this by adding ἡμέραι under the asterisk. On the other hand, the threefold repetition of ἡμέρας easily led to the omission of the second one (after δέκα) by the *b* Byz+ text, and of the third one, by *d*+.

11:20 V.20 contrasts with v.19, though no contrastive particle is used. MT begins with two asyndetic עד structures, with the second one explicating the first

---
35. See the discussion in Dorival 171–172.

one. For the first one Num adds a verb: "up to a month of days φάγεσθε," and hex has placed the verb under the obelus to make clear that MT lacks a verb. The phrase μηνὸς ἡμερῶν is a literal rendering of a Hebrew idiom meaning "a full month." The second ἕως clause is also a verbal one, but differs in that it represents a potential verbal notion: "until it would go out of your nostrils." This is clear from both the ἄν particle and the subjunctive verb ἐξέλθῃ. Num renders אפכם by the more logical plural, ἐκ τῶν μυκτήρων ὑμῶν; the singular אף is hardly suggesting that the food would be coming out from a single nostril, but rather "out of your nose." Cod G actually reads του μυκτηρου, which could be a hex reading, since G is a prime representative of the *O* text. V.a ends with και ἔσται ὑμῖν εἰς χολέραν. The noun translates זרא "something loathsome."[36] The Greek word is χολέρα "cholera,"[37] but here it is probably used in the same sense as the Hebrew word, "nausea"; comp Sir 37:30: καὶ ἡ ἀπληστία ἐγγιεῖ ἕως χολέρας, where the Hebrew has והמרבה יגיע אל זרא "and gluttony leads to nausea."[38] The use of εἰς modifying ἔσται is to be understood in the same sense as the Hebrew היה ל: "to become."

V.b gives the reason for the Lord's judgment, viz., meat to satiety, in a ὅτι construction containing two clauses, the second one explicative of the first one. It is because "you were disobedient to the Lord," and secondly, "and you wept before him ...." The verb ἠπειθήσατε is only seldom used to render the root מאס "to reject," (only three times; also at Lev 26:15 Isa 30:12); far more frequently used are ἀπωθέω (20 times) and ἐξουδενόω (11 times).[39] That the people were disobedient in the sense of doubting the divine word is clear from v.23.

This disobedience is made manifest by the Israelites' moaning (ἐκλαύσατε) before the Lord in their saying ἵνα τί ἡμῖν ἐξελθεῖν ἐξ Αἰγύπτου, a somewhat fancy way of translating למה זה יצאנו ממצרים "why did we leave Egypt?" It would have been much easier to render ινα τι εξηλθομεν as cod F, probably under the influence of one of The Three, has it. But the translator apparently

---

36. Tar^O renders by תקלא "a stumbling block, offence," whereas Tar^{JN} read ריחוק "something loathsome, abominable."
37. See the discussion in Dorival 149—150.
38. Instead of εἰς χολέραν Aq has εἰς ἀλλοτρίωσιν (retroverted from Syh), whereas Sym reads εἰς ἀπεψίαν. Aq understood זרא as equivalent for זרה, which was actually read by Sam. Kenn 17^c,193 also read זרה. Prijs 20—21 refers to various midrashic interpretations of זרא, but basically agreeing with Num in characterizing the word as referring to some form of sickness, such as אסכרא, בוטנא, דרריא or even צרעת.
39. According to the count in Dos Santos.

wanted to distinguish between למה and למה זה, and so used a dative pronoun of advantage, i.e. "for what benefit was the departure from Egypt for you." At 14:41 למה זה also occurs, but there it is followed by אתם, and so the translator simply used ἵνα τί (ὑμεῖς).

11:21 For πεζῶν referring to men of military age, men on foot, see the Note at Exod 12:37. The relative clause, ἐν οἷς εἰμι ἐν αὐτοῖς, parallels the ὅς ἐστιν ἐν ὑμῖν said of the Lord in v.20. Moses recognizes that the Lord is ἐν ὑμῖν, but says "I too am among them," with the recapitulative propositional phrase in imitation of the Hebrew אשר אנכי בקרבו; the plural αὐτοῖς renders the singular suffix of קרבו, with both οἷς and αὐτοῖς referring to "the people." Moses expresses scepticism of the Lord's proposal: "meat I will give them and they will eat a month of days"; for μῆνα ἡμερῶν, see comment at v.20. It might be noted that cod B uniquely added φαγειν after "I will give to them." This has no basis in MT; it is, in fact, borrowed from v.18, and illustrates the importance of not relying completely on the evidence of the oldest ms witness.[40]

11:22 The initial interrogative particle of MT is correctly interpreted by μή in Num; this particle expects a negative answer; what is implied is "should they slaughter sheep and cattle for them, would that satisfy them?" The Masoretes vocalized ישחט as a Ni, with "sheep and cattle" as subject. The indefinite plural active of Num is an acceptable rendering for the Hebrew passive. The αὐτοῖς refers to the 600,000 πεζῶν ὁ λαός of v.21. MT reads ומצא להם "and it would reach them," i.e. would it suffice them, and ἀρκέσει αὐτοῖς is precisely what is intended.

The correlative clause is parallel to v.a; this is even more obvious in MT where אם introduces the question (just as ה- did in v.1), but the correlative conjunction is an excellent translation, since the interrogative μή thereby carries over to v.b as well. Thus "or should all the fish of the sea be brought together for them, would that satisfy them?" It might be noted that in both parts of the verse an apodotic καί introduces מצא להם in imitation of MT.

The word for "fish," τὸ ὄψος, is a true hapax legomenon. דג is usually rendered by ἰχθύς (23 times), but only here by ὄψος. In fact, the variant ὄψον,

---

40. See THGN 134.

attested by M ol b+, is the word which occurs at Tob 2:2 7:9.⁴¹ The latter word refers appropriately to something that is cooked, here to prepared fish.⁴²

11:23 The Lord's reply to Moses' sceptical query is again put in question form by means of the particle μή, i.e. expectant of a negative reply. The question in MT reads היד יהוה תקצר, "will the hand (i.e. the power) of Yahweh be restrained?" Num renders the verb by οὐκ ἐξαρκέσει; by using οὐκ the negative μή becomes positive, i.e. "will the hand of the Lord not be sufficient to them?" The answer is "of course it will." The compound reflects the simplex word in v.23 which was used to render מצא; the compound with the negative interprets תקצר.

V.b gives divine assurance that "ἤδη γνώσει whether or not ἐπικαταλήμψεταί σε ὁ λόγος μου." The verb γιγνώσκω is unusual as a rendering for ראה; in fact, it occurs according to HR only six times; it usually (490 times) translates ידע. On the other hand, ראה is rendered by εἴδω 673 times, and by ὁράω 279 times.⁴³ Admittedly, the statistics for εἴδω may be somewhat skewed in view of the confusion between certain inflections of εἴδω and οἶδα,⁴⁴ but the general conclusion is clear; γνώσει as rendering for תראה is unusual. On the other hand, the distinction between "seeing" and "knowing" is in certain contexts slight, and the rendering here is defensible.

The second verb, ἐπικαταλήμψεται, is a hapax legomenon; it means "overtake," thus "whether or not my word will overtake you," an adequate rendering for יקרך "will happen to you."⁴⁵ The verb קרה occurs 30 times in the Hebrew Bible, and is translated by 19 different verbs in LXX, 14 of which occur only once each, and none is used more than five times.⁴⁶ It should be noted that this is to take place ἤδη "straightway, immediately," in fact, "now."

In the tradition, κυρίου in the phrase χεὶρ κυρίου is articulated in a popular V variant text. That this must be secondary is clear from the fact that the genitive

---

41. LS sub ὄψος simply says = ὄψον.
42. See LS sub ὄψον 3.
43. According to the count of Dos Santos.
44. See Walters 197—204.
45. Dorival points out that the use of the verb echoes that of συναντιλαμβάνεθαι in v.17; this is not impossible, though the meaning is substantially different there.
46. According to Dos Santos.

κυρίου occurs 125 times in Num, but is never articulated, and the variant text must here be judged to be secondary.⁴⁷

11:24 The verse introduces a new section. Moses goes out and speaks to the people. Presumably, he had been at the tent of testimony, and now informs the people who were outside of what the Lord had said, i.e. his promise of meat in abundance, in fact, to satiety.

Furthermore, he brought together the seventy men whom he had been ordered to assemble in v.16; comp comments ad loc. There he was told that "they should stand there with you." Here "he stationed them around the tent."

11:25 The verse reflects the fulfillment of the Lord's promise in v.17; he did descend⁴⁸ (in a cloud) and speak to him (i.e. to Moses). Furthermore, "he removed some⁴⁹ of the spirit which was on him and placed (it) on the seventy men, the elders."⁵⁰ This too reflects the promise in v.17. The verb περιείλατο literally means "to remove something that surrounds," thus to strip off, remove. It translates יאצל, which had been used at v.17, where it also occurred in the Hi. At v.17 it had been translated by ἀφελῶ, and the change in the compound element from ἀφ- to περι- should not be pressed. Furthermore, its occurrence in a middle inflection does not seem to change the meaning at all.⁵¹ For τὸ πνεῦμα, see comment at v.17.

The result of the reception of the spirit by the seventy elders was καὶ ἐπροφήτευσαν καὶ οὐκέτι προσέθεντο. The first verb is a translation of יתנבאו.

---

47. See THGN 104.
48. I.e. "revealed himself" according to the Tar.
49. The ἀπό is partitive; see SS 162.
50. Tarᴶ is careful to add ומשה לא הסיר מידעם "but Moses did not lose any" in the process of sharing the prophetic spirit.
51. The tradition concerning renderings of The Three is in some disarray. For Aq two readings have been given, but ἀπεσπάσατο "detach, turn away from" is almost certainly the true Aq reading. περιεῖλεν is also given in two mss as being Aq, and I suspect that reading to be a false tradition. It is probably simply a variant text within the LXX tradition, i.e. an active variant of the Num verb. The Theod tradition is a compound based on ἐσκίασεν, either with ἀπ- or ἐπ- as the prepositional element in the compound; it is based on misunderstanding אצל as formed from צלל "to overshadow." The reading of Sym is probably ἐπεσπάσατο. The attribution of ἐπισκίασεν to Sym in ms 321 is simply an error for Theod, based on an uncial confusion of Ε´ and Θ´. Were I rewriting the note in App.II I would now write: θ´ (σ´ 321) ἐπεσκίασεν ... 85´-321´, and omitted the note: θ´ ἐπισκίασεν entirely, as a more efficient statement.

The Hithp of נבא refers to speaking or prophecying in ecstacy. When the spirit fell on one, an individual would be stricken with ecstacy, and speak with a prophetic voice; see 1:Reg 10:5—13 and 19:20—24 for Saul; and for false prophets, see 3Reg 22:5—23. The Greek is to be taken in the same sense as the Hebrew. The gift of prophecy was, however, not permanent, "and was not repeated," i.e. it happened on this occasion for the seventy, but not again.⁵²

11:26 According to vv.24—25 Moses had gathered seventy elders and stationed them around the tent, whereupon the Lord placed some of Moses' spirit on them, with the result that they spoke ecstatically ("prophesied"). Our verse speaks of two others who did not join the seventy, though the spirit also rested on them, so that they too prophesied; Eldad and Modad remained in the camp. The spelling Μωδάδ follows the מודד of Sam rather than the מידד of MT. Since the graphemes *yodh* and *waw* were often confused in writing, as the Qumran mss abundantly illustrate, it is difficult to determine which is original, but one might take into consideration the Ἐλμωδάδ of Gen 10:26. In MT the word שם is bound in both cases to the next word, i.e. "the name of the one," and "the name of the second." Num has a dative in both cases, thus "the name to the one, ... to the second." LXX often renders by the dative of possession in such contexts.

It is said of them that οὗτοι ἦσαν τῶν καταγεγραμμένων "these were among those that had been registered (or inscribed)." This seems to imply that there was a register containing the names of the elders, i.e. of seventy-two elders. The perfect passive participle suggests a prior registration of these names.

Furthermore, MT says that לא יצאו האהלה "they did not go out to the tent," as though the tent were outside the camp. Num makes no such statement; it simply has οὐκ ἦλθον to the tent, leaving the location of the tent indeterminate. In the tradition, the *b*+ text has the Hellenistic inflection ηλθοσαν, but Num uses only the Classical form for this verb. The majority A M F text has εἰς instead of πρός, but the seventy elders did not go inside the tent, but simply האהלה.

11:27 Num's ὁ νεανίσκος is not further identified. That it is articulated is due to MT's הנער, but the Hebrew also fails to identify him.⁵³ Num subordinates וירץ to

---
52. The Tar understood יספו as derived from the root סוף, and translated by פסקן, i.e. "did not stop."
53. See Dorival 87—88.

a participle, καὶ προσδραμών, i.e. "And the young man running, announced to Moses." The dative Μωυσῆ and the genitive Μωυσῆ are only distinguished by the presence or absence of the iota subscript. The dative form occurs 29 times in the book, and except for 12:2 where the dative is assured by the μόνῳ modifying Μωυσῆ, the article is lacking only here. Only B V *b x* and two other mss lack the article in the tradition, and the critical text of Num should be emended to read τῷ Μωυσῆ.

Num has also added the direct quotation marker λέγων after εἶπεν, but MT lacks לאמר; accordingly, hex has placed λέγων under the obelus. It is indeed otiose, particularly after εἶπεν. The use of the present tense, προφητεύουσιν, is the usual pattern for rendering a participial predicate of a nominal clause. As in v.26, Num follows Sam in the spelling of the second elder, Μωδάδ.

11:28 The rendering καὶ ἀποκριθείς ... εἶπεν is the usual one for the coordinate ויען ... ויאמר. The transcription Ναυή for נון first occurs at Exod 33:11, and thereafter becomes standard for the name of Iesous' father. So too Ἰεσοῦς remains the standard rendering for יהושע throughout the LXX. For the rendering of משרת by ὁ παρεστηκώς, see Note at Exod 24:13; this rendering is limited to these two occurrences, and it seems likely that the Exod reference is the source here. The critical text reads Μωυσῆ, but it renders the free element of a bound phrase, and it should read Μωυσῆ, the genitive form of Μωυσῆς, and the text should be corrected to the genitive.

Another modifier of יהושע is מבחריו, which has been vocalized by the Masoretes to read as a hapax legomenon, but does occur in the feminine as בחור(ו)ת(י)ך in Qoh 11:9 12:1, where it means "your youth." The lexeme here means, according to NJPS, "from his youth," or as NIV "since youth." It might, however, also be taken as representing the word בחיר which means "a chosen one," and NRSV translates the structure as "one of his chosen men," i.e. taking the מן as partitive. Num with its ὁ ἐκλεκτός clearly understood the word in this sense, though disregarding both the initial *mem* as well as the plural inflection. In other words, Num reinterprets as though reading הבחור. I doubt that the Num interpretation was textual in origin, however; what Num is saying is that "being one of his chosen" makes him ὁ ἐκλεκτός. In the tradition, an αυτου has been added by the majority A B M text, which is probably hex in origin.

What Iesous said was "O Master Moses, restrain them."[54] The Hebrew reads אדני "my master," but Num correctly understood the word as vocative, and did not render the suffix. Hex has, however, added μου afer κύριε to render it.

11:29 Moses responded αὐτῷ, i.e. to Yesous with a μή question: μὴ ζηλοῖς σύ μοι "would you be jealous for me?" MT has a nominal clause with the participle המקנא as predicate preceding the pronominal subject. The use of a present tense is usual for rendering a participial predicate. The verb ζηλόω in Classical Greek is modified by an accusative, as in B x+ εμε, but the dative renders לי. In fact, the translator distinguished carefully between קנא ל and קנא את, rendering the former by a dative as here and at 25:13, but the latter by the accusative as at 5:14,30.[55]

The τίς δῴη is a calque for the Hebrew idiom מי יתן expressing a wish,[56] thus "would that ...." The structure only makes sense from the Hebrew point of view, and the Greek can only be understood as expressing a wish: "would that all the Lord's people might be prophets (when the Lord would put his spirit upon them)." In the tradition, the x text has added ειναι after προφήτας to make this somewhat clearer. Possibly one could approach the Greek clause by understanding the structure somewhat like: "and someone might set all the people of the Lord as prophets when ...." This at least takes the optative δῴη seriously. The ὅταν clause uses a subjunctive inflection δῷ as expected.

11:30 Num neatly captured the notion of the Ni יאסף "reentered," by using ἀπῆλθεν plus εἰς, i.e. "went away into (the camp)." According to v.16 Moses and the elders were stationed at (πρός) the tent of testimony. There the Lord came down and spoke to him (v.25). Reentering the camp meant going away from the tent, which was outside the camp, into the camp, a form of hendiadys for "leaving the tent and going into the camp."

11:31 MT states that "a wind set out (נסע) from Yahweh." The verb is the usual term for "pull up stakes, set out (on a journey), depart," and Num translates uniquely by ἐξῆλθεν. The verb is usually translated either by ἀπαίρω (83 times)

---

54. Tar^N has רוח קודשה (מנע מנהון), whereas Tar^J reads רוח נבואתא (כלי מנהון).
55. See THGN 109.
56. See GK 151a.

or by ἐξαίρω (39 times).⁵⁷ The verb ἐξῆλθεν "went out" is a colorless translation of the more vigorous נסע. It is probably an intentional toning down of the verb, thereby avoiding any notion of the רוח being the Lord's spirit as in v.29.

The wind then יגז שלוים "swept (or drove) quails (from the sea)." Num translated this by ἐξεπέρασεν ὀρτυγομήτραν. The verb occurs only here in LXX, and usually does not take an accusative modifier, i.e. it is intransitive "pass over, beyond," but here it must be transitive, i.e. made to pass over," referring to the wind making the fowl pass over (the land) from the Mediterranean (הים). The verbal form ויגז was vocalized by the Masoretes as a Qal, i.e. as an intransitive verb, though the consonantal text could represent a transitive Hi form as well. The noun is rendered by a singular collective ὀρτυγομήτραν, which is unexpected in view of MT's שלוים. Just how this bird differed from the ordinary ὄρτυξ "quail" is uncertain; it also occurs at Exod 16:13.⁵⁸

The final clause still has πνεῦμα as subject; it ἐπέβαλεν "cast" (the quail) "on the ground ὁδὸν ἡμέρας ἐντεῦθεν καὶ ὁδὸν ἡμέρας ἐντεῦθεν around the camp"; this differs only slightly from MT which has כדרך for ὁδόν 1° and 2°. The repeated locative is distributive; thus "a day's journey hither and yon (i.e. on all sides) around the camp." This, as Milgrom points out,⁵⁹ is in contrast to the manna which fell within the camp (v.9), thereby indicating "that the quail are a curse not a blessing." The abundance of the quail is signalled by ὡσεὶ δίπηχυ ἀπὸ τῆς γῆς "about two cubits from the ground," or as MT has it "about two cubits על פני הארץ. It might be noted that in this structure the preposition in כאמתים is recognized; Num has ὡσεί, "about, around, approximately."

11:32 Num subordinates the first clause by using a participle, καὶ ἀναστάς for ויקם, but then introduces the main verb συνήγαγον by a καί as well, in imitation of the parataxis of MT's ויאספו. Also in imitation of MT, the participle is singular, agreeing with the subject העם, which is then taken as a collective, with the next verb in the plural. The participle is modified by the timer "all the day and all the night and all the next day," though common sense dictates that this refers to the verb in the next clause. The ἀναστάς/יקם simply means that they

---

57. According to the count of Dos Santos.
58. Dorival (52) says: "Par ce substantif qui, selon Hésychius, désigne une caille de très grande taille, la LXX a sans doute voulu insister sur la grandeur du prodige opéré par Seigneur."
59. P.92.

were no longer sitting, but had become active. The Hebrew reads כל היום ההוא for the first timer mentioned, and hex has added an ἐκείνην under the asterisk to represent the untranslated pronoun.

V.a ends with an interruptive remark: ὁ τὸ ὀλίγον συνήγαγεν δέκα κόρους. The subject represents the articulated Hi participle הממעיט "the one gathering the least," which is what the Greek subject must also mean. The amount gathered, "ten cor," is enormous; it represents about 52 bushels; for the term, see Note at Lev 27:16.

V.b in MT states: "and they spread them all around the camp." Num apparently understood the purpose of spreading such an enormous amount of meat about the camp as a spreading out in the sun so as to preserve the meat in a dried form, and reads "and they dried out for themselves ψυγμούς around the camp." The cognate noun is difficult to translate; it represents an attempt to render the cognate free infinitive שטוח of MT, i.e. "(they dried out) dryings." Probably all that is intended is that they thoroughly dried out the fowl, which would be necessary if they wanted to preserve the meat. Vulg understood the verb in this way: *et siccaverunt eas (per gyrum castrorum)*. Sam read the text differently; by transposing the graphemes ט and ח, it has וישטחו להם שחוט "and they slaughtered them (or for themselves) a slaughter"; Pesh also read this. It is, however, not to be thought of as related to the reading of cod B 509, ἐσφαξαν.[60] That this reading is simply the result of palaeographic confusion, i.e. a misreading of ἔψυξαν, is clear from the fact that the cognate ψυγμούς is retained by both witnesses. In the tradition, a doublet developed in the *f* Byz+ text by which καὶ εσφαγαν was added before καὶ ἔψυξαν; this did make good sense: "they slaughtered and heaped up," but it is obviously secondary.

11:33 The first part of this verse is fully clear: "the meat was still between their teeth," but this is followed by טרם יכרת. The verb means "to cut," and so the collocation probably means "before it was chewed," i.e. cut up by the teeth. This is how NJPS: "not yet chewed" understood it. But in the Ni it usually means "be cut off, exterminated," and Num has taken it in this sense: πρὶν ἢ ἐκλείπειν. The Ni is usually understood by LXX in this way; in fact, ἐκλείπω renders נכרת 11 times, and is exceeded in frequency only by ἐξολεθρεύω (31 times).[61] What Num

---

60. As Prijs 39.
61. According to the count of Dos Santos.

means is "before life had left it," i.e. it was raw flesh that was being eaten. What is problematic is the use of the present infinitive. The majority A V text has εκλιπειν. Since the vowels ει and ι were both identical in sound in Hellenistic and Byzantine Greek, the choice should not be based on the oldest witness, because age is irrelevant here. Since the default form is the aorist, and there is no good reason for insisting on the process of dying, I would now change the critical text to read ἐκλίπειν.

V.b describes the outcome: "and the Lord was angered against the people, and the Lord smote the people with an exceedingly severe plague." The first clause in MT reads ואף יהוה חרה בעם, and hex has attempted to correct the Num text, a) by transposing κύριος ἐθυμώθη, and b) by adding οργη under the asterisk. This is a purely quantitative approach to translation; it puts the subject κύριος in the middle, and then adds a word to equal numerically the first three words. But to Origen what was important was to represent each Hebrew word and that in the proper order, even if this were bad Greek.

The second clause in MT has בעם as a modifier of the verb יך. This resulted in the Hebraic ἐν τῷ λαῷ; ἐπάταξεν in good Greek is usually modified by an accusative, and in the tradition, a B F majority text has changed the phrase to τον λαον. But this is a secondary stylistic improvement, and not original. That the Num text is not recensional is clear from its lack of support by any O or Byz mss. The popular accusative may well have been brought in under the influence of the τὸν λαόν of the previous clause.[62]

11:34 For the passive transform of the active ויקרא את שם, see the comment at v.3. Num translates the place name קברות התאוה by Μνήματα τῆς ἐπιθυμίας "sepulchre of desire." The ὅτι clause gives the folk etymology explaining the odd place name; it was so called "because there they buried the people who were seized by craving," a reference to the ἐπίμικτος ὁ ἐν αὐτοῖς of v.4; see comment ad loc.

11:35 This verse simply details the people's move to the next desert station, Ἀσηρώθ. In MT the verb is plural, נסעו, understanding העם, the subject, as comprising the plural "the people." Num renders the verb by the singular, which is

---
62. See THGN 110.

equally acceptable.⁶³ In the tradition, the B F V O n x+ text omits the article from the name of the place which the Israelites left, Μνημάτων τῆς ἐπιθυμίας, for which see comment at v.34; this must be a secondary omission. In v.34 the τῆς is present in all mss except cI plus two other mss; there it is obviously original, and it would be odd indeed for the translator to vary the name in adjacent verses.⁶⁴

The second clause is somewhat inappropriate as a conclusion to the chapter. It reads καὶ ἐγένετο ὁ λαὸς ἐν Ἀσηρώθ; this would be much more appropriate at the beginning of some episode. Both NJPS and NRSV have actually taken it as the introduction to ch.12, thus "When the people were in Hasaroth, Mariam and Aaron spoke ...." NIV has taken it as part of ch.11 with its "and stayed there," which rather stretches ויהי beyond its lexical parameters. The location of Haseroth is not certain, but see Note at Dt 1:1; there חצרת is translated by Αὐλῶν "courts, enclosures."

---

63. As does 4QNumᵇ with its נסע.
64. See THGN 106.

Chapter 12

12:1 V.b of the preceding verse, 11:35, is best read as the introductory clause for 12:1, and the period after ἐν Ἀσηρώθ should be changed to a comma in the critical text. It then reads "And when the people were in Haseroth, there spoke ...." MT lacks an equivalent for "the people," simply reading "and when they were in Haseroth." That the verbal predicate agrees with the nearer member of a compound subject is particularly clear from MT: ותדבר מרים ואהרן "and Miriam and Aaron spoke." Since Greek does not distinguish gender in the verbal inflections, it simply has καὶ ἐλάλησεν Μαριὰμ καὶ Ἀαρών, agreeing only in number.[1] The name מרים is vocalized as Miryam by the Masoretes, but Num has the older vocalization, with its Μαριάμ.

Moses' siblings spoke "κατὰ Μωυσῆ because of the Ethiopian wife whom Moses had taken." The rendering of תדבר ב by ἐλάλησεν ... κατά "spoke against" is unusual, but the ב is correctly understood as "against."[2] MT reads כשית, i.e. Cushite, but LXX consistently understands כוש as "Ethiopia," and thus כשית as an Ethiopian woman, for which see Notes at Gen 2:13. The apparent exception in the Table of Nations, at Gen 10:6—7, has כוש transliterated as Χούς, and seems to represent a different Cush, since its subclans comprise tribes from Southern Arabia to Moab; comp also v.8. How this is to be harmonized with the tradition of Moses' wife, Zipporah, a Midianitess, is not clear, but the fact that כוש in Gen 10 is located in the environs of Midian ought not be overlooked.[3]

The relative clause in MT is simply אשר לקח, i.e. without the repetition of משה as named subject, and hex has placed the (otiose) Μωυσῆς under the obelus.

12:2 What the siblings said constituted an attack on Moses' authority. The first question is introduced by an interrogative μή, i.e. anticipating a negative answer, whereas the second one is an οὐχί query anticipating a "yes" reply. In the former, the verb is perfect, λελάληκεν, but in the latter it is in the default aorist, ἐλάλησεν, though no such distinction obtains in MT, where דבר occurs for both.

---

1. See THGN 122.
2. See Johannessohn, Gebrauch 245.
3. Tar[N] solves this puzzle by identifying the Cushite wife of Moses as Zipporah.

What Num says is: "Has the Lord spoken only to Moses? Did not he speak to us also?" The distinction is an appropriate one, since what is implied is that the Lord has been speaking throughout to Moses, and the situation continues even up to the present, but in the past we too were addressed by the Lord. In this verse, ב modifying the verb דבר is understood in the normal sense of "spoke with," as over against v.1.

In the tradition, the Byzantine text has preferred the Classical second aorist ειπον instead of the Hellenistic εἶπαν, but Num throughout uses only the latter. For the first question it is not clear how Origen viewed the word μόνῳ; μόνος almost always represents some construction with the root בדד. But here it seems to be used to render רק אך, which is unique, but contextually appropriate. Admittedly, at Gen 7:23 it seems to interpret אך, and in Job ch.1 for רק אני לבדי LXX has ἐγὼ μόνος in its stead (vv.15—17,19), but the μόνος equals the לבדי structure, and the רק is not separately rendered. Furthermore, רק אך precedes במשה, whereas Num has Μωυσῇ μόνῳ. The hex text has placed μόνῳ under the obelus, but this disregards the particles of MT entirely. MS 426, which shows a remarkable degree of Hebrew influence not necessarily always hex, has transposed the two words as μονω μωσει, which is another possible solution.

12:3 MT characterizes "the man Moses" as "very ענו, beyond all people who are on earth." The positive πραΰς plus παρά with the accusative are used to express the comparative.[4] The word ענו means "humble," and it is rendered by ταπεινός six times in LXX. The word occurs only here in the Pentateuch, but obtains most often in Pss, where the word is frequently confused with עני "poor." This has resulted in an unclear picture. Furthermore, elsewhere it is always plural; the singular is unique to this passage. It is translated by πραΰς which means "gentle, mild, meek,"[5] whereas the Hebrew word rather intends humility, the unassuming, and certainly not the notion of the patient bearing of inflicted wrongs.[6] The rendering was, however, influential on later translators, and it is used nine times, mainly in Pss. That instead of ענוים the translators at times read עניים is clear from such translations as πένης and πτωχός (each occurring five times). Here the

---

4. See SS 149.
5. Field states that The Others also read πραῢς σφόδρα according to "codex unus" on the authority of Montef. I have been unable to identity this ms.
6. See Gray 123—124.

notion of "meekness, mildness" does make sense, even though that is not what ענו means.[7]

It might also be noted that the translator fully understood the meaning of האדם in the sense of "humanity." It is renderred correctly by the plural τοὺς ἀνθρώπους.

12:4 Num uses the adverb παραχρῆμα "suddenly, on the spot" to translate פתאם, for which see comment at 6:9. The statement that "the Lord said on the spot Go out, you three, to the tent of testimony" is occasioned by the Lord's hearing what Mariam and Aaron said about Moses in v.2. MT orders the addressees as "to Moses and to Aaron and to Miriam"; Num only has the preposition πρός before Μωυσῆν, and has transposed Aaron and Miriam, probably under the influence of Μαριὰμ καὶ Ἀαρών of v.1. Ms 426, probably representing hex, has changed the text to read προς ααρων και προς μαριαμ to equal MT exactly. It should be noted, however, that the text of Num is by no means certain. The order Μαριὰμ καὶ Ἀαρών is attested only by A B* 121, with all other witnesses transposing the two names. It is not impossible that the order of Num could be secondary, being influenced by v.1. Since the two uncials are, however, our oldest extant witnesses, the text of Num is certainly defensible.

The imperative is addressed to ὑμεῖς ὁ τρεῖς representing the שלשתכם of MT. Hex has transposed this to read ο τρεις υμεις to represent the order of MT. They are to go out to the tent of testimony. The final clause states that οἱ τρεῖς went out εἰς τὴν σκηνὴν τοῦ μαρτυρίου. This time the suffix of שלשתכם is not rendered, since it is obviously "you (three)."[8] The final prepositional phrase is repeated from the preceding clause. MT lacks an equivalent,[9] and hex has correctly placed it under the obelus. Note once again the insistence that the tent is outside the camp; they go out to the tent.

12:5 The theophany is described as the Lord coming down in a cloud pillar, and standing "at the door of the tent of testimony." Then "Aaron and Mariam were summoned and both went out." MT simply has "at the door of the tent," and hex

---

7. But see Dorival 80—81.
8. See SS 100.
9. Though 4QNum^b has been reconstructed as containing it, and the repeated prepositional phrase is probably textually based.

has placed τοῦ μαρτυρίου under the obelus. MT also has ויקרא, i.e. "(the Lord) called." Num uses a passive transform, which voids the direct involvement of the Lord: καὶ ἐκλήθησαν Ἀαρὼν καὶ Μαριάμ. This is probably an intentional change of MT's active ויקרא; there is a subtle difference between "he summoned them" and "they were summoned." This places the clause on the same level as the last one, καὶ ἐξῆλθον ἀμφότεροι, with Aaron and Mariam as subject for both clauses, whereas κύριος is the subject of the first two clauses, i.e. of κατέβη and ἔστη.

In the tradition, the two oldest witnesses, Codd A and B, along with four cursive mss, read εξελωοσαν, but Num always reads the Classical ἦλθον and its compounds. This illustrates how careful one must be in appraising even the oldest witnesses.

12:6 Num added the addressees: πρὸς αὐτούς (i.e. Aaron and Mariam). MT lacks this gloss, and hex has placed the phrase under the obelus. The subject of εἶπεν, being obvious. is not stated, but the Byz text added κυριος to make doubly sure.[10] MT added a polite נא after the imperative שמעו, and hex added δη under the asterisk to represent it.

The אם protasis is difficult. It reads אם יהיה נביאכם יהוה. It seems to say: "If your prophet should be Yahweh," which can hardly have been intended.[11] Modern translations all rewrite the text in part; NJPS and NIV interpret as "when a prophet of the LORD arises (is, NIV) among you," whereas NRSV takes יהוה with the apodosis, and paraphrases: "when there are prophets among you, (I) the LORD." Num does render נביאכם literally by προφήτης ὑμῶν, but then has the dative κυρίῳ for יהוה, thus "should your prophet be for the Lord," or possibly "should a prophet among you be for the Lord."[12] I would translate the line: "should a prophet of yours belong to the Lord." In other words, the dative is a dative of possession.

---

10. 4QNum^b added יהוה אלהים as subject.
11. The Tar were all troubled by the protasis as well. Tar^O read אם יהון לכון נביאין אנא (בחזין) יי. Tar^N also simplifies by הי נבייה ביניכון יהוי אין, whereas Tar^J refers it to the past: (היכמא דמתמלל עם משה) אין יהוון כל נביא דקמו מן יומת עלמא מתמלל עימהון.
12. Particularly astute is Milgrom's reconstruction of vv.6—8, in which he proposes an A:B:C:D::D′:C′:B′:A′ poem. But he suggests (p.309: note 23 to chapter 12), citing Freedman, that A is a "broken construct chain ... which gives the line this meaning: 'If either of you (Aaron or Miriam) is (or claims to be) YHVH's prophet.'" This does make wonderful sense. Unfortunately, Num did not understand the line in this way.

The apodosis follows with two clauses in the future tense: "in a vision I would make myself known to him, and in a dream I would speak to him." MT presents both verses asyndetically, which further emphasizes their poetic character. The future tense expresses potential, the timelessness of a condition.[13]

12:7 Vv.7—8a contrast with v.b. Ordinarily, the Lord reveals himself to prophets (as e.g. Mariam and Aaron?) in visions and dreams, but Moses ὁ θεράπων μου is a special case. The opening οὐχ οὕτως contrasts the Lord's relations with Moses with other objects of divine revelation, in this case with any "prophet of yours who belongs to the Lord." The rendering of עבד by θεράπων is particularly characteristic of Exod, where it occurs 28 times. It is only rarely used in the rest of the Pentateuch (twice in Gen, and four times each in Num and Deut). But Num also renders עבד five times by παῖς, the favored translation of עבד in Gen. It should be noted, however, that θεράπων is only used for the Lord's servant. On the other hand, παῖς is, except for 14:24 where God refers to Chaleb is "my παῖς, only used as a polite reference to the speakers as "your servants" (all addressing Moses in 31:49 32:4,5 and 27). Concerning "my servant Moses," the Lord said: "he is faithful ἐν ὅλῳ τῷ οἴκῳ μου. Usually, God's house refers to temple or shrine, but here the figure is that of one who is πιστός in God's household; he is a trustworthy servant. This becomes fully clear in v.8.

12:8 The prophetic character of Moses is unique; "mouth over against mouth will I speak to him," which is a graphic way of saying "face to face."[14] In fact, MT reads "mouth to mouth," using the preposition אל.[15] MT describes this by ומראה ולא בחידת. Presumably, מראה is to be taken adverbially, i.e. "visibly, clearly, plainly." Num has a prepositional phrase, ἐν εἴδει, "in visible form,"[16] and then understands the preposition ב as one of means, thus "through riddles."[17]

MT continues with the future sense in ותמנת יהוה יביט "and the likeness of Yahweh he will see." Num changed the tense to the aorist, thereby making it a reference to Exod 33:18—23, and comp 24:17. The fact that Moses had seen the

---

13. See Porter 421—423.
14. See Johannessohn, Gebrauch 249.
15. The Tar void the anthropomorphic figure by substituting ממלל for פה, thus "speech with (or to) speech."
16. This equals the במראה of 4QNum[b], which was probably the parent text of Num.
17. See SS 124—125.

Lord's glory, although only from the rear, gave him special status. This change in tense is probably an intentional correction of fact, since no further instance of Moses' seeing the Lord is recorded.[18]

In v.b, the Lord gives vent to his displeasure at Mariam and Aaron's daring to oppose Moses verbally. "And why were you not afraid to speak against my servant Moses?" The use of a κατα- compound infinitive plus a κατά phrase in modification stresses the opposition to Moses on the part of his siblings, which in Hebrew is shown by the use of a ב phrase modifying לדבר, for which see comment at v.1.

12:9 Num renders the verbal clause ויחר אף יהוה בם in unusual fashion by a nominal clause, using ὀργὴ θυμοῦ κυρίου as the subject, and ἐπ' αὐτοῖς as the predicate. Since ὀργή and θυμοῦ are synonyms, the combination intensifies the notion of anger; it means then "the fierce anger of the Lord (was upon them)." The use of ἐπί with the dative is locative; the anger was like a physical force resting on top of them. The αὐτοῖς refers to Aaron and Mariam.

The episode ends abruptly: "the Lord left." Note the use of the compound "went away from" to render the neutral וילך. The majority A F M V text reads the plural απηλθον, which would mean that the three siblings left. It is, however, a copyist error rooted in the similarity of the uncials E and O; in other words, ΑΠΗΛΘΕΝ was misread as ΑΠΗΛΘΟΝ.

12:10 Since the Lord had gone away (v.9b), the symbol of his presence, the cloud of revelation, also "removed from the tent." MT has סר "turned" from the tent. It was now also physically obvious to Mariam and Aaron that the Lord was no longer present.

The nominal clause והנה מרים מצרעת is literally rendered by καὶ ἰδοὺ Μαριὰμ λεπρῶσα; see Note at Lev 13:2. For ὡσεὶ χιών "as snow," see Note at Exod 4:6. That the flesh should become like snow means that it has lost the color of healthy skin, and become white.

V.b parallels v.1 in its repetition of the apodosis, though without repeating "Mariam" as subject of the ἰδού clause. Its "protasis" reads "ויפן towards Miriam," and Num renders this by καὶ ἐπέβλεψεν πρὸς Μαριάμ. So "when he

---

18. Tov 86 calls this a case of exegetical substitution, but this really does not explain anything. Why should the translator substitute?

looked towards Mariam, (behold she was leprous.)" A popular B V Byz+ variant text changed the preposition to επι, but this is a secondary adaptation to the compound element of the verb it modifies. The verb ἐπιβλέπω is frequently used to render the Qal of פנה; in fact, it occurs in LXX 30 times.[19]

12:11 Aaron does not approach God, but rather Moses; it was, after all, Moses whose authority had been questioned. According to MT he said בי אדני אל נא "O, my lord, do not, pray." Num correctly understood בי as a particle of entreaty. It occurs four times in the Pentateuch (also at Gen 43:20 Exod 4:10,13), and it is always rendered by δέομαι (or -μεθα). In later books it is rendered by the meaningless ἐν ἐμοί. Num, as usual, does not translate either the suffix of אדני, nor the נא particle of entreaty; hex does add μου after κύριε, as well as δη after μή, thereby representing the parent text fully. The rendering of תשת עלינו חטאת "do (not) hold sin against us" by Num has an interesting twist; it reads συνεπιθῇ ἡμῖν ἁμαρτίαν. The συν- compound occurs only rarely in LXX, and only once elsewhere for שית (at Ps 3:7), but there it is a middle participle "of those who have set themselves in concert round about me." Here it seems to mean "lay an extra charge of sin upon us." The συν- element adds the notion of "adding, joining," to that of "placing upon," and so "lay an extra charge upon."

This "sin" is described in MT by two relative clauses: "which we did foolishly (נואלנו) and which we committed (חטאנו)," i.e. which we foolishly committed. Num avoids the notion of folly, and pleads ignorance instead, and interprets אשר as causal: διότι ἠγνοήσαμεν καθότι ἡμάρτομεν. The use of καθότι to render ואשר is based on the intuition that the second clause is not coordinate in sense, but rather explicative. I would translate the Greek "because we were ignorant as to that we sinned," or more idiomatically "because we did not know that we had sinned."

12:12 Theoretically problematic is the subject of γένηται/תהי. Since the only feminine word in the immediate context is חטאת of v.11, it would be possible to make that the subject, but common sense dictates that Aaron is pleading on behalf

---

19. According to HR.

of the sister, i.e. the subject must be the Μαριάμ of v.10. It might be added that תהי could also be taken as second person verb addressed to Moses.[20]

The verb is modified by two ὡσεί structures, the second one illustrating the first one, thus "as one equivalent to death, as an ἔκτρωμα ἐκπορευόμενον from a mother's womb." MT simply has צאתו, with the suffix referring to מת, i.e. "as one dead, as it goes out of its mother's womb." Actually, Num clarifies MT's כמת by reading ὡσεὶ ἴσον θανάτῳ. In other words, Num makes clear that Mariam is not entirely כמת, but is like one who is similar to a dead person. Num has explained צאתו as an aborted fetus leaving a mother's womb, i. e. an ἔκτρωμα. Furthermore, the last clause of the verse, ויאכל חצי בשרו "and half of its flesh was eaten away" has a Ni verb as predicate with חצי בשרו as subject, and the suffix of בשרו refers to מת. Hex understood that MT had no equivalent for ἔκτρωμα, and placed it under the obelus. On the other hand, MT reads אמו "its mother," and hex added an αυτου under the asterisk after μητρός to represent the suffix.[21] Num has also understood the final clause differently in two respects. The Ni verb ויאכל was taken as an active verb, κατεσθίει, probably with ἔκτρωμα as its subject, whereas the suffix of בשרו, which could no longer refer to the dead one, has been changed to αὐτῆς, i.e. of the mother, or as Syh^ms which reads lh mrym instead of αὐτῆς, i.e. of Mariam. The noun itself is rendered by the plural τῶν σαρκῶν, since the "flesh" is dead; comp Gen 40:19 Lev 26:29 Deut 28:35.

12:13 Moses' intercession. The verb ἐβόησεν here indicates prayer; Moses called out to the Lord. Num has clarified the rather cryptic Hebrew אל נא רפה נא לה by paraphrasing the first נא particle by δέομαί σου, and omitting the second one. One ms, 767, which normally represents the n text, often witnesses to a hex reading as well. Here it alone added δη after ἴασαι, which equals the נא 2° of MT. Num has understood אל not as a negative particle, but as a vocative, ὁ θεός, which is confirmed by the Masoretic vocalization.

---

20. According to Milgrom, Rashbam took it in this way, rendering the verse "Let you be not like one dead, inasmuch as all who come from the same mother's womb partly die (when any brother or sister dies)." I find this possibility far-fetched, irrelevant in any case, since Num uses a third person verb.
21. SS 98—99 notes that Num omits the pronominal suffix far less frequently for bodily parts than in Gen Exod and Lev. This is clearly in line with the more literal character of Num as a translation document.

12:14 Num correctly interprets the first clause of the Lord's reply as the protasis of a condition: εἰ ὁ πατὴρ αὐτῆς (for ואביה). MT has a cognate verbal figure, ירק ירק with the first word as a free infinitive, intended to intensify the verbal idea, thus "had her father actually spit (in her face)." Num reproduces this by a present participle of the simplex cognate stem πτύων (ἐνέπτυσεν). The pattern is one commonly used in the Greek Pentateuch (and elsewhere) to represent the Hebrew cognate verbal figure as here, and it should be understood as a syntactic calque.

The future passive verb ἐντραπήσεται is regularly used (13 times) in LXX to translate the Ni of כלם. The verb means "to be turned about," and then metaphorically "to be put to shame," and so a good equivalent for נכלם. That such a daughter would be put to shame, i.e. isolated for a week, was apparently an expected practice. Indeed, to be separated for seven days outside the camp was demanded of anyone who was presumably cured of λέπρα; see Lev 14:8. Only afterwards, i.e. after the seven day period of isolation εἰσελεύσεται "might she enter (the camp)." This differs somewhat from MT, where the Ni of אסף obtains, i.e. "she may be collected," i.e. be brought in, readmitted (to the camp); in MT she is acted upon, but in Num she is active—"she may enter the camp."

12:15 Since Mariam was in isolation outside the camp for seven days, the people did not break camp during that period, i.e. they did not move on, until ἐκαθαρίσθη Μαριάμ. This is not what MT says: עד האסף מרים "until Miriam had been readmitted;" see comment at v.14. According to the laws of purification in Lev 13, one cured of ἀφὴ λέπρας had to undergo priestly examinations, as well as wash his or her clothes (vv.6,34), i.e. such a one must first be declared καθαρός before being readmitted to the camp. Num has insisted that Mariam must undergo such prescribed rituals; it was these rituals that held up the Israelites from moving camp.

Chapter 13

13:1(12:16) As at 11:35 נסעו העם is translated as a singular structure in Num: ἐξῆρεν ὁ λαός; see the discussion at 11:35. For ἐν τῇ ἐρήμῳ Φαράν, see comment at 10:12. There Φαράν was articulated as τοῦ Φαράν. Here only B* and five mss witness to the unarticulated proper name. The Byz text articulates with the dative article τη (wrongly masculine τω in 75′), and the overwhelming majority read του φαραν. I would now change the critical text to read the genitive article as original, i.e. as τοῦ Φαράν.[1]

13:3(2) The *s*ᵐᵍ and Syh text have added an appropriate introduction to the spy narrative based on Sam, which is in turn based on Deut 1:20—23; in this Moses urges the people to proceed with the invasion of Canaan. But some individuals first approached Moses, and suggested a cautionary dispatch of spies to bring in advice on how to take the land.

The reflexive pronoun modifying an imperative is difficult to translate. It serves apparently to call special attention to the addressee. It is in my opinion best left untranslated. The sense might be something like "do send off (men)!" ἀπόστειλον is really zeugmatic for "appoint and send off." In the context, what is intended is appoint and send off (some) men. The purpose of such appointment is κατασκεψάσθωσαν "let them scout out the land of the Canaanites." The verb means "to make a survey, to cover," and translates יתרו quite correctly. MT speaks of ארץ כנען "land of Canaan." This structure occurs 12 times in the book, and כנען is always transliterated as Χανάαν except here. This is the first occurrence of the structure in the book, and it is put into the descriptive context of "(which I am giving) τοῖς υἱοῖς Ἰσραήλ." The translator may well have wished to contrast peoples, i.e. "land of the *Canaanites*, which I am giving to the *Israelites* εἰς κατάσχεσιν." The purposive phrase at the end has no correspondent in MT, and is placed under the obelus in hex. So God is going to give to the Israelites for a possession land now belonging to the Canaanites. The relative clause recurs in the same form at Deut 32:49, and recalls the divine promises to

---

1. In spite of THGN 103.

give to Abraam and his seed the land of Canaan εἰς κατάσχεσιν αἰώνιον at Gen 17:8, and similarly to Iakob and his offspring, at Gen 48:4; see the Notes at Gen 17:8 and 48:4.

These appointments are designated by two norms: ἄνδρα ἕνα κατὰ φυλήν "one man per tribe," and uniquely κατὰ δήμους πατριῶν αὐτῶν. This occurs only here in the book, though κατὰ δήμους κατ' οἴκους πατριῶν αὐτῶν is common (20 times, and twice in reverse order), whereas κατὰ δήμους αὐτῶν by itself occurs 19 times. For the terms and their meaning, see comments at 1:20. Moses is instructed according to these norms: ἀποστελεῖς αὐτούς, an improvement on MT's תשלחו, which is not only plural but is also used absolutely, i.e. without a pronominal modifier; Sam does read a singular תשלח, though it is also used absolutely, whereas the Tar fully support MT's text. The text of MT seems somewhat deficient here. It also reads for the two norms: איש אחד איש אחד למטה אבתיו, i.e. it lacks an equivalent for κατὰ δήμους. Hex had some difficulty with this text, but did mark αὐτούς with an obelus, since תשלחו lacked a modifier, and also added a second ανδρα ενα under the asterisk to represent the repeated איש אחד.

The instructions end with πάντα ἀρχηγὸν ἐξ αὐτῶν. Probably intended was "everyone a leader out of them." The αὐτῶν must refer to τοῖς υἱοῖς Ἰσραήλ, as is clear from v.4.

13:4(3) Moses in obedience to the Lord's voice (διὰ φωνῆς κυρίου) "sent them out from the desert of Pharan." The phrase διὰ φωνῆς κυρίου avoids the anthropomorphism of the Hebrew על פי יהוה "according to the mouth of Yahweh."[2] The second clause is nominal, with πάντες ἄνδρες constituting the subject, and ἀρχηγοὶ υἱῶν Ἰσραήλ οὗτοι, the predicate. The predicate in turn has a clausal structure of its own in imitation of the Hebrew syntactic pattern, in which οὗτοι is the internal subject, and ἀρχηγοὶ υἱῶν Ἰσραήλ, the predicate. The general pattern may be seen by the rendering "as for all the men, they (were) chieftains of the Israelites."

13:5(4) Vv.5—17 constitute a list of those who were sent out on the surveying mission, along with their tribal origin. The list is superscribed by "and these (are)

---

2. Both Tar^JN retain "according to the mouth of," but Tar^J continues with מימרא דייי, and Tar^N, with דיי גזרת ממרה. Tar^O avoids פי entirely with its על מימרא דיי.

their names," after which the list is given. The first one sets the pattern which the remainder follows. First, the tribe is given inflected in the genitive (of source or origin): τῆς φυλῆς 'Ρουβήν, which renders a ל phrase: למטה ראובן; then follows the man's name and his patronymic: Σαμοῦ υἱὸς Ζακχούρ. For the spelling of 'Ρουβήν, see Note at Gen 29:32.

Σαμοῦ represents the Hebrew שמוע, but the majority M V text read σαλαμιηλ. This in turn led to the A+ reading σαμαλιηλ, the B reading σαμουηλ, as well as σαμιηλ, σαλαμουηλ and σαλαμηηλ. A revision of the original Σαμοῦ is attested as σαμμου in F f+, but the spelling with a single *mu* follows the translator's usual pattern. The compound name with a final -ηλ element was the name of the chief of the tribe of Simeon; see 2:12 7:36,41 10:19, and does not belong here. The shorter form is also supported by 963.[3] Whether Σαμοῦ or σαμμου is original is not certain.

The father's name, Ζακχούρ, also suffered in the tradition, as a list of the variant spellings in the Greek mss shows: ζακχυρ, ζαχουρ, ζαγχουρ, ζακουρ, σακχουρ, ζακχαρ, ζακχου, ζαχχου, ζαχηρ, ζαχαρ, ζαυχουρ, σακχουν, ζαχρου, ζαριχουρ, χακχουρ, χακχουρ and αχουρ, a total of 17 variant spellings; about half (eight) of these occur in single witnesses.

13:6(5) Representing the tribe of Simeon was Σαφάτ υἱὸς Οὐρί. The name Σαφάτ was relatively stable; the *b+* tradition changed the dental stop to *theta*: σαφαθ, and the *x* text produced σαφα. Other spellings include σαφαν, σαφαι and σαφοτ. Οὐρί, however, is supported only by C' f s+, all others attesting to the prefixing of a *sigma*. In MT, the name is חורי, and the *sigma* is an inner Greek error, a dittograph of the *sigma* of υἱός which precedes it.[4]

13:7(6) The appointee from the tribe of Iouda was Χαλὲβ υἱὸς 'Ιεφοννή. The name Chaleb was well known, and the spelling was stable, only χαλεφ (in six mss), and in individual mss: χαλευ, χαλε and χελεμ are deviant. His father's name suffered greatly, particularly from itacistic spellings, as well as by haplography of the *nu*. Disregarding these, there still remain change in vowel in ιεφανηη, ηαφωνι, dittography in ιεφοονηη, aphaeresis producing εφωνηη, εφονη and εφονι, and syncopation resulting in ιεφνη.

---

3. See THGN 116.
4. See THGN 116.

13:8(7) From the tribe of Ἰσσαχάρ came Ἰγαὰλ υἱὸς Ἰωσήφ. For variation in the spelling of Ἰσσαχάρ, see comments at 1:8. The name Ἰγαὰλ represents יגאל. That Ἰγαάλ would be unstable in its spelling is particularly clear from the uncial spelling ΙΓΑΑΛ, in which the last three letters all represent triangular forms. The most common variation is ιγαλ, to which most witnesses, including A F M, attest. Since the *aleph* begins the second syllable, it needs an *alpha* (or possibly an *epsilon*) to represent it. It should be said that no witness actually reads Ἰγαάλ, and it was restored by Rahlfs, in my opinion almost certainly correctly. The syllable יג when vocalized as *yig*, is always transcribed by ιγ, though the later recensors transcribed it by ιεγ. The non-initial syllable אל with an "a" vowel normally has three elements to represent it, resp. א, the vowel "a," and ל. The ms evidence promoting the reconstruction consists of ιλααλ in B x, in which Γ, however, was read as Λ, and ιεγααλ in 426. All others can be explained as corruptions of an original ιγααλ. These comprise ιεγλα, ιεγαλ, ιεγλαθ, ιγαδ, ηγαλ, γαλ, εχαλ, ιεγλαμ, ηγλαν, ηγλαμ, γαλαν, γαλαμ, γαλααχ, γαδ (Byz text), and the majority reading ιγαλ.[5]

13:9(8) "From the tribe of Ephraim, Αὐσὴ υἱὸς Ναυή." The name Αὐσή, representing הושע, "Hosea," became αυσης in V *ol* and Byz+, but for the rest is stable. The name Ναυή remains problematic, though it has become standard throughout the literature. The Hebrew reads נון, which can hardly equal Ναυή. Though no witness attests to it, the original transcription must have ended in a *nu*. In the uncial script the N and H are easily confused, and it is likely that the original transcription was NAUN not NAUH. But neither at Exod 33:11, where the name first occurs in the Pentateuch, nor at Num 11:28 nor here does the spelling ναυν occur in any extant witness, but see v.17 below (the spelling νουν in one ms is a later correction). I am not suggesting the change of name to Ναύν in the critical text, mainly because the name Ναυή is so entrenched, though I must admit to being sorely tempted. In the tradition, the *upsilon* became *beta* in a *d+* text, but this is due to the pronunciation of both β and consonantal υ as /v/.

13:10(9) The tribe of Beniamin was represented by Φαλτὶ υἱὸς Ῥαφού. The Hebrew reads פלטי בן רפוא, and Num transcribed both names accurately. Variant

---

5. The Others read Ἰεγάλ, which was apparently also read by Origen in hex.

spellings of Φαλτί are few, but include φαλτειν, φελτι, φαλτιας and φατι (badly corrected to φαιατι). 'Ραφού is also quite stable, though the following misspellings occur: ραφαν, ραφαν, ριαφου, ρειραφου, εριαφων and ραφουμ, all but ραφαν in b, being attested by single witnesses.

13:11(10) Appointed for the tribe of Zaboulon was Γουδιὴλ υἱὸς Σουδί, for the Hebrew גדיאל בן סודי. The misspelling of Γουδιήλ is almost entirely explicable on the basis of palaeographic confusion in the uncial tradition. Confusion of Δ and Λ produced the γουλιηλ of C'' s+; misreading of Γ as I resulted in ιουδιηλ in Byz, and reading Γ as Τ produced τουδιηλ in V and τουδηια (Λ read as A) of 120'. The γαδιηλ of oI+ may be due to confusion with the name Gad (to Gadi: to Gadiel). The spelling γουζιηλ is probably an auditory error, and γουδοηλ resulted by dissimilation of ιη to οη. Not easily explicable are σουδιηλ and γωμολ. The name Σουδί was obviously strange to Greek copyists, and resulted in σωδι, σοδι, σουδ, σουδιελ and σουαγ. The C'' s+ spelling σουρι need not depend on a misread *daleth* as *resh* in a Hebrew parent, since a cursive *delta* is more or less an upside down *rho*; i.e. it is explicable within the Greek cursive, copyist tradition.

13:12(11) MT identifies the next tribe doubly as למטה יוסף למטה מנשה. The translator changed this to read τῆς φυλῆς 'Ιωσὴφ τῶν υἱῶν Μανασσή "of the tribe of Ioseph, the Manassites." The other Joseph tribe had simply been characterized as τῆς φυλῆς 'Εφράιμ (v.9). In the tradition, both μαννασση (by dittography) and μαναση (by haplography) obtain.

The tribal representative was Γαδδὶ υἱὸς Σουσί. Γαδδί produced only a few variants: γαιδι, γαδι, γααδι and γαδ. Σουσί for סוסי was also quite stable, though a few mss misread the intervocalic *sigma* as a *delta*, thus σουδι, σουδει and σουδδη; apocopation also created σους in one ms.

13:13(12) The tribe of Dan was represented by 'Αμιὴλ υἱὸς Γαμαλί. Neither name created many problems, only αμεηλ occurring as a variant for 'Αμιήλ. Γαμαλί has resulted in some variant spellings, with γαμαλιηλ leading to γαμιηλ. Other misreadings are γαμαελει, γαμαδι (Λ as Δ), γαμασει, γαμαν, δαμαλη, γαμαι (ΑΛ as Α), and its itacistic variant γαμε.

13:14(13) Representing the tribe of Aser was Σαθοὺρ υἰὸς Μιχαήλ. Σαθούρ is misspelled as σατθουρ, αθουρ, θασουρ, σαρουθ and σαφουρ. His father's name, being a well known one, is quite stable, only μαχαηλ, μιχαιηλ, μιαηλ, μιηλ and χα obtaining.

13:15(14) The tribe of Νεφθαλί contributed Ναβὶ υἰὸς 'Ιαβί. For the spellings of Νεφθαλί, particularly of the majority reading with final *mu*, see comments at 1:15. Both Ναβί and 'Ιαβί were completely strange to Greek copyists, and misspellings abound. For Ναβί the β became υ in ναυι, ναυη and comp ναηι; change of vowel resulted in ναβα, ναβαυ, ναβια, ναο and note also νααβη and ναβιαμ; *beta* and *mu* were easily confused in certain cursive scripts, resulting in ναμι and αμι, and aphaeresis produced αβι, αβει, αυση, while dittography created νααβη. The father's name, 'Ιαβί, differs considerably from MT's וַפְסִי, and the parent text must have differed considerably from it. The name 'Ιαβί resulted in even greater confusion, with consonantal *iota* being corrected (by hex) to consonantal ου, thus ουαφει, ουαφση, ουαβη; final closure made ιαβειμ, ιαβιν, and aphaeresis created αβι, αβη, αυι, αβει, ακι. Note also σαβι, ιακει and δαβει.

13:16(15) Finally, the tribe of Gad had Γουδιὴλ υἰὸς Μακχί as its representative. The name Γουδιήλ also appeared as the name of the appointee of the tribe of Zaboulon in v.9, but with different parentage. The Hebrew name here also differs from that in v.9; it is גְּאוּאֵל. Only a hex ms, 426, and the *n* text revised the name to some approximation of the Hebrew name as γουιηλ or γουοιηλ. All other variant spellings are based on a Γουδιήλ original. which must have been due to the influence of v.9. Variant spellings include τουδιηλ (for which see comment at v.9), γουθιηλ, ουδιηλ, γοθδιηλ, ρουδιηλ and σουδιηλ. The name Μακχί was misspelled mainly in the intervocalic cluster, which became -χχ-, -χ-, -κκ- or -κ-. Other variants are βακχι, μαχειρ, ναχι, μακοσι, μοκοσι and μοσκωση.

13:17(16) After the subscription which Num translates word for word, it is said that Moses named (i.e. renamed) τὸν Αὐσή the son of Ναυή as 'Ιησοῦν. For Αὐσή and Ναυή see comments at v.9. It might be noted that ms 82 has the reading του ναυν instead of Ναυή. For the possibility of ναυν being original spelling, see comment at v.9. The name 'Ιησοῦν is the accusative of 'Ιησοῦς, and represents יְהוֹשֻׁעַ, which differs from הוֹשֵׁעַ in bearing the theophoric prefix.

13:18(17) Vv.18—25 describe the survey by the twelve tribal representatives. They were sent by Moses "to survey the land of Canaan." A popular M *ol* Byz+ gloss added εκ της ερημου φαραν after Μωυσῆς; this has no basis in MT, and was imported from v.4, where it occurs in a similar context. The Byz+ text reads εξαπεστειλεν instead of ἀπέστειλεν. Though there is no great lexical distinction between the two, ἀποστέλλω occurs for the Qal of שלח 431 times, whereas the double compound occurs only 66 times. For the Piel, however, the double compound obtains 159 times, but the single one only 71 times.[6]

Moses said to them "Go up ταύτῃ τῇ ἐρήμῳ." In MT this reads זה בנגב. The זה is here an adverbial indicating direction: "there," but Num has taken it as a pronoun modifying ἐρήμῳ, thus "to this desert." נגב can mean "south" or "the Negeb desert." What MT meant was that the twelve were first to go there into the Negeb, the area to the south of Canaan, and then to proceed into the hill country. Num by its ταύτῃ τῇ ἐρήμῳ probably also refers to this same barren, desert area. In fact, LXX usually translates נגב by νότος (52 times) or λίψ (35 times), and only nine times by ἔρημος.[7] The translation ἔρημος also occurs in v.23 and 21:1, but was already used in Gen (12:9 13:1,3) where it clearly refers to the desert area to the south. The word is never taken as a geographical name, Ναγεβ, in the Pentateuch.

13:19(18) Vv.19—21 give detailed instructions to the twelve as to what to look for in their survey. First of all, "you must see the land—what (or probably how) it is." The interrogative τίς ἐστιν can be taken as an adverbial modifying ὄψεσθε. Secondly, "and the people settled upon it, whether they are stronger or weak, whether they are few or many." τὸν λαόν is coordinate with τὴν γῆν, and so the τὸν λαόν structure also modifies ὄψεσθε. MT has no correlative conjunctions, but repeats the interrogative prefix ה- for הרפה, thus "is it strong, is it weak"; similarly אם obtains before רב. The renderings by ἤ are idiomatic and correct.

Unfortunately, the interrrogative particle εἰ and the correlative conjunction ἤ are homophonous (disregarding stress), and this has created confusion in the mss. In fact, most uncials (all but A) and half the cursives changed the second εἰ to η, but the balanced character of Num, i.e. εἰ ... ἤ, εἰ ... ἤ must be original.

---

6. Acording to Dos Santos.
7. According to the count in Dos Santos.

The use of (εἰ) ἰσχυρότερος for החזק might at first blush seem questionable, particularly since it is supported only by B and V, all other Greek witnesses reading the positive degree, ισχυρος. Its contrast, ἀσθενής is also positive, and it might be argued that both adjectives should be in the same degree. What the translator intends, however, is to begin with the comparative, i.e. whether the people are stronger (relatively speaking) or just weak. The more difficult reading of B V is, in my opinion, to be preferred as original text.

13:20(19) The query τίς ἡ γῆ is modified by an εἰς ἥν clause. The εἰς is used in the Hellenistic sense of "in (which they were dwelling on it)," as is clear from MT where ישב is modified by בה (rendered by ἐπ' αὐτῆς in Num). The question may best be rendered by "what about the land ... is it good or bad"? What is meant is Is the land productive, i.e. fertile, or not. For the confusion of εἰ and ἤ in both questions, see comment at v.19.

The second question poses the same query concerning cities: εἰς ἅς οὗτοι κατοικοῦσιν ἐν αὐταῖς, i.e. "in which they are dwelling." That εἰς ἅς means "in which" is clear from the ἐν αὐταῖς within the relative clause. MT's question is הבמחנים אם במבצרים "whether in camps or in fortified areas." What is asked is: Are the people nomadic or sedentary?[8] Num asks the question differently; it asks εἰ ἐν τειχήρεσιν ἤ ἐν ἀτειχίστοις "are they in walled (cities) or in unwalled (villages)?" Num has not only transposed the nominals, it has also asked a question as to the vulnerability of the cities; whether the cities are walled or unwalled is an important military question rather than a sociological one. Num asks the more pertinent query for those intending to invade the land.

13:21(20) The quality of the soil is also to be examined. Though the question τίς ἡ γῆ is repeated from v.20, it is now not the land in general, but the soil that is to surveyed, and γῆ should be translated by "soil, ground." The next question: "Is it rich or neglected"? MT has השמנה הוא אם רזה "is it fat or lean."? Num renders רזה by παρειμένη, the perfect middle participle of παρίημι, thus "has been disregarded, neglected." What is meant is Is the land so scrawny that it has not been thought sufficiently worthwhile to cultivate. Furthermore, "are there trees in it or not"? Num correctly understood עץ to be a collective, and uses the plural. As in v.20, εἰ and ἤ are confused in the tradition; see comment at v.19.

---

8. See Dorival 153.

The final instruction in MT reads "ולקחתם והתחזקתם some of the fruit of the land." The first verb urges diligence and might be rendered "and make a real effort (to take)." Num subordinates the first verb as a participle, προσκαρτερήσαντες "persist obstinately," which adequately renders what MT intends. Probably it might be translated "and make sure (to take along, i.e. to bring back)." The ἀπό is partitive, and fits well with the plural τῶν καρπῶν.[9]

The observation is then made that "the days are the days of spring, (even) forerunners of grapes," i.e. the time when the first ripe grapes appear. The Hebrew calls these the days of בכורי ענבים, but has no equivalent for ἔαρος, which hex has accordingly placed under the obelus. That Origen's use of the hex signs is largely mechanical, i.e. a quantitative one, is clear from the fact that the nominative πρόδρομοι is left unchanged. The word is an unusual choice for rendering בכורי "firstfruits"; in fact, it is unique in LXX.

13:22(21) The first two clauses of MT: ויעלו ויתרו are coalesced into a single clause as καὶ ἀναβάντες κατεσκέψαντο (τὴν γῆν) "and going up they surveyed the land." They surveyed from the southern limits, τὴν ἐρήμου Σίν, for צן, to the northern limit: 'Ραὰβ εἰσπορευομένων 'Εμάθ. The desert of Sin, apparently bordering the wilderness of Pharan to the south extended northward towards Canaan; this should not be confused with the desert of Sin, for סין, referred to in 33:11— 12 where the Israelites encamped afte leaving the Red Sea, before proceding to Raphaka. This is clear from 33:36 where our desert of Sin (צן) is between Gesion Gaber and Kades. It is unfortunate that the two deserts of צן and סין are both transcribed as Σίν. In the tradition, this latter was easily confused with Sinai (i.e. Σινά) supported by the popular V reading.

The northern limits of Canaan surveyed by the twelve are defined as 'Ραὰβ. This remains unidentified, but should not be confused with the 'Ραὰβ in the tribe of Aser (B text of Ios 19:28; and comp Iud 1:31 'Ροώβ). MT reads רחב, and the tradition has dealt badly with the name, with only the *rho* remaining as a constant element. The vowels -αα- are changed as -οο-, -οω-, -ωω-, -εω-, -ωα-, -ιω-, and -ω-. The final consonant is also unstable, the *beta* changing to a dental, either a *delta* or a *theta*. I suspect that this derives from a "Rehoboth" tradition, which Syh as well as Bohairic represent. This has resulted in ροωθ, ερωθ, ρωθ,

---
9. See SS 162.

ρωωθ, and even ρωωδ. MT, aware of possible confusion with the רחב In Aser, localized this Rehob more precisely as לבא חמת, i.e. (at) Libweh of Hamath. The translator did not recognize לבא as a place name, and took it to be the marked infinitive of בוא "to enter," and translated it by a genitive of place at which, as εἰσπορευομένων "at the entrances of Hemath."

Nor was 'Εμάθ known to Greek copyists. It was inexplicably confused with the Euphrates, and the Byz tradition read εφρααθ, probably from a badly written *mu* in 'Εμάθ, read as φ or φρ, which easily became εφρααθ. Variants developed further to εφααθ, εφρααт, ενφαθ, νεφαθ, νιφαθ, but only 'Εμάθ can claim to be original LXX.[10] Other misspellings of 'Εμάθ are εμαε, αιθαμ, εμμαωθ and σαμααθ; there is even an εγλααμ, corrected to εγφααμ.

13:23(22) For τὴν ἔρημον rendering נגב, see comment at v.18. The twelve "went up through (κατά) the desert,[11] and came up to Χεβρών," the famous cult site well known from the Abraam cycle; Hebron is first mentioned at Gen 13:18. At Hebron (i.e. ἐκεῖ) were 'Αχιμὰν καὶ Σεσὶ καὶ Θελαμίν. None of these individuals is known. The first one is a transcription of אחימן, and remains quite stable in the tradition, with three mss omitting the final consonant, and cod A oddly reading αχικαμ (as though אחיקם). καὶ Σεσί is ששי in MT; i.e. Num has added a conjunction. The name Σεσί is fairly stable in the tradition as well, though G and 376 add a *nu* at the end; B and V+ double the intervocalic *sigma*, particularly with an itacistic final -ει, i.e. ΣΕΣΕΙ becoming ΣΕΣΣΕΙ. Other spellings are σεσεσι and σεμει (in cod A). Furthermore, the Masoretes did not place a daghesh in the *sigma* either, and the majority tradition must be taken as original.[12] Less certain is the spelling Θελαμίν for MT's תלמי. Most witnesses lack the final consonant, which would be closer to MT, but the oldest witnesses A B G, as well as Philo, all read a final *nu*, as do Coptic and the Old Latin. The name was misspelled in a variety of ways, including θαλαμμειν, θαλαμι, θαλαμμει, θολομεει, θαλαβι, θαλμι, θολμι, θαλβει.

These three are called γενεαὶ 'Ενάκ "relatives, family members of Enak." MT is more specific; they were ילידי הענק "descendants of Anaq," i.e. Anaqites. The Anaqites were men of stature, in fact, γίγαντας, comp vv.29,34.[13] B F and

---

10. See THGN 116.
11. For κατά rendering ב, see Johannessohn, Gebrauch 247—248.
12. See THGN 116.
13. Tar^O actually reads גבריא instead of ענק; Tar^JN read ענק גיברא.

x+ transcribe עֲנָק as ενάχ, but this is wrong. The Hebrew *qoph* is always transcribed by *kappa* in Num.[14]

The last clause states that "Hebron was built seven years before Tanis of Egypt." That צֹעַן was identified as the Egyptian Tanis was well known in antiquity. Tar^J reads טאניס and Tar^NO have טנ(י)ס, and Vulg reads *Tanim urbem Aegypti*. Tanis was for long thought to be Avaris, but this is now discounted.[15] The name occurs in Egyptian sources as early as the Nineteenth Dynasty, and is located in the northeastern part of the Delta.

13:24(23) The נחל אשכל "the wadi Eshkol" is translated as Φάραγγος βότρυος "the wadi of (grape) clusters," understanding βότρυος as a collective. That ἦλθον, though attested only by B O n *x*+, is original is clear. The majority Hellenistic inflection, ηλθοσαν, is never used by Num.[16] The next clause, καὶ κατεσκέψαντο αὐτήν "and they surveyed (i.e. inspected) it (referring to Φάραγγος)" has no counterpart in MT, and was therefore placed under the obelus in hex.[17]

In accordance with the instructions in v.21 to bring back some of the fruits of the land, "they cut down from there (i.e. from the wadi) a branch and one cluster of grapes ἐπ' αὐτοῦ (i.e. on the branch)." The prepositional phrase has no counterpart in MT, and hex has placed the phrase under the obelus.[18]

"And they carried it ἐπ' ἀναφορεῦσιν." MT reads וישאהו במוט בשנים "and they carried it on a carrying frame by two (men)." The ἐπ' with the dative represents a ב of means.[19] Since Num translated by means of a plural noun, "on staves (or poles)," the בשנים became unnecessary and was omitted.[20] Hex has, however, added δυσιν under the asterisk after ἀναφορεῦσιν. Coordinate with αὐτόν, which must refer to βότρυν, are two ἀπό phrases, both of which are partitive,[21] καὶ ἀπὸ τῶν ῥοῶν καὶ ἀπὸ τῶν συκῶν "and some pomegranates and some figs."

---

14. See THGN 118.
15. See Levine ad loc.
16. See THGN 123.
17. From the length of the line, it would appear that 4QNum^b may be reconstructed as supporting it.
18. It is, however, probably textual in origin, since 4QNum^b has בה.
19. Theod and Aq change the noun to the singular, ἐν ἀναφορεῖ "by means of a pole," and Sym translates by ἐν ἀρτῆρι.
20. See SS 121.
21. See SS 162.

13:25(24) MT begins with למקום ההוא modifying קרא, but Num translates idiomatically by an accusative modifier τὸν τόπον ἐκεῖνον. Num did not translate קרא by a singular verb, because no subject is given, and so used the indefinite plural, ἐπωνόμασαν "they named," thereby following 4QNum^b and Sam, which is also supported by Tar^J and Pesh.²² The second modifier is, however, not inflected as an accusative. Since it is the name given to that place, it is placed in the nominative, Φάραγξ βότρυος. The majority text has an initial καὶ ex par, but Num translates accurately with no conjunction. The reason given for the odd name "Wadi of clusters" is the account which has been given of the cutting down of the cluster. As in v. 24, the singular βότρυος/βότρυν are collectives.

13:26(25) The twelve then "returned (ἀπέστρεψαν) from there, having surveyed the country." MT has "returned from surveying the country," i.e. does not have an equivalent for ἐκεῖθεν, though it does use the preposition מן in מתור.²³

13:27(26) Vv.27—34 deal with the report of the investigators to the Israelite assembly. The opening καὶ πορευθέντες ἦλθον "and going they came" represents the Hebrew "and they went and came in." וילך is often used in MT simply to indicate the onset of activity, something like "come" in English, e.g. "come, let's go," whereas in Hebrew one used "go," like in "go, let's go, come, etc." In Hebrew it is also normal to repeat prepositions, i.e. "to Moses and to Aaron," but in Greek the second "to" is otiose.²⁴ Hex, however, has added a προς before ᾿Ααρών to equal MT.

For Καδής see Note at Gen 14:7, where it is also called τὴν πηγὴν τῆς κρίσεως; this was in the wilderness of Pharan, where the Israelites were encamped; see v.1 and comp v.4. MT reads קדשה, i.e. with a *he* directive, thus "to Qadesh," but Num disregarded this; presumably the εἰς governing τὴν ἔρημον Φαράν is understood to govern Καδής as well. There according to MT ישיבו דבר "and they replied," literally "returned a word." Num understood its meaning, and used ἀπεκρίθησαν "they replied," but then added an unnecessary

---

22. Aq corrected this to the singular ἐπωνόμασεν. 4QNum^b had the plural קראו.
23. Theod and Aq read a different compound, καὶ ἐπέστρεψαν, and Sym used καὶ ἀνέστρεψαν. In view of these readings, the attribution of ἀπέστρεψαν to The Others cannot be correct.
24. But Tar^N also lacks a repeated conjunction before אהרן.

rate rendering for דבר in ῥῆμα. A more idiomatic rendering would have omitted ῥῆμα.

Furthermore, "they displayed the fruit of the land." MT has a pronominal suffix to the verb, ויראום, and hex has added αυτοις under the asterisk to represent it, thus "and they showed them."

13:28(27) Both MT and Num are agreed that the group reported "to him," i.e. to Moses. This seems to contradict v.27, where they replied "to them and all the assembly," but the official report was delivered to Moses; it was Moses who at the Lord's command had commissioned them in the first place; see vv.1—4. As often, the Hellenistic εἶπαν, which Num uses throughout for the third plural aorist, is changed in the tradition to the popular Classical ειπον. The reverse phenomenon obtains with ἤλθομεν, for which the B G C'+ text read the Hellenistic ηλθαμεν; see the comment on this verb at v.24.[25] "They said: we came to the land, to which ἀπέστειλας ἡμᾶς, γῆν ῥέουσαν γάλα καὶ μέλι." The ἀπέστειλας refers to Moses, and agrees with v.4, "and Moses sent them."[26]

Instead of "a land flowing with milk and honey," MT has וגם זבת חלב ודבש הוא "and it was flowing with milk and honey." Num tends to harmonize, to prefer recurring patterns rather than deviations from such, and here uses the usual pattern, which recurs in 14:8 16:13,14, and is common in Deut (6:3 11:9 26:10, 15 27:3 31:20). It had already appeared at Exod 3:8,17 13:5 33:3 and Lev 20:24.[27]

13:29(28) The report expresses a strong reservation: אפס כי "except that," which Num renders by ἀλλ' ἢ ὅτι "but that." This indicates contrast to the positive display of the "fruit of the land" of v.28. What they complain of is that "the people who dwell on it are audacious." This is not what MT says: "the people who dwell בארץ are עז." I would, however, question my earlier judgment that ἐπ' αὐτῆς

---

25. See also THGN 123.
26. Milgrom states: "A hint of the attitude of the scouts: It is not the land 'which the LORD promised.'" I find this suggestion specious. It would have been odd for the twelve to have said: "to which the Lord sent us."
27. Dorival maintains that γῆν represents וגם. He says: "En fait, elle n'ajoute pas le mot *gén*. En effet, ce mot doit être regardé comme le correspondant de la particule hébraïque *wegam*, de laquelle il est homophone." I am sceptical of this ingenious explanation. There is no evidence, as far as I can discover, that Num ever engaged in this kind of practice, one which later translators did follow, particularly Theod.

was original LXX. Its support outside of B and V is basically Byz, whereas the majority A F M text reads τῃν γην. Were this recensional, it would surely read εν τη γη, but την γην is idiomatic Greek, and I believe the critical text should be changed to read τὴν γῆν. This judgment receives added support from the reading θρασύ instead of עז. The Hebrew word means "strong," but θρασύ means "bold, arrogant, audacious," which word is fitting in a report obviously intended to make the people fearful.

Note also the freer nature of the nominal clause which follows. MT reads: "and the cities (are) בצרות and very large." Again Num interprets in exaggerated fashion, translating by ὀχυραὶ τετειχισμέναι; not only are they "fortified," but they are also "walled"; that this is an added feature was seen by hex, which placed τετειχισμέναι under the obelus. In the tradition, a popular V text joined the two by a και, which is an ad sensum gloss. On the other hand, the majority B V text omitted the καί after the participle, a case of haplography after -μεναι.

The final clause refers to the presence of τὴν γενεὰν 'Ενάκ. At v.23 the ילידי ענק were identified as γενεαὶ 'Ενάκ;[28] there the plural was taken literally, since it identified three specific individuals as relatives of Enak. Here the ילדי ענק refers to the clan as a whole, and the singular γενεάν is appropriate. For 'Ενάκ, but not εναχ, see comment at v.23.[29]

13:30(29) The verse is a series of nominal clauses in MT, each one repeating the participle יושב as its predicate. Participial predicates are normally rendered by the present tense, as κατοικεῖ here, or the imperfect. Actually, the imperfect would have been more appropriate in this verse. The verse thus makes a statement on the tribal inhabitants of Canaan, identifying in each clause the area of the country which they inhabited.

Num begins with καὶ 'Αμαλήκ, though MT is asyndetic. Actually, hex has omitted the καί and corresponds to MT.[30] The area which Amalek occupies is ἐν τῇ γῇ πρὸς νότον "in the land which is towards the south." MT has בארץ הנגב, which would hardly mean "the land τῆς ἐρήμου," as in vv.18,23 (and 21:1), but must refer to the south.

---

28. For the Tar on ענק, see footnote at v.23.
29. See also THGN 118.
30. So too The Others, which also omit καί.

The second clause reads "and the Chettite and the Hevite and the Iebousite and the Amorrite κατοικεῖ in the hill country." Num follows Sam's וההוי, which MT lacks, occasioning hex's placement of καὶ ὁ Εὐαῖος under the obelus. It should also be noted that Num throughout uses the singular predicate κατοικεῖ in imitation of MT; only the Byz+ text emends to the grammatically expected plural κατοικουσιν.[31] Of the tribes listed, only 'Αμορραῖος does not follow the Masoretic spelling, since the transcription has a doubled *rho* (for the Masoretes the *resh* may not be written with a daghesh). That both dittography and haplography should change the spelling is hardly surprising; thus αμμοραιος, αμοραιος and αμμωρραιος are all in evidence in the tradition.

The last clause locates the Cananite in two areas: "along the sea," i.e. the western part of the land, and "along the Jordan river" for the eastern part. MT simply has "the Jordan," and hex has omitted ποταμόν.[32] The omission is also attested by the Byz text and all the daughter versions. The word was probably intended by Num to contrast with θάλασσαν "sea," i.e. "west."

13:31(30) "Chaleb silenced the people πρὸς Μωυσῆν." The πρός reflects the Hebrew preposition אל. Precisely what either MT or Num meant by "to Moses" is not clear. Does it mean "before Moses," as Tar^N's קדם משה, or were the people rebellious over against Moses, and needed to be silenced?[33] This could be the basis for the על משה of Sam. Obviously, the πρός equals אל, and Num thus equals MT (and not Sam). Modern translations prefer "before Moses," and this could be what is intended,[34] though I would suggest that it means "towards"; the translator probably had in mind the eventual murmuring of the people, and here κατεσιώπησεν ... πρὸς Μωυσῆν stresses Chaleb's attempt at quelling an incipient revolt against the authority of Moses. I would render the phrase by "towards (or over against) Moses." In the tradition, the M *ol z*+ text included ιησους, reading

---

31. See THGN 122.
32. Theod reads καὶ παρὰ τὸν 'Ιορδάνην, i.e. also omits ποταμόν. Similarly, Sym translates by καὶ κατὰ τὸν 'Ιορδάνην. Aq has changed the noun to the genitive, τοῦ 'Ιορδάνου; undoubtedly, Aq had rendered על יד as well, which is suggested by the extant genitive noun, but only τοῦ 'Ιορδάνου is extant.
33. Note Tar^J which instead of אל משה has ואציתינון לות משה "and made them listen (or obedient) to Moses." Tar^O is ambivalent with its למשה.
34. That the meaning of אל is here uncertain is illustrated by Levine who translates "near Moses."

κατεσιωπησαν χαλεβ και ιησους. This reflects the tradition of the two spies bringing in a minority report; see 14:6.

Chaleb "said αὐτῷ Οὐχὶ ἀλλά we must certainly go up and possess it." MT has no equivalent for αὐτῷ nor for "No, but," and hex has placed the three words under the obelus. The αὐτῷ does, however, have a textual base in the לו of Sam. This pronominal gloss continues the notion that the report is formally directed only to Moses, as in v.28. The negative particle and conjunction are added for stylistic reasons; they make the contrast between Chaleb's urging and the majority statement in v.32 more striking.

MT uses the cognate pattern of free infinitive plus inflected verb twice in Chaleb's statement. The first one, עלה נעלה, is translated by a cognate participle plus a future verb, a common pattern used by translators, promoting the Hebrew sense of placing major stress on the verbal notion, thus "we must certainly go up"; what is meant is to go up into the land of promise. The majority A text reads κατακληρονομησωμεν, i.e. an aorist subjunctive verb. This is a possible interpretation, i.e. as a hortatory subjunctive, but it is not original. It is simply a misspelled future phonologically based, since the *omicron* and the *omega* were homophonous. It is, after all, coordinate to ἀναβησόμεθα, i.e. a future tense. Note also the future tense of the ὅτι clause.

The second instance is part of the כי clause, יכול נוכל. For this, the translator used the cognate adjective, δυνατοί, thus "we will certainly be capable over against them." What is meant is "we shall surely overcome, be victorious over them." The use of an adjective to render a cognate free infinitive is unusual, but fully effective.

13:32(31) Num renders the relative clause אשר עלו עמו "who had gone up with him" by the compound participle οἱ συναναβάντες (μετ' αὐτοῦ) "those who went up together with him," which is an elegant rendering. A popular A F M variant text has changed μετ' αὐτοῦ to μετ αυτων, thereby correcting the text to include the unmentioned ιησους.

The majority report advised against invasion. In fact, Num, by introducing their response by a rebellious οὐκ ἀναβαίνομεν, and making the MT report the reason for their refusal to invade by prefixing ὅτι, increased the negative character of the reaction. What Num says is "We are not going up because (we cannot go up against the people because they are much stronger than we)." Hex correctly placed οὐκ ἀναβαίνομεν ὅτι under the obelus. This blunt refusal in the present tense to go up gives added basis for the divine judgment against the ten bringing in the negative report in ch.14; see especially v.30. The reason given for not being able to invade is because ἰσχυρότερόν ἐστιν ἡμῶν μᾶλλον. Over against MT, the μᾶλλον is an exaggeration; it has no support in MT, and hex placed it under the obelus. The comparative degree in MT is expressed by the adjective plus מן, i.e. חזק הוא ממנו.[35] In the tradition, the F V majority text has transposed ἐστιν ἡμῶν, but the word order of Num is original. It both equals MT, and the oldest mss, A and B, support it.

13:33(32) MT says "And they brought out an evil report about the land, which they had surveyed (it), to the Israelites." Once again, the translator has exaggerated the statement by rendering דבת הארץ by ἔκστασιν τῆς γῆς "terror of the land." The structure "bring out an evil report" also occurs at 14:36,37, but there Num renders דבה more exactly by ῥήματα πονηρά and πονηρά resp.[36] I would translate "And they instilled terror for the land which ...."[37]

The surveyors no longer report to Moses, but spread their pessimistic opinions πρὸς τοὺς υἱοὺς Ἰσραήλ among the Israelites. What they said was "the land which we traversed to survey, is a land devouring those dwelling ἐπ' αὐτῆς." MT has an אתה after "to survey," which would be otiose in Greek, but hex has added αυτην under the asterisk to represent it. The prepositional phrase interprets the suffix of יושביה, for which see the comment on ἐπ' αὐτῆς at v.29 where MT, however, read בארץ.[38] In the tradition, the majority text has κατεσθίουσα rather than the κατέσθουσα of Num.[39] The majority text, as the more prosaic form, became popular in later times,[40] but the Num text is supported by all the uncial texts except V, and is probably to be preferred, though this is by no means certain.

According to MT, they reported that "all the people whom we saw in it (i.e. in the land) were אנשי מדות "men of measure," i.e. people of large size.

---

35. See SS 149.
36. Dorival 154 makes the point that Num understood דבה correctly, but intentionally changed it to ἔκστασιν here; in my opinion, he is exactly right.
37. Aq and Sym translate דבה by ψόγον.
38. The Others simply read αὐτῆς without the preposition.
39. As did The Others.
40. The Others read κατεσθίουσα as well.

Num understood the measure to refer to length, thus ἄνδρες ὑπερμήκεις "tall men." The Hebrew bound phrase is translated by an adjectival one.

13:34(33) Furthermore, "there we saw giants." The term τοὺς γίγαντας is the translation of הנפילים. Just who the Nephilim were is unknown. The translation γίγαντας is probably derived from Gen 6:4, where their description reads οἱ γίγαντες οἱ ἀπ' αἰῶνος, οἱ ἄνθρωποι οἱ ὀνομαστοί; see Note ad loc. Thus "they were famous men from antiquity," probably semi-mythical in origin. In any event, Num uses γίγαντας.[41] In MT, this is followed by בני ענק מן הנפילים, which the translator overlooked, probably due to homoioteleuton, i.e. jumping from the first הנפילים to the second one. Hex has supplied a translation of the missing words under the asterisk: υιους ενακ εκ των γιγαντων, undoubtedly taken from one of The Three, probably Theod.

V.b is much clearer in MT than in Num. It reads "and we were in our eyes as grasshoppers, but also were we thus in their eyes." The translator mistranslated בעינינו as ἐνώπιον αὐτῶν, thus "we were before them as grasshoppers, but also thus were we before them." The only sense I can make of it is that "we seemed like grasshoppers to them, but so we actually were," which is not an overly profound insight. Not only was the suffix mistranslated, but then Num tried to make sense out of it, and instead of the conjunction *waw* introducing the second clause, it was amplified as ἀλλὰ καὶ οὕτως. The ἀλλα was added to invite contrast, and οὕτως as an interpretive gloss intended to explain the contrast, but the attempt was not overly clear.

---

41. Sym renders the term by τεραστίους "monstrous ones."

Chapter 14

14:1 Chapter 14 continues the narrative of ch.13, by indicating Israel's response to the report of the twelve spies. MT begins with ותשא כל העדה ויתנו את קולם, with no indication of what all the assembly raised. Num renders ותשא by καὶ ἀναλαβοῦσα "and all the assembly taking up, gave voice." Dorival suggests as translation "et en accueillant ces propos,"[1] which is possible. Contextually at least, the report of the twelve has just been given, and it could mean "taking up the recommendation given, they gave voice," but it would be an unusual sense. I suspect that the Hebrew intended the את קולם to do double duty, thus "and they lifted up (their voice) and gave utterance," and the Greek should be taken in the same way. Num fails to render the suffix of קולם, and hex has added αυτων under the asterisk.[2] It should also be noted that Num has no equivalent for the preposition את either, and hex has accordingly added a την under the asterisk before φωνήν to represent it. The number of the verbs in MT is typically Hebrew in that when the verb precedes a collective noun (עדה), it is singular (תשא), but when it follows, it is plural (יתנו). Num uses the grammatically correct singular throughout.

Furthermore, "the people were weeping all that night." MT has בלילה ההוא as timer, i.e. has no equivalent for Num's ὅλον, and hex placed the word under the obelus. Since the weeping went on throughout the night, Num used the imperfect tense. MT has the plural verb ויבכו, even though its subject העם follows, presumably because העם has already been identified as כל העדה. In any event, Num continues with the singular.

14:2 MT has the Ni verb וילנו; LXX always renders the Ni or Hi of this verb either by διαγογγύζω or its simplex. Here Num has καὶ διεγόγγυζον (ἐπὶ Μωυσῆν καὶ Ἀαρών). The verb perforce has changed to the plural, since it is now υἱοὶ Ἰσραήλ that constitutes the subject. Since "murmuring, speaking rebelliously" is a process, Num correctly used the imperfect. MT, as usual, repeats the preposition על before Aaron as well, but in Greek this would be otiose, and hex did not add επι before Ἀαρών in spite of MT. In the tradition, εἶπαν appears in the

---

1. Pp.316—317.
2. See SS 99.

Classical second aorist inflection, ειπον, in V Byz+, but Num always uses the Hellenistic ending.

The people's complaint is given in two לו clauses; לו is a particle expressing unfulfilled wishes.³ This can be expressed in Greek either by εἰ plus an indicative in past tense, or by ὄφελον plus a past tense.⁴ Num used both; the first case is "ὄφελον we had died in Egypt land." The phrase ἐν γῇ Αἰγύπτῳ also occurs at 8:17 and 33:4. The structure בארץ מצרים also occurs at 3:13 where the bound structure is rendered more literally by ἐν γῇ Αἰγύπτου. The clause might be translated: Would that we had died in Egypt land." Then the correlative clause renders לו by εἰ, thus "or in this desert we had died."⁵

14:3 The first clause in MT is nominal, with the participle מביא as predicate. As usual, Num renders by a verbal clause using a present tense εἰσάγει to render the participle. The modifier εἰς τὴν γῆν ταύτην refers to the land of Canaan, about which they had received a pessimistic report. MT uses the common idiom לנפל בחרב as Yahweh's reason for bringing us into this land. Num interprets the figure "by the sword" correctly as a reference to warfare, ἐν πολέμῳ; "to fall by the sword" does mean to fall in warfare. The ἐν expresses instrument or means.⁶

The second clause does not repeat ἡμῶν for the τὰ παιδία; it is unnecessary in good Greek style, since the coordinate αἱ γυναῖκες is already modified by ἡμῶν. The majority A F V text has added ημων; the gloss is probably hex in origin. ἔσονται εἰς is a literal translation of יהיו ל, which means "will become; the Greek must take on this meaning as well, thus "our wives and children will become booty."

The last clause is a הלוא question in MT, i.e. it expects an affirmative answer. The Hebrew question says: "would not returning to Egypt be good for us"? Num makes this a strong affirmative statement. Instead of הלוא Num reads νῦν οὖν (βέλτιον): "Now then it is better for us to return to Egypt." This is no longer a question for discussion; it is a call for action.

14:4 The opening formula reads: "And they said איש לאחיו," i.e. "each one to his brother," which Num renders by ἕτερος τῷ ἑτέρῳ; this interprets what is

---
3. See GK 151e.
4. See Bl-D 359.1.
5. Aq, followed by The Others, repeats ὄφελον in place of εἰ.
6. See SS 121.

meant adequately.[7] Num does not represent the suffix of אחיו,[8] and hex has duly added an αυτου.

Num correctly renders the long forms נתנה and נשובה by hortatory subjunctives, δῶμεν (ἀρχηγὸν) καὶ ἀποστρέψωμεν. The word ἀρχηγόν "a chieftain," translates ראש.[9] The suggestion is clearly inciting to rebellion against the authority of Moses and Aaron; appointing a chieftain means a rejection of Moses and Aaron as their leaders, thus an ancient coup d'etat.

14:5 Num imitates MT by using a singular verb ἔπεσεν through attraction to the nearer element of a coordinate subject, thus "and Moses fell, and Aaron," or better, "and Moses and Aaron fell ἐπὶ πρόσωπον before all the assembly of Israelites," MT reads על פניהם, and hex has added αυτων under the asterisk after πρόσωπον. "Falling on one's face" is a symbol of complete despair and helplessness. This was done publicly, ἐναντίον πάσης συναγωγῆς of the Israelites. MT also has a doublet קהל עדה. The two words are synonyms, though קהל occurs only twelve times in the book, but in the other 11 cases it is always translated by συναγωγή. עדה, on the other hand, becomes συναγωγή 78 times. Actually, עדה is never translated in LXX by ἐκκλησία, whereas קהל is translated thus 75 times (and only 34 times by συναγωγή).[10] Which word was omitted by Num is unknown, but Origen thought that it was קהל,[11] and so he added εκκλησιας under the asterisk before συναγωγῆς.

14:6 The translator used a contrastive δέ, by which the actions of Iesous and Chaleb are contrasted with those of all the assembly of Israel in vv.2—5. In both cases, the parentage is described as ὁ τοῦ. This is exactly the same as the υιος

---

7. The idiom is variously rendered. Aq has καὶ εἶπεν ἀνὴρ πρὸς ἀδελφὸν αὐτοῦ, changing the plural verb to a singular to agree with the subject ἀνήρ. Sym translates as καὶ εἶπον ἕκαστος πρὸς τὸν ἀδελφὸν ἑαυτοῦ, whereas Theod has καὶ εἶπαν ἀνὴρ πρὸς τὸν ἀδελφὸν αὐτοῦ.
8. See SS 99.
9. Both Milgrom and Levine defend the NJPS rendering "Let us head back (for Egypt)" on the basis of Neh 9:17, but that is an echo of this verse, and so can hardly provide proof for the translation. Both NIV and NRSV support the interpretation of ראש as "head, chieftain."
10. The count is that of Dos Santos.
11. BHS states that Num omitted קהל, and orders "dl cf 7," but this fails to explain why קהל was present in the first place.

variant for the second case in the V b s^mg text. The genitive τῶν κατασκεψαμένων[12] represents the partitive מן of MT.[13] The tearing of garments is a token of extreme alarm, often attested in the Bible.

14:7 The Byz+ text has changed the Hellenistic εἶπαν to ειπον. What Iesous and Chaleb said to the entire assembly of Israelites was: "the land which we surveyed is extremely good." This is terser than MT's "As for the land which we traversed לתור אתה, good (is) הארץ extremely." MT uses the first part as a pendant construction, and then repeats הארץ as the subject of טובה plus מאד מאד. I have tried to represent the repeated adverb by using "extremely" for both MT and Num. The translator simplified the construction by omitting the second הארץ, and making the pendant of MT the subject of ἀγαθή ἐστιν. Hex fortunately did not add a translation of הארץ 2°, but did add παρηλθομεν εν αυτη και under the asterisk before κατεσκεψάμεθα to represent th Hebrew more precisely. This was in turn revised by Byz to read παρηλθομεν κατασκεψασθαι, a simpler, more elegant construction, and not another recensional rewrite on the basis of a Hebrew text.

14:8 The protasis in MT reads אם חפץ בנו יהוה "If Yahweh is pleased with us." The verb is usually rendered either by ἐθέλω (40 times) or by βούλομαι (21 times), but Num interprets uniquely by αἱρετίζει "to choose." This singular choice of lexeme places a somewhat different complexion on what God might do. The notion of choice stresses what would be the outcome of his satisfaction with Israel, viz. he would choose Israel. To the translator, the issue at stake is critical; the Lord might choose to reject his disobedient people; he might void the covenant he had made with them. Since the people had not lived up to their obligations, and were both disobedient and lacking in trust, he might cease choosing his people.[14] The verb is in present tense, and the apodosis is in the future; so: "if the Lord chooses us, he will bring us into this land and give it to us." The translator showed a good sense of style by not rendering the apodotic conjunction. For "land flowing with milk and honey," see comment at 13:28.

---

12. Aq and Sym read ἐκ τῶν κατασκόπων according to Montefalconius, as cited by Field, who, however, gives no source for the reading; nor was I able to find it.
13. See SS 169.
14. Instead of αἱρετίζει ἡμᾶς Theod has εὐδοκεῖ ἐν ἡμῖν; Aq reads βούλεται ἐν ἡμῖν, and Sym translates by εὐδοκεῖται ἡμῖν.

14:9 For ביהוה אל תמרדו "do not rebel against Yahweh," Num has ἀπὸ τοῦ κυρίου μὴ ἀποστάται γίνεσθε "do not become rebels (standing away) from the Lord." This is a fine interpretation of "rebel against"; it is an active turning away from, the antonym of "following after," of obedience. But hex, being excessively quantitative, and noting that two words were used to render תמרדו, placed γίνεσθε under the obelus, but a shorter μὴ ἀποστάται would be odd Greek.

On the contrary, "you must not be afraid of the people of the land, because they are food for us." Num contrasts this with becoming rebels, and uses δέ to stress the difference. Syntactically, ὑμεῖς serves as a nominative pendant, "but as for you." which is then followed by μὴ φοβηθῆτε "do not fear," a common pattern of encouragement. MT gives the reason for this in a כי clause: כי לחמנו הם. The הם refers to עם, and as often, Num uses the singular ἐστιν in agreement with λαόν, i.e. "they (it) are κατάβρωμα for us." The F *oII b+* text reads εισιν, which is hardly to be taken as a recensional correction; it is simply a variant ad sensum. The word κατάβρωμα occurs here for the first time, and is unique as a translation for לחם. Elsewhere it only translates derivatives from the root אכל. לחם occurs 273 times in the Bible, and usually (246 times),[15] it is translated by ἄρτος, and only once by κατάβρωμα (and once by its simplex).[16]

The next clause in MT is peculiar; it states סר צלם מעליהם "their shade has turned from upon them." This must be a metaphor for "protection" from the hot, burning sun of the East, and is usually interpreted as "their protection."[17] Since this contrasts with the next clause, ויהוה אתנו "and Yahweh is with us," the protection probably refers to their gods, i.e. their gods will turn from them, will be of no help when we invade their land. Usually, צל is translated either by σκιά (30 out of 49 cases) or by σκεπή (15 times).[18] The translator apparently did not know what to do with צלם, and contextualized by using ὁ καιρός, to which hex added αυτων under the asterisk, which once again shows how mechanically Origen went about his work in the hexapla. What the translator made of it was "the time has abandoned them." The term καιρός is difficult to translate; it refers to an appropriate moment, an opportune time. I suspect that what the translator

---

15. According to Dos Santos.
16. See the discussion in Daniel 138.
17. Tar⁰ interprets as תקפהון "their strength."
18. Theod and Aq translate צלם by ἡ σκιὰ αὐτῶν, and Sym, by ἡ σκεπὴ αὐτῶν.

wanted to say was that their moment in history has passed them by; after all, they are κατάβρωμα for us, "but the Lord is among us." Now our καιρός has arrived, so "do not fear them."

14:10 MT begins with ויאמרו with כל העדה as its subject. Since πᾶσα ἡ συναγωγή is singular, Num has used a singular verb (καὶ εἶπεν). The verb can mean "to think about," and the Greek must be understood in the same way. I would translate "And all the assembly had it in mind." The verb is modified by a complementary infinitive καταλιθοβολῆσαι αὐτοὺς ἐν λίθοις. The ἐν is obviously expressing means.[19] Both NJPS and NRSV render יאמרו by "they threatened." It should be said that hex "corrected" εἶπεν to the plural ειπαν to agree with the plural verb in MT.

But then "ἡ δόξα κυρίου appeared." What is meant by δόξα κυρίου is the visible presence of the Lord. Admittedly, no man can see God's face and live (Exod 33:20, and comp 16:7), but when the Lord reveals himself, it is his δόξα/כבוד that is seen, i.e. the shining effulgence, the glow that signifies the Lord's presence; in fact, NJPS translates the structure by "the Presence of the LORD." This then is "the glory of the Lord." Num, however, has added after the verb "ἐν νεφέλῃ (upon the tent of testimony)," which hex has placed under the obelus.[20] The gloss is not a false interpretation, since the "glory" usually appeared in "a cloud of fire." But in MT the glory of Yahweh appeared "in the tent of meeting," which Num renders by ἐπὶ τῆν σκηνῆς τοῦ μαρτυρίου ἐν πᾶσιν τοῖς υἱοῖς Ἰσραήλ "upon the tent of testimony among all the Israelites"; in other words, the glory appeared in the (pillar of) cloud over the tent. For the last phrase MT has "to all the Israelites," and the ἐν probably means "in the presence of."[21]

14:11 The verb ינאצני is vocalized by the Masoretes as plural, but the singular reading of Num is consistent with the consonantal Hebrew text. Hex, however, corrected the verb to the plural. The verb is often rendered in the Greek by παροξύνω, though the two are lexically not exact equivalents.[22] The Hebrew verb נאץ

---

19. See SS 121.
20. Pesh also reads "in a cloud," and Tar^J added בעננ י יקרא "in clouds of glory" as well.
21. As Dorival renders: "en présence de tous les fils d'Israël."
22. See Dorival 97–98.

means "to spurn, contemn, despise," whereas παροξύνω means "to exasperate."[23] The verbs following ἕως τίνος are both in the present tense, thereby stressing the process, thus "how long are they (the people) continuing to ...."

The verb יאמינו is modified by two ב phrases, but Num has πιστεύουσιν modified by the dative μοι, and by an ἐν phrase referring to the realm in which the failure to believe "in me" occurs, i.e. "in the face of all the signs which I performed in them." Incidentally, the relative clause modifying σημείοις has its pronoun οἷς also in the dative plural by attraction to its antecedent. This is atypical of Num,[24] in contrast to Deut, where attraction of case of relative pronouns to their antecedent was typical of that translator. Num usually inflects relative pronouns in accordance with the rules of grammatical relationships.

14:12 The use of the future tense contrasts with the present tense of v.11. God proposes πατάξω αὐτοὺς θανάτῳ, which is an odd statement if literally understood, i.e. as "I will smite them with death." But θάνατος has become a calque for דבר "pestilence," thus interpreted as a "fatal disease"; see Note at Exod 5:3.[25] In the tradition, the Byz text has introduced the divine statement by αφες με και "allow me and (I will smite)," presumably to mitigate the severity of the statement of divine intent.

The next clause in Num shows that θανάτῳ does not mean "death," but rather equals דבר, since "and I will destroy them" would otherwise be tautologous to the first clause. The Hi of ירש means "to dispossess," but a full dispossession usually means extermination. In fact, the most common rendering of הוריש is ἐξολεθρεύω (23 times), followed by ἐξαίρω (17 times), and by ἀπόλλυμι (8 times).[26]

In the final clause, God states "and I will make you καὶ τὸν οἶκον τοῦ πατρός σου into a nation greater and more numerous μᾶλλον ἢ τοῦτο." This expressed intent was also made at Exod 32:10, and particularly at Deut 9:14, for which see Note ad loc. The comparative μᾶλλον ἢ τοῦτο is exactly the same in

---

23. Aq translates by διασυροῦσίν με "they tear me in pieces," hence "disparage me." Theod and Sym accept Num, but read the plural παροξύνουσίν με, which is presumably in accordance with the reading tradition.
24. See THGN 99, where it is said that this is one of only two clear cases of such attraction noted in the book.
25. See also SS 125, as well as Dorival 98.
26. According to the count of Dos Santos.

the Deut passage.²⁷ Over against MT, Num includes as a coordinate accusative modifier of ποιήσω "and the house of your father," a phrase often found in the patriarchal promises; see e.g. Gen 12:1. Hex has placed the structure under the obelus as having no counterpart in MT.

14:13 With v.13 begins Moses' intercession on behalf of the people, and this continues through v.19. Rhetorically, the structures are extremely loose in this and the following verse, and are not always clearly connected; the translator at times had some difficulty in making good sense out of parts of it. The difficulty is that what Moses says is "and Egypt will hear that you (i.e. God) brought up by your power this people out of them (i.e. the Egyptians)." But of course Egypt, having experienced the plagues, the Exodus, etc., had experienced all of these things. The translation is, however, correct, and renders MT adequately. The final phrase, ἐξ αὐτῶν, must refer to the Egyptians, whereas its parent מקרבו with the singular suffix refers to Egypt, but the understanding that "Egypt" is not only a geographical, but also an ethnic concept is reasonable.

14:14 Num has a much clearer text than MT. The Hebrew begins with ואמרו אל יושב הארץ הזאת, i.e. the Egyptians will be reporting to the inhabitant of this land (referring to Canaan). This is followed by שמעו "they heard." I am not sure what this is supposed to mean. Num begins quite differently. It reads ἀλλὰ καὶ πάντες οἱ κατοικοῦντες ἐπὶ τῆς γῆς ταύτης ἀκηκόασιν "but also all those inhabiting this land have heard," which is fully clear. Whether or not Num had a different parent text is not known. If MT was its parent, Num did a good job of making sense out of it.

According to the accents placed by the Masoretes in the כי clause, אתה and יהוה both have disjunctive accents (a *munah* and a *zaqqeph qaton* resp), thereby making יהוה vocative, thus "you, o Yahweh," with בקרב העם הזה as predicate. Num has not understood it in this way. Its ὅτι σὺ εἶ κύριος makes εἶ κύριος predicate, i.e. "that you are the Lord among this people.²⁸

The relative clause has as its verb in MT נראה, vocalized as Ni third masculine singular suffixal form, thus "which appeared in plain sight (עין בעין), o

---

27. See SS 149.
28. Sym also takes יהוה as vocative: ὅτι σὺ εἶ κύριε.

Lord."²⁹ The antecedent of ὅστις must be the σύ of the ὅτι clause; this is apparent from the second person verb of the clause. Num has rendered the verb as though it were a participle, which the consonantal text does allow, i.e. it has used a second person present tense verb, ὀπτάζῃ, which is a hapax legomenon, presupposing a participle as parent text.³⁰ ὀπτάζομαι almost certainly means "is seen." The present tense might then well be translated as "you (who) are being seen ....," which the next clauses explain by the phenomena of ἡ νεφέλη σου and of the στύλῳ πυρός, both revelatory symbols.

Oddly, the translator rendered עמד as a past tense, though the Masoretes vocalized the word as a participle. What Num says is "and your cloud has stood over them," with the verb ἐφέστηκεν inflected in the perfect. This does make sense as a general statement of what has been and still is taking place; I would translate: "And your cloud has been standing over them (i.e. over the people as a constant protection), and you are going before them by day in a pillar of cloud, and in a pillar of fire by night." That means that the cloud standing over them is cloudy by day, but fiery by night. The accusatives τὴν ἡμέραν and τὴν νύκτα show extent of time, thus "during the day, during the night."

14:15 Num translates המתה (Hi of מות) "kill off" uniquely by ἐκτρίψεις "you would wipe out, erase," a colorful figure indeed.³¹ The clause sets the stage for the second one, and one might paraphrase the declarative clause as the protasis of a simple condition: should you wipe out the people as one person," or idiomatically, "in a single swipe," with the apodosis "then the nations ... would say." The ὅσοι clause uses the relative adjective in an absolute sense,³² i.e. "all who." The nominative is used thus, even though its antecedent, ἔθνη, is neuter; so "then the nations, all those who heard your name, would say, as follows."³³ The collocation ἀκηκόασιν τὸ ὄνομά σου really means "are aware of your reputation."

---

29. Aq translated the כי and אשר clauses as follows: ὅτι σὺ εἶ κύριος ἐν ἐγκάτῳ τοῦ λαοῦ τούτου ὃς ὀφθαλμὸν ἐν ὀφθαλμοῖς ὁρᾷ σὺ κύριε.
30. Milgrom defends the MT tense by having the verb refer "to the Sinaitic theophany beheld by the elders," i.e. a reference to Exod 24:10. I suppose it is possible to take it in this way, but it is far from obvious.
31. For the deliberative future, see Porter 424—425.
32. For which, see Bauer sub ὅσος,η,ον 2.
33. A neuter plural subject, here τὰ ἔθνη, occurs 39 times in the book, and 36 times the predicate is singular, which is good Classical usage. Here, however, ἐροῦσιν is used, probably to make the use of ὅσοι possible. See SS 197.

ὄνομα can mean "reputation," especially if it is something heard, and it can render שמע. That this does not presuppose a parent text שמך is clear when one examines how the noun שמע, which occurs 16 times in the Bible, is translated in LXX. Unique renderings by ἀγγελία, ἀκουστός, κλέος may be disregarded. Significant is the fact that the more literal ἀκοή is used only seven times, while ὄνομα occurs six times.³⁴

14:16 What the nations will be saying is: "because of the Lord's not being able to bring this people into the land which he swore to them, κατέστρωσεν αὐτούς in the wilderness." The מבלתי with the infinitive יכלת is elegantly rendered by a παρὰ τὸ μή plus infinitive, thus "by not being able" or "because of not being able." The translation of the verse is excellent except for the main verb. In MT this is וישחטם "he slaughtered them." Since καταστρώννυμι means "stretch out," it seems obvious that the translator mistakenly transposed the letters חט and read וישטחם "and he stretched them out."³⁵ Incidentally, hex pedantically added a και before the verb, thereby hardly improving the sense, but thereby numerically equalling the Hebrew word for word.

14:17 MT has Moses pray "And now יגדל נא כח אדני as you spoke saying." Num does not translate literally. Instead of יגדל נא it reads ὑψωθήτω "let ... be exalted," which is more specific than "pray, let ... be great." The rendering of יגדל by this verb does occur in Gen four times, and recurs once each in Ios and in LXX Dan.³⁶ Since it is unusual to speak of ἰσχύς being exalted, an A M Byz+ variant text has changed the noun to χειρ, which makes excellent sense, but represents a simplification of an original ἰσχύς.³⁷ Then Num changes כח אדני to ἡ

---

34. According to HR.
35. Whether this is an application of a rabbinic rule as Dorival suggests with his "il est possible aussi que le traducteur ait interprété la deuxième racine à la lumière de la première, par interversion des deux dernière consonnas" is indeed possible, but I suspect that the translator simply misread the word. After all, the Lord had proposed to Moses "πατάξω αὐτοὺς θανάτῳ καὶ ἀπολῶ αὐτούς in v.12, not simply to strew them in the desert.
36. According to HR.
37. Modern translators have mitigated the figure of "strength being great" in different ways. NRSV remains close to the Hebrew with "let the power (of the LORD) be great." Incidentally the word "LORD" must be a proof reader's error for "Lord," since MT reads אדני. NJPS has "let my LORD's (sic!) forbearance be great," while NIV translates "may the Lord's strength be displayed."

ἰσχύς σου κύριε, as though reading כחך יהוה.[38] Probably the reading σου is simply Num's adaptation to the direct address of Moses' prayer.

The verb in the ὃν τρόπον clause is εἶπας, but MT has דברת, which is usually rendered by ἐλάλησας. One may presume that the parent text read אמרת, which an early reviser changed in view of the לאמר following the דברת. This is admittedly speculative.

14:18 The ὃν τρόπον εἶπας (λέγων) of v.17 reflects Exod 34:6—7, but adapted to the present context. For the general meaning of the passage, see Notes ad loc. The first three items occur at the end of v.6, and the next three, ἀφαιρῶν ἀνομίας καὶ ἀδικίας καὶ ἁμαρτίας, obtain word for word in v.7. Num added καθαρισμῷ before οὐ καθαριεῖ, substituted ἀποδιδοὺς ἁμαρτίας (of fathers upon children) for ἐπάγων ἀνομίας. "Upon children" is followed in Exod by τέκνων ἐπὶ τρίτην μαὶ τετάρτην γενεάν, but more simply here by ἕως τρίτης καὶ τετάρτης. MT has no equivalent for καὶ ἀληθινός, but Num follows the ואמת of Sam.[39] Similarly, Num follows Sam's וחטאה with its ἁμαρτίας.[40] τὸν ἔνοχον has no basis in MT, and hex has placed it under the obelus. It was probably borrowed from Exod 34:7, which has γενεάν, though the precise genitive equivalent is found in the Ten Words (20:5).

V.b describes the negative characteristic of the Lord. I would translate v.b as "and in no way would he declare clean the culpable by repaying the sins of fathers upon children up to the third and fourth (generation)." This differs slightly from MT which reads "and in no way would he declare innocent, visiting the iniquity of ...." καθαρίζω does occur in LXX for the Pi of נקה five times, though ἀθῳόω and/or the adjective ἀθῷος are more frequent and more exact (11 times). I would understand καθαρίζω here as having a declarative sense as well. The majority A F M V text has added γενεας at the end of the verse, but this is an intrusion from the Exod passage.

14:19 Moses makes no apologies for his people; he simply asks God to forgive them. As usual, the translator disregards the נא particle, and hex made no attempt to recognize it. As in v.18 עון is translated by the noun ἁμαρτία, which might

---
38. Many mss do read יהוה instead of אדני.
39. Kenn 75,111,193 also added ואמת, whereas Kenn 109 added אמתו.
40. Kenn 18 also added וחטאה after פשע.

more exactly be used for the root חטא, but translators tended to be inexact on terms for wrongdoing. He prays that God might forgive the עון העם הזה, which Num translates by τὴν ἁμαρτίαν τῷ λαῷ τούτῳ. The dative is probably one of advantage, i.e. "forgive the sin for this people." The measure to be applied is κατὰ τὸ μέγα ἔλεός σου "according to your great compassion." The bound element of גדל חסדך is well rendered by an adjective.[41]

In the καθάπερ clause, ἵλεως ἐγένου "you were gracious" uniquely translates נשאתה. The verb נשא "to lift, carry," and so "take away, remove" in the sense of removing guilt, thus forgive, pardon, which is probably intended here. On the other hand, it could be understood in the sense of "carry, support," thus "as you gave support to this people," though in the context of סלח in both vv.19 and 20, probably "to remove guilt" is intended here. In any event, Num understood it in the sense of offering clemency for sin. Instead of לעם הזה, Num has αὐτοῖς which precedes ἐγένου; the majority A F V text has transposed the two words, which does come closer to MT, where "to this people" follows the verb. The variant text is, however, not recensional; neither O nor the Byz text support the variant word order.

14:20 MT has Yahweh say סלחתי "I have forgiven," which in effect means "I do forgive," i.e. a state of pardon has been achieved. Num has added the addressee πρὸς Μωυσῆν, which is admittedly not necessary, though factually correct. Hex has placed the phrase under the obelus. Num translates סלחתי by a verbal figure in present tense: ἵλεως αὐτοῖς εἰμι, again adding an αὐτοῖς to represent the recipients. This too has been placed under the obelus in hex. The use of ἵλεως plus linking verb was used in v.19 to render נשאתה, whereas סלח was rendered by ἄφες (imperative of ἀφίημι). The translator correctly understood סלח and נשא as synonyms.

14:21 MT begins with ואולם introducing vv.21—24; this signifies change of construction from what went before.[42] The section deals with reservations about what God had said in v.20. V.21 is an asseveration. What is meant is "but as certain as the fact that I live and that the glory of Yahweh fills all the earth." Then vv.22—24 present what will take place.

---

41. See SS 66—67.
42. GK 167b calls this an anacolouthon.

Num translates v.a literally, except for the initial *waw*, which it did not recognize, and the formula ζῶ ἐγώ "I am alive," must also be understood as an asseveration. It has, however, added a doublet, καὶ ζῶν τὸ ὄνομά μου "and my name is living"; this has no equivalent in MT, and hex has placed it under the obelus. The doublet illustrates how the Alexandrian understood ὄνομα as surrogate for the person. It may well constitute a forerunner of the common practice of reading השם "the name" wherever the tetragrammaton occurs.[43]

V.b is part of the asseveration formula as well. MT reads וימלא כבוד יהוה את כל הארץ. The Masoretes have vocalized the verb as Ni, which is a passive transform from a Qal or Pi. In the sense of "be filled," it can hardly have כבוד יהוה as subject. Num had no trouble with the clause, since it had only a consonantal text as parent, and translated: "and the glory of the Lord shall fill all the earth."[44]

14:22 The verse begins with an asseverative כי in MT, and its translation by ὅτι is a calque for כי. In other words, what is meant is "Assuredly, all these men who were seeing my glory." That the participle must be taken as past is clear from v.b where the verbal clause is in past tense. Num translates this word for word by ὅτι πάντες οἱ ἄνδρες οἱ ὁρῶντες τὴν δόξαν μου.[45]

Coordinate with τὴν δόξαν μου is καὶ τὰ σημεῖα ἃ ἐποίησα ἐν Αἰγύπτῳ καὶ ἐν τῇ ἐρήμῳ ταύτῃ. MT has a first singular suffix on the coordinate noun, ואת אתתי, for which hex added μου under the asterisk after σημεῖα. On the other hand, MT does not read a pronoun modifying במדבר, and so hex has placed ταύτῃ under the obelus to mark that fact. Presumably, the translator added ταύτῃ to remind the reader that the Israelites were still in the wilderness of Paran; see 13:4,27.

V.b with its καὶ ἐπείρασάν με for וינסו אתי put the divine criticism into a temporal perspective by past tense verbs. This is modified in Num by τοῦτο δέκατον "this tenth (time)." MT has a fuller זה עשר פעמים "these ten times."

---

43. Dorival 62 makes an interesting reference to Tar^N, which reads for v.a as follows: וברם חי וקיים אנא במימרי לעלם.
44. Aq tried to represent the Ni with his καὶ ἐμπλησθήσεται τῆς δόξης ΠΙΠΙ πᾶσα ἡ γῆ (retroverted from Syh), but he had to make the את phrase the subject as well.
45. Sym translates this by πάντες γὰρ οἱ ἄνθρωποι οἱ ἰδόντες τὴν δόξαν μου. For Theod and Aq only πάντες οἱ ἄνδρες οἱ ὁρῶντες is extant, which equals the Num text.

Whether "tenth time" or "ten times" are to be taken literally is not clear. NJPS, e.g. translates "these many times."[46]

This is followed by "and not εἰσήκουσάν μου τῆς φωνῆς," which renders שמעו בקולי. The choice of an εἰσ- compound is exactly right: "they did not listen to, i.e. obey my voice." The A F majority text which rearranges the modifier as της φωνης μου may well be recensional.[47]

14:23 ἦ μὴν οὐκ renders the אם introducing an oath formula, and can be rendered by "surely not." What is meant by ἦ μήν is well rendered by Dorival as "je le jure";[48] it does involve an oath, an "I swear it (that not)." What is sworn is that "not will they see the land which I swore to their fathers."[49] MT then continues with a parallel statement: "And no one of these who contemned me shall see it," which is an accurate translation, though with a contrastive δέ in the final clause of the verse in Num.

Num has added a corrective based on the information given later in the chapter (vv.29—35, and comp 32:11). The punishment is not to be applied across the board, "but their children, who are here with me, all those who (ὅσοι) have not known good nor evil, every inexperienced youngster (νεώτερος, i.e. younger person), to these I will give the land." This has no equivalent in MT or any other specific source, but is an addition on the part of Num. Hex has quite correctly placed this addition under the obelus. This is a creation of the translator, who apparently wanted to be sure that readers would not misunderstand God's intentions. The oath not to allow the Israelites to enter the land of promise is not to apply to children, and the death penalty, according to v.29, is to apply only to those ἀπὸ εἰκοσαετοῦς καὶ ἐπάνω.

This gives us a new perspective on the translator. On the whole, he was ready to render the Hebrew into Greek carefully, but he did not do so mindlessly. If the Hebrew might mislead the reader by an absolute statement on God's part, he believed called upon to interpret the mind of God, particularly when in

---

46. Dorival cites a fourth century writer's attempt to identify "les neuf mises à l'épreuve de Seigneur par les fils d'Israël antérieures à l'épisode de Nb 13—14," which to my mind is useless speculation.
47. As Sym did with της φωνης μου.
48. P.323.
49. Theod and Aq render אם יראו את הארץ by a word for word εἰ ὄψονται τὴν γῆν; Sym has a simple negative: οὐκ ὄψονται τὴν γῆν.

another context it was clear that God did not intend the absoluteness of his stated determination to destroy the recalcitrant people. In other words, the qualifications he made were correct; they just were not present in MT here.

This makes the contrastive δέ for the final clause sensible: "But all those who have provoked me shall not see it." In the tradition, a popular A F V text has changed the aorist participle παροξύναντες to a present one, παροξυνοντες, "who are provoking (me)," but this is unnecessary; the default aorist is fully satisfactory, in spite of τοῦτο δέκατον of v.22.

14:24 παῖς is used to render עבד as in Gen; it is also found in Num, it occurs seldom, for עבד only five times; cf comment at 12:7. Of Chaleb it is said that "there was another spirit ἐν αὐτῷ καὶ ἐπηκολούθησέν μοι." MT has עמו instead of "in me," but Num understands πνεῦμα as residing in a person, rather than with one. The following clause interprets וימלא אחרי; the idiom recurs at 32:12, where συνεπηκολούθησεν is used in a similar context; comp v.11 as well; this is normally understood as meaning "fully followed after (me)," i.e. it is zeugmatic for "fulfilled going after me."[50] See also Note at Deut 1:36, where the idiom is translated quite differently. Num translates the verb in this sense by using the compound verb ἐπακολουθέω "to follow closely," so to obey; the אחרי is then correctly rendered by a dative pronoun μοι.

The apodosis to the ὅτι clause is identifiable as such by the use of future verbs. Its introduction by καί is a crass Hebraism, imitating the והביאתיו of MT. In the tradition, the καί is omitted by a B V x+ text as a stylistic improvement. The καί can only have been based on the Hebrew, and constitutes original text.[51] The promise is twofold: a) "I will bring him into the land into which he had gone ἐκεῖ." The ἐκεῖ renders the שמה of the relative clause of MT "whither he had entered," and is also a Hebraism, which is best omitted in translation, since it is already expressed by εἰς ἥν. b) "and his offspring shall possess it." It might be noted as well that the amplification by the translator in v.23 also avoids any misunderstanding of the promise here that Chaleb's offspring was to possess the land of promise; see discussion at v.23.

---

50. See GK 119gg.
51. See THGN 101.

14:25 For the opening והעמלקי Num does not recognize the gentilic ending, and simply has ὁ δὲ ’Αμαλήκ. In the tradition, an O ms, 376, has αμαληκιτης, which may well be a hex correction. Num uses a plural present tense verb κατοικοῦσιν, in order to agree with the coordinate subject "Amalek and the Chananite." In MT, the clause is nominal, with the singular participle יושב serving as predicate.

V.b uses imperative verbal forms for פנו וסעו לכם. Num translates by ἐπιστράφητε ὑμεῖς καὶ ἀπάρατε. Num has rendered לכם by the nominative ὑμεῖς, but transposed it after the first verb. This created a great deal of activity in the tradition. The majority A F M text simply moved ὑμεῖς after ἀπάρατε. So did hex, which would have been sufficient, but Origen also added αυτοι under the asterisk. The Byz text merely added αυτους.[52] Their journey was to lead into the desert ὁδὸν θάλασσαν ἐρυθράν, which interprets המדבר דרך ים סוף. Since Num has εἰς τὴν ἔρημον for המדבר, it may have had the Sam text, המדברה, as parent text, though not necessarily so. At Exod 13:18 MT reads דרך המדבר ים סוף, which is translated by ὁδὸν τὴν εἰς τὴν ἔρημον εἰς τὴν ἐρυθρὰν θάλασσαν. In Exod ים סוף is always rendered in transposed order; see Note at Exod 10:19.

14:26 MT reads וידבר, which normally becomes καὶ ἐλάλησεν in Num, but here it has καὶ εἶπεν. This might well reflect a parent ויאמר, since the two translations ויאמר/εἶπεν and וידבר/καὶ ἐλάλησεν are regular in Num.[53]

14:27 MT divides the verse afer the first relative clause; i.e. it has עלי 1° under the *ethnach*. The עד מתי query thus includes the relative clause. Furthermore, some verb such as "shall I abide" must be understood. This is also true of its translation in Num where the accusative collocation has no verb expressed for it to modify; i.e. τὴν συναγωγὴν τὴν πονηρὰν ταύτην is anacolouthic. What it says is "how long—this evil assembly"? In MT, the אשר clause must be understood as referring to the assembly, thus "which are murmuring against me." One might then render MT by "how long (can I bear) this evil assembly (probably referring to those who brought in the evil report) which are causing murmurings against me"?

Num can not be understood in this way. The ἕως τίνος question pertains only to "this evil assembly." Then the ἅ clause must be taken, along with τὴν

---

52. See THGN 102.
53. See THGN 128.

γόγγυσιν of the Israelites along with its ἥν clause as two distinct, though asyndetic, modifiers of ἀκήκοα. In other words, v.a comes to an end with the question. V.b is the statement about what "I heard."

The first relative clause has no antecedent expressed; ἅ must be taken absolutely as "those things which they are murmuring before me." The reference of αὐτοί must be to the surveyors who brought in a negative report. This is clear from the way in which the second relative clause is interpreted. The ἥν refers to τὴν γόγγυσιν of the Israelites, which is also true of MT, i.e. אשר 2° refers to תלנות. But in MT the clause is again a nominal one, identical to the המה מלינים of the first clause. The first clause was rendered by the usual pattern of pronoun, αὐτοί, plus present tense verb as predicate, γογγύζουσιν. But here Num was troubled by the repetition of אשר המה מלינים, and so he makes a distinction by changing the second one. Instead of MT's "which they are creating murmurings against me," it omits המה, misrepresents both the participle as a past tense, ἐγόγγυσαν, and עלי, by his περὶ ὑμῶν. Thus two things are provoking the Lord: the rebellious attitude of the surveyors against me, and the rebellious stance which the Israelites have been taking over against Moses and Aaron.[54] Hex did add an αυτοι under the asterisk to represent the omitted המה,[55] but this really does not change the Greek so as to equal MT, except for this single word. Its omission by Num was clearly intentionally made to create two quite different matters which the Lord heard.

14:28 MT begins with an imperative אמר, which Num renders correctly by εἶπον.[56] For ἦ μήν, see comment at v.23. Here it appears positively, i.e. not for אם as at v.23, but for אם לא. The perfect tense form, λελαλήκατε is well chosen, since it suggests that what "you have spoken in my hearing (literally, in my ears)" remains alive in God's memory. The reference is to the rebellious

---

54. Tar^J also distinguished the two clauses by rendering the first relative clause by דמתחברין עלי "who were gathering themselves together against me," and the second one literally, by דהינון מתרעמין עלי.
55. As did The Others.
56. Not to be taken as first singular aorist as Dorival's "je leur ai dit" has it. The inflection could be analyzed in isolation in this way, since the aorist imperative and the first singular indicative are identical in form, but MT's אמר is here determinative. Dorival is not alone in this, however. The *d* text changed λέγει (in "says the Lord") to λεγω, which must have been rooted in misunderstanding εἶπον as well; this is particularly confusing, since the Byz text had also changed εἶπον to ειπε.

words of v.2; the Israelites' wish that "in this desert would that we had died" will return to haunt them; they will indeed die in this desert! This becomes clear in the following verse.

14:29 Num says "In this desert your κῶλα will fall." The word means "limbs," and is the most common rendering in LXX for פגרי "corpses" (seven out of 17 instances). It might be noted that the verb πεσεῖται is singular, which in Classical terms agrees with a neuter plural subject.[57] Coordinated with κῶλα are πᾶσα ἡ ἐπισκοπὴ ὑμῶν καὶ οἱ κατηριθμημένοι ὑμῶν "all your review and those which were numbered." The word ἐπισκοπή means "review," but with πᾶσα must refer to those reviewed. MT reads פקדיכם, which is usually rendered by ἐπεσκεμμένοι in Num (passim in ch.2). The singular was probably chosen in view of the לכל מספרכם which followed. What MT probably meant was "all those who were counted in your survey (or census)." But by distinguishing the two terms through using καί to render ל, it created some confusion. In fact, לכל simply became καί in Num, which hex tried to repair by adding παντες under the asterisk. The confusion arose from the fact that whose who were surveyed are those numbered;[58] in other words, the Num text is a hendiadys; the two words constitute a single concept, that of a census report, as a counting review.

The ἀπό phrase refers to κατηριθμημένοι, i.e. those numbered from twenty years (of age) and upward. These constituted ὅσοι ἐγόγγυσαν ἐπ' ἐμοί.

14:30 אם introduces a further part of the divine oath; it is a strong negative statement. Its translation by εἰ is in imitation of the Hebrew, and constitutes a real calque.[59] In fact, Dorival paraphrases by "j'en fais serment, vous, vous n'entrerez pas."[60] It should be taken as a further element of the oath based on the ζῶ ἐγώ of v.28. In other words, "As I live, ... if you will enter," i.e. "you will not enter."

The land is identified by a relative clause as that "on which I stretched out my hand to settle you (on it)." The divine stretching out of the hand is a meta-

---

57. See SS 197.
58. Actually, Kenn 69,128*,225 had וכל instead of לכל, which as possible parent text for Num would make the possibility for confusion even greater. And Kenn 17,181 read ולכל, which combines both readings.
59. For the oath formula, see Harl 76.
60. P.326.

phor for swearing an oath; what is meant is "which I had sworn to settle you on it." MT has בה for the prepositional phrase, and hex has corrected ἐπ' αὐτῆς to εν αυτη.[61]

Only two adults would escape the predicted fate of the people: Chaleb, the son of Iephonne, and Iesous, the son of Naue. For Naue, see the discussion at 13:9(8). Num varies the rendering of בן, the first one as υἱός, and the second one as ὁ τοῦ; the two are fully synonymous.

14:31 MT's וטפכם is obviously a collective, which Num understood by its καὶ τὰ παιδία. Hex has added υμων under the asterisk to represent the suffix.[62] The relative clause, ἃ εἴπατε ἐν διαρπαγῇ ἔσεσθαι, is a reference to v.3, which see. The infinitive ἔσεσθαι plus ἐν means "would become (booty)." The majority A F M text changes this ἐν phrase to εἰς διαρπαγην, which is what v.3 reads. Either phrase makes sense, but the ἐν construction was chosen, since it was supported by the earliest extant witness, cod B.

Instead of MT's "and ידעו the land which מאסתם, Num has κληρονομήσουσιν "they shall possess" the land. Num substitutes for the rather strange notion of "knowing" the land, the usual promise "they shall possess it." Similarly, Num renders מאסתם "you contemned, despised" uniquely by ἀπέστητε, i.e. "(which) you rejected." Num makes the contrast between what the people alleged in v.3 and what God now says even more decisive; it is a case of possessing vs rejecting, rather than knowing vs despising.

14:32 The opening ופגריכם אתם is peculiar; one would have expected ואתם פגריכם. In any event the אתם must be pendentive, i.e. "(and) as for you, your corpses." Num disregarded the pronoun entirely. For κῶλα, see comment at v.29.[63]

14:33 Num uses a contrastive δέ to set the τὰ κῶλα ὑμῶν of v.32 over against "your sons." νεμόμενοι "ranging" translates the Hebrew רעים "shepherds." The picture created is that of shepherds who roam about the desert. What is meant is

---

61. The Others also render בה by ἐν αὐτῇ.
62. Num tends to render suffixes less frequently than the earlier books of the Pentateuch; see SS 99.
63. Theod and Aq read πτώματα, and Sym has σώματα.

that the people will remain unsettled in the desert rather than be settled agriculturalists in the land of promise. ἔτη is an accusative of extent of time; this unsettled, seminomadic existence will continue for an entire generation, i.e. "forty years."

This type of existence is a case of the children bearing the sins of the fathers; "and they (your children) shall carry your prostitution." The term πορνείαν occurs only here in the Pentateuch as a characterization of the Israelite people, a term which was to become popular in the prophets, especially Hosea and Ezekiel. MT has a plural word זנותיכם "your acts of prostitution." The term is apt as a description of Israel's unfaithfulness to its Lord.[64]

This situation will remain "until your limbs are destroyed in the desert." MT reads "until your corpses are consumed in the desert." What is meant is until your carcasses which lie unburied will have disintegrated. תם means "to be finished, completed, come to an end." For κῶλα, see comment at v.29.[65] The O x text has changed the verb ἀναλωθῇ to εξαναλωθη, which apparently shows the influence of Theod on hex.

14:34 An explanation of the forty years. "According to the number of days which you surveyed the land, forty days—a day per year—you must take up your sins for forty years." MT repeats יום לשנה in order to display "an expressly *distributive* sense,[66] i.e. "a day per year," which Num has expressed by the genitive in ἡμέραν τοῦ ἐνιαυτοῦ. Hex has added a second ημεραν του ενιαυτου under the asterisk to show this repetition.

The last clause is difficult in MT. It reads וידעתם את תנואתי. The noun only occurs twice in the Bible; it is also found at Job 33:10, where the plural noun obtains, rendered as μέμψιν by LXX, signifying what God finds עלי. The parallel clause reads "he considers me לאויב לו (as an enemy to him)." Precisely what תנואה means is not at all clear. Since the verb הניא means "to hinder, frustrate," NJPS translates "what it means to thwart me," and NIV reads "what it is like to have me against you" (which sounds to me as though the translator was himself

---

64. Instead of ἀνοίσουσιν, Theod and Aq have the more literal ἀροῦσιν; Sym reads βαστάζουσι.
65. Aq translates by τελειωθῶσιν πτώματα ὑμῶν, and Sym reads συντελέσθη τὰ σώματα {ὑμῶν}. Theod has the verb ἐξαναλωθῇ.
66. GK 123d.

frustrated). NRSV cautiously supplies "my displeasure."[67] Num obviously did not understand the word either, and contextualizes by τὸν θυμὸν τῆς ὀργῆς μου.[68] Origen found Num to have one noun too many, and placed τῆς ὀργῆς under the obelus.

14:35 For ἦ μήν as translation for אם לא, see comment at v.28. Num omits the "all" in לכל העדה הרעה הזאת, possibly intentionally. After all, the punishment of "death in the desert" would not affect the entire assembly, since those under twenty years of age were excluded, as were Chaleb and Iesous. The omission of כל makes a more consistent text. Hex has, of course, added πασῃ under the asterisk to represent it.

This assembly is characterized as τῇ ἐπισυνεσταμένῃ ἐπ' ἐμέ. The compound recurs at 27:3, where it describes the rebellion of the assembly of Kore, in both cases representing הנועדים "those who banded together." The double compound is somewhat more conspiratorial in intent; it means "to join up, come together in a conspiracy."

The punishment is clear: "in this desert they shall be destroyed, and there they will die." The two verbs are synonyms, and reflect MT in their stress on the certainty of the penalty. It might be noticed that the verb תמם was rendered in v.33 by ἀναλωθῇ, but here it is rendered by the compound ἐξαναλωθήσονται; the intention is to intensify the verbal action, i.e. be fully destroyed.

14:36 The two verses, 36 and 37 can be read together, with the predicate, ἀπέθανον, not occurring until v.37. V.36 refers to the surveyors of the land who brought in an evil report. It is, however, also possible to read the two verses separately, in which case οἱ ἄνθρωποι plus the relative clause would constitute the subject, and the predicate introduced by καί would be παραγενηθέντες διεγόγγυσαν plus its modifiers. Then v.37 would have ἀπέθανον as predicate, with οἱ ἄνθρωποι—πονηρά constituting the subject, and the ἐν structure modifying the verb.

The predicate reduces the verb וישבו to an attributive participle, thus "on returning they murmured." It must be admitted that introducing the predicate

---

67. Levine 370 interprets by "punishment that the denial of God will bring upon them."
68. The Tar and Pesh all render the word by "you murmured against me." Vulg has *ultionem meam*, which is closer to Num.

with καί is unusual, but it patterns on the analogy of the apodotic καί. I would render the pattern as "and as for the men who ..., when (καί) they returned they murmured." The verb ילונו has been "emended" to read וילינו as a Qere reading, but the Kethib makes adequate sense, and is reflected by Num. MT has the phrase עליו modifying the verb, i.e. against him (i.e. Moses), but Num has κατ' αὐτῆς (i.e. "against the land"). What is meant is that they reported in muttering fashion against the land "to the assembly." MT reads את כל העדה. The את undoubtedly promoted the Qere reading, whereas the Qal would prefer an addressee given, as in the πρός of Num. Hex has inserted πασαν under the asterisk before "the assembly" to represent the omitted כל, for which omission, see comment at v.35.

The unmarked infinitive is explicative in character. Their murmuring against the land was concretized by ἐξενέγκαι ῥήματα πονηρὰ περὶ τῆς γῆς. The adjectival phrase "evil words" both here and similarly in v.37 translates דבה, which was interpreted quite differently at 13:33(32). Here, however, it renders דבה more literally; the report is a *ν* evil report.

14:37 The "men" are described as οἱ κατείπαντες κατὰ τῆς γῆς πονηρά "those speaking evil (words) against the land." In MT these are מוצאי דבת הארץ "those bringing out the land's דבה," in which "land's" would be an objective genitive. In the tradition, the Byz text has added εκεινοι after ἄνθρωποι; this is a typically Byz case of an explicating gloss, here showing that the ἄνθρωποι are the same as those of v.36. For דבת, see comment at v.36.[69] In the tradition, κατείπαντες appears in the Classical inflection in the majority F text as κατειπόντες, but Num always uses the Hellenistic inflection of the aorist for all forms of εἶπα.[70] In v.36 MT read דבה על הארץ, which Num rendered by ῥήματα πονηρὰ περὶ τῆς γῆς. Here MT reads דבת הארץ רעה, but Num simplifies by reading (in modification of κατείπαντες) κατὰ τῆς γῆς πονηρά, i.e. disregarding either דבת or רעה. The majority A F text has illustrated this uncertainty by transposing κατὰ τῆς γῆς and πονηρά. The penalty for speaking evil words against the land of promise was death "ἐν τῇ πληγῇ before the Lord."

---

69. Aq renders מוצאי דבת by οἱ ἐξενέγκατες διαβολήν.
70. See THGN 123.

14:38 The exception to v.37. Both "Iesous son of Naue and Chaleb son of Iephonne survived of those men who had gone out to survey the land." For Naue, see the discussion at 13:9(8). The translation "survived" reflects ἔζησαν "shall live" with a partitive ἀπό phrase modifying it.[71]

14:39 Moses communicated "these words" to all the Israelites. The reference of τὰ ῥήματα ταῦτα is probably to vv.27—35. In the tradition, hex has added παντα before "these words" under the asterisk. This means that the ms used by Origen read כל before הדברים.[72] The reaction of the people was ἐπένθησεν "mourned," for MT's plural ויתאבלו. As usual, העם is taken as a collective, and a plural verb is used, whereas Num has in strict grammatical concord used the singular. That the Israelites should mourn greatly, probably refers to the plague which killed off the ten who had brought in the evil report; see v.37.

14:40 Num has subordinated the first clause to the next one by changing the verb וישכמו to an attributive participle, ὀρθρίσαντες, and deleting the conjunction of ויעלו, thus "and rising early in the morning they went up." The subject must be πάντες υἱοὺς Ἰσραήλ of v.39.

What they say is ἰδοὺ οἵδε ἡμεῖς ἀναβησόμεθα "behold here we are going to go up," i.e. directly contrary to what the Lord had said. The demonstrative pronoun οἵδε has no counterpart in MT. Taken with ἡμεῖς it has the effect of separating the "we" from Moses distinctly by a "we who are here (will go up)."

The reason given for their change of mind is ὅτι ἡμάρτομεν. The verb in both Num and MT has the basic meaning of "making a mistake." I would understand both MT and Num to signify not so much a confession of sin as of having made an error in judgment, which the people would now rectify: in effect, they would nullify God's pronouncement of vv.27—35.

14:41 Moses reacts to the people's stated intention to invade contrary to the Lord's statement by asking ἵνα τί ὑμεῖς "why are you (transgressing the word of the Lord)?" Since MT has למה זה (אתם), hex has added τουτο after τί under the asterisk to represent the זה; see comment at 11:20. The interrogative clause is nominal in MT, אתם עברים, and Num follows its usual translation pattern by

---

71. See SS 159.
72. As did Kenn 1,4,144[vid],151,186.

ὑμεῖς plus a present tense verb, παραβαίνετε. Num correctly interprets the intent of פי יהוה by its ῥῆμα κυρίου. What פי means is that which goes out of the mouth, viz. the word.

Moses then warns the people: והוא לא תצלח "and it will not succeed." The pronominal subject היא (written as הוא) refers to the intention of the Israelites as expressed in v.40.[73] Num translates this freely by οὐκ εὔοδα ἔσται ὑμῖν.[74] The ὑμῖν has no counterpart in MT, and hex has placed it under the obelus.[75] The והוא also has no express equivalent in Num, but its omission constitutes no problem; οὐκ εὔοδα ἔσται can only refer to the intention of the Israelites, which Moses has already branded as παραβαίνετε. The feminine adjective was probably used in imitation of the feminine verb תצלח.

14:42 Moses bluntly warns the people not to attempt an invasion "because the Lord is not μεθ' ὑμῶν." This correctly understands בקרבכם "in your midst." If the Lord is not in your midst, he will then not be "with you," should you go up. The warning of disaster is expressed in a paratactic clause in imitation of MT: καὶ πεσεῖσθε πρὸ προσώπου τῶν ἐχθρῶν ὑμῶν, a warning similar to that expressed "if you should not obey me," at Lev 26:17, where the verb נגפתם is also rendered by πεσεῖσθε; see Note ad loc. The translation is free, but fully adequate.

14:43 For ὁ 'Αμαλήκ instead of the gentilic noun העמלקי, see comment at v.25. The popular A F M V has omitted the article, since proper nouns are commonly unarticulated in Greek, but the article is original text. Unusual is the nominal ὅτι clause in that no linking verb is used to indicate the predicate, but Num in imitation of MT has ὁ 'Αμαλὴκ καὶ ὁ Χαναναῖος as subject, and ἐκεῖ ἔμπροσθεν ὑμῶν as predicate. The next clause fails to render the preposition of בחרב, simply using the dative of instrument,[76] which is fully adequate. The b+ text does add an ἐν before the nominal, but this need not be recensional in origin.

The reason given for their falling by the sword is given in MT as כי על כן שבתם מאחרי יהוה. The כי על כן is rendered fairly by οὗ εἵνεκεν "seeing that," literally "on account of which." The שבתם is rendered as usual by ἀπεστράφητε,

---

73. See GK 135p.
74. See SS 74.
75. Tarʲ does read לכון as well.
76. See SS 121.

whereas מאחרי is not translated, but only paraphrased by ἀπειθοῦντες (κυρίῳ) "being disobedient to the Lord." Here the translator understood ושבתם as though it were followed by coordinate verb, in which case it would mean "again." What the Greek intends is "and you were again disobedient to the Lord." This then calls to mind 11:20's ὅτι ἠπειθήσετε κυρίῳ; see comment ad loc.[77]

The verse ends with "and the Lord will not be ἐν ὑμῖν." One might reasonably have expected μεθ' ὑμῶν, as at v.42, as equivalent for עמכם; there, however, MT read בקרבכם; see comment ad loc. But here ἐν ὑμῖν may well have been thought to be more appropriate; their God will not be in their midst, and will therefore not be their protection. A variant s^mg+ text does read μεθ υμων; the reading is almost certainly taken from one of The Three.

14:44 Unfortunately, the opening verb, ויעפלו, is a hapax legomenon, and remains unknown.[78] Its equivalent in Num is καὶ διαβιασάμενοι, which is also unique, though the simplex βιάζω is well known, and the compound is probably simply its intensive equivalent. The middle form usually means "to use force," and I would suggest that here it means "in stubborn fashion," I suspect that the translator was as in the dark about יעפלו as we are, and chose a contextually fitting word to say that "in total disregard of Moses and his warning, they proceeded."[79]

V.b makes clear that the people acted on their own, as the contrastive δέ shows. Neither the κιβωτὸς τῆς διαθήκης κυρίου nor Moses moved out of the camp. For the designation of the ark as τῆς διαθήκης κυρίου, see comment at 10:33. Elsewhere in the Pentateuch this designation occurs only in Deut (10:8 31:9,25,26). Later the term becomes common: in Ios it obtains 17 times; in 1— 3Reg, 10 times, and in Parap, 13 times.

14:45 For ὁ Ἀμαλήκ, see comment at v.25. For the popular omission of ὁ, see comment at v.43. The attributive phrase ὁ ἐγκαθήμενος ἐν τῷ ὄρει ἐκείνῳ "the one residing in that hill country," is in the singular, in imitation of MT. Sensibly,

---
77. See also Dorival 68.
78. The Targumists also had difficulty with this verb. Tar^O translated by ארשעו; Tar^N has כמנו, probably thinking of אפל rather than עפל, i.e. as "darkness," thus "secretly (they went)." Tar^J elaborated by his אזדרו (Ethp of זרז, hence "strengthened themselves") בחשוכא קדם קריצתא "in the darkness before dawn" (also reflecting אפל).
79. Dorival translates neatly "passent outre."

it should refer to both ὁ 'Αμαλήκ and ὁ Χαναναῖος, i.e. what is meant is Amalek and the Chananite who were residing. The singular is presumably used in attraction to the nearer antecedent, which is singular (in both Num and MT).

MT describes the outcome as ויכום ויכתום "and they smote them and beat them in pieces." Num describes their defeat differently: καὶ ἐτρέψαντο αὐτοὺς καὶ κατέκοψαν αὐτούς "and they made them flee and cut them down." The translator tried to differentiate between the two Hebrew verbs which are more or less synonymous by a colorful ἐτρέψαντο, but then cutting them down.[80] The slaughter followed the invaders as far as Ἑρμά, the location of which is unknown. In the tradition, B V C'+ read ερμαν, but MT has חרמה, and the final *nu* is secondary.[81]

The final clause "and they returned to the camp" is based on Sam. Hex placed it under the obelus, since it is lacking in MT.

---

80. The Targumists also found difficulty in distinguishing these verbs signalling destruction. Tar⁰ translated as מחונון וטרדנון "obliterated them and expelled them," while Tarᴺ read מחון יתהון ויכתתי יתהון. Tarᴶ typically elaborated by using three verbs: וקטלו יתהון ושיציאונון וטרודונון.
81. For a possible explanation of the B variant spelling, see THGN 118.

Chapter 15

15:1 For ἐλάλησεν, B V Byz x+ read ειπεν. But the usual rendering of ידבר is ἐλάλησεν, whereas יאמר normally becomes εἶπεν. There is really no good reason to adopt the minority variant, in spite of its support by cod B; see comment at 14:26.[1]

15:2 Vv.2—16 deal with regulations concerning sacrifices which will be offered in the promised land. V.2 is the temporal protasis, and concerns the future: ὅταν εἰσέλθητε εἰς τὴν γῆν τῆς κατοικήσεως ὑμῶν. MT has the plural מושבתיכם, but as Levine says[2] "Whereas the plural form of this verb may signify numerical plurality, here it expresses a qualitative plural, focusing on the *act* of settlement."[3] Num fully understood this, and refers to "the land of your settling" (i.e. your settlement). The relative clause is a common nominal one, "which אני נתן to you." As usual, Num translates this pattern by the pronoun ἐγώ plus a first singular present tense verb, δίδωμι.

15:3 Num has understood this verse as an apodosis to the ὅταν clause, as both the change to a future tense and to the singular number of ποιήσεις indicate. The apodosis is also introduced by an apodotic καί.[4] The verse then is an instruction: "then you shall perform a κάρπωμα," for which see Note at Deut 18:1.[5] In the tradition, only B V n x and 319 support the Num verbal form. All other ms witnesses read the plural, either in the subjunctive with A M C′ s+, or as indicative with the remainder.[6] This could be a recensional correction (possibly hex), or a rationalizing correction to agree with the plural εἰσέλθητε of v.2.

It should also be noted that אשה "a fire offering" is always rendered by κάρπωμα in Num.[7] Why אשה should be rendered by κάρπωμα is not fully clear.

---

1. See also THGN 118 for a fuller statement.
2. Pp.388—389.
3. P.388.
4. This is overlooked by Dorival, who renders by "et que tu feras."
5. The term אשה and its rendering in the Pentateuch are fully discussed in Daniel 155—164.
6. The Tar all witness to the plural verb as well.
7. See THGN 111.

Since it derives from a root meaning "to enjoy the fruit of," it may well simply be any sacrifice offered for God's enjoyment. Such an understanding certainly fits the description μεγαλῦναι εὐχὴν ἢ καθ᾽ ἑκούσιαν ἢ ἐν ταῖς ἑορταῖς ὑμῶν. In other words, it seems to be a generic term for a number of different sacrifices. Such a κάρπωμα may be either ὁλοκαύτωμα ἢ θυσίαν, which are the usual renderings for עלה and זבח resp.

In the tradition, considerable changes obtain. Instead of κάρπωμα, Origen's text read ολοκαρπωμα, and in hex he placed the ολο part under the obelus. The reading is certainly secondary, probably influenced by ὁλοκαύτωμα. Particularly odd is the B Byz x+ confused mixup of text.[8] First of all, the two words were transposed, and secondly, the plural ολοκαυτωματα was read, thus ending up in ολοκαυτωματα (κυρίῳ) ολοκαρπωμα. This should certainly not be taken seriously.[9]

What follows for the remainder of the verse explicates "you must perform κάρπωμα κυρίῳ, either burnt offering or sacrifice." μεγαλῦναι εὐχήν is an explicative infinitival structure "to make a great vow." This translates לפלא נדר. For the use of the root פלא with "vows," see comment at 6:2. Other possibilities explicating κάρπωμα include καθ᾽ ἑκούσιαν. The noun ἑκούσιος is the usual rendering for נדבה "a voluntary or free-will offering; this first occurs at Lev 7:6, which see. The vow and the voluntary offering are not always carefully distinguished. A further occasion given for performing a κάρπωμα is ἐν ταῖς ἑορταῖς ὑμῶν.

The ποιῆσαι structure is purposive, and defines why one might make great vows or voluntary offerings or festive sacrifices. These are done to make ὀσμὴν εὐωδίας κυρίῳ. For ὀσμὴν εὐωδίας, which is a calque for ריח ניחח, see Notes at Gen 8:21 and Exod 29:18.[10]

That the κάρπωμα, i.e. either ὁλοκαύτωμα ἢ θυσία, are all thought of as burnt offerings of some kind is clear from the alternative given at the end: "whether of cattle or of sheep." In other words, θυσία is here not to be understood as a cereal offering. The term θυσία differs here from its meaning in Lev 2.

---
8. Daniel 161—163 bases her discussion on the secondary text of cod B.
9. See THGN 112.
10. See also Daniel 118.

15:4 The δῶρον which the offerer offers refers to the various kinds of sacrifices listed in v.3. When one offers any of these, he must (also) offer a θυσίαν σεμιδάλεως. Here θυσίαν refers specifically to a meal or grain sacrifice as in Lev chapter 2, not as in v.3 to a burnt offering, viz. of cattle or sheep. This θυσίαν is to consist of "a tenth of an ephah." MT lacks an equivalent for τοῦ οἰφί, and so hex has placed this under the obelus. The gloss is ad sensum, and correct as to the measure intended. For "tenth of an ephah," see Note at Lev 5:11.[11]

The fine flour was to be ἀναπεποιημένης with oil. For the participle as a rendering for בלול, see Note at Lev 6:40, and comp 7:2. In MT, בלול modifies the preceding word עשרון, but Num more logically has a feminine participle modifying σεμιδάλεως; it is the fine flour that is made up with oil. In the tradition, the majority A M reading has the more common translation for בלול, πεφυραμενης "mixed," rather than ἀναπεποιημένης "made up, prepared." The oil to be used was to consist of ἐν τετάρτῳ τοῦ ἵν. In MT the measure precedes שמן, and hex has rearranged the structure to read εν τεταρτω του ιν (εν) ελαιω. Apparently hex also omitted the ἐν before ἐλαίῳ to equal שמן, though this is not certain. The ἵν was a liquid measure of approximately four liters, thus a quarter of a hin would be ca one liter; see Note at Exod 29:40.

15:5—6 Num has amplified the text considerably at the end of v.5, as well as after the initial καὶ τῷ κριῷ of v.6. With the exception of those initial three words of v.6, the entire text from ποιήσεις in v.5 through the first θυσίαν of v.6 has no correspondence in MT. Hex has shown this economically by placing all of this under the obelus, and then adding και τω κριω under the asterisk. By these one can correctly identify the text of MT.

V.5 continues the instructions of v.4: "and wine for the libation (or drink offering) a quarter of a hin ποιήσετε upon the burnt offering or upon the sacrifice." MT has the singular verb תעשה. Neither MT nor Num is consistent in the number of second person verbs throughout this section, and there seems to be little rhyme or reason for the confusion. In v.5 both ποιήσετε and ποιήσεις occur, and in v.6 similarly, ποιῆτε and ποιήσεις obtain. A possible attempt at

---

11. For modern equivalents for the ephah, see Bible Dictionaries sub "Weights and Measures."

rationalizing the text is seen in the M C' s y+ change of ποιήσεις to ποιησει. This could mean "one must make."[12]

In MT, the verb תעשה is modified by two different prepositional phrases: על העלה או לזבח, i.e. "you must sacrifice on the burnt offering or for the sacrifice." The distinction is voided by Num which uses ἐπί with the genitive for both phrases. העלה is rendered this time, not by ὁλοκαύτωμα as in v.3, but by τῆς ὁλοκαυτώσεως, which is a synonym.[13] In fact, עלה is most commonly rendered by ὁλοκαύτωμα in the Bible (163 times), whereas ὁλοκαύτωσις follows with 67 times. Other renderings include κάρπωμα (16), ὁλοκάρπωσις (12), with other nouns occurring in insignificant numbers (six or less times).[14]

After τῷ ἀμνῷ τῷ ἑνί the translator has added ποιήσεις τοσοῦτο "you shall perform in the same amounts." What Num says is that the amounts ordered in v.4 are to apply in the case of the one lamb. Then there follows another addition: κάρπωμα ὀσμὴν εὐωδίας κυρίῳ, which is taken over ex par, probably from vv.10,14; this also occurs at 28:13, as well as in exactly the same form in Lev 2:9 3:5 and comp v.16. At Lev 3:16 κυρίῳ is articulated, i.e. representing ליהוה; most witnesses also attest an article here as well, and this might actually be a hex addition.

V.6 begins with καὶ τῷ κριῷ, which stands for או לאיל of MT. The change in conjunction is due to the intervening glosses; in MT, it follows immediately after לכבש האחד ending v.5, in which case a correlative conjunction is appropriate, but not so in the Greek. Once again the translator made an addition. MT continues with "you shall make a grain sacrifice," But Num adds a temporal condition: ὅταν ποιῆτε αὐτὸν εἰς ὁλοκαύτωμα ἢ εἰς θυσίαν before it, i.e. it restates the occasion, not only unnecessarily, but in view of the definition of κάρπωμα in v.3 as ὁλοκαύτωμα ἢ θυσίαν in an unfortunate context. The θυσίαν is here not the grain sacrifice, but an animal sacrifice; immediately following on this addition, Num translates תעשה מנחה by ποιήσεις θυσίαν—but now θυσίαν for מנחה is a grain sacrifice as its definition as being "of fine flour" shows. In the tradition, the B O+ text adds an η "either" before εἰς ὁλοκαύτωμα, but Num only uses correlatives between nouns, never before the first noun of a series.[15]

---

12. Tar⁰ follows MT exactly, as does Tarʲ, but Tarᴺ uses the plural throughout except for its תקרב in v.10.
13. See THGN 112.
14. The count is that of Dos Santos.
15. See THGN 101—102.

For the offering of a ram, the grain sacrifice of fine flour consists of "two thirds (of an ephah, the flour) being made up with oil, a third of a hin." Here the two thirds is unidentified as to measure, but it must again be the ephah. For ἀναπεποιημένης, see comment at v.4. The tradition has, however, wrecked havoc with the word. V Byz+ attest to the neuter plural inflection, i.e. it is δέκατα which it modifies, which is hardly sensible. The A F M majority reading is αναπεφυραμενης, for which see comment at v.4.

15:7 The accompanying libation, as in v.5 consists of wine, but here "a third of a hin." The verb is προσοίσετε, but MT has the singular תקריב. For this change in number, see comment at v.5. In the tradition, Byz x+ articulate κυρίῳ. Hex does occasionally add τω under the asterisk to represent the preposition in ליהוה, but Num renders ליהוה by κυρίῳ, i.e. without an article.[16] MT has taken ריח ניחח as a direct modifier of תקריב; The Masoretes made the first cut in the verse before the verb, placing ההין under the *ethnach*. Num has simplified the text by adding εἰς before ὀσμήν.[17]

15:8 The previous offering had been a ram. Here a contrastive δέ introduces ἀπὸ τῶν βοῶν, as "what ποιῆτε for ὁλοκαύτωμα or for a sacrifice."[18] Since MT has the verb before the ἀπό phrase, the majority A F M text transposes them, following hex to equal MT. The preposing of the phrase is, however, original. MT has a singular verb here. The ἀπό is clearly a partitive, i.e. "one from the cattle herd." For μεγαλῦναι εὐχήν, see comment at v.3. The alternative to the vow is εἰς σωτηρίον "for a sacrifice for deliverance." This is the translation of שלמים, which when designating a sacrifice is always in the plural, but is translated by the singular σωτηρίον. For this type of offering, see Lev chapter 3.

15:9 Why the text should suddenly switch to a third person verb is puzzling, and Num simply follows MT's והקריב with καὶ προσοίσει. I would translate: "then one must bring alongside (ἐπί) the bullock an offering (i.e. a grain sacrifice) of fine flour." It is here quite clear that the grain sacrifice (the θυσίαν) accompanies

---

16. See THGN 104.
17. See Daniel 189.
18. Theod and Aq also use ὁλοκαύτωμα, but Sym translates עלה by εἰς ἀναφοράν.

the particular κάρπωμα of v.3 which is being offered. It is now obvious that from v.4 onwards, θυσίαν is an accompanying grain sacrifice that is being described.

In the case of a bullock being offered as one's κάρπωμα, the sacrifice of fine flour made up with oil is to consist of three tenths (of an ephah) of flour and a half hin of oil. It must be the relative size of the animal being presented that determines the size of the accompanying grain sacrifice. The animals are graded accordingly, beginning with a lamb (v.5), then a ram (v.6), and here a bullock. The amount of fine flour also increases in amount, from a tenth (v.4), to two tenths (v.6), and three tenths (v.9), with the oil increasing from a quarter of a hin (v.5), to a third (v.6), and here a half hin.

In the tradition, the V Byz text sensibly changes προσοίσει to ποιησεις, but this is influenced by the ποιήσεις of vv.3,5 and 6. The more difficult προσοίσει equals MT and is original text. For ἀναπεποιημένης, the Byz text reads the neuter plural, for which see comment at v.6. And as in v.6, the majority text has αναπεφυραμενης; see comment ad loc.

15:10 The accompanying libation is to be half a hin. MT has a second person singular verb rather than the nominal clause of Num. It reads "and wine תקריב for a libation," and hex has inserted προσοισει under the asterisk. Obviously, Origen used a third person singular verb to agree with הקריב of v.9, for which see comment at v.9. A reversion to the second person of earlier verses might have been expected. It is of course also possible that Origen's Hebrew text read יקריב rather than תקריב. For κάρπωμα ὀσμὴν εὐωδίας κυρίῳ, which has an equivalent structure in MT here, see comment at vv.5—6.

15:11 Num retains the second person which prevails in vv.2—8 with its οὕτως ποιήσεις, whereas MT continues with third persn יעשה (of v.9), though the Masoretes sensibly vocalized the verb as Ni, so "thus shall be done." The O x text, however, apparently represents hex in its continuing with a third person verb ποιησει; see comment at v.10 on the asterisked προσοισει for תקריב. The first dative modifier is τῷ μόσχῳ (τῷ ἑνί), here for לשור. It had been used for בן בקר in v.8, but after all, a בן בקר would be a שור. This also is to apply: "or to the one ram or to the one lamb." MT has no equivalent for the last τῷ ἑνί. The addition of τῷ ἑνί is undoubtedly a correct intuition. It might be noted that MT has לשה, which is usually rendered by πρόβατον (37 times, and only three times by ἀμνός, and once each by ποίμνιον and χίμαρος). The reverse is the case with כבש, for which ἀμνός is the LXX translation 82 times, but πρόβατον only 11 times.[19] It seems that Num has transposed the two for good sense. It is of course possible that Num had a different parent text.[20]

15:12 This verse, along with v.13, gives a general concluding statement: "according to the number of those which you would offer (ποιήσητε), so must you do (ποιήσετε) to the one (i.e. to each one) according to their number. This renders MT exactly.

15:13 MT says: "every native born must do thus את אלה"; instead of "these things" as modifier of "must do," Num has τοιαῦτα "in such a manner."[21] This is a free, but satisfactory interpretation, which accents the general character of what is being said.

The infinitive structure modifies ποιήσει, and explains the occasion for doing thus, viz. "on presenting καρπώματα εἰς (ὀσμὴν εὐωδίας) to the Lord." Num takes אשה as a collective, and translates by means of a plural noun. Actually, either singular or plural would be adequate. Num has also added a preposition before ὀσμήν, but MT simply has ריח, i.e. a second direct modifier of προσενέγκαι.

In the tradition, the Byz text changes the Hellenistic inflection of the aorist infinitive, προσενέγκαι, to the Classical second aorist inflection, προσενεγκειν. This reflects the later trend to pseudoclassicalism, which often characterizes the Byz text. Some witnesses, including Syh^L, omit εἰς, but this is unlikely to be recensional; it is rather ex par, e.g. vv.5,10,14.

15:14 The preceding verse concerned ὁ αὐτόχθων, but (δέ) here it concerns "the resident alien among you who might come into your land." The equivalent designation is a cognate expression: יגור אתכם גר; comp the more exact προσέλθῃ

---

19. According to the statistics of Dos Santos.
20. For לשה בכבשים Tar^O has אמר באמריא. Tar^J reads לאימר בר אימרי, but then uses בני גדייא to render בעזים, while Tar^N adds an extra או בגדיה after אמרה באמריה. See Dorival 127—128 for a discussion of the ways in which the Tar have handled the problem of the mixture of lambs and sheep. Certainly Num has simplified the text by transposing "sheep" and "lambs."
21. For the adverbial τοιαῦτα, see LS sub τοιοῦτος 6.

πρὸς ὑμᾶς προσήλυτος of 9:14. Here the translator uses προσγένηται as a contrast to the γένηται of the coordinate clause. MT has no equivalent for ἐν τῇ γῇ ὑμῶν, and hex has placed the phrase under the obelus. It is a further explication of ἐν ὑμῖν modifying προσήλυτος.

Not just the proselyte is concerned, but also ὃς ἂν γένηται ἐν ὑμῖν ἐν ταῖς γενεαῖς ὑμῶν "(or) who might be living among you in your generations," i.e. in future times. Those who are referred to are resident aliens, i.e. proselytes or any foreigners in times to come who might (temporarily) reside among you. In MT the relative clause is nominal, and Num has added the verb γένηται for good sense, which hex has placed under the obelus. Strictly speaking, the verb is added to conform to normal Greek discourse. The translator by his balance between προσγένηται and γένηται shows a fine sense of style.

The condition pertaining to these classes of people which is pertinent in this context is put into the future: "and he would perform a κάρπωμα ὀσμὴν εὐωδίας κυρίῳ." Actually, the conditional structure has two clauses as a protasis, and the καὶ ποιήσει clause is the apodosis. In turn, all of this is set up in anticipation of the general rule which follows.

V.b is then the general rule: "As you (yourselves) are doing, so shall the assembly do for the Lord." The ὑμεῖς, which I have translated by "(yourselves)," has no counterpart in MT, and hex has duly placed the pronoun under the obelus. It does, however, serve a useful purpose in stressing the contrast of ὃν τρόπον ... οὕτως .... The subject of the οὕτως clause is placed in v.15 in MT, i.e. a *soph pasuq* intervenes before הקהל. The κυρίῳ is not reflected in MT, and hex indicates that fact by placing it under the obelus. In fact, Num has changed the sense of the rule; MT had nicely contrasted "you" and "the proselyte," but Num made "the assembly" contrast with "you." The translator failed to understand the syntax of קהל. Milgrom is quite correct in his rendering "As for the congregation (i.e. the Israelites), there shall be one ..."; קהל belongs to v.15, rather than to v.14.

15:15 "One rule ἔσται to you and to the resident aliens who associate themselves ἐν ὑμῖν." In MT, this constitutes a nominal clause, and the majority F K M text omits ἔσται; this omission is almost assuredly recensional, though its source (possibly hex) is uncertain. Nor does MT have a counterpart for ἐν ὑμῖν, which is an ad sensum gloss, and hex has duly placed the phrase under an obelus. Num has interpreted MT's ולגר הגר as a collective, and translated it by the plural. As in v.14, Num has avoided rendering the cognate structure by a comparable Greek one as in 9:14, but translated the participle by τοῖς προσκειμένοις "those who associate themselves," which is actually the most frequently used rendering for the root גור (13 times), whereas the cognate προσέρχομαι is used in LXX only five times; in fact, the more neutral verb, κατοικεω, is more common than the cognate verb, occurring nine times.[22] On the 12 instances of πρόσκειμαι being used, ten occur in Lev and Num. In MT, this constitutes v.a; the Masoretes have placed הגר under the *ethnach*.

In Num, the next clause in MT, חקת עולם לדרתיכם, is not a separate clause, but is in apposition to νόμος (εἷς), thus "even a perpetual rule εἰς τὰς γενεὰς ὑμῶν," i.e. throughout the future. Cod B+ have omitted the article, but this phrase occurs seven times in exactly this form in Num, and nowhere else has the article been omitted or questioned. The omission is secondary.[23]

For Num, v.b reads "As you, even (or also) the resident alien shall be before the Lord." MT uses the Hebrew idiom ככם כגר, which Num correctly renders by ὡς ὑμεῖς καὶ ὁ προσήλυτος. No distinction is to be made between the Israelite and the proselyte.

15:16 Num reads: "one rule ἔσται, and one δικαίωμα there shall be for you and for the resident alien who has associated himself among you." MT has יהיה only after משפט אחד, which then does duty for both nouns; Num has an ἔσται after the first noun as well, and hex has omitted that one to conform to MT. More commonly, hex would have placed it under the obelus. It is possible that Origen's Hebrew text had been corrected by the omission of the linking verb, but there is no way of proving it.

The exact distinction between νόμος and δικαίωμα is dificult to describe. Dorival has rendered νόμος by "loi," and δικαίωμα by "règle."[24] I would prefer to consider the two terms when individualized by "one" as close synonyms, and would translate the one by "rule" and the other one by "regulation." It should be borne in mind that νόμος occurs twice in v.15, where MT has חקת, but in v.16 it

---

22. According to Dos Santos; actually, one of the 13 is incorrect, and the count should be 12.
23. See THGN 107.
24. Dorival 170—171 has given a fine discussion of δικαιώματα as used in Ptolemaic Egypt, which is most helpful.

occurs for תורה. In other words, "one torah" is the same as a חקה as far as the translator is concerned.

15:18—19 V.18 shows a couple of regular patterns, which recur not just in Num, but in the other books of the Pentateuch as well. Hebrew often expresses temporal concepts by means of a prepositional phrase in which ב governs a bound infinitive bound to a pronominal suffix as here בבאכם, where "in your entering" means "when you enter." Num translates this word for word by ἐν τῷ εἰσπορεύεσθαι ὑμᾶς. Another common pattern is the Hebrew nominal clause, in which a pronoun constitutes the subject, and a participle becomes the predicate, thus אני מביא. This pattern is translated normally by a verbal clause, in which the participle becomes a present tense verb, thus ἐγὼ εἰσάγω. Another common characteristic of translation Greek is the word for word translation of a relative pronoun plus an adverb (or prepositional phrase). Here אשר plus שמה, "whither," becomes εἰς ἥν ... ἐκεῖ; the ἐκεῖ is of course superfluous, but shows the parent text plainly.

In v.19, the temporal pattern referred to above recurs in באכלכם "when you eat," but Num does not use the literal pattern of a prepositional phrase here, but translates it by a temporal clause ὅταν ἔσθητε ὑμεῖς. Note, however, the use of ὑμεῖς, which is completely unnecessary for the sense, adds nothing, though it does serve to show the pronominal component of האכלכם.

The verb is modified by a partitive ἀπό phrase, ἀπὸ τῶν ἄρτων τῆς γῆς.[25] The parent text has a singular לחם, which Num renders by the plural. The intention of לחם הארץ, which is a unique phrase in the Bible, must mean the food of the land, which makes the plural τῶν ἄρτων sensible.[26]

. The apodosis in MT demands תרימו תרומה "you must lift up a dedicatory gift." For an understanding of the תרומה sacrifice and the root רום, see the Note at Exod 29:27. It is translated by ἀφελεῖτε ἀφαίρεμα; see Note at Lev 7:4, where the translation "dedicatory gift" is proposed for תרומה. But Num has a doublet rendering. Not only is it an ἀφαίρεμα, "something set aside, raised," but it is also an ἀφόρισμα "a separation," a term often used for תנופה; see Note at Exod 29:24.[27] Hex has noted the doublet rendering by placing ἀφόρισμα under

---

25. See SS 162.
26. Tar^J explains the phrase by מלחמא דעללתא דארעא.
27. See also Dorival 62.

the obelus. As at v.5, κυρίῳ is articulated by the majority text (though not by A and B); this is probably hex, which at times does render the preposition in ליהוה by the dative article; see comment at v.5.[28]

15:20 Vv.20—21 are explicative of "ἀφαίρεμα (ἀφόρισμα) which you must set aside to the Lord" of v.19. "As an ἀπαρχήν of your dough, a loaf, as a dedicatory gift you must set it aside." The αὐτό refers to the ἀφαίρεμα; it is otiose, has no equivalent in MT, and hex has placed it under the obelus. I would render ἀπαρχήν with NRSV as "first batch"; the term is usually rendered "first-fruit," but this is awkward with "dough." ἀπαρχήν renders ראשית. This equation occurs 19 times in LXX, though only six times in the Pentateuch. More frequently, it is used to translate תרומה, a rendering found 12 times in the Pentateuch out of 39 cases in the LXX; it became especially popular for Ezek, where 19 cases obtain, and only two for ראשית.[29] For ἀφαίρεμα, see comment at v.19.

The verb הרים is usually rendered by αἱρέω (15 times) or some compound of this verb (12 times), thus for simplex and compounds together, 27 times. But here ἀφορίζω is used, more commonly used for הניף in the Pentateuch, e.g. at 8:11.[30] But it does occur at 18:24 for הרים as well (and four times in Ezek).[31] In MT, the verb precedes תרומה, and hex has transposed ἀφαίρεμα ἀφοριεῖτε to equal the word order of MT.

It should be noted that תרימו occurs again in v.b, where the translator used the more usual ἀφελεῖτε. In v.b the ἀφαίρεμα is identified as "from the threshing floor" interpreting the bound phrase תרומת גרן. The word for threshing floor is ἅλωνος, from ἅλων, which is always used in the Pentateuch, not αλω from ἅλως, a synonym, which B x attest.[32]

15:21 MT begins with a partitive מן, i.e. מראשית, which the translator disregarded, but harmonized with the ἀπαρχὴν φυράματος ὑμῶν of v.20.[33] In

---

28. Incidentally, the Tar tend to render the preposition in the phrase by קדם, though Tar[N] here has לשמה דהי.
29. According to HR.
30. According to Dos Santos.
31. According to HR.
32. See THGN 128.
33. See SS 162.

Num, this modifies the last clause as part of v.20b, i.e. "so shall you lift up as a first batch of your dough."

In MT, the verse divides differently, with the *ethnach* marking תרומה, so that לדרתיכם by itself constitutes v.b. The apparent reason for this division is that "throughout your generations" is actually the only new information added by the verse. But this is not how Num understood it, as the καί introducing v.b proves; the conjunction separates "you must give a dedicatory gift to the Lord to your generations" (i.e. throughout the future), from the first part of the verse.

In the tradition, hex has changed φυράματος to φυραματων to agree with ערסתיכם of MT. In v.20 the Masoretes had vocalized ערסתכם as a plural as well, and Origen made no change, but here it can only be taken as a plural noun. Num had quite naturally harmonized with v.20.

15:22 Vv.22—29 deal with unintentional sins. First of all, unintentional sins involving the entire community (vv.22—26) are described; then vv.27—29 deal with such sins which concern individuals.

The condition or protasis is set out in vv.22—24 ἀκουσίως/לשגגה. MT describes the action by the verb תשגו, which Num defines uniquely here by διαμάρτητε, which means "to fail utterly," an intensive form which in the simplex means "to fail," i.e. "to sin," and is the usual translation for חטא. MT's verb means "to sin unknowingly," i.e. "by inadvertence," which contrasts with actions done ביד רמה rendered by ἐν χειρὶ ὑπερηφανίας (v.30). The translator probably chose this verb in the light of the coordinate verb μὴ ποιήσητε. Obviously, he does not translate here in isolate fashion, even though he tends to a word-for-word rendition, but he remains aware of the context, and takes it into consideration. What Num does is to substitute for the notion of inadvertence, a stronger stress on "your utter failure," which is then explained by the coordinate "and not do all these commandments which the Lord spoke to Moses." In other words, inadvertence pertains to sins of omission, in contrast to Lev 4:27: ἐν τῷ ποιῆσαι μίαν ἀπὸ πασῶν τῶν ἐντολῶν κυρίου ἣ οὐ ποιηθήσεται, which refers to doing what was forbidden.

15:23 Syntactically, this verse is part of the preceding clause. MT introduces this by את כל אשר "even all that which," which Num simplifies by καθά. Hex has changed this by substituting κατα for καθ, and adding παντα under the asterisk, resulting in κατα παντα α. It may also be noted that MT has a different syntagm; the את collocation explicates the את structure of v.22, not the אשר clause. The first συνέταξεν is explicated by a temporal clause: "from the day which συνέταξεν κύριος πρὸς ὑμᾶς and beyond throughout your generations." MT lacks an equivalent for the πρὸς ὑμᾶς phrase, and hex has placed it under the obelus. The translator simply harmonized with v.a, where exactly the same structure occurred, though there the prepositional phrase had a basis in MT.

15:24 The καὶ ἔσται introducing a protasis of some kind is a Hebraism, imitating והיה introducing אם or כי, and occurs elsewhere in Num five times (9:20, 21 10:32 15:19 21:8). It is best left untranslated. The protasis is completed with "if it happened unintentionally out of sight of the community." The verb is γενηθῇ, and is occasionally (26 times) used for the Ni of עשה.[34] The passive of γένομαι is a good free rendering, and avoids using the same verb twice in the same verse as is done in MT; see ועשו in the next clause. Though no subject for the verb is given either in Num or in MT, it has to be "the inadvertent sin," whatever that might be, i.e. the noun inherent in the verb διαμάρτητε/תשגו of v.22.[35] The apodosis is signalled by the change to a future verb. "The entire assembly must sacrifice (ποιήσει) one bullock from the cattle ἄμωμον for a burnt offering." MT has אחד after בן בקר, but Num has ἕνα before it, since it refers to μόσχον; it would be unusual Greek were it to follow the order of MT. The Hebrew has no correspondent for ἄμωμον, and hex has placed it under the obelus. It is an ex par gloss; only animals unblemished were allowed on the altar, and the gloss is not incorrect, though absent in MT.

Also to be offered as accompanying sacrifices for the burnt offering were the "θυσίαν τούτου and its libation according to custom." MT has מנחתו, and the demonstrative pronoun was used to make clear that the מנחה (as well as the נסך) were to accompany the עלה; it was the θυσίαν of the afore-mentioned ὁλοκαύτωμα.

The burnt offering was, however, not sufficient. A sacrificial ram from the goats was needed περὶ ἁμαρτίας, i.e. for a sin offering.

---

34. The count is that of Dos Santos. HR, however, (on which Dos Santos bases his count) is not always accurate. Thus at Ezek 36:3, the verb is תעלו, and not the Ni of עשה. Along the same line, it lists our passage incorrectly as well, as equalling the Qal of עשה.
35. For "sin by inadvertence," see Dorival 169.

15:25 For ἐξιλάσεται, see Note at Lev 1:4. The verb ἀφεθήσεται has no subject expressed, as was the case for γενηθῇ in v.24; see comment ad loc. The שגגה is translated by the neuter noun ἀκούσιον, derived from the adjective ἀκούσιος. The term occurs only here and in v.26 in the Pentateuch (it also occurs in Eccl 10:5), and always for שגגה. In v.b it occurs in the plural genitive, probably because the assembly is now referred to as αὐτοί, though the Masoretes vocalized שגגתם as a singular noun; in fact, the noun only occurs in the singular in the Bible, though theoretically MT could be vocalized as a plural noun.

The change in subject is indicated by καὶ αὐτοί for והם, followed by a change in tense, which follows on the ὅτι/כי clause introducing v.b. I would translate v.b: "because it was an inadvertent sin, and they did bring (or had brought) their gift as a κάρπωμα to the Lord, as their sin offering before the Lord concerning their inadvertent sins."[36] When חטאת is used in the sense of "sin offering" rather than as "sin," περὶ (τῆς) ἁμαρτίας is used. In MT, וחטאתם occurs; in other words, "their sin offering" is coordinated with אשה, but Num omits the conjunction, understanding the sacrifice for the Lord's pleasure, the κάρπωμα, to consist of περὶ τῆς ἁμαρτίας αὐτῶν. This is in accordance with the nature of אשה as an inclusive term for sacrifices. For κάρπωμα as its rendering, see the discussion at v.3.

15:26 MT has two coordinate ל phrases in modification of נסלח, but Num distinguishes between the two, the first one being translated by κατά plus an accusative, and the second one more exactly by a dative noun. I doubt whether Num was making a distinction between "pardon κατά the entire assembly" and "for the resident alien," i.e. "it will be forgiven for the entire assembly of the Israelites, and for the proselyte who associates himself with you." The only distinction being made here is between Israelites and the resident alien in the land. For προσκειμένῳ, see discussion at v.15. In the tradition, the majority A F M text reads προσπορευομενω, which may well be recensional in origin, since the participle הגר is cognate to לגר.[37]

---

36. The Tar had difficulty in distinguishing the two words קרבים אשה. Tar^JO made no distinction: קרבנהון קרבנא, whereas Tar^N simply omitted אשה.
37. Though Theod adopted προσκειμένῳ, i.e. the text of Num.

15:27 Vv.27—29 concern an individual who sins unintentionally. Num renders the initial conjunction appropriately by means of a contrastive δέ, thus "but if one person should sin unintentionally." The apodosis requires that he or she bring one year-old she-goat as a sin offering. MT has no equivalent for the μίαν, and hex has placed it under the obelus. MT introduces the apodosis with a conjunction, but Num omits it, thereby producing better Greek.

15:28 As in the case of the entire assembly of Israelites in v.25, "the priest must make atonement concerning the person τῆς ἀκουσιασθείσης and sins inadvertently before the Lord." The verb ἀκουσιάζω is a hapax legomenon; it renders the verb שגג. I would translate the participle as "who acts unintentionally."[38] In MT this is followed by an apparent doublet, בחטאה בשגגה "with an inadvertent sin," which Num renders by a coordinate structure, καὶ ἁμαρτούσης ἀκουσίως "and who sins inadvertently." The doublet does define the inadvertence of τῆς ἀκουσιασθείσης as "sin."

The verse ends with "to make atonement for him," to which MT added ונסלח לו. Hex has added και αφεθησεται αυτω under the asterisk to represent it. I suspect the omission to be an error on the part of the translator, whose eye jumped from one prepositional phrase, עליו, to another one, לו.

15:29 The syntax of MT is peculiar with the references האזרח and ולגר being coordinate. Num has levelled the two by coordinate datives; see note a in BHS. In MT, v.a is a unit outside the main clause, thus: "As for the native born among the Israelites and for the proselyte who resides in their midst." Then v.b constitutes the main clause: "One rule there shall be for you for the one acting in inadvertence."

Num has reworked this syntactically. Instead of a second person reference, לכם, everything is in third person. The relative clause at the end, ὃς ἂν ποιήσῃ ἀκουσίως "whoever might have done something unintentionally," is a pendant nominative, though in imitation of MT placed at the end. One might then render the verse for the sake of clarity as "As for anyone who might have acted unintentionally, to both the native born among the Israelites and the proselyte who

---

38. According to Dorival, the verb is attested elsewhere only once in a commentary on the Iliad by Eustathius.

attaches himself to them (i.e. to the Israelites), one rule shall apply (to them)." For τῷ προσκειμένῳ, see comment at v.15.

15:30 Num begins with καί in imitation of MT, though the person referred to here is not one who sins inadvertently, but ἐν χειρὶ ὑπερηφανίας, "with a hand of arrogance," an interpretation of ביד רמה "with a raised hand." What is meant by this is "intentionally." Num understands "with a raised hand" as a gesture of arrogance or defiance, thus blatantly; in any event, this contrasts with the ἀκουσίως of v.29. This in turn is modified by two ἀπό phrases, "from the native born or from the proselytes."[39] In MT, the nouns are in the singular, and the conjunction is *waw*. The Greek interprets these correctly as collectives.

Of such a one, MT says את יהוה הוא מגדף "Yahweh he is reviling (or blaspheming)." Num interprets by τὸν θεὸν οὗτος παροξύνει "God this one provokes." The translator not only renders the participle by a milder term "provokes, offends,"[40] but also avoids the tetragrammaton by substituting τὸν θεόν, a reading followed by all Greek witnesses. Normally, the את particle is rendered by the article, and the translator did so with his τόν, but was then faced with the problem of the tetragrammaton. If he were to render it in the usual way, it would result in τον κυριον, but this would be his rendering of את אדני; since יהוה could only be rendered by an unarticulated κύριον, he substituted θεόν. On the whole, it must be admitted that Num considerably mitigates the sin of arrogance by calling it a provocation of deity rather than a blasphemy of the Lord. The root גדף occurs only here in the Pentateuch; in fact, it only occurs seven times in the Bible, but only once elsewhere, at Isa 37:23, is it also rendered by παροξύνω, though in the parallel version, 4Reg 19:22, it becomes ἐβλασφήμησας, which was also used at v.6. I suspect that the translator did not feel that ἐν χειρὶ ὑπερηφανίας was necessarily blasphemy against the Lord; it was bad enough to brand it "provocation of the deity."

The apodosis as per usual is indicated by a future tense. In MT, it is introduced by *waw*, which Hebraism Num avoided. Apparently, hex had no such qualms, and added καί. The action was a capital offense; "that person must be

---

39. The prepositions are partitive; see SS 169.
40. As does Tar[N] with מחרף קדם הי׳, but comp Ps 44:17. The other two Targums use מרגז "angers."

destroyed from his people." In MT, the verb is נכרתה "must be cut off," commonly rendered by ἐξολεθρευθήσομαι.[41]

15:31 The reason for declaring ἐν χειρὶ ὑπερηφανίας to be a capital offense is given in a ὅτι clause; it is "because the word of the Lord he despised, and his commandments he has broken (or scattered)." Num follows Sam's משפטיו rather than the singular noun of MT.[42] The verb διασκεδάζω is the usual rendering for the Hi of פרר "to breach, break up."

The penalty is a variation of that given in v.30; "ἐκτρίψει ἐκτριβήσεται that person." The cognate free infinitive is rendered by a cognate dative noun: "that person shall certainly be wiped out," i.e. he will die. The verb ἐκτρίβω is used only four times to render כרת (in Ni or Hi); it is a vivid rendering of "be cut off," which is here used absolutely; there is no doubt that excommunication is fatal!

The verse concludes with ἡ ἁμαρτία αὐτῆς ἐν αὐτῇ, a nominal clause meaning "his sin is on him." The Hebrew has עונה "his iniquity," a word which also includes its attendant punishment for such iniquity. The rendering ἁμαρτία is typically inexact; words for evil, sin, iniquity, and the like are seldom rendered consistently in the Greek; the word ἁμαρτία is the most common word for sin, but is not overly specific as characterizing action "with an arrogant hand." Here the word is to be understood as involving the consequence of "sin"; i.e. "the wages of sin is death." The Byz text made the statement a γαρ clause, but the abruptness of Num is original text. The basis for the judgement had already been given in the ὅτι clause, and the nominal clause simply explicates the penalty in another manner.

15:32 Vv.32—36 deal with a violation of the Sabbath day. The occasion was a man collecting ξύλα on the day τῶν σαββάτων. ξύλα translates עצים, and means "pieces of wood, firewood." The plural τῶν σαββάτων is changed by the majority A F M text to the singular του σαββατου. But שבת was transliterated as σάββατα, i.e. the Aramaic emphatic form. σάββατα was easily misunderstood as the plural of a neuter word σάββατον. And in the Pentateuch only the plural obtains; see Note at Exod 16:23. In MT, "on the day" reads as ביום, and a

---

41. In fact, 74 times according to Dos Santos.
42. As does Pesh.

recensional εν was duly added by A n x+; this could be understood as hex in view of its support by ms 376 and Syh of the O group.

15:33 "Those chancing on him brought the one gathering firewood to Moses and Aaron and to the entire assembly of Israelites." MT also has a preposition before "Aaron which would be otiose in Greek; ms 426, an O ms, actually inserted προς before Ἀαρών, obviously on the basis of the Hebrew; the reading is, however, apparently not hex. Rhetorically a repeated προς would be out of place for the pair "Moses and Aaron," but is not objectionable before πᾶσαν συναγωγήν. In the tradition, a B M f n t+ text has added τη ημερα των σαββατων after ξύλα, but this is an error, a gloss taken over from v.32 where it is original.[43] Num also has a gloss; the identification of the assembly as υἱῶν Ἰσραήλ has no basis in MT, and hex has placed it under the obelus. The gloss is otiose; the entire assembly could only be "of Israelites."

15:34 "They put him away in custody, οὐ γὰρ συνέκριναν τί ποιήσωσιν αὐτόν." This differs somewhat from MT which reads כי לא פרש מה יעשה לו. The Masoretes vocalized both verbs as passive, thus "because it had not been decided what should be done to him."[44] By using plural active verbs, Num has a more consistent text, making "those who found you," which was the subject of v.33, the subject throughout. Dorival suggests that this reflects a Targumist tendency, but it is simply a matter of levelling the text.[45] The αὐτόν modifying ποιήσωσιν is unexpected, and an A F O b z+ variant αυτω is not surprising. This is hardly a recensional change, however, since the attraction of a dative of person as a modifier of ποιέω is a simplification of the text. I presume the τί structure means "how they should handle him."

15:35 MT begins with ויאמר, but Num has καὶ ἐλάλησεν. Since λαλέω is the standard rendering for the root דבר, whereas εἶπον is used for אמר, and Num has very few exceptions to these equations, the parent text for καὶ ἐλάλησεν may

---

43. See THGN 134.
44. Dorival 73 suggests that this illustrates the Targumist tendency of LXX. He bases this on the fact that both Tar^O and Tar^N have a singular passive verb, the Ithpeal of פרש, modified by להון, which modifier is absent from Tar^J.
45. Lee 78 translates συνέκριναν by "made a decision."

well have been וידבר.⁴⁶ Num has also added the signal for direct speech, λέγων; hex has placed this under the obelus, since MT has no לאמר.

The divine judgment is that "the man must certainly die." MT has מות יומת "he must certainly be put to death." Num again renders the cognate free infinitive by a cognate dative noun, in which the noun is used in the same sense as the free infinitive; i.e. it places special stress on the verbal notion.

The form of death is also prescribed. רגום is a free infinitive as well. When the free infinitive occurs in isolation, it simply puts out the verbal notion, i.e. "stone," which would be imperatival. But the free infinitive in context takes on whatever syntactic function is demanded by it. Since the actor for רגום is given as כל העדה, with אתו באבנים constituting verbal modifiers, what MT means is "the entire assembly must stone him with stones." Num did not understand this, and took רגום as in isolation rather than in context, and so rendered it by an imperative λιθοβολήσατε. This makes for an awkward syntagm, since πᾶσα ἡ συναγωγή can then only be taken as vocative, thus "stone him ..., you who are the entire assembly." The modifier λίθοις expresses instrument or means.⁴⁷

MT has added a locative expression, מחוץ למחנה, for the execution of the violator of the Sabbath rest, but Num has omitted this. Hex added εξω της παρεμβολης in order to equal MT. Since the locative is twice present in v.36, there is no obvious reason for its omission here. It might be noted that homoioteleuton does exist in MT; i.e. both העדה and למחנה end in *he*, and could have promoted an unintended omission.

15:36 Accordingly, the entire assembly carried out the divine order. They "brought him outside the camp, and πᾶσα ἡ συναγωγή stoned him with stones ἔξω τῆς παρεμβολῆς." Num rather carelessly repeated the subject as well as the locative phrase, both of which lack an equivalent in MT. Hex omitted both of these to conform to the Hebrew. MT, however, has וימת at the end of v.a. What hex did was to put και απεθανεν under the asterisk in the lacuna created by the omission of ἔξω τῆς παρεμβολῆς, thereby representing MT precisely. Hex also noted that MT had באבנים, and that Num had not translated the preposition; so hex added εν under the asterisk before the instrumental λίθοις.⁴⁸

---

46. See THGN 128.
47. See SS 121.
48. See SS 121.

V.b states that all this was done καθὰ συνέταξεν κύριος τῷ Μωυσῇ. MT has את משה modifying צוה, but συντάσσω does not take an accusative of person in modification. In fact, whenever the formula "as (or which) the Lord commanded Moses" occurs, the addressee is always the articulated dative, τῷ Μωυσῇ.[49] The majority A F M text reads πρὸς μωυσην, but this is never used by Num in modification of συντάσσω or ἐντέλλομαι. τῷ Μωυσῇ is original text. Instead of συνέταξεν, the majority A F M V text read ελαλησεν. Presumably, this is an attempt at harmonization; after all, according to v.35 the Lord ἐλάλησεν the judgement to be exacted, and the variant should be taken seriously. I would have taken it to be original text, except that O reads the variant text, whereas Cod B supports the Num text. It is then probably an early instance of rational exegesis, i.e. of influence of v.35's verb on this text.

15:38 What the Israelites are to do on the Lord's orders was: καὶ ποιησάτωσαν ἑαυτοῖς κράσπεδα ἐπὶ τὰ πτερύγια τῶν ἱματίων αὐτῶν. Since this begins with καί (for ועשו), it is coordinated with "and you shall say to them," and the verb is third plural imperative: thus: "and let them make for themselves." What they are to make are "fringes on the wings (i.e. the hems) of their garments." κράσπεδα is used for ציצת, which occurs only here and in v.39 in the Pentateuch, and is only translated by the plural of κράσπεδον, i.e. it is understood as a collective. It is also possible that Num had Sam as parent text, since it reads the plural ציציות. The word ציצת also occurs at Ezek 8:3 in the context of the prophetic transport through a יד תבנית by the ציצת ראשי. The translator rendered this by τῆς κορυφῆς μου, i.e. he omitted ציצת entirely; at least it was so interpreted by The Three who added a rendering of ציצת as a plus.[50] Since ציצת may well mean "tassels," it is possible that this was also intended by Num. Note that כנפי is also rendered by τὰ πτερύγια "wings"; what is meant is the hems (of their garments).

The next clause appears in second person plural future, whereas MT continues with the third person ונתנו. The third person is throughout a difficulty, and a second person for the two clauses would have been much clearer, but neither text supports such, though Num goes halfway, having ἐπιθήσετε for the second clause. Actually, the change to second person is made with the next verse. In any case, the Israelites are ordered, whether in third person or in second, to put a

---

49. See THGN 108.
50. Theod and Aq added τοῦ κρασπέδου, whereas Sym added τοῦ μαλλοῦ.

blue thread on these κράσπεδα. It should be noted that here Sam does not read the plural ציציות.

15:39 Num begins with καὶ ἔσται ὑμῖν ἐν τοῖς κρασπέδοις, referring to the blue thread of v.38, which will be in the fringes/tassels. MT has לציצת "(and it will be for you) for a tassel," which is not clear at all; nor is Sam with its plural noun clearer. Somehow the reference in היה must be the פתיל, which is how Num understood it.

The purpose of the κράσπεδα is then stated as "and you shall see them and recall all the Lord's commandments and do them (i.e. the commandments)." What is meant is "and when you see them, you will recall ...." This is also clearer than MT, where the modifier of עשיתם is the masculine singular אתו. This could be interpreted as referring to פתיל, but the "it" probably is an indefinite reference referring to the whole procedure, tassel(s) plus thread.

Num has πασῶν τῶν ἐντολῶν as modifier of μνησθήσεσθε. The Byz text has changed the modifier to the accusative; this is an attempt to invoke the Classical distinction in which the verb with the genitive means "to give heed to," and with the accusative, "to remember, recall." In Hellenistic times, the genitive was generally preferred throughout. The following coordinate clause is stylistically improved by the Byz text by changing it to a complementary infinitive structure, i.e. καὶ ποιήσετε becomes ποιῆσαι.

The negative counterpart is given in v.b. "And not may you turn aside after your thoughts and after your eyes, in (or by) which you are prostituting yourselves after them." This follows the Hebrew rather closely, in fact, at times too closely. MT has לבבכם, but the translator individuates by using the plural τῶν διανοιῶν. The last clause in the Greek is rather difficult to translate. In MT, this is a nominal clause: אשר אתם זנים אחריהם "after which you go whoring." As usual, Num translates by means of a pronoun and a present tense, but found אשר plus אחריהם difficult, and translated doubly by ἐν οἷς as well as by ὀπίσω αὐτῶν.[51] This could mean "by (means of) which you prostitute yourselves after them."[52]

---

51 Sym translates by οἷς ὑμεῖς πορνεύοντες ὑμεῖς ἀκολουθῶντες ὑμεῖς (retroverted from Syh).
52. See the discussion in Dorival.

15:40 Num renders word for word. The verbs μνησθῆτε and ποιήσητε are expressed coordinately, though the second one is the content of the first one. What is meant is "(in order that) you may remember to perform ...;" see the Byz variant text in v.39. Then v.b, again expressed paratactically, is actually the result of v.a. This is clear in the Greek from the change in verbal inflection to the future. What this meant is that "when you remember to perform all my commandments, then you will be holy to your God." Being ἄγιοι to God means being totally set aside to his service, i.e. committed to God.

15:41 The verse consists of two nominal clauses in both Num and MT. In each case ἐγώ/אני serves as subject. The first clause is not only a self-identification formula, but it also includes by means of an attributive participial structure a redemptive motif: "the one who brought you out of the land of Egypt," along with a covenantal purposive infinitival εἶναι ὑμῶν θεός. In MT this purpose reads להיות לכם לאלהים "to become God for you." In the tradition, the ὑμῶν only changes to υμιν in one Greek ms, which would be closer to MT. But the preposition in לכם can indicate possession as well. Note how the translator indicated word order as well by placing ὑμῶν before θεός. The second clause is a simple self-identification formula: "I am the Lord your God."

Chapter 16

16:1 MT begins with ויקח קרח "And Korah took," but the verb lacks a modifier, and no one, ancient of modern, has come up with a convincing explanation.[1] Num goes its own way, and has καὶ ἐλάλησεν Κόρε. I would take this to be singular by attraction to the nearest of the compound subject: "Kore ... and Dathan and Abiron ... and Aun." Then v.2 begins with καὶ ἀνέστησαν, thus "there spoke Kore and ..., and they stood up against...." I doubt that καὶ ἐλάλησεν must presuppose a parent וידבר; the translator could make no sense out of ויקח, and used his common sense to make a contextually fitting beginning to the story of the rebellion.[2]

Kore was the son of Ἰσαάρ, which transcribes יצהר. Though most copyists agreed with A B M V in spelling the name as ισσααρ, this cannot be original. The letter צ is not doubled, nor does ה assimilate to it. On the other hand, an initial *he* in a syllable is readily shown by *alpha*. Only Ἰσαάρ can be original.[3] The lineage of Kore is given, whereby it appears that Kore was a first cousin of Moses and Aaron; see Exod 6:16—21.

MT has אבירם for Ἀβιρών. It is of interest to note that the Qumran ms 4QNum^b reads אבירום, i.e. has an "o" vowel in the final syllable. Actually, ms G reads αβειρωμ, but this is coincidental. The nasals are easily confused in Greek script.

The name Αὐν for און is otherwise completely unknown. In the tradition, only B x and Cyr support the original spelling, all others reading αυναν or some derivative of it. This derives from Αὐνάν/אונן, the son of Judah (26:15 Gen 38:4,8,9 46:12). The father's name Φάλεθ/פלת is also rare, though it does occur once in 1Chr 2:33 as a descendant of Judah, which was also probably transcribed as Φάλεθ.[4] The two were, however, different individuals, since Φάλεθ, the father

---
1. Tar^O reads אתפלג "separated himself." Tar^N has פליג, whereas Tar^J followed MT with ונסיב, but then phantasized as to what he took on the basis of 15:38—39 by his גולייתיה דכולא תיכלא "a cloak which was entirely purple."
2. For a detailed discussion of the evidence, see Dorival 89—91.
3. See the discussion in THGN 115—116.
4. The reading Θαλεθ of B is obviously an error inspired by uncial confusion of Θ and Φ.

of Αὔν, was a Roubenite. The identification of Φάλεθ as υἱοῦ 'Ρουβήν follows Sam; MT reads בני ראובן, i.e. applying not only to Aun, but also to Dathan and Abiron.⁵

16:2 The four listed in v.1 "stood up before Moses, and 250 men τῶν υἱῶν 'Ισραήλ." The genitive translates a מן construction of MT, which is partitive in nature.⁶ These men are designated as ἀρχηγοὶ συναγωγῆς; this renders MT's נשיאי עדה only here in the Pentateuch, which otherwise uses ἄρχοντες (συναγωγῆς) for this structure (31:13 32:2 Exod 16:22). Elsewhere, ἀρχηγός occurs in the book to translate ראש, whereas ἄρχων is used for נשיא 58 times, but ἀρχηγός obtains only seven times in Num (though only twice for נשיא).

The next title is a unique translation. For MT's קראי מועד Num has σύγκλητοι βουλῆς. The term קראי only occurs three times in the Bible (also at 1:16 26:9 where it is rendered by ἐπίκλητος, whereas βούλη occurs only here in the Bible for מועד); in fact, it only occurs three times in the Pentateuch: at Gen 49:6 for סוד, and at Deut 32:28 for עצה, both in poetic contexts, and here. The term βουλή is a political term for a deliberating council, such as the Senate in Athens. Just what a βουλή would be to an Alexandrian Jew is not clear, but it must have been some kind of consultative group; what is clear was that it had standing in the community. In fact, it must have represented the συναγωγή, since it could summon leaders. As at 1:16 I understand the genitive as subjective. In 1:16 the ἐπίκλητοι are τῆς συναγωνῆς, i.e. those whom the assembly called. More relevant are the ἐπίκλητοι τῆς συναγωγῆς or קרואי העדה of 26:9, since this applies specifically to those who withstood Moses and Aaron "in the assembly of Kore." Here, however, the συναγωγή appears as a βουλή, which by its deliberation has called together, summoned the 250 men. In other words, the men had been especially called to leadership by the assembly acting as a βουλή. In fact, they are also ἄνδρες ὀνομαστοί, a rendering of אנשי שם, a collocation known from Gen 6:4, where οἱ γίγαντες of ancient times were called οἱ ἄνθρωποι οἱ ὀνομαστοί. In other words, they were renowned men, men of stature, of reputation. In Num this is coordinated with σύγκλητοι βουλῆς, but neither MT nor Sam has a conjunction. It is, however, attested by 4QNumᵇ which reads ואנשי שם, and this was undoubtedly the parent text for Num.

---

5. Though 4QNumᵇ apparently reads the singular בן, i.e. as in Sam.
6. See SS 168.

16:3 MT begins with ויקהלו על "and they gathered themselves together against." The Masoretes vocalized the verb as Ni, but Num translated it by συνέστησαν, an unusual rendering found elsewhere only at Exod 32:1 where the people συνέστη to Aaron. But here the verb is probably to be taken in a hostile sense "stood up together against (ἐπί)." MT has "against Moses and על Aaron, and they said אלהם." Greek normally does not repeat the preposition before coordinate nouns, though one O ms, 426, has added επι before 'Ααρών, undoubtedly an addition inspired by the Hebrew text. Num has also omitted אלהם, and an A F M majority text has added προς αυτους after εἶπαν; this is probably recensional (hex?).

What they say is ἐχέτω ὑμῖν ὅτι .... "Let it be held fast for you that." What this means is "Let it be understood that."[7] This idiom renders רב לכם "it is too much for you (that)."[8] What they aver is a given in "that all the assembly is fully holy and the Lord is in them (i.e. among those who are πάντες ἅγιοι)." The ὅτι clause is then to be taken as the subject of ἐχέτω; that is what is to be held fast, viz. that not just Moses and Aaron have authority, but the entire assembly is also holy, and the Lord is among its members as well.

V.b then raises the rebellious question: "and why are you standing up against the Lord's assembly"? I would take the verb to be a present indicative passive inflection. The translator has created a solid picture of complaint against Moses by using three compounds of ἵστημι on the part of the opponents to Moses: ἀνέστησαν (v.2), συνέστησαν and now κατανίστασθε in v.3. There is also a gradual increase in the level of opposition. The opponents rise up before Moses; they band together against; they complain that Moses and Aaron are rising up in opposiiton against the Lord's assembly.

16:4 Num subordinates וישמע to a participle καὶ ἀκούσας modifying the subject Μωυσῆς. The main verb then puts the stress where it belongs: "Moses fell ἐπὶ πρόσωπον." MT has על פניו as expected.[9] Hex has added αυτου to represent the suffix.[10] It should be mentioned once again that the Num translator tends to translate the suffixes, in fact, much more so than Gen, Exod and Lev, though not to

---

7. This is an unusual use of the verb ἔχω; see SS 182.
8. Theod and Aq render this in isolate fashion by πολὺ ὑμῖν, but Sym more idiomatically has ἀρκείτω "let it suffice."
9. See SS 99.
10. The Others added αὐτοῦ as well.

the extent that Deut does.[11] According to SS only 80 cases of an untranslated suffix occur in the book.

16:5 The opening word of God's statement is בקר, which the Masoretes have vocalized as "morning," Num understood as the verb בקר "to seek out, examine," and translated by ἐπέσκεπται. For this rendering, see Note at Lev 13:36. The verb is similarly rendered at Ps 26(27):4: "that I might see the delight of the Lord and ἐπισκέπτεσθαι τὸν ναὸν αὐτοῦ," as well as in Ezek 34:11: "Lo, I will seek out my sheep and ἐπισκέψομαι αὐτά." So instead of "in the morning" and of "ידע יהוה," Num reads "(God) has taken note and known." Num has ὁ θεός instead of יהוה, and has understood ידע as Qal, rather than the Masoretic Hi, in which the divine speech of v.a reads: "In the morning, even Yahweh will make known who belongs to him and the holy one (i.e. and who is holy), and will bring near to himself." Num understood בקר וידע as past tense, and changed Yahweh, the personal name of God, to "God." In Num this might then be translated: "God has examined and known those who are his and the holy ones and brought (them) to himself."[12] For Num the reference seems to be to Moses and Aaron; they are the ones whom God has examined, and brought to himself.[13] In the Greek the divine choice of Moses and Aaron had already been made; in MT that decision is to be proclaimed tomorrow.

This is confirmed by v.b, where the verbs of MT are all changed to past tense, thus ויקריב becomes καὶ προσηγάγετο; יבחר, ἐξελέξατο, and יקריב, προσηγάγετο. It involves both Moses and Aaron as the plural οὕς shows. In both cases of προσηγάγετο it is modified by πρὸς ἑαυτόν. To "bring near to himself" means to approach the altar, i.e. serve as priest.[14]

In the tradition, hex has transposed αὐτοῦ 1° after τὴν συναγωγήν to equal the order of עדתו. Ms 426 reads κυριος instead of ὁ θεός; obviously this reading is inspired by the Hebrew.[15] Furthermore, the majority A F M V text has omitted

---

11. See the count in SS, ch.8, especially pp.88,92,95,98 and 101.
12. This may well depend on a Hebrew text. N.b. that 4QNum[b] read הקריב instead of והקריב as well as ב]חר] rather than יבחר.
13. Both Tar[JO] interpret את אשר לו as "the one who כשר ל(י)ה, i.e. "the one who is acceptable, *kosher* to him." What is meant is one who is acceptable as the priest. Tar[N] renders literally by מן דמן דידה.
14. This is certainly made clear in Tar[J]; the first אליו becomes לפולחניה, and the second one, לשימושיה. Tar[O] also made the second one לשמושה.
15. The Others also read κυριος (retroverted from Syh).

the conjunction in καὶ προσηγάγετο, a stylistic improvement indeed. Another majority A F M reading has sought to make better sense by adding ουκ before ἐξελέξατο, but this is not how Num understood what God had said. The same exegesis inspired this majority text to add ου before the second προσηγάγετο. What this interpretation sought to say was "whom he had not chosen for himself, he did not bring to himself," but this is secondary.

16:6—7 The imperatival "this do, take for yourselves censers" is addressed to Κόρε καὶ πᾶσα ἡ συναγωὴ αὐτοῦ; this follows MT exactly. Of course, the sense of the vocative must be "Kore and all your assembly." The reflexive pronoun is ὑμῖν ἑαυτοῖς.[16] Hex found two pronouns rendering לכם one too many, and placed ὑμῖν under the obelus. The double form is, however, attested as early as the fourth century BCE. In MT, the instructions "and put on them (i.e. the censers) fire, and place on them incense" use two different verbs, תנו and שימו, which Num rendered in identical fashion "and ἐπίθετε on them"; admittedly, the two are synonyms, and here Num did not distinguish between them.

The judgment to be rendered on the morrow is καὶ ἔσται ὁ ἀνὴρ ὃν ἂν ἐκλέξηται κύριος οὗτος ἅγιος. The initial words introducing the relative clause are a pendent structure, which is then brought into the statement by οὗτος. What is said is "And there will be the man whom the Lord should choose—this one is holy." All that the introductory "and the man shall be" does is to place the structure into the future; this one will be holy. A better rendering might well be "As for the man whom ..., he (οὗτος) will be holy." What ἅγιος means is that οὗτος is the one acceptable to the Lord; he is the one who is set aside for special service. The issue will be decisive: it will be Aaron or you and your assembly.

MT repeats the רב לכם of v.3, but instead of ἐχέτω ὑμῖν, Num here translates by ἱκανούσθω ὑμῖν "let it be sufficient for you." This is the first instance of this verb being used for the רב idiom, but it became relatively popular among later translators (eight times; three in Deut).[17]

16:8 "Moses said to Kore," but addresses the group; the imperative εἰσακούσατε is plural, and υἱοὶ Λευί is vocative. Note that the verb is modified by μου, which

---
16. See the discussion on the reflexive pronouns in Mayser I,2,63—64.
17. According to HR.

is an ad sensum gloss. MT also has נא following שמעו, but Num never translates this particle. Or did the translator read שמעו נא as שמעוני as BHS suggests?

16:9 המעט מכם כי is a Hebrew idiom, literally "is it less than you that," which means "Is it too little (a matter) for you that." Num translates by μὴ μικρόν ἐστιν τοῦτο ὑμῖν ὅτι. The μή signifies a question expectant of a negative answer. The τοῦτο is a gloss presumably added for clarity; it, as well as the ἐστιν, has been placed under the obelus, since these have no actual counterparts in MT. In MT, the מן of מכם is comparative. This is here expressed in Num by the positive degree μικρόν plus a dative pronoun.[18]

τοῦτο refers to the ὅτι clause which follows. In Num, the verb is followed by ὑμᾶς ὁ θεὸς Ἰσραήλ, and in MT אתכם follows the subject "the God of Israel." The translator often preferred the pronominal modifier to follow the verb immediately, but hex transposed the order to that of MT.[19] MT ends v.a with a purposive infinitive להקריב אתכם אליו, i.e. "(he has separated you from the assembly of Israel) to bring you near to himself." In MT this ends v.a; i.e. the *ethnach* was placed under אליו by the Masoretes.

Num has a different view of things; in fact, it divides the verse at this point by changing the infinitive to a coordinate clausal structure: "and he brought you near to himself," plus two purposive infinitives. In other words, God did two things: he separated the Levites from the other Israelites, and he brought them to the tabernacle for a dual purpose. Why did the God of Israel "bring you near to himself," i.e. into the sanctuary complex where God himself was present? First of all, it was "λειτουργεῖν τὰς λειτουργίας of the tent of the Lord." Hex has prefixed the infinitive with an εἰς τὸ under the asterisk. This was intended to show that the infinitival marker ל was present in MT. λειτουργίας can refer to public service of any kind, but here it is defined as τῆς σκηνῆς κυρίου, i.e. as religious duties specifically assigned to Levites, for which see 4:4—33 and comp 8:5—26. In MT, this is described as לעבד את עבדת משכן יהוה "to perform the work of the tent of Yahweh."

The second purpose for the Lord's setting the Levites aside from the other tribes was "to stand ready before the assembly λατρεύειν αὐτοῖς." What this entails is that the Levites stand ready to assist members of the assembly of Israel

---

18. See SS 150.
19. See THGN 102.

in performing their religious duties. Note that the assembly is sensibly referred to as individuals, i.e. as αὐτοῖς. The infinitive in MT is לשרתם. This verb is usually rendered by λειτουργέω (68 times), and by λατρεύω only twice (also in Ezek 20:32).[20] Here λατρεύειν was chosen, since λειτουργέω had been preempted for עבד.

16:10 V.a is rendered word for word by Num, but v.b interprets MT's ובקשתם גם כהנה "and you seek to gain priestly status too"? Num has omitted גם entirely, and has changed the noun into an infinitive, ἱερατεύειν, thus "and you seek to be priests." MT has a noun rather than an infinitive; כהנה means "the priesthood, priestly status."[21] Hex has added και γε under the asterisk to represent the גם. Usually גם is rendered simply by καί (nine out of 14 times) in Num; it is apparently omitted four times, and once it is represented by μέν (22:33). It is never represented by και γε, which is characteristic of Theodotion; this was probably the source for hex here.

16:11 V.a is peculiar, and its syntax is not clear. There is no verb, and it reads word for word "So you and all your assembly ἡ συνηθροισμένη to God."[22] This obviously contrasts with v.b: "and who is Aaron that you should be murmuring against him"? The stress must then be on πρὸς τὸν θεόν, which I would understand to be the predicate of a nominal clause, with the subject as "you and your assembly which has been brought together." In MT, the corresponding predicate is על יהוה. Why the translator should have substituted τὸν θεόν for יהוה, as he did at v.5, is not clear. After all, the rebellious action is not first of all of man over against deity, but of Levites over against Israel's God, Yahweh. I can see no good reason for the change, and to say that the parent text must have been אלהים is no great help, since one would then ask, but why the change to אלהים when יהוה is clearly original and appropriate? Unusual also is the rendering of the preposition by πρός; since an επι would have been more obvious for showing opposition.[23] But πρός can be used in a hostile sense as well, and here must mean

---

20. The count is that of Dos Santos.
21. The Tar all define this as "high priestly status."
22. For the participle Aq read οἱ συντεταγμένοι, whereas Theod and Sym have οἱ συνηγμένοι.
23. Tar[N] renders the predicate by קדם הי.

"(brought together) against God."²⁴ Also problematic is the use of οὕτως "thus, so" for לכן "therefore." What the translator has apparently done, since לכן is not overly luminous anyway, is to disregard the preposition and take לכן as though it were כן. One might then provisionally translate v.a as "Thus you and all your assembly which has been brought together are against God."

V.b is a clear statement. It is poor Aaron who is really the object of rebellion on the part of Kore and his assembly; it is Aaron's priesthood that is at stake. The rendering of תלונו is correctly put into the present tense; they are murmuring against Aaron.

16:12 Vv.12—15 describe Dothan and Abiron's challenge to Moses' authority; this fits rather oddly in the context of Korah's challenge to Aaron's priestly status. When Moses summoned them, they refused, saying οὐκ ἀναβαίνομεν, using the present tense verb rather than a future, though נעלה does not distinguish between present and future. But the Greek translator uses the future as default rendering for the prefix inflected verb, and one must conclude that the choice of the present is deliberate; they declare themselves in rebellion. In v.14 this is repeated, but with reasons attached; cf comment at v.14. For the transcription Ἀβιρών for אבירם, see comment at v.1.

16:13 For μὴ μικρόν as rendering for המעט, see comment at v.9. As at v.9, Num has added τοῦτο as subject, and again hex has placed the pronoun under the obelus. That the Exodus should have been ἐκ γῆς ῥεούσης γάλα καὶ μέλι is particularly insulting, since this description is otherwise reserved for describing the land of promise. In the tradition, a V b n+ gloss has identified this land by adding ἐξ αἰγυπτου before the ἐκ phrase.²⁵ In fact, so fixed is this description for the land of Canaan, that the majority A B F M text has changed ἐκ γῆς ῥεούσης to read εἰς γην ρεουσαν, an obvious, but understandable mistake.

V.b constitutes a second ὅτι clause modifying μὴ μικρὸν τοῦτο. It reads ὅτι κατάρχεις ἡμῶν ἄρχων "that you are ruling over us as chief," an attempt to render the rare השתרר כי תשתרר עלינו גם. The verb is a Hithp of שרר, a denominative verb from שר "prince, chief." The free infinitive serves to stress the verbal

---
24. See LS sub πρός B.I.4.
25. So did Tarᴶ. Tarᴺ also felt the need to clarify MT and reads "from a land producing fruit pure as milk and sweet as honey."

idea. It thus means something like "that you should actually set yourself up as chief (or prince) over us." Note that Num has again used the present tense, thereby showing Dathan and Abiron's current dissatisfaction with the state of affairs. In the tradition, the Byz text has attempted to correct the noun ἄρχων so as to reflect the verbal idea of the free infinitive by reading συ αρχων ει.[26]

16:14 The initial אף לו as vocalized by the Masoretes is unique. Num probably revocalized לו to read *lu*, thus εἰ καί "if even," i.e. "even if." In the tradition, the majority A F M V text has added συ, for which see the text of Aq. It is, however, not original text in spite of its strong support. The verse expresses a contrary-to-fact conditional sentence in past tense; this is clear from the apodosis which consists of ἄν plus an aorist verb. What Num says is: "even if you had brought us into a land flowing with milk and honey, and given us an inheritance of field and vineyards, you would have cut out the eyes of these men (referring 'to us')." To which the rebels appended οὐκ ἀναβαίνομεν, for which see comment at v.12. The notion of "cut out the eyes" represents a Hebrew idiom meaning "to blind," i.e. to mislead.[27] Num interprets כרם as a collective noun, but not שדה; one might have expected the two coordinate nouns to be treated in similar fashion.

Num differs principally from MT in its rendering of the apodosis; in MT this is introduced by an interrogative prefix in העיני, but here Num has disregarded the ה-, and made it a statement, thereby making the complaint a direct challenge to Moses' authority, which is then made fully defiant by the final "we are not coming up."[28]

16:15 According to MT, Moses "became very angry," Num has made of Moses, who according to 12:3 was πραὺς σφόδρα παρὰ πάντας τοὺς ἀνθρώπους τοὺς

---

26. Aq renders v.b by ὅτι ἄρχεις ἡμῶν καίγε ἄρχων (by retroversion from Syh), whereas Sym has κατατυραννεῖς γὰρ ἡμῶν βιαίως (+ʿm hy Syh; this is puzzling; I find no basis of any kind for it in MT).
27. Milgrom compares the modern idiom "throw dust in one's eyes."
28. Aq renders the verse by καὶ σὺ πρὸς τὴν ῥέουσαν γάλα καὶ μέλι ἤγαγες ἡμᾶς, καὶ ἔδωκας ἡμῖν κληροδοσίαν (ʾyhybwt yrtwtʾ) χώρας καὶ ἀμπελῶνας (or -ώνων), οὐ (or μὴ καὶ) τους ὀφθαλμοὺς τῶν ἀνθρώπων τούτων ἂν ἐξέκοψας. οὐκ ἀναβαίνομεν; Sym translates ὅτι οὐδὲ εἰς γῆν ῥέουσαν γάλα καὶ μέλι εἰσήγαγες ἡμᾶς οὐδὲ ἔδωκας ἡμῖν κλήρους χώρας καὶ ἀμπελώνων, μὴ καὶ τοὺς ὀφθαλμοὺς τῶν ἀνθρώπων τούτων ἐκκόψεις. οὐκ ἀναβαίνομεν. (Both are retroverted from Syh).

ὄντας ἐπὶ τῆς γῆς, a man who "was very heavy of spirit," ἐβαρυθύμησεν σφόδρα.[29] This seems to be an intentional change to make Moses a more sensitive individual, one who instead of making a direct retort to the rebels speaks to the Lord.

What Moses said was "do not pay attention to their θυσίαν." MT has מנחתם.[30] The Greek verb is correctly read as προσσχῆς, not as in the majority A B F M V text προσχης. The verb is προσέχω, not προέχω.[31] The reason for asking the Lord not to regard the sacrifice of the rebels is that they have falsely accused Moses. He states: "not have I taken ἐπιθύμημα of anyone αὐτῶν, nor have I done harm to anyone αὐτῶν." The αὐτῶν are both examples of privative genitives.[32] MT has חמור, i.e. "I have taken no one's ass." Obviously, the translator misread the *resh* as a *daleth*. Various derivatives of the root חמד find their usual renderings in ἐπιθύμημα; see also ἐπιθυματός, and it is clear that Num read חמד.[33] The two consonants are easily confused, not only in the Aramaic script, i.e. ר vs ד, but they are also very similar in the old Canaanite scripts. ἐπιθύμημα/חמד also make good sense; according to Num, Moses said: "I have not taken a desirable object from anyone of them."[34]

In the tradition, hex has corrected the preposition εἰς in the phrase εἰς τὴν θυσίαν αὐτῶν to πρός, since MT reads אל.

16:16 What Moses said to Kore differs in Num from MT, except for v.b, where Num translated MT exactly. MT begins with אתה וכל עדתך, but Num substitutes an imperative ἁγίασον for אתה וכל, thus reading "sanctify your assembly." This must presuppose a different parent text. Num reflects some such occasion as that of Exod 19:14—15, where Moses ἡγίασεν αὐτούς (i.e. the people), and said to them γίνεσθε ἕτοιμοι. MT then continues with an imperative היו, which Num interprets by καὶ γίνεσθε ἕτοιμοι. The καί is made necessary in view of the

---

29. Comp באיש in Tar^N.
30. Aq and Sym translate the noun by δῶρον. Daniel 222 suggests that the anonymous τὰς προσφοράς came from Sym, probably correctly, in which case I would suggest that the attribution of δῶρον to Sym is an error for Theod; after all, the uncial designations Σ′ and Θ′ are very similar palaeographically.
31. See Walters 82—83.
32. See SS 168.
33. G.Veltri, Eine Tora für den König Talmi. Texte u. Studien zum Antiken Judentum 4 (Tübingen, 1994), 88—92 argues for חמוד as original Text.
34. Theod and Aq correct the rendering of חמור to ὄνον.

imperative being a second one, and therefore the clause is coordinate. Hex has placed ἕτοιμοι under the obelus, since MT has no equivalent for the adjective. But the imperative היו cries out for completion as a predicate, and "be prepared" could be taken as a free rendering for היו,[35] though presumably "be present (before Yahweh)," i.e. "present yourselves" is what MT intends.

16:17 The Lord's orders take up those of vv.6—7a in detail. "Each one" is defined as including the 250 men as well as σὺ καὶ 'Ααρών. ἕκαστος throughout explicates the second person plural subject of the verb; e.g. "and λάβετε, each (of you) individually his censer," etc. The four individuals of v.1 are here presumably included in the 250. In the tradition, the C' s text add αυριον after ἔναντι κυρίου, but this is an import from v.16, and has no justification in MT.

16:18 MT begins with ויקחו, but Num has the singular καὶ ἔλαβεν in order to be grammatically congruent with the subject ἕκαστος.[36] Only after the initial clause does Num change to the plural with MT.[37]

V.b reads "and there stood near the doors of the tent of testimony, Moses and Aaron." This differs considerably from MT, which reads ומשה ואהרן, i.e. "they stood ..., along with Moses and Aaron."[38] By omitting the conjunction before משה, only Moses and Aaron stood near the doors of the tent. Num reads παρὰ τὰς θύρας, though MT simply has פתח. The preposition is, however, necessary, but hex did change the plural to the singular τὴν θύραν to equal MT. In MT, פתח is always singular when referring to the tent of meeting, but Num is inconsistent, using the plural four times in the book, and the singular nine times. From v.19 it is clear that the entire group of rebels stood near the door, and in v.20 it becomes obvious that Moses and Aaron are also there; see discussion ad loc.

---

35. Both Tar[JO] have הוו זמינין "be prepared" as an interpretation of היו.
36. Theod and Aq follow MT with καὶ ἔλαβον. Tar[N] has the singular ונסיב, whereas Tar[JO] read the plural.
37. Sym subordinates v.a by means of participles, and thereby makes the verb in v.b the main verb. It reads for v.a λάβοντες δὲ ἕκαστος πυρεῖον ἴδιον καὶ ἐπιθέντες εἰς αὐτὰ πῦρ, and of course then omitted the καί introducing v.b.
38. Kenn 196 also reads משה.

16:19 Num changed v.a by adding an αὐτοῦ after "the entire assembly"; what Num says is "and Kore gathered together his entire assembly against them near the door (singular) of the tent of testimony." MT could be understood to refer to the entire assembly of Israel, and Num made certain that the text would be understood to refer only to his followers. This is not what MT intended, however, as is clear from the narrative that follows. It is there presupposed from both vv.22 and 24 that the assembly of Korah was distinctive. Hex, however, placed αὐτοῦ under the obelus in strict adherence to MT's העדה. The phrase ἐπ' αὐτούς must refer to Moses and Aaron, i.e. the gathering is a hostile one over against them. In the tradition, the A V Byz x+ text changed τὴν θύραν to the plural τὰς θύρας, for which see the discussion at v.18, which is probably the source of the variant text.

Num renders MT v.b accurately. The δόξα of the Lord appeared to all the assembly. This δόξα was presumably the luminous cloud which signified the presence of the Lord.

16:20 As often, Num does not repeat the preposition before a second coordinate noun, whereas Hebrew does have אל before Aaron, as well as before Moses.

16:21 Num renders הבדלו in vivid fashion by ἀποσχίσθητε "split yourselves (out of the midst of the assembly)." The verb recurs in v.26, but there it represents סורו. V.b has ואכלה; the Masoretes vocalize the verb as the long form of the verb, which after *waw* commonly indicates a result clause. Num renders the conjunction in the usual way by καί, and the verb as ἐξαναλώσω, which I would take to be an aorist cohortative subjunctive, correctly representing the long form of the verb. I would translate the clause: "so that I may annihilate them εἰς ἅπαξ. This phrase occurs only here, and means "once for all." It translates כרגע "in an instant" adequately.

16:22 For ἔπεσον a popular A B F M text reads the Hellenistic επεσαν. On the whole, it would seem that the translator preferred the Classical second aorist spelling.[39] Only for εἶπαν is the Hellenistic spelling assured throughout. For other verbs, including πίπτω, the Classical form is preferred.[40] The subject must be

---
39. Aq reads ἔπεσαν, but both Theod and Aq retain the ἔπεσον of Num.
40. See THGN 124.

Moses and Aaron. They address God as "θεὸς θεός of the spirits and of all flesh." The coordinate genitives represent הרוחת לכל בשר, rather than coordinate nouns. The "spirits for all flesh" would be better rendered by a second genitive, since the spirits refer to the breath of life for all flesh.[41] The Num text could even be understood as distinguishing the spiritual and the physical aspects of human life, which obviously cannot be understood for the Hebrew.

The prayer itself is a complaint: "if one person sinned, is the anger of the Lord on all the assembly"? This differs from MT where the apodosis reads ועל כל העדה תקצף "against all the assembly will you be angry"? Note that "all the assembly" must refer to the Israelite assembly, not just to the followers of Korah; see v.19. Num softens the anthropopathism of Yahweh being angry against the assembly to a third person nominal structure: "will the anger of the Lord be on all the assembly."

16:23—24 After the usual introductory statement "and the Lord spoke πρὸς Μωυσῆν λέγων,"[42] Moses is ordered to speak to the assembly as follows Ἀναχωρήσατε κύκλῳ ἀπὸ τῆς συναγωγῆς Κόρε.[43] The choice of ἀναχωρέω to translate העלו is unique, but it does come up with exactly what MT intends, i.e. the assembly is told to withdraw, move away from. This together with κύκλῳ ἀπό gives the means to withdraw altogether from around. Unusual is the use of למשכן קרח דתן ואבירם. Precisely what does משכן mean here? A משכן can hardly be shared by all three, and modern versions illustrate the difficulty.[44] They take משכן as a collective. Num has a different understanding. According to v.16, Moses had ordered Kore to appear on the morrow together with his συναγωγήν before the Lord. Accordingly, Num reads τῆς συναγωγῆς Κόρε, i.e. has omitted דתן ואבירם, probably as a rationalization in which the translator noted his own τὴν πᾶσαν αὐτοῦ συναγωνήν in v.19. Hex has tried to "correct" Num by adding (και) δαθαν και αβιρων under the asterisk, a reading which easily became the majority A M reading, particularly in view of v.25, which see.

---

41. The vocatives become ἰσχυρὲ θεέ in Theod, but θεὲ ἰσχυρέ in Aq and Sym (both readings retroverted from Syh).
42. Aq read πρὸς Μωυσῆν τῷ λέγειν. For Theod and Sym only λέγων is extant.
43. For The Three following texts are extant. Theod reads λάλησον πρὸς πᾶσαν συναγωγὴν λέγων ἀναχωρήσατε; Aq has λάλησον πρὸς τὴν συναγωγὴν τὸ λέγειν, and Sym has λάλησον πρὸς τὴν συναγωγὴν λέγων ἀναχωρήσατε κυκλόθεν.
44. NJPS translates by "abodes"; NRSV has "dwellings," and NIV reads "tents."

16:25 Vv.25—35 deal with the punishment of the rebels. That this begins a new section in the narrative is clear from Moses' action in going to Dathan and Abiron, together with all the elders of Israel. MT lacks "all," and hex has placed πάντες under the obelus. According to MT, Moses took the initiative, i.e. he "stood up and went to Dathan and Abiram," and then the elders ילכו אחריהם. Num smoothes out these details by its συνεπορεύθησαν μετ' αὐτοῦ "they accompanied him."

16:26 Again Moses spoke to the assembly (i.e. of the Israelites). As in v.21, ἀποσχίσθητε "to split off" is used, but now it occurs for סורו נא "to turn aside." Here Num uses the verb in a new context, ordering the Israelites, not Moses and Aaron as in v.21, to make a sharp division between themselves and "the tents of these callous people." As usual, Num does not translate נא. The use of σκληρῶν to interpret רשעים is unique and unexpected. For the translator, the wickedness of the rebels consists of their callous, hardhearted refusal to be subject to Moses' authority. Hex has changed the verb to a more conventional rendering of סורו, απελθατε, and has added δη under the asterisk to represent the נא particle, which Num normally does not translate. Similarly, hex preferred πονηρων to σκληρῶν for translating רשעים, as a more accurate equivalent.

Furthermore, the assembly is ordered not to "touch πάντων ὅσα belong to them." In the tradition, the B M V Byz x+ text has ων instead of ὅσα, i.e. the relative pronoun is attracted to its antecedent πάντων in number, gender and case, a phenomenon particularly characteristic of the Deut translator. Num, however, always uses ὅσα when its antecedent is πᾶς (with the exception of πᾶς ὅς at 19:16 and παντὸς οὗ at 19:22), and the ων is secondary, possibly Byz in origin.[45]

The μή structure represents a פן clause, and refers specifically to the warning not to touch anything belonging to the rebels "lest you should perish by all their sins." פן is better rendered by μήποτε, and hex has duly added a ποτε under the asterisk. The ἐν is one of means; the sins are the means by which those involved will be punished all together (συναπόλησθε). Note that Num has rather unexpectedly rendered כל חטאתם by a singular πάσῃ τῇ ἁμαρτίᾳ αὐτῶν; it must

---

45. See THGN 99.

of course be taken as a collective. The verb in MT is more colorful; the Ni of ספה means "be brought to an end, be terminated," which of course does involve "perishing."

16:27 In MT, the people "moved away from the משכן of Korah, Dathan and Abiram round about."[46] The Ni of עלה is only rarely used in the sense of "to distance oneself." Its rendering by ἀπέστησαν is unique in LXX, but not incorrect. But then "Dathan and Abiram went out standing at the door of their tents." Num found the distinction between three rebels and the action of two rebels somewhat contradictory, and so made the first clause include only Kore, thus "and they stood away from the tent of Kore round about, And Dathan and Abiron went out and stood ...." Hex has "corrected" Num by adding καὶ δαθαν καὶ αβιρων under the asterisk after Κόρε, thereby resstoring the apparent contradiction.

Num makes no distinction between משכן in v.a, which is translated by σκηνῆς in Num, and the אהלי of Dathan and Abiron in v.b, also translated by σκηνῶν, a correct intuition. The משכן and the אהלים as secular dwellings are tents. In the tradition, σκηνῶν is changed by the majority A F M text to σκηνωμάτων. It might be argued that the majority tradition is original, made to differentiate between the different Hebrew nouns, but in v.25 אהלי was translated by σκηνῶν as well, with only *b* and ms 392 reading σκηνωματων. The fact is that σκήνωμα is never used in Num at all, and σκηνῶν must be original.[47]

Num simplifies נצבים by making it a verb coordinate to ἐξῆλθον, thus "went out and stood," whereas MT reads "went out, arraigning themselves." The only semantic difference lies in the use of a participle as a process; i.e. it means "were stationing themselves (near the door)." Num rendered פתח by the plural, παρὰ τὰς θύρας, since each tent had its own entrance. As subjects coordinate to Dathan and Abiron are listed "and their wives and their children and their ἡ ἀποσκευή." MT has טף, a collective meaning "little ones, infants." In the Tetrateuch, טף occurs 21 times, and in 11 cases it is translated by ἀποσκευή, a translation found only in the Tetrateuch. The word ἀποσκευή usually means "baggage, household stuff," but it can include dependents as well; see Note at Exod 10:10;[48] that here it refers to people is clear; baggage can hardly go out and stand

---

46. For ἀφίστημι in the sense of "stand back, aloof," see Lee 35—36.
47. See THGN 128.
48. See Lee 104—106, where the rendering "family" is proposed.

by tent doors. Since it is coordinate with αἱ γυναῖκες and τὰ τέκνα, it can only mean "little ones" here. This semantic usage is limited to the Tetrateuch.

16:28 Moses now addresses the people and presents the challenge: "ἐν τούτῳ you will know that the Lord sent me." The ἐν is one of means: "by means of this."[49] The τούτῳ is proleptic; it refers to vv.29—30, the test which is to authenticate Moses' authority. Num has ἀπέστειλεν, the default past tense. A C+ text has refined this by changing the aorist to the perfect απεσταλκεν, but this is unnecessary; the aorist is quite sufficient. Precisely what πάντα τὰ ἔργα ταῦτα refers is not stated, nor is it necessary to specify. The works that Moses has done were done by divine authority; "the Lord sent me to do" all these works. In fact, ὅτι οὐκ ἀπ' ἐμαυτοῦ. This ὅτι clause, like the first one, modifies γνώσεσθε, and is the obverse of its counterpart. MT has כי לא מלבי. Since לב is the seat of reason, its translation by the reflexive pronoun is sound. The source of Moses' authority is not his לב, the rational source of human action, the self, but "the Lord sent me to do all these works."

16:29 V.a consists of two εἰ clauses. The first one reflects MT exactly: "if these should die according to the death of all (i.e. common) humanity." What is meant is clear; if these rebels die in normal fashion. MT changes the construction of the second clause to a passive one as "and the visitation of common humanity should be visited on them," i.e. and the fate of all men befall them. Num changed this by prefixing a second εἰ to introduce the condition, and then followed the syntactic pattern of the first one by a κατά phrase as modifier of ἔσται "according to the visitation of all humanity," followed by ἐπισκοπὴ ἔσται "their visitation should be," a stylistic pattern placing the two clauses in exact parallelism.

The apodosis reads οὐχὶ κύριος ἀπέσταλκέν με. Here the perfect verb is more appropriate, since what שלחני means is that "Yahweh had not sent me." The commission was a past event, but the validity of the commission remains with Moses. The majority A F text has changed the verb to the default past, απεστειλεν, which as a contrast to v.28 is not fully appropriate.

16:30 MT has a second conditional structure to contrast with v.29, in which v.a has four conditions, and v.b presents the apodosis: "and you will know that these

---

49. See SS 126.

men had rejected Yahweh." Num has a substantially different pattern. Instead of ואם, it has ἀλλ' ἤ, as though reading כי אם. Instead of conditions following, the verbs are inflected in the future (except for the second one which has been subordinated as a participle). In other words, Moses predicts the disastrous end for the rebels.

The first clause following on the adversative particle "but," reads ἐν φάσματι δείξει κύριος "but the Lord will show by means of an omen (i.e. a sign from heaven)." This is a far cry from MT, which has ואם בריאה יברא יהוה "but if Yahweh should create a (new) creation," i.e. something never before seen or experienced.[50] It is possible that Num did not understand the first clause, but it is more likely that once the conditions were removed in favor of judgment, that the translator simply created an appropriate introduction to the terrible fate which the Lord had in store for them. All these will be revealed as a heavenly sign. What Num has done is to present the outcome as a certainty, not simply as an either (v.29) or (v.30). In other words, v.29 is thereby set aside as quite beside the point, as only possible in theory, but not as a real possibility at all. In the tradition, hex has changed φάσματι to χασματι "chasm, gulf."[51] One suspects that this meaning is based on the account of what happened in v.31 ותבקע האדמה אשר תחתיהם, rather than on the term בריאה. The second clause "and the ground opened its mouth" is subordinated by Num to an attributive participial construction: "And the earth opening its mouth swallowed them ...."[52] MT simply has "and swallowed them and all that they had," but Num inserts after "them," καὶ τοὺς οἴκους αὐτῶν καὶ τὰς σκηνὰς αὐτῶν. Hex placed both of these insertions under the obelus to indicate that no counterpart existed in MT. The addition is only found in part in v.32, where "and their houses" does occur, but there is no reference to "their tents." Here οἴκους probably means "households," whereas σκηνάς refers to their dwellings. The noun שאל is usually rendered by ᾅδης (61 out of 70 cases),[53] and it simply means the same as שאל, i.e. it is a calque.

V.b is a final prediction which concerns the Israelites: "and you shall know that these people have irritated (or exasperated) τὸν κύριον." Only here in the book is κύριον for the tetragrammaton articulated, but the article represents the את

---

50. The Three translate accordingly. Theod has καὶ εἰ κτίσμα κτίσῃ κύριος, which Aq revised by changing εἰ to ἐάν. Sym reads ἐὰν δὲ κτίσμα κτίσῃ κύριος.
51. According to Milgrom, note 65, the meaning "chasm" was also attested by Ibn Ezra.
52. For καὶ ἀνοίξασα Sym has ὡς ἤνοιξεν (retroverted from Syh).
53. According to HR.

governing יהוה.⁵⁴ It should, however, be noted that the C′ b s^mg text has τον θεον.

16:31 MT begins with an otiose ויהי "and it happened," which Num omits, as it did at 11:25, and comp 10:35. ויהי also occurs another 13 times in the book, but these are with timers, and so not otiose. Num simply begins with ὡς δέ (ἐπαύσατο) to represent ככלתו, which is quite sufficient. The δέ does represent the conjunction of ויהי; it could equally well have been και ως.

The judgment is immediate: "as he finished speaking all these words (vv.28—30), the ground under them was split." MT has "ground אשר under them," but this was not corrected by hex, though the V t text did add η afer ἡ γῆ, which could be recensional, but is probably a stylistic gloss, or simply a dittograph after γῆ. Similarly, a majority A F M V text added των ποδων before αὐτῶν, i.e. "under their feet," a sensible but unnecessary gloss.

16:32 MT begins with "and the earth opened its mouth," but Num uses a passive transform by which "its mouth" is lost; it reads "and the earth was opened up." The earth "then swallowed them ... and all the people who were μετὰ Κόρε," but MT has לקרח, "who (belonged) to Korah." Dorival suggests⁵⁵ that Josephus (IV, 51—56) is probably right in understanding "all the people who were with Kore" to exclude Kore himself. This is possible, since according to vv.16—17, he was part of the 250 men, who according to v.35 were not swallowed up by the earth, but consumed by fire. It might also be noted that in v.27 "both Dathan and Abiron went out and stood near the doors of their tents," as did their families. Admittedly, this is a great deal of exegetical ingenuity to heap on the preposition μετά. See comment at v.35.⁵⁶

16:33 "And they went down, they and whatever was αὐτοῖς ζῶντα to Hades." In the tradition, cod B reads αυτων instead of the dative pronoun. This does not change the sense; it is merely a stylistic improvement. In vv.26,30 the same Hebrew expression, כל אשר להם, occurs, and the dative was unanimously supported. Here only one Greek ms reads the genitive, and it must be secondary.⁵⁷

---

54. See THGN 103.
55. P.352.
56. See also the comment in SS 59.
57. See THGN 109—110.

In the tradition, the majority A F M V text added παντα before ὅσα; since cod G and 426 do not add the παντα, it is probably not hex in origin, though it must be an early correction towards the Hebrew text. In MT, "they went down חיים," i.e. the adjective modifies the subject. Num makes this neuter plural, ζῶντα, agreeing with the nearer of the compound subject, ὅσα. A popular A M V text has changed this to ζωντες, the expected masculine plural form.[58]

The last clause renders MT literally by καὶ ἀπώλοντο ἐκ μέσου τῆς συναγωγῆς. To perish from the midst of a group is really a zeugma for "perish and disappear," but Num simply translates ויאבדו.

16:34 "All Israel" is understood as a collective, and אשר is rendered by the plural οἱ. They fled ἀπὸ τὴν φωνῆς αὐτῶν, i.e. "from their outcry." The reason given, ὅτι, quotes what they actually said; this explains the unusual use of λέγοντες by itself for the finite verb אמרו. λέγοντες normally presupposes לאמר introducing direct speech, plus some verb of saying introducing it. One might translate the ὅτι structure by: "because—lest the earth swallow us." It should occasion no surprise that the majority A F text added ειπαν before λέγοντες, but the more difficult shorter text must be original.

16:35 Here the fate of the 250 men, for whom see v.2, is described separately from those swallowed up alive in vv.32—33. For these "fire went out from the Lord and it devoured the 250 men who were offering incense." What is not settled, either in Num or MT, is the fate of Kore. He was part of the 250 men according to v.17, i.e. Kore is addressed and told "take each his censer ... 250 censers." The event is again referred to at 26:10, where the phrase καὶ Κόρε is coordinate with αὐτούς whom the earth swallowed, but that was ἐν τῷ θανάτῳ τὴν συναγωγῆς αὐτοῦ ὅτε κατέφαγεν τὸ πῦρ τοὺς 250." And incidentally, Sam omitted καὶ Κόρε entirely. The fate of Kore remains uncertain.

16:36—37(17:1—2) MT reads "and Yahweh spoke to Moses לאמר." Then v.2 begins with what he said: אמר אל אלעזר "say to Eleazar." For וידבר interpreted as καὶ εἶπεν, see comment at 14:26. Num omits לאמר, and hex has added λεγων. But this makes little sense if no direct speech then follows, as it does in MT.

---

58. The Others also read ζῶντες.

Instead of an imperative אמר Num has καί, i.e. it reads "And the Lord said to Moses and to Eleazar."[59]

In Num both Moses and Eleazar are addressed, and the singular verb ירם "let him remove" becomes a plural imperative ἀνέλεσθε "raise," hence remove. What they are to remove are τὰ πυρεῖα τὰ χαλκᾶ "the copper censers" MT has only את המחתת, but Num has harmonized with v.39, where MT also has "copper censers." Hex placed τὰ χαλκᾶ under the obelus. The removal is מבין השרפה "from among the burning," which Num rendered by "from the midst of τῶν κατακεκαυμένων," i.e. those things or persons which had been burned." The reference seems to be to v.35, i.e. to the charred remains of the 250 who were devoured by the divine fire.

Furthermore, τὸ πῦρ τὸ ἀλλότριον τοῦτο σπεῖρον ἐκεῖ. The imperative has now changed to the singular like the Hebrew זרה.[60] MT refers only to האש, and hex has placed τὸ ἀλλότριον τοῦτο under the obelus. Apparently Num is harmonizing with the account in Lev 10:1; see Note ad loc, and comp also Num 3:4. The adverb ἐκεῖ translates הלאה "at a distance"; for the equation, see also Gen 19:9 and the Note ad loc.

Versification differs between MT and Num at this point. MT ends with כי קדשו, which constitutes v.b, but Num takes the את מחתות החטאים האלה בנפשתם of the next verse as modifier for ἡγίασαν, thus "they sanctified the censers of these sinners by their ψυχαῖς," which probably refers to their corpses.[61] What is meant by ἡγίασεν is that the censers had been rendered unfit for ordinary use; they were defiled and had to be reassigned to sacred use and presented to the Lord; see v.38. MT is also difficult, since the verse starts with את, thus requiring some verb to modify. But possibly the את structure should be taken as an apposite for the את המחתות of v.a, thus "even the censers of the men who sinned at the cost of their lives."[62] This would be an analcolouthon, possibly best separated by dashes.

16:38(17:3) Num changes to the singular imperative ποίησον, i.e. addresssing Eliezar, over against MT's plural עשו with an indefinite subject, "and let them

---

59. Theod has εἶπον τῷ Ἐλεαζάρ, whereas Aq and Sym read εἶπον πρὸς Ἐλεαζάρ (both retroverted from Syh).
60. Aq translates by λίκμα (retroverted from Syh), and Sym, by σπόρπισον.
61. As Dorival: "par leurs cadavres."
62. As translated by NIV.

make." The "hammered plates" are to serve as "περίθεμα for the altar." The term περίθεμα is a fine choice for צפוי "covering," since the plates are to serve something placed around the altar, i.e. an enclosure.

ὅτι introduces the reasons for the protective covering for the altar, which are shown by three clauses. First of all, "προσηνέχθησαν before the Lord." The plural passive refers to the αὐτά (i.e. the πυρεῖα) which were brought before the Lord.[63] This is a passive transform of הקריבם "they brought them," in which the suffix "them" becomes the subject, which then makes the next verb intelligent, "and they (i.e. the censers, which were transformed into hammered sheets) were sanctified." Finally, "and they became a sign for the Israelites." The translator understood ויהיו as a past tense, but the Masoretes with acute exegetical insight vocalized it as a future, i.e. "so that they might become a sign to the Israelites."

16:39(17:4) Num follows Sam's identification of Eleazar as בן אהרן הכהן by its υἱὸς Ἀαρὼν τοῦ ἱερέως. MT simply has הכהן, in which case it is Eleazar who is the priest. In Num, the genitive τοῦ ἱερέως can only refer to Ἀαρών. Hex placed υἱὸς ἱερέως under the obelus. Whether hex also changed τοῦ ἱερέως to ο ιερευς is uncertain, since only cod G of the *O* group supports this necessary change in case, once υἱός ἱερέως is declared secondary by the obelus sign.

In any event, Eleazar carried out the orders of v.38, and took the copper censers which οἱ κατακεκαυμένοι had presented, and προσέθηκαν them as an enclosure for the altar. The participle refers to the 250 men who were killed by the fire from the Lord (v.25).[64] In the tradition, the *O b* s^mg+ text has changed the perfect middle participle of Num to the aorist passive, a reading also attested by Sym.

For the last clause, MT has the verb וירקעום "and they hammered them," in which the subject must be taken to have changed to the indefinite plural; the text is at first glance confusing, since the subject of the coordinate clause was given as השרפים, which would make no sense as subject of ירקעו. The intent is probably best shown by a passive "they were hammered." This is also true of the Greek, but the verb is quite different. Instead of "were hammered," Num is best translated by "and they were added (as an enclosure)," a free interpretation

---

63. Not the λεπίδας ἐλατάς as in SS 198.
64. Theod translates השרפים by οἱ ἐμπυρισθέντες; while Aq reads οἱ ἐμπεπρησμένοι. Sym retains the root of Num by οἱ κατακαυθέντες.

removing the process of hammering the copper into other forms (i.e. into sheets to surround the altar), and simply stating that the products of the process were added, put in place.

In the tradition, a popular O text tried to improve the verb by changing it to περιεθηκαν, i.e. the cognate verb to περίθεμα. A still further exegetical rationalization on the part of the Byz tradition obtains in the singular cognate verb περιεθηκεν, which would make fine sense by making Eleazar the subject, but it is not original.

16:40(17:5) The verse begins with μνημόσυνον, which serves as an apposite to περίθεμα of v.39, i.e. "(they were added as an enclosure for the altar) even as a reminder." By means of the copper sheet surrounding the altar the Israelites are reminded "so that no stranger who is not ἐκ the seed of Aaron might approach." The ἐκ is unique in the book as translating a partitive מן.[65] In the tradition, the majority A F M V text reads the Classical μηδεις rather than the Hellenistic μηθείς, which was dominant in the last three centuries BCE.[66] The Hellenistic form was completely replaced by μηδεις in the early years of our era.[67]

The exclusivity of the priesthood is stressed by the definition of μηθείς as ὃς οὐκ ἔστιν ἐκ τοῦ σπέρματος Ἀαρών. In Num the ἔστιν represents הוא, i.e. in Num the relative clause is a nominal clause, with הוא coming at the end. Hex recognizes the difference in word order, and transposed ἔστιν after Ἀαρών to equal MT. What was limited to the Aaronic lineage was "ἐπιθεῖναι θυμίαμα before the Lord." In MT, this is a cognate structure להקטיר קטרת, but Num avoids this and clarifies that הקטיר involves placing the incense on the altar, not just "incensing incense," or waving a censer with incense, but actually putting the incense in place.

This μνημόσυνον will avoid a repetition of such a case "as that of Kore and his ἡ ἐπισύστασις, as the Lord spoke by means of (literally, by the hand of) Μωυσῆ." MT has עדתו "his assembly," but Num makes it clear that this assembly was a "coalition," an ἐπισύστασις. MT also differs from Num in that the verse ends with לו, thus "as the Lord spoke to him (i.e. to Eleazar)." This con-

---

65. According to SS 159.
66. See Mayser I,1,448—449. For the μηθείς form, see the explanation of J.Wackernagel, Kleine Schriften II, 1054.
67. See THGN 128.

stricts the order to Eleazar, whereas Num leaves it open as a general order. Hex added αυτω to represent the unrendered לו.[68]

16:41(17:6) The "following morning כל עדת of the Israelites murmured against Moses and against Aaron." Num simply has οἱ υἱοὶ Ἰσραήλ as subject, and also omits the second "against." Hex has added πασα η συναγωγη under the asterisk, and changed οἱ υἱοί to υιων.[69] What they murmured was "you ἀπεκτάγκατε the people of the land." The use of the perfect tense is intentional and appropriate.[70] In the tradition, the O d+ variant text changed the verb to the default aorist απεκτεινατε, but the perfect is more fitting and original.

16:42(17:7) Since the ויהי introduces a timer, it is translated by καὶ ἐγένετο; see comment at v.31. The timer reads ἐν τῷ ἐπισυστρέψεσθαι with τὴν συναγωγήν as the accusative subject of the infinitive, thus "when the assembly had reformed (or regrouped) itself." MT has בהקהל "when (the asembly) had been gathered together."[71] As usual, Num does not repeat the preposition for ועל אהרן, simply reading "against Moses and Aaron."

The next clause states "and ὥρμησαν upon the tent of testimony." What is not certain is the subject of the verb "they rushed, hurried"; is it the συναγωγήν or is it Moses and Aaron? Either is possible, but the nearer possible antecedent is Moses and Aaron. Furthermore, the subsequent dialogue involves the two brothers as well. ויפנו אל means "and they turned towards." The Greek verb is, however, quite different. The use of ὁρμάω to interpret פנה occurs uniquely here, but contextually, it does make good sense. The assembly murmur against the two brothers, who immediately hurry to the place where God meets man, the tent of testimony.

And the desired end was achieved: "And as for it (i.e. the tent), the cloud covered it; and the glory of the Lord appeared." MT begins with והנה "and behold," which is in unusual fashion rendered by καὶ τήνδε. I find no special sig-

---

68. Theod and Aq also added αὐτῷ, whereas Sym more elegantly added περὶ αὐτοῦ.
69. (τῶν) υἱῶν is also read by The Three (retroverted from Syh).
70. Theod and Aq translate by ἐθανατώσατε, and Sym read ἀνείλατε.
71. Dorival points out an interesting progression in the translation of the root קהל. At v.3 it was rendered by "se lève contre," συνέστησαν; in v.19, the community "s'organise en coalition," ἐπισυνέστησεν, and here the community "s'organise en troupe militaire."

nificance in this change from the usual καὶ ἰδού; it simply varies the diet, though admittedly, καὶ ἰδού is the usual rendering for והנה. Both renderings, however, serve the same purpose, viz. to call particular attention to what follows. For "glory of the Lord," see comment at v.19. The cloud covering the sanctuary was the cloud of revelation, symbolizing the presence of the Lord.

16:43—44(17:8—9) Moses and Aaron entered κατὰ πρόσωπον of the tent of testimony; MT has them entering אל פני "to the front" of the sanctuary, and one might have expected εἰς πρόσωπον, but prepositions are notoriously difficult to translate idiomatically. The verb occurs 22 times in Num, and is usually modified by an εἰς phrase.

According to MT Yahweh spoke only to Moses, but, since Aaron also entered the sanctuary, and what is ordered in v.45 is plural, Num added καὶ Ἀαρών, which hex dutifully placed under the obelus.

16:45(17:10) The address is to both: "withdraw from the midst of this assembly." MT reads הרמו, which is the Ni of the root רמם, a variant of the root רום, thus "lift yourselves up," i.e. "remove yourselves."[72]

The remainder of the verse is an exact repetition of the last clause of v.21 and the first one of v.22, both in Num and MT. In fact, the only difference between the text of v.21 and v.45a is the initial verb. In v.21 it is ἀποσχίσθητε, but here it is ἐκχωρήσατε. See the discussion both at vv.21 and 22a.

16:46(17:11) Moses orders emergency measures in view of the plague. The crisis is considered desperate as the series of imperatives shows: λάβε ... ἐπίθες ... ἐπίβαλε ... ἀπένεγκε ... ἐξίλασαι. Only slight differences between Num and MT obtain. For שים קטרת "put on incense," Num has ἐπίβαλε ἐπ' αὐτὸ θυμίαμα "throw incense upon it"; the ἐπ' αὐτό is an ad sensum gloss, which hex has placed under the obelus. For הולך "cause to go," hence "bring," Num has ἀπένεγκε "take, carry away." And instead of העדה, Num has the unique reading τὴν παρεμβολήν "the encampment." παρεμβολή is calque for מחנה in the Pentateuch, occurring 98 times out of a 100 cases of חנה, and only twice (also at Exod 17:1, where it renders מסע) does it not represent מחנה. Actually, out of

---

72. See GK 72dd.

202 instances of מחנה in the Bible, 193 of them are rendered by παρεμβολή.[73] It may, I would suggest, be safely concluded that the parent text here read המחנה, not העדה.

V.b gives the reason for the urgency: "Because anger had gone out from before the Lord; it (i.e. the anger) had begun to shatter the people." MT has "the plague had begun," and hex has placed τὸν λαόν under the obelus, since MT does not mention "the people." Num makes the anger of the Lord the agent, whereas MT leaves the agent undefined, though the free interpretation of Num is not unwarranted; a נגף certainly could be said θραύειν the people, though one might have expected something like "to kill off, decimate" rather than "to break up, shatter."[74]

16:47(17:12) Aaron carried out Moses' orders as he (had) spoken αὐτῷ. MT has no correspondent to the pronoun which was added ad sensum, and hex has placed it under the obelus. Num does not have him run into the תוך of the assembly, but simply εἰς τὴν συναγωγήν. Hex added μεσην under the asterisk, but failed to change τὴν συναγωγήν to the genitive case. A reader would have found it difficult to understand this text, particularly if, as was usually the case, the hex signs were not present.

MT then continues with "והנה the plague had begun among the people." Num improved on the sense by its καὶ ἤδή "and already." Then Aaron ἐπέβαλεν the incense, and made propitiation for the people. The verb ἐπέβαλεν has יתן for its parent, an unusual translation (in fact, occurring elsewhere only at Exod 7:4). But this is exactly what Moses had ordered in v.46: ἐπίβαλε ἐπ᾽ αὐτὸ θυμίαμα, and Num simply adapted his text accordingly. For the translator this is what תן really should mean here! For ἐξιλάσετο, see Note at Lev 1:4.

16:48(17:13) As usual, the Hebrew repeats prepositions before coordinate nouns. MT reads "And he (i.e. Aaron) stood between the dead and between the living." Num does not repeat the "between," and hex has added ανα μεσον under the as-

---

73. According to the count of Dos Santos.
74. The Tar seemed to have some trouble with הנגף as well. Tar⁰ has מותנא, whereas Tar ʲ reads לקטלא, and Tar ᴺ has a doublet חבלה מחבל בעמא.

terisk before τῶν ζώντων. Aaron's standing between the dead and the living constituted an effective wall of atonement.[75]

16:49(17:14) The plague ws responsible for the death of 14,700 people, outside of those who died ἕνεκεν Κορε. This refers to the 250 men of v.2.

16:50(17:15) וישב is rendered by its most frequent translation, καὶ ἐπέστρεψεν. In the tradition, C' f read a different compound, απεστρεψεν. The former occurs somewhat more frequently in the Bible as translation of שוב (300 times), whereas ἀποστρέφω occurs 203 times.[76] The ἀπ- compound is more frequently used in Num (12 times), since ἐπ- obtains only three times. But all the uncials and most minuscules (all groups except C' and f) support Num, which must be original LXX here. Hex has also made a change; since MT reads המגפה נעצרה, Origen reordered ἐκόπασεν ἡ θραῦσις by transposing the verb to the end.

---

75. Tar[J] explains it as בצלו במצע ועבד מחיצותא במחתייתא; presumably, the partition was created by waving the censer. Tar[N] explains as "between the dead בעי רחמים for the living."
76. The count is that of Dos Santos.

Chapter 17

17:2(17) Moses is ordered to take from the Israelites ῥάβδον ῥάβδον, which is a word for word rendering of MT. The repetition of a noun has a distributive sense in Hebrew,[1] as is clear from what follows, i.e. "by rods"; what is meant is a rod for each tribal leader. This is what Num must mean as well. The use of ῥάβδον ῥάβδον is an example of a syntactic calque. These rods are to be taken κατ' οἴκους πατριῶν "according to paternal houses," for which see comment at 1:2. Here, however, the term is used somewhat differently as a synonym for the tribe. Thus the rods are to be twelve in number, "from all their chieftains (ἀρχόντων) according to their paternal houses." Not surprising is the omission of ῥάβδον 2° either by dittography or for simplification by C'⁾ Byz s+, but the repeated ῥάβδον imitates MT, and is original. Similarly, the majority A F M V tradition has added αυτων after πατριῶν 1° under the influence of πατριῶν αὐτῶν occurring later in v.a, but Num follows MT exactly. For πατριῶν αὐτῶν, see comment above; it too is equal to "tribes."

V.b is introduced by καί, though MT does not have a conjunction, but the clause is coordinate, a second command, and the καί is a sensible addition. Since תכתב had not been rendered by the default future, but by another imperative, a conjunction became advisable. Num correctly understood איש as a pendant "as for each one, (his name you must write)."[2] Num shows this by rendering איש by the genitive ἑκάστου, thus "of each one, his name ἐπίγραφον on his rod." The imperative "inscribe" interprets תכתב "you shall write." The compound is more appropriate here than the usual simplex verb "write," since it refers to inscribing a name on a rod.

17:3(18) Specifically, "the name (of) Aaron ἐπίγραψον on the rod of Levi." For ἐπίγραψον, see comment at v.2. Since MT has תכתב, hex has corrected the imperative to the more literal future επιγραφεις.[3] The reason for the order is given in MT's כי clause as "because there is (to be) one rod לראש of the house of their fathers." This seems somewhat at odds with an earlier understanding of

---

1. See GK 123a,d.
2. See GK 139c.
3. The Others also render תכתב by ἐπιγράφεις.

organizational structures as given in ch.1, where tribes are a larger social structure than a בית אבות whose ראש might be chosen to be the chieftain of the tribe. At v.2 it was pointed out that בית אבות was used in a different sense from that in ch.1; here it is synonymous with "tribe," but Num seems disturbed by the usage in ch.1. Accordingly, he attempts to correct this by substituting for ראש κατά φυλήν, thus "according to the tribe of their paternal house." Num has also added δώσουσιν at the end, which not only has no counterpart in MT, but does not fit into the context overly well. I would understand this as having an indefinite plural subject which is then best translated by a passive transform, thus "according to the tribe of their paternal house shall it be given (or presented)." What is referred to is the assignment of a rod to a particular individual. In other words, Num is making a general rule to fit the case of Aaron's rod. Hex has placed δώσουσιν under an obelus to show that it has no basis in MT.

One O ms, 426, has obviously been separately influenced by the Hebrew, since it has simply changed φυλήν to κεφαλην so as to conform to the ראש of MT.

17:4(19) θήσεις αὐτάς translates הנחתם "make them to rest" correctly. τίθημι is often used to render the Hi of נוח in the Bible (20 times); in fact, only αἴρω occurs more frequently (29 times). Other renderings include ἀφίημι (17 times), καταλείπω (nine), and ἀποτίθημι (eight).[4] αὐτάς refers to the ῥάβδους of v.2. Moses must place them in the sanctuary κατέναντι τοῦ μαρτυρίου. The term τοῦ μαρτυρίου renders העדות, and is a short or abbreviated form for ἡ κιβωτὸς τοῦ μαρτυρίου, for which see 4:4, but see also comment at v.10 below. The ark of the testimony was in the adytum, and "over against the testimony" means that the rods are to be placed there. κατέναντι is found only six times in the Pentateuch, and only here in Num. For לפני one would have expected the simplex ἔναντι (or ἐναντίον)[5]

The relative clause in MT reads אשר אועד לכם שמה, which also occurs at Exod 29:42, as well as at 30:6 but with לך instead of לכם. In both cases LXX reads ἐν οἷς γνωσθήσομαί σοι ἐκεῖθεν, and in both cases a popular tradition reads εκει instead of ἐκεῖθεν. It is obvious that Num has simply taken over this text from Exod, but from the more popular εκει tradition, not the ἐκεῖθεν/שמה text;

---

4. According to Dos Santos.
5. The semi-prepositions ἔναντι, ἐναντίον and ἐνώπιον are fully dealt with by Sollamo.

see especially the Note at 29:42. It should be noted, however, that the singular σοι is also attested by the לך of Sam,[6] possibly under the influence of the Exod passages.[7] The singular readings σου/לך are probably inspired by the fact that the Lord spoke to Moses (v.1), not to Moses and Aaron.

17:5(20) The opening καὶ ἔσται ὁ ἄνθρωπος ὃν ἂν ἐκλέξωμαι αὐτόν is the same pattern as in 16:7, except for the resumptive pronoun αὐτόν/בו (which is otiose in Greek); i.e. it is a pendant structure which is then taken up in the main clause through the pronoun αὐτοῦ; in other words, "his rod" refers to the rod of the person whom I would choose. The καὶ ἔσται imitates MT, and is also otiose in Greek. The person whom I would choose will turn out to be Aaron. The sign of the Lord's choice is the blossoming of the chosen one's rod.

V.b outlines the hoped-for result of the choice. השכתי is the Hi of שכך, which occurs only here in the Bible. In the flood story of Gen (8:1) the Qal of שכך is used of the recession of the waters. Here the causative means "I will make to recede (from me את תלנות of the Israelites)." Num used περιελῶ "I will remove." The plural modifier תלנות occurring only in the plural in the Pentateuch (twice in this chapter and five times in Exod 16), is always translated by a singular noun γογγυσμός. The term occurs only for תלנות in the Pentateuch. The singular means "murmuring" in general, whereas the plural would presumably refer to individual instances of murmuring. It is the former which the Lord will remove; in other words, there will be no more murmuring.

In the tradition, the majority A F M V text reads απο σου rather than ἀπ' ἐμοῦ modifying περιελῶ, but MT reads מעלי. The reading is secondary, influenced by the relative clause identifying the murmuring as ἐφ' ὑμῖν, which renders עליכם. But the Lord wanted to remove from himself the murmuring of the people. The απο σου is incorrect and secondary.

17:6(21) Moses carried out the Lord's orders given in v.2. The second clause can be interpreted in two ways in the Num version. MT says "all their chieftains gave him a rod." The consecution οἱ ἄρχοντες αὐτῶν ῥάβδον could be interpreted in the same sense as MT, but the αὐτῶν could be taken as referring to ῥάβδον as well, i.e. as "all the chieftains gave him their rod." Presumably, the translator

---

6. As well as by Kenn 95ª,151 and 600.
7. Tar^J, but not Tar^NO, reads the singular לך as well.

intended the former. MT then specifies clearly "per chieftain one rod for one chieftain (according to the house of their fathers)." The translator was understandably a bit confused with the phrase נשיא אחד recurring, and omitted the second אחד. Num then has "one rod per chieftain according to an ἄρχοντα according to their paternal houses." Hex has added ενα under the asterisk after ἄρχοντα to represent the omitted numeral. For κατ' οἴκους πατριῶν αὐτῶν, see comment at 1:2. In sum, then, these constituted twelve rods.

The final clause adds a thirteenth: "and the rod of Aaron was among their rods." It should be remembered that in the book (see 1:4—46 and vv.47—49) the twelve tribes include Manasseh and Ephraim, but not Levi; his rod then becomes an extra.

17:7(22) MT uses the same verb as in v.4, the Hi of נוח, i.e. וינח. There the simplex θήσεις was used, but here the compound ἀπέθηκεν obtains. The two are synonyms, and no distinction was intended. In the tradition, an F f n+ text substitutes επεθηκεν, but again this is a synonym. Moses simply does what he was told to do in v.4, except that here the deposit is "before the Lord in the tent of testimony."[8] V.4 had been more specific on the placement of the rods; see comment ad loc. It should be noted that ἐν is used in modification of ἀπέθηκεν; it must then have the same intent as εἰς would have; he placed them in the tent.[9]

17:8(23) MT begins with ויהי plus a timer, for which see comment at 16:31. Num translates ממחרת correctly by a dative τῇ ἐπαύριον; thus "and it happened on the next day (that Moses and Aaron entered the tent of testimony)." The paratactic nature of MT is reflected in the καί which I translated by "that." According to MT, only Moses entered the sanctuary, and hex has duly placed καὶ 'Ααρών under the obelus. I would argue, however, over against the notes in BHS, that the shorter text was original. In the next verse it is Moses who brought out all the rods from the sanctuary, and in v.10 it is Moses alone who is told to place Aaron's rod before the testimonies for safekeeping. Only at the end of the tale is Aaron brought back into the story, where he and Moses did as the Lord

---

8. Theod retains the ἔναντι κυρίου of Num, whereas Aq changes to εἰς πρόσωπον κυρίου, and Sym, to ἔμπροσθεν κυρίου.
9. See SS 136.

had commanded, but see comment at v.10. In the Greek version, however, the two are involved in the narrative; see 16:9 and the comment ad loc.

The sign of the Lord's choice predicted in v.5 is now realized; it is Aaron's rod, which represented the tribe of Levi (εἰς οἶκον Λευί) that had blossomed. The εἰς phrase renders MT word for word, and means "for the house of Levi," i.e. represented it. At v.5 a compound verb, ἐκβλαστήσει, was used; in the realization of the sign here, the simplex, ἐβλάστησεν, was deemed sufficient.

The growth on Aaron's rod was revealed in three stages: it brought out buds (βλαστόν), grew flowers (literally, and flowered flowers), and produced nuts; thus a graduated growth of buds, flowers and nuts. The term κάρυα is a general term for "nuts," but MT has the more specific term שקדים "almonds."[10]

17:9(24) Num translated MT word for word. In the tradition, attempts to improve the Greek were made. A V Byz+ text articulated υἱούς, so as to read παντας τους υιους ισραηλ. The lack of articulation in Num is probably a rather painful Hebraism. The V majority text has changed ἔλαβον (ἕκαστος) to the singular ελαβεν, thereby expressing grammatical concord with the subject ἕκαστος.[11] This text, however, retained the coordinate εἶδον, which has υἱοὺς Ἰσραήλ as its subject. What the variant text says explicitly is "they saw and each one took his rod." Of course, Num says this too, but in terms of the Hebrew idiom "and they took, each one his staff." What is presumably meant, but not stated, is that the chieftains of the tribes, representing the Israelites, did the actual taking of the tribal rods.

17:10(25) According to MT, Yahweh ordered Moses to return (השב) Aaron's rod to the front of the testimony. The translator found the consecution השב plus לפני awkward, and probably on the basis of v.7 changed השב to ἀπόθες, thus "place Aaron's rod before the testimonies." The use of ἐπιτίθημι for השיב is unique in LXX, but it is sensible here. Of course, they had been removed ἀπὸ προσώπου κυρίου (v.9), so that their placement before the testimonies was a replacement, but Num stresses the positioning rather than the return of the rods. Note that Num understood העדות to refer to the tablets of the testimony, and uses the plural. The term העדות occurs 12 times in the book, in 10 of which it obtains as

---

10. The Others translate more exactly as ἀμύγδαλα.
11. Cod B also witnesses to the singular with its εβαλεν.

the free element of a bound phrase (with אהל, משכן or ארן), and only here and at v.4(19) is it governed by לפני. In v.4(19) this follows אהל מועד which is always rendered by σκηνὴ τοῦ μαρτυρίου, and so by attraction לפני העות became κατέναντι τοῦ μαρτυρίου, but see comment ad loc for another possible explanation. Since the ark contained the tablets with the Ten Words, the rendering ἐνώπιον τῶν μαρτυρίων is fully justified.

MT gives the reason for the return of Aaron's rod to be למשמרת לאות, which Num renders by εἰς διατήρησιν σημεῖον "for safekeeping as a sign." The majority A F M text added εἰς before σημεῖον, which equals MT exactly, and also makes good sense. It is fully possible that an εἰς could have been dropped in the tradition through copyist error, but I would suggest that the reverse took place. The translator rendered לאות by a second accusative modifier to ἀπόθες, and a recensor (hex?) added the preposition as a correction of the Num text to equal MT. The freer rendering is probably original text. The σημεῖον is for τοῖς υἱοῖς τῶν ἀνηκόων, here used uniquely to translate בני מרי, a phrase meaning "rebels." ἀνηκόων refers to those who do not, or are unwilling to, hear. For such people only a visible sign could communicate as a constant warning, viz. the presence of Aaron's rod set in front of the ark in the sanctuary.

This warning is expressed in the last two clauses, which, though paratactically ordered, serve as the hoped-for result: "(so that) their murmurings may cease from me and they not die." This is a possible understanding of the consonantal text of MT, but the Masoretes vocalized ותכל as a Pi. This could be taken in either of two ways, as a second singular verb with Moses being addressed, thus "that you might stop their grumbling," or as a third feminine singular verb with אות as a feminine noun as subject, thus "that it might stop ...." The Num interpretation is simpler.[12]

17:11(26) MT refers the obedient carrying out of Yahweh's orders to Moses alone, whereas Num adds καὶ 'Ααρών; comp comment at v.8. In the tradition, the A F M majority text has changed καθά to ὅσα, but Num correctly rendered כאשר by καθά. The change to ὅσα is no improvement, but would presuppose a parent כל אשר, which would also make perfectly good sense. To make the narrative consistent with v.10 "and the Lord said to Moses," אתו is interpreted as τῷ

---

12. The Tar all read ויסופן, "(that) they should stop (their murmurings)."

Μωυσῆ.¹³ Hex has placed καὶ ᾿Ααρών under the obelus, because this is not supported by MT. Since Num included Aaron in the carrying out of the Lord's orders, the final כן עשה had to be turned into the plural (οὕτως) ἐποίησαν as well. Hex, however, changed this to ἐποίησεν to correspond to the singular עשה.

17:12(27) Vv.27—28 are an apparently independent snippet of text in which the Israelites utter a cry of despair. Its context is not at all clear. It could be taken as a prelude to 18:1—7, i.e. a cry of despair to which the following verses give some relief. On the other hand, it might also be understood as the Israelites' response to the Korah episode, the death of the 250 men by fire, and then the plague killing thousands.¹⁴ The Israelites address Moses with a threefold cry: "we are utterly destroyed, have perished, are spent." The three verbs all belong to the same semantic field, but the first and last verbs are different compounds of the verb ἀναλίσκω. MT has גוענו for the first verb, i.e. "we expire," and for the next two uses the same verb אבדנו "we perish," but distinguishes the two by adding כלנו "all of us" before the second אבדנו, thus "we perish, all of us perish." Num has no equivalent for כלנו, and hex has added παντες ημεις under the asterisk before the last verb, παρανηλώμεθα.¹⁵

17:13(28) MT speaks of "everyone who in any way comes near the tabernacle of Yahweh." If the tale was intended as prelude to 18:1—7, the הקרב הקרב, might refer to approaching the sanctuary to bring a sacrifice, i.e. in the sense of "even approaching the sanctuary to bring a sacrifice could be fatal." The repeated participle is indeed unusual, and is difficult to translate; in fact, a single participle would seem to me to suffice.¹⁶ Num has indeed interpreted this by a single participle, πᾶς ὁ ἁπτόμενος "anyone who touches (the Lord's tent must die)." No attempt was made in the tradition to correct the text by repeating the participle.

The question with which the verse ends is the unusual interrogative האם, introducing תמנו לגוע, i.e. the simple interrogative particle -ה is prefixed to the

---

13. The Others render MT literally by συνέταξεν κύριος αὐτῷ.
14. See the sensible explanation proposed by Milgrom in his note at v.28.
15. Tar^JN have defined the three outcries as referring to recent calamities, viz. death by the plague, the earth swallowing up others, and fire coming out to devour still others. Tar^J lacks reference to the first one, the plague.
16. Tar have tried to make sense of the repeated participle by using a participle plus cognate infinitive, but "anyone who approaches to approach" is no better in Aramaic than it is in English.

interrogative אִם, thus "shall we never come to an end with dying"? In other words, will this process of dying, beginning with the earth swallowing Dathan and Abiron with their families, then of Kore and the 250 being killed by fire, and now the plague killing 14,700 men, never come to an end?[17] Num has tried to capture this sense by its ἕως εἰς τέλος αποθάνωμεν "are we to be dying forever"?[18]

---

17. For הַאִם see BDB sub אִם 2.c.
18. For εἰς τέλος, see Bauer sub τέλος 1.d.γ.

Chapter 18

18:1 Num had added the direct speech marker λέγων after "The Lord said to Aaron," which hex has placed under the obelus, since there is no לאמר in MT. The syntactic pattern of what the Lord said in v.a consists of a nominative pendant "as for you and your sons and your paternal house," followed by the clause in which the pendant is brought into the clausal structure in the subject of the second person plural verb, λήμψεσθε; the predicate has τὰς ἁμαρτίας τῶν ἁγίων as a direct modifier of the verb. This pattern is similar to that of v.b in which again a pendant, σὺ καὶ οἱ υἱοί σου, is set out, and again the clause pattern is like that of v.a.

Num's ὁ οἶκος πατριᾶς σου "the house of your paternity" has as counterpart in MT: בית אביך אתך "the house of your father with you." Since Num does not translate אתך, hex has added μετα σου under the asterisk after πατριᾶς σου. In v.b אתך again recurs, and again Num omits it; there too hex has added μετα σου under the asterisk after the nominative pendant.[1] Num rendered עון המקדש "the iniquity of the sanctuary" by plural nouns: "the sins of the sacred objects (or places)."[2] In the context of the preceding verse, the "taking of the ἁμαρτίας τῶν ἁγίων probably refers to the priestly responsibilities for the encroachments on the sacred precincts—note "the one touching the tent of the Lord must die" in 17:13. One might well render Num: "you must bear responsibility for the errors (or mistakes) regarding sacred objects." This differs from MT which reads את עון המקדש "the guilt connected with the sanctuary."[3] In the tradition, a popular B M text has changed ἁμαρτίας 1° to απαρχας. This can only be described as rooted in a careless scribal mistake; the "firstfruits" of the sacred objects makes little sense, and should not be taken seriously.

V.b is a precise parallel to v.a, but has τῆς ἱερατείας ὑμῶν instead of τῶν ἁγίων. So the priests must also bear the responsibility for any errors which concern their priesthood; presumably the various rules and regulations which govern the conduct and performance of the priests are intended by τῆς ἱερατείας. The

---
1. Kenn 96,196 also omit the אתך.
2. The Three translate by τὴν παρανομίαν τοῦ ἁγιάσματος (retroverted from Syh).
3. Levine thinks that the עון refers to defilement (of the Sanctuary), which is possible.

priests are then doubly responsible for τὰς ἁμαρτίας τῶν ἁγίων and τῆς ἱερατείας ὑμῶν; they must bear the final responsibility for both.[4]

18:2 The initial וגם is simply rendered by καί, not only here, but throughout the Pentateuch. Only in later translators and recensors was καιγε ever used. The term ἀδελφούς is best rendered by "kinsmen, relatives"; a wider group is intended than "brothers," as the apposites φυλὴν Λευί and δῆμον τοῦ πατρός σου show. Both of these apposites refer to a social unit. In MT, the former is מטה, which can mean "tribe" or "rod," but here means "tribe."[5] The second one represents שבט אביך. Unfortunately, שבט is a synonym; in fact, can also mean both "tribe" or "rod."[6] The structure here means "tribe of your father." The translator understandably wanted to distinguish the two words in Greek as well, and so he rendered שבט by δῆμον, possibly best rendered by "familial deme." The term designating a deme in ancient Athens applied to a social unit with hereditary membership, hence my suggestion "familial deme." As for these, i.e. your kinsmen, "bring them to yourself"; this represents an attempt to render MT's "bring near אתך," i.e. "with you."[7] The general sense is that the Levites must come close to the priests; this is clear from the next two clauses: "and let them be added to you and serve you," with both verbs in the subjunctive mood. προστίθημι "to add" is used to render ילוו "they shall be associated with," thus be joined with. The Hebrew verb is cognate with the tribal name לוי; see Gen 29:34 and the Note ad loc, where a folk etymology for the name לוי is given. The point of these directions is to define how far the Levites are to share priestly responsibilities for the defence of the purity of the sanctuary. The basic distinction between priests and Levites is that the former bear the primary responsibility for cultic activity, whereas the Levites, though joined to the priests, are to minister to the priests.

Meanwhile, in v.b the priestly station is defined by a nominal clause, in which the predicate is "ἀπέναντι τῆς σκηνῆς τοῦ μαρτυρίου." I would render the clause by "while (καί) you and your sons with you are in front of the sanctuary."

---

4. It might be noted that the Tar use the plural חובי for the singular עון of MT in both parts of the verse as does Num with its τὰς ἁμαρτίας.
5. In fact, Aq translates by ῥάβδον, though Theod and Sym more sensibly read φυλήν.
6. Neither Tar^O nor Tar^N distinguish between the two words; both use שבטא.
7. The Tar all use לותך, which is similar to Num.

18:3 The cognate structure φυλάξονται τὰς φυλακάς σου "they shall perform your guard duties" correctly renders שמרו משמרתך, since the noun is a collective, and the plural φυλακάς is precise. The use of the middle φυλάξονται is hardly to be distinguished lexically from the active, φυλαξουσιν, which is witnessed by O f+ in the tradition; this could possibly be construed as a hex correction.[8] The Levites then are to effect your guard duties and the guard duties of τῆς σκηνῆς σου. MT has כל האהל "of all the tent." I am now deeply suspicious of the σου, which could so easily have intruded from the φυλακάς σου. Earlier,[9] I defended the σου as original because it was placed under the obelus in Syh[T]. This does mean that the σου had entered the text before Origen, who attests to its presence. But the σου is not really all that sensible. To refer to the tent as "Aaron's" is presumptuous, and I would now remove it from the critical text. The witness of B V x z+, which lack the σου, is, I believe, correct for the original text; in other words, the σου should be removed from the critical text.

This protective guard of the sanctuary is not without exceptions. The omission of כל by Num may well have been rooted in the fact that excluded from the φυλακὰς τῆς σκηνῆς was the further instruction that "to the sacred vessels and to the altar they may not come near." MT does not use an adjectival phrase, but has a bound phrase כלי הקדש, but such phrases are often rendered in LXX by adjectival phrases.[10] Oddly, Origen did not add a rendering for כל in his hex.

Such encroachment by the Levites is not only forbidden; it is actually punished by death, not only of the Levites, but also of the priests, i.e. "they may not approach ... and not will they die, both they and you." In other words, the priests are also responsible for the Levites keeping their distance. Note the different uses of the future tense; the second one is related to the first one as result, i.e. "so that they will not die."

18:4 For προστεθήσονται as rendering for נלוו, see comment at v.2. In the tradition, the Byz text has added an exegetical gloss, και ουτοι, after the verb to ensure a correct understanding of the subject; this was probably done as a balance to the πρὸς σέ which follows. It is obviously secondary. The verse restates v.3 in

---

8. Bauer sub φυλάσσω 2.b states: "OT infl. is prob. felt in the use of the mid. for the act...., i.e. in the sense of *"keep* a law, etc. fr. from being broken, hence *observe, follow."*
9. In THGN 98.
10. See SS 65.

similar terms, but without the negative reservations. The Levites are to perform guard duties for the tent of testimony κατὰ πάσας τὰς λειτουργίας τῆς σκηνῆς. MT said לכל עבדת האהל "for all the work connected with the tent." The plural λειτουργίας is not an incorrect understanding of the Hebrew, since עבדה refers to the labors connected with the sanctuary.

The last clause forbids the ἀλλογενής from approaching σέ. MT has the plural אליכם, referring to "you and your sons." Num is, however, consistent with the עליך modifying the first verb; this is a good illustration of Num's striving for a consistent text. The term ἀλλογενής "foreigner" is often used (17 times) to render זר, which would be more exactly translated by ἀλλότριος (30 times).[11] The intent is, however, the same; outsiders have no right of approach to the sanctuary.

18:5 This verse contrasts with the previous clause, but also excludes the Levites. The subject of φυλάξεσθε is the priests.[12] These guard duties, which v.3 stated were forbidden the Levites, are here explictly assigned to the priests, viz. τῶν ἁγίων and τοῦ θυσιαστηρίου; cf comments at v.3.

V.b in MT is a clear reference to the outburst of anger, the קצף which went out from before Yahweh resulting in הנגף, killing 14,700 people; see 17:14 (=Num 16:49).[13] Num had rendered קצף there by ὀργή. Num, however, with full intention avoids such a reference. This is clear from two facts. First of all, Num has disregarded עוד.[14] Admittedly, the majority A F M V text added ἔτι, but this must be recensional. Its omission would be difficult to explain palaeographically; the shorter text is clearly original LXX. And secondly, the translator chose θυμός to translate קצף rather than the ὀργή used at 16:46. I would suggest that the translator wanted to dissociate this statement from the plague which had such disastrous results. Note also the difference in prepositions; in MT the קצף was על the Israelites, i.e. "against." but in Num the θυμός was ἐν, i.e. "among (the Israelites)."

---

11. The count is that of Dos Santos.
12. The Others read the active φυλάξετε. See comment and footnote at v.3.
13. As Tar^J makes clear with its רוגזא דהוה.
14. As did Tar^N.

18:6 MT begins with ואני הנה, and then continues with a first person verb. Num shortened this by omitting הנה, which hex represented by an added ἰδού.[15] The shorter text of Num may be due to the translator's wish to contrast with καὶ σύ beginning v.7. It is the Lord who has taken "your kinsmen the Levites from the midst of the Israelites." This represents the end of v.a in MT.

V.b continues in MT with two designations for these Levites: 1) לכם מתנה "for you a gift," and 2) נתנים ליהוה "given (i.e. dedicated) to Yahweh."[16] Num has disregarded לכם entirely, and joined the two parts together as δόμα δεδομένον κυρίῳ. This can only be interpreted as a rewrite of the Hebrew; after all, the plural נתנים can hardly be taken as modifying the feminine singular מתנה. The neat double assignment of Levites to the priests (as fellow-guardians) on the one hand, and to the Lord (i.e. for the Lord's work) on the other, is thereby lost. The translator was obviously misled by the cognate מתנה נתנים as though what was meant was ^a"a gift given to the Lord." Hex did add ὑμῖν under the asterisk in front of δόμα to represent the untranslated לכם, though the resultant text must have confused its readers considerably.

The Levites were then "to perform the works of the tent of meeting." Here the cognate structure is relevant, and was rendered accordingly by λειτουργεῖν τὰς λειτουργίας (τῆς σκηνῆς τοῦ μαρτυρίου).

18:7 The καὶ σὺ καὶ οἱ υἱοί σου μετὰ σοῦ contrasts with the καὶ ἐγώ of v.6. The Lord said: I have taken ... Levites to do the works of the sanctuary; now you ... "must maintain (διατηρήσετε) your priesthood according to every custom (or usage) of the altar and that which is inside the curtain." What constitutes the priestly service is what was forbidden the Levites, all matters that concern the use of the altar (κατὰ πάντα τρόπον of the altar), and the sacred objects which are within, i.e. behind the curtain; for the καταπέτασμα, see Note at Exod 26:31. Specifically what was behind the curtain was the ark as the symbol of the divine presence.

MT then continues with an odd text. The last word in v.a is ועבדתם "and you must serve." This word is marked by an *ethnach*. Then it continues with עבדת מתנה אתן את כהנתכם "(as) a work of dedication (or of a gift) I will put your priesthood." Somehow there seems to be an extra verb. BHS considers

---

15. As did Theod and Aq with their καὶ ἐγὼ ἰδού. Sym read differently with ἐγὼ γάρ.
16. This is made crystal clear by Tar[N] which added אינון before יהיבון.

ועבדתם a dittograph, since it is followed by עבדת מ(תנה); most modern scholars follow this suggestion, but Num does not support this, witnessing to the word by its καὶ λειτουργήσετε.[17] Num has "fixed up" the text by dividing the verse differently; the καὶ λειτουργήσετε introduces v.b, and then it disregards the other verb אתן; עבדת is then read as a free form; so what Num says is "and you must do the works (τὰς λειτουργίας) as a δόμα (gift) of your priesthood."[18] Hex has taken account of the unrepresented אתן by adding δωσω under the asterisk after δόμα. The double accusative modifier of λειτουργήσετε does create an odd text: "you must perform works as a gift," but that is what Num seems to mean. The verse ends with a reference to "the foreigner who encroaches"; he must die; cf comment at v.4.

18:8 Vv.8—19 deal with priestly benefits. These are granted by the Lord to Aaron and his sons. That it is not just the high priest, Aaron, but the priests as a whole who are involved, is immediately made clear by Num which changed MT's opening statement to Aaron "I have given לך" to "I have given ὑμῖν." The overall statement calls what is given τὴν διατήρησιν τῶν ἀπαρχῶν "charge over the first fruits." This translates משמרת תרומתי "charge over my offerings." תרומה is most often rendered by ἀπαρχή (39 times in the bible). but also by ἀφαίρεμα (28 times),[19] of which half (14 according to HR) are found in Num; for ἀφαίρεμα, see Note at Exod 29:27, and for ἀπαρχή as rendering for תרומה, see Note at Exod 25:2—3. The term ἀπαρχῶν is here a cover term for all those offerings from which the priests receive a first portion. The A F M majority text has added μου after ἀπαρχῶν; since this equals MT, the plus is probably recensional (hex?).

V.b then explains what this giving charge of the firstfruits involves. It means that "from all those (offerings) consecrated μοι by the Israelites, to you I have given αὐτά for a perquisite (γέρας 'a share, measure') and to your sons μετὰ σέ as a perpetual prescription." The ἀπό is probably to be understood as partitive; this is not really what the preposition in לכל of MT means. This either

---
17. Nor do the Tar, which have both verbs.
18. Daniel 86 makes the following interesting point: "On a de même λειτουργεῖν λειτουργίας au verset 7, ou ʿ-b-d et ʿăbhôdhâh s'appliquant exceptionnellement, non aux Lévites, mais aux prêtres."
19. The count is that of Dos Santos.

intends "as for all …," or as Levine "including all."[20] The phrase is somewhat ambiguous, and Num has made good sense out of it. Furthermore, MT has a bound construction: "the holy things of the Israelites," which Num interprets by τῶν ἡγιασμένων (μοι) παρὰ τῶν υἱῶν Ἰσραήλ, i.e. "the (offering) consecrated to me by the Israelites," a fine exegesis of MT. The μοι has no basis in MT, and hex has placed it under the obelus. This also applies to μετὰ σέ; the gloss is ex par. The αὐτά must refer to "the consecrated (offerings)" i.e. τῶν ἡγιασμένων.

18:9 The initial καί has no correspondence in MT. The verse now specifies in particular from which ἀπαρχῶν/תרומת the priestly perquisites are to come. It is headed by καὶ τοῦτο ἔστω ὑμῖν "and let this be for you," which is modified by a partitive ἀπό construction which serves as a general title for a list of the offerings which will contribute a γέρας for the priests. This is what MT intended by its placement of האש under the *ethnach*. These γέρας are referred to as ἀπὸ τῶν ἡγιασμένων ἁγίων i.e. "from the dedicated holy things (offerings)."[21] This is followed by τῶν καρπωμάτων, for which MT reads מן האש. The מן is a partitive preposition, which is marked by a simple genitive;[22] Num intentionally left out an ἀπό, showing that "the offerings" was not coordinate with the four ἀπό phrases defining "the offerings." The phrase was understood by Num as מן האשה, "one from the fire offerings" (or better "from the offerings"). For the אשה sacrifice, see Note at Lev 1:9. Num always renders אשה by κάρπωμα. To make all this somewhat clearer, I would suggest that the comma after καρπωμάτων in the critical text be changed to a colon.

There follows a list of four ἀπό phrases, all of which explicate the καρπωμάτων which constitute the sources for the priestly benefits. The first is taken ἀπὸ τῶν δώρων αὐτῶν. This represents the general term כל קרבנם, which is rightly understood as a collective. MT has no preposition, but Num has ἀπό throughout. It is probably significant that MT lacks a preposition only for the first one in the list, viz. the קרבנם, since thereby it becomes clear that the list of four explicates האש, rather than being coordinate with it.

---
20. In comment on this verse.
21. Theod reads ἀπὸ τῶν ἁγίων τῶν ἁγίων, while Aq has ἀπὸ ἡγιασμένου τῶν ἁγίων, and Sym, ἀπὸ τοῦ ἁγίου τῶν ἁγίων.
22. See SS 168.

The next three are all introduced by ל in MT, but in Num these are all represented by a partitive ἀπό.²³ One might well understand each one as introduced by some such word as "a portion" or "a share" from, since each one produces a γέρας; see v.8. The next source was "from all the θυσιασμάτων which represents the מנחתם of MT, i.e. "their grain sacrifices." This equation only occurs twice in LXX; see also Lev 2:13. The usual rendering of מנחה in Num is θυσία. I doubt that any distinction between θυσίασμα and θυσία should be maintained here.²⁴ This is followed by ἀπὸ τῆς πλημμελείας αὐτῶν, and finally, ἀπὸ πασῶν τῶν ἁμαρτιῶν, to which hex has added αυτων under the asterisk, since MT has חטאתם. These last two are transposed from MT, which has ולכל חטאתם ולכל אשמם "and for all their sin offering and for all their trespass offering."²⁵ It will be noticed that only τῆς πλημμελείας is singular, but then the word is always singular in the Pentateuch. Oddly, the B Byz x+ text has omitted the article, but all the sacrifices listed are articulated, and the omission of τῆς is almost certainly secondary.²⁶ It might be noted that in the list of sacrifices, all except the first one, τῶν καρπωμάτων, repeat the preposition ἀπό. Since Greek commonly omits the preposition before coordinate nominals, the repetition is probably an intentional deviation. It serves to stress the fact of each class of sacrifice contributing its share as coming "from" the sacrifices presented. The list is followed by ὅσα ἀποδιδόασίν μοι. This represents אשר ישיבו לי in MT, i.e. "which they must return to me."

MT concludes with קדש קדשים לך הוא ולבניך "very holy to you is it and to your sons." Num has a different statement: "from all the holy (offerings) there shall be (a share) to you and to your sons." Num has summarized neatly the fact that the priestly share will be yours and your sons' from all τῶν ἁγίων, another cover term for what the verse has ordered as sources for the priestly perquisites.

18:10 The verse begins with a locative ἐν τῷ ἁγίῳ τῶν ἁγίων "in a most holy area," i.e. within the sanctuary. The αὐτά refers to πάντων τῶν ἁγίων of the preceding clause; it is "the holy portions which you (the priests) are to eat." πᾶν ἀρσενικόν is defined by σὺ καὶ οἱ υἱοί σου, which has no counterpart in MT, and

---

23. See Daniel 303—304, note 22.
24. But see Daniel 204—206.
25. For a full discussion of the root πλημμελ— in Greek, see Daniel, Excursus III, pp.341—361.
26. See THGN 107.

which hex has omitted, thereby equalling MT. Thus only priests may eat the γέρας of these various offerings. The final statement is "they shall be holy to you." The singular ἔσται is in concord with the neuter plural subject αὐτά. This renders קדש יהיה לך. Origen's LXX must have had ולבניך in his Hebrew text, since hex added καὶ τοῖς υἱοῖς σου at the end.[27]

18:11 This verse gives further sources for priestly benefits. MT begins with a nominal clause, which Num clarifies by the future ἔσται. Hex insists on placing this under the obelus, though it is a correct interpretation of what MT intends, although it has no actual correspondent to the verb. For ἀπαρχή, see comment at v.8. The majority A B F M text reading απαρχων is secondary, being attracted to the δομάτων (αὐτῶν) which follows it. Num interprets מתנם as a collective, i.e. renders it by a plural noun, δομάτων (αὐτῶν).

The priestly benefits are from "all the deposit offerings of the Israelites." For ἐπιθεμάτων as rendering for תנופת, see the Note at Lev 7:20(30). In distinction from the very holy sacrifices of vv.9—10, which only males might eat, daughters might also eat from the deposit offerings. In fact, every member of the priestly household who was καθαρός could eat αὐτά, which in view of the ἐπιθεμάτων is more logical than the singular אתו of MT, which must refer to the opening וזה.

18:12 MT refers to "all חלב יצהר and all חבל תירוש ודגן, (even) ראשיתם which they may present to the Lord." The use of חלב "fat" with reference to new oil, wine and grain, means the best or choice parts. Num renders חלב by ἀπαρχή, i.e., firstfruits. The term יצהר is rendered simply by ἐλαίου, and similarly, תירוש, by οἴνου. Num combines the notion of "newness" and of "fatness" in the single term ἀπαρχή. To complicate matters still further, a summary term for the three is added with ראשיתם "their beginning," i.e. their "firstfruits," which Num also renders by ἀπαρχὴ αὐτῶν. One might then render Num as "all firstfruits of oil and all firstfruits of wine and grain, (even) their firstfruits which they might present to the Lord, to you I have given them."

---

27. The Others also attest to the gloss καὶ τοῖς υἱοῖς σου. Obviously, the Hebrew text known to the recensors had ובניך at the end of the verse. Note that Tar[N] reads להון instead of לך.

In the tradition, all Greek witnesses except b 319 support an articulated κυρίῳ. The Hebrew has ליהוה, and the article presumably represents the preposition. But a review of all cases of the translation of ליהוה by Num convincingly demonstrates that the translator never used τω. In a few cases (six), hex added τω under the asterisk to represent the ל, but never did the translator do so.[28]

18:13 MT uses בכורי rather than ראשית here. MT vocalized the word as "firstborn," a term more common for the animal world. Num uses πρωτογενήματα, a term limited, except for two instances in Ezek where it is used to render ראשית, to translating בכורים "firstfruits." The bound phrase, בכורי כל "the firstborn of all" become τὰ πρωτογενήματα πάντα "all the first produce," or "products." The noun is modified by two ὅσα clauses: "whatever are in their land; whatever they might bring to the Lord." The predicate is in the singular: σοι ἔσται, in concord with a neuter plural subject. The last clause is an exact copy of the concluding clause of v.11; see comment ad loc.

18:14 The noun חרם has been rendered uniquely by the passive participle ἀνατεθεματισμένον "(everything) that has been anathemized," or "that has been devoted." The term is usually rendered by ἀνάθεμα. Num has the far more numerous term "(among) the Israelites" for בישראל, a typical case of harmonization on the part of Num.

The verse gives one an insight to the nature of the חרם. It does not necessarily mean that something is devoted to destruction; as a negative concept, it is removed from any secular or profane context, thus devoted either to destruction, or to the sanctuary; thus anything, πᾶν ἀνατεθεματισμένον, whether meat, grain or wine, when rendered anathema, becomes devoted to the sanctuary, and so can be used by priests.

18:15 Num begins with καί, but MT is asyndetic. For the tabu nature of all firstborn ("those opening the womb"), see Note at Exod 13:2. The relative clause "which they bring to the Lord" is introduced by ἅ. Since its antecedent is πᾶν διανοῖγον, it ought to be singular, and it is plural only ad sensum, i.e. everything that opens sensibly includes all those that open. The lack of strict concord did

---

28. See THGN 104.

trouble copyists, and the majority A M V text changed ἄ to οσα. A similar impulse inspired the Byz variant text, which changed the present indicative προσφέρουσιν to a subjunctive αν προσφερωσιν, making the verbal idea potential "(which) they might offer," but the presentation of the firstborn was not an option; the firstborn automatically belonged to the Lord, and had to be presented, whether human or animal (ἀπὸ ἀνθρώπου ἕως κτήνους). The subjunctive is not only secondary; it is wrong.

The adversative structure, which comprises v.b, presents an interesting distinction. It concerns the redemption of the firstborn of people vs the firstborn of unclean cattle. For the former, the predicate is λύτροις λυτρωθήσεται, but for the cattle, it is λυτρώσῃ. The human firstborn "must actually be redeemed," but for cattle, "you may redeem." The distinction made is that for the former, the redemption is mandatory, but for unclean cattle, it is permissive. MT has the same active verb, תפדה for both, but for the human firstborn, the verb is preceded by a cognate free infinitive, i.e. פדה תפדה "you must actually redeem." Num's rendering is adequate, i.e. as a cognate dative noun plus a passive verb.

In MT, the subjects are singular, בכור האדם and בכור הבהמה, which Num correctly understood as collectives, and translated by plural throughout.

18:16 Num is terser than MT; it reads "And as for its redemption from a month (i.e. at the age of one month), the rate is five shekels according to the sacred shekel; (they) are twenty obols." The antecedent for αὐτοῦ is the πᾶν διανοῖγον μήτραν of v.15. MT is more detailed; it has a verb, תפדה, after מבן חדש, for the opening, i.e. "you shall redeem its redemption at the age of one month, at the cash rate of five shekels according to the sanctuary shekel (which) is twenty gerahs." Hex has tried to "correct" Num by adding λυτρωσῃ under the asterisk after μηνιαίου as well as by adding αργυριον after συντίμησις under the asterisk to represent MT's כסף (ערכך). The term ערכך is morphologically unclear; it must be a fossilized form of which the second masculine singular suffix is irrelevant; it occurs quite often in Leviticus, where it is always rendered by τιμῆς. Here it is translated by ἡ συντίμησις "valuation," hence "rate." The bound phrase, (ב)שקל הקדש "shekel of the sanctuary," is understood as an adjectival phrase, τὸν σίκλον τὸν ἅγιον, which is a possible understanding of the consonantal text, though the Masoretes vocalized it as a bound phrase. For the shekel equalling twenty obols, see comment at 3:47, where, however, שקל was translated by δίδραχμον.

18:17 Redemption was an alternative for the first born of unclean cattle, but for clean cattle, i.e. for μόσχων, προβάτων and αἰγῶν, this was not permitted. MT lists these by singular nouns throughout, as e.g. בכור שור, and connects each one with the correlative conjunction או, whereas Num translates the nouns by the plural, thus as πρωτότοκα μόσχων,[29] and renders או by καί throughout. The reason for this stricture is ἅγιά ἐστιν. The subject is the three cases of πρωτότοκα, i.e. plural nouns. Concord of neuter plural nouns with singular predicates is fully consonant with Classical Greek syntax.[30]

V.b states what must be done with these firstborn. This is stated asyndetically, but Num begins with καί.[31] For clean animals, a) "their blood you must pour out πρός the altar"; probably "towards" the altar is meant. The choice of πρός was undoubtedly conditioned by the verb προσχεεῖς which it modified. MT has על, i.e. "on, (or against) the altar."

b) "And the fat you must offer up as a κάρπωμα for a pleasant odor to the Lord." MT has a suffixed חלבם, and hex has added αυτων under the asterisk after στέαρ to represent it. The verb ἀναφέρω also occurred for הקטיר at 5:26; cf comment ad loc. κάρπωμα renders אשה throughout the book; for its probable rationale, see Notes at Lev 2:9 and Deut 18:1. For εἰς ὀσμὴν εὐωδίας, see Note at Exod 29:18. The rendering εἰς ὀσμὴν εὐωδίας is a calque for the Hebrew לריח ניחח.

18:18 τὰ κρέα always occurs in the plural when it renders בשר, which is sensible. The meat ἔσται σοί. The collective neuter plural uses a singular verb. Hex has added αυτων under the asterisk after κρέα, since MT reads בשרם.

V.b refers to the analogy of the sacrifices for deliverance of Lev 7:31—34. The two analogies are introduced in MT resp by כ, but in Num the first one is presented as καθὰ καί, and the second by κατά. The first one thus reads "according as also (καί) the breast of the deposit offering," for which see comment at v.11. The second refers to the "right shoulder." In MT this is a bound phrase שוק הימין, which Num renders by an adjectival phrase.[32] For the render-

---
29. Tar^N also uses plural nouns throughout, thus בכורי תוריה, etc.
30. See SS 197.
31. Though many Hebrew mss do read ואת instead of (דמם) את. Tar^J also reads וית, but Tar^{NO} do not.
32. See SS 6.

ing of שׁוֹק "thigh" by βραχίονα "shoulder," see Note at Exod 29:22. This peculiar interpretation is limited to Exod (twice), Lev (eight times) and Num (twice; also 6:20).[33] שׁוֹק is correctly rendered five times by κνήμη, and once each wrongly by κωλέα "thigh bone," and σκέλος "leg."

18:19 For ἀφαίρεμα "dedicatory gift" as rendering תרומה, see Note at Lev 7:4. In MT, however, the term is plural, and Num uses a singular, though πᾶν ἀφαίρεμα does include all ἀφαιρέματα![34] And since the genitive modifier τῶν ἁγίων is plural, the rendering is not incorrect. The cognate structure תרומת ירימו is neatly reproduced by ἀφαίρεμα ... ἀφέλωσιν; I would translate: "Every dedicatory gift of sacred things which the Israelites might dedicate to the Lord."

Num then says "σοὶ δέδωκα and to your sons and your daughters with you as a νόμιμον αἰώνιον," for which see v.11, of which, except for an αὐτά after the verb, it is an exact copy. MT has נתתי לך, and the majority A F text has transposed σοί after the verb to agree with MT; the change is probably due to hex. At v.11 MT read לך נתתים, which was exactly reproduced by Num.

For MT's ברית מלח עולם "an everlasting covenant of salt," Num has διαθήκη ἁλὸς αἰωνίου. One would have expected αἰωνίου to have referred to διαθήκη rather than to ἁλός; i.e. "a covenant of eternal salt" is somewhat bizarre,[35] and I suspect that the translator made a mistake here. On the other hand, no copyist or textual group has changed it to make αἰωνίου modify διαθήκη. The "eternal salt" must reflect the "salt of the Lord's covenant" at Lev 2:13; see Note ad loc. Presumably, the salt as a preservative was thought to make the διαθήκη eternally valid.

Num also differs from MT in the final prepositional phrase. MT speaks of "your seed אתך," i.e. "with you." Num has changed the phrase to μετὰ σέ, a far more common modification of "seed," but MT also makes good sense. Even though one's seed comes after one, the covenant is valid with one's generations as well.

---

33. According to HR.
34. Pesh also uses the singular. It should be noted that תרומת is defectively written, and the consonantal text can be taken either as a singular or a plural noun.
35. SS 64 says about this structure: "In Num 18:19 ist das Adjektiv mit einem falschen Substantiv verbunden: διαθήκη ἁλὸς αἰωνίου (statt αἰώνιος) ἐστιν."

18:20 ויאמר is rendered here not by ειπεν, but rather by καὶ ἐλάλησεν, the usual rendering for וידבר, and the rendering probably has a textual basis; see comment at 15:35. Though v.20 introduces a new section, the pronoun αὐτῶν connects it with v.19, since it refers to οἱ υἱοὶ Ἰσραήλ of that verse. V.20 is a good illustration of parallelism in prose; "you shall not inherit" and "you shall have no portion" mean the same.

This negative statement of v.a contrasts with v.b which MT presents asyndetically: "I am your portion and your inheritance ...," whereas Num introduced this with ὅτι. What the Greek is saying is that your having no share assigned when the land of Promise is parcelled out among the tribes is due to your being wholly dedicated to the service of the Lord; he will be your heritage. The introduction of ὅτι simply makes explicit what is implicit in MT.

18:21 The Levites are to receive "every ἐπιδέκατον in Israel as a share." The term ἐπιδέκατον is first introduced by Num to render מעשר when it means "tithe," and is used in this sense only in the rest of the Bible, except at Isa 6:13 where it translates עשריה "a tenth."[36] They are assigned tithes in exchange for their λειτουργιῶν "public services." The plural noun correctly interprets עבדתם as a collective noun. In the tradition, the Byz text has added υιοις before Ἰσραήλ, but MT merely has בישראל, and the variant text is ex par.

These services are then explained by a ὅσα clause syntactically unconnected; it explicates the λειτουργιῶν by the descriptive "whatever they (i.e. the Levites) perform (as a) service in the tent of testimony."[37] One might express this unconnectedness by means of a dash. In MT the אשר clause is nominal: הם עבדים, which Num renders as usual by a pronoun and a present tense. The O f+ change to the future λειτουργησουσιν is obviously secondary.

18:22 A warning to laymen: "not may Israelites come into the tent of testimony anymore λαβεῖν ἁμαρτίαν θανατηφόρον," "to incur death bearing sin" (or better "guilt"). This renders לשאת חטא למות "to incur sin so as to die." I would understand the second infinitive as an apposite to לשאת חטא, thus "to incur guilt" is "to die." Num understands למות as modifying חטא, not לשאת חטא. The adjec-

---

36. See the discussion in Dorival 170.
37. See THGN 100.

tival phrase actually interprets MT correctly; the guilt of encroachment is fatal; it bears the seeds of death.

18:23 This verse deals with the Levites, but first in the singular as αὐτός/הוא and then in the plural as αὐτοί/הם. At first blush, one might understand the change to the plural pronoun to refer to the Israelites, but it is clear from the last clause that the plural also refers to the Levites.[38] For λειτουργήσει τὴν λειτουργίαν, see v.21. This λειτουργίαν of the tent of testimony belongs to the Levites. That the Levites bear their sins is a further reflection on the "death-bearing guilt" which encroachment on the sacred tent would involve, and which the Levitical guard was supposed to prevent. Num makes the νόμιμον αἰώνιον "the perpetual rule" apply to the latter statement only, since it is εἰς τὰς γενεὰς αὐτῶν, i.e. plural, even though as in MT, both clauses are included in the חקת עולם. This is clearer in MT, since it is to apply to לדרתיכם "to your generations," i.e. the suffix is second person.[39]

18:24 The reason for the last clause of v.23 is given by a כי clause. The statement ending v.23 is then restated in a διὰ τοῦτο clause in v.b. The language is greatly repetitive.

The verse begins with the accusative modifier of δέδωκα, viz. "the ἐπιδέκατα of the Israelites which they would set aside as a dedicatory gift to the Lord." Here מעשר is rendered by the plural; comp the πᾶν ἐπιδέκατον of v.21 which actually means the same thing, i.e. "every tithe" equals "the tithes." For ἀφορίσωσιν ἀφαίρεμα, see comments at 15:18—19,20. It might be noted that ἐν κλήρῳ is the usual rendering for לנחלה. The change by the Byz text to κληρονομια is simply for variation; at v.21 Byz does not change ἐν κλήρῳ. In the διὰ τοῦτο clause the cognate ינחלו נחלה is not rendered by a cognate expression as in v.23, but by a different noun, κλῆρον, though retaining the κληρονομήσουσιν of v.23.

18:26 The a:b::b′:a′ opening pattern imitates MT's "and to the Levites you shall speak, and you shall say to them." The modifiers are אל phrases in MT, but the

---
38. The Tar simplify all this by using a consistent plural.
39. Though Tar[N] also supports the third person by its לדריהון.

first one is rendered by a dative, τοῖς Λευίταις, and the second one, by πρὸς (αὐτούς).

The protasis presupposes reception of the tithe by the Levites, a tithe "which I have given you from them (i.e. the Israelites) ἐν κλήρῳ," though MT does not read לנחלה as in v.24, but בנחלתכם. Hex has supplied υμων under the asterisk to represent the untranslated suffix.

The apodosis is introduced by an apodotic καί in imitation of MT, and is signalled by the change to the future tense. For ἀφελεῖτε as the usual rendering for the Hi of רום, see comment at 15:20. For the rendering of ἀφελεῖτε ἀφαίρεμα, see comment at 15:18—19. The verb is followed by ὑμεῖς which has no basis in MT, and hex has accordingly placed it under the obelus. It functions as a contrast to the Lord's δέδωκα ὑμῖν; i.e. the Lord assigned the tithe to you; now it is your turn, and "you must dedicate as a dedicatory gift to the Lord a tithe from the tithe." The preposition ἀπό occurs twice in the verse, and both cases are partitive.[40]

18:27 The verse reads "and your dedicatory gifts shall be reckoned for you as grain from ἅλωνος and ὡς ἀφαίρεμα from the press (i.e. the wine press)." In the tradition, B x+ read αλω instead of ἅλωνος. The two, i.e. ἅλως and ἅλων, are synonyms, but only ἅλων occurs elsewhere in the Pentateuch. Cod B also reads αλω at v.30 (with only two other mss in support) as well as at 15:20, with only three other mss. ἅλωνος must throughout be the original LXX.[41] Cod B (together with x+) also omits the ὡς before the coordinated ἀφαίρεμα. This is probably merely an internal stylistic improvement. Num often repeats the preposition, though good Greek style would not follow the normal Hebrew practice of such repetition. The omission here is secondary.[42] What is more difficult to understand is the unique use of ἀφαίρεμα to represent מלאה, a word that occurs only twice elsewhere in the Bible: at Exod 22:29(28) it refers to the fullness of the harvest and the juice from the presses. At Deut 22:9 it has a similar meaning; see Notes at Exod 22:29 and Deut 22:9. But why use ἀφαίρεμα here? Dorival[43] refers to

---

40. See SS 168.
41. See THGN 128.
42. See THGN 130—131.
43. P.376.

Tar^N as approaching the sense of Num, but this is unlikely.⁴⁴ Why use "as a dedicatory offering from the press" as a coordinate to "as grain from the threshing floor." One might have expected something like "the full flow from the press." I can see no exegetical reason for the term, and can only suggest that the translator was inattentive at this point; the word had already occurred twice in the context, once in v.26, and again in the plural in v.a. It was also to appear both in vv.28 (twice) and 29; I suspect that he made a mistake.

18:28 MT says: "So must you dedicate, even you, the dedicatory gift of Yahweh from all your tithes." Num not only uses a plural τῶν ἀφαιρεμάτων to render תרומת, which is a possible reading of the consonantal text, but has also introduced it by a partitive ἀπό. In turn, "from all your tithes" modifies ἀφαιρεμάτων; in other words, Num interprets as "some of the Lord's dedicatory gifts from all your tithes." In the tradition, the majority A F M text read παντων in modification of (τῶν) ἀφαιρεμάτων which is clearly secondary, an importation from ἀπὸ πάντων ἐπιδεκάτων which follows. The rendering of תקחו in the relative clause is interpreted as ἂν λάβητε, i.e. understanding תקחו as a potential notion, "whatever you might receive from the Israelites," rather than a future.

Coordinate with the initial clause, "so must you dedicate," is the last clause, "and must give ἀπ' αὐτῶν a dedicatory gift κυρίῳ for Aaron the priest." MT has ממנו "from it," though the reference must be to the כל modifying מעשרתיכם which is plural. Presumably, it might otherwise possibly refer to תרומת, but that is a feminine (singular). Num has the more logical plural, referring to ἐπιδεκάτων. Since MT reads את תרומת, hex found ἀφαίρεμα a deficient rendering, and so prefixed the article το to represent את. The translation of (תרומת) יהוה by a dative, presumably one of possession, is rhetorically unfortunate, since it is followed by another dative indicating indirect object, 'Ααρὼν τῷ ἱερεῖ. A genitive κυριου would have been clearer, and one ms, 72, actually reads κυριου, but I doubt that this is due to Hebrew influence.

18:29 The δομάτων refers to the tithes which the Levites receive. For ἀφελεῖτε ἀφαίρεμα, see comment at v.19. MT, however, has את כל תרומת, and hex has

---

44. Tar^N reads ותתחשב לכון אפרשותכון כאפרשות עיבורא מן אדרא וחמרה מן מעצרתא "And your offering shall be reckoned to you as the offering of grain from the threshing floor and wine from the press."

prefixed παν under the asterisk to ἀφαίρεμα. חלבו, literally "its fat" means "its best parts," which Num translates by τῶν ἀπαρχῶν "the first fruits." For the use of ἀπαρχή to translate חלב, see comment at v.12. Num has not translated the suffix, and hex has supplied an αυτου under the asterisk to make up for it.

As a second accusative modifier of ἀφελεῖτε, Num has τὸ ἡγιασμένον (ἀπ' αὐτοῦ). This represents את מקדשו, but without an equivalent for the suffix, which hex took care of by adding an αὐτοῦ under the asterisk. The Hebrew word is, however, problematic as vocalized by the Masoretes. Apparently, they wanted to avoid understanding the noun as "his sanctuary," which admittedly, would make odd sense. They then vocalized it in unique fashion, creating thereby modern confusion. Num understood the word vocalized as a Pu passive participle, thus "that which has been sanctified (from it)." The pronoun must refer to ἀφαίρεμα. The rendering is not overly luminous; just what is meant by that which has been sanctified from the dedicatory gift may be clearer than the את מקדשו ממנו of MT, but it is not immediately clear what the translator meant by it. What v.b seems to say is "from all its first fruits that which has been sanctified by it."

18:30 The temporal ὅταν clause correctly renders the Hebrew prepositional phrase with bound infinitive plus pronominal suffix, thus "whenever you might dedicate the first fruit from it." Num uses τὴν ἀπαρχήν to translate חלבו, to which hex has added αυτου under the asterisk to represent the untranslated suffix; for ἀπαρχήν, see comment at v.12.[45] Num correctly used the present subjunctive verb within the ὅταν clause, which is far superior to the default aorist αφελητε of the O group.

The apodosis is identified as such by its use of the future tense; it is also introduced by an apodotic καί in imitation of MT. For ἄλωνος appearing in B+ as αλω, see the comment and footnote at v.27. Both cases of γένημα "produce" are modified by ἀπό phrases, though MT has two bound phrases.[46] In fact, the omission of both cases of ἀπό by n+ is, I suspect, recensional in origin.[47]

---

45. SS 100 makes the astute comment that the ἀπ' αὐτοῦ which follows both here and in v.32 makes the suffix superfluous.
46. Though 4QNum^b has מן היקב, and may have had (מן הגורן) originally as well. In other words, the ἀπό phrases may well have a textual base in their parent text.
47. The tradition that The Others adopted the Num text is quite incredible. The attribution o' οἱ λ' for the two ὡς phrases is probably mistakenly amplified to include οἱ λ' from the o' οἱ λ' attribution of the καὶ ἐρεῖς πρὸς αὐτούς reading immediately above it on the margin of the ms (344).

18:31 The subject of ἔδεσθε is ὑμεῖς (i.e. the Levites) καὶ οἱ οἶκοι ὑμῶν, which equals MT. Actually, MT reads a singular noun, וביתכם, though 4QNum^b reads the plural (ה)ובתיכמ. The majority A V text, however, adds και οι υιοι υμων between the two, but this has no claim to being original text; it was added under the influence of the oft-recurring "you and your sons" throughout the book. Num has a modifier of the verb in αὐτό (i.e. ἀφαίρεμα of v.29), which equals MT. A popular F V text reads the plural αυτα, which probably refers to δομάτων.[48]

The reason given for this is "because it is payment to you for τῶν λειτουργιῶν ὑμῶν τῶν in the tent of testimony." MT has a singular noun עבדתכם, though it is rightly understood as a collective noun. The second τῶν has no counterpart in MT, though it does make for a smoother text.

18:32 V.a is a promise that "you will not take on ἁμαρτίαν on account of it when you dedicate the firstfruit from it." For αὐτό see comment at v.31. The plural variant αυτα would refer to δομάτων of v.29, but is clearly secondary. The term ἁμαρτίαν, like its parent חטא, here means the guilt associated with "sin, error." The "firstfruit from it" renders חלבו, for which see the discussion at v.30. As in v.30, hex has added αυτου under the asterisk to ἀπαρχήν. By ἀπαρχήν is meant the tithe of the tithe, so what is being said is that as long as the tithe of the tithe has been dedicated, no guilt is incurred in the handling and eating of the tithe. In the tradition, the majority A B F M text has οτι αν instead of ὅταν. This is simply a palaeographically inspired error; i.e. the insertion of an *iota* between *tau* and *alpha* is easily made. As the temporal collocation בהרימכם proves, only ὅταν fits; οτι does not;[49] compare the ὅταν clause of v.30 which it repeats exactly; see comments ad loc.

V.b gives a warning: "τὰ ἅγια of the Israelites you may not profane, lest you should die." The warning about τὰ ἅγια "the sacred gifts" need not refer only to the tithes, though they do constitute the immediate context. The warning can be taken as a subscription, and might simply be a general warning against defiling sacred things of the Israelites. The rendering of the paratactic ולא תמות by a ἵνα μή structure is precisely what MT must mean.

---

48. 4QNum^b reads או(ת)ימה.
49. See THGN 129.

Chapter 19

19:2 Vv.2—10 concern the ritual of the red heifer. The opening statement identifies what is to follow: αὕτη ἡ διαστολὴ τοῦ νόμου, which represents זאת חקת התורה "this is the prescription of the law." The term διαστολή as a rendering of חקת is unique. I would suggest that what it means is "This is the stipulation of the law." Dorival renders this by "voici la disposition de la loi."[1] The term basically means "separation," and so the separate distinctions made within the νόμος, hence the understanding what the regulation (νόμος) stipulates. The word only occurs four times in the LXX as a whole; see also 30:7 Exod 8:23(19), where the notion of "separation, parting" is intended. "What Yahweh ordered" presumably modifies התורה. Its translation uses ὅσα which is neuter plural in form, but is actually used as a fossilized relative adjective used as a relative pronoun "whatever." It too modifies what precedes, viz. τοῦ νόμου.

What the Israelites are to do is: λαβέτωσαν πρὸς σὲ δάμαλιν πυρρὰν ἄμωμον. MT has פרה, which says nothing about the age of the animal; it simply means "a cow," but Num, noting that it had never had a yoke placed on it, sensibly used δάμαλιν "heifer." Incidentally, פרה is translated elsewhere by δάμαλις five times, though, as is proper, 18 times by βοῦς. Num follows Sam in its reading καὶ ᾗ, whereas MT lacks a conjunction.[2]

Why the heifer should be πυρράν is unknown, though speculation is rife. Gray suggests on one page[3] that "red is the colour of life," but on the following page he suggests that it may have been "because red is the colour of blood." As with any animal sacrifice, it had to be ἄμωμον "spotless"; in fact, it is unnecessarily redefined as ἥτις οὐκ ἔχει ἐν αὐτῇ μῶμον. The verb ἔχω is often used in the context of rendering an אשר בו structure.[4]

---

1. He defends the use of διαστολή as a choice which is "heureux, car, dans les *papyri*, διαστολή signifie: «ce liste détaillée, liste d'impôts, disposition particulière d'un contrat» (378)." This is then followed by a valuable and full summary of the ways in which חק is translated in the Pentateuch.
2. But 4QNum^b also supports the אשר of MT.
3. P.247.
4. See SS 59.

The red heifer had to have the further qualification καὶ ᾗ οὐκ ἐπιβλήθη ἐπ' αὐτὴν ζυγός. In other words, the heifer had never been used for secular purposes; comp Deut 21:3.

19:3 Num with its καὶ δώσεις is addressing Moses, i.e. continuing the singular λάλησον of v.2. The conflict between the singular and the Lord speaking "to Moses and Aaron" is not easily explicable. Suffice it to say that it is normally Moses alone who is the oral intermediary between the Lord and Israel. MT, however, with better rationale, has the plural ונתתם, since this is part of what Moses is saying to the Israelites; see v.2.[5] In any event, the heifer is to be given to Eleazar, the priest.

V.b continues in third person, MT in the singular, and Num in the plural.[6] The plural is sensible as an indefinite plural, which is best translated by a passive transform: "And it (i.e. the heifer) shall be brought outside the camp εἰς τόπον καθαρόν and be slaughtered before him (i.e. before Eleazar)." The singular is more difficult, since the verbs are not only singular but also active, and the most natural rendering would be "and he shall bring out ... and slaughter," but this is followed by לפניו, which must refer to Eleazar. In other words, the singular verbs can not refer to him, but must also be taken as indefinite, thus "and one must bring it ... and slaughter it before him." The Greek with indefinite plural verbs follows the more usual course for indefinite subjects. The change to the plural is undoubtedly intentional; thereby Num avoids any possible suggestion that Eleazar might be the subject. Num makes a smoother text, removing any possible ambiguity.[7] The phrase "to a clean place" is a case of harmonization with v.9, where it also occurs, but there with Hebrew support. Hex has correctly placed the phrase under the obelus.

19:4 Num has shortened the text in two cases: instead of "Eleazar הכהן," it simply reads Ἐλεαζάρ; this is followed by "from its blood," to which MT had added באצבעו. In both cases hex has added an equivalent under the asterisk: ο

---

5. On the other hand, the singular is supported by 4QNum^b which reads ונתתה; this reading must have been parent text to Num.
6. Probably based on a plural verb as in 4QNum^b, which has ושחטו.
7. Tar^J solves the problem by called Eliezar סגן כהניא, and having כהניא אוחרן as subject of ויכוס.

ιερευς after "Eleazar," and τω δακτυλω αυτου after "its blood." The ἀπό here, as well as later in the verse, is partitive.[8]

Though it is unstated, Eleazar must then go to the tent with some of the blood, since he must sprinkle "before the face" of the tent. The heaping up of ἀπέναντι and τοῦ προσώπου is meant to indicate in precise fashion where the sprinkling is to take place, viz. on the door side of the tent; this accords with the אל נכח פני of MT. The sevenfold sprinkling indicates that this was a purification ritual.

19:5 Num continues with an indefinite plural active verb, καὶ κατακαύσουσιν, for MT's singular verb ושרף, for which see comment at v.3. The modifier in MT is את הפרה "the cow," which Num simplifies by the pronoun αὐτήν, as in v.3, and had continued by αὐτῆς in v.4. Presumably, MT's use of the noun was intended to introduce the parts of the cow that are to be burned up, viz. את ערה ואת בשרה ואת דמה "its skin and its flesh and its blood." In fact, the Masoretes have divided the verse at this point; i.e. לעיניו is placed under the *ethnach*. This means that שרף only governs את הפרה לעיניו, with ישרף governing the remaining prepositional phrases, and I would take Num as reflecting this understanding as well. Since Num had referred to "the cow" simply by a pronoun, it introduced the first unit of v.b with a καί, i.e. "καὶ τὸ δέρμα," to which hex has added αυτης under the asterisk to represent the untranslated suffix. That the introduction of a καί to introduce "the skin" might simply be due to dittography in the parent text, the preceding word being לעיניו, is also possible, though as suggested above, not necessarily. The second unit, "its flesh," is rendered by τὰ κρέα αὐτῆς. The plural is used, since the meat has been slaughtered, and "dressed meat" is usually represented by the plural κρέα.

The verse is to be divided after αὐτοῦ. Though what follows explicates the αὐτοῦ, a new syntagm is introduced to modify the final verb κατακαυθήσεται, a singular passive verb with a compound subject: "even the skin and its flesh and its blood σὺν τῇ κόπρῳ αὐτῆς ('with its dung')." MT has the same verb as at the beginning, but here it is translated by a passive, whereas MT's ישרף is again active with an indefinite subject "one shall burn." The Greek correctly understood this, as its passive transform indicates. The compound modifier of

---

8. See SS 162.

ישרף has become the compound subject of the passive verb. In other words, the nouns, τὸ δέρμα, τὰ κρέα and τὸ αἷμα are not in the accusative, but rather in the nominative.

19:6 For the list of purifying elements for use in the burning up of the heifer, comp Lev 14:4, where, however, the last two are reversed; see comments ad loc. Here only one word, κόκκινον, is used to represent שני תולעת, whereas in Lev 14:4 (and in Exod passim) two words are used, κεκλωσμένον κόκκινον. See also comment at 4:8 where the Hebrew words are transposed, but the single word κόκκινον is also used to translate the pair. In fact, the two words are apparently synonyms.

According to MT, it is the priest who will throw these elements into the burning of the cow, which is sensible, since it is the priest who must take them and השליך. Num, however, changes to the indefinite plural of earlier verses (vv.3,5).[9] This is probably due to the distinction made in vv.7,8 between the priest and the one doing the burning, another case of rationalizing the text.

19:7 Num translates word for word, except for rendering במים by an instrumental dative ὕδατι, i.e. without a preposition.[10] After laundering and bathing, the priest may reenter the camp; though not stated, these had to be performed outside the camp. One might have expected the verb טמא to be rendered by a verb, but Num uses the equally valid rendering of ἔσται plus a verbal adjective. This remains the pattern throughout the chapter, except for v.20a, which see.

19:8 The same regulation as in v.7 is mandatory for "the one burning it (i.e. the heifer), except that in MT במים occurs with both verbs of v.a, i.e. with כבס and with רחץ, but Num lacks an equivalent in both cases.[11] Hex has added εν υδατι under the asterisk in both cases. Note the difference between the rendering of במים in Num in v.7, and the more exact rendering by Origen here, who also translated the prepositions. One might note that the majority A M V text added υδατι after "his body," an obvious case of harmonization with v.7.

---

9. See Dorival 110.
10. See SS 118.
11. Kenn 69 does support the omission of the first במים.

19:9 A third party is introduced as ἄνθρωπος καθαρός, "who is to bring together the ashes of the heifer, and put them away outside the camp in a clean place." These ashes are to be stored, i.e. εἰς διατήρησιν "for safekeeping." This preservation or safekeeping is defined as ὕδωρ ῥαντισμοῦ ἅγνισμά ἐστιν, which I would translate as "water of sprinkling; it is a cleansing." What is meant is that the water of sprinkling serves as a means of cleansing. MT has למי נדה חטאת הוא. The term ἅγνισμα occurs uniquely as a rendering for חטאת, but ἁγνισμός is found twice for חטאת, at v.17 and at 31:23. In all three cases, חטאת is understood as a purification rite by which the guilt of sin is removed. Relevant to the understanding of this interpretation is 8:7 where the ceremonial cleansing of the Levites is ordered. To accomplish this, περιρρανεῖς αὐτοὺς ὕδωρ ἁγνισμοῦ. Since the abstract ἅγνισμα defines the "water of sprinkling," it is clear that the water of נדה is here to be understood as the water which is sprinkled for the removal of נדה, i.e. the impurities of the menses are removed by the sprinkling of the water which has become a cleansing agent by the ashes of the red heifer—note that the burning of the heifer specifically included τὸ αἷμα αὐτῆς (v.5). This then also makes sense of the safekeeping of the ashes. Cf especially the discussion at 8:17.[12]

19:10 The washing of garments is also mandatory for the one gathering the ashes of the heifer. Num renders בגדיו simply by τὰ ἱμάτια, which hex corrects by adding αυτου.[13] It should also be noted that this is placed immediately after the verb πλυνεῖ, with the subject, ὁ συνάγων τὴν σποδιὰν τῆς δαμάλεως, following. In MT את בגדיו follows the subject,[14] and hex has also transposed τὰ ἱμάτια (αυτου) after δαμάλεως to agree with the word order of MT. It might be noted that for variation Num renders את אפר by τὴν σποδιάν, rather than by τὴν σποδόν as in v.9. There is no difference in meaning. As might be expected, an A F majority text reads την σποδον under the influence of v.9. It might also be noted that a popular A F M text transposed the subject before the predicate, i.e. before πλυνεῖ; comp the transposition in hex noted above.

That v.10 ends a section seems clear from the concluding clause with its definition of what has been said as a νόμιμον αἰώνιον. It is to be a perpetual

---
12. See also the discussion in Dorival 124.
13. See SS 99.
14. See THGN 102.

prescription, not only for the Israelites, but also τοῖς προσκειμένοις προσηλύτοις. For this as a rendering for the singular לגר הגר, see discussion at 15:15. MT, however, had added בתוכם, and hex has added εν μεσω αυτων to represent the untranslated phrase. This led in turn to the majority A F M reading εν μεσω υμων; the reading εν υμιν of b is based on 15:15.

19:11 Vv.11—13 describe how the red heifer ritual affects the one who touches a corpse. The rule is that "the one who touches the corpse of any ψυχῆς ἀνθρώπου shall be unclean for seven days." The Greek structure renders literally the נפש אדם of MT. The word נפש/ψυχῆς means "a person," and the person of a human being is tautologous. One can do no better than to translate "(corpse of) a human being." Why the Byz+ text should have begun the section with και is puzzling; it is neither original nor logical.

The Greek is straightforward, but MT is peculiar. V.a is syntactically a pendant, since v.b begins with a conjunction וטמא "even he will be unclean." What MT says is "As for the one who touches the corpse of a human being, he will be unclean for seven days." Sam has יטמא instead of וטמא, which makes a simpler syntactic structure. The waw and the yodh are very similarly made, and it is possible that יטמא became וטמא through a copyist error (or the reverse!). Num apparently follows the Sam text.

19:12 "He (the one who has touched a corpse) must cleanse himself בו on the third day"; the antecedent of בו is not certain, but probably the מי נדה is intended.[15] Num has disregarded the בו, leaving the means to be used for cleansing undefined. Hex has added εν αυτω under the asterisk to render the בו. This presupposes ὕδωρ as the antecedent, not σποδίαν which is feminine.

MT then continues with "and on the seventh day he will be clean." Num divides afer "seventh day," after which it reads καὶ καθαρὸς ἔσται, almost certainly based on Sam's וטמא, rather than MT's יטמא. This is also supported by Pesh and Vulg, and may well be the better text.

V.b states the obverse of this proposition: "and if he should not be cleansed on the third and on the seventh day, he will not be clean." That in v.a וטמא is the

---

15. Though Milgrom suggests אפר as the antecedent, which strikes me as unlikely. According to v.9, the ashes had been gathered for safekeeping למי נדה; it was this water which Num understood as "water of sprinkling," and which in turn is described as being ἄγνισμα.

earlier text seems to be secured by v.b, where reference is made to cleansing on both the third and the seventh day. Note that a passive verb is used in v.b, ἀφαγνισθῇ, rather than a middle, though MT repeats the Hithp יתחטא. This represents a fine insight; if someone fails to cleanse himself, he has done nothing; it means that he is not cleansed.

19:13 The verse concerns someone who has touched a human corpse, and has failed to undergo a cleansing ritual. "Every one touching a corpse" is followed by ἀπὸ ψυχῆς ἀνθρώπου, which I would understand as a partitive phrase modifying ἁπτόμενος, thus "any part of a human being," i.e. the touching of any part of the corpse contaminates a person. For ψυχῆς ἀνθρώπου, see comment at v.11. MT does articulate האדם, but Num follows v.11 which does not. Admittedly, Sam also reads אדם, but this need not be the parent text of Num, since Num tends to harmonize his text.

The essential component of the condition is put into an ἐάν clause with two coordinate verbs. This renders a text which is much clearer: אשר ימות ולא יתחטא "which is dead and he does not cleanse himself." By rendering אשר which modified נפש האדם by ἐάν, and then placing the two verbs as coordinate within the structure, potential confusion is created, since common sense dictates that the subjects of the two verbs must differ, i.e. "if *it* has died, and *he* has not been cleansed"; for ἀφαγνισθῇ, see comment at v.12. The apodosis is in the default aorist tense, "he defiled the tent of the Lord." This is a plausible rendering of טמא, though a present tense might have been a more exact reflection of what MT intended. Incidentally, the majority F text has articulated κυρίου, which is certainly secondary. Num never articulates κύριος when it represents the tetragrammaton, unless the Greek text requires it, viz. when κύριος is accompanied by δέ, it perforce reads ὁ δὲ κυριος, or when it is governed by את, the accusative τὸν κύριον obtains. That κύριος in all cases is rendered by the unarticulated noun as its default rendering is clear.[16]

The general verdict for the uncleansed individual is given as "that person shall be wiped out from Israel." The rendering of the Ni of כרת by the verb ἐκτρίβω is unusual, occurring elsewhere only at 15:31 and Gen 41:36, the usual rendering being ἐξολεθρεύω (31 times according to Dos Santos). Num fortunately

---

16. See THGN 103—104.

did not translate the initial *waw* of MT's clause though the V *b+* text did add a καί, which I suspect is not recensional, but ex par.

The reason for this harsh judgment is given in a ὅτι clause: "ὕδωρ ῥαντισμοῦ was not sprinkled on him; he is unclean; his uncleanness is still on him (ἐν αὐτῷ ἐστιν)." MT lacks the final ἐστιν, and hex has placed it under the obelus.[17] For ὕδωρ ῥαντισμοῦ as rendering for מי נדה, see comment at v.9. The verb περιρραντίζω occurs here and at v.20, for the Pu of זרק which only occurs in the Bible in these two places. The Hebrew root has the notion of "dashing, throwing," and the use of the Greek verb meaning "to sprinkle" is contextually determined.

19:14 The remainder of the chapter deals with details concerning the carrying out of the red heifer ritual of purification. In fact, v.14 begins with καὶ οὗτος ὁ νόμος "and this is the regulation." MT begins with זאת, but Num follows Sam's וזאת, and hex placed the καί under the obelus to show that it had no equivalent in MT. The use of ἄνθρωπος before the conditional particle reflects the common Hebrew pattern of אדם כי. "Should a person die באהל," is updated by Num to read ἐν οἰκίᾳ. Alexandrians lived in houses, not in tents. After all, this contrasts with ἐπὶ προσώπου τοῦ πεδίου of v.16, which see.

The regulation applicable in such a case is that "everyone who enters the house and whatever is in the house shall be unclean for seven days." MT differs only in its use of אשר for both cases, i.e. "whoever enters ... and whoever is ...." One might have expected ὅς rather than ὅσα, but the ὅσα may have been impelled by the כל preceding the אשר, although πας ος would have been a better equivalent for MT. Hex has supplied παντα under the asterisk to render the כל.[18]

19:15 Open vessels in the house where a dead person lies are unclean as well. Such vessels are defined in MT as אשר אין צמיד פתיל עליו, which is difficult to understand, since the usual meaning of צמיד "bracelet" and of פתיל "thread" can hardly have been intended here. Moderns interpret the clause to mean "which had no cover (or lid) secured on it." What is meant then is vessels which are not securely sealed. Num follows a similar understanding: ὅσα οὐχὶ δεσμὸν

---

17. The Others also omit it.
18. For καὶ ὅσα—fin Sym has καὶ ὁ ἐν τῇ σκηνῇ ἀκάθαρτος ἔσται ἑπτὰ ἡμέρας (retroverted from Syh). Apparently, Sym disregarded the כל as well.

καταδέδεται ἐπ' αὐτῷ "which does not have a tie bound upon it," in other words is not firmly sealed.¹⁹

19:16 Anyone who touches something dead outside the house, i.e. ἐπὶ προσώπου τοῦ πεδίου "on the plain," viz. השדה, is also unclean for seven days. Such a one is defined as τραυματίου ἢ νεκροῦ ἢ ὀστέου ἀνθρωπίνου ἢ μνήματος, all of which modify ἅψηται. τραυματίου "someone slain" contrasts with νεκροῦ "a cadaver," i.e. one who died a natural death. MT has בחלל חרב for the first one, and hex has added ρομφαίον under the asterisk to represent the חרב, thus "one slain by the sword." The third one represents בעצם אדם, and a popular A text has changed ἀνθρωπίνου to ανθρωπου.²⁰ The adjectival structure adequately renders the bound phrase of MT. That a grave also defiles is clear from the principle underlying vv.14—15, in which anything or anyone in an enclosed space with a corpse is thereby contaminated. Num does not follow the word order of MT's יטמא שבעת ימים, but has ἀκάθαρτος ἔσται after ἑπτὰ ἡμέρας; hex has changed the word order to equal MT.

19:17 The verb of the first clause is plural with an indefinite subject; it has τῷ ἀκαθάρτῳ as an indirect object: "for the unclean (person)." What is to be taken is "ἀπὸ τῆς σποδιᾶς (of that which was burned of the cleansing)." The ἀπό is a good example of a partitive, i.e. "some of the ashes."²¹ MT has מעפר "some of the dust"; one might well have expected מאפר. The interpretation σποδιᾶς is of course correct; see vv.9—10. For τῆς κατακεκαυμένης τοῦ ἁγνισμοῦ, see the discussion at v.9. The ἁγνισμοῦ is the same in meaning as the ἅγνισμα. Here the ashes are from what had been burned up of the red heifer, called "the cleansing." The "cleansing" renders החטאת "the purification rite."

V.b states "and they shall pour out on it living water in a vessel." MT has a singular verb ונתן, and Num follows Sam which has the plural.²² The Hebrew

---
19. The recensors interpret in similar fashion. All Three render ὅσα οὐχὶ δεσμόν by ᾧ οὐκ ἔστιν πῶμα (i.e. hw dlyt 'ayt lh ksy'), but for καταδέδεται ἐπ' αὐτῷ they differ. Aq reads στρεπτὸν ἐπ' αὐτῷ "a turning about on it," and Sym has συννημένον πρὸς αὐτό "joined to it "; Theod has συνδεδομένον ἐπ' αὐτῷ "tied up on it." All readings are retroverted from Syh.
20. This reflects the reading of Aq: ἀνθρώπου. Theod and Sym adopted the Num rendering.
21. See SS 66.
22. As do Pesh and Vulg.

says "one shall put into a vessel," which Num interprets by ἐκχεοῦσιν ... εἰς σκεῦος. Since what is put into the vessel is ὕδωρ ζῶν, "pour into a vessel" is a good contextual translation. Admittedly, ἐκχέω occurs only twice in LXX to represent נתן; it also occurs at Exod 30:18 in a similar context; see comment ad loc.

19:18 The rite of cleansing is described. "A clean man must take hyssop and dip (it) into the water and sprinkle." The verb is modified by four ἐπί phrases. For τὸν οἶκον, see comment on τὴν οἰκίαν at v.14. Both render the noun אהל. The other phrases summarize the unclean mentioned in vv.14—16, i.e. "the vessels, the persons whoever were there, and the one who touched ...." MT has כל הכלים, and hex has added παντα under the asterisk before τὰ σκεύη to represent the כל, Num having followed the text of Sam which lacks כל.

This last phrase reads ἐπὶ τὸν ἡμμένον, which is modified by the four referred to in v.16 as found on the face of the plain (or open field), but in a different order. The first one, τοῦ ὀστέου τοῦ ἀνθρωπίνου, is a case of harmonization with v.16, since MT has only בעצם. Accordingly, hex placed τοῦ ἀνθρωπίνου under the obelus. Instead of the νεκροῦ of v.16, here τοῦ τεθνηκότος is used. Both, however, contrast with "the one slain," and refer to one who died a natural death. For the inclusion of μνήματος, see comment at v.16.

19:19 The καθαρός shall besprinkle the ἀκάθαρτον. The subject was called ἀνὴρ καθαρός in v.18. As in v.12, the ritual is to be performed on the third and the seventh days, to which MT added וחטאו "and he shall cleanse him." Num has changed this to a passive construction "καὶ ἀφαγνισθήσεται (on the seventh day)." MT states that after the washing of his garments and his bathing with water, וטהר בערב "and he will be clean in the evening." This statement is unique in the chapter; the usual conclusion (vv.7,8,10,21,22) is "and he shall be unclean until evening," and Num has used this; whether this was a case of intentional harmonization, or simply an unconscious ex par adaptation is not known. In view of Num's preference for set patterns, I suspect that the former was the case.

18:20 The verse begins with a nominative pendant, καὶ ἄνθρωπος ὃς ἂν μιανθῇ καὶ μὴ ἀφαγνισθῇ "and as for the person who is defiled and is not cleansed." MT is slightly different in that the second verb is Hithp, i.e. "and has not cleansed himself," but see comment at v.12.

The penalty for such an individual is given in the main clause, which refers to the pendant by ἡ ψυχὴ ἐκείνη: "that person shall be destroyed from the midst of the assembly." In v.13 a different verb was used to render נכרתה; here the usual rendering ἐξολεθρευθήσεται is used. And instead of ἐξ Ἰσραήλ, here ἐκ μέσου τῆς συναγωγῆς obtains. Of course, "the assembly" is "Israel," and the Byz text has changed τῆς συναγωγῆς to των υιων ισραηλ, and the b text has simply added ισραηλ.

Two reasons for the penalty are given in two ὅτι clauses; the first reason is "because the ἅγια of the Lord he has defiled." MT has מקדש "the sanctuary (of Yahweh)." For the use of "holy places (or objects)" as an interpretation of מקדש, see comment at 18:1.

The second ὅτι has no basis in MT, and hex has placed it under the obelus. For ὕδωρ ῥαντισμοῦ οὐ περιερραντίσθη ἐπ' αὐτόν, see comment at v.13, of which this is an exact copy. In fact, Num has taken over the entire ὅτι clause from v.13.

19:21—22 That this section is coming to an end shortly is clear from the mention of νόμιμον αἰώνιον "a perpetual prescription." The remainder is more or less repetitious, a final dotting of the "i" and crossing of the "t." "The one sprinkling the ὕδωρ ῥαντισμοῦ must also wash his clothes," and the one touching it shall be unclean for the rest of the day.

So contagious is the unclean one that anything he touches will be unclean, and the person who touches him will also be so until evening. The only thing unusual is the παντός which introduces the relative clause: "which the unclean one touches it." Since the verb ἅψηται governs the genitive, its modifier αὐτοῦ (for בו) is genitive, and the introductory παντός is genitive by case attraction. One might have expected either πᾶς "everyone" or πᾶν "everything." Possibly the genitive was used to preserve the ambiguity of כל of MT.

Chapter 20

20:1 This new section has the Israelites on the move; they, i.e. all the assembly, came to the wilderness of Σίν; this place is not to be confused with Σινά, though a number of witnesses do so. This confusion is only possible in the Greek tradition. In Hebrew the latter is סני, whereas Σίν represents צן. For the location of this wilderness, see comment at 13:22. The proper noun is unarticulated, which is the usual pattern in the book when governed by "the desert of."[1] Their arrival is dated "in the first month," but the year is not indicated, which creates a chronological problem. The problem is, however, one for MT; Num simply translates MT.

According to MT, "וישב the people in Καδής." Num renders the verb by κατέμεινεν, a verb occurring only seldom in LXX, and only twice elsewhere for ישב (22:8 Josh 2:22). That this is unusual is clear from the usual renderings of this verb: e.g. κατοικέω (502) times, καθίζω (167), and ἐνοικέω 129 times.[2] But that they "stayed" there is clear from the context, which states that "Mariam died there, and was buried there." Nothing is said about the usual forty day period of mourning. The name Καδής is the transcription of קדש "Qadesh," and created very little difficulty for copyists. Two mss omitted the final consonant, and a number of scattered witnesses doubled the *delta*, but the spelling is certain.

20:2 The narrative continues with the story of the rebellion of the people against Moses and Aaron because of the lack of water to drink (vv.2—13). Num does not render the repeated preposition על before Ἀαρών, which is indeed better Greek.

The Byz tradition has amplified the text of the first clause by two glosses. It reads "and there was no water (+ εκει) for the assembly (+ πιειν)." These are added under ex par influence, the first one probably from v.b where the adverb does occur, and the second is a case of harmonization with v.5. In the second clause, the A F M V majority text read the compound συνηθροισθησαν instead of the simplex verb of Num. The Ni יקהלו is translated by the simplex only here,

---

1. See THGN 103.
2. According to Dos Santos.

whereas the compound is used to render it only at Ios 22:12. Either makes good sense, and Num simply follows the text of the oldest witness, cod B.

20:3 The reaction of the people is described by καὶ ἐλοιδορεῖτο ὁ λαὸς πρός "the people railed against." This translates וירב העם עם "and the people entered into a controversy with." The verb ריב has as its base meaning the juridical sense of laying a charge against. Of course, here it has no such sense, since Moses was himself the final court of appeal, but the translation makes good sense in the context. See Note at Exod 17:2 for a similar situation, where the Israelites also engaged in a violent quarrel with Moses.

MT introduces their specific charge by ויאמר לאמר, which Num reduces to λέγοντες, and hex has added καὶ ειπαν before it under the asterisk to equal the ויאמר of MT.

The quoted speech is introduced by ולו, which is translated by ὄφελον, a fossilized form meaning "oh that"! Here it occurs with the aorist, and refers to what is not attainable in past time.³ MT expresses this wish by a cognate expression: ולו גוענו בגוע אחינו "oh that we had perished when our brothers perished," a reference to ch.16, the account of the rebellion of Korah, Dathan and Abiram. Num breaks up the cognate pattern, probably merely for variation, by its ὄφελον ἀπεθάνομεν ἐν τῇ ἀπωλείᾳ τῶν ἀδελφῶν ἡμῶν "oh that we had died in the destruction of our brothers"! In the tradition, a popular A F reading created a cognate pattern by its απωλομεθα for ἀπεθάνομεν. The latter verb is much more common in LXX as translation for גוע (six times vs twice for ἀπόλλυμι). The temporal structure with a bound infinitive is nominalized, though dictionaries do not recognize a noun גוע.

20:4 The complaint is similar to that of 16:13, where ἀποκτεῖναι ἡμᾶς is also used, whereas MT has the Qal infinitive למות שם, i.e. "that (we and our cattle) should die there." This is probably a fine example of Num harmonizing with the 16:13 passage; cf comment ad loc. In fact, the Num text actually makes the accusation against Moses considerably more vicious, as though Moses had brought the people into the desert with murderous intent. Num also omits the שם, which hex makes up for by adding εκει under the asterisk after ἀποκτεῖναι. Also

---

3. See Bl-Debr 359.1.

in the tradition, is a change in the introductory interrogative ἵνα τί, for which oI' C'' s read διὰ τι, which is a synonym.[4]

20:5 Num here reads καὶ ἵνα τί τοῦτο, though MT has ולמה as at v.4. Obviously, the parent text read ולמה זה, which is a variant of ולמה.[5] Since MT lacks מה, hex has placed the τοῦτο under the obelus. The rebellious assembly asked "why did you bring us up out of Egypt παραγενέσθαι," to which MT had added אתנו, which, in view of ἀνηγάγετε ἡμᾶς, is strictly speaking, unnecessary in Greek. Hex has, however, added ημας under the asterisk to represent the אתנו.

The assembly described "this nasty place" as "a place where nothing is sown, nor are there figs, ... nor is there water to drink." MT phrases this rather differently: "not a place of grain and figs and vines and pomegranates, and there is no water to drink." Though the structures differ considerably, the Num version does give the sense of the Hebrew adequately. The major difference is the rendering of the noun זרע "of grain" by a verbal clause οὗ οὐ σπείρεται "where nothing is sown."

20:6 As usual, a singular verb obtains as congruent with the nearer element of a coordinate subject which follows the verb. When the verb precedes, the singular is used; thus καὶ ἦλθεν is normal. Movement from one place to another is expressed by ἀπὸ προσώπου ... ἐπί plus an accusative. According to MT, the brothers "entered the door (of the tent)" ויבא ... אל פתח. Num, however, translates by καὶ ἦλθεν ... ἐπὶ τὴν θύραν; they did not enter, but "came to the door." It was then at the door of the tent of testimony that ἔπεσον ἐπὶ πρόσωπον. The singular is used, since each of them had a face. MT does add a suffix, פניהם, and hex added αυτων under the asterisk to represent it. The suffix is often left untranslated.[6] In the tradition, the Hellenistic επεσαν occurs in an A B F popular variant,[7] but the Hellenistic inflection is used consistently only for εἶπαν, whereas for other verbs Num uses the Classical form throughout.[8]

---

4. Aq also makes a change with εἰς τί, whereas Theod and Sym retain Num.
5. See BDB sub מה 4d for a discussion of the "strengthened" form למה זה.
6. See SS 99.
7. Aq also read ἔπεσαν, but Theod and Sym used ἔπεσον.
8. See the discussion in THGN 124.

For the appearance of ἡ δόξα κυρίου, see discussion at 14:10. Num renders אליהם literally by πρὸς αὐτούς, but apparently hex, along with Byz+, changed the preposition to read επ αυτους. I fail to see why the change was made.[9]

20:8 The verse begins with λάβε τὴν ῥάβδον. Though the address is to σὺ καὶ Ἀαρών, both λάβε and ἐκκλησίασον are in the singular, since they precede the vocatives, and therefore are in the singular. See the discussion in v.6. Similarly, after the vocative occurs, the verbs become plural in Num.

Which rod is meant is debatable, though in view of Exod 17:5—7, it probably was Moses' rod, rather than Aaron's, which was intended.

For ἐκκλησίασον rendering the Hi of קהל, see Note at Lev 8:3. Though the verb following the vocatives reads ודברתם, which would presuppose a future verb in Num, the translator continues the use of an imperative with καὶ λαλήσατε. This was probably done to contrast with the verb in the next clause, καὶ δώσει (τὰ ὕδατα αὐτῆς). The change from the plural imperative to the third person singular future makes the relation between the two clauses intimate: "speak ... and it shall yield its waters." The second clause can be understood as the result of the speaking, and it would not be incorrect to render: "speak to the rock before them, that it might yield its waters."

V.b changes to second singular verbs in MT; it is thus Moses alone who is to effect the bringing out of water from the rock and laving the assembly and their cattle. Num, however, changes the singular verbs to the plural: ἐξοίσετε ... ποτιεῖτε, which accords with its common practice of plural verbs after the subject; but probably of greater import, this renders this verse consistent with v.12, in which the Lord punishes both Moses and Aaron, because οὐκ ἐπιστεύσατε ἁγιάσαι με ἐναντίον υἱῶν Ἰσραήλ. Once again, Num is careful to make an account consistent throughout.

Just why the translator should translate מימיו by the plural ὕδατα αὐτῆς, but מים by the singular ὕδωρ is not clear. I suspect it is merely a matter of variation, since Num is erratic in the use of ὕδωρ vs ὕδατα.

20:9 So Moses took the rod τὴν ἀπέναντι κυρίου which was before the Lord," whereas MT simply has מלפני יהוה. Does this mean that Moses' rod had been

---

9. The Others read πρὸς αὐτούς, which makes the variant all the more puzzling.

deposited in the tabernacle? All of this was done καθὰ συνέταξεν κύριος. MT lacks an equivalent for κύριος, and hex has placed it under the obelus. In the tradition, the Byz b+ text added αυτω after the verb, which is simply an ad sensum gloss.

20:10 The opening verb, ἐξεκκλησίασεν, illustrates clearly that Num follows a deliberate pattern with compound subjects. The subject is Μωυσῆς καὶ ᾿Ααρών, and it follows the verb. Therefore, Num uses a singular verb, even though MT has ויקהלו, i.e. a plural inflection. Nor does Num translate the cognate ויקהלו את קהל by a Greek cognate structure, although this is quite possible in Greek. The noun קהל is usually rendered by συναγωγή in Num, whereas the cognate verb is normally rendered by ἐξεκκλησιάζω or ἐκκλησιάζω, and Num follows the more usual course. In fact, though ἐκκλησία is the more common rendering in LXX for the noun קהל (69 times, whereas συναγωγή occurs 37 times),[10] ἐκκλησία is never used in Num. The noun does not actually occur in the Pentatuech, except in Deut.

Note that though the first clause has a compound subject with a singular verb, the next clause also has a singular verb, καὶ εἶπεν, not a plural. But there the subject is no longer "Moses and Aaron," but only Moses. This is clear from the μου of ᾿Ακούσατέ μου.[11] MT does not support the μου, although it does read שמעו נא, and it is possible that Num read the Hebrew as שמעוני, which would produce ἀκούσατέ μου. It should be said that Num does not otherwise render the נא particle; later translators did render it by δή, and hex often supplies a δή, though not here. The assembly is addressed as "disobedient ones," ἀπειθεῖς, which inteprets MT's המרים "rebellious ones."

Moses then asks a μή question, which would expect a negative answer: "Is it from this rock we must bring out for you water"? The use of μή to render the neutral interrogative prefix -ה, does slant the question. It raises some doubt in the minds of hearers; after all, it was the wrong question; it was not Moses and Aaron who were to bring out water from the rock, but rather the divinely ordered word. The question in Greek expects the reply: no, *we* should not bring out water from the rock. In other words, Num improves on the question in MT!

---

10. According to the count of Dos Santos.
11. See THGN 122.

20:11 Num subordinated the first clause by means of a participle, and eliminated the conjunction of the second clause in MT; thus "and raising his hand, Moses struck the rock." This correctly places the stress on ἐπάταξεν. The smiting is τῇ ῥάβδῳ, which is a good example of a dative of means or instrument.[12] MT reads במטהו, and hex has added αυτου under the asterisk to render the suffix. Furthermore, Moses struck the rock δίς "twice," with the desired effect that "much water came out and the assembly and their (αὐτῶν) cattle drank." The word συναγωγή is rightly understood as a collective, making the plural pronoun necessary (both in MT and Num).

20:12 As usual for Hebrew, MT repeats the preposition "to Moses and to Aaron," but the Greek does not. Ms 426 of the O group has added προς before Ἀαρών, a reading clearly based on the Hebrew. The divine word to the brothers is patterned as a ὅτι clause plus a διὰ τοῦτο one, which correctly reproduces the יען and the לכן structures; thus "because οὐκ ἐπιστεύσατε ..., therefore οὐκ εἰσάξετε ὑμεῖς ...." MT has האמנתם בי "you did (not) trust me," but Num omitted "me," possibly because the modifier להקדישני also had a first singular pronominal modifier, which Num did translate by (ἁγιάσαι) με. In other words, Num absolutizes the verb. It is not "believe in me," but "did not have faith, trust." In any event, hex has added εν εμοι under the asterisk to render the untranslated בי. It should also be noted that the M V Byz+ text added μοι, which may well simply be an ad sensum gloss, and not a recensional text.

The exact intent of "you did not trust (or believe) so as to sanctify me" is not immediately clear. First of all, Moses and Aaron could hardly make the Lord holy, and ἁγιάσαι με must mean "to display my holiness" or "to recognize my holiness." What is at stake is that Israel's God should be recognized as God before the Israelites. The main verb then probably ought to be contextually rendered by "you did not have enough faith (to demonstrate my holiness)."

In the tradition, υἱῶν Ἰσραήλ, which occurs 78 times in the book, is articulated by a popular A M V Byz text. Usage shows no pattern, since by my count τῶν occurs in 43 cases, but is lacking in the other 35. Whenever the problem of articulation is textually uncertain for υἱῶν Ἰσραήλ, it would then seem wise to follow the oldest witnesses, here that of cod B.

---

12. See SS 121.

The divine judgment in the "therefore" clause addressed to Moses and Aaron is "οὐκ εἰσάξετε ὑμεῖς τὴν συναγωγὴν ταύτην into the land which I have given them." MT has no equivalent for ὑμεῖς, which is unnecessary to the sense, and hex has placed it under the obelus. It was probably added by the translator to give the sense that it is not you, but someone else, who will lead the Israelites into the Promised Land. In the tradition, the A M V majority text has εδωκα instead of δέδωκα, but the change is secondary. The perfect and the default aorist are easily confused, but the perfect is here the preferred text. The Lord had given it and the gift remains valid.

20:13 MT says המה מי מריבה "those are the Waters of Meribah," i.e. the מי מריבה is taken as a place name; at 27:14 they are called מי מריבת קדש "the Waters of Meribat Qadesh."[13] Num, however, translates the name, both here and in ch.27, here by ἀντιλογίας "strife," thus "this (was) the water of strife." This is modified in MT by a relative clause which describes the relevance of the name מריבה, i.e. "where they quarreled with Yahweh, but he was sanctified among them." This is translated as a ὅτι clause, which is sensible, thus: "because the Israelites railed against the Lord, and he was revealed as holy among them." For the meaning of ἡγιάσθη ἐν αὐτοῖς, see the comment on ἁγιάσαι με in v.12, and comp also 27:14. For ἐλοιδορήθησαν as an interpretation of רבו, see discussion at v.3, though here the verb is used absolutely, being modified only be ἔναντι κυρίου.

20:14 Vv.14—21 describe Moses' attempt to gain permission to travel through Edom. V.a simply states that "Moses sent messengers from Kades to the king of Edom λέγων." The λέγων has no correspondent in MT, though apparently hex did not call attention to this lack by an obelus. Since the message begins with "Thus says your brother Israel," the direct address indicator is not really necessary.

The actual message continues through v.17. The title "your brother," a polite term used in diplomacy for one supreme head of state addressing another, i.e. Moses to the king of Edom, recalls the tradition that Edom's genitor was Esau, the twin brother of Jacob, the genitor of Israel. For μόχθον as rendering for

---

13. For the nominal structure, see SS 78.

329

תלאה, see Exod 18:8, where Moses told his father-in-law about "all the μόχθον that had happened to them on the way"; cf Note ad loc. The relative clause אשר מצאתנו is translated by an attributive participle τὸν εὑρόντα ἡμᾶς "which overtook us" (literally "found us").

20:15 Since Israel is simply recalling their past history, the default aorist is used both here and in v.16a. The second clause used "παρῳκήσαμεν (in Egypt ἡμέρας πλείους)." MT has the neutral נשב, which is usually rendered by the verbs κατοικέω, ἐνοικέω or κάθημαι, καθίζω. The translator, however, used παροικέω with its emphasis on temporary residence.[14] In fact, it is used only here in the Pentateuch for ישב (though at Gen 24:37 whre οἰκῶ obtains in Gen, the majority A M 961 text does read παροικω), and only six times elsewhere in the Bible. They were πάροικοι, resident strangers, in Egypt. Origen's text apparently read this in third person as παρωκησαν, but this is a mistake; it continued the third person of κατέβησαν with our fathers as its subject, but MT had changed to ונשב. There they remained for πλείους days. The comparative πλείους means "numerous, many."[15]

The third clause refers to the Egyptians. The Masoretes voalized מצרים as "Egypt," but οἱ Αἰγύπτιοι is a fully possible rendering of the consonantal text, and it need not presuppose the המצרים of Sam.

20:16 Num repeats the subject of εἰσήκουσεν with its κύριος. Hex placed the word under the obelus, since MT does not have it, it being unnecessary in view of the first clause: "and we called out πρὸς κύριον." The third clause in MT, "and he sent a מלאך," is reduced to a subordinate participial structure, since the stress quite rightly rests on the fourth clause, "and he brought us out from Egypt"; thus "and sending an ἄγγελον, he brought us out of Egypt." The reference to a messenger is undoubtedly to "ὁ ἄγγελος τοῦ θεοῦ, the one going before the camp of the Israelites, and went behind" of Exod 14:19, i.e. to Israel's guardian angel. See other references in the Note ad loc.[16]

V.b speaks of the Israelite's present location. Num says "and now we are in Kades, a city on the edge of your borders." MT has a clause modifier והנה "and

---

14. Aq used ἐκαθίσαμεν, whereas Theod translated by κατῳκήσαμεν. Sym read διετρίψαμεν.
15. See Bauer sub πόλυς II.
16. Not so Rashi, who says about "angel" זה משה מכאן שהנביאים קרואים מלאכים.

behold" instead of the timer "and now." The νῦν brings the message up to date, contrasting with the aorists which had preceded. Furthermore, MT has a nominal clause in which אנחנו is subject and בקדש is the predicate, followed by an appositie structure "a city on the edge of your border." גבולך is a singular noun, which Num renders by the plural τῶν ὁρίων σου, i.e. understanding גבול as a collective. Num has made the clause a verbal clause by its ἐσμεν for אנחנו, which is fully legitimate.

20:17 The proposal: "Let us pass through your land"—is stated along with a number of promises of care not to harm anything or make use of anything belonging to Edom. The first two clauses in MT use the same verb, i.e. the first plural of עבר, both in the long form נעברה "let us traverse," and for the next one, לא בעבר "we will not traverse." Num uses two different compounds: for the first one, παρελευσόμεθα "we would go along," and for the second, "we would not go through."[17] Both often occur as renderings for עבר; the παρ- compound occurs 106 times, whereas the δι- compound is used 59 times.[18] Both are modified by διά phrases, and one must conclude that the translator thought of the two as synonymous. For the second clause, the modifiers are δι ἀγρῶν οὐδὲ δι ἀμπελώνων, i.e. with plural nouns, to render singulars of MT, בשדה ובכרם, which are rightly taken as collectives.

MT then follows with "and we would not drink well-water." Num translates מי באר by ὕδωρ ἐκ λάκκου σου. Since באר has no suffix, hex placed σου under the obelus. The rendering of "well-water" by "water from your cistern(s)" is reasonable in view of the arid land of Edom.[19]

V.b then designates the road they would follow. "(By) the ὁδῷ βασιλικῇ we would journey." The adjectival structure, "the royal road," translates a bound phrase in MT,[20] giving assurance that "they would deviate from it, neither to the right nor to the left ἕως ἂν παρέλθωμεν τὰ ὅριά σου." The translator reverts to the first rendering of העבר by using the verb παρέρχομαι again. As in v.16, the singular גבולך is rendered sensibly by a plural noun.

---

17. I would understand the futures here throughout as deliberative; see Porter 424—425.
18. Acording to Dos Santos.
19. Tar[N] also has מי גובין, and Tar[O] reads מי גוב. Presumably, באר was read as בור.
20. See SS 66.

20:18 Edom answered with a point blank refusal. In fact, Edom uttered a threat: "εἰ δὲ μή, ἐν πολέμῳ I will go out to meet you." The protasis is a free rendering of פן "lest." What is meant by εἰ δὲ μή is "otherwise."[21] MT has בחרב "with the sword," which is metonymic for "war," which Num realized.[22] In the tradition, the text of Origen, represented by O plus Syh, read the plural, εξελευσομεθα, which is not supported by MT.

20:19 Num uses the historical present καὶ λέγουσιν for ויאמרו, since the narrative imitates dialogue. According to MT, the Israelites said "we will go up by the מסלה." The noun derives from the root סלל, thus "a raised, or heaped up road." So by extension, it refers to a highway or a public road.[23] Num has a unique interpretation: παρὰ τὸ ὄρος παρελευσόμεθα "we would go along the mountainous area." A possible explanation is given by Dorival[24] who suggests that since Esau dwelt ἐν ὄρει Σηίρ according to Gen 36:8, what was meant by Israel was that they would travel "le long de la montagne," i.e. "de longer la frontière." This is not impossible, and the suggestion is furthered by the understanding of מסלה as a raised, heaped up route. The use of the verb παρέρχομαι to translate עלה is unique in the Bible, and is here chosen as a thematic verb in the narrative, the verb occurring five times within it (vv.17,17,19,19,21).

This is followed by a conditional statement, the protasis of which reads "and if we should drink τοῦ ὕδατός σου, even I and τὰ κτηνή." The genitive is a partitive, "any of your water," and could presuppose Sam's ממימיך, though not necessarily so; after all, MT does not mean "all your water," whereas "some of your water" is a good interpretation of MT as well. The parent text also has מקני "my cattle," and the majority A F M tradition adds μου; I suspect that the μου is a recensional gloss.[25] MT introduces the apodosis with a conjunction, ונתתי, but Num, in the interest of better Greek, omitted it. MT said "and I will give מכרם "their price." Num does not render the suffix, but added σοι, as an ad sensum gloss. Hex has made no attempt to correct the text at all.

---

21. Dorival translates "dans le cas contraire."
22. Theod Aq and Sym read ἐξέλθω an aorist subjunctive instead of ἐξελεύσομαι, thereby stressing the potential nature of the action.
23. Both Tar^JN read "by the road of the king."
24. Pp.142—143.
25. Tar^N reads "I and our cattle," i.e. בעירנן.

V.b is also rendered freely. MT's רק אין דבר probably means "it is only a small matter," i.e. "there is nothing else, only ...." This Num renders by an adversative structure ἀλλὰ τὸ πρᾶγμα οὐδέν ἐστιν "but the matter is nothing," which is a good attempt to render what MT intended. But the remainder of what they said is a paraphrase of the Hebrew. MT says "let us pass through on foot." Num, instead of translating ברגלי, repeats the original request, παρὰ τὸ ὄρος παρελευσόμεθα, for which see comments supra. Why the translator should have avoided translating ברגלי is puzzling; after all, how else would they cross, if not on foot?

20:20 ὁ δὲ εἶπεν, i.e. Edom, replied. MT simply has "you may not pass through," to which Num added δι' ἐμοῦ; this harmonizes with v.18. Hex has placed the phrase under the obelus. Edom suited action to their word. "Edom went out to meet him (i.e. Israel) ἐν ὄχλῳ βαρεῖ and ἐν χειρὶ ἰσχυρᾷ." MT has בעם כבד וביד חזקה. The word ὄχλος means "a crowd," and as a rendering for עם occurs only here in the Pentateuch, and occurs elsewhere only twice (in Jer). What is meant is "with a heavily armed crowd." The second phrase is exceedingly rare in LXX, occurring elsewhere only at Isa 8:11 and 1Macc 11:15. The usual rendering for חזקה (ביד) is κρατειᾳ. I would suggest the translation: "with a strong force."

20:21 Num renders וימאן "and he refused," by the milder καὶ οὐκ ἠθέλησεν, thus "and Edom did not want (to allow Israel to go along through its borders)." The rendering διὰ τῶν ὁρίων αὐτοῦ is a case of harmonization with v.17, which see. Note also that Num simplifies the compound preposition, מעליו, by ἀπ' αὐτοῦ.

20:22 Vv.22—29 narrate the death of Aaron. The narrative begins by Israel pulling stakes from Kades, and arriving in its entirety, i.e. "all the assembly," at Ὥρ τὸ ὄρος, i.e. "at Hor the mountain." This represents הר ההר, i.e. were Ὥρ translated it would mean "mountain, the mountain." Its location is completely unknown. All that is known is that it was not at Kades, though it was at the borders of Edom. The designation "Hor the mountain" is an unusual one; one would expect the two terms to be reversed as in Mt. Sinai, Mt. Carmel, etc. The unusual order is probably due to "Mountain" being taken as the name of "the mountain." It would be possible to understand the consonantal text as an elative, "the mount of mountains," in the sense of God of Gods, Lord of lords, thus "the height of, or the top of the mountain." But LXX throughout takes הר as a proper name.

In the tradition, the Byz+ text has the singular απηρεν rather than the ἀπῆραν of MT. The subject reads οἱ υἱοὶ Ἰσραὴλ πᾶσα ἡ συναγωγή; presumably the variant text refers to συναγωγή, but this cannot be original. πᾶσα ἡ συναγωγή is simply an apposite to "the Israelites," and not the reverse, as the Byz text seems to imply.

20:23 The divine orders come to Moses and (to) Aaron. As usual, Num does not render the על before Aaron, though hex pedantically added πρός under the asterisk. The text gives the only information we have as to the location of "Hor the mountain." It is ἐπὶ τῶν ὁρίων γῆς Ἐδώμ. This gives a great deal of latitude as to its exact location. MT has the singular גבול, which Num correctly understands as a collective.

20:24 Num understands the Ni יאסף as a precative, and translates by a third singular imperative, προστεθήτω "let there be added," instead of "let there be gathered." A more common rendering would be the verb συνάγω, "bring together," (used 42 times), whereas προστίθημι occurs only ten times.[26] The translation is due to the confusion of the roots יסף and אסף, but it occurs sufficiently often so that no textual conclusions should be drawn from it. In fact, הוסיף is common, although the passive Ho does not occur in the Bible. The collocation "be added (or be gathered) to one's people" means to die a normal death, usually in old age. Num has πρὸς τὸν λαὸν αὐτοῦ, which might be thought to presuppose the עמו of Sam, rather than the עמיו of MT, but this would be quite unjustified, since one would hardly expect a rendering προς τους λαους αυτου.[27]

The ὅτι clause gives the reason for the (premature) death of Aaron. MT says that it was "because not יבא (may he enter) the land which I gave to the Israelites." This is sensible, but Num "corrects," or better "harmonizes," the account by changing יבא to εἰσέλθητε; both Moses and Aaron were denied passage to the Promised Land. The reason for the denial is "because παρωξύνατέ με at the water τῆν λοιδορίας." The use of the second plural verb εἰσέλθητε is

---

26. The count is that of Dos Santos.
27. Oddly, Tar⁰ has עמה, while Tar^JN have עמיה.

almost certainly due to attraction to the παρωξύνατε in the διότι clause later in the verse, although the fact that "the Lord said πρὸς Μωυσῆν καὶ 'Ααρών" may have been a contributing factor. It should be observed that the Byz+ text has modified the verb to equal MT, i.e. as εισελθη. Num also interprets the verb of the relative clause by the perfect δέδωκα. The Lord had given the land to the people by his promise in the past. The popular A V variant aorist εδωκα is secondary. The basis for the Lord's not allowing entrance to the land of promise is "because you exasperated me at the water of railing." The collocation "exasperated me" is an interpretation of מריתם את פי "you rebelled against my word." The term את פי "my mouth" is metonymic for "my word," i.e. what comes out of my mouth. Num completely voids any such anthropomorphism by using με. The rendering of מריתם by παρωξύνατε is unique as well. In the tradition, a popular A F M V gloss, εν κατασχεσει, occurs after "to the Israelites"; this has no basis in MT, but is well known ex par.

That מי מריבה is not understood as a place name by the translator is clear from its translation by τοῦ ὕδατος τῆς λοιδορίας "water of railing." The same term occurred at v.17, but there מריבה was translated by τῆς ἀντιλογίας, which an ol b+ text also reads under the influence of v.17. Obviously, the מריבה is simply understood as a descriptive term.

20:25 Moses is told to take τὸν 'Ααρὼν καὶ 'Ελεαζάρ. In MT, both names are governed by the preposition את; in fact, throughout this section (vv.25—29), except when either is the subject of a clause, they are always thus governed. And throughout the section, the translator has rendered the את by the article τόν before 'Ααρών, but not before 'Ελεαζάρ. The reason for the distinction is that the fact that 'Ελεαζάρ is in accusative is assured, since the name is throughout modified by τὸν υἱὸν αὐτοῦ. A popular A M V gloss has identified 'Ααρών as τον αδελφον σου but this has no basis in MT, and is ex par.

At the end of v.b, Num has added ἔναντι πάσης τῆς συναγωγῆς, which is not attested in MT, and is therefore placed under the obelus by hex. This is a case of harmonization with v.27 where ἐναντίον πάσης τῆς συναγωγῆς follows εἰς Ὢρ τὸ ὄρος. Instead of ἔναντι, the majority A F M V text has εναντιον. Whether ἔναντι or ἐναντίον is original is problematic. I would suggest that, since the origin of the gloss could hardly be the εναντίον πάσης τῆς συναγωγῆς of v.27, but rather the לעיני כל העדה of MT at v.27, the εναντιον of the majority text is a secondary adaptation to v.27 of Num.

20:26 Num renders the contrasting verbs הפשט "strip" and הלבשת "you must dress" neatly by related imperatives: ἔκδυσον and ἔνδυσον "unclothe" and "clothe." That this is an intentional ploy is obvious, since normally the translator would render the second verb by a second singular future inflection. The modifier of הפשט is את בגדיו, but since the clothing intended was the priestly vestments, the translator used τὴν στολήν αὐτοῦ rather than the more usual τα ιματια αυτου; in other words, it was "his robe" that was to be taken off and put on Eleazar. Num failed to render the suffix of והלבשתם, and hex has added αυτην, referring to στολήν, under the asterisk to represent it.

MT then states "and Aaron shall be gathered up and die there." Num makes a single clause out of it by subordinating the first clause into an attributive participle, προστεθείς, thus "let Aaron having been added, die there." For the use of προστίθημι for the Ni יאסף, see the discussion at v.24; what is obviously meant is "having been added (or gathered) to his fathers."

20:27 Moses then did as he was divinely ordered. The order had been to take Aaron and Eleazar, "and bring them up to Hor the mountain (before all the assembly)." MT changed this here to ויעלו "and they went up to (Hor ...)." The translator, however, recorded Moses' action exactly as the Lord had ordered, and reads καὶ ἀνεβίβασεν αὐτοὺς εἰς Ὡρ τὸ ὄρος ἐναντίον πάσης τῆς συναγωγῆς, a more precise carrying out of the orders of v.25 than that of MT. Since συνέταξεν is normally modified by a dative indicating the person(s) commanded, the urge to add (or prefix) an αυτω was almost irresistible; in fact, all Greek witnesses except B V and 319 succombed, but MT simply has צוה, not צוהו, and the absolute use of συνέταξεν is original text.

In the tradition, the B V O f n+ text read αυτον instead of αὐτούς. It has been suggested that this reading was original LXX based on the ויעלהו of Sam. But, as suggested above, the orders in v.25 had been to bring αὐτούς, not just Eleazar, and the B text is secondary.[28]

20:28 As at v.26, the verbs ἐκδύω and ἐνδύω are used for the removal and donning of garments; see comments at v.26. The δύω compounds can be modified

---

28. See THGN 113.

either by one accusative or two; with one accusative a person removes (or dons) a garment, and with two, the verb is transitive, and a person removes (or dons) the garment of another person. MT names משה as the subject after ויפשט; it is of course unnecessary in view of ויעש משה of v.27, and Num omitted it. Hex, has, however, added μωυσης under the asterisk after ἐξέδυσεν. In the tradition, a B b d+ text has omitted the τόν before Ἀαρών. That את before "Ααρον" was rendered throughout this section had already been noted at v.25, but here it was also semantically necessary. Without the article, the clause would mean that Aaron removed his garments, which is plainly incorrect.[29] It might further be noted that בגדיו is here rendered by the usual τὰ ἱμάτια αὐτοῦ rather than by the τὴν στολὴν αὐτοῦ of v.26. Once it was clear from v.26 that it was the priestly vestments that was intended by בגדיו, the word could be translated by the more common (and literal) plural noun.

And then "Aaron died שם at the top of the mountain." Num disregarded the שם, since it was otiose, but hex added εκει under the asterisk to represent it.

20:29 Since according to v.28, only "Moses and Eleazar had come down from the mountain," it was obvious that "all the assembly recognized that Aaron ἀπελύθη." The passive of ἀπολύω means "was released," a Classical and gentle rendering for גוע "had expired."[30] The verb is usually rendered either by ἀποθνῄσκω (eight times) or ἐκλείπω (six),[31] but only here by ἀπολύω. It might also be noted that MT's plural verb ויראו, with כל העדה as subject, was rendered in strict concord with συναγωγή by the singular εἶδεν "saw, recognized." Either number would have been defensible.

---

29. See THGN 107.
30. Theod translated by ἐξέλιπεν, and Aq used ἐδαπανήθη.
31. According to the count of Dos Santos.

Chapter 21

21:1 MT clearly refers to the king of Arad as הכנעני "the Canaanite," which Num has taken as a proper noun, ὁ Χανανίς; this was quite intentional, being confirmed in v.3 where את הכנעני becomes τὸν Χανανίν; see also 33:40 where the king of Arad is once again referred to as ὁ Χανανίς. There, however, he was dwelling in Canaan.[1] That this was an intentional change is clear from the fact that elsewhere where הכנעני occurs in the book, it is rendered by ὁ Χαναναῖος. In the tradition, the A *f n*+ text also reads χαναναιος, whereas a *t z*+ text reads χαναυι, and the *d* group has χανααν. Scattered readings include χαναναι, χανι, χαναιος, χανις, χααυης and χαχανης. The translator may have avoided using "the Canaanite" to characterize the king of Arad here, since Arad was outside the Promised Land which Israel was not yet occupying.[2] The king was ὁ κατοικῶν κατὰ τὴν ἔρημον, i.e. "inhabiting the desert." Note that ישב הנגב is translated using a cognate structure, with a cognate preposition, which may be subsumed within the compound verb; i.e. κατοικεῖν κατά means the same as κατοικεῖν. This is then a good translation of MT. To the translator, the desert dwelling king of Arad could not possibly be an actual Canaanite, so his name must be Chananis.

MT has it that the king heard כי בא ישראל דרך האתרים "that Israel was coming the way of Atharim." Num, however, took וישמע in an absolute sense: "And he heard the news," and then translated כי by γάρ, within a new clause, thus "For Israel came ὁδὸν Ἀθαρίμ." It should be pointed out, however, that the majority A F M V text read οτι ηλθεν rather than ἦλθεν γάρ, but the much more difficult γάρ structure must be original. The accusative ὁδόν is used here as a preposition "by way of," a usage apparently found only in LXX.[3] The place name Atharim is completely unknown. In the tradition, B Byz+ change the final *mu* to a *nu*; confusion between the two nasals in final position is often attested in the tradition, but here the Hebrew should be determinative.[4] The name is often understood as התרים "the spies," as referring to the route that the

---

1. The Others have ὁ Χαναναῖος.
2. Not surprisingly, Tar^J identifies him as עמלק, as does Rashi.
3. As Dorival 185 points out, citing as other examples Deut 1:9 and Isa 9:1.
4. See THGN 116.

κατασκεψάμενοι took in ch.13.⁵ Copyists also were unfamiliar with the name, and this resulted in numerous misspellings. Aside from itacisms, note the following: ναθαρειμ in b, θαρειμ, αθαρσιμ, αθαριν, αθαρρειν, αηθαριμ, αβαρειμ, αβαριν (Byz), βαρειμ (n), αβαρη and αβαριθ.

So Chananis "made war against Israel וישב ממנו שבי." The noun שבי occurs 43 times in the Bible, and is always translated by a derivative of the stem αἰχμαλω-; in 36 cases αἰχμαλωσία is used as here. The verb is translated in similar fashion; it is usually rendered by αἰχμαλωτεύω (26 times) or αἰχμαλωτίζω (seven times).⁶ But Num avoids a cognate pattern, and uses a unique translation for the verb, κατεπρονόμευσαν "carried off booty," thus "and carried off booty from them (i.e. Israel) into captivity." This was probably done because of ממנו viz. (to make booty) from Israel. The ἐξ αὐτῶν is a partitive construction; I would translate the clause: "and they carried off some of them as booty into captivity." The change to a plural verb does make sense, though MT continues with a singular. Num had the king make war, but "they" (i.e. his people) carried off prey. Hex apparently corrected the verb to κατεπρονομευσεν to conform to MT.

21:2 The condition which Israel placed in its vow to the Lord was ἐάν μοι παραδῷς τὸν λαὸν τοῦτον ὑποχείριον "if you would deliver to me this people in subjection." This is a free rendering of MT's אם נתן תתן את העם הזה בידי "if you would actually give this people into my power."⁷ Num apparently had no free infinitive in its parent text, and interpreted בידי by μοι ... ὑποχείριον. Hex has attempted to adapt Num to MT by the following changes: omission of μοι, and the addition of παραδιδους in its place (for נתן), and the change of ὑποχείριον to υπο χειρα μοι (for בידי).⁸

Num is also inexact in the rendering of the apodosis. MT has והחרמתי את עריהם "then I will anathematize their cities." Num does not use an apodotic καί, which apparently hex added, and the translator also increased the modifier of the verb to read αὐτὸν καὶ τὰς πόλεις αὐτοῦ. What Num is doing is in line with

---

5. This must reflect the parent text of Aq and Sym who translate τῶν κατασκόπων. This is also supported by Tar, Pesh and Vulg.
6. According to the count of Dos Santos.
7. See SS 100.
8. Instead of ἐάν ... λαόν, Theod has ἐὰν παραδόσει παραδῷς τὸν λαόν; Aq translates as ἐὰν διδοὺς δῷς σὺν τὸν λαόν, whereas Sym has ἐὰν δῷς τὸν λαόν.

v.1, i.e. it was the king of Arad who made war, and it would hardly have been virtuous to overlook the one directly responsible for the attack on Israel. Since αὐτόν was added, adjustment also had to be made in עריהם, and the suffix was changed to αὐτοῦ.[9] I would suggest that Num tried to improve MT, i.e. make it a more appropriate statement. Not only would Israel undertake to put the cities of the Araclites under the ban, but would also deal convincingly with their king. Actually, what Num did was to harmonize the apodosis with v.3; see below. Apparently, hex placed καὶ αὐτόν under the obelus, i.e. the obelus in Syh^L is erroneously placed before καὶ τὰς πόλεις, which can hardly be correct.

21:3 The vow was successful; the Lord delivered up Chananis into subjection to it (i.e. to Israel). ὑποχείριον αὐτοῦ has no counterpart in MT, but is based on Sam's בידו; hex has placed the phrase under the obelus. In the tradition, the majority A F M V text has changed αὐτοῦ το αυτω, and I suspect that the dative is original text, and that the B f z+ text has simplified the original αὐτῷ to αυτου. After all, the protasis of Israel's vow had been "If μοι you would deliver this people into subjection." I would suggest changing the critical text to read αὐτῷ instead of αὐτοῦ.

In the tradition, the inflected (τὸν) Χανανίν was not appreciated by many copyists. A popular A M(vid) text dropped the final consonant and made it χανανι. Another group of texts, O f n+, probably hex in origin, corrected Χανανίν to χαναναιον, which equals MT, whereas the d text made it χανααν as in v.1.

MT then continues with ויחרם אתהם ואת עריהם. The most natural understanding of this clause, since the preceding clause read "and he delivered up the Canaanite," is to take the subject as unchanged, thus "and he (i.e. the Lord) rendered them and their cities anathema." One might also understand ויחרם as declarative, thus "and he declared the Canaanite and their cities anathema." But in view of Israel's promise in v.2 "then I will anathematize their cities," it seems preferable to understand an unstated change of subject, i.e. to "Israel." Num has changed the pronouns אתהם and the suffix of עריהם to the singular, thus referring to the king, which had already been the vow in v.2 for Num. Again, the change

---

9. BHS obviously considered Num a superior text, as its imperative "lege ואת-אתו" implies. But to read אתו ואת עריהם would make an odd text indeed; one would also have to read עריו. The note is far too simplistic.

is an intentional rewriting of the text to make a consistent picture, in which the king of Arad is throughout the responsible individual, not only for the attack, but also for the inflicted ban.

The final clause continues with a third singular verb, ויקרא; once again, common sense dictates another change of subject, this time to an indefinite third singular, "and one called (the name)," i.e. the name was called. The translator fully understood this, and used an indefinite plural καὶ ἐπεκάλεσαν. In the tradition, the A s^{mg} z+ text read the singular, probably a correction from one of the Revisers. According to MT the place was called חרמה. The name also appeared at 14:45 where it was transcribed as Ἑρμά. There Amalek and הכנעני chased the disobedient invading Israelite troup to "Herma." But the translator does not identify the חרמה of 14:45 as the same place. Here a different situation obtains; it was not the Canaanite, but Chananis, the king of Arad, who was involved. Accordingly, Num translates the name by Ἀνάθεμα.[10]

21:4 MT has ויסעו as the main verb of v.a, which is modified by a purposive infinitive לסבב, thus "and they moved camp ... in order to go around (the land of Edom)." Num has changed the pattern, making περιεκύκλωσαν "they went around" the main verb, and subordinated ויסעו to an attributive participle, thus "and pulling up stakes ... they skirted around." MT describes the route as דרך ים סוף "by way of the sea of reeds." The sea of reeds is, as usual in the Pentateuch, rendered by "the red sea." Since the "red sea" is in the direction around the land of Edom, the Red Sea may actually be intended here. It could hardly refer to the ים סוף of the Exodus. On the other hand, it could simply refer to the way they had come, i.e. in the direction of ים סוף, in which case it would be consistent with Exodus. Num renders דרך in doublet fashion, i.e. by ὁδὸν ἐπί "route over against (the red sea)." For ὁδόν used as a preposition, see comment at v.1. Uncertain is the syntax of τὴν γῆν Ἐδώμ. It could be rendered "the land Edom," i.e. Ἐδώμ is in the accusative. But in MT (את) ארץ אדום is a bound phrase, which would be "the land of Edom." In the tradition, two attempts to simplify the syntax obtain. Cod B plus three mss omitted τήν; this is obviously secondary, since the τήν represents the preposition את.[11] The Byz text omitted γῆν, probably

---

10. See Dorival 144.
11. See THGN 107.

an error due to homoioteleuton, but it does create a simpler text. I suspect that the translator thought of Ἐδώμ as genitive, i.e. as "the land of Edom."

V.b states that "the people became discouraged on the way." This is not really what MT says, which reads ותקצר נפש העם "that the people became impatient, restive." The verb ὀλιγοψυχέω makes it clear that it was not so much impatience, as discouragement that affected the people.[12]

21:5 MT begins with וידבר העם באלהים ובמשה "and the people spoke against God and against Moses." Num translates by κατελάλει ὁ λαὸς πρὸς τὸν θεὸν καὶ κατὰ Μωυσῆ. The use of the imperfect is well-considered, since the "speaking against" was a process; they were verbally abusing both God and Moses. But why use πρός with God, and the expected κατά with Moses? At v.7 where the same verb is used with the same modifiers, Num has the expected κατά for both phrases. Modified by a κατά phrase, the structure must mean "were railing against," but why "towards God"?[13] The translator apparently wanted to make a distinction of some kind. The speaking was not simply a murmuring against Moses; the people were also rebellious over against God.[14] I would translate "And the people were railing over against God and against Moses.[15] This is followed by the direct speech marker λέγοντες, for which MT has no equivalent, and which hex has placed under the asterisk.

The rebellious generation, according to the Masoretes, addressed both God and Moses, "Why did you (plural) bring us up (from Egypt)," but Num follows Sam's הוצאתנו with its ἐξήγαγες ἡμᾶς "you (singular) brought us out (from Egypt)," i.e. addressed only to Moses. It is quite possible to read a singular verb from the consonantal text. The avoidance of the plural tradition, however, may well have been theologically inspired. To accuse God (along with Moses) of

---
12. For the lexical background of the verb, see Lee 76.
13. Johannessohn, Gebrauch 268—269 describes the use of πρός as "bei feindlichem Vorgehen"; comp πόλεμον πρός (for ב) at Gen 32:25.
14. The Tar all avoid putting God and Moses on the same level as well, not only by means of different prepositions, but also by using different verbs. Tar⁰ reads ואתרעם עמא במימרא דיי ועם משה נצו "And the people rebelled against the word of Y. and quarreled with Moses." Tarᴶ has ורהרהו עמא בלבבהון ואישתעיאו על מימרא דייי ובמשה נצו "And the people complained in their heart and spoke against the word of Y. and quarreled with Moses." Tarᴺ interpreted as ומליל עמה בתר ממרה דהי ועל משה אשרעמו "And the people spoke after (i.e. against) Y. and against Moses they murmured."
15. Dorival translates: "et le peuple parla mal vers Dieu et contra Moïse."

having effected the exodus from Egypt for evil, rather than for redemptive, ends was going too far. On the other hand, MT simply has למות "to die (in the desert)," whereas Num goes much further with its ἀποκτεῖναι ἡμᾶς "to kill us," for which see 16:13, with which it harmonizes.[16] Since MT simply has למות, hex has placed ἡμᾶς under the obelus, but did not change the transitive verb ἀποκτεῖναι.

The ὅτι clause gives the reason for the complaint: "because there is no bread nor water, ἡ δὲ ψυχὴ ἡμῶν προσώχθισεν ἐν τῷ ἄρτῳ τῷ διακένῳ τούτῳ." The Hebrew has ונפשנו קצה בלחם הקלקל "Our person has (i.e. we have) come to loathe the miserable bread ('food')." The term הקלקל is a hapax legomenon, an adjective based on the root קלל "be light, trifling," thus "worthless, miserable." διακένῳ is Num's attempt at a literal rendering, hence "empty, thin, meagre."[17] MT has no actual equivalent for τούτῳ, and hex has placed the pronoun under the obelus. The word is an ad sensum gloss, and was omitted by B z+, but this is not original; probably it was omitted by mistake due to homoioteleuton.[18] The verb προσώχθισεν means "to be irritated," and so "to be weary of." It differs somewhat from the Hebrew "to feel a loathing for," but it also occurs for it at 22:3.[19]

21:6 The Lord sent "venomous" serpents, i.e. τοὺς θανατοῦντας, "death dealing." This intepretes השרפים "fiery, burning," referring to the burning sensation caused by the bite of poisonous snakes. These "bit the people, and there died λαὸς πολὺς τῶν υἱῶν Ἰσραήλ." The collocation "much people of the Israelites" interprets MT's עם רב מישראל. The מן is partitive, and is rendered by the genitive, with the necessary addition of τῶν υἱῶν to show the partitive nature of מישראל.[20] This is not a textual matter presupposing מבני ישראל, but an attempt to show partitiveness.

21:7 The opening two clauses in MT, "and the people came to Moses and they said," is changed into a single syntagm by Num: "and the people coming ...,

---

16. But Tar[N] also reads למקטלה יתן.
17. The Others render by κούφῳ.
18. See THGN 132.
19. There is disagreement in the tradition as to the reading of Aq, some witnesses attesting to the present σικχαίνει, and others to the aorist passive ἐσικχάνθη. Since MT has קצה, the past tense verb is probably the better reading. Sym read ἐνεκάκησεν.
20. See SS 168 which calls this a "Quantitätsausdruck."

were saying that." The use of the imperfect is lively in narration, but the ὅτι introducing what they were saying has no basis in MT, and was omitted by hex, thereby equalling the Hebrew. What they said was ἡμαρτήκαμεν.[21] In the tradition, a popular B V text has changed the perfect tense to the default aorist, but the perfect is contextually more exact, and is original.[22]

For κατελαλήσαμεν κατὰ κυρίου καὶ κατὰ σοῦ, see the discussion at v.5. Here, however, a single verb with two κατά phrases is used in Israel's confession of sin.[23] In the tradition, the majority A B F V text has articulated κυρίου. Examination of usage in Num, however, shows articulation of the divine name in the genitive to be attested in the tradition only rarely. The genitive occurs 120 times in Num, and in only five cases is the articulation possibly questionable from the tradition. It appears that the translator never articulated κυρίου when it represented the tetragrammaton.[24]

The request is εὖξαι οὖν πρὸς κύριον "so pray to the Lord." The οὖν has its basis only in the context, not in MT. The substance of the prayer is put into third person imperative, (καὶ) ἀφελέτω, reflecting a correct understanding of the short form ויסר, "that he might turn aside."

Moses did so; he "prayed πρὸς κύριον on behalf of the people." Hex placed πρὸς κύριον under the obelus, since it has no equivalent in MT. It is strictly speaking unnecessary to the sense, but it does assure that the prayer was properly directed.

21:8 The Lord ordered Moses: "make for yourself a שרף and place it on a נס." Most moderns are agreed that a שרף was some kind of snake. The verb means "to burn," and probably some kind of poisonous (i.e. burning) snake was intended.[25] Num has the safe reading ὄφιν. The term נס, which means "sign, signal," is also rendered unimaginatively by its usual rendering σημείου, but in the context it should mean something like a pole, or better "a signal pole," since Moses is to

---

21. Theod and Sym not only omitted the introductory ὅτι, but also changed the verb to the default aorist, ἡμάρτομεν.
22. See THGN 104.
23. But the Tar distinguished as at v.5; cf footnote at v.5.
24. See THGN 124.
25. NRSV translates by "poisonous serpent"; NJPS has "a *seraph* figure," and NIV makes it "a snake." Milgrom explains: "a winged snake similar to the winged Egyptian uraeus (cobra)."

place the snake on it, and it was to be visible to the people in the camp.[26] An early popular M gloss added χαλκουν after ὄφιν, under the influence of v.9, where it is original.[27] Here it is secondary, even though it was placed under the obelus by hex. What one can conclude from this fact is that the intrusion into the text was preOrigen, since Origen's text already had the gloss.

MT continues with "and it shall be כל הנשוך, when he sees it, he shall recover (literally 'live')." Num found "everyone bitten" to be unclear as subject, and added before it the condition ἐὰν δάκῃ ὄφις ἄνθρωπον. What Num says is "and it shall be if a snake should bite someone, everyone who is bitten ἰδὼν αὐτὸν ζήσεται." Ms 426 has omitted the added protasis to equal MT; the omission is obviously a revision inspired by the Hebrew. The gloss is based on the ὅταν clause of v.9.

In the tradition, a V b n+ text has added και before ἰδών; this formally equals MT's וראה, but is probably not to be taken as recensional.

21:9 So Moses made an ὄφιν χαλκοῦν, "a copper snake." In MT this is a cognate structure, נחש נחשת, which can hardly be simulated in Greek. Undoubtedly, the notion of the snake being copper is due to the Hebrew word play. Then he ἔστησεν it ἐπί a signal pole. In the tradition, the Byz text changed the verb to the compound επεστησεν as a stylistic improvement, since the preposition is cognate to it; but see v.8.

Precisely what v.8 had predicted, now took place. After Moses had placed the copper snake on a signal pole, "καὶ ἐγένετο ὅταν ἔδακεν ὄφις ἄνθρωπον, καὶ ἐπέβλεψεν ἐπὶ τὸν ὄφιν τὸν χαλκοῦν, he recovered." The ὅταν clause is clearly the source of the ἐάν clause of v.8.[28] The use of ἐπιβλέπω is contextually determined. It only renders the Qal of ראה 10 times (as opposed to εἴδω 673 times, and ὁράω 279 times),[29] but here it is exactly right. The bitten person had to "look upon" the bronze serpent in order to be cured.

In the tradition, the B ol Byz+ text has the imperfect εδακνεν instead of the original ἔδακεν.[30]

---

26. Sym understood this and used ὕψους, both here and in v.9.
27. As also in Tar[JN], but not in Tar[O].
28. Instead of ἐπέβλεψεν, Theod reads ἐπέβλεπεν; Aq and Sym retain the aorist.
29. According to Dos Santos.
30. See THGN 124 for the originality of the aorist inflection.

21:10 The place name 'Ωβώθ for אבת is not known. It was also unfamiliar to copyists, who produced a number of misspellings: αβωθ, ωβωδ, ωφωθ, εβωθ, σωβωθ, ωκωθ and ωκωβ.

21:11 Since the stress is on the next place of encampment, Num subordinates the first clause to a participial construction καὶ ἐξάραντες ἐξ 'Ωβώθ. The next place was called עיי העברים, for which Num has 'Αχελγαὶ ἐκ τοῦ πέραν. Just how עיי became 'Αχελγαί is problematic. Only the γαί equals עיי. The name recurs at 33:44, but there the name becomes Γαὶ ἐν τῷ πέραν. The origin of 'Αχελ is the real problem. I suspect that the parent text read בנחל עיי העברים, and that the original text was ΕΝΝΑΧΕΛΓΑΙ. The second νυ was dropped by haplography, thus producing ἐν 'Αχελγαί. Since this is merely a conjecture of mine with no extant witness except possibly Syh,[31] I would not emend the critical text, except to read two words for 'Αχελγαί, thus 'Αχὲλ Γαί. The origin of the double name is in my opinion a doublet with "valley, wadi" modifying Γαί. What is then meant is "the Gai valley on the other side."[32] The Israelites are now "on the other side (of Edom; see v.4) in the desert over against Moab eastward (literally, towards the sunrise)." The B M ol ƒ+ text reads κατα instead of the elided form κατ'. The elision of final vowels of prepositions is common in Hellenistic prose, particularly in frequently occurring phrases such as κατ' ἀνατολάς, but are otherwise avoided in Num; see also 23:7.[33]

21:12 The verse begins asyndetically, rendering משם נסעו ויחנו word for word.[34] The wadi Ζαρέδ (for זרד) is well-known as the modern Wadi-l-Hesa, which separates Edomite territory from that of Moab. The B Byz+ text misspelled the name as ζαρετ, and a b+ spelling reads ζαρεθ, but only Ζαρέδ can be original. The *daleth* of MT is always and only transcribed by *delta* in Num.[35]

---

31. Which reads bnḥl' g'y' mn 'br'
32. Sym reads ἐν τοῖς βουνοῖς "in the hills" instead of 'Αχελγαί.
33. See THGN 97.
34. The Others, according to a marginal reading of ms 344, read καὶ ἐκεῖθεν ἀπάραντες παρενέβαλον. This is a highly suspicious attribution. I can hardly credit Aq (nor Theod) as having added καί over against MT, nor of subordinating ו נסעו to a participle. It could be Sym, but what is clear is that it is the text of Num in v.13.
35. See THGN 117.

21:13 For the subordinating participle ἀπάραντες, see the comment on ἐξάραντες at v.11. As at v.11, Num begins with καί over against MT, possibly in agreement with Sam. On the other hand, throughout this section (ending at v.20) whenever the movement of peoples is introduced, MT lacks an initial και only here and at v.12. At v.12 the MT text is strongly supported, but here the majority B text lacks και, and the original text is by no means certain.

Their next encampment was εἰς τὸ πέραν Ἀρνών "beyond the Arnon." The Arnon is the modern Wadi-l-Mujib, the northern border of Moab. Num then reads ἐν τῇ ἐρήμῳ for אשר במדבר. Hex has added ο εστιν under the asterisk to represent the untranslated אשר. This is followed by "τὸ ἐξέχον from the borders of the Amorrites"; τὸ ἐξέχον is in apposition with τὸ πέραν Ἀρνών. Thus the area beyond the Arnon is "that which runs from the borders of the Amorrites." In MT, this modification is not certain; היצא "that which goes out" can best refer to מדבר, which immediately precedes the participle, though עבר ארנון is not impossible. In Num, the modification can only be to τὸ πέραν Ἀρνών.[36] It will have been noticed that גבול האמרי "the border of the Amorite" is rendered by the plural in Num.

This geographical description is justified by a γάρ clause which reads "For the Arnon ὅρια of Moab between Moab and between τοῦ Ἀμορραίου". גבול is again taken as a collective, but האמרי is now rendered as a singular. Why Num should vary between the plural "the Amorrites" and the singular is unknown; possibly it was simply done for variety's sake. In any event, it constitutes the northern border of Moab.

21:14—15 MT begins with "Therefore it is said in the book of the wars of Yahweh." Num took מלחמת יהוה as the title of the book, and understood מלחמת as a singular. It reads διὰ τοῦτο λέγεται ἐν βιβλίῳ Πόλεμος κυρίου. This is a possible understanding of the consonantal text of MT. There follows in MT some lines of poetry, largely incomprehensible. Num has tried to make some sense out of the Hebrew. The remainder of v.14 reads "he (or it) has inflamed the (area of) Zoob and the wadies of Arnon." Since the book is called "Πόλεμος κυρίου," I would take the subject of ἐφλόγισεν to be κυρίου. τὴν Ζωόβ renders את והב misread as את זהב. The article represents את, and since it is feminine probably means "the

---

36. See also Dorival 145.

land of." The name is unknown, and was confusing to copyists as well. The final consonant became voiceless in some mss, creating ζωοφ or ζουφ. The Byz text transposed the consonants so as to read βοαζ, and a few mss read βοοβ. The verb is a reconstruction of בסיפה. Since the Syriac (Aramaic) verbal root ספף means "to burn up," the translator may well have thought of some form of this Northwest Semitic verb. καὶ τοὺς χειμάρρους Ἀρνῶν stands for ארנון הנחלים ואת, though understood as ארנון נחלי ואת. The majority B F M V text articulated κυρίου, but see comment at v.7.

V.15 is also uncertain. MT seems to say "and the slope of the wadies which reach to the settlement (שבת) of Ar, and it leans on (or towards) the border of Moab." Once again, Num has made a stab at making sense. It reads "And the wadis he established for Er to inhabit (or 'to settle Er'), and it lies adjacent to the borders of Moab." Num has taken הנחלים ואשד without regard to אשר, simply reading καὶ τοὺς χειμάρρους. Apparently, Num could make no sense out of נטה "to stretch, reach out," and contextualized by using κατέστησεν "he established"; after all, God was the creator God, and he set down, established the wadis. לשבת is presumably meant as a preposition governing a noun, but Num took it as a marked infinitive, κατοικῆσαι (Ἤρ) "for Er to inhabit." In the tradition, A B M+ read κατοικίσαι. This would also make sense; as a transitive verb it would mean "to settle Er," though only the Num text could equal שבת.[37]

The last line, καὶ πρόσκειται τοῖς ὁρίοις Μωάβ, is a fully possibly interpretation of MT. Once again, גבול is taken as a collective, and translated by the plural ὁρίοις.[38]

21:16 Num begins with καὶ ἐκεῖθεν τὸ φρέαρ, which is even more abrupt than the Hebrew ומשם בארה, which at least has a *he* directive.[39] Whether or not באר is a place name, or as in Num, is intended as "the well" is not known. In any event, it is identified in v.b by "τοῦτο ἐστιν τὸ φρέαρ ὃ εἶπεν κύριος πρὸς Μωυσῆν Bring together the people καὶ δώσω them water πιεῖν." MT reads הוא הבאר, i.e. a nominal clause, which Num clarified by a linking verb. In the tradition, a B F *f*

---

37. See THGN 129.
38. Sym has rendered these two verses by διὰ τοῦτο εἴρηται ἐν καταλόγῳ τῶν πολεμούντων κύριος πρὸς μὲν Αὐξάβ ἐν λαίλαπι. τῶν δὲ φαράγγων πρὸς Ἀρνῶν· ἡ γὰρ ἔκδοσις τῶν φαράγγων ἔκλινεν μέχρι τῆς κατοικίας Ἄρ, καὶ ἐπίκειται τῷ ὁρίῳ Μωάβ (retroverted from Syh).
39. Tar make a verbal clause by adding להון אתיהיבת.

n+ text omits the ἐστιν, which would be closer to MT, but this need not be taken as recensional; Num commonly renders such nominal clauses by adding an ἐστιν. Incidentally, a majority B F text has also omitted the article, which omission admits of a double explanation. It may have been omitted to make the noun indefinite, i.e. "this is a well about which ...," or, if this omission was created subsequent to the omission of ἐστιν, it would be a case of haplography after τοῦτο. καὶ δώσω translates ואתנה, though the long form after the conjunction actually expresses result or purpose, "that I may give." A more accurate rendering would have used ὥστε or ἵνα instead of καί. As for πιεῖν, this is an ad sensum gloss with no basis in MT, and hex has rightly placed it under an obelus.

21:17 The poetic lines of vv.17b—18 are identified as τὸ ᾆσμα τοῦτο "this song" which Israel sang. This song is characterized as ἐπὶ τοῦ φρέατος "about the well." This renders MT's עלי באר, and makes better sense in my opinion than the vocalization proposed by the Masoretes making עלי an imperative from עלה, i.e. "go up, o well," i.e. produce water. It must be admitted, however, that Num is unique in this rendering; all other ancient witnesses have an imperative plus a vocative.

In Num the song begins with ἐξάρχετε αὐτῷ. MT reads ענו לה "sing to it." The verb ἐξάρχω means "to begin," and in the context I would understand it as "start (to sing)," or "begin (the song)."[40] Comp Note at Exod 15:21, where the same verb is used with reference to the Song of Mariam.[41] Num uses the present imperative, which a V *b n*+ text tried to improve by changing it to the aorist, εξαρξατε, possibly since the semantics of the verb are difficult to understand as a process. Precisely for that reason, the present must be original. No reviser would change the aorist to the more difficult present.

21:18 The Song of the Well then begins with a pendant nominative, φρέαρ, "As for the well"; this simply imitates MT. The first clause in both MT and Num then reads "rulers dug it." ἄρχοντες is by far the most common rendering for the Hebrew שרים (254 times).[42]

---

40. Schl renders the verb inter alia by *cantu praeeo*, quoting "Hesych. ἐξάρξατε, ἄρξατε μελῳδίας, ὑμνήσατε, προκατάξατε, καταλέξατε."
41. Aq and Sym translate by καταλέξατε "recite, chant."
42. According to Dos Santos.

The second line in MT reads כרוה נדיבי העם "the nobles of the people dug it." The verb כרה is parallel to חפר of line one, both meaning "dig," though חפר is somewhat broader, "to dig for" in the sense of "to search out, explore." Num renders the verb by ἐξελατόμησαν "hewed out." The subject, however, is βασιλεῖς ἐθνῶν "kings of nations (or peoples)." The translator wanted to avoid translating העם by the usual τοῦ λαοῦ, since this would be taken to be the people of Israel, whereas this was hardly intended by the העם of the poem. By using the plural, ἐθνῶν, the reference can only be to foreign peoples or nations. Furthermore, the use of βασιλεῖς for נדיבי probably accords better with the realization that the Edomites, Moabites and Ammonites were all kingdoms, and βασιλεῖς fits well as a parallel to ἄρχοντες of line one.[43]

The final line has also been reinterpreted. MT has two ב phrases indicating instrument: במחקק במשענתם. The second phrase is easily understood; it means "with their staffs," and the first one is a Poel participle of חקק "to inscribe, etch." Since it belongs to נדיבי העם, it is something similar to a "staff," possibly a sceptre. But Num goes its own way, abandoning the Hebrew in favor of a different understanding.

Since it had spoken of foreign kings as responsible for the digging of the well(s), it took the two ב phrases as containing verbal elements, such as bound infinitives descriptive of royal activity. Thus the second phrase was understood as meaning "when they wielded the sceptre," and there was created ἐν τῷ κυριεῦσαι αὐτῶν "when they were masters."[44] The first one was then interpreted similarly in the sense of when they were issuing חקות "decrees," and ἐν τῷ βασιλείᾳ αὐτῶν was produced. I would render the two by "in their kingly rule, when they were masters (in control)."

That the Well Song was an interruption is clear from the next stage in their desert travels which is recorded as καὶ ἀπὸ φρέατος εἰς Μανθαναίν. In MT the stage is described as "from the desert to Mattan." Here the translator simply corrected what he took to be a misleading statement. V.16 had said that τὸ φρέαρ was the last stage. It was indeed in the desert, but Num specifies that it was "the well" located there. How Num understood מתנה is unclear. The dissimilation of "ττ" to "νθ" is clear enough; it could easily be argued that מתנה is an assimilated

---

43. See also Dorival 151.
44. Theod translated במשענתם by ἐν ταῖς ῥάβδοις αὐτῶν, and Aq, by ἐν τῇ βακτηρίᾳ αὐτῶν.

form of *mantanah*, but the -αιν ending seems to represent a dual ending, such as in מהנים "Mahanaim." In the tradition, some witnesses attest to an -αιμ ending. The Greek seems to be dependant on some such name as מתנים, but no such place is known. In fact, the tradition created a large number of misspellings: with the last syllable appearing as -νιν, -ναιμ, -ναειλ, -ναι; or the first syllable as μαθ-, μανδ-, μαν-, ματθ-, μαθν- or μανθ-. Also attested is the syncopation of the middle syllable in μαναιν and μαθναι as well as the Hebraic correction of ms 426 as μαθθανα.

21:19 The next two stages: "and from Manthanain to Naaliel, and from Naaliel to Bamoth." For Μανθαναίν (or should it be accented Μανθανάιν?), see comment at v.18. Νααλιήλ was unknown to copyists (as well as to moderns), and resulted in a welter of misspellings: νααδιηλ, μααλιηλ, μανιηλ, ναλιηλ, ναδιηλ, νααλλιηλ, ααλιηλ, νααυιηλ, νααυηλ, νεανιηλ, μαναηλ, ναχαιηλ, ναχεηλ, αναχαιηλ, μανααναηλ, μαθαναηλ and μανθαναηλ; in fact, not even the final -ιηλ was immune from change, since the corrector of one ms misread it as μαθαναην.[45] The name Βαμώθ (meaning "hill" or "high place") was also puzzling to copyists, who misspelled it as βαιμωθ, βαμωβ, μαμωθ, μαβωθ, βαθωμ, βαθ, βαθμωβ and καμωθ.[46]

21:20 "And from Bamoth to הגיא," which means "valley," and is translated by νάπην.[47] Presumably, νάπην was taken by copyists as a place name, as the tradition shows. The following variants obtain: σιανα ναπην, ιαννα ναπην, ναπαν, ναγην, ιαπην, ιαννα, αννα, ιανα, ιανην, ναπην ιαννα and ναπην ηανα. The intrusion of the inexplicable reading of Theod has created havoc with the translation of גיא by νάπην.

The "valley" is then localized as that "which is in the πεδίῳ of Moab." πεδίον is a common rendering for שדה (85 times), though not as frequent as

---

45. Aq translated נחליאל as two words: (εἰς) χειμάρρους ἰσχυρῶν (retroverted from Syh), for which comp נחלין מתגברין of Tar[N].
46. Aq translated by a plural (εἰς) ὑψώματα; Sym read (εἰς) βουνόν (retroverted from Syh).
47. Which both Aq and Sym accept. Theod, however, read ιαννα, which I cannot explain. The only suggestion I can make is quite far-fetched. Could it have anything to do with γεεννα, i.e. with גיא הנם? That the graphemes Γ and Ι are easily confused is well-known; from *γεεννα to *ιεεννα to ιαννα is not an impossible progression. The reading of Theod, or some variant of it, has affected the text tradition as well.

ἀγρός (210 times).⁴⁸ The term שדה probably simply means "region, area" or "land," when it refers to Moab, Edom, Aram, etc., and I would render πεδίῳ as such as well.

This is then further located as "from the top of τοῦ λελαξευμένου." The participle is a translation of הפסגה, usually understood as a proper noun. For this rendering of "the Pisgah," see Note at Deut 3:27. This is described in MT as ונשקפה על פני הישימן "and looking out over the wasteland." The Ni participle is feminine, and modifies הפסגה; it is the Pisgah range that overlooks the desert area.

Num has understood this last section differently. Instead of ונשקפה of MT, it read נשקפה of Sam, as its τὸ βλέπον shows.⁴⁹ Nor does it modify λελαξευμένου, but rather πεδίῳ, and the critical text would be improved by placing a comma after λελαξευμένου. It is then the land of Moab which βλέπον κατὰ πρόσωπον τοῦ ἐρήμου "which looks out over against the desert."

21:21 The remainder of the chapter describes their military encounter and defeat of Seon and Og. According to MT, ישראל sent מלאכים to Sihon, king of האמרי. Num has Μωυσῆς rather than "Israel" who did the sending.⁵⁰ Num is then in line with 20:14, where it was Moses who sent messengers to the king of Edom; this was his prerogative as leader of the Israelites. Num thereby follows protocol; it was Moses, as representing Israel, who actually did the sending. He sent πρέσβεις "elders, ambassadors," rather than ἀγγέλους, i.e. a higher grade of messenger. This is also used at 22:5 for "messengers" of Balak sent to Balaam. Elsewhere in the Bible this rendering occurs only at Deut 2:26, which is probably based on the account here. That this is rare is clear from the fact that by contrast, ἄγγελος renders מאלך 197 times in the Bible.⁵¹ The singular האמרי is quite correctly taken as a collective and rendered by the plural Ἀμορραίων, though unarticulated. Num also adds over against MT λόγοις εἰρηνικοῖς "with peaceful words"; this follows the דברי שלום of Sam, for which see Deut 2:26. Hex has placed these words under the obelus, since they have no basis in MT.

---

48. The count is that of Dos Santos.
49. As do Pesh and Vulg, which, however, do modify the participle.
50. The Others read Ισραηλ. This reading has crept into the text tradition where ισραηλ has replaced Μωυσῆς in the F f s^{mg}+ text; the reading could be hex, since ms 58 and Syh both support it.
51. According to Dos Santos.

21:22 The message sent is similar to that sent to the king of Edom at 20:17. It begins with a plural verb παρελευσόμεθα (διὰ τῆς γῆς σου), though MT has the singular; this equals 20:17. The next clause is τῇ ὁδῷ πορευσόμεθα, which is a gloss with no support either at 20:17 or in MT. Hex has placed it under the obelus. Sam, however, has בדרך המלך אלך, which is probably the basis for Num, though it misses a rendering for המלך.

The next promise is "not will we incline οὔτε into a field οὔτε into a vineyard"; this renders MT exactly. The Byz text has glossed the verb by δεξια ουδε ευωνυμα, which is taken over from 20:17, though Sam also witnesses to the longer text here. The use of οὔτε ... οὔτε gives stylistic balance, and is not textual. The following clause reads "we will not drink water ἐκ φρέατός σου." MT has a bound phrase, מי באר, and Num renders the free element by a prepositional phrase, i.e. for "well water," Num has "water out of your well."[52] Hex has placed σου under the obelus, since באר is without a suffix. The Byz text has changed φρέατος to the plural φρεατων, a rationalizing change. For ὁδῷ βασιλικῇ πορευσόμεθα, see comment at 20:17. The adjectival phrase renders a bound phrase, דרך המלך, of MT.[53] The final ἕως clause is exactly the same in 20:17; see comment ad loc.

21:23 Not only did Seon not permit (ἔδωκεν) Israel to pass through his borders (plural for גבלו as a collective), he also "brought together all his people, and went out παρατάξασθαι τῷ Ἰσραήλ in the desert." MT simply has לקראת ישראל "to meet Israel"; of course, meeting Israel meant "to engage in battle with Israel." This is clear from the last clause, where וילחם בישראל is translated by the same idiom: καὶ παρετάξατο τῷ Ἰσραήλ. The battle took place at יהץ, for which see Note at Deut 2:32. Num renders "(he came) יהצה" by εἰς Ἰάσσα. The *-he* directive is doubly rendered, by the preposition as well as by the final *alpha*. Transcriptions in the Pentateuch often reflect this custom. In the tradition, Ἰάσσα, which should be changed to read Ἰάσα, as at Deut 2:32, since the grapheme ה does not assimilate, but is transcribed either as a vowel or be zero.[54] The spelling suffered greatly, often through confusion with the name

---

52. See SS 69. For the renderings in Tar^NO, see footnote at 20:17.
53. See SS 66.
54. See the disscussion in THGN 115—116.

'Ισάαρ/יצהר, for which see 3:19 16:1; this resulted in such spellings as ιασσαρ, σααρ, ααρ, σιασωρ, σισσααρ, as well as σιασσα.

21:24 For φόνῳ μαχαίρας as a rendering for לפי חרב, see Note at Exod 17:13. This rendering also occurs at Deut 13:15(16) 20:13. It means "by the slaughter of the sword," thus "in battle." The rendering of ויירש "and he (i.e. Israel) took possession" is uniquely, but idiomatically, translated by κατεκυρίευσαν "they gained mastery"; the point being made is that Israel now took over his land as their own land, as though this were the first step in gaining control of the Promised Land. The land gained was Israel's first inheritance, and comprised the land between the two large wadies, the Arnon and the 'Ιαβόκ. A number of mss mistakenly misread the name as ιακωβ, i.e. as Jacob. This northern limit is identified as being ἕως υἱῶν 'Αμμάν "as far as the Ammanites."

The ὅτι clause supposedly gives the reason for the limit. It reads "because 'Ιαζήρ is the borders of the Ammanites." The town 'Ιαζήρ was a border city, which was later spied out and taken according to v.32; cf Bible Dictionaries sub "Jaser." This would presuppose יעזר, but that is not what MT has here. It reads only the two middle graphemes עז, so that the כי clause reads "because the border of the Ammonites was strong," which makes even better sense. Here, however, the parent text of Num must have read יעזר. In the tradition, 'Ιαζήρ also appears as αζηρ, ιαζη, ιεζηρ, ιναζηρ and even as αζ in one ms.

The name 'Αμμάν occurs twice, and represents an older pronunciation of עמון. Some witnesses do read αμμων, but the older pronunciation is dominant, and original.[55] In the tradition, the O text has οριον instead of ὅρια, which could be a hex correction, though I am sceptical about it. Hex did place ἐστιν under the obelus; that certainly had no equivalent in MT.

21:25 Not only did Israel take all their cities; it also "settled in all the cities of the Amorrites, in Hesobon and in all its neighbouring villages." Israel has finally secured land of its own. חשבון is vocalized by the Masoretes as *Heshbon*, i.e. as a bisyllabic name, but throughout the LXX it is transcribed as a trisyllabic 'Εσεβών; possibly this reflects an older pronunciation on the analogy of עקרון "Ekron," always appearing in LXX as 'Ακκαρών. In the tradition, it does appear

---

55. See THGN 117—118. For the pronunciation of עמון as 'Αμμάν, see the discussion in THGD 62.

as εσσεβων in a number of witnesses, as well as σεβων, both easily explicable by the similarity of epsilon and sigma in the uncial script; individual mss witness also to εισεβων, ευσεβων and εβων.

Num interprets בנתיה "daughter villages" by συγκυρούσαις αὐτῇ "those which are near to it," which is an acceptable interpretation,[56] for which see discussion at 35:3, where it renders מגרשי. The "daughters" of a city refer to the villages surrounding it and in a sense within its sphere of influence, and so depending on it.[57] In the tradition, αὐτῇ is changed to the plural αυταις by an A M popular text. This is an error by inadvertence, which barely makes sense, in that it must refer to πόλεσιν. MT's suffix is in the singular, and the reference has to be to Ἐσεβών.

21:26 Num begins with ἔστιν γὰρ (Ἐσεβών) with "city of Seon the king of the Amorrites" as the predicate nominative. MT, however, begins with חשבון (כי) as subject, with עיר סיחן מלך האמרי הוא as predicate. Since this type of nominal clause in which the predicate in turn is an SP clause with הוא as subject and the remainder as predicate of the predicate often obtains, LXX commonly uses a linking verb to render the pronoun. Hex has recognized the reordering in Num, and transposed ἔστιν to the end, and reversed γὰρ Ἐσεβών to begin the clause; this then equals MT.

The second clause says: "and οὗτος (i.e. Seon) engaged the former king of Moab in war." This correctly renders MT, but the next clause does not. It reads: "and ἔλαβεν all his land ἀπὸ Ἀροήρ as far as the Arnon." The B F f+ text has changed the verb to the plural ελαβον, but this cannot be taken seriously, since the subject was defined by the οὗτος of the preceding clause.[58] MT, however, does not support "from Aroer"; it reads מידו "from his hand." In other words, MT reads: "and he took all his land from him (i.e. from his hand) as far as the Arnon." I doubt that this is a textual matter; an emendation מיבק based on v.24 has also been proposed,[59] but Num is merely conforming to Deut 2:36 which reads ἐξ Ἀροήρ. This makes fine sense, since according to Ios 13:25, Aroer was located κατὰ πρόσωπον Ῥαββά.[60]

---

56. The Three render the term in isolate fashion by θυγατράσιν αὐτῆς.
57. As understood by Tar which render by כפרנהא "her villages."
58. See THGN 123.
59. See note in BHS.
60. The Three all translate by ἐκ χειρὸς αὐτοῦ.

21:27 Just what the המשלים did is not fully clear. They are people who speak or compose משלים, i.e. proverbs, riddles, allegories, even extended poetic compositions. Num called them οἱ αἰνιγματισταί "those who compose dark sayings, who speak enigmatically."[61] What is clear from various attempts at translations is that they were performers of verbal artistry.

The poem continues through v.30; it celebrates the victory of Hesebon over Moab, and its use here was probably impelled by v.26 recounting Hesebon's conquest of Moab during the reign of an earlier Moabite king.

The poem begins with an invitation: "come to Hesebon." In MT the city is described by "let the city of Sihon be rebuilt and well-founded." Note that the Masoretes have placed the *ethnach* on חשבון, which is odd. One would expect parallel structures with תבנה referring to חשבון, and תכונן, to עיר סיחון, which is how the translator understood it. Num refashions the verse as an invitation to "come to Hesebon ἵνα it may be built up, and (to) the city of Seon (that) it may be well-established." Since, according to v.25, Israel now occupied and dwelt in Hesebon, an invitation to come to the city in order that it might be built up and well equipped might be considered more appropriate for the addressees (understood as the Israelites).

21:28 Lines one and two render MT word for word, thus "for fire went out from Hesebon, a flame out of the city of Seon." The terms "fire" and "flame" are figurative for war. Lines three and four differ from MT. καὶ κατέφαγεν ἕως Μωάβ reflects a misreading of ער "Ar" as עד, i.e. as ἕως, as well as the addition of an initial conjunction, which MT lacks. The final line in MT reads בעלי במות ארנן "the masters of Bamoth of Arnon" or "the owners of the heights of Arnon," i.e. the heights along the Arnon. These too would be devoured along with Ar of Moab. Num constructed a verb to parallel κατέφαγεν of line three, and chose κατέπιεν "swallowed up," probably reading בלעה instead of בעלי. The verb בלע is often translated by καταπίνω (28 times out of 45 occurences), followed in frequency by καταποντίζω (seven times).[62] Num also understood במות not as a place name, but as illegitimate cult places, and substituted στήλας, "pillars"; see 22:41

---

61. Instructive are the attempts of modern translators at translating המשלים. NJPS has "the bards"; NIV chose "the poets," and NRSV reads "the ballad singers."
62. Accordig to Dos Santos.

and 33:52; see also Note at Lev 26:30. The lines may be rendered as "And it (i.e. the fire/flame of warfare) devoured as far as Moab, and swallowed up the pillars of the Arnon."

21:29 Lines one and two render MT literally as "Woe to you, Moab; you were destroyed, people of Chamos." The Byz text prosaically connect the two lines by οτι, which has no basis in MT; in fact, the gloss misinterprets the intent of the text, the two poetic lines being strictly parallel. The term λαὸς Χαμώς refers to Moab; Chamos was its national God.

The third line in MT reads נתן בניו פליטם "he has rendered his sons fugitives." The subject is Chamos. Num has made a passive construction out of this: ἀποδόθησαν οἱ υἱοὶ αὐτῶν διασῴζεσθαι "their sons have been sold to be kept alive." What is meant is that their sons have been sold as slaves, thereby being safely preserved, rather than being killed off. This rendering avoids giving Chamos any such powers; afer all, to Num Chamos was a heathen god, a powerless idol. The next line is parallel to line three: "and their daughters are captives," with line five completing both lines three and four: "to Seon, king of the Amorrites." The fourth hemistich of MT differs in that the נתן of the previous line is held over, thus "and his daughters, into captivity." Both sons and daughters had been taken into captivity by the Amorrite king.

The αὐτῶν in lines three and four refer to λαός of line two. MT has singular suffixes, but the plural is a correct interpretation, since λαός/עם are collective concepts.

21:30 The verse in MT defies interpretation. It remains to see what Num made of it, and how the translator operated. The first line reads "And their seed will be destroyed, (from) Hesebon up to Daibon." The first word of MT, נירם, was read as נינם "their offspring," for which see Note at Gen 21:23. אבד was probably read as יאבד; at least, it is rendered by a future tense, ἀπολεῖται. Presumably, "their offspring" is then identified geographically as encompassing the area of Hesebon up to Daibon. The pronoun αὐτῶν must refer to λαός or Μωάβ of v.29, since the geographical reference involves Moabite cities.

The next line also constitutes an attempt at making sense out of MT's ונשים עד נפח אשר עד מידבא. The first word was read as "and the women," which is a possible rendering of the consonantal text. The next word, עד, was translated by ἔτι, also possible on the basis of the consonantal text of MT. נפח was then read as a plural verb, προσεξέκαυσαν. The verb means "to blow," and with "fire" it becomes "to stoke up, to stir up fire," probably "to engulf with flames," for which see Ezek 22:20. MT reads נפח אשר; obviously the translator read אשר as אש, thus producing προσεξέκαυσαν πῦρ. The final phrase in MT reads עד מידבא "up to Madaba," but Num has ἐπὶ Μοαβ, as though the text read על מואב. What Num did was to try to make sense. The verse might be translated: "And their seed will be destroyed, even Hesebon up to Daibon, and women have again stirred up fire over Moab."

In the tradition, the A F M majority text added αυτων after γυναῖκες. There is no justification in MT for the pronoun, which was added under the influence of (τὸ σπέρμα) αὐτῶν in line one.[63]

21:31 Num repeats word for word the second clause of v.25, except for changing the καί to a δέ construction. So instead of dwelling "in the land of the Amorites," as MT, Num reads "in all the cities of the Amorrites." Sam does read בערי instead of בארץ as well.

21:32 Moses sent off κατασκέψασθαι τὴν Ἰαζήρ. The infinitive is well-chosen, since it means "to reconnoiter, examine closely." It translates לרגל "to spy out." The verb ἀπέστειλεν is used absolutely; implied is that he sent out "some men." The feminine article shows that more than a single town is meant; it is the area of Yazer, which, according to v.24, constituted ὅρια υἱῶν Ἀμμάν. For Ἰαζήρ, see comment at v.24.

The result follows in the next two clauses. First of all, "and they took possession of it and all its villages." MT has "and they captured its daughter villages," for which term see comment at v.25. The Num text is somewhat more exact; obviously, the Israelites did not take possession only of the daughter villages of Yazer, but also the city itself.

The next clause adds the necessary complement to capture: "and they cast out the Amorrite who was there." Num followed the text of Sam: ויורישו, rather than the singular of MT.[64] The verb ירש means "to inherit, possess," and LXX

---

63. See THGN 98.
64. The Kethib has the Qal ויירש, which the Qere corrects to ויורש. The plural is a simpler text.

usually translates it by κληρονομέω (101 times), or by its κατα- compound (25 times).⁶⁵ But it is often used in the opposite sense of "to disinherit," as here, hence such renderings are found as ἀγχιστεύω, ἀπόλλυμι, ἐκτρίβω, κυριεύω, λαμβάνω or παραλαμβάνω. Here it is uniquely, though correctly, understood as ἐξέβαλον.⁶⁶ Instead of ὄντα, a popular B V text reads κατοικουντα, which is a secondary adaptation to the context.⁶⁷

21:33 V.a in MT reads: "and they turned and went up the road of Bashan." Num makes a single clause out of these clauses by rendering יפנו by a participle, thus καὶ ἐπιστρέψαντες ἀνέβησαν. The subject remains Ἰσραήλ of v.31. The bound phrase, דרך הבשן is interpreted by using a recapitulating pronoun plus a prepositional phrase, thus "ὁδὸν τὴν εἰς Βασάν."⁶⁸ The article of הבשן is omitted, since the case of Βασάν is determined by the governing preposition. The Greek makes clear that the Basan way is the one that leads to Basan.

According to MT, "Og, the king of Bashan came out to meet them, הוא and all his people." The translator found the הוא otiose, and omitted it. Hex added αυτος before "and all his people" to represent the pronoun.⁶⁹ The peoples met for battle εἰς Ἐδράιν, which equals אדרעי in MT. The preposition is added ad sensum. The name is correctly reproduced only by hex with εδραι, Num having added a final νν. The name was misspelled by some witnesses as εδραειμ, σεδραιν, εδρασιν, εδραν, εδρυιν and εδρασι, itacisms having been disregarded.

21:34 The divine reassurance to Moses is given as a reason for not fearing Og. It states: "into your hands I have delivered him ...." MT has בידך, but Num uses the plural noun; there is no semantic difference intended; both numbers mean "into your power." The Greek normally uses εἰς in this context.⁷⁰ Note the use of the perfect tense rather than the default aorist in παραδέδωκα. Though victory is still in the future, the outcome of the coming battle has been divinely determined, and is certain. The V ol b n+ text has παρεδωκα, but the perfect is original text. The Lord had already delivered him and all his people and πᾶσαν his land to

---

65. According to the count of Dos Santos.
66. Also supported by the דהוון שרין of Tar^N.
67. See THGN 129.
68. See SS 69.
69. Se SS 73.
70. See SS 136.

Israel. MT has no equivalent for πᾶσαν, but it was easily added in view of "all" his people immediately preceding it.

V.b is a good rendering of MT by Num. Note that the participle in the relative clause, which constitutes the predicate of a nominal clause, is well-rendered by the imperfect κατῴκει; Seon *was* dwelling in Esebon, but not any more in spite of the κατοικει of the z+ text.

21:35 Num translates the opening plural verb ויכו by a singular καὶ ἐπάταξεν, but the subject can hardly be Moses, but must be the Ἰσραήλ of v.31. Israel "smote him and his sons and all his people until there was not left of him a ζωγρίαν," i.e. "a living remnant." The popular B spelling, ζωγρειαν, is secondary.[71] The Hebrew parent is שריד.[72] Num does translate the last verb by a plural, an ad sensum adjustment referring to the people of Israel. Here the ויירשו is rendered by its usual counterpart ἐκληρονόμησαν, for which see the discussion at v.32. In MT ארצו refers to the land of Sihon, but the translator's αὐτῶν makes Seon's land the land of the Amorrites.

---

71. See Walters 37.
72. Theod translated by ὑπόλειμμα, and Aq has λεῖμμα. Sym read λείψανον.

Chapter 22

22:1 Usually when MT uses ויסעו, a point of departure is also given, but here it is lacking. Num simply reads καὶ ἀπάραντες οἱ υἱοὶ Ἰσραήλ, and then continues with the main clause: "they encamped on the west of Moab along the Jordan over against Jericho." MT simply has ירחו "Jericho," i.e. without a preposition. This is always rendered in Num (nine times) by κατὰ Ἱεριχώ "over against Jericho," and in MT it is preceded either by לירדן (twice) or על ירדן (seven times). The term ערבות was vocalized by the Masoretes to mean "steppes, plains," thus "on the plains of Moab." Num understood the consonantal text to be vocalized to mean "west." The word δυσμῶν means "setting (of the sun), and so "west."

22:2 Vv.2—21 describe the summoning of Balaam by Balak, king of Moab. V.2 has been made subordinate to v.3 by Num, i.e. וירא has been made into a participle, ἰδών, thus "and when Balak saw ... all that Israel did to the Amorites." Syntactically, however, v.2 is unrelated to v.3 which has Μωάβ for subject. V.2 is a nominative pendant in the form of an absolute construction. One might more commonly have expected a genitive absolute structure.

Unusual for Num is the rendering of לאמרי by the singular τῷ Ἀμορραίῳ. Elsewhere the translator understood the gentilic noun as a collective, but here he apparently intended it to refer to the Amorrite, Seon, the king. The name Βαλάκ is misspelled by some witnesses (f+) on the analogy of Βαλαάμ as βαλαακ. His father's name Σεπφώρ (for צפור) was also dealt with inconsistently in the tradition; thus σεφφωρ, σεφωρ, σεμφωρ, σεπφων and επφωρ are all attested.

22:3 The main clause represents the setting for the narrative; "(and) Moab was very afraid of the people (i.e. of Ἰσραήλ v.2), because they were numerous." The plural refers to λαόν as a collective. For the verb προσώχθισεν as translation of יקץ, see comment at 21:5. The subject Μωάβ is repeated for the last clause, but a C' s+ variant changes this to βαλακ; it is then Balak who is weary of the presence of the Israelites.

22:4 Moab communicated its fears τῇ γερουσίᾳ Μαδιάν "the eldership of Madian." This renders אל זקני מדין. The term γερουσία "council of elders, senate" also occurs at v.7, but elsewhere זקנים is always translated by πρεσβύτεροι in Num. The term γερουσία may be intended in ch.22 to refer to some "ruling council" of Madian, though it is dangerous to attempt to distinguish the two translations; see Note at Exod 3:16. In the tradition, Μαδιάν has been changed to μαδιαμ by almost all witnesses, but the final *mu* spelling is secondary, and the final *nu* is to be preferred.[1]

MT has as subject of ילחכו the noun הקהל to which Sam added הזה. Num supports Sam with its ἡ συναγωγὴ αὕτη.[2] Num also uses a singular verb ἐκλείξει, from ἐκλείχω, again following the singular ילחך of Sam, though it must be said that since the verb precedes the noun, the singular conforms to the more usual pattern of Num. Num also differs from MT in its interpretation of the modifier את כל סביבתינו "all that is around us," by its πάντας τοὺς κύκλῳ ἡμῶν "all those around us"; i.e. Num makes it refer to people.

The ὡς structure uses an optative mood, thus "as the ox might lick up the greenery from the field"; ὡς ἐκλείξαι represents כ plus the bound infinitive לחך "as the licking up of (the ox)." Num has correctly understood the intent of MT.[3]

The final clause identifies Balak, son of Sepphor, as "the king of Moab at that time." This is a nominal clause in MT, but is verbalized by Num through the addition of ἦν, thus "Balak ... was king of Moab." The word עת "time, occasion" is particularly well rendered by καιρόν; the latter is the usual rendering (197 times) as opposed to ὥρα (31 times) or ἡμέρα (10 times).[4]

22:5 The final clause of v.4 makes it unnecessary to identify the subject of ἀπέστειλεν; it is of course Balak. According to MT, he sent מלאכים "messengers," which Num translates by πρέσβεις "elders, ambassadors," probably to harmonize with v.7, where they are called זקני מואב וזקני מדין. At v.7 the reference becomes ἡ γερουσία of Moab and ἡ γερουσία of Madian, and for two councils of elders, here the cover term πρέσβεις might have been deemed more appropriate. Balaam is identified as the son of βεώρ, which name is relatively stable in the tradition, only βεω, βεων, βερωρ, βεαν and σεπφωρ being attested as variants. This is followed by Φαθούρα, representing פתורה, with the final

---

1. For a discussion and presentation of the evidence, see THGN 117.
2. As do Pesh and Vulg.
3. For the use of the optative in similes, see J.Joosten, Biblica 77(1996), 230—231.
4. According to the count of Dos Santos.

vowel to be taken as the *he* directive, thus "to Pethor." Origen must have taken it in this way, since hex has prefixed the name with εἰς under the asterisk. The name baffled many copyists, and misspellings are numerous: πατουρα, φαθυρα, φαθουρρα, φαθουρας, φαθαρα, φθθουρα, παρα, βαθουρα, βαθουρω, βαθυρα, βαιθουρα and φαβουρα.

The place was located (ὅ ἐστιν) ἐπὶ τοῦ ποταμοῦ γῆς υἱῶν λαοῦ αὐτοῦ "at the river of the land of his compatriots," which hardly identifies the location geographically. MT has על הנהר ארץ בני עמו "beside the River, (in) the land of his compatriots." הנהר must here refer to the Euphrates. What the land of his relatives means is not known. Incidentally, Sam reads עמון instead of עמו, which reading would make sense, i.e. "land of the Ammonites."⁵ In that case the river would either be the river Jordan or the river Jabbok. But Num read MT.

The purpose of the delegation was to summon Balaam. The message was "behold a people has come out of Egypt, and behold it covered the visage of the earth, and it is dwelling beside me." The consecution of tenses is quite intentional. The perfect ἐξελήλυθεν represents יצא as antecedent to the status of the aorist κατεκάλυψεν; the last verb ἐγκάθηται renders the participle יושב, and refers to the present situation. MT does not support "and behold," but has הנה, but Num follows Sam's והנה.⁶

In the tradition, the majority A F M text read ὅς instead of ὅ (ἐστιν) for אשר. This cannot be correct, since it would mean that instead of Phethoura being located by the river, it would refer to Balaam son of Beor. The variant arose because of the similarity of *omicron* and *sigma* in uncial script, i.e. ΟΕΣΤΙΝ easily became ΟΣΕΣΤΙΝ; it was a simple mistake. On the other hand, why Φαθούρα should be taken as neuter is also mysterious; if it were masculine, the correct ὅς reference would be most confusing. If the place was a city, one might have expected a feminine ἡ.

22:6 The actual request of the delegation: "curse for me this people because ἰσχύει οὗτος ἢ ἡμεῖς." This represents a nominal clause in MT with an adjective plus a comparative מן i.e. עצום הוא ממני.⁷ A popular A M text reads the com-

---

5. Also read by Kenn 80*,84,136*211*,325,355*,597*,569* and 612, Pesh and Vulg. There is now some evidence from fragmentary remains at Deir Alla which refer to Balaam, which make the reading most attractive.
6. But numerous Hebrew mss also read the conjunction.
7. See SS 81 and 149.

parative adjective ισχυτερος instead of the verb. This correctly interprets the Num text, but represents a simpification or clarification, and must be considered secondary. It is, however, not to be understood as a recensional text. Since it is Balak's message, ממני is used, though Num makes it plural, ἡμεῖς (or did Num read ממנו?).

MT introduces the following structure with אולי, i.e. "perhaps I might be able to smite them and chase them from the land." Num has rendered this by a conditional structure; "if we would be able to smite among them, then I will chase them out of the land." The fluctuation of singular and plural might seem odd, but it reflects the identification of king and people. The plural is hardly the royal "we" or plural of majesty, but is simply a case of the king viewing himself as absolute monarch, and therefore incorporating in himself the will and action of the people. Particularly daring in this respect is the consecution אוכל נכה "I might be able, we would strike," i.e. I (or we) would be able to strike." Num has neatly encapsulated this by using the plural δυνώμεθα plus an infinitive πατάξαι in the protasis, but the singular ἐκβαλῶ in the apodosis.

The ὅτι construction of v.b is a piece of Oriental flattery, attributing magical powers to Balaam: "because I know whomever you might bless σύ, he is blessed, and whomever you might curse σύ, he has been cursed." Num has added an unnecessary pronoun to both relative clauses, and hex has placed both cases of σύ under the obelus to show that they are absent from MT. The change in tense for εὐλόγηνται to κεκατήρανται shows an attempt to represent MT more precisely. The present tense renders the participle, whereas the perfect passive renders the inflected Ho (or Qal passive) יואר.[8]

In the tradition, copyists felt the sudden introduction of ἐάν to be overly abrupt, and the Byz text revised it as εανπερ, whereas the F C'+ tradition added δε. Both variants are stylistic in nature. The same could be said for the popular A V gloss οτι after οἶδα; it too is clearly a secondary smoothing out of the text.

22:7 MT begins with a plural verb וילכו with a compound subject "the elders of Moab and the elders of Midian." Since Num renders both cases of זקני by ἡ γερουσία, the compound subjects are both singular. Accordingly, Num followed its usual pattern of using a singular verb when the verb precedes compound

---

8. See GK 52e.

singular subjects, i.e. ἐπορεύθη.⁹ For the use of γερουσία to render זִקְנֵי, see comment at v.4.

This is followed by a puzzling καὶ τὰ μαντεῖα ἐν ταῖς χερσὶν αὐτῶν, rendering וקסמים בידם. The noun means "divinations," but what was precisely in their hands is not at all clear, nor does the Greek translation help. It was, after all, Balaam who was the expert diviner, who could be expected to have means of divination on his own. It has often been suggested that it refers to the moneys to pay for divination, i.e. the divination fees, which could be a possible understanding. In any event, it was something they could carry in their hands; comp 1Reg 9:7—8 καὶ τί οἴσομεν τῷ ἀνθρώπῳ τοῦ θεοῦ; and note the reply of the παιδάριον "Behold there is present in my hand a quarter shekel of silver, which you may give to the man of God." The plural "hands" is used by Num, since the delegation members all had hands. The singular obtains in MT.

When the delegation arrived, "εἶπαν to him (i.e. to Balaam) the words of Balak." In MT, the verb is וידברו, which is normally translated by καὶ ἐλάλησαν, and it is quite possible that Num's εἶπαν presupposes a parent ויאמרו.¹⁰ Actually, the majority text has the Classical second aorist, ειπον, instead of εἶπαν, but Num always used the Hellenistic form.¹¹ It should also be noted that εἶπαν ῥήματα is rarely attested, whereas λαλέω ῥήματα is common. Thus the former occurs (including modification by κατὰ τὰ ῥήματα) three times in the Pentateuch (and six elsewhere), whereas with λαλέω the Pentateuch has 17 cases and there are 29 elsewhere.¹²

22:8 Balaam suggested to the delegation that they remain αὐτοῦ overnight. The αὐτοῦ is an adverb meaning "right here," for פה, and is not the genitive of αὐτός.¹³ Num does not name the subject, since it is obvious from the context, but the Byz text added βαλααμ, even though a singular verb could only refer to Balaam. During the interval he will await divine instructions, which he would then pass on to them. For הלילה Num quite correctly has the accusative τὴν νύκτα, i.e. "tonight." In the tradition, the Byz+ text added ταυτην, thereby

---

9. See THGN 122.
10. See THGN 128.
11. See THGN 123.
12. According to my count from HR.
13. See LS sub αὐτοῦ.

making doubly sure that only "tonight" could be read. The gloss simply makes what is implicit explicit.

Balaam goes on to say: "and I will respond (with) the message (ῥήματα) which the Lord might speak to me." The intent of the clause is to show the reason for staying overnight, i.e. "that I might respond ...." The word ῥήματα correctly renders the singular דבר; the Hebrew "and I will bring back word" is interpreted by ἀποκριθήσομαι ῥήματα; strictly speaking, the modifier is not necessary; to "bring back word" means "to reply, respond," but the translator included ῥήματα as an antecedent for the relative clause which follows. The term דבר can mean "word" or "matter," depending on the context. Here it involves speaking, and only ῥήματα is appropriate, and not the πραγματα of the majority B F V (and A which reads πραγμα) text.[14]

The Byz+ text read the simplex εμειναν instead of the more Hellenistic κατέμειναν of Num. The Byz text often prefers somewhat more Classical readings than those of Num. In the tradition, the *b n*+ text substitutes "Balak" for Μωάβ; the chieftains are, however, of Moab as MT states, not of Balak.

22:9 "And God came to Balaam," presumably in a dream. The change from κύριος in Balaam's statement in v.8 to ὁ θεός follows the deliberate change of MT in vv.9—12; comp also the same change from v.19 to vv.20—22. "And he (i.e. God) said αὐτῷ." The pronoun has been placed under the obelus by hex to mark its absence from MT.[15] In MT, God asks: "מי these persons with you"? Num does not ask "who," but τί. In other words, Num asks "Why are these persons with you"? The change avoids any risk that a reader might think that God did not know who these people were.[16] The text of Num may have been inspired by Sam's מה, but if so, it used τί, which can mean either "what" or "why."

22:10 Balaam's reply in MT simply states: "Balak ... שלח אלי," after which the message Balak sent is given in v.11. Num smoothes out the text by adding the modifiers αὐτούς to the verb ἀπέστειλεν, as well as the direct speech indicator λέγων at the end, thereby introducing v.11. Hex placed the αὐτούς under the

---

14. See THGN 129.
15. Though 4QNum^b has אליו before מי as well, and the parent text probably had אליו.
16. Theod and Aq translate literally by τίνες οἱ ἄνδρες οὗτοι, but Sym retains the text of Num.

obelus, though λέγων was not marked thus. Ms 426 of the O group did omit λέγων, undoubtedly due to MT, i.e. probably through one of the recensors.[17]

22:11 What Balaam quotes the messengers as saying is almost word for word what vv.5—6 had reported. The only changes are κεκάλυφεν instead of κατεκάλυψεν, and I am sceptical about its originality. The perfect tense is supported by only three mss, and except for the Byz reading κατεκαλυψεν taken over from v.5, all others read εκαλυψεν, which I would now regard as original LXX. The Num reading is based on the perfect tense of the preceding clause; the addition of a *kappa* before εκαλυψεν is a secondary one. That the middle verb was the default aorist was argued at v.5, and should apply here as well. The critical text must read ἐκάλυψεν. As in v.5, so here λαὸς ἐξελήλυθεν does not represent the articulation of MT's העם היצא. This may well have a textual basis, since 4QNum^b reads עם יצא, though how a secondary העם הוצא developed is not clear. Possibly the article of העם is a case of dittography, since the preceding word is הנה. Presumably, the participle would then have been secondarily articulated by attraction to העם.

For the next clause, καὶ νῦν δεῦρο ἄρασαί μοι αὐτόν equals the first clause of v.6, except for changing τὸν λαὸν τοῦτον to αὐτόν. The critical text would be improved by changing the punctuation after αὐτόν from a comma to a colon.[18] The clause καὶ οὗτος ἐγκάθηται ἐχόμενός μου has no counterpart in MT, and is imported from the end of v.5. This is also true here of 4QNum^b which has והואה יושב]... Neither MT nor Sam attest to it here, though both have it at v.5.

The אולי structure is somewhat more straightforward than at v.6. Instead of the peculiar plural verb נכה modifying אוכל, v.11 has להלחם, which makes much better sense. At v.6 the verb of the apodosis was also modified by מן הארץ. Num has changed ἐάν to εἰ ἄρα, thereby changing the conditional structure of v.5 to a "perhaps" collocation. εἰ ἄρα equals the אולי of MT precisely. It thus reads "perhaps I will be able πατάξαι αὐτόν and chase αὐτὸν ἀπὸ τῆς γῆς." Num has kept πατάξαι of v.6 rather than translating להלחם, but made better Greek by its αὐτόν modifier than the ἐξ αὐτῶν of v.6. The ἀπό phrase is a variation of the ἐκ

---

17. The λέγων was probably textually based, since 4QNum^b attests to לאמור at the end of the verse.
18. I find Dorival's critique of the inconsistency of my punctuation in these two verses (in his discussion of 22:6) fully justified. The ὅτι clause, which intervenes at v.6, does not really change this perception.

phrase in v.6, but has no equivalent in MT, and hex has placed it under the obelus.[19] And instead of αὐτούς of v.6, Num here keeps close to MT with its αὐτόν.

22:12 God refuses permission: "you may not go with them οὐδέ may you curse the people." MT does not introduce the second לא by a conjunction, but Num follows Sam's (ולא (תאר).[20] The reason given for the second prohibition is a statement of fact ἔστιν γὰρ εὐλογημένος. The participle is a literal rendering of ברוך.

22:13 Num makes the coordinate ויקם ... ויאמר into a single syntagm by reducing ויקם to a participle: καὶ ἀναστὰς Βαλααμ τὸ πρωὶ εἶπεν. τὸ πρωί may well be regarded as a calque for בקר(ב), which it renders 247 times in the Bible,[21] whereas other renderings are extremely rare.

What Balaam said to the chieftains of Balak was: "Return to your κύριον. οὐκ ἀφίησίν με ὁ θεὸς πορεύεσθαι with you." This is a somewhat free paraphrase of MT, which had ארצכם "your land," whereas Num ordered the delegation to return to "your master."[22] MT is not overly fitting, since throughout the dialogue, it was Balak whose words are being quoted, and it was he who had sent them. MT then has a כי clause, explaining why they should return. It is "because Yahweh has refused לתתי to go with you." Num omitted the כי, and has changed יהוה to ὁ θεός, rendered מאן "has refused" by a negative particle plus a present tense οὐκ ἀφίησιν "is not allowing," and for לתתי translated only the suffix by με. What Num made of it was "Return to your master. God is not allowing me to go with you." Ms 426 changed ὁ θεός to κυριος, obviously on the basis of the Hebrew; so did the b s^mg+ text; the reading probably derives from one of the Revisers.

22:14 For καὶ ἀναστάντες rendering ויקומו, see comment at v.13. The "chieftains of Moab came ... and εἶπαν Οὐ θέλει Balaam to go with us." As at v.7, the

---

19. But 4QNum^b has מן האר(ץ). The letter ץ is fully clear in Plate XLI, line 5.
20. As do Kenn 1,4,17,18,69,75,84,193,225,226,232 and 294. Tar^JN both read ולא, as do Pesh and Vulg (neque).
21. According to the count of Dos Santos.
22. The editor has transcribed 4QNum^b by אדונ(י)כמה, but quite rightly has dotted all the letters. Actually, the first letters of ארציכמה seem to be an equally possible transcription based on the Plate.

Hellenistic εἶπαν is supported only by a minority of witnesses, whereas the A F M V majority text read the Classical ειπον. Num, however, consistently uses the Hellenistic inflection for this verb.[23] The opposite is the case with ἦλθον. For this verb Num always uses the Classical second aorist form, and the reading of s^{mg}, ηλθοσαν, is secondary. The majority A F M V text has added αυτω after "they said," and 4QNum[b] also witnesses to אליו, though neither MT nor Sam do. The reading of B+ is probably original Num text nonetheless. What they reported was "οὐ θέλει to go with us." MT has מאן "refused," as at v.13, where it was also rendered by a present tense, but by οὐκ ἀφίησιν. What they said was "Balaam does not want to go with us," which was not quite accurate, since Balaam was simply following the orders of God. The charge of arrogance by Rashi against Balaam is unfortunate.[24]

22:15 The collocation (καὶ) προσέθετο ἔτι plus infinitive is a Hebraism, more particularly it is a Hebraic syntactic calque, representing ויסף עוד plus a bound infinitive (here unmarked). "And he added again (to send)" simply means "and he sent a second time," literally "again added a sending." This time the delegation was more impressive: ἄρχοντες πλείους καὶ ἐντιμοτέρους τούτων. The comparative degree governs the genitive, which represents the comparative מן of Hebrew.[25] The chieftains were "more numerous and distinguished than these." The pronoun refers to the first delegation of chieftains.

22:16 Num promotes a more lively style of dialogue by its use of the historical present in "(and they came to Balaam) and λέγουσιν to him." MT has a past tense ויאמרו. τάδε λέγει also has a present tense, but that structure is a calque for כה אמר. The message from Balak transmitted by the second delegation is 'Αξιῶ σε μὴ ὀκνήσῃς ἐλθεῖν πρός με.

The first clause 'Αξιῶ σε "I pray you" is an idiomatic rendering for the נא particle of entreaty, which Num normally disregards. But here the translator wants to record the pleading character of this second invitation. Note that ἀξιόω is now regularly used, not in the Classical sense of "consider worthy," but as "request, ask."[26] What MT says is "Please do not hold yourself back from going

---

23. See THGN 123.
24. Rashi speaks of his בלשון נסות.
25. See SS 149.
26. See Lee 68—69.

to me." Num translated MT well. Origen, however, placed σε under the obelus, which betrays how mechanically he worked in hex. Of course, the נא particle does not include the σε, but see comment above. After all, neither does ἀξιῶ equal נא.

22:17 Num renders the Hebrew pattern: cognate free infinitive plus a finite verb in unusual fashion, by using a cognate adverb to render the infinitive, ἐντίμως ... τιμήσω. The intent of the Hebrew pattern is, however, reflected in the Greek as well; both stress the verbal notion: "I shall greatly honor (you)," to which MT added מאד; since Num omitted the intensifier, hex added σφοδρα under the asterisk.

Furthermore, he said: "and whatever you might say, I will do for you." This is not what MT says; it has אלי after the verb תאמר, but has no counterpart to the σοι following ποιήσω.²⁷ What MT says is "I will obey all your instructions," but Num has the structure explicitly referring to the opening statement, i.e. in greatly honoring you, whatever you might demand (in the matter of reward for services rendered), I will do for you. In other words, Balak offers Balaam a blank signed cheque. Over against MT, Num does not actually render כל, though ὅσα does generalize. The addition of παντα by the majority A F M text before ὅσα (or simply as α) is probably a hex correction. Similarly, hex is the majority F M V text that added μοι after εἴπῃς; this represents the לי which Num did not render. Over against this, hex placed σοι under the obelus, since MT lacked its equivalent.

And finally, he repeated the original request of v.6 "and come, curse for me this people," but changed the simplex ἄρασαι of v.6 to the compound ἐπικατάρασαι. This was intended to reflect the change from ארה in v.6 to קבה here. In v.11, however, where Balaam is informing God what Balak had said, MT also used קבה, but Num quite probably corrected Balaam's report by using the ἄρασαι (for ארה), which Balak's ambassadors had used. The use of the compound is intended to make a stronger imprecation. Apparently, the two verbs in Hebrew are synonymous, and קבה of v.11 could reflect the ארה of v.6, but here Num is making a distinction; here the compound is an intentional variation. Possibly one might translate the compound by "damn," and the simplex, by "curse," thereby

---

27. But 4QNumᵇ does have לכה after אעשה. It, however, also attests to אלי after תאמר.

showing the intended difference. It should be said, however, that Num is not consistent; see e.g. v.12 where καταράσῃ renders ארה.

22:18 Balaam's reply is given "τοῖς ἄρχουσιν of Balak"; this agrees with the usage of vv.8,13,14,15, where MT has (ם)שרי. But here MT has changed to עבדי, which is never rendered by ἄρχων in the Bible (except here). In fact, עבד simply does not equal שר, and the change to ἄρχουσιν "corrects" MT, by harmonizing with the narrative's designation of the status of the delegation; they were not "slaves, servants," but "chieftains" whom Balak sent.

Balaam refuses to yield to temptation, but avows his strict conformity to the word of the Lord God, to the extent of expressing inability to deviate even mentally in anything from what deity has said. What he says is: "if Balak were to give me his house full of silver and gold, not would I be able to transgress the word of the Lord τοῦ θεοῦ by doing αὐτό, small or large in my mind." The use of παραβαίνω to render עבר here is quite correct, though LXX only uses this equation 11 times. Much more common are διαβαίνω (104 times) and διέρχομαι (59 times),[28] but these represent the core meaning of עבר "to pass through, cross over," whereas here, it is used in a moral sense "to transgress."

The protasis reflects MT adequately, but the apodosis does not. In MT, Balaam refers to the word (פי) of יהוה אלהי, i.e. disregards the suffix, which hex then supplies by adding μου after τοῦ θεοῦ.[29] This omission neutralizes the reason for Balak's invitation. After all, as a diviner or prophet who worshipped Yahweh as his God, Balaam's blessing or curse would be more powerful or effective against Israel, the people of Yahweh. This is the first indication of the translator's antipathy towards the diviner Balaam. The αὐτό is a gloss, and grammatically must refer to ῥῆμα; hex has placed it under the obelus. Though the neuter pronoun must refer to ῥῆμα, its real intent is a more general one; "it" in sense refers to "transgressing the word," and the ποιῆσαι structure shows the means which could be used. The contrast μικρὸν ἢ μέγα is a typical merism, i.e. from one extreme to the other, and means "anything." The final prepositional phrase ἐν τῇ διανοίᾳ μου also has no basis in MT, but is based on the מלבי of 24:13, and is placed under the obelus by hex. There, however, Num renders the phrase by παρ ἐμαυτοῦ. The addition constitutes Num's attempt at making Balaam strictly

---

28. Acording to the count in Dos Santos.
29. As attested also for The Others.

obedient to the word of God. What the ποιῆσαι structure means to say is "by mentally affecting it in any way." Even in mind I would not act in any deviant fashion over against what God has said.

22:19 For שבו Num used the unique rendering ὑπομείνατε; elsewhere (v.8 20:1) Num used καταμείνω to render ישב when it meant "to stay, remain." In spite of the piety expressed in v.18, Balaam does not suggest an immediate departure of the delegation, but bids them "remain here, even you, τὴν νύκτα ταύτην" and "I will find out what the Lord will again speak to me." MT has הלילה as at v.8 with no added pronoun, and hex has placed ταύτην under the obelus to indicate that fact. For a possible understanding of the pronoun, see the discussion on the Byz gloss at v.8. For the use of προσθήσει plus infinitive, see the explanation at v.15.

In the tradition, hex has added δη under the asterisk after ὑπομείνατε to represent the נא particle of entreaty in MT. Num hardly ever pays attention to this particle, though see comment at v.16 on ἀξιῶ σε.

22:20 It was God, rather than κύριος/יהוה who "came to Balaam νυκτός and said to him."[30] For the use of "God" in the Balaam narrative, see the comment at v.9. Num simply follows the usage of MT. The genitive νυκτός expresses time within which something takes place, thus "during the night." What God says is "If to summon you, πάρεισιν οἱ ἄνθρωποι οὗτοι, ἀναστὰς ἀκολούθησον them." The present tense verb πάρεισιν "are present" interprets באו "have come." Of course, if someone has come, he is then present. MT has no counterpart for οὗτοι, simply having האנשים as subject. Hex has dutifully put οὗτοι under the obelus to indicate the absence of a demonstrative.

The apodosis in MT reads קום לך אתם "arise, go with them." Rendering the first word by an attributive participle is a frequent phenomenon in Num, but "go with them" is idiomatically translated by "follow them."

Balaam is, however, strictly warned: "but whatever word I will speak to you, τοῦτο you must do." MT simply has אתו "it." rather than "this."

22:21 For ἀναστάς, see comment at v.13, and for τὸ πρωί, also see comment at v.13. The verse introduces the story of Balaam and his she-ass, a story which

---

30. But not in the Tar, where it was the *Memrah* from before Y. which came.

continues through v.35. It will be noticed that the שרי reappear here; cf the עבדי of v.18, and the comment ad loc. The ass was a she-ass as the Hebrew אתון shows. A male ass is a חמור, but both of these are rendered by ὄνος with the sex indicated by the gender of the article, so here τὴν ὄνον.

22:22 In v.20 God had ordered Balaam: "follow them (i.e. the delegation)," but now God is furious that ἐπορεύετο αὐτός. This arbitrary change in attitude on God's part has exercised commentators from early times onward. Moderns tend to explain this by insisting on a change in source at this point, i.e. that a different source begins at v.22. But Num simply translates MT without apology.[31] The Hebrew idiom ויחר אף "and anger burned," (or literally "and the nostril became hot") was fully understood by Num: καὶ ὠργίσθη θυμῷ "and was angered by wrath," i.e. "was furious." Incidentally, only MT and Num witness to "God," both Sam and Tar reading the personal name of Israel's God. The imperfect ἐπορεύετο represents the participial predicate of the nominal clause הוא הולך.[32] In the tradition, the B V O Byz f+ text read επορευθη, which would not conform to the translator's usual rendering of a participial predicate either by a present or an imperfect tense.[33]

The next clause in MT says: "ויתיצב מלאך יהוה in the way לשטן to him." Instead of "angel of Yahweh," Num has ὁ ἄγγελος τοῦ θεοῦ. The use of "God" instead of "the Lord" is part of the translator's attempt to minimize the role of Israel's God in the story in favor of the general term ὁ θεός.[34] The verb is also changed to ἀνέστη, i.e. the angel stood up.[35] The Hebrew verb means "to station oneself," and ἀνίστημι is not a bad translation. Num has, however, disregarded the next word, בדרך, and hex has added εν τη οδω under the asterisk (mistakenly as an obelus in Syh) to make up for it. The phrase לשטן "for an adversary" is interpreted as a marked infinitive, which the consonantal text does allow. Num has the present infinitive ἐνδιαβάλλειν, which here probably means "to play the role of a διαβολός" i.e. "an adversary" a Satan.[36]

---

31. Tar^J explains by ארום אזיל ללטוטינון "since he had gone to curse them."
32. Sym adopts the Num text, but Theod and Aq use the present tense πορεύεται.
33. See also THGN 124—125.
34. Instead of τοῦ θεοῦ, The Others read κυρίου (retroverted from Syh) as do the Tar.
35. Sym preferred the simplex ἔστη, but Theod, followed by Aq, read ἐστηλώθη.
36. Aq understood this by his transcription σαταν. Theod translates by ἀντικεῖσθαι.

The verb ἐπιβεβήκει is perfect, but here renders a participle רכב. This does not really violate the usual pattern for rendering participial predicates, since semantically the perfect means "was riding (since he has mounted on) his she-ass." The term נעריו "his lads" is rendered here by παῖδες (αὐτοῦ), which is also used to render עבד (14:24 31:49 32:4,25,27). Elsewhere, נער only occurs at 11:27 where it is more specifically translated by νεανίσκος. For עבד, θεράπων occurs four times (11:11 12:7,8 32:31), and at 32:5 it becomes οἰκέτης.[37]

22:23 The verse begins with a lengthy nominative pendant: "and the she-ass seeing the angel τοῦ θεοῦ ἀνθεστηκότα in the road and τὴν ῥομφαίαν drawn in his hand." Num throughout calls the angel, "the angel of God," but MT has מלאך יהוה (see also vv.23,25—27,31,35, but see v.34 for "angel of the Lord"), which is in line with Num's avoidance of the notion that Balaam was Yahweh's prophet; this then extends to his angel as well. The participle represents נצב, and is particularly appropriate in the compound form, ἀνθεστηκότα "standing against," i.e. in opposition. MT has חרבו, but Num did not render the suffix, it being unnecessary in the context; it would hardly have been someone else's sword which the angel had in his hand. Hex has, however, added αυτου to represent the suffix.

The main clause is introduced by καί in imitation of MT. The subject ἡ ὄνος is given, thereby demonstrating that the first part of the verse, which also has ἡ ὄνος given as its subject, is a pendant structure outside the main clause. The coordinate clause oddly has an imperfect verb, ἐπορεύετο, whereas its coordinate ἐξέκλινεν is aorist, and the O text, possibly hex, changed the verb to the aorist επορευθη. There is no good reason exegetically for the imperfect; it probably was taken from v.22, where the imperfect ἐπορεύετο was fitting; see comment ad loc; here MT has וילך, i.e. it is a past tense for which the aorist of the O text would have been more appropriate.

V.b begins in MT with ויך בלעם, but Num omits the subject, thereby creating possible confusion, though common sense would dictate that it must be Balaam; hex has duly added βαλααμ under the asterisk.

---

37. Tar^J identifies the lads as ינים וימריס. For the Jannes and Jambres legend, see A.Pietersma, The Apocryphon of Jannes and Jambres the Magicians. Papyrus. Chester Beatty XVI. With New Editions of P.Vindob. Greek inv. 29456+29828verso and BL Cott Tib B. v.f.87. 1994.

The modifier reads: τὴν ὄνον τῇ ῥάβδῳ τοῦ ευθῦναι αὐτὴν ἐν τῇ ὁδῷ.[38] MT has no equivalent for τῇ ῥάβδῳ, and hex has placed it under the obelus. Its origin must have been v.27, where Balaam struck the she-ass במקל, translated by τῇ ῥάβδῳ. The marked infinitive, showing purpose, is contextually particularly appropriate: "in order to straighten (her) out, to redirect." MT says to "bend her (on the way)." The verb renders the Hi of נטה elsewhere only at Ios 24:23: εὐθύνατε τὴν καρδίαν ὑμῶν πρὸς κύριον.

22:24 Then "the angel of God ἔστη in the furrows of the vineyard with a fence on either side."[39] For τοῦ θεοῦ, see comment at v.23.[40] MT has the angel standing במשעול of the vineyards. The term משעול is a hapax legomenon, and its exact meaning is unknown. It is probably related to שעל "hollow (of the hand)," and so may well be some kind of ditch or hollowed out area. Vines are usually planted in rows in the vineyards with only small space between the rows, which space is cultivated, and the term αὔλαξιν was used by Num, referring to these narrow spaces between the vines; the term usually refers to "furrows" in a plowed field, so here the plowed space between rows of vines. This is clear from φραγμὸς ἐντεῦθεν καὶ φραγμὸς ἐντεῦθεν which follows. The vines grow on fences of a sort, and such passages would be narrow. The word ἀμπελώνων renders כרמים, and the variant B V ƒ+ text αμπελων "vines" cannot be original.[41]

22:25 For ἰδοῦσα, see v.23. For τοῦ θεοῦ, see comment at v.22. The she-ass squeezed herself towards the wall, and squeezed Balaam's foot. MT uses the same verb, but in different stems. For the first clause, it has תלחץ vocalized in the Ni, but in the second one, as a Qal. Num has cleverly used different compounds of the one verb θλίβω. The Ni verb is translated by προσέθλιψεν ἑαυτήν, but the Qal form becomes ἀπέθλιψεν (plus an accusative modifier). MT, however, repeats אל הקיר for the second verb as well, and hex has added προς τον τοιχον under the asterisk to remedy the omission.

---

38. Theod has τὴν ὄνον αὐτοῦ ἐκκλῖναι αὐτὴν εἰς τὴν ὁδόν; Aq translates τὴν ὀνάδα αὐτοῦ ἐκκλῖναι αὐτὴν τὴν ὁδόν, while Sym reads τὴν ὄνον μετακλῖναι αὐτὴν εἰς τὴν ὁδόν.
39. For καὶ ἔστη, Sym read ἀντέστη δέ, but Theod and Aq followed Num.
40. For τοῦ θεοῦ, Theod (cod^L has The Others) has κυρίου (retroverted from Syh).
41. See THGN 129.

For the stereotype προσέθετο ἔτι, see comment at v.15. It should be noted, however, that here MT lacks the עוד of v.15, i.e. has no counterpart to ἔτι.

22:26 For προσέθετο, see comment at v.15, and for τοῦ θεοῦ, see comment at v.23.[42] MT states that the angel "again proceded (עבר) and stood in a narrow place." Num pictures the movement as "καὶ ἀπελθὼν ὑπέστη in a narrow place." The bound infinitive עבר was interpreted by the participle "going away (he stood fast)," and the conjunction before יעמד was rendered by a καί placed before the participle. This was made necessary in view of Num's restructuring of the syntax. The narrow place where he stood fast is then defined as εἰς ὃν οὐκ ἦν ἐκκλῖναι δεξιὰν οὐδὲ ἀριστεράν. MT has "where there was no דרך to turn right or left." Hex has added ὁδος to represnt דרך. The word is unnecessary for the sense, but it had not been rendered as such by Num.

22:27 For ἰδοῦσα ἡ ὄνος τὸν ἄγγελον τοῦ θεοῦ, see v.23 and the comments ad loc. The she-ass responded by "συνεκάθισεν underneath Balaam." The verb is a good rendering for ותרבץ, though it is used uniquely; in fact, the verb occurs but rarely in the Bible, and only here for רבץ; Like the Hebrew lexeme, it means "to cower, crouch." Balaam's reaction was once again to be angry. At v.22, the same Hebrew idiom ויחר אף had occurred, but here no attempt is made to render the idiom word for word; Num simply said ἐθυμώθη. Hex was dissatisfied with this rendering, and added οργη under the asterisk; comp the rendering ὀργίσθη θυμῷ at v.22, which transposed the two roots; see comment ad loc. In the final statement, "And he beat the she-ass τῇ ῥάβδῳ," MT has במקל "with a club.[43] Hex has placed an εν before the article to equal the Hebrew preposition.

22:28 Num continues with its use of ὁ θεός as substitute for יהוה, for which see comment on "angel of God" at v.23. The she-ass λέγει. For the use of the historical present in dialogue, see comment at v.16. A popular A M text has changed λέγει to ειπεν, but the lively historical present is appropriate. She asks: τί πεποίηκά σοι that you have struck me τοῦτο τρίτον; The verbs are both in the perfect tense, though the default aorist would have sufficed; The B O Byz+ text

---

42. The Others read κυρίου (retroverted from Syh).
43. See SS 121.

actually read ἐποίησα instead of πεποίηκα.⁴⁴ But this could only suffice if both verbs were aorist.⁴⁵ Instead of the ordinal τρίτον, MT uses the cardinal שלש רגלים, which is a matter of style, not one of content.

22:29 Balaam's reply to the question "Why," is ὅτι ἐμπέπαιχάς μοι. For the verb as rendering התעללת, see Note at Exod 10:2.

V.b begins with καί, but MT has no conjunction. The protasis has יש as its verbal element, "if there were a sword in my hand," which Num interprets by εἶχον "if I had a sword ...."⁴⁶ MT makes use of the desiderative particle לו.⁴⁷ The apodosis of this contrary to fact condition (ἄν ἐξεκέντησά σε) is introduced by ἤδη, whereas MT has כי עתה. The כי is to be taken as asseverative: "indeed (now). Num disregarded the כי, and translated עתה by ἤδη "already (I would have pierced you through)." The verb occurs only here in the Pentateuch, and is a unique, though picturesque, rendering, appropriate for הרגתיך "I would have killed you."⁴⁸

22:30 Again the reply of the she-ass is indicated by a historical present; see comment at v.16. The nominal clause, οὐκ ἐγὼ ἡ ὄνος σου, has ἐγώ as subject,⁴⁹ and the introductory οὐκ introducing a question expecting an affirmative answer: Am I not your ass? ὄνος is then further characterized by a relative construction: "On which ἐπέβαινες from νεότητός σου up to the present day." The verb is an imperfect inflection, i.e. "you were riding." Problematic is the MT text as parent for νεότητός σου. MT reads מעודך, a highly uncertain text. עוד apparently means "continuance," but is normally used as an adverb in the sense of "still, yet, again," and the Num text is simply a contextual rendering. Since its context is "from ... up to the present," the guess "youth" makes excellent sense.⁵⁰ Pesh has also understood it this way.⁵¹ The use of σήμερον plus an unnecesssary τῆς ... ἡμέρας does not occur often in LXX. In the Pentateuch, it is limited to five cases (out of 23) in Gen, one in Num, and once (out of 66 cases) in Deut.

---

44. The Others also read ἐποίησα.
45. See THGN 125.
46. See SS 185.
47. See GK 151², note 1.
48. Aq, Sym and Theod all render in more plebeian fashion by ἀπέκτεινά σε.
49. See SS 78.
50. Both Tar^JN also read מן טלותך "from your youth."
51. Vulg paraphrased by translating the phrase by *semper*.

The she-ass continued with a μή question, i.e. one expecting a negative answer. MT has a Hi verb הסכנת with a cognate free infinitive, הסכן, introducing it, i.e. "have I actually been in the habit (of doing thus to you)." Num has interpreted this by a different syntagm: ὑπεροράσει ὑπεριδοῦσα in modification of ἐποίησα which represents the marked infinitive לעשות of MT. The cognate collocation has become a dative noun plus a cognate participle. The root means "to overlook," i.e. to neglect. Num thus interprets by "Have I (ever) acted thus to you by actually neglecting (you and your needs)?"

22:31 Num indicates the intervention of "God" as a third party by means of a contrastive δέ. In MT, the subject is יהוה,[52] for which change see comment at v.23.[53] God now opened Balaam's eyes; actually the verb used is ἀπεκάλυψεν, the verb used for "to reveal"; with τοὺς ὀφθαλμούς I would rather translate: "Then God uncovered the eyes of Balaam (and he saw)." What he saw with his now-seeing eyes was "the angel τοῦ θεοῦ standing in opposition in the road, and the sword drawn in his hand." Once again, τοῦ θεοῦ is substituted for יהוה, for which see comment above. A popular B text, possibly hex in origin, reads κυριου, which is not original.[54] MT has חרבו, but Num fails to render the suffix.

The final clause reads "and bowing he prostrated himself on his face." This represents two clauses in MT. The second verb, וישתחו, is used to indicate a response of obeisance, here of worship, and the verb προσκυνέω is a calque for it; in fact, out of 152 cases of the Hebrew verb in the Bible, 149 are translated by προσκυνέω.[55] Obviously then, it must be translated in the Hebrew sense: "and bowing down, he did obeissance." The verb is modified by לאפיו, literally, "to his nostrils"; Num correctly understood this as a case of *pars pro toto*, and rendered the phrase by τῷ προσώπῳ αὐτοῦ. Since obeisance involved τῷ προσώπῳ αὐτοῦ, one might render the dative structure with κύψας, i.e. "and bowing down to the ground, he worshipped."

22:32 The A M C⁾ s y+ text has changed εἶπεν to the present λεγει as in vv.28,30, but the present tense is used in this tale only for the she-ass. For τοῦ

---

52. Milgrom makes the interesting observation that יהוה, rather than the "angel of Yahweh," intervenes only twice, at v.28 and here, both times "to effect a miracle."
53. The Others read κύριος (retroverted from Syh).
54. See THGN 129—130.
55. Acording to Dos Santos.

θεοῦ, see comment at v.23.⁵⁶ For τοῦτο τρίτον, see comment at v.28. For הנה, Num reads καὶ ἰδού. The use of ἐγώ/אנכי before the inflected verb, is probably intended as an introduction of the third party; *you* struck *the she-ass*, but it was *I* who came out εἰς διαβολήν σου. In MT, the equivalent is לשטן "for an adversary";⁵⁷ MT has no equivalent for σου.⁵⁸

The reason for the angel's appearance is given in a ὅτι clause: "because ἡ ὁδός σου was οὐκ ἀστεία before me." Num follows Sam's דרכך rather than the absolute הדרך of MT. In MT, the predicate is a verb ירט, but this is a hapax legomenon, the meaning of which is unknown. It also puzzled Num who made a contextual adaptation; that the reason for the angel's opposition was the fact that Balaam's way was "not acceptable, well-pleasing" could not be too far from the mark.⁵⁹

22:33 Num reduces the first clause, ותראני האתון, to a subordinate syntagm "καὶ ἰδοῦσά με ἡ ὄνος, which may best be understood in a temporal sense "and when the she-ass saw me." This correctly interprets MT. Num reads "and she turned away ἀπ' ἐμοῦ," which follows the מלפני of 4QNumᵇ and Sam rather than the לפני of MT. For τρίτον τοῦτο, see the comment at v.28, where, however, the two words are transposed. An A V *b t+* text actually reads τουτο τριτον.

V.b begins asyndetically in MT, but is introduced by καί in Num. MT begins with אולי "perhaps," but Num has (καὶ) εἰ μή which equals לולי; this is also presupposed by Pesh and Vulg.⁶⁰ Num has shortened the protasis by omitting מפני after נטתה, but the majority A F M V text added απ εμου; the reading is probably hex in origin.

The apodosis is in two parts, i.e. a μέν ... δέ construction. This differs from MT where this is a כי clause: "For even you I would have killed, and her I would have kept alive." Num, however, has disregarded the כי entirely. The μέν structure reads "now you μέν I would have killed." In the tradition, the B *b x* text

---

56. The Others read κυρίου (retroverted from Syh).
57. As at v.22 Aq has transliterated as σαταν (retroverted from Syh), whereas Theod read αντικεῖσθαι, and Sym has ἐναντιοῦσθαι.
58. But 4QNumᵇ does have לכה[... before כיא. Presumably, the lacuna before it had לשטן.
59. The parent text could not have been the רעה הדרך of 4QNumᵇ. Note that Sam reads הרע דרכך.
60. Milgrom (note 80) calls this "*Ulai* in the sense of *lula'*."

has added ουν after νῦν. MT does have גם after עתה, but this is irrelevant; גם is normally disregarded, and is never rendered by ουν, which is in reality a palaeographically inspired error, a partial dittograph of νῦν.[61] An interesting variant text is the popular addition of the particle αν in both the μέν and the δέ structures; though probably not original text, the particles do stress the potential nature of the contrary to fact apodosis.

22:34 Elsewhere in the narrative מלאך יהוה is always rendered by ἄγγελος τοῦ θεοῦ, but here Num has τῷ ἀγγέλῳ κυρίου.[62] Why once, and only once, Num should depart from his regular rendering baffles me. In the next verse, he reverts to ὁ ἄγγελος τοῦ θεοῦ again. Since only one Greek witness, ms 54, reads του θεου here, it would be overly capricious to go against such overwhelming support for Num, and adopt it as original text.[63] The only possible reason that occurs to me is that Balaam's admission, ἡμάρτηκα, as a confession of sin, is properly directed to Israel's God, the Lord; i.e. Yahweh's own messenger is a more fitting recipient of such confession than would an unidentified deity. Admittedly, this is not an overly compelling basis for the translator's deviance from his normal usage, but it is not impossible that to the translator it was important that Balaam should confess his sin to the Lord's angel.

The reason for Balaam's confession is given in a γάρ clause: "for I did not know that you had stood against me on the way to meet (me)." MT does seem awkward; it says "because I did not know that you were standing to meet me in the way." Hex has reordered and changed the text to equal MT more precisely; it omitted μοι, then added μοι after συνάντησιν, and also transposed ἐν τῇ ὁδῷ to the end, i.e. has changed "against me on the way to meet" to "to meet me in the way." The transposition in particular makes much better sense. In fact, this hex text became the majority A F M text in the tradition.

V.b expresses a willingness on Balaam's part to go back home if the angel of the Lord so desires: "and now if (this) does not please you, I shall return." The subject of ἀρέσκει is not stated, but what is probably intended is Balaam's confession along with its γάρ clause. MT puts the protasis somewhat differently. Instead of μή σοι ἀρέσκει, MT has רע בעיניך "it is evil in your eyes," or more

---
61. See THGN 134.
62. The Others read ΠΙΠΙ (retroverted from Syh).
63. See THGN 130.

idiomatically as NJPS "(if) you still disapprove." In any event, Num avoids the anthropomorphism of בעיניך by its rendering. Num rather neatly allows for the לי of the final אשובה לי by the use of a future passive verb ἀποστραφήσομαι "I will turn myself back," i.e. I will return.

22:35 The angel of God completely disregards the suggestion that Balaam return home. Note again the return to the usual τοῦ θεοῦ instead of יהוה, for which see the remarks in v.34. The angel said "accompany the men." Num's συμπορεύθητι is more precise and colorful than the neutral לך of MT; it is an excellent translation. In the tradition, the Byz text has added an ad sensum τουτων after ἀνθρώπων.

MT continues with "and only the word which I might speak to you, it you may speak." Num does not begin with a conjunction, and instead of "I might speak (אדבר) has ἂν εἴπω. Since Num with consistency renders the root דבר by λαλέω, and אמר, by εἴπω, the parent text may well have read אמר rather than אדבר.[64] Num does not follow MT's אתו תדבר, but rather the text of Sam: אתו תשמר לדבר; it has τοῦτο φυλάξῃ λαλῆσαι "this you must be careful to speak."

22:36 Num renders the first clause by a subordinate participial structure, which might well be translated: "And Balak on hearing that Balaam had arrived"; the main verb which follows is ἐξῆλθεν (to meet him). The place of meeting is "at the city of Moab which is on the borders of Arnon at the edge of the borders."[65] What city of Moab was intended by the location on the borders of Moab is not certain, but it probably would be Aroer, i.e. the Ἠρ of 21:15. Incidentally, this has led some scholars unnecessarily to emend the עיר of MT meaning "city" to ער, i.e. the place name Er.[66] Num can be cited in defence of the עיר of MT; this also makes perfectly good sense, if it is understood that the Moabite city, rather than being named, is described geographically as being on the southern borders of the Arnon, which incidentally were the northern borders of Moab as well; in

---

64. See THGN 128 at 15:1.
65. For ἐκ μέρους in the sense of "limit or edge," see Lee 72—76.
66. Both NJPS and NRSV transcribe as "Ir-Moab," which is quite unnecessary; it simply means "a city of Moab"; which city is meant is not stated; all that is said is that it was "a city of Moab which is on the borders of the Arnon." Tar^N reads לארעהון דמואבײ "to the land of the Moabites," which avoids any identification of the place to which Balak went.

other words, Balak went as far in the direction from which Balaam was coming as he could within the territory under his control.

22:37 Balak addresses Balaam impatiently. In MT, his first question reads הלא שלח שלחתי אליך לקרא לך "did I not actually send (i.e. a delegation) to you to summon you"? Num omitted the cognate free infinitive, possibly through haplography; at least, there seems to be no exegetical reason for omitting it, though see v.38. Hex has added a participle (either present or aorist) under the asterisk before ἀπέστειλα to make up for the omission. Both αποστελλων and αποστειλας occur in the tradition, and it is uncertain which one hex represents.[67] Balak followed this with a second question: למה לא הלכת אלי "why didn't you come to me"? Num put the verb into the imperfect tense, ἤρχου, since the verb is one of movement, i.e. involving a process.

V.b is a sarcastic query: Am I actually not able to pay you (literally to honor you)"? Num has omitted the interrogative prefix האמנם, and hex has added η before ὄντως to represent it.

22:38 As in v.37, the translator ignores the cognate free infinitive. MT reads היכול אוכל "will I really be able," which Num translates by the verbal figure δυνατὸς ἔσομαι, "will I be able." Balaam has just said: "Behold, I have come to you; now will I be able to speak anything"? Num has disregarded היכול entirely. The only recensional activity recorded in the tradition is the rendering of the interrogative prefix to the free infinitive by μη in the Byz text. The μη anticipates a negative answer: "now will I be able .... No!" But the Byz text fails to render the free infinitive. The presence of a μη does, however, help in understanding the passage. It is then followed by Balaam's "the word which God would cast into my mouth, this will I speak," which must be understood adversatively. After the query with its No!, comes "but the word, etc." What the Byz text makes explicit is that the question "will I now be able to speak something (i.e. on my own)," expects a negative answer. The omission of the infinitive is unfortunate; it would have stressed Balaam's inability to say anything on his own initiative: "would I really be able to say anything?" Presumably, the translator felt that the infinitives in the dialogue of vv.27—38 interrupted the flow of the discourse: "would I not be able ... now would I be able."

---

67. Because the evidence is in Syh; it is not certain which form is parent for its *mšdrw*.

The verb βάλῃ "cast" is somewhat stronger than שׂים "put, place"; this is clear from the ways Greek renders this verb. Though βάλλω is used to translate שׂים six times, as is the compound ἐπιβάλλω, ἐπιτίθημι is used 69 times, and its simplex, 244 times.[68] To Num, what God does when he wants to transmit a communication by a prophetic medium is to throw the word into his mouth. Only such a message should then be spoken. An A b f s+ text changed λαλήσω to φυλαξω λαλησαι; this corresponds to Sam, but its source is v.35, which see; this is another case of harmonization of the text on Num's part.

22:39 Balaam and Balak went up together to a place called קרית חצות, which is otherwise completely unknown. The translator translated the words by πόλεις ἐπαύλεων "cities of encampments." The term ἔπαυλις can mean "unwalled village, encampment," or even military quarters.[69] It is possible to read קרית in the consonantal text as a plural noun, but ἐπαύλεων hardly equals חצות, which would actually mean "streets." though a possible parent might be חצרות; the word חצר usually refers to a courtyard, and in that sense is normally rendered by αὐλή (125 times in the Bible). But another חצר means "settlement, an unwalled area of occupation," and LXX uses ἔπαυλις 16 times in the Bible in this sense.[70] I suspect that the translator had this חצרות in mind here.

22:40 "And Balak sacrificed πρόβατα καὶ μόσχους." These are reversed in MT as בקר וצאן, both terms being collectives, and therefore rendered by plural nouns. The work μόσχος is usually reserved for פר, and only seldom occurs for בקר, which is more commonly translated by βοῦς. There is, however, no reason to doubt that μόσχος is intended for בקר. Hex has transposed the two nouns to equal the order of MT.

The second clause creates some difficulty for interpreters. It reads: "And he sent to Balaam and to the chieftains who were with him." What makes this difficult is the use of ἀπέστειλεν/ישלח in an absolute sense, whereas these verbs are both transitive. What was it that he sent to Balaam and the delegation which brought him to Moab? Presumably, it was some of the meat which had been sac-

---

68. According to the count of Dos Santos.
69. Dorival translates the name as "Villes-des-Domaines."
70. The statistics are those of Dos Santos.

rificed. One would have expected a different verb as well, such as "he served, gave, dealt out," and "send" remains an odd choice.[71]

22:41 For τὸ πρωί as a calque for בבקר, see comment at v.13. Unique for Num is the use of the passive ἐγενήθη together with a timer; in fact, it occurs only here in the book. Elsewhere it is ἐγένετο that is used with a timer (7:1 10:11,34 16:42 17:8 21:9 and 26:1).

Num has subordinated ויקח to an attributive participle, thereby placing the stress quite correctly on the next clause: "And Balak taking along Balaam, brought him up ἐπὶ τὴν στήλην τοῦ Βάαλ." MT reads במות בעל, apparently a place name, but its location is completely uncertain. The word במות means "high places," and the translator must have read the word spelled without a vowel letter, i.e. as במת, since he rendered it by the singular τὴν στήλην, adding a preposition for good sense. The term means "stele, pillar," and occurs for במה at 21:28 33:52; see comment at 21:28, and more particularly, the Note at Lev 26:30 for the rendering of במה in the Pentateuch;[72] the word was apparently not understood by the Pentateuch translators. Copyists were troubled by the reference to Βάαλ, and the following misreadings obtain: βουαλ, βαλαλ, βαλααλ, βαλααμ, βαλαμ, βαλακ and βαλαακ.

V.b of MT says: "And he (i.e. Balaam) saw from there a part of the people." The word קצה means "extremity," and is so understood by Num with its μέρος τι "some part." Hex has placed τι under the obelus, as having no actual equivalent in MT. Num has a somewhat different view of the matter, making Balak the subject, and the verb transitive, i.e. ἔδειξεν αὐτῷ "showed him." The change is a sensible one, in that it makes Balaam somewhat more passive in the matter, and makes Balak the host on the tour.

---

71. Modern transations all emend the text. NJPS has "and had them served to," and NRSV reads "and sent them to," while NIV interprets as "and gave some to." All are troubled by the transitivity of the verbs in question.
72. Interesting is the way the Targums render the phrase. Tar[N] remains close to MT with לבמתה דבעלה. Tar[O] has לרמת דחלתה "to the high place of his God," and Tar[J] has לרמת דחלתא דפעור "to the high place of the God of Peor."

Chapter 23

23:1 Balaam said to Balak "Build for me here seven βωμούς." The Hebrew מזבחות is more commonly rendered by θυσιαστήρια, but LXX in general distinguishes between pagan altars (βωμοί) and legitimate Israelite altars (θυσιαστήρια).[1] The choice of βωμούς here is deliberate. An altar built by Balak is non-Israelite, pagan, and therefore illegitimate by definition.[2] Furthermore, he also told him to prepare seven bullocks and seven rams; presumably, to prepare them, meant to make them ready for sacrifice.

23:2 Balak did as εἶπεν αὐτῷ. In MT, the text reads "as דבר," which would usually become ἐλάλησεν in Num.[3] Hex placed αὐτῷ under the obelus, since the indirect object is not indicated in MT. According to Num, he (i.e. Balak) offered up a bullock and a ram on the altar (βωμόν). For the significance of βωμόν, see comment at v.1. Num does not specify the subject, but MT does; it was בלק ובלעם, and hex has added βαλακ και βαλααμ under the asterisk after the verb. By omitting the named subjects, Num rids Balaam of sacrificing animals on heathen altars.[4] What they did is, however, described in some detail at v.4, for which see comment ad loc, and see vv.14 and 30 as well.

23:3 Num has Balak told to stand alongside τῆς θυσίας σου, for which MT has עלתך. Though עלה is usually translated by ὁλοκαύτωμα, the translator uses the general word for "sacrifice" as well. No difference is intended, as is clear from v.6 where in the same context עלתו occurs, and Num has τῶν ὁλοκαυτωμάτων αὐτοῦ. But in v.15, it is again τῆς θυσίας σου, and in v.17 the same word becomes τῆς ὁλοκαυτώσεως.[5]

---

1. This distinction is not carried through by the Recensors; Aq, Sym and Theod all read θυσιαστήρια here.
2. On the distinction between βωμός and θυσιαστήριον in LXX, see Daniel 18.
3. See THGN 128 sub 15:1. Kenn 5,181 read אמר instead of דבר, and אמר was probably parent text for Num.
4. Kenn 185 also omits ובלעם.
5. See Daniel 245.

The next clause is καὶ πορεύσομαι. In MT, the verb is the long form, ואלכה, but it is doubtful that the long form means more than ואלך would; a cohortative intention would hardly be fitting here. The majority A V text has ἐγὼ δὲ instead of καί, which may well be simply a stylistic change. On the other hand, 4QNum[b] reads ואנוכי אלך, and I suspect that ἐγὼ δὲ (πορεύσομαι) is original text, and would suggest that the critical text be changed accordingly. This means that the B F M popular reading καί is probably a hex correction, since it is supported inter alia by O and Syh as well. The use of πορεύσομαι in isolation is intended to contrast with παράστηθι; i.e. Balak will go off (by himself) to seek divine direction.

The conditional structure which follows differs in a number of ways from MT. MT begins with אולי, and continues with יקרה יהוה לקראתי "Perhaps Yahweh might chance to meet me." As usual, Num substitutes ὁ θεός for יהוה.[6] For יקרה Num has φανεῖται "should appear," and has μοι in modification, but omits the first singular suffix of לקראתי. What Num says is "If God should appear to me in a meeting (ἐν συναντήσει)." Hex has made some attempts at changing the text to correspond to MT. μοι has been transposed to follow συναντήσει, and in its place (i.e. after the introductory εἰ) has added πως.[7]

The apodosis consists of two parts. In MT, these are ודבר מה יראני "and whatever word he might show me," and והגדתי לך "and I will relate to you." Num translates word for word, except for the second "and," which is fortunately omitted.[8]

MT then ends the verse with וילך שפי. The word שפי occurs only here and at Job 33:21 which is unfortunately a difficult text shedding no light on the passage here. The word may mean "a bare place, a barren height," but remains quite uncertain. In its place, Num has added a two clause insertion before it, detailing that both Balak and Balaam carried out what Balaam had ordered. Num reads: "And Balak stood alongside his sacrifice, and Balaam ἐπορεύθη ἐπερωτῆσαι τὸν θεόν, καὶ ἐπορεύθη εὐθεῖαν." Hex has placed all but the final clause under the obelus, as having no counterpart in MT. In other words, the rendering for וילך

---
6. Sam also reads אלהים, but the Num text did not necessarily have this as parent text.
7. Sym also read εἴ πως, which constitutes a nice attempt at rendering אולי.
8. See SS 34.

שפי must be the καὶ ἐπορεύθη clause "and he went a direct (or straight) road."[9] I understand the feminine adjective to presuppose some such noun as ὁδός.

But is the καὶ ἐπορεύθη a doublet interpretation? Is the "straight road" one in which Balaam seeks a divine oracle? If so, that is not immediately apparent. I would suggest that, as the first ἐπορεύθη clause reflects the carrying out of the order to Balak: παράστηθι ἐπὶ τῆς θυσίας σου, so the καὶ ἐπορεύθη clause reflects the carrying out of καὶ πορεύσομαι along with the εἰ structure which follows. Admittedly, it is not clear how this fits with εὐθεῖαν, which seems far removed from שפי, but that the translator misread the word as ישר is textually quite far-fetched.[10] I suspect that the straight road is similar to the lonely one which Tar⁰ suggests, one which the prophet walked to meet deity in search of instructions.

23:4 "And God appeared to Balaam, and Balaam said to him."[11] MT once again has the Ni of קרה as in v.3, which see, but did not name "Balaam" as the subject of the verb "said." Common sense dictates that it could hardly be אלהים, but Num makes this explicit. A V t z+ text has changed "Balaam" to βαλακ. This accords with vv.1—2; it was indeed Balak who built seven altars and then offered up a bullock and a ram on (each) altar. Somehow the obvious rendering of MT (and Num) "Seven altars (βωμούς) I prepared and offered a bullock and a ram on (each) altar" does not make sense, in fact, it contradicts vv.1—2; I would suggest that the verbs are to be taken as doubly transitive, i.e. "I had (an altar) prepared and had a bullock and a ram offered up on each altar." What is meant is then in line with vv.1—2, where Balaam ordered Balak both to build and to offer up.

23:5 Num throughout this chapter renders שים, the verb in the idiom "he put a word into the mouth (of Balaam)" by the verb ἐμβάλλω "cast, throw in," a picturesque way of putting it; cf comment at 22:38. What that word is is not clear

---

9. The Tar all had difficulty with שפי as well. Tar⁰ read אזל יחידי "he went alone." Tar^N expands this by its בלב יחידי שפי למילוט ית יסשאל "with singlemindedness, satisfied (i.e. ready) to curse Israel." Tar^J reads גחין כחויא "crawling like a snake" (reflecting the curse of Gen 3:14?).
10. But to speak of this doublet as a later gloss as Daniel 245—246 does is even more unacceptable.
11. It might be noted that Sam reads וימצא מלאך אלהים את בלעם. This avoids the notion that God himself should have appeared to Balaam.

until v.7. Once again the subject יהוה is changed to ὁ θεός. What God says is "returning to Balak, thus shall you speak." The imperative שוב is deemphasized by changing it to a subordinate participle, thus "when you return to Balak, thus must you speak." Usually when כה occurs with a verb of speaking, what is to be said follows, but here the οὕτως refers to the ῥῆμα which God cast into Balaam's mouth.

23:6 On his return to Balak, "והנה was standing by his burnt offering, הוא and all the chieftains of Moab." Since נצב has no apparent subject, Num has substituted for והנה the demonstrative pronoun ὅδε, thus "this one (i.e. Balak) stood by his τῶν ὁλοκαυτωμάτων." This then made הוא superfluous, and Num omitted it, but added μετ' αὐτοῦ at the end.[12] The plural noun is unexpected, since at v.3 Num read ἐπὶ τῆς θυσίας αὐτοῦ, but it reflects v.2, where more than one animal, μόσχον καὶ κρίον, were sacrificed. The translator thereby makes the account more consistent.

The verse ends with καὶ ἐγενήθη πνεῦμα θεοῦ ἐπ' αὐτῷ. This has no equivalent in MT, but at 24:2 this same clause serves as an introduction to the καὶ ἀναλαβὼν τὴν παραβολὴν αὐτοῦ of the following verse. The translator must have had the ותהי עליו רוח אלהים of 24:2 as parent text here as well. That this is not a borrowing from the Num text, and therefore secondary, is clear, since ותהי is here rendered by καὶ ἐγενήθη, whereas in ch.24 it became καὶ ἐγένετο. Hex placed the clause here under the obelus, since it was absent from MT. For its relevance, see comment at 24:2.

23:7 The term משל, which occurs in the Bible 37 times, is most commonly rendered by παραβολή as here (29 times).[13] In fact, παραβολή is used only to translate משל, and it may well be called a calque, i.e. it must have the same sense as the Hebrew word משל. Since in the Balaam narrative it is used throughout as something which God was speaking through him, the term "oracle" comes to mind. The first of such παραβολαί is introduced by καὶ ἀναλαβὼν τὴν παραβολὴν αὐτοῦ εἶπεν, representing two coordinate clauses in MT. The first clause in MT reads וישא משלו. The notion of "lift up, raise" implies "and he raised his

---

12. SS 73 characterizes these differences as representing an "ungewöhnliche Übersetzungsweise."
13. According to HR.

voice to speak (a משל)." The reading ἀναλαβών is a somewhat plebeian rendering, i.e. it simply says "taking up his oracle"; "taking up" must include "lifting up one's voice to speak."

Μεσοποταμία occurs 18 times in the Bible, of which 14 are in the Pentateuch, mainly in Gen. It is unique as a rendering for ארם.[14] In Gen it usually occurs for פדן or for פדן ארם, and once for ארם נהרים (24:10). Whether the Alexandrian translator had a clear geographic picture of the area is uncertain. It only occurs here in the book, and I doubt that any valid geographic identification can be drawn from its use here, particularly since the gentilic form ארמי is usually rendered by Συροῦ "the Syrian." In the next line the region is called (ἐξ) ὀρέων ἀπ' ἀνατολῶν "the mountains from the East." In MT, this is a bound phrase הררי קדם, and the omission of ἀπ' by the b f+ text equals MT more precisely, though the omission is hardly recensional.[15]

Since the next two lines constitute what Balak actually said, Num has added λέγων to introduce it, though MT does not have the direct speech indicator, and hex has placed the word under the obelus. The couplet reflects the prose invitations of 22:6,17. It reads "come, ἄρασαι for me Jacob, and come, ἐπικατάρασαί μοι Israel."[16] It might be noted that ἄρασαι/ארה here contrasts with ἐπικατάρασαι/זעמה, whereas in 22:6 and 22:17 these reflected the Hebrew ארה vs קבה; cf comment at v.8 on זעם. MT has no equivalent for the μοι of the second line of the couplet, and hex has placed it under the obelus to indicate that fact.[17] I would render the last line by "and come, damn Israel for me."

23:8 In Balaam's protest, the equivalences are again different. In line one ἀράσομαι—ἀρᾶται reflect אקב and קבה resp., but at v.7 ἄρασαι represented ארה, and at 22:17 ἐπικατάρασαι was used. It reads "how shall I curse whom the Lord does not curse"? Line two uses a different verb, זעם "denounce," and hence

---

14. Though at Jdg 3:8 where ארם נהרים occurs in MT, the Greek has Συρίας ποταμῶν, but hex inserts μεσοποταμιας under the asterisk between the two.
15. It is rather a case of omission due to homoiarchon: (ἀπ') ἀνατολῶν.
16. For ἄρασαι, Syh quotes The Three as reading k'y. Precisely what Greek imperative this renders is problematic. The Pa verb means "rebuke severely," but that it was chosen to represent ארה over against, and to contrast with, the זעמה of the second line is strange indeed. I suspect that the index in Syh is over the wrong "curse," i.e. that it really belongs to ἐπικατάρασαι, in which case the reading interprets זעמה, and I could then suggest the Greek ἐμβριμῶ; comp Field at Pss 7:12 and 37:4.
17. The evidence is based on Syh, which, however, lacks the metobelus in the ms.

"to curse," which in v.7 was translated by ἐπικατάραομαι. Num uses καταράομαι "pronounce a curse, to execrate." The line reads "or how shall I execrate whom God does not execrate"? MT does not have the correlative conjunction, but introduces the line by ומה. The Byz text has changed ἤ to καί, which equals MT. One peculiarity of Num is that it has κύριος for אל in line one, but ὁ θεός for יהוה in line 2. The use of κύριος might at first blush appear contrary to the general attitude of the translator, but at 22:19 he had also used κύριος as naming the one whom Balaam sought out: προσθήσει κύριος λαλῆσαι πρός με. It was certainly true that κύριος had not cursed Israel!

In both lines Num has clarified MT by making the second clause within each line a relative clause. MT actually reads: "How shall I curse—God has not cursed him; and how shall I denounce—Yahweh has not denounced." The first line is correctly understood; the relative pronoun represents the suffix of קבה, i.e. the "him." The second line sound somewhat cryptic, and Num has simplified it by understanding the זעם as also implying a suffix, and has quite correctly interpreted the line as fully parallel to the first line.[18]

23:9 The first couplet reads: "Because from the top of mountains, I shall see him (i.e. Israel); and from the hills I shall regard him." This differs from MT only in the understanding of צרים "rocks" as ὀρέων "mountains." The translation is unique, though understandable. Since it is parallel to גבעות, צרים probably is to be taken as referring to rocky heights; certainly, ὀρέων is a better parallel to βουνῶν than πετρῶν would be.

The last two lines predict a unique future for Israel. They read: "Behold a people shall dwell alone; not will it be reckoned together among nations." To dwell μόνος means "by itself, safely, without external alliances." This is reaffirmed in the last line. The "nations" are the non-Israelites; Israelites constitute the λαὸς μόνος. The two lines complement each other neatly; being συλλογισθήσεται would involve external alliances, but these are not to characterize Israel's future.

23:10 The first couplet reads: "Who has reckoned precisely the seed of Jacob; and who may number the citizenry of Israel"? The first line reflects MT's מי מנה

---

18. The Tar all add a pronoun after the last verb as well.

עפר יעקב "who has counted the dust of Jacob"? The interpretation of עפר as τὸ σπέρμα reflects the promise made to Abram at Gen 13:16: "I will make τὸ σπέρμα σου ὡς τὴν ἄμμον τῆς γῆς." In fact, "if anyone can count the dust of the earth, also your seed may be counted." In the tradition, the ol b x+ text reads εξηκριβωσατο, which is a synonym of the verb in Num. Also witnessed is the verb εξιχνιαζομαι, either in the present tense by C'' or in the aorist by s; the verb means "to track down, trace out," but neither of these is an improvement on Num.

The second line is not as easily explained. MT's text reads ומספר את רבע ישראל. Obviously, the translator made the first word to read ומי יספר "and who may number."[19] But just what the רבע of Israel means is difficult to determine. The word רבע means "a quarter." Can this possibly mean "even a quarter of Israel's people"? Then it could be a true parallel to line one: "Who has counted the dust of Jacob; and who shall number (even) one quarter of Israel's descendants"? If this interpretation be granted, the rendering of רבע by δήμους can at least be understood. δῆμοι basically means "clans," but is often used to refer to people in general, to the citizenry of a land. In other words, Num is probably a reasonable interpretation of its parent text.[20]

The second couplet reads "and may my person (ψυχή) die among the persons (ψυχαῖς) of the righteous, and may my seed be like their (τούτων) seed." I have avoided translating ψυχή/נפש by "soul," since נפש refers to the "self," not to a "soul," and the line simply means "may I die among the righteous ones." MT reads differently; it has "May I (נפשי) die the death of the upright (ישרים)."

For the last line MT has ותהי אחריתי כמהו "and may my latter end be like his (i.e. Israel's)." The term אחרית means "end, that which comes afterwards," and it can then mean in a concrete sense "posterity." The rendering σπέρμα μου for אחריתי is thus a reasonable interpretation. The repetition of τὸ σπερμα in the ὡς structure is then an ad sensum addition, since MT simply has כמהו. Presumably, the τούτων of Num could refer to Ἰσραήλ, though more likely its antecedent is δήμους.

---

19. It should be noted that Sam reads ומי ספר. I would suggest that by dittography יספר was read; this would explain the change in tense to a future from an aorist in line one.
20. Theod read for line two καὶ ἀριθμὸν ἑνὸς ἐξ τεσσάρων τοῦ Ἰσραήλ, and Aq has λογισμὸν ἑνὸς ἐξ τεσσάρων τοῦ Ἰσραήλ (both retroverted from Syh).

23:11 Balak was quite unhappy. "What πεποίηκάς to me"? The majority A F M text has the aorist ἐποίησα instead of the perfect, but the perfect is original text. Since the aorist is the default tense, it occurs commonly; here, however, it is the perfect that shows the lasting effect of a past action, and it is used intentionally.

The use of κέκληκά σε instead of לקהתיך is a case of harmonization. In chapter 22 where Balak sent a delegation to Balaam, it is καλέσαι Balaam (vv.5, 20,37), not "to take" him, and Num creates a more consistent narrative. By contrast, Balak says καὶ ἰδοὺ εὐλόγηκας εὐλογίαν "and behold, you have blessed (i.e. uttered) a blessing." MT has the verb ברכת followed by a cognate free infinitive, thus "you have actually blessed (them)." This is an unusual order, since the free infinitive usually precedes the noun,[21] but it also stresses the verbal notion from this position.

23:12 Instead of ויען ויאמר, Num states "and Balaam said to Balak"; the identification of speaker and addressee is simply a matter of keeping straight who is talking to whom. It should be noted that this is characteristic of the dialogue form of the Balaam narrative as a whole; comp 22:9,10,29,30,34,35,37,38 23:2,3,13,15, 25—27,29 24:10,12.

What Balaam says is put in the form of an οὐχί question, i.e. a question requiring an affirmative answer. It reflects what he had told Balak earlier at 22:38, but now stated even more strongly: οὐχί ... τοῦτο φυλάξω λαλῆσαι "this must I not be careful to speak"? Cf also comment at 22:35. Once again, Num substitutes ὁ θεός for יהוה, for which see comments at 22:9,22, and especially v.23.

23:13 According to MT, Balak now says to Balaam לך נא "pray go (with me)"; normally Num does not render the particle נא, but here he substitutes ἔτι "yet, still," thus "go with me to yet another place," which has nothing to do with נא, but is an ad sensum gloss. The word "place" is modified by a relative clause: ἐξ ὧν οὐκ ὄψῃ αὐτὸν ἐκεῖθεν. The use of the plural relative pronoun is unexpected, and can only be some kind of ad sensum reference to "heights" or "vantage points." One would expect a singular οὗ, and all witnesses, except B V plus four mss and Syh, attest to οὗ. But this must be a simplification of the text. If οὗ were

---

21. See GK 113r.

original, it would be difficult to understand how ὧν would develop, and here the more difficult reading must be original. In any event, the statement by itself would not make good sense, but it is explained in the next two clauses: ἀλλ' ἢ μέρος τι αὐτοῦ ὄψῃ, πάντας δὲ οὐ μὴ ἴδῃς "but some part of it (i.e. of Israel) you will see, though not will you see all (the parts)." πάντας is plural, and translates כלו "all of it," and Num naturally did not translate the suffix, but used the plural instead,[22] which also substantiates the originality of the plural ὧν; cf comment above.

V.b states: "and execrate for me him (i.e. Israel) from there."[23] MT reads וקבנו לי, and ms 426 and C'' have transposed μοι αὐτόν, thereby equalling the word order of MT. This could be understood as a recensional correction.

23:14 According to MT, Balak then brought him to שדה צפים "field of watchers," or probably "field of Ṣophim." To the translator, this did not make a great deal of sense, so he translated it by reversing the two terms, i.e. by εἰς ἀγροῦ σκοπιάν "to a watchtower of the field." By retaining the word order of MT, i.e. ἀγροῦ before σκοπιάν, Num attempted to show the Hebrew text, but the case inflections show the syntactic relations. In the context, this makes sense, since it is located ἐπὶ κορυφὴν λελαξευμένου "on the crest of the Hewn Rock." This odd rendering for הפסגה "Mt. Pisgah" was already seen at 21:20; for the translation, see Note at Deut 3:27.

For v.b, see comments at vv.1—2. Here, however, ויעל is translated not by καὶ ἀνήνεγκεν "and he offered up," but by καὶ ἀναβίβασεν and he brought up." Admittedly, עלה in the Hi means "made to go up," but it also means "to offer up, to sacrifice." The rendering here seems to me wooden; common sense would dictate that what Balak did was to sacrifice a bullock and a ram on the altar.

The subject of ᾠκοδόμησεν remains Balak. Num has added ἐκεῖ, which parallels the ἐνταῦθα of v.1, but it has no counterpart in MT.

23:15 MT continues without stating the subject: "And (he) said to Balak," which Num clarifies by added Βαλαάμ after εἶπεν.[24] I suspect that Num here represents original text; see the remark on ויען ויאמר at v.12, a remark which might well

---

22. See SS 100.
23. For the rendering "execrates" for κατάρασαι, see comment at v.8.
24. As do Kenn 69,206 and Pesh.

apply here as well. Num repeats the command of v.3: παράστηθι ἐπὶ τῆς θυσίας σου, but MT added כה after the imperative. Hex has accordingly added αυτου under the asterisk after παράστηθι. Num had followed Sam, which also lacks כה. In fact, MT uses כה again in the next clause: ואנכי אקרה כה "and as for me, I will meet (God) yonder." The two cases of כה are used in the sense of "here ... yonder." Num has disregarded both, but interpreted it here as he did in v.3, where Balak went ἐπερωτῆσαι τὸν θεόν, while Balak remained at his sacrifice; cf discussion ad loc. So instead of אקרה כה, Num has (ἐγὼ δὲ) πορεύσομαι ἐπερωτῆσαι τὸν θεόν. This does make clear what the mysterious אקרה "I will encounter" intends. Over against Balak, who must stay by his sacrifice, Balaam will go off to seek a divine oracle.

23:16 Once again, it is ὁ θεός who met with Balaam, rather than the יהוה of MT. Instead of ἀποστράφητι, the majority text has αποστραφηθι, which can not be correct. The imperative is active, not passive. It does, however, show that Byzantine copyists easily confused the *theta* and the *tau*, even though they are phonemically distinct; the confusion did not extend to any of the uncial texts, however, i.e. the confusion is found only in late Byzantine mss, with the oldest ms supporting the variant text, 407, written late in the tenth century. For the rendering of וישם by καὶ ἐνέβαλεν, see comment at v.5.

23:17 Rather than translate MT, Num took over his own translation of v.6, except for correcting the plural τῶν ὁλοκαυτωμάτων to a singular τῆς ὁλοκαυτώσεως.[25] MT does differ, however, in the initial verb which reads ויבא "and he came in" rather than καὶ ἀπεστράφη; the latter is contextually more fitting. MT also has no equivalent for πάντες, and hex has placed it under the obelus.[26]

For v.b it should be noted that Balak's question is correctly rendered by τί ἐλάλησεν κύριος. Balak naturally knew Balaam's God to be Yahweh; it would then be quite proper for Balak to speak of Balaam as Yahweh's prophet; it is the translator who prefers to regard Balaam, a non-Israelite, as a prophet of God, not of Israel's God, κύριος.

---

25. See Daniel 252.
26. The obelus is wrongly placed in Syh[L].

23:18 For v.a, see comment at v.7. In the tradition, the Byz text added βαλααμ after ἀναλαβών. The gloss is correct, though unnecessary, but avoids the possible understanding that Balak was the subject; after all, it was Balak who was the subject of v.17b.

The couplet beginning the second oracle of Balaam, vv.18b—24, is a call to attention. "Stand up, Balak, and hear; give ear as a witness, O son of Sepphor." The second line is somewhat different in MT. It reads האזינה עדי, i.e. "give ear to me (O son of Sippor)." Num has misread עדי "to me," as עד "witness." The use of עדי as preposition modifying האזינה is strange, though it is not impossible; cf Job 32:11 where עד תבונתיכם modifies אזין.

23:19 The first couplet reads "Not like a person is God in that he should be deceived; nor like a human being in that he might be threatened." The translator has rendered the structure *waw* plus a verb with prefix inflection in both lines by a passive infinitive showing how the deity is not to be perceived. In both lines the translator has added ὡς; in other words, he has avoided any notion of God being human in any way; rather he is "unlike" a person. Even a negative statement: "is not איש," is avoided by changing איש to ὡς ἄνθρωπος. איש means "a man, a male," an ἀνήρ, but Num has chosen the generic term which I have translated by "person," since ἄνθρωπος has no sexual connotation. The infinitive διαρτηθῆναι is aorist passive of διαρτάω. MT is, however, active ויכזב "that he might tell a lie."[27]

The infinitive in line two is ἀπειληθῆναι, an aorist passive infinitive of ἀπειλέω "to threaten," thus "that he would be threatened." MT has ויתנחם "and he would repent, change his mind." The translator avoided a literal translation. Not only does God not repent, he cannot be coerced in any way.[28]

The second pair of lines reads "would he, having said, not act; speak, and not carry through"?[29] The translator correctly understood that the interrogative particle of ההוא applied to the entire couplet. Why the translator varied the struc-

---

27 Theod and Aq read καὶ διαψεύσεται, whereas Sym has ἵνα (δια)ψεύσεται. It is not certain whether the compound is to be read or the simplex, since it depends on the exact placement (and its interpretation) of the index sign in the text.
28. Sym has ἵνα μετανοήσῃ.
29. For the first line, Aq has οὐχὶ οὗτος εἶπεν, καὶ ποιήσει (retroverted from Syh). What Aq has made of it is: "Is it not the case that when he has said something, then he will do (it)"?

tures for the two lines is not clear. For the first one, he subordinated the first verb to a participle εἴπας, but in the second one he used a future verb, though omitting the conjunction of ודבר; i.e. he followed the text of Sam, דבר.

23:20 The first line in MT reads: Behold, to bless I have received (orders). The verb is לקחתי, which Num understood as passive, παρείλημμαι, the perfect passive of παραλαμβάνω "to take, receive." What Num says is "Behold, to bless I have been taken," i.e. "been invited."

The second line is clear in MT. It reads: "And when he blesses, I cannot turn it back." In other words, what God does I cannot undo. Num has understood the first word, וברך, not as a third masculine singular verb, but as a contextual free infinitive, which the consonantal text allows (though omitting the conjunction). Such an infinitive takes on the inflectional meaning of its context; since it is both preceded and followed by first singular inflected verbs, it too is understood as a first singular verb. On the other hand, instead of וברך, Sam reads אברך, and this may well have been the parent text of Num. Since the second verb is future, אשיבנה, our translator has rendered line two by εὐλογήσω καὶ οὐ μὴ ἀποστρέψω "I will bless and will not turn aside (or reverse)." Num has made the verb absolute, not rendering the suffix. Hex has added αυτην under the asterisk to represent it, thereby forcing a transitive meaning for the verb.

23:21 Num had some difficulty with the first couplet of MT. The verbs are in third person singular, viz. הביט and ראה. Presumably, they are best taken as indefinite, and the lines probably mean: "Not has one observed mischief in Jacob, nor seen trouble in Israel." The exact meaning of the nouns און and עמל is difficult to define, but something like "mischief and trouble" (as connected with toil) was probably intended. Num misunderstood the couplet as a pronounced blessing, and so used future verbs. Though the Hebrew verbs are synonyms, this itself created difficulty for the translator. The second line was rendered by a passive transform in which עמל as πόνος "toil, distress" was changed to the subject of a passive verb: οὐδὲ ὀφθήσεται πόνος ἐν Ἰσραήλ "nor shall distress be seen (i.e. appear) in Israel."

That left line one, in which the translator boldly abandoned the notion of seeing entirely and stated flatly "οὐκ ἔσται μόχθος ἐν Ἰακώβ "nor shall there be hardship in Jacob." Once the notion that the line is a blessing is adopted, the interpretation that "one shall not see" can simply mean "there will not be."

For line three MT was rendered literally by Num: "the Lord his God is with him." In both lines the αὐτοῦ refers to Israel/Jacob.

But in line four Num does not render literally. MT reads ותרועת מלך בו "and the acclaim of a king is in it (i.e. in Israel)." Num interpreted תרועת as a plural τὰ ἔνδοξα "glorious things or acts." Admittedly, תרועה is a difficult word to define. It is something audible, a joyous cultic shout, or a trumpet blast (see σημασίαν at 10:5—6), or an outcry. Translators range from σημασία (9 times), ἀλαλαγμός (8), κραυγή (8), φωνή (3), ἐξομολόγησις (2). On the other hand, ἐνδόξος is a unique rendering (as are ἀγαλλίασις, ἐξηγορία, and σάλπιγξ).[30] But the rest of the line ought to have given no trouble, except that the term מלך constituted a red flag to the translator. For Num the only king for Israel was Yahweh/κύριος, and accordingly, he substituted ἀρχόντων (ἐν αὐτῷ).[31] So Num changed the line to read "the glorious deeds of chieftains (or rulers) are in it (i.e. in Israel)." Obviously, this departure was an intentional avoidance of the notion of a king in Israel. It certainly is not what MT meant or said.

23:22 Though the verse is poetically a couplet, it is best understood as a single syntagm. I would suggest that the colon after Αἰγύπτου should be deleted from the critical text. I would then translate Num: "The God who brought them (the people) out of Egypt is like the glory of the unicorn for him (i.e. Israel)." What is meant by the simile is that the redeemer God is as resplendent as the fabled unicorn, understood as a beast celebrated for its ferocity and power. In other words, Israel's God is gloriously invincible.

Whether this more or less interprets MT correctly is not certain, since the second line, i.e. the simile, is difficult to understand. It reads כתועפת ראם לו. The word that is unclear is תועפת. It is bound to ראם "wild ox," which is almost always rendered by μονοκέρως in the Bible, and for which see Note at Deut 33:17. What is almost certain is that it does not mean δόξα. Modern translators have simply guessed at its meaning. NRSV has "strength," whereas NJPS and NIV have "horns." I refuse to take part in this guessing game.

In the tradition, a number of variants merit comment. Cod B plus one ms omit the article at the beginning of the verse. This is a purely palaeographically

---

30. The statistics are from Dos Santos. This diffusion (or confusion) is also evident among the recensors. Aq rendered by ἀλαλαγμός; Sym, by σημασία, and Theod, by σαλπισμός.
31. The Three all read βασιλέως ἐν αὐτῷ.

inspired error. In the uncial text the letters ΟΘΕΟΣΟΕ are all much alike, and the omission by haplography of the first ὁ is almost unavoidable. What is remarkable is that it does not happen more often. In Num the nominative θεός is always articulated.[32] The pronoun αὐτούς refers to the people of Israel, but at the end of the verse αὐτῷ also refers to Israel. It is then not surprising that a majority A F M text has αυτον instead of αὐτούς, but Num has followed MT meticulously here. MT reads "them" and "to him," and so does Num. A popular reading has changed ἐξ (Αἰγύπτου) to εκ γης,[33] but again Num reads ממצרים literally and correctly.

23:23 The first couplet reads "For there is no portent in Jacob, nor divination in Israel." This sets the stage for the next couplet: "in due course (or at the proper time) there will be said to Jacob and Israel, what God will do." Num with its future makes a more appropriate reaction to the first couplet than the פעל "has done" of MT. After all, augury and divination are both intent on predicting what is going to happen. But neither οἰωνισμός nor μαντεία are permitted in Israel; neither one will (or can) say what God will be accomplishing, ἐπιτελέσει. What God has done needs no prediction, but what God will accomplish will be told when the time is opportune (κατὰ καιρόν) by means of a prophetic word.

In MT, both "Jacob" and "Israel" are each governed by ל, but only Ἰσραήλ is articulated by τῷ. Hex has added a τω under the asterisk before Ἰακώβ as well to represent the preposition. The two names do not refer to distinct entities; both refer to the same people. I would make this clear by rendering καὶ τῷ Ἰσραήλ by "even to Israel."

23:24 The oracle uses the simile of the lion's cub and the lion for the people of Israel. The first couplet reads "Behold, a people like a lion's cub will rise up, and as a lion will show itself proudly." The renderings, σκύμνος and λέων are attempts to distinguish between לביא and ארי, both of which mean "lion," though לביא may also be taken as "lioness." MT has "shall rouse itself," יתנשא, for the second verb. But the general picture is not incorrectly shown.

---

32. See THGN 107.
33. As does Tar[N].

The next couplet is rendered literally; it continues the figure of the people as a lion: "he will not lie down until he will have eaten prey, and (until) he will have drunk the blood of the slain."

23:25 Better to say nothing is Balak's reaction: "Neither with curses curse μοι him, nor blessing bless him." The μοι has no correspondent in MT, but corresponds to Balak's original order to Balaam ἄρασαί μοι τὸν λαὸν τοῦτον at 22:6. The translator was faced with two גם negative clauses, and neatly used οὔτε ... οὔτε to translate them. MT has two clauses with cognate free infinitives introducing inflected verbs: קב לא תקבנו and ברך לא תברכנו, which are exactly parallel, but Num renders them differently. In the first one he translated the infinitive by a plural dative noun, κατάραις, but in the second one, by a present participle, εὐλογῶν. Thus "neither curse him with curses, nor actually bless him." Furthermore, though in MT a לא precedes the verb in both clauses, in Num the second clause has as its verb μή plus a subjunctive, whereas in the first clause, the verb is future, καταράσῃ, and therefore without μή. Of course, both clauses are introduced by οὔτε, which suffices to negate the future of the first clause.

23:26 In Gen ויען ויאמר was always (12 times) translated by a participle plus verb structure as here; in Num the Hebrew pattern occurs only four times; twice (also at 11:28) it is translated by the above structure, once (22:18), by καὶ ἀπεκρίθη καὶ εἶπεν, and once, by a completely different pattern; see v.12. The ἀποκριθεὶς εἶπεν pattern is good Greek style.

Balaam's reply is put into an οὐκ question, i.e. one expecting an affirmative answer: "did I not speak to you as follows"? In MT, the quoted speech reads כל אשר ידבר יהוה אתו אעשה "everything which Yahweh will speak, it I must do." Num has a slightly different statement; כל is rendered by τὸ ῥῆμα as at 22:20; cf Sam's כל הדבר, which is, however, probably irrelevant; the translator simply stayed close to Yahweh's original order to Balaam at 22:20. As usual, יהוה becomes ὁ θεός, though this time Sam does read האלהים, which is probably irrelevant as well. אתו is translated by τοῦτο, as at v.12 and 22:20.

In the tradition, a popular A F text has changed the initial καὶ ἀποκριθείς to ἀποκριθεὶς δέ. This is a stylistic change, since the reply of v.26 contrasts with Balak's orders to desist in v.25, but the Hebraic pattern is original.

23:27 The richness of Greek vocabulary is neatly illustrated by the translation of אקחך "I will take you" by the compound verb παραλάβω σε "I will take you along." The particle נא, which precedes it in modification of לכה, is, as generally throughout the book, disregarded. אולי "perhaps" is always translated in Num by an "if" particle, i.e. by εἰ or ἐάν; see v.3 and 22:6,11,33. So אולי יישר בעיני האלהים "perhaps it would appear right in the eyes of God" is translated by εἰ ἀρέσει τῷ θεῷ "if it should please God." The Greek idiom is a good interpretation of the Hebrew, i.e. "to be right in the eyes" does mean "to please."

The final clause is put into the imperative "and execrate for me αὐτόν (i.e. Israel) from there." MT has a second singular וקבתו "and you may execrate him." Hex has transposed μοι αὐτόν to conform to the word order of MT.

23:28 Then Balak "took Balaam along to the crest of Φογόρ, τὸ παρατεῖνον to the desert." MT refers to the ראש הפעור הנשקף על פני הישימן "to the top of Peor, which over hangs the face of the desert," i.e. which borders on the desert; comp 21:20. The transcription Φογώρ demonstrates that the ע grapheme did double duty for Classical Hebrew; it represents either a *ghayin* or an *ʿayin* phoneme, and the translator was aware of the distinction, which was still active in the Hebrew of his community. Examples of the *ghayin* pronunciation are Γάζα—עזה, Γαιβάλ—עיבל, Γασιών—עציון, Γόμορρα—עמרה, Γοθολία—עתליה and cf also Γελμών—עלמן at 33:46.

The syntax of τὸ παρατεῖνον is not obvious. It apparently describes Phogor, but that is in the genitive. I would take the neuter to represent an understood τὸ (ὄρος), which would then intend τὸ παρατεῖνον as an apposite of (εἰς) τὴν κορυφὴν Φογόρ," thus "to the crest of Phogor, on the (mountain) bordering (or extending along) on the desert", literally "on the one stretching out into the desert."[34] Unfortunately for the grammarian, the translator is repeated careless in referring to antecedents not expressly stated but simply implied. Alternatively, the apposite structure might be understood as "even on (Phogor) bordering on the desert."

---

34. Dorival 185—186 offers another explanation. He takes it as an adverbial phrase, along with τὸ ἐξέχον (21:13) and τὸ βλέπον (21:20) "sont sans doute des tournures à valeur adverbiale et de sens géographique," and translates it by "à proximité." This is not impossible, but see my comments at 21:13,20.

In the tradition, the Byz+ text has changed παρέλαβεν ... ἐπί to παραλαβών ... ανεβιβασεν αυτον επι. This has no textual basis in MT, but is imported from 22:41, which see.

23:29—30 MT repeats the text of v.1 word for word, and Num makes only two changes. In v.1 בזה is twice rendered by ἐνταῦθα, but here the translator uses ὧδε. Num also reads πρὸς (Βαλάκ) rather than τῷ. Num also repeats v.2 with one exception; instead of ὃν τρόπον, v.30 uses the synonym καθάπερ. That the translator actually cites his own vv.1—2 rather than retranslating the Hebrew text of vv.29—30 is clear from the differences between the MT of vv.2 and 30. At v.2 MT read דבר, whereas at v.30 this becomes אמר; furthermore, at v.2 MT had ויעל בלק ובלעם, i.e. had identified the subjects as "Balak and Balaam"; this Num had changed to καὶ ἀνήνεγκεν, which equals the ויעל of v.30; cf comment at v.2. Similarly, both vv.2 and 30 added αὐτῷ after εἶπεν, which has no basis in MT in either verse. It is thus the text of Num at v.2, not that of MT, that is the basis for Num here.

Chapter 24

24:1 Vv.1—2 constitute an introduction to a third oracle, but this time fully divorced from Balak's instigation. The opening clause of MT is subordinated to a participle: "and Balaam seeing ... went ...." What Balaam said was "that καλόν ἐστιν ἔναντι κυρίου εὐλογεῖν τὸν Ἰσραήλ." This represents a nominal structure in MT, i.e. the Hebrew has no linking verb, and hex has consequently placed ἐστιν under the obelus. The conclusion that Balaam had arrived at was that it was useless to try to persuade the Lord to change his mind, as Balak had hoped for (23:27), since he was determined (it was καλόν ... ἔναντι κυρίου) to bless Israel.

The main clause then has it that "he did not go κατὰ τὸ εἰωθός to meet (i.e. seek to find) omens." The κατά phrase, "according to custom," is a correct interpretation of כפעם בפעם "as on occasions (i.e. on previous occurrences)." What the κατά phrase means is "as he was accustomed to do." The departure from his usual practice is then described in the coordinate clause "and he ἀπέστρεψεν his face towards the desert." The verb used is unique as a translation for וישת "and he set"; the translator, by choosing this verb, presupposes that Balaam had been facing Moab, i.e. internally in response to Balak's importunities. Now he acts on his own, turning towards the desert. It is of course possible that the translator mistakenly thought of וישב which in the Qal is translated by ἀποστρέφω 202 times in LXX.[1]

It will have been noted that in view of the changed circumstance, יהוה in the כי clause had not been changed to τοῦ θεοῦ, but is rendered by the usual κυρίου. The unusual לקראת נחשים "to meet divinations" is rendered literally by εἰς συνάντησιν τοῖς οἰωνοῖς "to meet with omens." Presumably, what is meant by this is "to look for and find."[2]

24:2 Num reduces the first clause to an attributive participial structure: καὶ ἐξάρας Βαλαὰμ τοὺς ὀφθαλμοὺς αὐτοῦ. MT then continues with וירא which he does not translate by the usual ὁρᾷ, but uniquely by καθορᾷ "looked down," i.e.

---

1. According to the count in Dos Santos.
2. Sym, however, also renders literally by εἰς ἀπάντησιν τοῖς οἰωνοῖς (retroverted from Syh).

"he saw from a higher position"; in other words, he now stood on a height from which he saw Israel, not in part, but having encamped according to tribes." MT has שכן לשבטיו "dwelling according to its tribes." Hex has added αυτου under the asterisk after φυλάς. Num renders the participle by a perfect participle, which is reasonable. The Hebrew's "dwelling" means that the Israelites had formed their encampment, and were now dwelling.

The final clause, καὶ ἐγένετο πνεῦμα θεοῦ ἐπ' αὐτῷ, also occurs at 23:6 with one change, viz. ἐγενήθη for ἐγένετο, to introduce the first oracle; this had been paralleled at 23:16 with respect to the second oracle (vv.18—24) by καὶ ἐνέβαλεν (i.e. with ὁ θεός) ῥῆμα εἰς τὸ στόμα αὐτοῦ (of Balaam). That the divine spirit happened on Balaam attributes the oracle (vv.3—9) to divine inspiration, and not to τοῖς οἰωνοῖς which he had sought. In this way, the narrative ensures the authenticity of the oracle.

In the tradition, ἐπ' αὐτῷ was transposed with πνεῦμα θεοῦ, by a majority A F text. This change in word order is almost certainly hex in origin; all the usual supporters of the hex text, O'′ Arab and Syh, support this order which accords with MT's order עליו רוח אלהים. Note that θεοῦ is unarticulated, not only here, but throughout this chapter (five times) as well as in the borrowed text at 23:6, but elsewhere it is with one exception (6:7) always articulated throughout the book. And the B b text has changed ἐπ' to εν, which hardly reflects עליו; it must be secondary.[3]

24:3 For v.a, see comment at 23:7. The passive participle נאם is used in reference to prophetic oracular statements. It means "something uttered, oracled," and φησίν is its active counterpart. MT normally uses it as the bound element of a bound phrase. Thus in line one it means "an oracled (word) of Balaam," which Num rendered by "Balaam utters." What he actually utters begins at v.5.

The second line is parallel to line one, though MT joins the two lines with *waw*, but in Num line 2 is asyndetic. Parallel to Βαλαάμ is ὁ ἄνθρωπος ὁ ἀληθινῶς ὁρῶν "the person who truly saw," i.e. the person with true vision. The ἄνθρωπος translates הגבר "the strong man." The adverb describing ὁρῶν is Num's rendering for שתם, which appears only here and in the same context at v.15. The word is unknown, though Aramaic does recognize the verb in the sense

---

3. See THGN 97.

of "to unseal, to open," which would fit contextually. But another שתם, a hapax legomenon occurring at Lam 3:8, means "to shut out sound," thus "to close," where LXX reads ἀπέφραξε (προσευχήν μου) for שתם תפלתי, i.e. "he has blocked up, sealed off my prayer." Presumably, the translator hedged his bets. One could understand the line as "The utterance of the man with eyes open," or "with eyes (i.e. physical eyes) closed," but seeing with inner vision. With either understanding the prophet is ὁ ἀληθινῶς ὁρῶν, one who truly sees.[4]

24:4 "One who hears the λόγια of God utters." The λόγια is perhaps best rendered by "sayings," and renders אמרי.

Lines two and three should in my opinion be read together. The reference is still to Balaam, the man who truly sees. He both utters the sayings of God, and is one "who saw a vision of God in a dream, his eyes having been uncovered." The word "God" is the translation of שדי, often rendered by "the Almighty." Num does not differentiate between שדי, אל and אלהים, all three being rendered by ὁ θεός.

MT has a somewhat different understanding. It has "who sees (יחזה) a vision of שדי, falling with eyes opened." Num did not necessarily have a different text. The participle נפל is understood as "falling in a prophetic trance," i.e. "in a dream, or ecstatic state."[5] In the translator's view, the divine revelation comes ἐν ὕπνῳ, but differs from the ordinary dream state in that the eyes remain open, which might be thought of as a ancient description of the visionary state.[6]

24:5 The actual oracle begins with a descriptive praise of Israel: "how beautiful (are) your houses, o Jacob, your tents, o Israel." Since σου οἱ οἶκοι represents אהליך, the majority A F M text's transposition of σου and οἱ οἶκοι may well be recensional (probably hex). That "your tents" should become "your houses," and משכנתיך, "your tents" is mere poetic license, though the notion of dwelling in "tents" must have been unreal to an urban Alexandrian.

---

4. See Dorival 138—139.
5. Note Tar^O: שכיב ומתגלי לה "he laid down and it was revealed to him." The verb שכיב renders נפל in the sense of "laid himself down to sleep," hence falling into a dream state.
6. Theod and Aq translate גלוי עינים by ἐμπεφραγμένου ὀφθαλμοῦ αὐτοῦ, but Sym has the plural ἐμπεφραγμένων ὀφθαλμῶν αὐτοῦ (retroverted from Syh). This accords with the reading for The Others as ἐμπεφραγμένοι in Procopius. The recensors must have understood Balaam to have seen a vision of Shaddai with closed eyes, i.e. "in a dream."

24:6 This verse presents a series of four similies for the dwellings of Israel. The first line reads כנחלים נטיו "like wadies they stretch out." This puzzled the translator, and for נחלים he substituted νάπαι, possibly under the awareness that wadis lie in river bottoms, hence "glens, vales, valleys." The extension of such glens seems irrelevant as a figure for the protection of Israelite dwellings, but wadis lay deep below the ground level, as travellers who have had to cross such crevices as the Wadi-l-Mujib or the Wadi-l-Hesa know, since the actual stream is usually shadowed by the tall banks of the wadi which may extend hundreds of feet upward. And so he contextualized with σκιάζουσαι, thus "like glens giving shadow," so are "your tents, o Israel" (v.5).[7]

Line two reads "and ὡσεὶ παράδεισοι ἐπὶ ποταμῶν." MT lacks an initial conjunction, and also has נהר, i.e. "river" in the singular. The simile is clear; Israel's dwellings are luxuriant, "like gardens besides rivers." Thus just like gardens which are well-watered, so Israel will dwell secure from any danger of lack of nourishment. The value of water to sustain life was particularly acute in the Near East with its dry seasons, and certainly in the Egypt of the translator which was completely dependent on the Nile for its survival.

Line three reads "and like tents which the Lord pitched." As at line two MT lacks an initial conjunction. The line represents an attempt to understand MT's כאהלים נטע יהוה. It seems clear that אהלים does not mean "tents" here, but something that could be planted. The Masoretes did not vocalize it as "tents," but as a kind of tree, probably the agallochs or aloes, a resident tree of Indic origin, whose wood when burnt is sweet-scented. The word is not a native Semitic word, but borrowed. The translator, however, understood it vocalized to mean "tents." But tents are hardly planted; they are pitched. The simile is, however, not a particularly good one; that the tents of Israel are like the tents (which the Lord pitched) is somewhat tautologous, though it does, I suppose, add a sense of security. If the dwellings are like those which the Lord created, they must stand firm. The verb נטע, however, does not mean "pitch," and here 4QNum[b] reads the expected נטה, which is commonly rendered by πήγνυμι as here. Whether or

---

7. Dorival 139 quite rightly states that "La LXX n'offre pas une traduction, mais une exégèse où se trouve introduite l'idée d'ombrage qui, dans *Nombres*, évoque la protection divine."

not one should read נטה or נטע is another matter. What is clear is that Num presupposes the reading of the Qumran text.

The last line creates no problems of translation. Both MT and Num read: "like cedars beside waters." The simile is somewhat grotesque, since cedars flourish on the mountains of Lebanon, and not besides waters, but what is symbolized is clear. Well-watered cedars stand firm and secure against attack.

24:7 The opening couplet in MT continues the figure of trees, but with lines three and four there is an abrupt change. These lines read: וירם מאגג מלכו ותנשא מלכתו "And may its king rise more (i.e. higher) than Agag, and may its kingdom be exalted." The pronominal reference in the "its" is to Israel. The reference to Agag is to Agog king of the Amalekites during the reign of Saul. Sam, however, reads גוג instead of אגג, which probably gave rise to Num's interpretation: καὶ ὑψωθήσεται ἢ Γὼγ βασιλεία αυτοῦ καὶ αὐξηθήσεται ἡ βασιλεία αὐτοῦ.[8] In MT the מן of מאגג is comparative. The ἢ used after ὑψωθήσεται is an attempt to unite the notion of "to be high, be raised" with the particle ἢ.[9] It will be noted that Num has substituted for מלכו the translation of מלכתו, i.e. read ἡ βασιλεία αὐτοῦ in both lines, thereby avoiding a direct reference to a king for Israel. "Kings" are allowed for non-Israelite principalities, but for Num, as for Deut, the term βασιλεύς is avoided when referring to Israel's rulers.[10] Only the Lord is to be recognized as Israel's king; such a one may be called an ἄρχων, but not a βασιλεύς.

The change of אגג to Γὼγ has, however, far-reaching interpretative implications. The reference is no longer to a historical figure in the early days of Israel's kingship but to the eschatological hopes embodied in the (mythical) figure of Gog from the land of Magog in Ezek chh.38 and 39. In the distant future, Israel shall rise beyond that of the great destroyer and emperor of the east whom the Lord opposes and will overcome when it attacks Israel in some great eschaton.

---

8. For line three all Three attest to Agag. All read καὶ ὑψωθήσεται ὑπὲρ ᾽Αγὰγ βασιλεὺς αὐτοῦ (retroverted from Syh).
9. See SS 149, which rightly suggests that "strictly speaking, ὑψωθήσεται does not indicate any comparison, ..., but its use with ἢ is not entirely irregular."
10. See my "The LXX Translator of Deuteronomy," Section 8.1 (p.87), IX Congress of the International Organization for Septuagint and Cognate Studies Cambridge 1995, ed by Bernard Taylor, Septuagint and Cognate Studies 45. (Atlanta, 1997).

Now to return to the opening couplet. MT's text is not fully clear, but probably means something like: "Water shall flow from its buckets, and its seed shall have (literally shall be in) many waters." The term מים רבים usually refers to the underground waters, and the line apparently means that the seeds of the tree will be well supplied with moisture. Possibly the couplet refers both to an abundance of water from above and from below.

Num has abandoned the figure of trees entirely, and created a new context for the eschatological promise of the second couplet, a context somewhat modelled on v.17: ויקם שבט מישראל/καὶ ἀναστήσεται ἄνθρωπος ἐξ Ἰσραήλ, which see. Num has also introduced an ἄνθρωπος (instead of מים) by his ἐξελεύσεται ἄνθρωπος ἐκ τοῦ σπέρματος αὐτοῦ καὶ κυριεύσει ἐθνῶν πολλῶν "A person shall come out of his issue, and become lord over many nations." The eschatological hopes of the people are now centered in an individual, an ἄνθρωπος. Whether these hopes were intended to reflect realization in the reign of David, as is sometimes suggested,[11] or is projected into the distant future, cannot be determined. In view of the adoption of Γώγ rather than Ἀγάγ in line three, the latter does seem to be the more likely. Such eschatological hopes did involve Jewish hopes in a future figure, not at all limited to the Alexandrian Jews of the third century BCE.[12] There is little point in trying to reconstruct a different parent text, as is done e.g. in BHS. Num constitutes a complete reinterpretation, and has little to do with a parent text. The impetus for the rewrite may, however, have been stimulated by the similarity of במים and בעמים, whereas ἐκ τοῦ σπέρματος αὐτοῦ may reflect וזרעו.[13]

24:8 Line one in MT is a nominal clause with מוציאו ממצרים as predicate; thus "God is the one bringing him (i.e. Israel) out from Egypt." Num has followed

---

11. See Dorival 139—140, and comp J.Lust, Messianism and Septuagint, Suppl.VT 36 (Leiden 1985), 174-191.
12. This is clear from Tar, as their rendering of the couplet readily demonstrates. Tar⁰ has יקום מלכיהון מן בינייהון; Tar^N has יסגי מלכא דיתרבא מבנוהי וישלוט בעממין סגיאין ופרוקהון מנהון יהוי יכנש להון גלותהון מן מדינת בעלי דבביהון ובנוי ישלטון באומין סגין. Tar^J reads יקום מנהון מלכהון ופרוקהון מנהון ובהון יהוי וזרעיית בנוי דיעקב ישלטון בעממין סגיאין. For a discussion of Tar, see Dorival 139.
13. The Recensors read the MT couplet as follows (as retroverted from Syh): Theod renders by ἐξαντληθήσεται ὕδωρ ἐκ τῶν λεβήτων (qds') αὐτοῦ καὶ τὸ σπέρμα αὐτοῦ ἐν ὕδασιν πολλοῖς; Aq has ἀπορρεύσει ὕδατα ἐκ τῶν λεβήτων αὐτοῦ· καὶ σπέρμα αὐτοῦ ἐν ὕδασιν πολλοῖς; Sym reads ἐποχετεύσει ἐπὶ τοῖς παραφυαίσιν ἑκάστης· τῷ δὲ σπέρματι ἑκάστης ἐντὸς ὑδάτων πολλῶν.

Sam's נחהו "led him out" with its ὡδήγησεν αὐτόν. Had Num read MT, he would have used either a present or an imperfect inflection.

Line two I would analyze as having αὐτῷ as subject "there was to him," i.e. "he had," and ὡς δόξα μονοκέρωτος as predicate; thus "he had the glorious appearance of a unicorn" (literally, "like the glory of a unicorn"). This differs considerably from MT which has כתועפת ראם לו; both it and its translation are an exact copy from 23:22b; cf comments ad loc. Here, however, its parallel line is a different syntagm, and therefore is to be understood as an independent structure.

Lines three and four are interpreted in cannibalistic fashion. The subject is not ὁ θεός, but the αὐτόν/αὐτῷ of lines one and two, i.e. Israel. Line three reads "he shall eat the nations of his enemies," which represents MT's "he shall eat nations, even his enemies." The word צריו is in apposition to גוים, whereas Num apparently read גויי צריו. Then the next line reads "And he shall suck out their fat (or marrow)," whereas MT says "he shall crunch their bones." Actually, crunching bones is done in order to get at the marrow, a fact apparently known to the translator. Israel will devour its foes completely.

The final line reads "and he shall shoot the enemy with its (i.e. Israel's) missiles," or "pierce with darts." The Hebrew actually says "he shall smash his arrows." MT has no equivalent for ἐχθρόν, and hex has placed it under the obelus.

24:9 The opening verbs כרע שכב are reproduced by a participle plus an aorist verb, κατακληθεὶς ἀνεπαύσατο "having stretched out he slept (like a lion and like a lion's cub)," which is followed by τίς ἀναστήσει αὐτόν "who would dare rouse him"? The translator probably felt that חציו was the instrument, not bizarrely, the object of ימחץ, and so provided an ad sensum gloss to fill out the text, thereby making it more meaningful.

The rendering ἀνεπαύσατο for שכב is unique, though not inappropriate. The Qal verb is usually translated by κοιμάω (151 times) or καθεύδω (25 times), but in view of the next line with ἀναστήσει, ἀνεπαύσατο was wisely chosen.[14] This is a fitting conclusion to lines three to five of v.8. For the same figure, see 23:24.

---

14. The statistics are those of Dos Santos.

The final couplet is directly addressed to Israel. MT has two nominal clauses מברכיך ברוך and וארריך ארור, in which subject and predicate do not agree in number. The singular predicates are to be understood in a distributive sense: "may each one be blessed, ... cursed."[15] Num had no difficulty with this usage, but simplified it by making the verbs and their subjects plural throughout. What the Greek says is "May those blessing you (i.e. Israel) be blessed, and those cursing you, be cursed."

24:10 Num interpreted ויחר אף idiomatically by its καὶ ἐθυμώθη. The Hebrew ויחר אף occurs ten times in the book, and is usually rendered by two words: by ἐθυμώθη ὀργῇ (11:1,10); ὠργίσθη θυμῷ (25:3 32:10,13), and by two nouns ὀργὴ θυμοῦ at 12:9. Here and at 11:33 22:27 no attempt at reproducing the Hebrew idiom in a literal word for word fashion is made, but a simple verb ἐθυμώθη obtains: "and he was enraged, became angry." Hex has, however, in each case added an οργη under the asterisk to represent the אף. The verb is modified by an ἐπί phrase, thus "he was angered over against (Balaam)." Since MT has Balak's anger directed אל Balaam, the n+ reading προς could be a correction towards MT, but I doubt that the variant is anything more than a stylistic one.

The verb συνεκρότησεν (ταῖς χερσὶν αὐτοῦ) refers to the physical clapping or striking of hands together. The verbal idea is itself neutral, but here it is intended as an angry gesture. The verb as a συν- compound is modified by a dative, but correctly renders the Hebrew יספק את כפיו.

Balak's angry words to the seer are a royal rebuke: "to execrate my enemy I have summoned you, and behold, you actually blessed this third time." The Masoretes vocalized איבי as a plural noun, "my enemies," but the consonantal text can be either singular or plural. The perfect tense κέκληκά σε is fully appropriate as an interpretation of קראתיך; MT's past tense is neutral.

A substantial change made by Num is in the interpretation of MT's הנה clause. In MT, the timer reads זה שלש פעמים "these three times." This modifies a verbal structure ברכת ברך in which the free infinitive follows its cognate verb. This order may indicate a continuity of verbal action, i.e. "you kept on blessing (these three times)," though comp comment at 23:11. But Num changed the timer to an ordinal τρίτον τοῦτο "this third time." Num then changed the word order of

---

15. See GK 145 l.

the verbal structure as well. The present participle renders the infinitive, but precedes the verb, and the clause now clearly reads with special stress on the verbal notion, hence, the translation: "you actually blessed (this third time)." Hex has made two changes in word order to imitate that of MT: it transposed both εὐλογῶν εὐλόγησας as well as τρίτον τοῦτο.

24:11 Num renders the opening ועתה "and now" neatly by νῦν οὖν "now then"; Num also does not render the לך of ברח לך. This common use of the prepositional phrase with an imperative is peculiarly Hebraic, and is in my opinion best left untranslated.[16] With ברח it is a crude kind of "beat it, you." Num fortunately does not add a σεαυτῷ (but see 10:2 13:2 21:8). This usage is particularly common with λάβε (e.g. Lev 9:2) or with πρόσεχε (as often in Deut). In some contexts such a σεαυτῷ may express advantage. Num simply has φεῦγε. The aorist εἶπα in context intends a pluperfect sense: "I had said," contrasting with καὶ νῦν. The Byz text substituted the more Classical second aorist ειπον, but with no semantic difference.[17] What Balak had intended was "I would honor you," whereas MT read כבד אכבדך "I will really honor you," but Num disregarded the free infinitive; hex, however, supplied τιμων under the asterisk to represent it.

Num has changed the הנה clause modifier meaning "behold" into a timer, which is contextually a fine change; καὶ νῦν constitutes a good contrast with εἶπα, which is thereby voided. "And now the Lord has deprived you of any δόξης," i.e. of the τιμήσω σε I had intended.[18]

24:12 Num preserves the unusual word order of MT by which "to your messengers whom you sent to me" precedes the main verb ἐλάλησα. The statement is introduced by οὐχὶ καί, which represents הלא גם. This order is intentional, and places the stress on the dative phrase, thus: "Was it not already to your messengers whom ... (that) I said λέγων"?

24:13 Up to τὸ ῥῆμα κυρίου, this verse is an almost exact repetition of what Balaam said to the chieftains of Balak in 22:18, except for the δῷ μοι, which is

---
16. GK 119s speaks of this as "an apparently pleonastic *dativus ethicus*." I have often wondered why grammarians hide their confusion by putting it into Latin; this makes it actually sound profound!
17. Num consistently uses the Hellenistic inflection for this verb; see THGN 123.
18. The genitive represents a partitive מן; see SS 162.

here reversed. Since MT has יתן לי, hex has transposed μοι δῷ to the Hebrew order. Just why Num placed μοι before the verb is puzzling; possibly it was to place more stress on the pronoun, although this is not at all evident.

As at 22:18, Num has added an αὐτό after the infinitive ποιῆσαι, which is then here modified by πονηρὸν ἢ καλὸν παρ ἐμαυτοῦ. Hex has placed the αὐτό under the obelus, since it has no counterpart in MT. Num has reversed MT's nouns in טובה או רעה, and the majority A F M text has reordered the Greek text to equal that of the Hebrew; the reordering is almost certainly hex in origin. The Byz text has a doublet here, having added μικρον η μεγα before the pair; this is a secondary import from 22:18. The prepositional phrase translates מלבי "from my own will." Since the לב is the central driving force of a person, the reflexive pronoun is a fine rendering.

The final statement in Num of the quoted speech included in the λέγων at the end of v.12 differs from MT. Num says "whatever God εἴπῃ, this ἐρῶ." The verb "to say" is twice used, but MT does not use the root אמר, but דבר for both clauses. MT reads "What Yahweh speaks (ידבר), it I must speak (אתו אדבר)." In view of the regularity with which Num translates the verbs דבר and אמר resp. by λαλέω and εἴπω, a different parent text is a reasonable suggestion.[19] The prejudice of the translator against Balaam as a prophet of Yahweh, also appears from his use of ὁ θεός, which has been noted throughout the Balaam narratives.

24:14 Balaam's reply begins with "and now ἰδοὺ ἀποτρέχω εἰς τὸν τόπον μου." MT has a nominal clause, הנני הולך. Usually, Num renders such a structure with a pronoun ἐγώ plus an inflected present tense, but here he has not included the otiose pronoun, and the Byz+ text has added an εγω afer ἰδού; its source is almost certainly one of The Three. αποτρέχω is not the usual rendering of הלך, though it does occur 13 times in LXX; here it is, however, fitting. The prepositional phrase "to my place" corresponds to Balak's orders in v.11, "flee εἰς τὸν τόπον σου," but here MT has "to my people." The Num text does fit the context, but it does not equal MT, where τον λαον σου would have been more accurate. The change to τόπον once again reflects Num's preference for a consistent text.

In v.b Balaam says to Balak, as a kind of consolation prize, "come, I will give you counsel (as to) what this people will do (to) your people ἐπ' ἐσχάτου

---

19. See THGN 128.

τῶν ἡμερῶν." This statement is a watershed in the Balaam narrative. V.a has concluded the account of Balaam and his oracles in response to Balak's overtures. V.b then introduces a new section, which is tied to what has gone before by the slimmest of connections. In fact, v.b constitutes an artificial join between the Balaam narratives and the oracles which follow.

An unusual rendering is the accusative τὸν λαόν σου for לְעַמְּךָ. In fact, scattered mss actually change this to the easier dative, τω λαω σου, but here the more difficult accusative must be original. I suppose what Num really made of it is "in what way this people will affect your people." This is modified in MT by באחרית הימים. The phrase is somewhat ambiguous, and has led to various interpretations. In some contexts, it has an eschatological sense, but others think of it as "a reference to the near future from the point of view of the speaker."[20] Num has made of it ἐπ' ἐσχάτου τῶν ἡμερῶν "at the end of days," which is also ambiguous; what are τῶν ἡμερῶν? Does it refer to the end of "time," or to the end of a specific period?[21] The V Byz+ text makes the phrase even more ambiguous by its επ εσχατων των ημερων, though I suspect that εσχατων is subvariant of εσχατω.

24:15 V.15 is an exact copy of v.3; see comments ad loc.

24:16 Num lacks φησιν for נאם, and hex has supplied it under the asterisk. For the rest, line one is an exact copy of v.4's line one; see comment ad loc. Since each line is a nominal clause in apposition to the subjects of φησίν of v.15, the lack of a rendering for נאם is no impediment for understanding the line. Line two begins asyndetically over against MT. It reads "one who knows the knowledge of the Most-High"; this translates MT word-for-word, even to the extent of preserving the cognate structure ידע דעת by its ἐπισταμένοι ἐπεστήμην. The genitive ὑψίστου is a subjective one; the source of the knowledge is the Most High. Theoretically, it could be an objective genitive, i.e. knowledge about God,[22] but this is made unlikely by the parallel constructions, λογία θεοῦ and ὅρασιν θεοῦ. Copyists were aware of the distinction, and ensured a "correct" interpretation by the B V Byz f+ gloss παρα added to govern ὑψίστου, but this is secondary.[23]

---

20. Milgrom 206.
21. For באחרית, Theod and Sym have ἐπ' ἐσχάτῳ, but Aq translates by ἐν ἐσχάτῃ.
22. See Milgrom 207, which, however, inteprets the terms "subjective" and "objective" in unusual fashion.
23. See THGN 134.

Line three is introduced by καί, though MT lacks an initial conjunction. Num continues the pattern of using a participle plus accusative modifier, though in reverse order; this does not correspond to MT, which uses an inflected verb יחזה, as at v.4; see comment ad loc. Accordingly, Num reads καὶ ὅρασιν θεοῦ ἰδών. I would understand θεοῦ as a subjective genitive; the source of ὅρασιν is God.

The last line is an exact copy of the last line in v.4, both of MT and of Num; see comment ad loc.

24:17 The Masoretes have vocalized אראנו as a Qal: "and I will see it, thus "and what I see (is not now)." I would understand the ולא עתה as referring to the suffix of אראנו. So MT states that the seer's vision is about the future. Num has understood the consonantal text as a Hi verb, which is indeed possible. Num translates the first word by δείξω αὐτῷ "I will show him, (but not now)." The dative presumably refers to Balak, though this is not certain.[24]

Line two in MT reads אשורנו ולא קרוב "I will behold it, and (i.e. but) it is not near." This is an obvious parallel to line one.[25] Num misread the verb, i.e. as אשרנו, but analyzing the verb as from the root אשר. Num has μακαρίζω "I declare blessed." The second part was also rendered by a present tense verb, καὶ οὐκ ἐγγίζει "and it is not nearby." This so-called misreading is surprising in view of the context. After all, at 23:9 lines one and two of MT read אראנו and אשורנו resp., but there Num read ὄψομαι αὐτόν and προσνοήσω αὐτόν; from this, I would conclude that he read the lines here to contrast with 23:9. There the seer refuses to curse Israel because he will see/behold him from the hills. Here, the emphasis has shifted to the "not now" and the "not nearby." Furthermore, lines three through six follow, and the "I will show him" and "I declare blessed," may well be intentional departures from MT, i.e. possible reinterpretations of the Masoretic tradition to set the stage for the predictions to come. It must be remembered that μακαρίζω is not a future, but a present tense inflection, possibly used in the sense of "I am on the point of, am about to declare blessed," and that in an

---

24. Aq translates ὄψομαι αὐτὸν καὶ οὐ νῦν; Sym reads a present tense verb, ὁρῶ.
25. Aq translates by προσκοπῶ αὐτὸν ἀλλ' οὐκ ἐγγύς. According to Eusebius, Sym also reads this, but with ὁρῶ as verb. There is something wrong with this tradition. According to Procopius, Sym read ὁρῶ for the verb in line one; it is unlikely that a good translator like Sym would have used the same verb for both lines one and two, and that for different verbs.

absolute sense. i.e. the failure to recognize the suffix of אשורנו is hardly a palaeographically inspired matter; it is part of the reinterpretation.

Lines three and four constitute a couplet, but are not fully clear in MT. The second stich means "a sceptre from Israel shall arise," but the first refers to a star from Jacob as subject of דרך. The verb usually means "to march, tread," which hardly fits in this context. I suspect that here דרך is a denominative verb from the noun דרך "road, path, way," and so "to make its way, travels," and reflects the notion of the route of a star as it appears in the sky, i.e. appear on the horizon. The inflection is a neutral one; i.e. the old *qatala* inflection is neutral as to tense and aspect, and takes on the character of its context. Since the context of lines one and two is future, the Num translation ἀνατελεῖ ἄστρον ἐξ Ἰακώβ is an accurate one: "there shall rise up a star from Israel." Presumably, the term ἄστρον is a personification of an individual ruler; the person of David has often been suggested.[26] MT then goes on to show that the star is a royal figure in MT, i.e. a שבט "a sceptre (from Israel shall stand up)."[27] At first glance, the Num interpretation seems strange; it reads καὶ ἀναστήσεται ἄνθρωπος ἐξ Ἰσραήλ "and there shall stand up a person from Israel," but substituting a "person, an ἄνθρωπος," for שבט is not really far-fetched; it makes certain that both כוכב and שבט refer to an individual (royal) figure.[28] After all, the figure of a sceptre standing up does need interpretation. By substituting ἄνθρωπος for sceptre, Num avoids the notion that the person is a royal figure, a king.

The final couplet in MT is difficult; it reads "and he shall crush פאתי of Moab, and קרקר all the sons of Seth." Moderns understand פאתי as a dual noun referring to "the temples" of a man's head. Then קרקר is usually changed to Sam's קדקד "skull." Num, however, understood it differently. It reads "and he will break in pieces the leaders of Moab, and take as booty all the sons of Seth."[29] The Tar all understood the פאתי מואב as referring to the leaders of

---

26. Tar⁰ reads כד יקום מלכא מיעקב "when a king shall arise from Jacob." Tar^JN have a similar text.
27. Tar⁰ renders ויתרבא משיחא "and the Messiah shall be anointed (from Israel)." Tar^J agrees, but amplifies with ושיבט תקיף "and a strong ruler." Tar^N identifies the שבט as ופרוק ושליט "a redeemer and a ruler."
28. Sym renders שבט by σκῆπτρον.
29. Sym translates the first line of this couplet as "καὶ παίσει κλίματα Μωάβ "and he will smite the slopes of Moab."

Moab.³⁰ It is clear that not only Num, but the Tar all had difficulty with פאתי as well as with קרקר. The Num interpretation is clearly an old Jewish understanding of these words, which is then later reflected in all three Targums.³¹

24:18 Vv.18—19 no longer deal with Moab, but with Edom, though the second line of v.19 is uncertain. V.18 in MT reads "And Edom shall be a possession; and Seir, his enemies, shall be a possession, but Israel has acted with strength." Num has translated more or less word for word, but has identified שעיר as Ἡσαύ, for which see Gen 33:14 36:8—9; see Notes at Gen 36:8,9. The Masoretes vocalized עשה as a participle, but Num interpreted the consonantal text by ἐποίησεν, which is also possible. Furthermore, the identification of Seir as "his enemies" has been simplified by changing the noun to the singular ὁ ἐχθρὸς αὐτοῦ. And the adverbial use of חיל has been rendered by a prepositional phrase ἐν ἰσχύι.³²

24:19 MT reads the first line as "may one rule from Jacob," or better "may one from Jacob rule."³³ I would then translate the second stich as "so that he might destroy the survivors of the city." The term שריד I would take as a collective. Num apparently did not understand ירד; at least, its ἐξεγερθήσεται "shall be aroused" can hardly render ירד, either as representing רדה or ירד. It is most commonly used to represent the root עור. Since the last word of the second line reads מעיר, it is possible that some kind of word play involving יעיר or יועד instead of ירד lies behind Num. Admittedly, this is pure speculation, but it is an interesting possibility, since obviously Num does not translate MT. What it says is "and one shall be aroused out of Jacob."

Line two does translate MT. It reads "and he (i.e. the one from Jacob) shall destroy the one who has been rescued from a city." What appears to be intended

---

30. It might be instructive to see their texts. Tarᴼ has ויקטול רברבי מואב וישלוט בכל בני אנשא; Tarᴶ reads ויקטול רברבי מואבאי וירוקן כל בנוי דשת "and he shall kill the rulers of the Moabites, and drain off all the sons of Sheth." Tarᴺ interprets in similar fashion: "And he shall kill the strong ones (תקיפי) of the Moabites, and destroy (ישיצי) all the sons of Sheth."
31. Sym translated the verb קרקר by ἐξερευνήσει "he shall search out."
32. The Tar all interpret חיל as wealth; thus Tarᴼ has אצלח בנכסין "has prospered with possessions."
33. This is often interpreted as messianic. Thus Tarᴶ has שליט ויקום, while Tarᴺ reads עתיד מלך למקום.

is that anyone who has gone into a city (of Edom) for protection will, however, not survive.

24:20 The usual introduction for a new oracle, for which see comment at 23:7, is preceded by another subordinate structure, καὶ ἰδὼν τὸν ᾿Αμαλήκ, which translates a coordinate clause וירא את עמלק. The stress is quite rightly placed on the main clause, i.e. on εἶπεν.

The first line of the oracle is straightforward: "The beginning of nations is Amalek." This probably intends to put Amalek's origins in the most favorable light, and to contrast with the second line in MT: ואחריתו עדי אבד, which is obscure. The first word contrasts with ראשית, and must mean "its end." The predicate then must be עדי אבד and a verb must be understood, something like "leads", thus "its end (leads up) to a destroyer," which is not overly luminous. Num has rendered אחריתו as τὸ σπέρμα αὐτῶν "their offspring," for which see comment on the last line of 23:10. It then paraphrased עדי אבד by the verb ἀπολεῖται, thus "their seed shall perish." In any event, the verb does reflect the root אבד, probably as יאבד (by dittography). Num has made good sense out of a difficult line.

24:21 Num reads Καιναῖον for קיני. This spelling is probably not original; since in Byzantine Greek the "αι" and the "ε" were homophonous, both were realized as /ε/. The name also occurred at Gen 15:19, where it was transcribed as Κεναίους. Since the oldest witness, cod B, also reads κεναιον here, it would seem judicious to change the critical text to read Κεναῖον. For the syntactic pattern of the introduction to the oracle, see comment at v.20.

The oracle also included v.22, where the text of MT is obscure. V.21b reads "your dwelling is strong, and if you set your nest in the rock." Another protasis is to follow, and the apodosis is finally given in v.22b. The word ἰσχυρά is Num's rendering of איתן "secure, enduring," but the interpretation is plausible, though it only occurs here.

In MT, the next line is clear: "and your nest is set (שים) in the rock (or in Sela?)." שים is here to be taken as a Qal passive participle.[34] Num was obviously confused as to the intent of ושים; in its place, it has καὶ ἐὰν θῇς. In other words,

---

34. See GK 73f.

it does not take the two lines of the couplet as parallel (as in MT), but as parallel with the first line of v.22.

24:22 The text of MT is difficult; in fact, I can make no sense out of the second line at all. The first stich apparently says "but Qayin shall become a burning." The term קין is a pun on הקיני "the Kenites." This then contrasts with v.21, which describes the strong, if not impregnable, position of the Kenites. Though the Kenite is usually thought to be a Midianite clan of smiths, the reference to its nest being set in סלע makes a confusion with Edom a real possibility; comp v.18 where Edom and Seir are identical.

The second stich begins with עד מה "how long"? It continues with אשור תשבך, possibly meaning "Asshur will take you into captivity." Num has read עד מה as ערמה "deceit," and made it part of the first stich. Instead of כי אם it seems to have read ואם as its καὶ ἐάν presupposes. The translator then took לבער as a preposition plus a proper noun, thus τῷ Βεώρ. This is most peculiar, since Beor was the father of Balaam. It probably was intended to refer to Βεώρ, the father of Bala, an early king of Edom, according to Gen 36:32. This might be taken to add support to the understanding of the Κεναῖον being an Edomite clan in this ancient oracle. What the translator made of the verse was: "And if there should be a nest of deceit for Beor, the Assyrians shall take you into captivity."[35] I am not sure what is meant by "a nest of deceit for Beor," nor why this should lead to Assyrian captivity. On the other hand, the relation of v.21b to the last line of the oracle is fully clear, even though it misrepresents MT.

24:23 MT lacks an equivalent for Num's opening καὶ ἰδὼν τὸν Ὤγ, but then continues with the usual introduction, for which see comment at 23:7. One would, in view of vv.20,21, have expected some addressee being named. For Og, see 21:33—35. A popular F V text (possibly hex in origin) has omitted the opening reference to an address; the omission equals MT, and may well be recensional in origin. On the other hand, it could easily be a case of homoioteleuton leading to parablepsis.

---

35. Theod translated the verse by ὅτι ἐὰν γένηται εἰς ἁρπαγὴν (lḥṭwpy') ἕως τινὸς Ἀσσοὺρ αἰχμαλωτεύσει σε; Aq rendered it by ὅτι ἐὰν γένηται εἰς τὸ ἐπιλέξαι (lmgb') Καὶν ἕως τινὸς Ἀσσοὺρ αἰχμαλωτεύσει σε, whereas Sym made of it καὶ ἐὰν ᾖ καταβοσκόμενος ὁ Κεναῖος ἕως τινὸς τῷ Ἀσσοὺρ ἡ αἰχμαλωσία σου. (All were retroverted from Syh).

The oracle is quite obscure in both MT and Num. It begins with "O, o! Who can survive (literally live) when God would set (i.e. determine) these things"? The initial ὦ ὦ reads אוי "alas" in MT. Apparently, it constitutes a repeated transcription rather than a translation of the Hebrew. The "when clause" is an attempt at making sense out of the Hebrew משמו אל, which has never been satisfactorily explained. What the translator did was to divide the prepositional syntagm into component parts, i.e. ὅταν representing מ, θῇ stands for שים, and ταῦτα rendering the suffix.[36] What ταῦτα refers to is not immediately clear, and I would suggest that it refers to the general afflictions of v.24, but see comment at v.24 on ἐξελεύσεται. In the tradition, the Byz text has tried to clarify the sense by adding επι της γης at the end; this would help to ease the intent of the verb, i.e. "whenever God would set these on the land," but it is merely an explanatory gloss.

24:24 The opening syntagm of MT is best understood as a pendant construction: "and as for ships from the side of Kittim," with the next line constituting the principle clause: וענו אשור וענו עבר "even they shall afflict Asshur and shall afflict Eber." The צים is then taken up in the last stich "And even it עדי אבד," which is also found at the end of v.20, where it is simply rendered by ἀπολεῖται. It is obvious that there are obscurities in the text which do not admit of ready solution, and various scholars have tried to reconstruct a meaningful original. I shall not add to their number.

It is a quite sufficient task to make sense out of Num itself. It reads for the first stich καὶ ἐξελεύσεται ἐκ χειρὸς Κιτιαίων. The verb reflects a rewrite of צים as though it were the root יצא.[37] The subject is probably the ταῦτα of the preceding stich, though this in turn creates a problem as to what the pronoun refers to.[38]

The next stich renders the verbs of MT literally by καὶ κακώσουσιν for the וענו of both clauses. The subject must be the Κιτιαίων of the preceding stich. MT has אשור for the modifier of the first clause, and עבר "Eber," for the second. The translator took עבר as though it were a gentilic, and made it Ἑβραίους, which is certainly not what עבר intended. But in the time of the Alexandrian

---

36. This is similar to what Tar⁰ did: כד יעבד אלהא ית אלין.
37. Pesh similarly understands such a verb by its *npqn* "they are going out." Num probably follows the text of Sam: יוציאם.
38. This is similar to what Tar⁰ did: כד יעבד אלהא ית אלין.

translator, the Kittin attacking the Hebrews may have been a possible reconstruction. What the oracle meant by עבר remains, however, still unknown; it certainly did not refer to the Hebrews.[39]

The final stich in MT reads וגם הוא עדי אבד. What הוא refers to is unclear, since possible references in the oracle are all plural. Num makes excellent sense by changing it to the plural. So וגם הוא becomes καὶ αὐτοί, and refers to the Κιτιαίων, who afflicted both Asshur and the Hebrews, but "also they (with one accord shall perish)." The predicate in Hebrew, עדי אבד, also occurred at v.20, where it was translated by ἀπολεῖται. The adverb ὁμοθυμαδόν has no actual equivalent in MT, and was added by Num to suggest that the Kittians would die together, i.e. in concert. In any event, the Alexandrian made their fate absolute; no one of Israel's enemies, i.e. the Kittians, are to escape destruction.

24:25 Num renders the three clauses, ויקם בלעם וילך וישב, in an unusual manner, by subordinating the first and third verbs to attributive participles: thus "and Balaam standing up, departed, returning (to his place)." This places the main stress on "departed," rather than on "returning," as might have been expected. This difficulty was felt by copyists as well, and an *ol t+* text transposed ἀπῆλθεν ἀποστραφείς to the more usual order. The *d* text solved the problem by omitting ἀποστραφείς.

V.b of MT reads וגם בלק הלך לדרכו "and also Balak went on his way." The translator assumed that לדרכו must have referred to למקמו, since he translated the sense by πρὸς ἑαυτόν "to his own," i.e. to his own place. From v.b it now becomes clear why the translator placed the stress in v.a on ἀπῆλθεν; it was meant to contrast with Balak's action. Thus "Balaam ἀπῆλθεν ... to his place, and Balak ἀπῆλθεν to his own."

---

39. Tar⁰ interprets by לעבר פרת.

Chapter 25

25:1 The chapter describes how the Moabites led the Israelites into idolatry. The verb κατέλυσεν means "to lodge," and is more commonly used to render the root לון "to stay the night, lodge;" in fact, it is unique for the Qal of ישב. It does occur once for the Ni, but not in the Pentateuch. The verb ישב is most often translated by κατοικέω (502 times), followed by καθίζω (167), κάθημαι (129), and οἰκέω (61 times).[1] Num chose to accent the fact that they halted, hence spent the night.[2] 25:1 5location of Σαττίμ is not known, but must lie somewhere east of the Jordan on the plains of Moab, probably north of the Arnon. The place was also strange to copyists who misspelled the name in many ways: by haplography the -ττ- became a single *tau*; the vowel *alpha* became -ε- or -ι-, whereas the *iota* was changed to -ε- or -υ-; the -ττ- became -βετ-, -τγτ-, -ντ- or -τμ-; furthermore, the initial *sigma* was lost in αττιν, αττι, and ατην. And the apocopation of the *mu* resulted in σαττι, σατμη and αττι. At 33:49, the name appears in Βελσαττίμ. Actually, the majority A B M V text changed the final labial to a dental, but the final -*mu* equals MT, and is likely to be original.[3]

The Masoretes vocalized ויחל as a Hi of the root חלל meaning "to begin," thus "the people began to commit adultery with the daughters of Moab." But the same consonants can represent the Ni of חלל "to profane oneself," which is how Num took it, with its καὶ ἐβεβηλώθη "and the people profaned themselves by having illicit sexual relations with the daughters of Moab." The root πορν- occurs 67 times as rendering of זנה,[4] and only twice was another root chosen; obviously it refers to playing the harlot, engaging in harlotry.

25:2 The subject of ἐκάλεσαν is the θυγατέρες Μωάβ of v.1. Num has αὐτούς as the modifier of the verb; its antecedent is ὁ λαός of v.1; actually, MT has לעם, i.e. identifies those who were summoned as "the people." MT has a second modifier in לזבחי אלהיהן, which Num translates by ἐπὶ τὰς θυσίας τῶν εἰδώλων αὐτῶν. The majority A F M text has simplified this by using the preposition εἰς,

---
1. The count is that of Dos Santos.
2. For the development of this intransitive sense, see Bauer sub καταλύω 2.
3. See THGN 116.
4. According to the statistics of Dos Santos.

whereas the B V O+ text changed τὰς θυσίας to the dative plural. Both of these variants are plausible, but Num's text best explains the development of both variants, and should be retained as original text.[5] The translator makes a religious judgment by interpreting אלהיהן as τῶν εἰδώλων αὐτῶν. From an Israelite perspective, these are idols.[6]

MT continues with "and the people ate, and worshipped their gods." In Hebrew, it is clear that the people did not eat their gods by the change in number. When the verb precedes a subject which is a collective, it is singular, but when the verb follows, as is the case with וישתחוו, it is plural. Though Num imitates the matter of change in number, the translator added τῶν θυσίας αὐτῶν after ὁ λαός to make it clear that it was of the sacrifices the people ate. The genitive is a clear case of a partitive genitive; they ate some of their sacrifices. Hex placed the explanatory gloss under the asterisk.

The verb προσκυνέω is a true calque of the Hebrew השתחוה. Out of 151 cases of this verb, 149 are rendered by προσκυνέω.[7] Similarly, προσκυνέω is used almost exclusively to render this Hebrew verb (and its Aramaic synonym סגד); in fact, the only certain exception is נשק at 3Reg 19:18, where the Lord said to Elijah that there were 7000 men "whose knees had not bent to Baal," and "every mouth which οὐ προσεκύνησεν αὐτῷ." The Hebrew term is colorful, since it means "to make oneself bow down," and so "to worship."

25:3 MT describes Israel's idolatry by the Ni verb ויצמד "and (Israel) attached herself to, joined up with, Βεελφεγώρ." The name is quite stable in the tradition; in fact, only the following variants occurred: βελφεγωρ, φεελφεγωρ, βεελγωρ and βεελφεβωρ. Num interpreted the verb in more concrete terms, καὶ ἐτελέσθη "was initiated into the cult, or mysteries (of Beelphegor). As Dorival has pointed out,[8] Num did not try to render the Hebrew literally, but used an equivalent of the Moabite religion, which "would actualize a Hebrew term for Greek readers."[9] As to Beelpeor, nothing further is known of this deity than what is said here. What is clear, however, from the Greek transcription is that the middle consonant

---

5. See THGN 110.
6. NJPS understood אלהיהן as a singular, i.e. "their God." Either the singular or the plural can be defended, but Num is quite clear about it; they are "their idols."
7. According to Dos Santos.
8. Pp.173—174.
9. Theod and Aq render the Hebrew literally by ἐζευγίσθη "was yoked, joined."

was not an *'ayin*, but a *ghayin*; both phonemes are represented by the ע grapheme. The two phonemes as well as their voiceless parallels,[10] were obviously still distinct phonemes in Alexandria in the third century BCE.

For Num's rendering of the Hebrew idiom ויחר אף, see comment at 24:10. The divine reaction to the idolatry of Israel is a recurrent theme throughout the Scriptures.

25:4 The Lord ordered Moses to "take τοὺς ἀρχηγούς of the people." MT has את כל ראשי. Num omitted כל, possibly in the interest of fairness; after all, not all the chieftains were necessarily involved in the idolatry at Baalphagor; at least, the text does not say so. Hex has, however, added παντας, and this text influenced Cod B, as well as *O* and Byz+. It is, however, not original.[11]

In the next clause, MT reads והוקע אותם ליהוה. Unfortunately, the meaning of this Hi imperative of יקע is not at all certain. The Qal apparently means "to dislocate" at Gen 32:26, which describes Jacob's experience at Peniel with respect to his thigh. The Hi seemingly refers to some form of execution, and various renderings have been suggested: "impale, hang, dismember," but it remains uncertain.[12] Num is wary of decision, and chose a neutral παραδειγμάτισον "make an example of." The verb is modified by a locative prepositional phrase: ἀπέναντι τοῦ ἡλίου, which renders נגד השמש literally; its meaning is clear: "over against the sun" means "in public, publicly." In the tradition, the majority A F M V text reads κατεναντι instead of ἀπέναντι. נגד appears only seven times in the Pentateuch, and only once in Numbers. It is impossible to determine which one the translator chose, and so one can only follow the text of the oldest witness, cod B, which reads ἀπέναντι.

The next clause is in the future. When an imperatival clause is followed syndetically by a future, that clause commonly expresses the result of the imperatival clause. I would translate: "so that the anger of the Lord's wrath might be turned away from Israel."

---

10. Cf J.W.Wevers, Ḥeth in Classical Hebrew, in Essays on the Ancient Semitic World, Toronto Semitic Texts and Studies (1970), 101—112. See also J.Blau, On Polyphony in Biblical Hebrew, The Israel Acad. of Sciences and Humanities, Proceedings VI,2 (1982) 43—70.
11. In fact, it was read by Theod, which was probably the source used by Origen; see THGN 135.
12. Aq translates by ἀνάπηξον "impale," and Sym, by κρέμασον "hang."

In the tradition, a popular A M text reads προς μωυσην for τῷ Μωυσῇ; since the addressee after εἶπεν/אמר can be expressed either by a dative or a πρός phrase, it seems wisest to follow the oldest witness, cod B, which reads the dative.

Sometimes, Origen felt constrained to represent the preposition in ליהוה by τω, though usually he does not add the article. Here, hex has added τω under the asterisk before κυρίῳ, a reading which was eventually supported by the A F M majority text.

25:5 The Masoretes vocalized שפטי, the addressees, as an active participle, i.e. "the judges," but Num apparently read שבטי "tribes," though see Exod 18:25—26, in which various ranks of leaders were appointed within the tribes to act as judges. The speaker is Moses, who interprets v.4, by applying the divine orders of v.4 as involving capital punishment.

MT reads הרגו איש אנשיו הנצמדים לבעל פעור. The verb is in the imperative, thus "kill each one of you his men who have joined up to Baalpeor." Num interprets הנמצדים as in v.3, again using the root τελέω, but instead of the blanket plural אנשיו, uses the singular τὸν οἰκεῖον αὐτοῦ "his relative," i.e. a member of his household who has been initiated into the rites of Baalphegor.[13] The averting of the divine wrath (v.4) can only be effected by each one cleansing his own household of all idolators.

25:6 An ἄνθρωπος/איש is modified by τῶν υἱῶν Ἰσραήλ, which is a partitive genitive rendering מבני ישראל.[14] According to MT, this Israelite person brought to his brothers the Midianite woman." What MT apparently means is that the Israelite brought his Midianite bride to his family. This is not what Num says. It reads "he brought his brother to the Midianite woman, presumably for prostitution, probably having transposed אל and את.[15] This was done לעיני before κυρίῳ, Num used ἐναντίον to render לעיני. In the tradition, cod B n+ read the more popular εναντι in the second case, but extra support is sparse. For the first one, cod A O n y+ read εναντι. It is not likely that Num would have changed

---

13. Sym interpreted הנמצדים by τοὺς μυηθέντες "those initiated into the mysteries."
14. See SS 169.
15. See Dorival 94.

from the one to another in an adjacent phrase. Incidentally, these three cases are the only cases in Num which involved לעיני.[16]

The last clause is a nominal one in MT with a pronoun, המה, as subject, and a participle, בכים, as predicate. Num follows his usual pattern by his αὐτοὶ rendering the pronoun, and an imperfect tense verb, ἔκλαιον, to show the notion of process in past tense. The introductory conjunction is rendered by a δέ construction; this is hardly a contrastive δέ, and probably simply shows attendant circumstance. That the Israelites were weeping at the door of the sanctuary was presumably occasioned by the wholesale slaughter of relatives who had been led into idolatry through the Moabite women.

In the tradition, τὴν θύραν becomes plural τας θυρας in a popular F V variant text. There is, as far as I have been able to determine, no rhyme nor reason for singular vs plural with respect to the door(s) of the tent of witness, and the reading of the oldest ms has throughout been followed. In MT the word פתח is always singular when referring to the tent of testimony or any part of it throughout the Pentateuch.

25:7 Num reduces וירא to a subordinate participle; after all, seeing what happened is simply the occasion for Phinees, Aaron's grandson, to rise up from the midst of the assembly. Φινεές is the transcription of פינחס. The ח is transcribed by an unstressed *epsilon*. His father's name was Ἐλεαζάρ (for אלעזר), again the pharyngeal ע is transcribed by a vowel, but since the next vowel is an *alpha*, the pharyngeal character of ʿayin is shown by vowel change, i.e. also to *epsilon*.

The final clause of MT, "and he took a spear in his hand," is also reduced by Num to a subordinate participial structure to modify v.8a; Num reads "and taking a σιρομάστην in the hand." A σιρομάστης is some kind of spear, possibly a barbed one,[17] and occurs four times in the Greek for רמח "spear," as well as once for the synonym חנית.[18] This is apparently the first use of this word; it is a strange word, and its etymology is of no help in understanding the word.[19] I have no idea how this compound can be intended as some kind of spear. Num has also failed to render the suffix of ידו, since it is completely unnecessary to the sense;

---

16. See THGN 96.
17. See LS sub σιρομάστης.
18. Aq preferred to render by κοντόν, and Sym has δόρυ.
19. According to Dorival, who translates the word by "une sonde à silo"; see comment ad loc, p.463.

Phinees could hardly have taken the spear in someone else's hand! Hex has, however, duly added αυτου under the asterisk to represent the suffix.

25:8 In Num vv.7—8 must be read together. Since the last clause of v.7 had been changed to a participial structure subordinate to the opening clause of v.8, the introductory "and" of MT was necessarily omitted in the interest of good Greek. The verse begins with εἰσῆλθεν, of which Phinees is the subject. Note that "the Israelite man" is an articulated adjectival phrase, necessarily articulated, since v.6 had already designated an ἄνθρωπος τῶν υἱῶν Ἰσραήλ. According to MT, ויבא אחר "and he went in after (... אל הקבה)." The word קבה is a hapax legomenon, and is usually thought to be the same as the Arabic *qubba* meaning "dome." But just what a dome was doing at Sattim is a mystery.[20] It must have been a place into which the couple went, presumably to consummate their illicit union. It is usually thought to be descriptive of a certain kind of tent, presumably shaped like a dome, and that is as good a guess as any in the context. Unfortunately, Num also had trouble with the word, as its rendering τὴν κάμινον shows. This word occurs in the Pentateuch only four times. At Gen 19:28 and Exod 19:18 the word is used for כבשן "kiln," and at Deut 4:20, for כור "furnace." The Greek term became popular in the later volumes of the LXX, particularly in Daniel, for the furnace stoked to intense heat into which the Three Friends of Daniel were thrown. Here the word must be a chamber of some sort, but why it is called a κάμινον is puzzling. Dorival argues that "il faut songer à une tente ou à une partie de tente au forme voûtée ou conique, à un type spécial de chambre destiné aux couples." He bases this on the fact that in Rome prostitutes i.e. *fornicariae* "tirent leur nom du mot *fomix* "voute," car elles se tenaient dans des cellules voûtées."[21] Accordingly, his rendering "chambrette" might be taken as a sufficiently neutral term to be used here, i.e. "small room."

On the other hand, the choice of κάμινον is odd. One possibility that should be considered is that it does mean "kiln, oven." Apparently, the Hellenistic oven was a domed structure of some height in which bread was baked.[22] Already in

---

20. The translations by Aq: τὸ τέγος and by Sym: τὸ πορνεῖον, both meaning "brothel" are clearly judgmental renderings, and are hardly to be taken seriously as linguistic evidence for the meaning of הקבה, in spite of wide acceptance of such an interpretation, e.g. by Dalman and Jastrow.
21. P.464.
22. According to a suggestion of my colleague, Prof. J.S.Holladay, the archaeologist who has been digging a number of years at Tell-el-Muskouta in the delta.

Pharaonic Egypt, community-based bread ovens were huge, and are pictured in the monuments as being dome-shaped, and there is no good reason for such ovens not to have been known in Hellenistic times, and to an Alexandrian the only domed structure which he might well be acquainted with would have been such an oven, which could be thought to be the size of a small room. I would thus simply translate κάμινον by "oven."

There he (Phinees) pierced them both, the Israelite man, and the woman διὰ τῆς μήτρας αὐτῆς "through her womb"; MT has אל קבתה, an obvious word play with הקבה, though the words are unrelated. Presumably, what is implied is that the pair were killed while cohabiting.[23]

The direct action by Phinees was successful: "and the plague was stayed from the Israelites."

25:9 The number killed ἐν τῇ πληγῇ was 24,000. The reference to "the plague" is to the order by Moses to the tribes to kill relatives who worshipped Beelphogor. The narrative is not at all clear how the action of Phinees constituted the conclusion of that slaughter.

25:11 According to MT, God says that Phinehas "turned away (השיב) my wrath from upon the Israelites." To turn away wrath is undoubtedly correctly interpreted by Num's κατέπαυσεν "stopped, made to cease." His action averted possible further wrath on the people. For Φινεές and 'Ελεαζάρ, see comments at v.7.

This is then described somewhat ambiguously in Num by ἐν τῷ ζηλῶσαί μου τὸν ζῆλον ἐν αὐτοῖς. What makes it ambiguous is the failure on the part of the translator to translate the suffix of בקנאתו. The next word קנאתי is rendered by μου τὸν ζῆλον. Hex has changed this by adding αυτον after the infinitive and reordering μου after ζῆλον to equal MT exactly. Cod G had wrongly noted αυτον as under the obelus, an obvious error for an asterisk. The Greek is just not as clear as it could be. One might, however, translate Num: "by being zealous for my honor among them." Translating into acceptable English automatically voids the cognate expression, "being zealous for my zealousness." It should be noted that the use of the accusative τὸν ζῆλον in modification of ζηλόω is good Classi-

---

23. As Rashi suggests: כוון בתוך זכרות של זמרי ונקבות שלה וראו כולם שלא לחנם הרגם.

cal usage; the verb usually takes an accusative of person,[24] but not consistently so in Num. When the verb is modified by a ל phrase in MT, Num uses a dative, as in v.13. Here, however, the Hebrew has את קנאתי.[25]

V.b describes the result: "and I did not utterly destroy the Israelites in my zeal." What is meant is that this resulted in my not destroying .... Again, the same root is used; the divine "zeal, jealousy, honor" is thematic for the passage.

25:12 MT begins with לכן אמר "therefore, say." Num reads οὕτως εἶπον "Thus say." The Greek does at times treat לכן as though it were כן. The form εἶπον as aorist imperative is homophonous with the first singular or third person plural aorist indicative.[26] The command is probably a shortened form of an oath by the Lord to be quoted to the people. It is introduced by an ἰδοὺ ἐγώ/הנני, and this introduces a nominal clause in MT in which a first singular pronominal suffix serves as subject of a participial predicate, נתן, which Num renders, as usual, by ἐγώ plus a first singular present indicative verb: "Behold, I am giving (αὐτῷ διαθήκην εἰρήνης)." The αὐτῷ refers to Phinees. But MT reads את בריתי שלום, which is unusual Hebrew. Is שלום in apposition to בריתי, i.e. "my covenant, even peace," or can one take it as meaning "my covenant of peace"? Num has solved the problem by disregarding the suffix entirely with its διαθήκην εἰρήνης.[27] Hex has added την μου under the asterisk before διαθήκην to represent both את and the suffix of בריתי. This has in turn led to a number of amplifications, but the most popular is that of A M majority reading την διαθηκην μου before διαθήκην.[28] This is obviously an attempt to make better sense of the Hebrew, i.e. first rendering בריתי, and then by repeating ברית, reading the διαθήκην εἰρήνης of Num.

25:13 Phinees is promised a perpetual priesthood, one which will be his and his descendants. Specifically, this is called a διαθήκη ἱερατείας αἰωνία. Since αἰωνία

---

24. See LS sub ζηλόω.
25. See THGN 109.
26. Pesh was here probably influenced by Num, since it reads 'mrty "I said."
27. See SS 100.
28. Theod has διαθήκην μου εἰρήνης, whereas Aq reads τὴν συνθήκην μου εἰρήνης. The tradition has only εἰρήνην for Sym, which is meaningless in isolation. Since the word is in the accusative, Sym may, however, have taken MT literally as "(my covenant,) even peace."

is nominative, it modifies διαθήκη; in other words, it is the covenant which is eternal, not the priesthood. Of course, the covenantal promise, being eternal, must involve a perpetual priesthood, but precisely what this means is not clear; whether the high priesthood or an ordinary priesthood is meant is not stated. MT reads כהנת עולם, which may have promoted the F V b f n+ change of αἰωνία to αιωνιας, or to d t's change to αιωνιου. A genitive would render the free element of a bound phrase more accurately, but that is not what Num says.

Two reasons are appended to this promise: ἀνθ' ὧν ἐζήλωσεν τῷ θεῷ αὐτοῦ καὶ ἐξιλάσατο περὶ τῶν υἱῶν Ἰσραήλ. Acting zealously for his God refers to vv.7—8. The second clause is unusual; that the slaughter of the mismatched couple should constitute an atonement sacrifice is a peculiar notion. It must be viewed as a ransom paid for Israel's safety which is what is really meant.[29]

25:14 The name of the Israelite man involved was Ζαμβρί, which represents זמרי of MT. MT reads איש ישראל, which Num renders as though "Israel" were a gentilic: τοῦ ἀνθρώπου τοῦ Ἰσραλίτου. The transcription of the name Ζαμβρί attests to the consonantal cluster -μβ closing a syllable, rather than an expected -μ; in fact, an expected ζαμρι is not witnessed even by a single Greek witness.[30] Actually, even ζαβρι occurs in the tradition; also attested are ζαμαρ, ζαμβριος and even γανβρη.

The father's name was Σαλώ for סלוא. This, being a totally unfamiliar name to the copyists, suffered extensively in the tradition. Confusion of the uncials Λ-Δ easily created σαδω in z. The popular F V text change to σαλωμ is due to the influence of the well-known שלום. Other related spellings are σαλων and even σαλμων. By haplography (after υἱός), the variants αλω, αλωμ, αλων were created, and two mss even read ααρων.

The fate of the man is described in MT as המכה who was הכה, both words being Ho inflections of the root נכה. These were rendered by Num as τοῦ πεπληγότος (ὃς) ἐπλήγη. Since for the active, the verb πλήσσω occurs only five times over against πατάσσω which obtains 253 times, this might seem an unusual rendering, though semantically it is acceptable. On the other hand, the Ho of נכה

---
29. For the use of the dative after ζηλόω , see THGN 109.
30. In fact, only Syh witnesses to zmry, but this is almost certainly based on Pesh, not on the Greek tradition.

occurs only 14 times in MT, and in nine of these the verb πλήσσω is used, as well as once the noun πληγή occurs.³¹

Ζαμβρί was identified as ἄρχων οἴκου πατριᾶς τῶν Συμεών "chieftain of the paternal house of those of Simeon." For οἴκου πατριᾶς, see comment at 1:2. MT for τῶν Συμεών is לשמעני, and the τῶν is an attempt to render the gentilic.³² Most witnesses in the tradition omit τῶν as otiose, whereas the Byz text has changed it to των υιων, but the unusual τῶν, though supported by only four mss, is probably original text.³³

25:15 The name of the woman involved is also given. She is described as τῇ γυναικὶ τῇ Μαδιανίτιδι τῇ πεπληγυίᾳ, following the pattern of τοῦ ἀνθρώπου τοῦ Ἰσραηλίτου τοῦ πεπληγότος. MT, however, had changed the order of the modifiers for the woman with its האשה המכה המדינית. Hex has accordingly reordered to τη πεπληγυια τη μαδιανιτιδι to agree with MT. One might have expected a better parallel by the use of the genitive; the dative is, however, acceptable usage, though MT has a bound phrase שם האשה.

Her name is given as Χασβὶ θυγάτηρ Σούρ, which renders כזבי בת צור. One might have expected zeta for zayin, which is its normal Greek transcription, but the name is probably taken from Gen 38:5, where the name also occurs (for כזיב). The cluster -זב- is exceedingly rare in proper names; I found only two more: אזבי in 1Chron 11:37 and עזבוק in Neh 3:16. For the former, codd A N and two mss read αζβι; cod B plus one ms have αζωβαι; cod S has αζωβε. Other spellings are ασβαι, ασβαηλ, ασβι and αβδι. LXX (Esdr II. 13:16) has Ἀζβούχ for עזבוק, with negligible variants, though cod B reads αζαβουχ and S, αζαβου. The evidence for Χασβί here is incontrovertible, with the variant spellings χαυσβι, χαζβει, γασβι and χασκι attested only once each in the mss. For Σούρ, see 31:8 where he is called one of the five kings of Midian. The name is quite stable in the tradition; single mss attest to σσουρ, ασσουρ, σου, σουρι and σουρει. In MT, he is called ראש אמות בית אב במדין הוא "head of a clan, a paternal house in Midian." Num has taken אמות as the name of the paternal house; in fact, it first translated the word by ἔθνους, and then transliterated it. What Num says is "chieftain of the tribe (or clan) Ommoth, a paternal house it is of those of

---

31. The count is that of Dos Santos.
32. Tar⁰ reads לבית שמעון; Tarᴶ has לשיבט שמעון and Tarᴺ, דבנוי דשמעוני.
33. See THGN 107–108.

Madian." Hex has placed the transcription 'Ομμώθ under the obelus, i.e. as being an extra word in Num. Whether one should take it or its translation ἔθνους as the gloss, is debatable. Num has ἐστιν for הוא, and hex has transposed it to the end of the verse to agree with its position in MT.

It should be noted that, as in v.14, τῶν introduces the proper name, Μαδιάν. It serves a similar purpose, i.e. of understanding the proper name as referring to the people, here thus to "the Madianites."[34]

In the tradition, 'Ομμώθ becames ομωθ by haplography, εμμωθ, by uncial confusion of O/E, and σομμωθ by dittography (after ἔθνους). Other spelling variants include σομωθ, σομωχ, σομωβ, σαμμωθ, σαμμαωθ, σομμων, ομθομ and ομμοον.

25:16 MT simply reads "And Yahweh spoke to Moses saying." Num translates this, but then adds Λάλησον τοῖς υἱοῖς 'Ισραὴλ λέγων, which hex has quite rightly placed under the obelus. Its source is ex par; comp 5:6,12 6:2 9:10 15:2,18.

25:17 MT begins with the bare free infinitive. This is similar to English usage, for which the bare mention of a verbal infinitive constitutes an imperative: thus "treat as an enemy." The verse says: "treat the Midianites as an enemy, and smite them." Num translates the verse word for word, except that the future והכיתם is also rendered by an imperative. In fact, the translator makes an interesting distinction; the first imperative is in the present tense, since it betrays a state of mind, but the second one is in the default aorist, i.e. simply "smite them."

25:18 The כי clause with which this verse begins is a nominal clause with הם as the subject, and the participle צררים as predicate. Num renders this by its usual pattern of pronoun plus present tense inflected verb: "because they are treating you as an enemy in deceitful fashion, with which they were deceiving you on account of Phogor, and on account of Chasbi, the daughter of the chieftain Madian, their sister." Since ἐν δολιότητι, i.e. an abstract noun, renders בנכליהם "by their acts of craftiness," hex has added αυτων under the asterisk to represent

---

34. See THGN 107.

the suffix. For τὴν πεπληγυῖαν rendering המכה, see comment at v.14. For Φογώρ, see comment at v.3, and for Χασβί, see comment at v.15. Χασβί is further described as τὴν πεπληγυῖαν ἐν τῇ ἡμέρᾳ τῆς πληγῆς διὰ Φογώρ. The ἐν indicates time when,[35] "in the day of the plague on account of Phogor," a reference to vv.1—5.

The fragmentary v.19 of MT is taken with the following verse in Num; see comment at 26:1.

---

35. See SS 110—111.

Chapter 26

26:1 A second census of Israel of able bodied men is ordered, preparatory to the occupation of the land of promise. This verse incorporates the fragmentary 25:19: ויהי אחרי המגפה as a temporal introduction to this new section: "and it happened after the plague (καί that)." Since Num reads ἐλάλησεν, it seems likely that its parent text was not the ויאמר of MT, but rather וידבר.[1]

The addressees are now both Moses and Eleazar τὸν ἱερέα. Note that Num repeated the πρός before the second name as well. Greek usually does not repeat the preposition in such a context, whereas Hebrew usually does. Actually, the F V M majority text omits the preposition as a stylistic improvement. MT, however, inserts בן אהרן before "the priest." Hex has also added υιον ααρων to represent the longer MT text.[2]

26:2 For the structure λάβε τὴν ἀρχήν in the sense of "take a head count," see the discussion at 1:2. Here the verb is, however, singular, not plural as at 1:2. This is surprising, particularly since both Moses and Eleazar are addressed, and MT actually has the plural; comp also v.3. For κατ' οἴκους πατριῶν αὐτῶν, see comment at 1:2. The last item, "every one going out צבא in Israel," was rendered at 1:3 by ἐν δυνάμει, but here it is taken, not as the noun צבא, which is how the Masoretes vocalized it, but as a complementary infinitive, as though it were לצבא, becoming παρατάξασθαι "to stand ready for battle array," for which see comment at 1:45.

26:3 MT has אתם in modification of וידבר, which Num has understood as μετ' αὐτῶν, i.e. the parent text must have been defectively written as in MT. The text reads "and there spoke Moses and Eleazar the priest with them." The Greek is somewhat ambiguous. Does μετ' αὐτῶν modify ὁ ἱερεύς, i.e. "the priest with them," or the verb ἐλάλησεν? In the tradition, a majority M text understood it as modifying the verb, as its change to αυτοις demonstrates. But cod B plus four

---
1. See THGN 128.
2. The Others also added υἱὸν Ἀαρών.

mss omitted the phrase. Only μετ' αὐτῶν as original text could explain both variant texts.[3]

This was done בערבת מואב "on the steppes of Moab." Num, however, transcribed ערבת by 'Αραβώθ.[4] For the translator, ערבת apparently represented a particular location in Moab (possibly some village or town). As at 22:1, this was near the Jordan across from Jericho.

26:4 V.a concludes the introductory statement of vv.1—3 with "From twenty years and upward, as the Lord commanded Moses," probably to be taken as the content of the λέγων at the end of v.3; for the raison d'etre of the age limits, see comment at 1:3.

V.b is a kind of superscription to the rest of the chapter, i.e. the record of the census. Num reads: "Even the Israelites who were going out of Egypt": MT has מארץ מצרים, but hex apparently did not correct the text. The Byz text added ησαν after the initial conjunction, which was added as a clarifying gloss. An odd gloss obtains at the beginning of v.b, but it is palaeographically explicable. B V O n x plus a number of versions read συ before καί, thus "you and the Israelites who were going out of Egypt." It is, however, merely a mistake, a dittograph from the preceding word Μωυσῆ. The last two letters -ση are repeated as a homophonic spelling: συ.

26:5 Vv.5—11 constitute the census report of the Roubenites. The first report has the superscription 'Ρουβὴν πρωτότοκος 'Ισραήλ, after which begins the account of its census report with υἱοὶ δὲ 'Ρουβήν. The δέ particle has no counterpart in MT, but it does equal Sam. The name 'Ρουβήν is quite stable, except for the usual rōbēl of Eth and the rūbīl of Arab Syh. The first descendant is given as 'Ενὼχ καὶ δῆμος τοῦ 'Ενώχ. This deviates from the pattern which then follows, viz. τῷ plus name, δῆμος plus the articulated gentilic. MT has חנוך משפחת החנכי. There is no equivalent for the καί in the Hebrew. Its omission by b+ is probably ex par rather than recensional.

The second item is τῷ Φαλλού, δῆμος τοῦ Φαλλουί, thereby initiating the pattern to be followed throughout. The name is relatively stable, with haplog-

---

3. See THGN 132.
4. Aq translated by ἐν ταῖς ὁμολόταις (retroverted from Syh), but Sym, by ἐν τῇ πεδιάδι.

raphy creating φαλου/φαλοvι, with cod B reading φαυλου. Other spellings include φαλλους and φαλους. For the gentilic, a final *sigma* was a popular variant as φαλλουεις, φαλλους, φαλους,and even φαλλως show; for these, see Note at Gen 46:9, where an original Φαλλούς is defended in place of Φαλλού.

26:6 The name חצרן is transcribed as 'Ασρών. A popular A V spelling has changed the final nasal to *mu*, thus ασρωμ (or εσρωμ), but only the Num spelling can be taken as original, since the gentilic 'Ασρωνί never appears as ασρωμι in the tradition. A variant reading by x z mss has transposed -σρ- to read αρσων. More significant is the Byz introduction of a και before δῆμος, but this stylistic gloss is not carried through in later verses, and is probably merely a copyist error. The Byz text also omits both cases of τῷ in the verse, but does not do so later on. It must be an error, since a marker for the dative is needed for the tribal name. The tradition does betray some uncertainty about the gentilic form 'Ασρωνί. The Byz text has rejected the gentilic form entirely in favor of ασρων or ασρωμ.

For the next offspring, Χαρμί, the tradition, aside from the usual itacistic variants, has produced only a few oddities: χαμειρ, χραμει and μαρχι, but is otherwise stable. The Byz text again added και before δῆμος, as in v.a.

26:7 Num disregards the gentilic הראובני, and simply reports ούτοι δῆμοι 'Ρουβήν. The Byz text does prefix 'Ρουβήν with the article του, which might be thought of as possibly recensional in origin. Their "review (ἐπίσκεψις) or census report," for which terms see comment at 1:21, amounted to 43,730; this contrasts with the report of the earlier generation in 1:21 2:11, of 46,500. In the tradition, a popular A text has 50 instead of 30, but this cannot be correct.[5]

26:8 The use of υἱοί (plural) even when only one is listed demonstrates that υἱοί throughout the report in this chapter simply means "offspring." The Greek is a calque for the בני of MT. For Φαλλού, see comment at v.5. The offspring of Phallou was 'Ελιάβ. In the tradition, this name is surprisingly volatile, ελιαμ, ελιαφ, εδιαβ, αλιαβ all receiving some support.

---

5. See THGN 115.

26:9 The offspring of Eliab are Ναμουήλ and Dathan and Ἀβιρών. The name Ναμουήλ becomes ναβουηλ in some mss; the confusion of β and μ is common in the thirteenth and fourteenth century mss where the two graphemes are similar in the cursive script. Also attested are λιαμουηλ and αμουηλ. Ἀβιρών represents אבירם of MT. The spelling with final *nu* is attested in the entire Greek tradition, and represents an -ων ending rather than the -רם ending of MT. Since רם is a well-known root in Hebrew, the transcription is unexpected, but Num probably thought of the root אבר to which an -ων ending would make better sense than an -ωμ ending.

V.b then follows with οὗτοι ἐπίκλητοι τῆς συναγωγῆς "these are the ones called by the assembly," i.e. the genitive is a subjective one; it is the assembly that did the calling or naming. MT has singled out דתן ואבירם as the ones who were named, which is correct; Namouel was not part of the group who led the revolt against the authority of Moses, for which see 16:1—3. This is lackng in MT, and hex has added δαθαν και αβιρων under the asterisk to equal the text of MT, though adding no equivalent for the introductory הוא.

This is followed by another οὗτοι structure; it reads "οὗτοί εἰσιν those who formed a coalition (οἱ ἐπισυνιστάντες) against Moses and Aaron in the assembly of Kore in the revolt κυρίου." This misrepresents MT, which had pinpointed הוא דתן ואבירם as the coalition, whereas in Num's account the οὗτοι must refer to the three opponents listed in v.a. MT has no actual equivalent for οὗτοί εἰσιν, and hex has placed the words under the obelus. The articulated participle has a relative clause as background in MT, which reads אשר הצו. The verb, Hi of נצה, only occurs once elsewhere, in Ps 60:2. It is likely that the parent text here was that of Sam which read הועדו as well as reading בהועדתם instead of בהצתם; comp 14:35 27:3 where ἐπισυνίστημι also occurs in similar contexts, but for the root יעד.[6] In the structure ἐπισυστάσει κυρίου, κυρίου renders על יהוה. Clearly, the genitive must be an objective one; it constituted a revolt against the Lord. Hex made this clear by adding κατα before κυρίου under the asterisk to equal the על of MT.

26:10 The reference to the fate of Kore's group is to 16:32—35, which see. Num subordinates the first clause to a participle, thus "and the earth, opening its

---

6. Tar⁰ uses a neutral term as well: דאתכנשו and באתכנושיהון. The same verb is used by Tarʲ, but Tarᴺ goes its own way with the verb פלגו.

mouth, swallowed them and Kore." This is followed in MT by במות העדה "when the assembly died." The translator took מות, not as an infinitive, but as a noun for "death," and made it ἐν τῷ θανάτῳ τῆς συναγωγῆς αὐτοῦ "in the death of his assembly," i.e. at the time of the death of his assembly. The addition of αὐτοῦ serves to define the assembly as being that of Kore, and also thereby avoids any possible misunderstanding that the entire assembly had died, which would be absurd, though grammatically a possible understanding. It, however, has no basis in MT, and hex has placed the pronoun under the obelus. The death is then given a temporal setting; it took place "when fire devoured the 250." MT defines the 250 as איש, and hex has added ανδρας under the asterisk to represent it.[7]

MT ends with a good example of the use of היה plus ל in the sense of "to become." The clause reads ויהיו לנס "and they became a sign, a signal." Num, however, used an ἐν phrase: καὶ ἐγενήθησαν ἐν σημείῳ. Presumably, this is an example of ἐν being used in the sense of εἰς.[8]

26:11 This verse contrasts with the foregoing, and the translator chose a δέ construction to stress this: "But the sons of Kore did not die." This serves as a possible corrective to v.10 in which "his assembly" would normally be taken as including his sons.

26:12 Vv.12—14 detail the affairs of the Sumeonites. Over against MT Num begins with καί. MT reads "The Simeonites according to their clans," but Num represents a different text; it has "and the Sumeonites; the clan of the Sumeonites." Sam's text reads בני שמעון למשפחת השמעוני, and may have been the parent text to Num, though the preposition is not represented by Num.

The first clan reads "to Namouel, a clan the Namouelite." In the Gen 46:10 parallel the name is Ἰεμουήλ; which form is the earlier cannot be determined. One ms actually reads ιαμουηλ here, but the gentilic remains Ναμουηλί. The name is misspelled in various ways in the mss: ναμωηλ, ναμοηλ, αναμουηλ, αμουηλ, αμαηλ and μουηλ. In the tradition, the Byz text reads του for ὁ, i.e. "the clan of the Namouelite," which constitutes an attempt at smoothing out the text. Throughout the chapter, the pattern δῆμος ὁ plus a gentilic noun is main-

---

7. The asterisk is wrongly placed before καὶ διακοσίους in Syh^L.
8. See SS, ch.11, pp.131—140; this example is, however, not given there.

tained, i.e. the gentilic is articulated. For v.12 what this means is "Namouel has (dative of possession) a clan, the Namouelite."

The second clan reads "to Ἰαμίν, a clan the Yaminite." The name is stable in the tradition, though the following do occur: ιαβειμ, ιαμειμ and αμειν. As for the first clan, so for the others, the Byz text reads του before the gentilic, i.e. for the second and third clans as well.

The third clan is "τῷ Ἰαχίν, a clan the Yachinite." In the tradition, the final nasal became a labial in b C+, i.e. ιαχειμ, ιιαχειμ. Other misspellings include αχιν, ισχιν, ισχειλ, ιαχει and ναχιμ. The gentilic also suffered badly, as a list of misspellings in the tradition shows: ιασχινει, ιαχινιει, αχεινι, διαχινι, ιαχονι, ιαχιν, ιαχει, ιαχειλ and ιαζιν.

26:13 The remaining Sumeonite clans are Zara (for זרח) and Saoul. Instead of Ζαρά, the C' tradition reads ζωρα and ζωραει resp., whereas Byz has ζααρ for both clan name and gentilic. Other variants include ζαραι, ζαραβ, σασααρ and ναζαραιν. In the parallel Gen 46:10 the name is Σάαρ for צהר. As usual for these verses, instead of the nominative article for the gentilic, Byz has του in both cases. Similarly, for the last case, that of Σαούλ, Byz reads του σαουλ for the gentilic. The tradition misspelled Saoul as σαουηλ, σαου and even as σαμουηλ, but the gentilic remained stable.

26:14 "These are the clans of Sumeon, according to their review: 22,200." In the first census, the review consisted of 59,300, for which see 1:23 2:13. In the tradition, Συμεών is articulated by a genitive pronoun in Byz (singular in d t; plural in n). This probably reflects MT, which has משפחת השמעוני "clans of the Simeonite." MT also has no equivalent for ἐκ τῆς ἐπισκέψεως αὐτῶν; beginning with the next tribe, MT does include לפקדיהם for the remaining tribes, but here it is lacking. Hex does not place the phrase under the obelus, and it seems likely that the parent text did have the word.

26:15(19) Vv.15—18 report on the tribe of Judah. MT reports on Gad before Judah, but Num has Gad at vv.24—27, i.e. the order of vv.15—27 in Num is Judah, Issachar, Zaboulon and Gad. Hex has throughout transposed the text to follow the order of MT.

Num introduces the sons of Judah with a δέ structure, which has no equivalent in MT. Both MT and Num list only Er and Aunan, after which they state that Er and Aunan died in the land of Canaan. The majority A F M V text added to the list και σηλων και φαρες και ζαρα, which is not surprising, since these three are given in v.16 as the sons who survived the death of Er and Aunan, who both died without offspring. The added list is, however, secondary.

26:16(20) Num uses a δέ structure to introduce the Judaites according to their clans. This is neatly justifiable as contrastive to the sons of Judah who died without issue, viz. Er and Aunan. The first one is listed as "לשלה" was the clan of השלני." One might have expected a σηλω for the son's name, but Num has Σηλών, undoubtedly because the gentilic for the name is ὁ Σηλωνί. In the Gen 46:12 account, the name is given as Σηλώμ, and the majority F text actually also reads σηλωμ here. There is no real certainty as to which nasal is original, and so one follows the text of the oldest witnesses, A and B, which read Σηλών. The Byz text reads ο σηλωμ for the gentilic, which is obviously secondary.

The next one reads τῷ Φάρες δῆμος ὁ Φάρες, though MT reads the gentilic form הפרצי. Only the *f* text changes Num to read ο φαρασι. The last son was Ζάρα (for זרח), and the gentilic name is given as ὁ Ζαραΐ. The V Byz+ text changed the gentilic to ζαρα; in fact, the Byz text throughout the chapter rejects the gentilic form entirely in favor of the tribal name. The name is most stable, only ζαραι, ζαρες and ζαραρα being attested, with no more than two mss supporting a misspelling.

26:17(21) As in Gen 46:12 the sub clans of Φάρες are also given as part of the Judah account. The first one gives no problem; "to Hasron, a clan the Hasroni." This also occurred as a Roubenite clan, for which see comment at v.6. The second son of Phares was τῷ Ἰαμουὴλ δῆμος ὁ Ἰαμουηλί. Their parent text probably was the לחמואל and החמואלי of Sam, rather than the לחמול and החמולי of MT.

In the tradition, cod B plus six mss read ιαμουν (and ιαμουνι resp.), but this is secondary.[9] Related readings are ιαμων and ιαμμουν. Other readings include ιαμαηλ, ιεμουηλ and αμουλ.

---

9. For a palaeographic explanation of the development of this secondary text, see THGN 118.

26:18(22) The summary statement for Judah: "these are the clans for Judah according to their review: 76,500." This contrasts with the first census report (of 38 years previous) of 74,600, for which see 1:27 2:4. Instead of τῷ "for," the A x+ text reads του "of," which is closer to the bound phrase of MT.

26:19(23) Vv.19—21 deal with the tribe of Issachar. Num begins with a καί, which has no support in MT, and which the n+ text omits; the omission does equal MT, but is probably ex par, and not recensional, in origin. For variant spellings of the name Ἰσσαχάρ, see Note at Gen 30:18. For the first member's name, BHS reads תּוֹלָע, but Sam has לתולע.[10] Num follows the Sam text with τῷ Θωλά. In the tradition, some mss (f+) change the *omega* by attraction to *alpha*, (i.e. to θαλα.) This also obtains in the gentilic form as θα(λα) in a few mss, but the Hebrew spelling ensures the *omega* as original; cf also Gen 46:13 which reads Θωλά as well.

The second clan is named Φουά for פוה. The gentilic is then formed as Φουαί as expected, but MT reads פוני. The Num transcription is probably based on Sam's פואי (which also reads the member's name as פואה).[11]

26:20(24) The first name, Ἰασούβ for ישוב, is expected, though the Byz text has voiced the interconsonantal *sigma*, thus as ιαζουβ; it also has ιαζουβ for the gentilic. The name did give trouble to copyists, however, especially for the gentilic, which became ισουβι, ασουβι, ασσουβει, ιασουβειμ, ιασουβ and ιασουφ, but the correct spelling is assured as Ἰασουβί.

The second name represents שמרן and its gentilic השמרני. These are transcribed as Σαμράμ and (ὁ) Σαμραμί resp. The translator reads *mu* instead of the Hebrew *nun*. The two nasals are often confused, especially in final position. It might be noted that final *nun* of Aramaic, e.g. as a plural nominal inflection, usually becomes *mem* in Hebrew. The reading with *mu* is, however, certain; cf also Ζαμβράμ in Gen 46:13.[12] The name is bisyllabic, not trisyllabic (as uniquely in B*; B* also has σαμαρανει uniquely for the gentilic.)[13] The name gave a great deal of trouble to copyists, as the following list of misspellings shows: ζαμβραμ,

---

10. As do Kenn 75* 191; Kenn 286 has לתולה.
11. 4QNum[b] also attests to the spelling with א.
12. Theod and Aq also read (τῷ) Σαμράμ, and Sym reads (τοῦ) Σεμρώμ.
13. See THGN 118.

σαμβρειμ, σαμβραμ, σαμραν, σαμβραν, αμραμ, αραμ, αμβραν, αβρααμ, αβραμ, αβραν and αμβραμ. A similar list might be given for the gentilic.[14]

26:21(25) The summary statement gives the count as 64,300 for the second census. This contrasts with the first census of 1:27 and 2:6 where the tribal count was 54,400. In the tradition, the 64,000 is almost universally followed, but the majority A F text reads τετρακοσιοι instead of τριακόσιοι. This may well have been influenced by the τετρακόσιοι of the first census, but is secondary, since MT reads ושלש מאות.[15]

26:22(26) Vv.22—23 concern the Zaboulonites. The sons of Zaboulon are three: Σάρεδ (for סרד), ʼΑλλών (for אלון), and ʼΑλλήλ (for יחלאל). The first son is called Σέρεδ at Gen 46:14. In both traditions, the first vowel is unquestioned. One may then conclude that the translator of Num transcribed the names independently of Gen; The copyists were also not influenced by the Gen transcription; though the misspellings are numerous, the first vowel is secure; note σαρεα, σαραι, σαρε, σαρυιδ, σαδρι (Byz), αδρι and ζαμβρη.

The second one, ʼΑλλών, also contributed a number of misspellings: αλων, αλωμ, ααλων, αλαων, αλλαων (Byz) and αλλω.

The last name listed reads τῷ ʼΑλλὴλ δῆμος ὁ ʼΑλληλί. The Hebrew reads ליחלאל משפחת היחלאלי.[16] The transcriber disregarded the initial *yodh*, but the hex text revised it; (cf ιαλληλ, ιαλλη, ιαλιηλ and ιαηλ). Outside the hex tradition, the name is very unstable; note αδδηλ, αληλ, αλληδ, αληδ, αλλι, αλι, αλλην, αλληα and αιηλ (Byz). It might be noted that in Gen 46:14 the name is also transcribed without regard to the initial *yodh* as ʼΑλοήλ.

26:23(27) The summary count for the clan Ζαβουλών according to their review: 60,500. MT has a gentilic הזבולני rather than the tribal name, which is unique for the chapter. Num follows the usual pattern, which is also attested in Sam. This review differs from the earlier census, in which the tribe numbered 57,400; see 1:29 2:8.

---

14. Theod and Aq read ὁ Σαμραμεί, and Sym has ὁ Σεμρωνίτης.
15. See THGN 114.
16. The Others read τῷ ʼΙαλὶλ δῆμος ὁ ʼΙαλιλεί.

26:24(15) Vv.24–27 deal with the Gadites. The first son is Σαφών for צפון, also written in the tradition as σαφουν, σαμφων and ασαφων. Instead of the gentilic Σαφωνί, the Byz text as usual has the tribal name σαφων.

The second son is 'Αγγί, which transcribes חגי, with no change for the gentilic, except for its articulation. This is also true for the third son, Σουνί (for שוני), which appears as ὁ Σουνί for the clan name. In Gen 46:16 'Αγγί and Σουνί appear with Hellenized endings, i.e. as 'Αγγίς and Σαυνίς resp.

26:25(16) Here 'Αζενί and 'Αδδί occur for both the sons and the clan names. In MT these are האזני/אזני and הערי/ערי resp. For the second one, Num follows the העדי/עדי readings of Sam.[17] In the tradition, 'Αζενί becomes αζουνι, αζανι, αζανιει, αζωνι, αζινι, αζενε, αζνει, αζαν (in Byz), ζανει and αζε. In the parallel Gen 46:16 list this is Θασοβάν (but אצבן in MT); cf Note ad loc. The name 'Αδδί is quite stable, only αδι, ανδι, αδιδει and αδδειει occurring as variant spellings. In Gen the name is Hellenized as 'Αηδίς.

26:26(17) 'Αροαδί is both the son's name and the tribal name, which follows Sam's ארודי and הארודי, whereas MT has ארוד for the tribal name; (it is 'Αροηδίς in Gen 46:16). The name was badly misspelled by copyists; note αρουαδει, αοραδι, αροδει, αροηδι, αροιδι, αραδι, αροαδ (Byz), αοραδ, αροαρ, αρωδ and αροα.

The final son was 'Αριηλ (for אראלי), also spelled αριηδ, αροηλ and αροηλι.[18] The clan name was 'Αριηλί, also misspelled as αριηδει, αριλι, αριαλι, αηριηλι, αοαριηλι, αροηλι, αηλι and αριηλ (Byz+).[19] In the parallel Gen record, the name became 'Αριηλίς.

26:27(18) The total count for the second census for the Gadites was 40,500. In the tradition, only the 500 was stable. A popular B F M V text has an extra four thousand, i.e. 44,500. I suspect that this is explicable as a partial dittograph, i.e. τεσσαρες και τεσσαρακοντα χιλιαδες developing from an original τεσσαράκοντα χιλιάδες.[20] The count contrasts with the earlier census of 45,650, for which see 1:37 2:15.

---

17. The Pesh also reads עדי, but the Tar all follow MT, as does Vulg.
18. 4QNum[b], however, reads אר(י)אל, i.e. the parent text for Num.
19. 4QNum[b] read האריאלי, which assures the vocalization 'Αριηλί.
20. See THGN 115.

26:28(44) Once again Num has reordered the tribes, dealing with the tribe of Aser here rather than after the Danites. Hex has transposed vv.28—31 after v.47, to equal the order of MT. Vv.28—31 deal with the count of the Aserites.

The first member was Ἰαμίν/ὁ Ἰαμινί; MT reads הימנה/ימנה. The parallel account in Gen 46:17 has Ἰεμνά. There is no evidence of hex interference correcting Ἰαμίν to the Ἰεμνά of Gen, which would equal MT more exactly. In the tradition, only a few variants spellings (outside of itacistic spellings of course) obtain; these include ιαμμειν, ιαμβειν, ιαμειμ and αμιν. The Byz text again uses the tribal name ιαμιν, rather than the gentilic.

The second member is Ἰεσουί (for ישוי[ה]). Variant spellings are ιεσσουι (F y+), ιασ(σ)ουβ (Byz), ιασουν, ιεσουνι, ιασου and ιεσου (B V b), as well as ισουι and ιασουνει, only for the gentilic. The Gen 46:17 parallel text reads Ἰεσουά (for ישוה).[21]

The third member given was Βαριά/ὁ Βαριαί for הבריעי/בריעה. The Byz text reads βερι for both. Other misspellings in the tradition include βαρειαει, αβαρεια, βαριω and βαρα. For the gentilic, note also βαρια and βαραι (A y+).

26:29(45) Over against the parallel text of Gen 46:17, where Χόβορ and Μελχιήλ are given as subclans, i.e. as sons of Βαρία, here Χόβορ and Μελχιήλ are a fourth and fifth son of Aser. MT also names these as לבני בריעה, and hex has added των υιων βαρια under the asterisk at the beginning of the verse. Num follows the text of Sam which also has the shorter text.[22]

How the Hebrew חבר was originally pronounced is not clear. The Masoretes vocalized the name with *seghol* in both syllables, probably presupposing an earlier monosyllable *ḥabr*. One ms actually reads χαβερ (and χαβερι). Except for the Byz reading χοβορ for the gentilic as well, the tradition is very stable.

Μελχιήλ correctly transcribes מלכיאל. In the tradition, a few misspellings do occur, but throughout are only attested in single witnesses, except for the usual failure of the Byz text to recognize the gentilic ending, i.e. reading μαλχιηλ. These include μελλιηλ, μεχιηλ, μελχηλ and μεχχιηλ.

---

21. Gen has an extra son, Ἰεούλ, but MT has ישוי, which is probably a doublet reading for ישוה.
22. The shorter text is hardly original; note the consecution הבריעי לבני בריעה. The omission is caaused by the recurrence of בריע.

26:30(46) The name of Aser's daughter was Σάρα, indistinguishable from the name of her great-grandmother Σάρα, later changed to Σάρρα, for which see Gen 17:15. In Hebrew, however, the name differs; here MT has שרח, whereas Abram's wife's name was שרי. It might be noted that V Byz s+ read σαρρα, i.e. the name later given to Abraham's wife.

26:31(47) The summary statement for the review of the clan of Aser is given as 53,400. Note that MT has בני אשר "the Asherites." Hex has added υιων before 'Ασήρ to equal MT.[23] In the reports of the first census at 1:41 and 2:28, the count ws 41,500. Only the hex+ text reads πεντήκοντα (χιλιάδες), all others reading the τεσσαρακοντα of the first census, i.e. 43,500. Here only the hex reading can be considered original;[24] alone the numbers of MT can be original, since the totals for the Israelites in v.52 given in Num equal the totals in MT.[25]

26:32(28) Vv.32—41 detail the review of the offspring of Joseph, with vv.33—38 dealing with Manasse, and vv.39—41, with Ephraim. V.32 simply gives the names of the sons of Joseph according to their clans as being Μανασσὴ καὶ Εφράιμ. For other spellings of Μανασσή, see Note at Gen 41:51.

26:33(29) The V Byz text begins with και, but MT (and all the other ancient witnesses) begin asyndetically. The offspring of Manasse was Μαχίρ for מכיר. In turn, Machir fathered Γαλαάδ; for Γαλαάδ, see Bible Dictionaries. That υιοί is better rendered by "offspring" is particularly clear here, since only one "offspring" is again mentioned, though vv.33—36 give a number of descendants for Galaad. In other words, υιοί refers not only to "sons," but to the next generations as well; cf also comment at v.8.

26:34(30) MT begins asyndetically, but Num introduces οὗτοι with a καί. The first descendant of Galaad is 'Αχιέζερ, whose clan was ὁ 'Αχιεζερί. MT, however, has האיעזרי/איעזר. The usual pattern for the Hebrew is the name governed by ל followed by the articulated gentilic; this becomes τῷ plus the name

---
23. Sym is also attested as reading υἱῶν 'Ασήρ.
24. Which is also substantiated by The Others.
25. See also THGN 114.

(representing the predicate of the noun clause), followed by ὁ plus the gentilic (representing the subject). A popular A B F M text, however, omits τῷ. Here, MT also omits the ל.[26] Furthermore, at Josh 17:2 the name is אביעזר;[27] see also 1Chr 7:18. The Greek name presupposes a parent Hebrew אחיעזר/אחיעזרי, and the Qumran text represents the parent text of Num.

A second offspring was Χελεκ/Χελεκί for the Hebrew חלק/חלקי. The name created difficulty for copyists, producing χαλεκ, αχελεκ (n), χελεχ, χελεγ (B+), as well as χελεδ (z), χελεβ, χελεεγ ανδ αχελει. For the gentilic even greater confusion reigned, with the Byz text as uusual, not recognizing the gentilic ending.[28]

26:35(31) In both vv.35—36 MT does not introduce the offspring's name with ל, whereas Num uses τῷ in all four cases, which illustrates once again this translator's love of patterns of translation.[29] Ἐσριήλ and its gentilic represent אשריאל and אשראלי, though the Masoretes vocalized it as Asriel(i). Copyists found the name strange, and created εσρεηλ, ιεσριηλ, εξριηλ or εσδριηλ (Byz), σεριηλ (b), σερεηλ, σαριηλ, εριηλ, εστριηλ, εσσριηλ and εξεριηλ.

The next name is Σύχεμ/Συχεμί, representing שכם(י). Since the name "Shechem" was well-known, the tradition was stable for its spelling; as usual the Byz text also read συχεμ for the gentilic word as well.

26:36(32) "For Συμαέρ (there was) a clan, the Συμαερί." MT introduces the verse with a conjunction, which Num disregarded. MT, however, reads שמידע and השמידעי. Num read *resh* instead of *daleth*, and transposed it with *'ayin*, thus as *שמיער* and *השמיערי*. There is no evidence of correction to the Hebrew of any kind in the tradition.

---

26. 4QNum^b has לאחיעזר, which must be parent to Num's τῷ Ἀχιέζερ.
27. Gray 392 suggests that איעזר is an abbreviation for אביעזר, and that Ἀχιέζερ is a mistake for the latter, but see previous f.n.
28. For a defence of the Num text as original, particularly over against the impossible reading of cod B with a final *gamma*, see THGN 118.
29. BHS maintains in each case that the tribal name be introduced by ל, which somehow presupposes that the Num translator only translated mechanically in isolate fashion, which is simply not true.

The second name is Ὄφερ for חפר. The name is stable in the tradition, only εφερ and αφερ (each supported by only two witnesses) obtaining. As usual the Byz text retains οφερ for the gentilic as well.[30]

26:37(33) The son of Hophir was Σαλπαάδ (for צלפחד). An initial צ is always transcribed by *sigma* in Num (except fo צען which became Τανίν at 13:23). In the tradition, Σαλπαάδ is misspelled in various ways: σαλπαδ, σαλπααλ, σααλπααλ, σααλπαδ, σαλφααδ and σαλτααλ. Each of these is palaeographically explicable. "He had no sons, but (had) daughters."

V.b begins with καὶ ταῦτα τὰ ὀνόματα, for which the parent text was clearly the reading of 4QNum^b ואלה שמות. MT has no equivalent for ταῦτα, simply reading ושם, and hex omitted the pronoun to equal MT. The presence of ταῦτα changes the syntax. In MT, the subject of the clause is "the names of the daughters of Zalophehad," with the list of names which follows constituting the predicate. In Num the subject is ταῦτα, and its predicate is "the names of the daughters of Salpaad"; the list is then in apposition with ταῦτα.

The five names are connected by καί throughout, whereas in MT only the first and the last pair are connected by *waw*, with the third one, חגלה completely asyndetic.[31] The first name is Μααλά, which transcribed מחלה. Intervocalic ח is represented by a double vowel, whereas in CV or VC position, MT uses a single vowel. The name also occurs at 27:1 36:11, and the double vowel is original throughout in spite of A B+ reading μαλα both here and at 27:1. On the other hand, at 36:11 both 963 and B read Μααλά.[32]

Νουά stands for נעה, and only νουσα and νουαλ obtain as variant spellings. Ἐγλά represents חגלה. It too is quite stable, and only the uniquely supported misspellings, αιγαλ, αγλα, αιχλα, εγαα and αιγλαν, obtain. Μελχά for מלכה gave no trouble to copyists, only μελκα, μελχαλ and μελχθα appearing in single witnesses. The last name is θερσά for תרצה. Variant spellings in the tradition are limited to θαρσα, θρεσα, θηρσα, θερεα and θελσα, with no more than two mss witnessing to any particular misspelling.

---

30. The *omicron* is assured by 4QNum^b, which reads וחופר and החופרי resp.
31. It should be noted, however, that many mss do read ומלכה for the fourth name.
32. For a fuller statement, see THGN 118—119.

26:38(34) According to the review for the clan of Manasse, there were 52,700 counted. A popular A text has changed the 52,000 to 62,000, but this does not agree with MT's חמשים,[33] and there is no obvious reason for the variant.[34] The first census reported a much smaller count of 32,200 according to 1:33 2:21. Num has the usual ἐξ construction for ופקדיהם. The parent text is that of Sam, which also occurs in 4QNum[b] as לפקודיהם. Cf comment at v.45.

26:39(35) Vv.39—41 concern the other son of Joseph, the Ephraimites. Num begins with "καὶ οὗτοι the sons of Ephraim," whereas MT begins asyndetically. MT, however, adds למשפחתם, and hex has added κατα δημους αυτων under the asterisk to represent it. The first offspring was Σουταλά with the clan name as ὁ Σουταλαί representing השתלחי/שותלח. This contrasts with Σουθάλααμ of Gen 46:20, but this had no counterpart in MT. The origin of this spelling is therefore unknown. The majority text has σουθαλα, but there seems to be no pattern for the transcription of ת vs ט. The *tau* is used for both graphemes, and is far more common than the *theta*, but *theta* also occurs for both. This seems to be the case regardless of position. E.g. for initial position תרצה became Θερσά at v.37, but in v.39 תחן becomes Τάναχ; see below. Accordingly, Num simply followed the oldest witness, cod B, though it must be admitted that a good case for the *theta* can be made. At Gen 46:20 the oldest ms, 962, does read a *theta*, though that is the product of another translator. Furthermore, for the name Τάναχ/Ταναχί only ms 426 reads a *theta*, but actually, ms 426 often witnesses to secondary Hebrew influence. As expected, the name was misspelled in a variety of ways in the tradition: σαταλ, σουθαλαδ, σουλαθα, θουσαλα, σουθαλασει and θωσουσαλα (cod A).

In MT, the second clan attributed to Ephraim reads לבכר משפחת הבכרי, which Num omitted. Hex added τω βαχαρ δημος ο βαχαρι under the asterisk to represent the omitted clan.

The last descendant of Ephraim is Τάναχ for the Hebrew התחני/תחן. Obviously, the parent text presupposed transposed consonants and read תנחי/תנח. Here the ח grapheme represents an original velar ח, rather than the laryngeal, as its transcription in *chi* demonstrates.[35] In the parallel Gen 46:20 text the name

---

33. The Others also read πεντήκοντα.
34. See THGN 115.
35. See J.W.Wevers, Ḥeth in Classical Hebrew, Essays on the Ancient Semitic World, edited by D.B.Redford and J.W.Wevers (Toronto: 1970), 101—112.

appears as Τάαμ, but without a correspondent in MT. The name is quite stable in the tradition, with the usual exception of the Byz text reading ταναχ for the gentilic form as well as for the patronymic, although some misspellings in single mss do occur: ναχ, θαναχ, ταναει, ταμαχιηλ and αχαμ.

26:40(36) Num follows Sam, in not representing the initial *waw* of MT, but the Byz text supplied a και. On the meaning of υιοί, see comment at v.8. A subclan is attributed to Soutala, viz., Ἐδέν/Εδενί. MT has הערני/ערן. The name ערן occurs only here, whereas עדן is a well-known Hebrew root; in fact, עדן occurs both as a personal name as well as a geographical one in the Hebrew Bible. Which is here original cannot be determined. In the tradition, the Byz text read εδεμ (for both). Also attested are εδιν (*C'*), ουδεν(ι) as well as εδιεν and εδωμ.

26:41(37) MT reads "These are the clans of בני אפרים," for which Num has Ἐφράιμ. Hex has added υιων before Ἐφράιμ to represent the untranslated בני. The count amounted to 32,500, which is considerably less than the count at the first census of 40,500 according to 1:31 2:19.

V.b constitutes a subscription: "these are the clans of the sons of Joseph according to their clans." MT lacks "the clans of," and ms 426 and Syh probably represent hex by changing δῆμοι υἱῶν to υιοι, thus "these are the sons of Joseph."

26:42(38) Vv.42—45 concern the Benjaminites. Vv.42—43 list four descendants of Benjamin: Βάλε, Ἀσυβήρ, Ἀχιράν and Σωφάν, whereas Gen 46:21 lists only three: Βάλα, Χόβορ καὶ Ἀσβήλ. These represent בלע ובכר ואשבל in MT. The Gen text then continues with six sons of Bala and one subclan (i.e. Γηρά fathering Ἄραδ). In MT, there are a further seven descendants of Benjamin. There would seem little point in comparing these with the names given in vv.42—44, which are substantially different.

The first offspring is Βάλε representing בלע. The Byz text has βαλακ for both the tribal name and the gentilic. This name is of course well-known from the Balaam narratives of chh.22—24, but see also βαλακ as the majority reading for Βαλά at Gen 14:2,8 36:32,33.

The second was Ἀσυβήρ/ὁ Ἀσυβηρί, though MT has האשבלי/אשבל. Mediate Hebrew influence is clear in the reading of ms 426: ασβηλ/ασβηλει. Confusion of liquids /r/ and /l/ is well-known in Egyptian, e.g. in the Merneptah

Israel Stele where Canaanite leaders greeted the Pharaoh by *sharom*.³⁶ This is particularly well-documented in Coptic dialects; in fact, in Memphitic every /r/ has become /l/. Incidentally, this probably shows that the /l/ and /r/ phonemes were pronounced as velar consonants in Alexandria. In the tradition, the name was variously spelled as ασσυβηρ, ασουβηρ, ασιβηρ, ασοβηρ and ασβηρ.

The third son of Benjamin was Ἀχιράν for אחירם with corresponding gentilics Ἀχιρανί for אחירמי. The hex text corrected the *mu* to *nu*, i.e. as αχιραμ and αχιραμι resp, but the forms with *nu* are original. The confusion between the two nasals is well-documented for LXX in general. Also secondary is the spelling with an initial *iota* as in B V+. This is simply a case of dittography based on a parent uncial, since the word Ἀχιράν is articulated by the dative τῷ, which in uncial writing would appear as ΤΩΙ.³⁷ Other misspellings include αχραν, αχιρων, αχειρα and αχειρ.

26:43(39) A final offspring for Benjamin is given as Σωφάν/Σωφανί, but MT has השופמי/שפופם. I presume that the parent text for Σωφάν was שופם, and not the odd שפופם of MT. Once again, the confusion of nasals is evident as in the case of Ἀχιράν. Hex did change the *nu* to *mu* for both patronymic and gentilic as in the case of the third clan (in v.42), but made no further change to approximate MT.³⁸ Also found in the tradition are σωφαρ, σωφαι and σαφαν.

MT has a fifth member which Num omits. It reads לחופם משפחת החופמי. The omission was accidental, due to homoioteleuton. The translator's eye skipped from one ופמי- to the second one. Hex has added τω ουφαμ δημος ο ουφαμι under the asterisk to represent the omitted text. The Byz text has added τω αραδι δημος ο αραδι; for its source see comment on the hex addition in v.44.

26:44(40) Two names are given as sons of Bale: Ἀδάρ καὶ Νοεμάν. MT has ארד for the first one. There is an obvious confusion of the order of *resh* and *daleth*, but whether ארד or אדר as at 1Chr 8:3 was the original order cannot be determined. In any event, Num read Ἀδάρ. The second offspring was נעמן in the parent text.³⁹

---

36. I am indebted to my colleague Ronald Leprohon for this reference.
37. See THGN 117.
38. See THGN 117.
39. See THGN 135.

Num then disregards the first son, and continues with "to Noeman, a clan, the Noemanite." MT only partially fills in with a parallel for the first offspring with its משפחת הארדי, which seems to me to be a defective text; one would expect an introductory לארד, as in Sam, which, however, omits v.a entirely. Hex has added τω αδαρ δημος ο αδαρι under the asterisk; clearly the hex text is here based on the longer text of v.b of Sam rather than MT, i.e. one with the expected ל phrase at the beginning before משפחת.⁴⁰

In the tradition, the majority A F V text has αδερ instead of 'Αδάρ. Num simply adopted the vocalization of the oldest extant witness, cod B.

26:45(41) V.b begins with ופקדיהם, which Num omits, having rendered למשפחתם by its usual pattern with ἐξ ἐπισκέψεως αὐτῶν. In other words, Num treated the ופקדיהם as an unnecessary doublet to the ל phrase. It should be noted that ἐπίσκεψις regularly renders both words throughout this chapter, so that a shortened version was a sensible solution. Note that hex made no attempt to "correct" Num to fit the text of MT.

The count is given as 45,600. This contrasts with the earlier census figures of 35,400 at 1:35 2:23. The majority A B F M V text read the 30,000 of the first census instead of the 40,000 of the second, but this cannot be original. It not only disagrees with MT, it also does not fit the summary statement of the complete census report in v.51.⁴¹ The 600 is also not stable in the tradition; the Byz text reads 300, and the majority text has 500, but only 600 can be original.⁴²

26:46(42) Vv.46—47 concern the offspring of Dan. Only one descendant (υἱοί) is given, Σαμί, for השוחמי/שוחם. In the parallel account, Gen 46:23, the (single) offspring is 'Ασομ for חושם. What parent text the translator read is not certain; it may have been שחמי, i.e. with a scramble of consonants, and the *waw* read as *yodh*. Note that the name in Gen also shows transposition: חושם vs שוחם (Num). The name is variously spelled in the tradition: σαμε, σαμεει, σαμειν, σαμεν, σαμ, σαμιει, σαμειδη, σαδι, σωμαν, as well as the σουαμ in ms 426, which is due to mediate Hebrew influence.

---

40. See THGN 135 as well.
41. See THGN 114.
42. See THGN 115.

MT begins the verse asyndetically, and Num with its καί equals the Sam text. MT begins with אלה, which Num omits. A Byz text restores ουτοι; this is either recensional or ex par; see vv.7,9,14,18,21,23,27,31,34,38,40 and 45; I suspect that it was ex par.

26:47(43) The review of "all the clans of Sami" (representing the δῆμοι Δάν) is counted as 64,400. The C' s text closed the final syllable of Σαμί by the dental nasal, σαμ(ε)ιν, and ms 426 shows Hebrew influence by its σουαμει (for שוחמי), as it did in v.46.

In the tradition, the cI text read τριακοντα instead of ἑξήκοντα (thousand), and the majority A B F M V text read εξακοσιοι instead of τετρακόσιοι. This cannot be original, since MT reads the same as Num. Nor is the majority reading due to the influence of the first census which read 62,700 at 1:39 2:26. The variant remains inexplicable.[43]

26:48 The last tribe to be surveyed is the υἱοὶ Ναφθαλί (vv.48—50). For the majority spelling of Ναφθαλί with a final *nu* in vv.48—50, see Note at Gen 30:8. The first offspring is 'Ασιήλ/ὁ 'Ασιηλί for יחצאלי/היצאל. At Gen 46:24 the name is given as 'Ιασιήλ for יחצאל. It must be admitted, however, that the majority text reads ασιηλ, and since the name there immediately follows Ναφθαλί in Gen, haplography/dittography was at work; in other words, the spelling of Gen is not certain. Here the tradition does show a variant reading ιασιηλ/ιασιηλι, but supported by only two O mss, 58 and 426; in other words, the variant is probably a hex correction. Why the translator should have transcribed the syllable יח by an *alpha* rather than by *iota alpha* is not clear. As it does throughout the chapter, the Byz text does not transcribe the gentilic ending; it reads ασιηλ. The name is variously realized in the tradition: as ασεηλ, ασαηλ, ασηλει, σιηλ, σαηλ, ασηλ, βασιηλ and δασιηλη.

The second offspring is Γαυνί for גוני. The Gen translator transcribed this by Γωυνί. Either is a possible transcription of the consonantal text. In the tradition, the A M popular text also read γωυνι. Also attested are γουνει, γααυνει, γωυινι, γωννει, γαυει, ωγαυη and ωγυνι.

---

43. See THGN 115.

26:49 The third Naphthalite was Ἰέσερ/ὁ Ἰεσερί for היצרי/יצר, which in the Gen parallel was Ἰσααρ (not Ἰσσααρ as printed; see Note ad loc) for יצר (as though it were יצהר). In the tradition, the Byz text read ιε(σ)σααρ. Also occurring are the spellings ιεσσερ, ισεερ, εσερ, ιεσσερει, εσρι (A oI y), ιεσσρι, νεσσερ, θερι and ιασιει. Other misspellings for the gentilic include ασσερι, ιεσσρι, ιεσρι, εισσερεει, ιεσσουρι, ισερι and ισσερι.

The last descendant is Σελλήμ/ὁ Σελλημί for Hebrew השלמי/שלם. In Gen 46:24 the name is spelled Συλλήμ. In the tradition, the name was badly treated, appearing as σελημ, συλλημ (Byz), σελλη, συλημ, σηλωμ, σελει, σεαλημ and σεληλ. The gentilic underwent similar treatment.

26:50 The summary statement of the review of the Naphthali clans: 45,400, which contrasts with the 53,400 of the first census report at 1:43 2:30. MT reads: "These are the clans of Naphthali למשפחתם ופקדיהם (were) fifty and forty thousand and four hundred." Num has reduced this to ἐξ ἐπισκέψεως αὐτῶν, i.e. it omitted למשפחתם, and treated ופקדיהם as at vv.38 and 45, i.e. the pattern followed throughout the chapter; see comment at v.45. Instead of τετρακόσιοι, the majority A B F M V 963 text reads τριακοσιοι; this is an error, disagreeing with MT. The text of Num is original; it alone fits the total count of v.51. The source of the majority variant is unknown.[44]

26:51 The total count of the review of the Israelites, which amounted to 601,730. This is the sum total of the twelve reviews given in vv.7—50 of Num and MT, and insures the Num text as correct over against variant texts. Num does not imitate the plural of MT: אלה פקדי, but correctly interprets by the singular αὕτη ἡ ἐπίσκεψις; see also comment at 1:44.

MT also has no conjunction before שבע; i.e. it reads "600 thousand and a thousand, seven hundred and thirty." Num follows Sam by reading καὶ ἑπτακόσιοι. The first census had been a somewhat larger count; the total had been 603,550 according to 1:46 2:32.

26:53 τούτοις refers to the twelve tribes listed in the chapter as surveyed. The land of promise "will be apportioned κληρονομεῖν according to the number of

---

44. See THGN 115.

names." The infinitive translates the prepositional phrase בנחלה "for a possession," i.e. "by inheritance," and is probably intended as a complementary infinitive, i.e. "apportioned to inherit (or possess)." The division is to be made according to the population count of the second census; i.e. to the tribe with the largest number of names, the largest portion was to be assigned.

26:54 This principle is clearly stated in v.54. "For the more numerous you must increase the inheritance, and for the less numerous you must decrease their inheritance." MT has נחלתו for "the inheritance," as well as for "their inheritance," i.e. the translator uses the genitive pronoun only for the second case, which is then intended to do double duty.[45] Hex has added a genitive pronoun for the first κληρονομίαν to equal MT more precisely. Num correctly understood the nouns רב and מעט as collectives, and translated them by the plural comparatives, πλείοσιν and ἐλάττοσιν.

V.b enunciates the principle "to each (i.e. tribe) as they were surveyed, their inheritance shall be assigned (δοθήσεται). What is meant by the καθώς clause is "according to the findings of the census report."

26:55 A second principle for assignment of the land of promise is introduced in vv.55—56, viz. διὰ κλήρων. MT has בגורל אך, but Num disregarded the אך, and has rendered the ב phrase by διά plus the plural noun, i.e. "through lots";[46] it is through the sacred lot that the land is to be assigned. This seems to contradict the principle enunciated by vv.54—55, viz., that size of population was to be the determining factor for assignment of land. This need not be the case, however. What the lot was to determine was geography, not the size of the land assignment.

"They shall inherit according to the names (τοῖς ὀνόμασιν a dative of means or instrument) in accordance with the tribes (κατὰ φυλάς) of their paternal ancestry." MT reads the "tribes of their fathers."

26:56 Num interprets the תחלק of MT as a Qal, which is a possible understanding of the consonantal text. The Masoretes, however, vocalized it as a third feminine singular Ni with נחלתו as its subject, i.e. "(according to the lot) his

---
45. See SS 100.
46. See SS 121.

inheritance shall be apportioned," whereas Num understood it as a command to Moses: "you must apportion his (i.e. each tribe's) inheritance."

This apportionment is to be ἀνὰ μέσον πολλῶν καὶ ὀλίγων "between (the) many and (the) few." This adequately renders בין רב למעט, and it attempts to harmonize the two principles, that of number and that of lot. The two nouns are here rendered by the positive degree, rather than the comparatives of v.54, but the rendering is fully adequate. As suggested in a comment at v.55, the size of the inheritance was determined by "number," but the particular location was determined ἐκ τοῦ κλήρου.

26:57 Vv.57—62 deal with the Levites, who were not to be assigned a portion of land among the tribes. MT begins with "and ואלה פקדי of Levi," which Num changed to "and the υἱοί of Levi," which together with κατὰ δήμους αὐτῶν, follows the pattern of vv.19,22,24,28,32,42 and 46. Hex has added ουτοι επεσκεμμενοι under the asterisk after the opening καί to represent MT, but it did not omit (as ms 426 did), or mark υἱοί with an obelus, to indicate its lack of correspondent in MT.

The pattern of a dative name followed by δῆμος plus an articulated gentilic found throughout this chapter is also used for the sons of Levi here. The first "son" was Γεδσών, who was the ancestor of the Γεδσωνί clan. MT has הגרשני/גרשון. For a reasoned defence of Γεδσών for גרשון, see Note at Gen 46:11. Hex has corrected the name as γηρσων/γηρσωνι.

The second Levite was Καάθ/ὁ Κααθί for הקהתי/קהת. For Καάθ, see Note at Gen 46:11. The name is completely stable in the tradition.

The third son was Μεραρί for המררי/מררי. For the name, also see Note at Gen 46:11. The name is stable in the tradition, only μαραρει, μαρερει and γεραρει occurring as misspellings, and for the gentilic, a further μεραει and μεραapι obtain.

26:58 MT reads "These are the clans of Levi," whereas Num speaks of the clans of the Levites; hex has placed υἱῶν under the obelus to indicate its lack of a correspondent in MT. The clans are throughout registered as δῆμοι plus the articulated gentilic. The first clan is ὁ Λοβενί, for which see 3:18, where it was assigned to Gedson. In MT, it is vocalizes as "Libnite." In the tradition, it is variously spelled as λεβενι, λοβεννι, λευενι, λουβενι, λομενι and λοβερνυη.

The second tribe is ὁ Χεβρωνί, which is followed in MT by משפחת המחלי; this was omitted by Num, probably by parablepsis due to the repetition of משפחת; hex added δῆμος ο μοολι under the asterisk to represent the omitted clan. The name Χεβρωνί also occurs in the tradition as χεβρενει, χευρωνι, χεβρωενι, λεβρωνει, χεβρων and χευρων.

The last two clans are given as δῆμος ὁ Κόρε καὶ δῆμος ὁ Μουσί. The names are transposed in MT as משפחת המושי משפחת הקרחי. The majority A F M text follows the order of MT, but since both B and 963 follow the Num order, this is probably original text; this is the order of Sam as well, which also supports the καί joining the two, though it should be noted that Sam joins all the items with conjunctions, not just the last pair as in Num. At 3:20 Μουσί is said to be a subclan of the Merarites. The name did suffer in the tradition, as the following show: βουσι, ομουσι, μοσι and ομοουσι.

V.b states "and Kaath fathered Ἀμράμ"; comp 3:27. The majority A text reads αμβραμ. The M tradition has αμραν, and many scattered witnesses read αμβραν; others read αβραν or αβραμ, but the transcription Ἀμράμ for עמרם is original.

26:59 Most witnesses change the initial καὶ τό to τὸ δέ, but the two oldest witnesses, B and 963, read the Num text, which is thus probably original. The change to a δέ construction is stylistic, indicating change of subject, viz. to the name of Amram's wife, Ἰωχάβεδ, for the Hebrew יוכבד. The name created a great deal of confusion among copyists, who spelled it in a variety of ways: ιωχεβεδ, ιωχαδεβ, ιωχαχαβεδ, ιωχαβερ, ιωχαβελ, ιωχαβουθ, ιωχαβεβ, ιωχαβετ, ιωχαβιθ, ιωχαφεθ, ιαχαβεθ, ιωχαμεθ, ιωχαβθυ, and as a majority A M spelling, ιωχαβεθ. Jochabed is identified as a daughter of Levi, i.e. as the aunt of her husband, Amram.

This is followed in MT by אשר ילדה אתה ללוי, which does not make much sense, since it says: "who (i.e. the daughter) bore her to Levi in Egypt." The translator changed the אתה to τούτους. At first blush, this seems grotesque; the pronoun seems to reflect vv.57—58, which is impossible. So what does this mean?

I would suggest that this only makes sense as referring to a procedent, rather than to an antecedent, i.e. to the next clause, which is fully clear. It reads: "And she bore to Amram: Aaron, and Moses, and Mariam their sister." When the preceding clause says "who bore them to Levi in Egypt," it means that she produced greatgrandchildren to Levi, namely the three whom she bore to Levi's grandson, Amram. The translator did not write gibberish, but simply attributed offspring directly to the ancestral parent, a common Hebrew practice. In other words, the last clause explicates the preceding relative clause. I would translate the last clause as "even (or namely) she bore to Amran, Aaron and Moses and Mariam their sister."

In fact, copyists had no difficulty with these clauses. The only changes of significance to be noted in the tradition are the addition of accusative articles before Μωυσήν and before Μαριάμ. These were probably added by hex; in fact, the την before Μαριάμ is under the asterisk. The articles represent Origen's attempt to render the את introducing both names in MT.

26:60 MT begins with a singular Ni verb ויולד, which Num changes to the plural καὶ ἐγεννήθησαν, since the subject is compound. The majority A F M text read ετεχθησαν, which is a synonym. For the active ילד τίκτω is far more common than γεννάω/γίνομαι (182 vs 36 times), but for the Ni the occurrences are 15 vs 26.[47] Since the oldest witness read ἐγεννήθησαν, it was probably original. In MT, the four sons are given in two pairs: Nadab and אביהוא, Eleazar and Ithamar, which Num renders in the pattern a+b+c+d.[48]

Num differs from MT only in the second name, which throughout LXX becomes 'Αβιούδ; see Note at Exod 6:23. In the tradition, the names are stable. For Ναδάβ, ναδαμ, ναιδαμ and ναβαδ occur. For 'Αβιούδ, αβιουθ and αβουδ are found, whereas the variant αβιου is due to Hebrew influence. The third name suffered apocopation in one ms as ελεαζ, and the fourth son is spelled as ιαθαμαρ in a single ms.

26:61 The premature death of the two eldest sons occurred "ἐν τῷ προσφέρειν αὐτοὺς πῦρ ἀλλότριον ἔναντι κυρίου in the desert of Sina." The incident referred to is found in Lev 10:1–2. MT has no equivalent for "in the desert of Sina," which is a case of harmonization with 3:4 where ἐν τῇ ἐρήμῳ Σινὰ occurs. Hex has placed the structure under the obelus to indicate its lack of an equivalent in MT.

---

47. The count is that of Dos Santos.
48. Many Hebrew mss, however, also read ואלעזר for the third item.

26:62 MT begins with ויהיו פקדיהם, as predicate and subject, with the number "23,000" comprising the modifier or complement of יהיו. Num has a different syntactic pattern. Throughout the second census report the usual reference to the census survey occurred as לפקדיהם, which was rendered by ἐξ ἐπισκέψεως αὐτῶν, and Num uses this phrase here as well. The number τρεῖς καὶ εἴκοσι χιλιάδες becomes the subject of ἐγενήθησαν, and the prepositional phrase modifies the verb. The subject then has an apposite following: "every male from one month old and above." The number of Levites has increased by a thousand since the first census; cf 3:39.

The reason is given in a γάρ clause, in turn followed by a ὅτι clause. The γάρ clause explains that the Levites had not been included in the survey (συνεπεσκέπησαν "had been surveyed along with") ἐν μέσῳ υἱῶν Ἰσραήλ.[49] In turn, the reason for their not having been included in the second census is given as "ὅτι οὐ δίδοται αὐτοῖς κλῆρος in the midst of the Israelites."

26:63 MT begins with אלה פקודי משה ואלעזר, but Num adds καί at the beginning, and makes the structure singular, thus "and this is the survey of Moses and Eleazar (the priest)." This is then modified by a relative clause which explicates the ἐπίσκεψις; it is the survey "which they surveyed the Israelites." Structurally the clause is in apposition, i.e. it is introduced by the nominative relative pronoun οἵ, and might be best translated as "by which they surveyed the Israelites."

This is followed by exactly the same three locatives as at v.3: in the Ἀραβώθ of Moab, at the Jordan, and over against Jericho. For the Ἀραβώθ of Moab, see comment at v.3.

26:64 The genitive τῶν ἐπεσκεμμένων is partitive, translating a מן phrase of MT.[50] V.a reads "and among these, there was not a person of those who had been surveyed (or reviewed) by Moses and Aaron," to which MT added הכהן. Hex has represented this by adding του ιερεως under the asterisk.

V.b is an anacoluthon: "whom they surveyed, even the Israelites in the desert of Sina." The οὕς ... τοὺς υἱοὺς Ἰσραήλ is syntactically difficult to

---

49. Which was accepted by Theod and Aq, but Sym has ἐν τοῖς υἱοῖς Ἰσραήλ, which a popular A M text also read.
50. See SS 169.

defend." The pronoun refers to the τούτοις, and the clause would have been simpler without the τοὺς υἱοὺς 'Ισραήλ; it would then read "whom they had surveyed." It does, however, imitate MT's אשר פקדו את בני ישראל. One might render this as "—even the Israelites whom they had surveyed in the desert of Sina."

26:65 The reason for this lack of survival is given in a ὅτι clause. It was "because the Lord had said of them: they shall certainly die in the wilderness," for which comp 14:29—30. It is clear that the αὐτοῖς modifying εἶπεν does not denote the addressee, but is rather a dative of respect, i.e. "the Lord had said of (or about) them."

This statement by the Lord was indeed carried out. "And not was there left ἐξ αὐτῶν anyone, except Chaleb ... and Iesous υἱὸς Ναυή." The preposition ἐξ is partitive,[51] as the οὐδὲ εἷς shows. Unusual is the nominative following πλήν. This would normally be genitive, but here πλήν is used as a conjunction.

In the tradition, Χάλεβ is stable, only χαλευ, χαλεφ, καλεβ and χαβελ obtaining as variants. His father's name, 'Ιεφοννή, created more difficulties. The following spellings obtain: ιεφονη, ιεφθοννη, ιεφθονη, εφοννη, εφονη and φθοννι. 'Ιεσοῦς was בן נון, but Num has υἱὸς Ναυή. For the transcriptions of both names, see comments at 11:28. Ναυή is spelled otherwise in the mss as ναβη, ναβι and ναη. Instead of υἱός (Ναυή), a popular B V text reads ο του, but υἱός was chosen as critical text because the oldest Greek witness, 963, reads υἱός.

---

51. See SS 169.

Chapter 27

27:1 Syntactically, vv.1—2 of Num must be taken together, in which the verbs תקרבנה and תעמדנה are reduced to participles, with an intervening nominal clause defining the subject more precisely, with the participial structures subordinate to, the verbal predicate λέγουσιν (for לאמר) at the end of v.2. This reverses the pattern of MT which has the two verbal clauses (also separated by a nominal clause) plus לאמר as the marker introducing the direct speech of vv.3—4. V.a reads "and (when) the daughters of Salpaad, son of Hopher, son of Galaad, son of Machir, of the clan of Manasse, the sons of Joseph, approached (προσελθοῦσαι)." For Σαλπαάδ and his genealogy, i.e. Ὀφερ, Γαλαάδ, Μαχίρ, Μανασσή, and Ἰωσήφ, see 26:32—37, together with comments on the names involved.

The text of v.a in MT is also longer than than of Num; Num has omitted בן מנשה, which followed "Machir," and hex has inserted υιου μανασση under the asterisk before τοῦ δήμου to represent the omitted text. The omission was not unreasonable, and the translator may have felt that two Manasse phrases בן מנשה למשפחת מנשה was overly repetitious.

Furthermore, instead of בן יוסף, which refers specifically to Manasse, Num has the plural τῶν υἱῶν Ἰωσήφ, i.e. the entire genealogy is included as sons of Joseph, not just Manasse as in MT, but his descendants as well.

V.b is a nominal clause which interrupts the two participial structures. Num has "and these are their names," while MT has "and these are the names of his daughters." Hex did not correct the Num text; after all, the opening participial structure had identified them as αἱ θυγατέρες Σαλπααδ, and αὐτῶν is not only an ample reference, it is a stylistic improvement. The names of the five daughters are given exactly as at 26:37, also joined severally by καί; in MT the pattern followed is 1 2+3+4+5, whereas that of Sam is 1+2 3 4+5.[1] For the names of the daughters, see comments at 26:37.[2]

---

1. 4QNum[b] reads ונועה, and so do Kenn 1,109 as ונעה, instead of נעה. This would then represent the parent text of Num.
2. For Μααλά as original transcription of מחלה, see also THGN 119.

27:2 The στᾶσαι structure parallels the προσελθοῦσαι one of v.1, for which see comment at v.1. The change in syntactic patterns for these two verses as described in v.1 seems to change the central thrust of the passage to where it belongs. What is important is not so much that the five sisters approached and appeared before the leaders and the people, but rather the judicial complaint or inquiry which they presented. This is much clearer in the Num version where λέγουσιν is the main verb than in MT, where the case is presented under לאמר.

The locatives in Num consist of four ἔναντι phrases plus one ἐπί unit governing the genitive. In MT, there are only three לפני structures followed by the noun פתח used adverbially. The difference between the two consists of 1.) MT does not repeat לפני before "all the assembly," i.e. לפני הנשיאם וכל העדה is a single locative phrase. Hex has placed ἔναντι 4° under the obelus, and 2.) Num translated פתח by the prepositional phrase ἐπὶ τῆς θύρας (of the tent of testimony).[3] Hex, followed by Byz, has changed τῆς θύρας to την θυραν, but the reason for the change in case is not obvious. The predicate λέγουσιν is in the present tense, which is unexpected, particularly as substitute for the direct speech marker לאמר. Various attempts were made to improve the Greek, all of them involving a change to λεγουσαι, either by itself in ms 426+ equalling MT, or preceded by an aorist verb, ελαλησαν in *f* or by ειπον in *O* Byz. It may be noted that λεγουσαι and λέγουσιν are similar in sound, but λεγουσαι could not be original text; the participial structures of v.1 and 2 need some kind of predicatival resolution, i.e. an inflected verb is required. I suspect that the translator realized that לאמר was not really the predicate in the Hebrew, and the choice of an unusual present tense as predicate constituted his compromise. I suspect that the choice may be due to its unusual use to render לאמר; the direct quotation marker is by nature timeless, and is here being treated in the same way as participial predicates are.

27:3 The daughters present the case of their father who "died in the wilderness ... and had no male offspring." What makes this case have judicial significance lies in the distinction which the plaintiffs made between those who died as part of the generation covered by 26:65, and those who took part in the ἐπισυστάσης "insurrection" engendered by Kore; the assembly of Kore was destroyed, including his entire family, for which see ch.16.

---

3. Theod has παρὰ τὴν θύραν, and Sym, πρὸς τὴν θύραν.

Apparently, neither of these applied to the father; rather Salpaad died διὰ ἁμαρτίαν αὐτοῦ. Precisely what "his sin" was is not stated, but presumably it refers to the general reaction on the part of the Israelites to the report of the spies; see particularly 14:29—30. But the text does not make mention of this point. The pronoun הוא is here rendered literally by αὐτός. More commonly, the Pentateuch translators use ουτος; in fact, the F z+ text actually substitutes ουτος, but the strongly supported αὐτός is here original text. In the tradition, the majority F K M V 963 text follows the common Hellenistic practice of using the elided preposition δι' instead of the full διά before an initial *alpha*. But Num on the whole avoided this practice.[4]

27:4 MT argues the case for daughters as potential heirs by means of a question: "Why should the name of our father be removed from the midst of his clan because he had no son"? Num makes this a plea: "let the name of our father not be wiped out ... because he had no son," which is what is actually the point of the question asked; the rendering is free, but fully adequate. The use of ἐξαλείφω to render גרע is unique, but the verb is variously rendered in LXX, most frequently by ἐξαιρέω (seven times),[5] and here in the context of the loss of name, it is well-chosen.

What is requested is a κατάσχεσιν "a holding, a possession" among our paternal relatives. MT uses a singular verb תנה; i.e. Moses is addressed as the final court of appeal; this would be a ῥῆμα τὸ ὑπέρογκον which Moses would have to decide personally; see Exod 18:22,26. Num, however, in view of the plaintiffs appearing before Moses, Eliazar, the rulers and the entire assembly (v.2), used a plural imperative, δότε. This is a clear case of rationalization on the part of the translator.

27:5 The case was even too great for Moses to decide on hs own; he "brought their case before the Lord." It should be noted that in spite of the plural δότε in v.4, it is Moses alone who now takes action.

27:6 Num does not render ויאמר by the usual και ειπεν, but has καὶ ἐλάλησεν, which presupposes וידבר. Both verbs occur frequently in the book; in fact, וידבר

---

4. See the discussion in THGN 97.
5. According to HR.

occurs 57 times in Num, of which 48 have יהוה as subject. I suspect that the parent text of Num was וידבר rather than ויאמר.⁶

27:7 The opening clause in MT is nominal, with the participle and its modifer כן serving as predicate. One might have expected the translator to use a present tense to render the participial predicate, which does constitute its default rendering, but he chose the contextually more pertinent perfect λελαλήκασαν. The statement in the perfect, "correctly the daughters of Salpaad have spoken," gives the basis for the judgment which follows. The rendering of כן by ὀρθῶς is unique, but is precisely what is meant. Actually, ὀρθῶς occurs only seldom in LXX; it is used for היטיב five times and twice for טוב, all but one occurring in the Pentateuch.⁷

The judicial order is given in MT as נתן תתן, with the cognate free infinitive serving to give additional stress to the verbal notion. What is meant is "you shall actually assign." Num has rendered this in unusual fashion by a cognate accusative noun preceding a second singular future verb, which is the translator's attempt to put extra stress on the verbal idea: "you shall give a giving," i.e. you must really (or indeed) assign." What is to be assigned to them (i.e. to the daughters) is a "κατάσχεσιν κληρονομίας among their paternal relatives." MT has אחזת נחלה, i.e. "a possession of an inheritance." I would render the Greek by "a hereditary holding (or title)"; what the daughters are thereby entitled to is full standing as heirs. The property of Salpaad will be retained by his actual offspring, i.e. his name will not disappear.

In other words, "and you shall transfer (περιθήσεις) their father's share (i.e. heritage) to them." This divine instruction in turn, gives rise to a more detailed set of instructions on inheritance laws in cases of a person dying without male heir in the following verses (vv.8—11).

27:8 Vv.8—11 constitute a law of succession occasioned by the incident described in vv.1—7. V.8 makes a general rule that when a man dies without having a son, "you must transfer his inheritance to his daughter."

---

6. See THGN 128.
7. According to HR.

In the tradition, the Hebraic υἱὸς μὴ ᾖ αὐτῷ is stylistically improved by the K f s z+ text as υιους μη εχη.[8] Hebrew perforce expresses "to have" by the verb "to be" plus a dative nominal. Since this is part of the protasis, the verb must be in the subjunctive.

The C'⁾ s+ text has added και before περιθήσετε, which equals MT's apodotic conjunction. The reading may well betray mediate Hebrew influence. The variant τον κληρον for τὴν κληρονομίαν in the F K f s z+ text is part of the stylistic rewrite which introduced the εχη reading; see above.

27:9 But (δέ) should there not be לו בת? Num has θυγάτηρ αὐτῷ. The popular hex text has transposed the words to follow the Hebrew word order. The protases in vv.9—11 are all introduced by ἐὰν δέ, i.e. with a contrastive δέ.

Tha apodosis is asyndetic in Greek, though not in MT, and reads "δώσετε τὴν κληρονομίαν to his brother." Here, as well as in vv.10,11, the suffix of נחלתו is disregarded; it is of course quite unnecessary, since the αὐτοῦ does appear in v.8, and would be otiose in the succeeding verses;[9] the majority V 963 text, almost certainly hex in origin, has added αυτου to represent MT more precisely.

27:10 "But if he should have no brothers, you must give τὴν κληρονομίαν τῷ ἀδελφῷ of his father." Hex has added αυτου after κληρονομίαν under the asterisk; see comment at v.9. The use of the singular ἀδελφῷ for אחי represents an inferior vocalization of אחי; after all, there may well be more than one paternal uncle who could inherit; see v.11 אחים. The Masoretes would have the inheritance shared among the surviving brothers of the father of the deceased. Or is the singular an intentional reading of אחי as singular, thereby avoiding a division of the land to be inherited? It is indeed possible to understand ἀδελφῷ as "a brother," but the Num text does not then deal with the possible difficulty of determining which surviving uncle would inherit, if more than one had survived.

27:11 Finally, "but if his father had no brothers"; here only the plural "brothers" can be understood. As in vv.9—10, נחלתו is rendered by τὴν κληρονομίαν, and

---

8. For a discussion of the use of the verb ἔχειν in the Septuagint, see I. Soisalon-Soininen, VT XXVIII (1978), 92—99, and reprinted in SS 181—188.
9. Se SS 100.

again hex has supplied an αυτου under the asterisk to represent the untranslated suffix. "You must give the inheritance to the relative who is nearest him (i.e. the deceased) ἐκ his tribe." This is a highly unusual rendering for משפחה; in fact, φυλή occurs here for the first time in Num (also at 33:45 and twice at 36:1). One would expect δῆμος which is used to render משפחה 145 times in the book.[10] On the other hand, it must be an intentional change, since the two cases of its use at 36:1 also refer to this same case. It clearly gives much greater latitude. What seems to be intended in Num is the preservation of tribal boundaries rather than the smaller clan unit; what is at stake then is the tribal lands as inviolable. The ἐκ renders a partitive מן of MT.[11] Thus the property must at least remain within the tribe. The following clause in MT reads: "and he shall inherit אתה (referring to נחלתו)." Num does not render the opening conjunction, and renders אתה by τὰ αὐτοῦ "his goods," which is more idiomatic than a literal αυτην would have been, which is, however read by K f s+.

V.b constitutes a subscription to vv.8—11a: "And this shall be δικαίωμα κρίσεως for the Israelites, according as the Lord commanded Moses." The term recurs at 35:29, but as δικαίωμα κρίματος. It translates לחקת משפט.[12] The Byz text has added an εις before δικαίωμα, which represents the ל of MT. Incidentally, MT simply begins the subscription by והיתה "and it shall be." Num makes better sense by adding τοῦτο, i.e. καὶ ἔσται τοῦτο.[13]

27:12 Vv.12—23 deal with the succession to Moses. In MT Moses is ordered: "go up to הר העברים הזה." There is no indication as to what "this mountain of the Abarim" is, though the demonstrative pronoun would presuppose a specific mountain already identified. Num translates the bound phrase by an articulated prepositional phrase, τὸ ἐν τῷ πέραν,[14] but then identifies what is meant by הזה by an anacolouthon, τοῦτο ὄρος Ναβαύ. I would prefer to change the critical text by omitting the parentheses, and using a dash and a comma in substitution; this would more accurately indicate that the statement has its impulse in the הזה of

---

10. According to HR.
11. See SS 168.
12. Milgrom translates this by "the law of procedure," and contrasts it with חקת התורה "the ritual law" as at 19:2; i.e. the latter is "followed in the sanctuary," whereas the former "relates to the procedure followed by the judiciary."
13. See GK 144b.
14. See SS 69.

MT. The locative ἐν τῷ πέραν presumably refers to the other side of the Jordan, i.e. to Transjordan; cf 32:19,32 35:14, and further defined at 34:15 as κατὰ Ἰεριχὼ ἀπὸ νότου κατ' ἀνατολάς. At 21:11 πέραν is identified as ἐν τῇ ἐρήμῳ, and at 33:44 the phrase is defined as ἐπὶ τῶν ὁρίων Μωάβ. Hex has placed ὄρος Ναβαύ under the obelus to indicate that this has no counterpart in MT. In the tradition, Ναβαύ is misspelled both as ναβαβ and ναυαυ, which is due to the fact that consonantal *upsilon* and *beta* were homophonic in Byzantine Greek, both being pronounced as /v/. Other spellings include ναβων, ναγαυ and ναβαν. The identification is taken from Deut 32:49 which reads הר העברים הזה הר נבו. Deut translated this by τὸ ὄρος τὸ Ἀβαρὶμ τοῦτο ὄρος Ναβαύ, from which it is obvious that the source for the Num passage was not the Greek text of Deuteronomy, but rather the Hebrew.

V.b continues the Lord's statement to Moses: "and see the land of Canaan, which I am giving the Israelites for a possession (ἐν κατασχέσει)." This is not quite what MT says, which has neither the identification of the land as Χαναάν, nor does it call the gift of the land as being ἐν κατασχέσει, and hex has placed both of these ad sensum glosses under an obelus. Num has also changed the tense of the verb in the relative clause. MT reads נתתי, i.e. "(which) I gave (the Israelites)," but Num, possibly because the conquest of the land was still future, interpreted the verb by ἐγὼ δίδωμι, which is the regular translation pattern: pronoun plus participle, used to translate a nominal clause. But here I suspect the translator, who was not above making changes in the text when it suited his purpose, is trying to say: "which I am about to give (the Israelites for a possession)." Once again, the translator is not mindlessly translating, but is trying to say what he believes the MT is really saying (in spite of itself).

26:13 The clauses of v.a are to be understood as successive, i.e. "and you shall see it (i.e. the land), and then be added to your people, even you."[15] The idiom "be added to your people" simply means "die." MT has the plural עמיך, but Num's τὸν λαόν σου is a collective; in fact, the plural would be odd in Greek. The Hebrew usually uses the plural עמיך in this idiom, though at Gen 49:29 the Masoretes vocalized עמי as a singular.

---

15. Sym adopted καὶ σύ, but Aq read καί γε σύ.

In the καθά clause of v.b,[16] one again sees the translator amplifying the text; after "as was added Aaron your brother" he inserted a locative ἐν Ὤρ τῷ ὄρει "at Mount Hor," for which see 20:22—29. Admittedly, the text of MT is rather abrupt; the absolute use of נאסף is disconcerting, and one automatically adds a mental "to his people," but the locative is an obvious gloss, and hex placed it under the obelus.

27:14 The rendering of כאשר by διότι is unusual, and it is possible that the translator read the אשר of Sam as parent text. The use of כאשר with causal force is, however, attested in MT.[17] Here the meaning "because, since" seems demanded by the context. Moses also had to die before the people entered Canaan, because "παρέβητε τὸ ῥῆμά μου in the desert of Sin." The words "you transgressed my word" well renders the Hebrew מריתם פי, since "my mouth" is metonymic for "what I said, ordered," i.e. my word. The plural verb is used since it was Moses and Aaron who disobeyed the Lord, according to 20:10—11, over against vv.7—8.

The occasion for Moses' (and Aaron's) sin was "ἐν τῷ ἀντιπίπτειν τὴν συναγωγὴν ἁγιάσαι με οὐχ ἡγιάσατέ με "when the assembly was failing to sanctify me, you did not sanctify me." The verb ἁγιάζω here is probably best rendered by "upheld (my) sanctity." What it means is to recognize throughout the "Godness" of the Lord. Failure of the brothers to carry out the Lord's command to speak to the rock meant substituting their own will for the Lord's; by this they failed to recognize the Lord as the God who was in control. This is a simplification of MT, which reads במריבת העדה להקדישני; this is an awkward construction which must mean something like "when the assembly was rebellious—so as to sanctify me"; i.e. the marked infinitive must modify מריתם פי, and not מריבת. Hex has tried to show the text of MT by placing οὐχ ἡγιάσατέ με under the obelus, which is technically correct, but actually muddies the waters considerably. Apparently, Origen took ἐν—ἁγιάσαι με to represent MT correctly.

It is clear from the prepositional phrases that follow, ἐπὶ τῷ ὕδατι ἔναντι αὐτῶν, that the marked infinitive of MT cannot modify מריבת העדה. The translator was fully aware of the problem, and so he added οὐχ ἡγιάσατέ με before the locative phrases. Hex's placing these words under the obelus was a purely

---

16. Instead of καθά, Aq has καθώς, and Sym, ὃν τρόπον.
17. See BDB sub כאשר, on p.455, as well as KB sub כ 8.b.

mechanical reflex, and is hardly an aid to understanding the passage. In other words, Num understood what MT meant to say, but had said it badly.[18] The ἐπί plus dative must here be understood as a locative;[19] it means "at the water." The second phrase, also locative, is unique in Num, since Num throughout avoided using ἔναντι before pronouns. I am, however, sceptical about the originality of the preposition. True, the majority B F K V 963 text does read εναντι, but the popular A text read ἐναντίον. Note that at 20:8 25:6 ἐναντίον was taken as Num's rendering for לעיני, even though weakly supported, simply because cod B read it. Since Num obviously avoided using ἔναντι before pronouns, I would now read ἐναντίον here as well rather than ἔναντι.[20]

For the construction ὕδωρ ἀντιλογίας, see the comment at 20:13.

27:15 Since Num reads εἶπεν, the parent text was probably not ידבר as MT, but יאמר. MT also ends the verse with the direct speech indicator, לאמר, which is not translated by Num. Hex added λεγων at the end under the asterisk to represent it.

27:16—17 Moses' words are a plea for a successor to be appointed: ἐπισκεψάσθω "let him appoint," with κύριος ὁ θεὸς τῶν πνευμάτων καὶ πάσης σαρκός as the subject. This characterization of κύριος also occurred at 16:22; see comment ad loc. There too, καὶ πάσης σαρκός interpreted לכל בשר. The translator again changed the notion of "the spirits of all flesh," i.e. as both the source and sustainer of all life. The translator distinguishes between "the God of the spirits and of all flesh." The distinction between πνεῦμα and σάρξ became more meaningful in later Judaism.[21] The plea is for the appointment of a "person ἐπὶ τῆς συναγωγῆς ταύτης "over this assembly." Since MT simply has על העדה, hex has placed ταύτης under the obelus.

V.17 further defines such a person. V.a has four ὅστις clauses as renderings for four אשר clauses. They divide into two pairs. The first pair contrasts two verbs, εξελεύσεται and εἰσελεύσεται, i.e. "whoever would go out (or go in) before them," representing the Qal verbs יצא and בוא. The second pair again con-

---

18. Tar^J neatly clarified the text by rendering (העדה) במריבת by במי מצות כנישתא "at the waters of contention (in) the assembly," as though reading במי מריבת.
19. See SS 123.
20. See THGN 05—96 for the ms evidence.
21. For the contrast, i.e. of spirit understood as part of the human personality, see Bauer, sub πνεῦμα 3.a.

trast two verbs, ἐξάξει and εἰσάξει "bring out" vs "bring in." In Hebrew these are the Hi verbs of the first pair, i.e. יוציא vs יביא. Thus in the Hebrew nos.1 and 3 use the same root, as do nos. 2 and 4, whereas in Greek nos.1 and 2 use compounds of the same verb, simply varying the prepositional element, as do nos.3 and 4.

V.b, though presented coordinately, details the reason for the plea: "and (i.e. so that) the assembly of the Lord may not be like sheep for whom there is no shepherd." Fortunately, Num does not translate the recapitulating pronoun להם within the relative clause, but see the αυτοις added after ἐστιν by ms 426, which is obviously Hebraic in origin.

27:18 The verbs of the opening clause are in direct contrast to v.15, i.e. ἐλάλησεν vs יאמר. The parent text probably read ידבר as at v.6.[22] Since the clause is followed by direct speech, Num has included a λέγων, which hex placed under the obelus, since MT has no לאמר.

What the Lord spoke to Moses is translated word for word with only the following differences: as usual the father of Ἰησοῦν/יהושע is written as Ναυή. For the Greek transcriptions of these names, see comments at 11:28. The structure אשר בו is at times rendered idiomatically by the verb ἔχειν.[23] In the last clause, Num has "and you shall place τὰς χεῖράς σου on him," whereas MT has ידך. It is doubtful that this is a textual matter, since throughout the Pentateuch the number of יד with suffix is not observed strictly by the translators. Note that in v.23 both MT and Num record Moses' obedient response by "and he placed his hands on him," and Num may well have harmonized v.18 with v.23.

In the tradition, a popular Byz text reads εαυτον instead of σέαυτον. The neutral reflexive pronoun does not change the meaning of the text. Note that Ἰησοῦν is articulated; the τόν represents את, and its popular omission must be secondary.

The reference to Iesous as someone "who has πνεῦμα in himself" is not as concrete as one might wish, since πνεῦμα is not defined. All that can be said as to its meaning must come from his performance as Moses' successor. He was not a second Moses, but he did serve as leader who brought the Israelites successfully into the Promised Land, and kept them faithful to the Lord their God during his

---

22. See THGN 128.
23. See SS 58—59.

lifetime. It might then be best understood as "the spirit of leadership" which was in him. In the tradition, this lack of concreteness was also felt, and the M V Byz+ text added θεου after πνεῦμα.[24]

27:19 MT is a much clearer text than Num. It reads "and make him stand before Eleazar the priest and before the entire assembly, and command (i.e. commission) him in their sight." Num renders the first part up through the word "priest" word for word, but then inserts ἐντελῇ αὐτῷ before the next "before." This creates a doublet text, i.e. both "and give orders to him before the entire assembly, and "and give orders about him before them (i.e. the assembly)." Apparently, Num is trying to distinguish between the commission of Yesous ("command before") and the notion of procedure for the new leader ("command concerning"), which is then outlined in v.21. In other words, the two aspects covered are the installation, and then the subsequent actions incumbent on Yesous. The text of V O b z+ omitted ἐντελῇ αὐτῷ, which was probably hex inspired (though the textual evidence is uncertain, since ms 376 and Syh also omitted the καί before it). Hex did place περὶ αὐτοῦ under the obelus, and added an αυτω before it; this would equal MT. A popular A M text has changed the second ἐντελῇ to the aorist imperative εντειλαι. Either reading is possible in the context.

It might be noted that ἔναντι occurs twice, rendering לפני, but that its synonym, ἐναντίον, occurs before a pronoun, i.e. αὐτῶν; see comment at v.14.[25]

27:20 Moses is told: "δώσεις τῆς δόξης σου on him." The genitive modifier is a clear case of a partitive genitive;[26] he is told to put some of his δόξα on him. The word "glory" renders הוד, a word commonly rendered by δόξα in LXX, but appearing only here in the Pentateuch. What is probably intended by the word is "authority," i.e. Moses is to transfer some of his authority to Yesous. No instruction as to how such a transfer was to be effected is given. In the tradition, an F+ text has changed τῆς δόξης to the accusative την δοξαν; that would mean that all of Moses' authority was to be transferred, but this variant text should not be taken seriously, since MT has a partitive מן in מהודך.

---

24. Tar[JO] both interpret the spirit as רוח נבואה, but Tar[N] has רוח קדש מן קדם יי שרייה עלוי.
25. See also THGN 96.
26. See SS 162.

The purpose of the transfer is ὅπως ἂν εἰσακούσωσιν αὐτοῦ οἱ υἱοὶ Ἰσραήλ "that the Israelites might obey him." MT's text is somewhat different: למען ישמעו כל עדת בני ישראל; Num did not translate the כל עדת, and added an accusative modifier, αὐτόν, ad sensum. Actually, כל עדת does not add anything substantial to the text; a simple "the Israelites" is more concise and just as meaningful as "all the assembly of the Israelites." The translator showed fine sensibility in choosing the εἰς compound to translate the verb; the Israelites would not just "hear" Yesous, but would "listen to, obey" him. Oddly, Origen apparently made no effort to add an equivalent for the untranslated כל עדת in his hex.

27:21 Here the procedure for Yesous' leadership under the Lord is ordered. He is to "set himself before Eleazar the priest." The use of the middle is a fine choice on the part of the translator; MT simply says יעמד "he shall stand," but this is something that Yesous is to do; in v.19 Moses is to set him before the priest; here he operates on his own. MT then continues with ושאל לו במשפט האורים לפני יהוה "and he (i.e. Eleazar) shall inquire for him according to the judgment of the Urim before Yahweh." Num renders the verb in the plural. The translator was puzzled by the coordinate singular verbs, (for which the subject must have changed), and so he rendered the שאל by the indefinite plural modified by two accusatives; thus the αὐτόν for לו probably means "about him" (i.e. about Iesous), and the second accusative for במשפט is the judgment (or decision) τῶν δήλων before the Lord.[27] Alternatively, one can also understand αὐτόν as referring to the priest, i.e. "and they shall have him inquire (i.e. seek) the judgment," i.e. understanding שאל as a doubly transitive verb. The term δήλων is Num's attempt to render the puzzling אורים, which is usually paired with תמים. Why only the one term is used here is a mystery, since the two terms are otherwise always paired. Precisely what a decision of "Manifestations" means is unclear. See Note at Exod 28:26, where, however, the pair is rendered by τὴν δήλωσιν καὶ τὴν ἀλήθειαν. In any event, the term(s) must refer to a form of priestly divination, a way of ascertaining the will or direction of deity.

V.b then states "ἐπὶ τῷ στόματι αὐτοῦ shall go out, and ... go in, he and the Israelites with one accord and all the assembly." At v.14 the metonymic character of פי was realized as ῥῆμα, but here the figure of "mouth" is retained.

---

27. Theod reads φωτισμῶν instead of δήλων.

One might have expected an avoidance of such an anthropomorphism, but it occurs twice within the verse. MT has "he and all the Israelites with him, and all the assembly." The αὐτός must refer to Yesous himself. Hex has added παντες before οἱ υἱοὶ Ἰσραήλ to render the untranslated כל. Unusual is the rendering of אתו "with him" by ὁμοθυμαδόν "with one accord," though it is not incorrect.

27:22 Moses carried out the Lord's orders, i.e. "as commanded αὐτῷ κύριος." MT has יהוה אתו, which impelled hex to transpose to κυριος αυτω. MT says ויקח את יהושע ויעמדהו. The translator subordinated the first clause to a participle, "and taking Yesous, he set him," thereby placing the stress on positioning Yesous. This positioning was "ἐναντίον Eleazar the priest and ἐναντίον all the assembly." Since the translator used εναντίον in the first case, in spite of the fact that εναντι was the more popular preposition, he naturally used it in the second case as well.[28] The more popular εναντι is well represented in both cases in the tradition, but ἐναντίον seems to have been original.

27:23 Moses placed τὰς χεῖρας αὐτοῦ on him, as ordered at v.18. MT has the plural here as well, though not at v.18, where Num harmonized with this verse. The second clause reads ויצוהו "and he commissioned him." This verb had been rendered by ἐντελῇ in v.19, which is the usual rendering for צוה,[29] but here Num has the unusual συνέστησεν, which occurs only twice in LXX for צוה (also in a similar context at 32:28, which see). It is used here in the sense of "to establish in office,"[30] i.e. with the same meaning as the simplex. This would thus be a good contextual rendering. All this was done "καθάπερ the Lord had ordered Moses." MT has דבר as the verb in the כאשר clause, but Num must have had צוה as parent text.[31] Incidentally, καθάπερ occurs only here in Num for כאשר,[32] though it is fully correct. MT also has ביד משה, i.e. "had spoken through Moses." But it seems likely that the parent text read את משה.[33] Whenever συντέλλω is modified by a designation of the one(s) ordered (23 cases in Num), a

---

28. See THGN 96.
29. According to Dos Santos ἐντέλλομαι occurs 339 times for the Pi of צוה.
30. See J.A.L.Lee, Melbourne Symposium on Septuagint Lexicography, ed. by T.Muraoka, SCS 28(1990), 11—12.
31. As Kenn 69.
32. See THGN 127.
33. As Kenn 69.

dative modifier obtains 21 times, and only twice is the modifier formed by πρός plus an accusative. Four times the verb is used absolutely.

Chapter 28

28:2 Chh.28—29 concern the calendar for the public sacrifices required. In a general introduction the Israelites are ordered to be attentive in bringing the proper offerings at the festivals. Moses is told to order the Israelites "and say to them λέγων." The direct speech marker is not present in MT, and hex has placed λέγων under the obelus.

The preposed accusative modifiers of προσφέρειν are τὰ δῶρά μου δόματά μου καρπώματά μου plus the prepositional phrase εἰς ὀσμὴν εὐωδίας. For the first one, the Masoretes have vocalized קרבני as a singular, but the consonantal text can be read as plural as well.[1] The second item, δόματά μου, also means "my gifts," and stands for לחמי. Already in Lev the notion of God's bread or food was scrupulously avoided, and was rendered by δῶρα throughout, but here that term had already been used to render קרבני, and a synonym, δόματά μου, is substituted, but see v.24, where δῶρον does occur as the rendering for לחם.[2] For this scruple, see the discussion at Note at Lev 21:6.[3]

The third sacrifice is called καρπώματά μου which renders לאשׁי. The Masoretes vocalized אשׁי as a plural bound form; the rendering of Num as a plural noun plus μου is a possible interpretation of the consonantal text. The sacrifice אשׁה is a general term for sacrifice, but is always rendered by κάρπωμα in Num.[4] For the term κάρπωμα, see Note at Exod 29:25. In MT, the term is the bound element of the phrase אשׁי ריח ניחחי, but the translator renders the ריח ניחחי by an εἰς phrase, probably because לריח ניחח is a common fixed phrase. Note also that the suffix was disregarded, and that hex added μου to make up for it; in fact, ניחחי occurs only here in LXX.

The general occasion for such offerings is given in MT as במועדו "at its appointed time," which, however, Num renders by ἐν ταῖς ἑορταῖς μου "at my festivals." במועדו would more properly have been translated here by εν καιρω

---

1. But see Daniel 121.
2. For God's לחם, see Daniel 139—140.
3. The Targ et around the notion of God's food by identifying לחמי as the לחם סדור "the bread of arrangement," i.e. the bread of the presence which was placed on the table in the tabernacle.
4. See THGN 111.

αυτου; cf 9:3,7,13. Num renders מועד by ἑορτή again at 29:39 (as well as at 10:10 15:3). The word is used for חג at v.17 and 29:12. In other words, Num does not distinguish in this section between "stated times" and "festivals" as MT does, translating both by ἑορτή. That here Num must refer to festivals is made clear both by the change of the third person singular suffix to μου, as well as by the plural number of the noun.

28:3 MT identifies the offerings to be made by the singular: "This is the אשה which you must bring." Since the אשה is to consist of two lambs, Num made this plural: ταῦτα τὰ καρπώματα. One could, I suppose, suggest that אשה is a collective, were it not for the fact that in v.2 the plural אשי occurred; see comment ad loc. Num has made a consistent statement. These are ὅσα προσάξετε to the Lord.[5] Here MT's תקריבו is rendered by προσάξετε, but in v.2 להקריב became προσφέρειν. The two verbs are synonyms, and no distinction was intended by Num.

The offering of two year-old lambs without blemish was meant as τὴν ἡμέραν for a perpetual sacrifice. The accusative shows extent of time, thus "daily"; what is meant is "every day." The term עלה תמיד is here rendered by εἰς ὁλοκαύτωσιν ἐνδελεχῶς "for a burnt offering perpetually." At v.6 עלת תמיד is, however, rendered by ὁλοκαύτωμα ἐνδελεχισμοῦ, reflecting the bound phrase by a genitive modifier; no difference in meaning was intended by the translator.

28:4 The order to sacrifice (ποιήσεις) is now in the singular, probably since only one priest could be involved; Num simply follows MT's תעשה. A popular A F K M text changes both instances of ποιήσεις to the plural ποιησετε. The reason for the daily sacrifice consisting of two lambs is now clarified; one is to be used τὸ πρωί "early," i.e. in the morning, and the second one, τὸ πρὸς ἑσπέραν "at eventide." The Hebrew has the picturesque בין הערבים "between the two evenings," i.e. at vesper time.

---

5. Instead of ὅσα Theod and Aq have a singular pronoun ὅ, which is what אשה rendered by a singular would demand; Sym, however, has the plural ἅ.

28:5 MT simply lists the ingredients for the daily sacrifice, but Num sensibly supplies the verb ποιήσεις, which hex quite properly placed under the obelus. The verb is, however, a correct interpretation, and is occasioned by its double use in v.4.

For the οἰφί as a dry measure, see Note at Lev 5:11.[6] The fine flour is to be used "for a sacrifice made up with a quarter of a ἴν of oil," for which see Note at Exod 29:40.[7] MT characterized the oil as שמן כתית "beaten oil," but Num follows Sam which lacks כתית. Hex has supplied κεκομμενω under the asterisk after ἐλαιῷ to represent it.

28:6 This verse is anacoluthic as the nominative shows, and for sense I would add "it is," i.e. "it is a perpetual sacrifice which came into being (γενομένη) at Mount Sina for a sweet smelling savour for the Lord." Num does, however, present a grammatical difficulty. The word for sacrifice, ὁλοκαύτωμα, is neuter, but the relative clause translates העשיה, the feminine singular passive participle of עשה, which may well have influenced the translator; in MT this modifies עלת, which is feminine. I suspect the translator was careless, possibly having the feminine noun ὁλοκαύτωσιν (ἐνδελεχῶς) of v.3 in mind. This carelessness extends to the omission of אשה which occurs in MT after ניחח, and which Hex has corrected by adding κάρπωμα under the asterisk after εὐωδίας.[8] Unusual, though not incorrect, is the rendering γενομένη for the participle.

28:7 "and its libation" probably refers to the ὁλοκαύτωμα of v.6, i.e. the libation accompanying the perpetual holocaust. Hex apparently read εἰς σπονδην.[9] The "quarter hin with the one lamb" identifies the size of the libation; a quarter hin would be cir. one quart or liter in quantity. The text is somewhat cryptic, since nothing is said as to what the libation consisted of. A popular gloss identifies the ἴν as ιν οινου. The gloss was probably based on the identification of the quarter hin for the one lamb as being οἴνου at v.14. Concerning the libation, "in the sanctuary you must pour (it) out as a libation of σίκερα to the Lord." Why a liba-

---

6. Tar^{JO} identify the Ephah as "three seahs," whereas Tar^N consistently renders the word by מכלתה.
7. The ἐν is instrumental, not locative; see SS 123. This is the case throughout this section for ἐν ἐλαιῷ.
8. But see also Daniel 163.
9. Aq also read εἰς σπονδήν. Presumably the parent text must have read ולנסכו.

tion of strong drink should be poured out is not clear. For σίκερα, see comment at 6:3.[10]

28:8 V.a is an exact repetition of v.4b, which see. V.b in Num reads "according to its (i.e. the first or morning sacrifice) meal offering and according to its libation, you must offer (ποιήσετε) for a sweet smelling savour to the Lord." MT has for "according to its meal offering," כמנחת הבקר, which is clearer than κατὰ τὴν θυσίαν αὐτοῦ. Furthermore, MT has the singular תעשה in both v.a and b, whereas Num changes to the plural for v.b. The plural had occurred in v.2 as a general command to be observant, but the change to the plural in v.b is unexpected. MT begins v.b with כמנחת הבקר וכנסכו "according to the morning sacrifice and according to its libation (you must sacrifice)," but Num makes no reference to הבקר, simply alluding to it by a genitive pronoun, αὐτοῦ. MT then continues with תעשה אשה ריח ניחח. Num, however, has ποιήσετε εἰς ὀσμὴν εὐωδίας κυρίῳ, omitting any reference to אשה as it did at v.6, and again hex has added κάρπωμα under the asterisk before the εἰς phrase to represent the disregarded אשה.[11]

28:9 Vv.9—10 concern the Sabbath day's offerings. For the plural τῶν σαββάτων, see comment at 15:32. Though MT lacks a verb in v.9, one must be understood, and Num has supplied προσάξετε as in v.3, thus "and for the day of the Sabbath you must bring." For two year-old lambs without blemish, see v.3. Also to be brought are "two-tenths (presumably of an ephah) of fine flour, made up with oil for a meal offering and a libation." MT has a different order. For εἰς θυσίαν it reads מנחה, but this comes before בלולה בשמן, i.e. it reads "two-tenths of fine flour (as) a meal offering mixed with oil ונסכו." The majority A F M text has transposed "made up with oil" after θυσίαν, which equals the MT order; this reordering is clearly a hex correction. Num also failed to render the suffix of נסכו, and hex added an αυτου under the asterisk at the end of the verse to represent it.

---

10. Aq read μεθύσματος (retroverted from Syh).
11. But see Daniel 163.

28:10 Presumably, σαββάτων ἐν τοῖς σαββάτοις means "each and every Sabbath." MT has שבת בשבתו, whereas Num follows Sam, which lacks the suffix. On the other hand, the suffix is difficult, since שבת is usually feminine, though at Isa 56:6 it does appear as masculine. The MT reading is the *lectio difficilior*, and is probably to be preferred. Hex, however, does read σαββασιν αυτου, thereby supplying a rendering for the suffix. The heteroclitic dative plural is shared by *s* *x*+, but is rare in LXX, occurring only at 1Macc 2:38.

These Sabbath offerings are alongside (i.e. besides ἐπί) the regular burnt offering and its libation. Here the holocaust of התמיד is not rendered by ἐνδελεχισμοῦ as at v.6 or ἐνδελεχῶς as at v.3, but by τῆς διὰ παντός. No distinction in meaning is intended, however.

28:11 Vv.11—15 deal with the offerings at the new moons. MT reads ראשי חדשיכם "at the beginnings of your months" or "at your new moons." Num rendered this by a single noun (ἐν) ταῖς νουμηνίαις, but failed to recognize the suffix; hex supplied a υμων to make up for it. MT requires that "you must bring an עלה to Yahweh," but since ten animals are required, Num made this plural, ὁλοκαυτώματα. Or does the plural reflect the holocausts of all the new moons,[12] rather than the עלה for each new moon sacrifice? Num lists the required holocausts exactly as MT does: two bullocks from the herd, and one ram, seven year-old lambs without blemish.

28:12 Num begins asyndetically over against MT, and hex has added an initial και to equal MT. WIth respect to the two bullocks, it requires "three tenths of fine flour made up with oil for the one bullock, and two tenths ... for the one ram." In both cases, MT has מנחה after "fine flour," which the translator disregarded. In both cases, hex has added εις θυσιαν under the asterisk after each σεμιδάλεως to make up for the omitted מנחה.

28:13 Num begins with "δέκατον δέκατον of fine flour made up with oil." MT begins with a conjunction, and has מנחה after "fine flour." Hex has inserted εις θυσιαν there to represent it, whereas the Byz text has added και at the beginning to equal MT. The repeated δέκατον is in imitation of MT, which repeats עשר(ו)ן,

---

12. As Dorival suggests.

presumably in a distributive sense, thus "for each a tenth," though it actually adds little in sense. I would simply render: "a tenth (of fine flour)."¹³ Not surprisingly, the majority B F text reads only one δέκατον. The repeated δέκατον occurs five times in Num, and only here could its originality be called into question. One must conclude that the popular reading is a case of haplography.¹⁴ This is intended τῷ ἀμνῷ τῷ ἑνί, which in view of the distributive δέκατον I would translate here by "for each lamb." עלה is here rendered by θυσίαν, which is unusual; in fact, it occurs for עלה elsewhere in the book only at 23:3,15. The more general term for sacrifice contrasts with the more usual rendering ὁλοκαυτώματα of v.11.¹⁵

28:14 Num begins the verse asyndetically over against MT. The αὐτῶν of "their libation" has ὁλοκαυτώματα of v.11 as its antecedent. The Hebrew has the noun in the plural, נסכיהם, which is sensible in view of the αὐτῶν, but Num uses a singular, ἡ σπονδὴ αὐτῶν, i.e. for each one, one libation. The sizes of the libations are summarized for the offerings of the new moons. For the one bullock the libation must be a half of a hin. For the one ram ἔσται the third of a hin, and the fourth of a hin ἔσται for the one lamb, (even) of wine. For each animal the designation τῷ ἑνί is given. MT lacks such in all three cases, but Sam has האחד modifying both פר and כבש, but not for the second one, איל. 4QNumᵇ has האחד only for כבש. Hex placed only the third case of τῷ ἑνί under the obelus.¹⁶ Presumably the οἴνου applies to each case of τοῦ ἵν. MT does not repeat יהיה for the second and third quantity, and hex has placed both cases of ἔσται under the obelus to show that MT has no correspondent for them.

V.b is a summary statement that "this is the burnt offering month by month for the months of the year." The accusative μῆνα denotes extent of time; thus μῆνα ἐκ μηνός means "each month." Obviously ὁλοκαύτωμα does not refer to the σπονδή, but rather to the entire section, vv.11—14, i.e. the offerings which would include the holocausts as well as "their libation."

---

13. Theod and Aq have δέκατον δέκατον σεμιδάλεως εἰς θυσίαν ἀναπεποιημένης ..., whereas Sym has καὶ ἀνὰ δέκατον σεμιδάλεως δῶρον πεφυραμένης ἐν ἐλαίῳ.
14. See THGN 114.
15. See Daniel 244—245.
16. It should be noted that BHS has cited Sam incorrectly.

28:15 For χίμαρον ἐξ αἰγῶν, see Note at Lev 4:23. The word χίμαρον is, however, often used to designate a male goat, and the collocation χίμαρον ἐξ αἰγῶν is a calque for the Hebrew שעיר עזים which probably means "a kid." The accusative is used, since it is still governed by προσάξετε of v.11. This was to serve περὶ ἁμαρτίας, which phrase refers to the "sin offering." The phrase is common in the book of Num, occurring 34 times, whereas in Lev it is found 44 times. In Lev the prepositional phrase was nominalized by articulation,[17] to distinguish it from "sin." The περὶ ἁμαρτίας is here distinct from the noun which would mean "sin" as well; see also Note at Lev 4:3.

V.b is a separate syntagm in the Greek, with a preposed prepositional phrase, "besides the regular holocaust," modifying the verb, ποιηθήσεται. This has as its subject (καὶ) ἡ σπονδὴ αὐτοῦ, with the antecedent for the pronoun as χίμαρον, thus "even (or also) its libation shall be performed."

28:16 Vv.16—25 deal with the passover festival. Specifically, v.16 speaks of the fourteenth day of the first month as the actual πάσχα to the Lord. MT repeats the preposition ב before "fourteenth," but in Num ἐν covers both "month" and "fourteenth." The Hebrew idiom usually has "(day) to the month," which Num correctly renders by the genitive τοῦ μηνός.

28:17 With the fifteenth day of this month, the ἑορτή of the ἄζυμα is introduced. For the date formula, see comment at v.16. There remains an awareness that the passover and the feast of the unleavened bread were in origin distinct, though in practice they had become fused. It is on the 15th day τοῦ μηνὸς τούτου (i.e. of the first month), thus the day after the actual passover, that there is to be "a feast," for which see comment at v.2 on ἑορταῖς μου, and the order states that "for seven days ἔδεσθε unleavened bread." Num has made this a direct command: "you must eat," rather than the Ni third masculine singular "shall be eaten" of MT; Num followed the תאכלו of Sam.[18]

28:18 Over against MT Num begins the verse with καί. It has also restructured the syntax of v.a, which in MT reads "On the first day there is (i.e. is to be) a

---

17. See the discussion at THGL 117.
18. Kenn 9 also reads תאכלו. The reading may well be based on Lev 23:6.

sacred convocation." Num has changed ביום הראשון to a nominative ἡ ἡμέρα ἡ πρώτη,[19] and added ἔσται ὑμῖν, probably to harmonize with v.25, which see.[20] Hex has treated the two words differently; it omitted ἔσται, but placed ὑμῖν under the obelus.

The rendering ἐπίκλητος for מקרא is found only in Num (also at 29:1, 7,12). It is a diptote adjective, here nominalized, and is intended in the same sense as the noun κλήτη which is used elsewhere to render מקרא in the Pentateuch (Exod 12:16 and ten times in Lev 23).

V.b is a formulaic clause occurring 13 times in the Pentateuch. The notion of the bound phrase מלאכת עבדה, rendered by an adjectival phrase, ἔργον λατρευτόν,[21] refers to festivals, and contrasts with ἔργον which is forbidden on the Sabbath as well as on the day of atonement (see 29:7). The term ἔργον λατρευτόν probably refers specifically to one's ordinary work, whereas ἔργον refers to any kind of work.[22]

28:19 "You must bring ὁλοκαυτώματα κάρπωμα to the Lord." MT reads אשה עלה. Num has transposed the two words; it always renders אשה by κάρπωμα. The B K Byz+ text has changed κάρπωμα into the plural by attraction to the plural ὁλοκαυτώματα, but the singular is original.[23] The plural ὁλοκαυτώματα has understood עלה correctly as a collective. What Num is saying is "you must bring burnt offerings as a sacrifice." In MT the three offerings to be brought are connected by conjunctions, but not so in Num, which reads μόσχους ἐκ βοῶν δύο, κριὸν ἕνα, ἀμνοὺς ἐνιαυσίους. Hex has added καὶ before κριόν,[24] but not before ἑπτά; the b text phrases formed an a b+c pattern, by adding καὶ before ἑπτά.

28:20 V.a is a nominative pendant, i.e. "and as for their meal offering, (even) fine flour made up with oil." The αὐτῶν refers to the ὁλοκαυτώματα of v.19. V.b then follows with preposed accusatives τρία δέκατα ... δύο δέκατα modi-

---

19. See SS 110.
20. Kenn 17,107 also added יהיה לכם here.
21. See SS 66.
22. For a discussion of ἔργον λατρευτόν in LXX, see Excursus I in Daniel 329—334.
23. See THGN 111—112.
24. As did The Others.

fying ποιήσετε. The dative structures modifying δέκατα 1° and 2° read τῷ μόσχῳ τῷ ἑνί and τῷ κριῷ τῷ ἑνί resp. MT lacks an equivalent for τῷ ἑνί in both cases, but Num harmonizes with v.14; cf comment ad loc. The B F V oII f z+ text has omitted the verb, which can not be original.[25]

28:21 Num renders MT word for word. For the δέκατον δέκατον, see comment at v.13. The singular verb is anomalous in the context of consistent plurals from v.8b to the end of the chapter, but Num simply follows MT's תעשה. The omission of the verb in Sam is a secondary attempt at greater consistency.

28:22 Num follows Sam, again harmonizing by adding ἐξ αἰγῶν after χίμαρον; see vv.15,30 29:5,11,16,19 and 25; hex has placed the phrase under the obelus.[26] Hex has also transposed ἕνα after περὶ ἁμαρτίας, thereby equalling the word order of MT. For περὶ ἁμαρτίας, see comment at v.15. For a discussion of the meaning of ἐξιλάσασθαι, see Note at Lev 1:4.

28:23 The opening word πλήν is here used as a preposition with the genitive; it usually occurs as a conjunction meaning "except, only," but here it means "outside of, besides"; what is meant is that the offerings prescribed for the festival of unleavened bread do not substitute for the regular (διὰ παντός) holocaust of the morning, for which see vv.3—4, but are additional sacrifices. The phrase διὰ παντός has no correspondent in MT, and hex has placed it under the obelus.[27] Since it is defined by the relative clause, ὅ ἐστιν ὁλοκαύτωμα ἐνδελεχισμοῦ, the phrase is indeed otiose. MT ends the verse with תעשו את אלה, but Num has omitted the verb and then attached ταῦτα to the next verse for good sense. Hex has added ποιησετε under the asterisk before ταῦτα to correspond to MT.

28:24 Since ταῦτα representing את אלה from v.23 has been joined to v.24, it begins with ταῦτα κατὰ ταῦτα, Num begins with "these according to these you shall perform per day for the seven days." See comment on ταῦτα at v.23. What is meant is that you must perform these in the same fashion; in other words, there

---

25. See THGN 125—126, which has analyzed v.b as a nominal clause, but the alternative analysis offered above is more likely to have been intended by Num.
26. Kenn 80,129,193 also add עזים.
27. But see THGN 112.

is to be no variation in the number of sacrifices to be offered up, as e.g. in the feast described in 29:12—38. The accusative τὴν ἡμέραν renders ליום and must mean "per day," i.e. daily. For לחם, Num has δῶρον, avoiding as did Lev, the notion of "food of God." See the discussion at v.2.[28]

V.b begins with a preposed prepositional phrase, ἐπὶ τοῦ ὁλοκαυτώματος τοῦ διὰ παντός, which translates על עולת התמיד. For the structure, see comment at v.15b. Usually עולה is rendered by ὁλοκαύτωμα, but when modified by τοῦ παντός, the synonym ὁλοκαύτωσις is preferred (11 times), whereas ὁλοκαύτωμα occurs only three times (also v.31 29:6). I doubt whether any distinction was intended. The verse also ends differently in Num. MT ends with יעשה ונסכו "it shall be performed and its libation," and the verb is modified by the על phrase. Num would have been better off by repeating its rendering at v.15b: ποιηθήσεται καὶ ἡ σπονδὴ αὐτοῦ, but instead he misconstrued יעשה, a Ni inflection, and tried to continue with a second person instruction, using a singular as at v.21, and omitting the conjunction, thus "you shall perform its libation." See comment at v.21 on the unfortunate singular verb.

28:25 MT begins with a temporal ב phrase, and Num treats it exactly as at v.18, which see. In fact, it differs from v.18, except for "seventh" instead of "first," in only two matters. At v.18 Num used the nominalized adjective ἐπίκλητος to render מקרא, but here the more usual κλητή obtains,[29] though only here in Num; see comment at v.18. Secondly, Num has added ἐν αὐτῇ at the end of the verse; this has no basis in MT, and hex placed it under the obelus. The gloss is ad sensum; see also 29:35 Exod 12:16 Lev 23:11. In the other nine cases of the formula in the Pentateuch, no ἐν phrase obtains.

28:26 Vv.26—31 deal with the day τῶν νέων, known in MT as the day of הבכורים, "the day of the first fruits." The rendering is unique; the term is a nominalized use of the adjective νέος "fresh, new," and is here intended to refer to the new grain products of the field; in other words, the translation is not incorrect, but merely unusual. בכורים is usually rendered by πρωτογενήματα (11

---

28. See also Daniel 139—142.
29. See SS 110.

times). On the other hand, the noun νέος is used to translate the month called אביב seven (out of eight times), i.e. interpreting the word as "new shoots," the month in which seeds normally sprouted. One might render the term as "(the day) of the new growths." In the ὅταν clause νέος occurs in its usual adjectival sense in θυσίαν νέαν, where it renders חדשה (מנחה). The ὅταν clause translates the prepositional phrase בהקריבכם idiomatically, "whenever you would bring." What you bring is a "new sacrifice to the Lord, of weeks." The term τῶν ἑβδομάδων refers to the feast of weeks, i.e. it is an abbreviated form for ἑορτὴ ἑβδομάδων, for which see Exod 34:22. MT, however, has בשבעתיכם, and hex has added ὑμων under the asterisk to represent the untranslated suffix. Hex has also added the article under the asterisk before κυρίῳ to show the presence of the preposition in ליהוה. Hex makes this "correction" only sporadically, for which there seems to be no rhyme or reason. For ἐπίκλητος—ποιήσετε, see comments at v.18, where exactly the same text obtains.

28:27 According to MT, it is an עולה that you must bring, but Num, in view of the list of animals of which the עולה is to consist, translates it by the plural, ὁλο-καυτώματα. The M 963 oI' C' x+ text has the singular, which technically equals MT, but עולה is surely to be understood as a collective. The variant text is simply the result of parablepsis due to homoioteleuton. The list of animals is exactly the same as in v.11, except for omitting καί before κριόν, and for the position of ἑπτά before "year old lambs" rather than after it as in v.11. The majority A F M text, however, has the same word order as at v.11, and the original word order is by no means certain. MT has no equivalent for ἀμώμους, but Num harmonizes. Hex has placed the word under an obelus. Sam does have תמימם, but also adds יהיו לכם, which is an import from v.19.

28:28—29 Num begins asyndetically, therein following Sam over against MT. V.28 is an exact copy of v.20, except for the lack of an introductory καί, as well as the omission of the verb ποιήσετε at the end of the verse. The lack of a verb means that the syntax of vv.28—29 differs radically from that of vv.20 and 21. The opening ἡ θυσία αὐτῶν is the subject of a nominal clause, with "fine flour made up with oil" as its predicate. The predicate is then further defined by a series of three apposites, including v.29 as the third one. For the first two, see comments at v.20.

V.29 renders MT word for word; it also finds its parallel in v.21, where, however the verb ποιήσεις occurs; cf comments ad loc.

28:30 As at v.22, Num begins with καί in which it follows Sam rather than MT.[30] The verse is an exact copy of v.22, including περὶ ἁμαρτίας, which BHS lacks, but which is present in Sam as לחטאת.[31]

28:31 For πλήν, see comment at v.23. For τοῦ ὁλοκαυτώματος τοῦ διὰ παντός, see comment at v.24. V.a ends with the verb ποιήσετέ (μοι); this is preceded by καὶ τὴν θυσίαν αὐτῶν, which refers directly to ἡ θυσία αὐτῶν of v.28; it makes sense out of the unusual syntagm of nominals in vv.28—30 as being cultic activity, i.e. "even their sacrifice" which ποιήσετέ μοι. MT has no equivalent for the μοι, and hex has placed it under the obelus. It is an exegetical gloss indicating for whom all the sacrifices are intended.

The verse ends with καὶ αἱ σπονδαί αὐτῶν. This is amply clear as to its syntactical position from 29:6,11,16,19,22,25,28,31,34 and 38; it is coordinate with ἡ θυσία αὐτῶν of v.28. In the tradition, this easily became και τας σπονδας αυτων as in the B V Byz x+ text, but this is a simplification making the construction coordinate with τὴν θυσίαν αὐτῶν. The *lectio difficilior* is original text.[32]

---

30. But Kenn 17,75,107,128 and 181 also read ושעיר.
31. Kenn 9*,17,95 and 615 also added לחטאת after אחד.
32. See THGN 110.

Chapter 29

29:1 Vv.1—6 concern the "day of the signal." This day is the first day of the seventh month, thus is actually the seventh new moon festival; here it is called ἡμέρα σημασίας. In MT this is called the יום תרועה "day of the trumpet blowing." For σημασία rendering תרועה, see comments at 10:5—7; there the sounding of the תרועה was the σημασία for the breaking up of camp.[1] In the Pentateuch, the rendering of תרועה by σημασία is found only in Num, and only for תרועה. Obviously, it must have been an audible signal of some kind, since other interpretations of תרועה suggest this as well (except for Lev 13 where it is used to render ספחת or מספחת as a mark or spot on the skin), such as ἀλαλαγμός (eight times), κραυγή (also eight times). Even unique renderings reflect some kind of oral expression; cf σάλπιγξ, ἀγαλλίασις, ἔνδοξος, ἐξηγορία, ἐξομολόγησις. But here there is no indication what kind of signal the תרועה is supposed to be. The יום תרועה eventually became identified with the beginning of the agricultural year, and today the sounding of the trumpet signals Rosh haShana, the Jewish New Year's Day.

That this was a special day is clear from the ban on πᾶν ἔργον λατρευτόν, for which see comment at 28:18. In fact, it is called an ἐπίκλητος ἁγία, for which see comment at 28:18 as well.

29:2 The offerings to be brought differ from those demanded on the (other) new moons (v.11), when two bullocks from the herd were to be offered; on this seventh new moon, only one bullock was to be sacrificed. In MT, the פר is circumscribed by בן בקר אחד, which in Num is recorded as ἕνα ἐκ βοῶν. Num took עלה as a collective, and translates by the plural ὁλοκαυτώματα; after all, nine animals were to be sacrificed, a bullock, a ram and seven lambs.

29:3 Num does not render the initial conjunction, but otherwise translates MT word for word. The prescription is exactly the same as those for the new moons in 28:12: "three-tenths ... for the one bullock, and two-tenths for the one ram."

---

1. See Dorival 148—149.

Num harmonized with that passage by adding τῷ ἑνί for both the τῷ μόσχῳ and the τῷ κριῷ, though MT lacks equivalents. Hex has placed the second one under the obelus.

29:4 This verse is paralleled by 28:13a, though here it is modified by τοῖς ἑπτὰ ἀμνοῖς, thus a tenth for each lamb of the seven lambs. MT, however, reads עשרון אחד "one tenth," whereas Num follows Sam in harmonizing with the δέκατον δέκατον of 28:13,21 and 29. Furthermore, Num has no equivalent for the initial conjunction; the Byz+ text corrects this by adding και at the beginning.

29:5 This verse is exactly the same as 28:22,30 in Num, and represents MT exactly. The phrase περὶ ἁμαρτίας has חטאת as Hebrew counterpart, i.e. without a preposition; in fact, MT has לחטאת only at 28:15, but elsewhere in chh.28—29 simply has חטאת, which is throughout these two chapters rendered by the περί phrase; after all, it does not mean "sin," but "sin offering."

29:6 For πλήν, see comment at 28:23. Now it becomes obvious why only one bullock is required for the day of signal. Since it is the seventh new moon, these nine animals which are to be sacrificed according to v.2, are extras; the regular burnt offerings of the new moons, for which see 28:11—15, are also required. Note again the rational use of the plural ὁλοκαυτωμάτων rather than the singular עלת of MT. This use also leads to the interpretation of ומנחתה "and its meal offering" as plural καὶ αἱ θυσίαι αὐτῶν, i.e. with both noun and pronoun in the plural. The next coordinate, καὶ αἱ σπονδαὶ αὐτῶν, has no equivalent in MT. It should noted that these are all in the nominative, and not genitive. In other words, these are not governed by πλήν, but are syntactically nominal clauses. I would take the verse to mean: "besides the burnt offerings of the new moon, both their meal offerings and their libations, and the regular holocaust, both their meal offerings and their libations (must be) according to their constitution, for a sweet smelling savour for the Lord." In MT, however, אשה occurs after ניחח, and this, as at 28:6,8, which see, is omitted by Num, and hex has added καρπωμα under the asterisk before κυρίῳ.[2] Comp v.11 where in a similar context Num does render the אשה. The language is on the whole very repetitive, and follows MT

---

2. See Daniel 163 for the omission.

quite closely. MT, however, does read ומנחתה ונסכיהם after התמיד, which Num levels to "both their meal offerings and their libations." In MT, the suffix of מנחתה refers to the perpetual holocaust, but that of ונסכיהם refers to both the perpetual holocaust and that of the new moon. Sam solved this by using singular suffixes for both nouns.[3]

The term σύγκρισιν renders משפט "judgment," and "their constitution" probably refers to "their customary ritual." The phrase כמשפט means "according to specification"; it also occurs at 9:3, where κατὰ τὴν σύγκρισιν is coordinate with κατὰ τὸν νόμον; see comment ad loc.

29:7 Vv.7—11 concern the tenth day of the seventh month, elsewhere known as the "day of atonement"; cf Lev 23:27 25:9. Num does not repeat "seventh," simply referring to the tenth τοῦ μηνὸς τούτου. Hex added του εβδομου after μηνός under the asterisk to equal the השביעי MT. On this day, which is to be "an ἐπίκλητος ἁγία for you, you must maltreat yourselves (κακώσετε τὰς ψυχὰς ὑμῶν)." The verb is a rendering of עניתם "you must humble yourselves," which is most commonly rendered by ταπεινόω (31 times in LXX), but by κακόω 12 times.[4] The former is, however, not used in Num; in fact, in the Pentateuch, ταπεινόω is used to translate the Pi or Pu of ענה 14 times, and κακόω 12 times (four times in Num; twice in 24:24, and once at 30:14). Num understood ענה in the sense of "to distress, afflict" rather than "to humble oneself."[5]

The last clause is introduced by καί, following Sam rather than MT. Note that it is not "all ἔργον λατρευτόν" that is to be avoided, but simply "all ἔργον." The day of atonement is on the same level as the Sabbath; all work, not just one's regular work, is to be avoided; that clause may be rendered by "and you shall not do any (kind of) work."

29:8 The structure καὶ προσοίσετε ὁλοκαυτώματα renders והקרבתם עלה.[6] In the tradition, a popular F text substituted προσαξετε, i.e. the reading of Theod and Sym, but προσοίσετε must be original text. Once again, Num translates the sin-

---

3. In direct contrast to Num.
4. According to Dos Santos.
5. Milgrom neatly rendered the verb as "you shall practice self-denial"; see particularly his explanatory note.
6. Instead of προσοίσετε, Theod and Sym read προσάξετε.

gular עלה by the plural in view of the nine animals which are to be sacrificed.⁷ That the majority A F M text read the singular need not be taken seriously; it was almost certainly formed because of homoioteleuton, and not in order to equal MT. Hex has added τω κυριω to render the ליהוה, which Num did not translate, though it added κυρίῳ after καρπώματα, which an A F M popular reading omitted. This apparently was an old reading, since O and Syh also lack it. In other words, it was absent from Origen's LXX text.⁸ Num also has added καρπώματα after εὐωδίας ex par, i.e. καρπώματα κυρίῳ are both additions in Num over against MT. The word, whether in the singular or in the plural, occurs either before or after εἰς ὀσμὴν εὐωδίας 11 times in the book; in fact, the A F majority text changed it to the singular καρπωμα. Hex also corrected the word order. MT has described the prescribed bullock as בן בקר אחד, but Num has ἕνα ἐκ βοῶν; hex placed ἕνα at the end so as to conform to MT, as was done at v.2; cf comment ad loc.

29:9 Num begins the verse asyndetically over against MT. The verse is an exact copy of v.3, which see. MT, however, has "three tenths לפר," followed by שני. Num had added τῷ ἑνί after μόσχῳ ex par, and has καί before δύο, in conformity to v.3; in other words, the translator simply repeated v.3 rather than translate MT's v.9 himself.

29:10 This verse equals v.4, except that it reads εἰς τοὺς ἑπτὰ ἀμνούς instead of the τοῖς ἑπτὰ ἀμνοῖς of v.4. As at v.4, the Byz+ text introduced the verse with καί; at v.4 this could have been interpreted as recensional, but here MT is also asyndetic (over against Sam).

29:11 Num follows Sam in its reading of καί at the beginning of the verse.⁹ V.a is exactly the same as in v.5, which see. The ἐξιλάσασθαι περὶ ὑμῶν has no counterpart in MT, and hex has placed it under the obelus. It seems obvious that Num has harmonized its text with v.5.

For πλήν, see comment at 28:23. Num here uses the fuller designation for the "sin offering," which Lev had created, viz. τὸ περὶ τῆς ἁμαρτίας. Here it is

---

7. The Others read the singular plus τῷ κυρίῳ.
8. Which is probably what o´ means; it represents the "Seventy" text of Origen. This lacked κυρίῳ as well.
9. As do Kenn 17,69,109,181 and Tar^N, Pesh and Vulg.

the sin offering τῆς ἐξιλάσεως, which identifies this day as the day of atonement; the Hebrew has הכפרים. The word ἐξιλάσεως is a hapax legomenon in LXX, although its meaning is clear. The Hebrew word is elsewhere rendered by the related ἐξιλασμός (four times) or ἱλασμός (twice). Its choice was probably facilitated by the occurrence of the infinitive ἐξιλάσασθαι in v.a.

As at v.6, after the πλήν structure, the verse continues with nominatives after the πλήν structure: "even the regular holocaust, its (referring to ὁλοκαύτωσις) meal offering and its libation (shall be) according to constitution (or customary usage), for a sweet smelling savour κάρπωμα for the Lord." MT has "and" before "its meal offering," and in the tradition, the Byz text has added a καὶ before ἡ θυσία; this is probably recensional in origin. Instead of αὐτῆς modifying σπονδή, MT has the plural noun and suffix, ונסכיהם, i.e. the libation pertaining to both the regular holocaust and the meal offering. Num limits it to the θυσία.

What follows has no correspondence in MT, and is in the main taken over from v.6, which, however, read an αὐτῶν after σύγκρισιν, and lacked κάρπωμα; cf comments ad loc. Hex has placed all of κατά—fin under the obelus to show its absence in MT.

29:12 Vv.12—38 deal with the offerings on the eight days of the ἑορτὴν κυρίῳ, elsewhere called ἑορτὴ σκηνῶν, Lev 23:34, i.e. the Feast of Tents or Tabernacles. Actually, the feast is said to be ἑπτὰ ἡμέρας, but vv.35—38 deal with the eighth day as "a holy convocation for you." V.12 begins with "and on the fifteenth day of this seventh month, there shall be a holy convocation for you." Num follows Sam, rather than MT which lacks הזה, i.e. an equivalent for τούτου.[10] Hex has placed the τούτου under the obelus. For ἐπίκλητος ἁγία, see comment at 28:18.

No ordinary work may be done on this day, but "you shall celebrate (literally feast) αὐτήν as a festival to the Lord for seven days." MT has no equivalent for αὐτήν which must refer to ἐπίκλητος.[11] Hex placed αὐτήν under the obelus. The ἑπτὰ ἡμέρας is quite properly in the accusative, since it shows extent of time.

---

10. Kenn 9 and 190 also had הזה, as did Pesh.
11. Only Tar^N with its יתי recognizes the pronoun, though Kenn 18,80 and 99 do read אתו, referring to חדש.

29:13 Here הקרבתם is translated by προσάξετε, whereas at v.8 it became προσοίσετε. The two are synonyms, but see comment at v.8. As usual, Num renders עלה by a plural noun, as e.g. v.8; see comment ad loc.[12] The sacrifices to be brought are defined by MT as thirteen bullocks out of the herd, two rams, yearling lambs fourteen. But this is intended only for the first day, since successive days are separately prescribed, thus v.17, "on the second day," v.20 "on the third day," etc. Num makes this clear by adding τῇ ἡμέρᾳ τῇ πρώτῃ before listing the animals, thereby avoiding any possible confusion; hex has put the words under the obelus to indicate that there is no equivalent in MT. It might also be noted that κυρίῳ represents ליהוה. Usually κυρίῳ is not articulated, but occasionally, as here, hex has added the article under the asterisk to represent the preposition ל;[13] see comment at 28:26.

The pattern followed in the teen numbers in Num are throughout in the order of the Hebrew, thus τρεῖς καὶ δέκα, not δεκα τρεις as the Byz text has it, and τέσσαρας καὶ δέκα, not the popular δεκα τεσσαρας of B V 963+.[14] The verse ends with the clause ἄμωμοι ἔσονται. Its subject is not the entire list of animals, but only refers to the ἀμνούς; this is clear from the parallels for the next days, vv.17,20,23,26,29,32 and 35, where ἀμώμους modifies ἀμνούς throughout.

29:14—15 The pattern which occurred at 28:20,28 and vv.3,9 is again used here, though now in the plural. Note that over against MT, it does not and never does begin with a conjunction (vv.18,21,24,27,30,33,37), though in all cases MT has ומנחתם. It is not clear why Num uses the plural αἱ θυσίαι here, but not at v.18, though for the remaining days it reverts to the plural. Num follows Sam's הפרים rather than the indefinite פרים of MT by its τοῖς ... μόσχοις. For τρισὶν καὶ δέκα, most witnesses read τρεισκαιδεκατα, but throughout, Num uses the inflected numbers, i.e. τρισίν rather than τρεῖς, so the Num form is probably original. The writing of the three words as a compound is immaterial; the old uncials wrote without space between words. The real difference would be known only through stress patterns.[15]

---

12. See also THGN 111.
13. See THGN 103—104.
14. See THGN 115.
15. See THGN 115.

Over against MT, Num is asyndetic; though the majority A F text does add και at the beginning, this is not a hex correction, since O and Syh both follow Num. At vv.4,10, the Byz text added και as well. For τέσσαρας καὶ δέκα, see comment at v.13. As for v.14, the noun (ἀμνούς) is articulated as in Sam, but not in MT. The majority A B F M text has changed τέσσαρας to the nominative τεσσαρες, which in later Greek was often used for the accusative as well.[16] According to Thackeray,[17] the assimilation of the accusative to the nominative form τεσσαρες did not become common until the first and second centuries of our era. That it became the majority text in the mss of the LXX is then not surprising, but it is not the original third century BCE text.

29:16 There is also to be offered χίμαρον ἐξ αἰγῶν ἕνα περὶ ἁμαρτίας πλὴν τῆς ὁλοκαυτώσεως τῆς διὰ παντός. This is similar to the prescriptions throughout ch.28; see vv.15,22—23,30—31, and comp 29:5—6. MT then continues with מנחתה ונסכה "its meal offering and its libation." The suffixes clearly refer to the daily holocaust. Num felt that all the offerings for the day should be included in a nominative summary statement, and reads αἱ θυσίαι αὐτῶν καὶ αἱ σπονδαὶ αὐτῶν. This might well be translated: "(these are) their meal offerings and their libations."

29:17 Over against MT, Num does not begin with και. In spite of the fact that only 963 b and ms 509 support the shorter text, the translation pattern demands that, regardless of the fact that MT begins the daily sections with וביום (except for the eighth day), Num should only begin with καί for the first day (v.12), and thereafter consistently begin with τῇ ἡμέρᾳ.[18]

MT follows the pattern of 28:11,19,27 and vv.2,8,13 of adding בני בקר after פרים, after which it no longer adds such designation. Num omits it already here, and hex adds εκ βοων under the asterisk to equal MT. The number of bullocks to be brought is decreased by one to δώδεκα, a pattern of decrease which obtains through the seventh day. The animals to be sacrificed are throughout in the accusative; in other words, the προσάξετε of v.13 carries over for all seven days. For the popular F variant τεσσαρες, see comment at vv.14—15.

---
16. See Bl-D 46.2.
17. Pp.148—149.
18. See THGN 101.

29:18 MT reads ומנחתם ונסכיהם. Num omits the opening conjunction, and changes the second noun to the singular, i.e. it reads ἡ θυσία αὐτῶν καὶ ἡ σπονδὴ αὐτῶν. The pronouns refer to the sacrificial animals of v..17. Thus according to MT, a single meal offering is to be offered but libations are in the plural. Num has made the pair consistent by using the singular throughout; contrast v.19. This change should occasion no surprise, since Num throughout these two chapters makes the nouns consistent in number whenever "sacrifice(s)" and "libation(s)" appear coordinately; a similar consistency obtains for the genitive pronouns modifying the pair.

The animals for which these are intended are characterized by κατὰ ἀριθμὸν αὐτῶν, i.e. according to the number specified in v.17, as well as κατὰ τὴν σύγκρισιν αὐτῶν, for which hex has placed the αὐτῶν under the obelus, since MT reads כמשפט. For σύγκρισιν. see comment at v.6.

29:19 This verse is an exact copy of v.16; cf comments ad loc. MT differs only in reading ונסכיהם instead of the ונסכה of v.16.

29:20—22 The third day. The instructions are exactly the same as for the second day, except for the adjustment of the number of bullocks to eleven. MT, however, has no equivalent for ἐξ αἰγῶν in v.22. MT also has חטאת before אחד, and hex has transposed ἕνα after περὶ ἁμαρτίας to equal MT.

29:23—25 The fourth day. The number of bullocks required is reduced to ten. In v.24 the opening nouns are now in the plural: αἱ θυσίαι αὐτῶν καὶ αἱ σπονδαὶ αὐτῶν. Note that Num throughout writes both nouns in the same number regardless of MT, which here has מנחתם ונסכיהם. In fact, for each of the seven days both nouns are plural throughout, regardless of the Hebrew, for which see comment at v.16, where the pattern first occurs. The final αὐτῶν is placed under the obelus as in v.18, which see.

29:26—28 The fifth day. Except for the reduction of bullocks required to nine, the prescriptions are exactly the same as those for vv.23—25. In v.27 ἐξ αἰγῶν has no equivalent in MT, and hex has placed it under the obelus. As in v.18, the αὐτῶν after σύγκρισιν is placed under the obelus; cf comment at v.18.

29:29—31 The sixth day. The bullocks prescribed are again reduced by one, to eight. For the rest, the text is the same as that of vv.26—28. As in that section, both the final αὐτῶν of v.30 and the ἐξ αἰγῶν of v.31 are placed under the obelus, neither being represented in the MT text.

29:32—34 The seventh day. The required bullocks are now down to the ideal seven. The Num text for the rest is exactly the same as for vv.29—31. MT, however, now has a suffix at כמשפטם, and the final αὐτῶν of v.33 has here an equivalent in MT. As for ἐξ αἰγῶν in v.34, it has again been placed under the obelus by hex, since MT has no equivalent for it.

29:35 As at v.17, the lack of an initial και is original text. In fact, here MT also begins asyndetically. The shorter text has survived only in V 963 plus six other Greek witnesses (mss), but Num is consistent in its practice of not introducing the successive days (i.e. after the initial one at v.12) with a και.[19] The eighth day is separate from the seven days of the festival; in fact, it is called an ἐξόδιον, a word signifying the final day, the closing celebration of a religious festival.[20] For a fuller discussion of the word and the Hebrew עצרת which it represents, see Note at Lev 23:36. Except for Jer 9:2 where עצרת is used in a non-technical sense, it is always translated by ἐξόδιον. As for the opening day of the festival (v.12), "you may not do any ordinary work ἐν αὐτῇ." MT has no prepositional structure at the end of the clause, and hex has placed ἐν αὐτῇ under the obelus. In the tradition, the verb is changed to the third singular future pasive ποιηθησεται in a C s reading, but this is secondary; it may well be a derivative of the itacistic reading ποιησεται.

29:36 For the closing celebrations, "you shall bring ὁλοκαυτώματα εἰς ὀσμὴν εὐωδίας κάρπωμα." MT reads עלה אשה ריח ניחח. Once again, Num, being aware that more than one animal is to be presented for the holocaust, renders עלה by the plural ὁλοκαυτώματα. In the tradition, the F O Byz+ text read a singular. This could be understood as a hex correction, but it was not corrected in earlier

---

19. See THGN 101.
20. Aq translates the Hebrew word by ἐπίσχεσις "stoppage," hence probably "conclusion," viz. the concluding feast.

instances, and I suspect that this is a palaeographically inspired reading, rather than a recensional one.

Since the word κάρπωμα regularly renders אשה in the singular, two observations may be made. The A B 963ᶜ y z+ reading of the plural καρπωματα is secondary, and secondly, the present text must have read אשה after ריח ניחח. The hex text did transpose κάρπωμα before εἰς to fit the text of MT.

29:37 This verse follows the pattern of v.33, except for perforce changing ταῖς μόσχοις and τοις κριοῖς to the singular in view of μόσχον ἕνα and κριὸν ἕνα of v.36. Over against MT, it has καί before τῷ κριῷ as in the earlier pattern of vv.21—33. Hex placed the final αὐτῶν under the obelus, since כמשפט of MT has no pronominal suffix.

29:38 The text of Num is exactly the same as at v.34. The phrase ἐξ αἰγῶν follows the text of Sam, but has no correspondent in MT, and hex has placed it under the obelus. Num also followed Sam's אחד לחתאת, but MT has the two words reversed. Accordingly, hex reordered Num's text to read περι αμαρτιας ενα.

29:39 The subscription to chh.28—29. "All these you must perform to the Lord in your festivals." For the unexpected ἐν ταῖς ἑορταῖς ὑμῶν for במועדיכם, see comment at 28:2. Num does not distinguish in this calendar of cultic occasions between "stated times" (מועדים) and "festivals" (חגים).

V.b in MT reads לבד מנדריכם ונדבתיכם "besides any of your vows and your voluntary offerings." I have taken the מן as partitive, i.e. "any of." The text then goes on with four ל phrases which define the vows and voluntary offerings, i.e. "whether your burnt offerings and (or) your meal offerings and your libations and your offerings for deliverance." This would imply that vows, etc. had been listed as extras; note the לבד structures at 28:23,31 and at vv.6,11,16 et al; the difficulty with MT is that vows, voluntary offerings and sacrifices for deliverance had not been mentioned; after all, these are offerings by individuals rather than by the community. Num has dealt with this by dividing sharply between ταῦτα, which refers to all the public cultic observances dealt with in the cultic calendar of chh.28—29, and the six private offerings, i.e. by individuals, by using πλήν governing the genitive "your vows," and then stringing along paratactically the next five in the accusative. I would translate v.b by "besides your vows, as well as (performing) your voluntary sacrifices and your holocausts and your meal offerings and your libations and your sacrifices for deliverance." These last five are accusative, thus further modifiers of ποιήσετε.

Chapter 30

30:1 V.1 is best understood as part of what preceded rather than as introducing ch.30, which is what v.2 does. Num begins with καὶ ἐλάλησεν, but MT has ויאמר. It seems reasonable to assume that Num's parent text read וידבר; see v.2.

30:2 Vv.2–17 discuss the validity of vows, particularly those made by women. V.2 also begins with καὶ ἐλάλησεν Μωυσῆς, and could easily be taken as a doublet of v.1, though see comment at v.1. Here MT does read וידבר. MT reads לבני ישראל after אל ראשי המטות, which Num renders by omitting לבני, thus "(to the chieftains of the tribes) of Israel." Hex has added (των) υιων before Ἰσραήλ. Whether the article is hex or not is uncertain. It is not clear why Moses should communicate the Lord's word to the tribal chieftains rather than directly to the Israelites, who are more commonly the recipients of the Lord's instructions.

In both vv.1 and 2 the relative clause אשר צוה יהוה occurs, but v.1 uses the verb ἐνετείλατο, whereas in v.2 the verb συνέταξεν obtains. As far as I can determine, there is no distinction intended by the two, though the former is used far more often than the other as rendering for צוה. The verb συντάσσω occurs 79 times, but ἐντέλλομαι is used 339 times to render the Hebrew verb.[1]

30:3 Num begins with ἄνθρωπος ἄνθρωπος, but MT has a single איש. Hex has duly placed the second one under the obelus. Since either ἄνθρωπος or ἄνθρωπος ἄνθρωπος can occur as a pendant nominative before ὃς ἄν with no difference in intent, it seems likely that Num's parent text must have read איש איש rather than a single איש. In the tradition, the Byz text has limited the application of the demands of this verse to the Israelites, either by substituting for, or adding to, the second ἄνθρωπος, των υιων ισραηλ, but this has no support in MT nor is it necessary in view of the addressees signalled in v.2, "the chieftains of the tribes of Israel."

In MT the כי clause is the protasis, with a coordinate verbal, i.e. with ידר נדר ליהוה as the first structure, well rendered by (ὃς ἄν) εὔξηται εὐχὴν κυρίῳ

---

1. The count is that of Dos Santos.

"should vow a vow to the Lord." Its correlative has a contextual free infinitive plus a cognate modifier: או השבע שבעה. In context a free infinitive takes on the syntactic color of the context, in this case of ידר נדר, thus "or should swear an oath." The translator fully understood its syntax as his rendering ἢ ὀμόσῃ ὅρκον shows. In MT, this structure is modified by a marked infinitive defining the context of the שבעה; it reads לאסר אסר על נפשו "to bind a binding on himself." The translator has quite a different construction; he has a third correlative: ἢ ὀρίσηται ὁρισμῷ περὶ τῆς ψυχῆς αὐτοῦ "or should bind himself with an obligation for himself" i.e. he takes on himself a voluntarily imposed obligation for himself. The translator may well have considered the oath as consisting of taking on a voluntary obligation as better expressed by an alternative, thus "would swear an oath or would bind himself with a limitation on his person," thereby more completely defining the full range of promises made to the Lord. No attempt at changing this interpretation obtains in the tradition. The B 963 Byz x+ text has changed the word order to read ορισμω η ορισηται, which is not at all an improvement.

The apodosis demands that "he may not profane his word." The verb βεβηλόω is regularly used in the Pentateuch for the root חלל, either in the Pi or the Hi (as here). To render something profane means that it becomes βέβηλος "common, trodden underfoot like trash." The Byz text has tried to improve the text by changing τὸ ῥῆμα to the plural τα ρηματα, but the singular does not mean " the one word," but that which he spoke, i.e. it already means "words," as the ὅσα clause modifying it implies.

Actually, what is meant is further clarified by πάντα ὅσα ἂν ἐξέλθῃ ἐκ τοῦ στόματος αὐτοῦ ποιήσει, i.e. a man's word must be his bond, "everything which procedes out of his mouth, he must perform."

30:4 MT begins the verse with a conjunction, but Num has a δέ construction, which represents a finer Greek style. The vow is made κυρίῳ.[2] For ὀρίσηται ὁρισμόν, see the comment at v.3 on ὀρίσηται ὁρισμῷ. The change in case is insignificant, though it should be noted that C'+ text changed ὁρισμόν to ορισμω to agree with the dative of v.3.

The Byz text has substituted the more literal και for the ἤ of Num, probably mediated through one of The Three. The modifier ἐν τῇ νεότητι αὐτῆς refers to

---

2. The Others read τῷ κυρίῳ, with the article rendering the preposition ל.

the time when the woman was not yet married, i.e. remained in her father's house.

30:5 The coordinate protasis in Num reads "and her father should hear her vows and her obligations which she laid upon herself, and the father should remain silent." That this is coordinate with v.4 is clear from the continued use of the subjunctive mood: ἀκούσῃ ... παρασιωπήσῃ. Num follows Sam's את נדריה ואסריה rather than the singular nouns of MT.³ MT has for the second clause: והחריש לה אביה "and there remained silent for her, her father." Num has αὐτῆς ὁ πατήρ, which hex rewrote by changing αὐτῆς to αυτη,⁴ and then adding αυτης under the asterisk to equal MT exactly. The Byz+ text transposed αὐτῆς after ὁ πατήρ as the more usual representation of אביה (but left the לה out of consideration). Clearly Byz was simply making an internal stylistic change.

Num signals the apodosis by the change to a future verb, which is introduced by a καί in imitation of the Hebrew. The apodosis in MT consists of two clauses, the first in the plural, and the second one in the singular. Num makes both plural as does Sam, which, however, also adds a suffix to the second subject, i.e. אסריה. The Byz+ text also added αυτης afer ὁρισμοί, but this is merely a stylistic gloss; it is not recensional.

According to MT, the second clause reads "every אסר ... יקום. Note that MT uses the same verb as was used for the the first clause, i.e. קמו. Num changes the verb, reading μενοῦσιν αὐτῇ "shall remain (in force) for her." The verb is of course plural in view of the subject ὁρισμοί, but αὐτῇ is an ad sensum gloss, which hex placed under the obelus.

30:6 "But if her father should actually negate (i.e. refuse to acknowledge) at the time that he heard all her vows and the obligations that she imposed on herself, they shall not stand." Num follows the text of Sam, which has הנא יניא rather than MT's הניא. The cognate free infinitive is rendered by a participle, which is also intended to place particular stress on the verbal idea. Hex has placed the participle ἀνανεύων under the obelus, since it is not supported by MT. What the expression means to convey is that her father simply cancels or annuls the action of his daughter. MT indicates this by the modifier אתה; it is "her" that he ne-

---

3. As does Pesh.
4. The Others also read αὐτῇ.

gates. Num has no equivalent, since an accusative of person cannot occur with ἀνανεύω, which is either used absolutely or with an accusative (or genitive) of thing. Hex added a dative αυτη under the asterisk after "her father," i.e. "for her" to equal אתה, which is sensible. MT has a suffix for אסריה, which Num does not translate, since it is otiose in Greek, particularly in view of the limiting nature of the relative clause modifying ὁρισμούς. Hex has added αυτης under the asterisk to represent the suffix.

Not only will the young woman's undertakings not "remain," but the Lord καθαριεῖ αὐτήν "will consider her blameless." This is an interpretation of יסלח לה "will forgive her," which is not quite the same. According to Num, the woman has not committed a sin; she was a minor, and pardon is inappropriate. Rather she remains in a pure state, i.e. she is blameless. As in the protasis, Num used ἀνένευσεν in an absolute sense, i.e. did not translate the modifier אתה, and again hex added αυτη under the asterisk accordingly.

30:7 Vv.7—9 concern a woman who is married while her vows or obligations are still valid. The Hebrew for the marriage condition is ואם היו תהיה לאיש, which is rendered word for word by Num as ἐὰν δὲ γενομένη γένηται ἀνδρί, literally, "but if she should actually become a man's." Once again a cognate participle is used to render the cognate free infinitive. I would translate: "but if she should actually be married."

Furthermore, καὶ αἱ εὐχαὶ αὐτῆς ἐπ᾽ αυτῇ κατὰ τὴν διαστολὴν τῶν χειλέων αὐτῆς "and her vows (are) upon her according to the utterance of her lips."[5] The κατά structure is highly problematic. MT has או מבטא שפתיה. The word מבטא occurs only here and in v.9, and it probably means a rash or thoughtless utterance; comp the comment at Lev 5:4 on διαστέλλουσα for לבטא. The problem is made worse by the relative clause that follows: אשר אסרה על נפשה "which she had imposed on herself." Obviously, the מבטא שפתיה is the same as the אסריה of v.6; at least, that is how Num understood it, since it has οὓς ὡρίσατο κατὰ τῆς ψυχῆς αὐτῆς. Furthermore, in v.9 ואת מבטא שפתיה is translated by καὶ οἱ ὁρισμοὶ αὐτῆς, though it seems more likely that at v.9 a different parent text is involved. The syntax is simply wrong here, and I suspect that the οὕς is sec-

---

5. For ἐπ᾽ αὐτῇ, Theod has ἐπ᾽ αὐτήν, while Aq retains Num, and Sym has καθ᾽ ἑαυτῆς.

ondary, and that ὅσα should be read.⁶ The secondary οὕς is taken from vv.5,6, where exactly the same οὕς clause occurs, an early copyist error which B V O x+ perpetuated, but it simply cannot have been intended by the translator. The translation then makes sense; "according to the (thoughtless) utterance of her lips which she imposed upon herself." I suggest the notion of thoughlessness, since διαστολή of the lips really implies the opening, the expanding of the lips; it refers to that which just fell out from the lips. The ὁρισμός was unplanned; it was a מבטא.

30:8 The conditions are similar to those of the first case; see v.5. Num has reordered the clauses of MT so that the relative clause "at which time he heard" follows the second condition rather than the first. Hex has transposed καὶ παρασιωπήσῃ αὐτῇ to follow the relative clause, thereby equalling the order of MT. The change in word order in Num makes excellent sense, since her husband not only heard his wife making her vows but he kept silent at the time. The Hebrew order states the obvious; of course, he heard it at the time she spoke; when else would he have done so? The real point is made by the Greek; i.e. he kept silent at the time instead of immediately cancelling the vow; see also v.9.

V.b constitutes the apodosis, and is introduced by καὶ οὕτως, whereas MT has only a conjunction. Hex placed the οὕτως under the obelus.⁷ Num follows Sam in its reading כל נדריה.⁸ Similarly, Num reads the plural καὶ οἱ ὁρισμοὶ αὐτῆς for MT's ואסרה.⁹

30:9 Num has a substanatially different text from MT, and has harmonized in part with v.6. MT begins with ואם ביום שמע אישה יניא אותה "and if on the day that her husband hears, he negates her (i.e. disallows her)," but Num follows the pattern of v.6 exactly, only substituting ὁ ἀνήρ for ὁ πατήρ, thus "but if her husband should actually negate on the day that he should hear." Hex has placed ἀνενεύων ἀνενεύσῃ under the obelus, and transposed ὁ ἀνὴρ αὐτῆς after ἀκούσῃ, and

---

6. Both Theod and Aq read ὅσα ὡρίσατο, whereas Sym has ὃ ἔδησεν καθ' ἑαυτῆς (for על נפשו).
7. Both cod G and Syr wrongly include the καί as well; the obelus belongs between the words καὶ οὕτως.
8. But Kenn 4,9,75,80,94 and 166 also add כל.
9. Num's parent text is reflected in 4QNumᵇ: ואס(ריה).

then added ανανευση αυτη, all of which then equalled MT, but it also means a substantial rewriting of the text.

MT then reads והפר את נדרה אשר עליה ואת מבטא שפתיה אשר אסרה על נפשה "and should dissolve her vow which was on her and the rash utterance of her lips which she had imposed on herself." Num has in its place πᾶσαι αἱ εὐχαὶ αὐτῆς καὶ οἱ ὁρισμοὶ αὐτῆς οὓς ὡρίσατο κατὰ τῆς ψυχῆς αὐτῆς οὐ μενοῦσιν ὅτι ὁ ἀνὴρ ἀνένευσεν ἀπ' αὐτῆς. Possibly, a different parent text lay behind the Num text, though some harmonization with v.5 may underly it. In fact, for the source of this text up through μενοῦσιν, see that verse which only differs in that πάντες is added before οἱ.[10] For the ὅτι clause, see the similar statement at the end of v.6. Here, however, ἀνέσευσεν is uniquely modified by ἀπ' αὐτῆς, and may best be rendered by "because her husband had cancelled (it) from her." Here too, one suspects that the translator harmonized the text with v.6, simply transposing the two clauses, and adding an ἀπ' αὐτῆς as a modifier to ἀνένευσεν.

Origen had quite a time trying to "fix up" this text to fit MT. First of all, "all her vows and her obligations" was placed under the obelus; it had no counterpart in MT. Then he added under the asterisk και διασκεδαση την ευχην αυτης την επ αυτης η την διαστολην των χειλεων αυτης, after which he read οσα (not οὕς). This, Origen almost certainly took from Theod. This then does equal MT, except for η instead of the coordinate conjunction, but see או in v.7. The remainder, i.e. οὐ μενοῦσιν to the last αὐτῆς of the verse was placed under the obelus, since this too was lacking in MT.

All that remained was καὶ κύριος καθαριεῖ αὐτήν, which does equal MT, and for which see comment at v.6.

30:10 The vow of a widow and of a divorcee (or better, a divorced woman; the word ἐκβεβλημένης means "a woman who has been cast out"; see Note at Lev 21:7) cannot be annulled. In MT such a vow is defined as כל אשר אסרה על נפשה "everything which she has imposed upon herself." The verb אסר has throughout not been used for the execution of a vow, but rather for אסרים (or of מבטא שפתים); for vows, only the cognate verb נדר was used. Similarly, in Num εὐχή demanded εὔξηται (not ὡρίσατο, e.g. v.8). This must have dictated the use of

---

10. 4QNum^b reflects the πάντες; it reads כול נדריה. Note that this substantiates the plural noun of Num as well. The Qumran text also read ואסריה; this is parent text to the καὶ οἱ ὁρισμοὶ αὐτῆς of Num, but it is lacking in MT.

εὔξηται here for אסרה. Note the awkwardness of the modifier κατὰ τῆς ψυχῆς αὐτῆς used with εὔξηται, presumably, what is meant is "vowed for herself"? Num disregarded the כל as well, and hex added παντα under the asterisk before ὅσα. The predicate reads μενοῦσιν αὐτῇ, whereas MT has the singular verb. The plural can only be justified by the intervening ὅσα ἄν clause, understood as plural. Oddly enough, no copyist changed the verb to the singular μενει. I suspect that the translator was influenced by the μενοῦσιν αὐτῇ of v.5 as contrasting with the οὐ μενοῦσιν of v.9.

30:11 Vv.11—13 concern the husband's role in the case of a wife's vow or self-imposed obligation. V.11 presents the protasis: "If her vow or obligation (imposed) on herself by an oath (be undertaken) in the house of her husband." The syntax of MT is much clearer: "If in the house of her husband אסר אסרה או נדרה upon herself by an oath." The syntax of the verse in Num is highly unusual in that it is constructed without any verbs; as a nominal clause it is not luminous either; presumably what is predicated is the ἐν phrase: "in the house of her husband." Num has misunderstood the third singular verbs as nouns with third feminine singular suffixes, and in consequence omitted the אסר which should have clarified the structure. Hex has partially "repaired" the text of Num by substituting for ὁ ὁρισμός the structure ον ωρισατο ορισμον under the asterisk, but leaving ἡ εὐχὴ αὐτῆς as it is. The Byz text simply added αυτης, which is a stylistic gloss based on the coordinate "her vow." Byz then omitted κατὰ τῆς ψυχῆς αὐτῆς, which in view of the αυτης added immediately before the phrase may simply be a case of homoioteleuton occasioning an accidental omission. On the other hand, its omission does simplify the text considerably. Unusual is the μεθ' ὅρκου, presumably referring only to the ὁρισμός. It renders בשבעה uniquely, though correctly, taking the preposition as instrumental.[11]

30:12 The first three clauses are all syndetic and are part of the protasis, but the third one in MT is asyndetic. So in MT the first two condition the third one, thus "and (when) her husband hears and remains silent for her, then he did not negate her (i.e. not annul her actions)." In Num the three clauses are on the same level:

---

11. See SS 125.

"and her husband should hear, and remain silent for her, and not negate for her." That they belong to the protasis is clear from the subjunctive mood of the verbs. That all three clauses constitute the protasis is, however, also true of MT; note that the Masoretes divided the verse by placing אתה under the *ethnach*.

The apodosis is introduced by καί in imitation of the Hebrew, and is identified by the change to a future verb. It consists of two clauses, the first following MT word for word: "then shall stand all her vows." The second clause is in the singular in MT: "and every obligation which she imposed on herself shall stand." The translator made the clause plural as a more precise parallel to the first one. It reads "and all her (αὐτῆς) obligations which she imposed on herself shall stand (στήσονται κατ' αὐτῆς)." Hex placed the αὐτῆς as well as the κατ' αὐτῆς, neither of which had a correspondent in MT, under the obelus. The additions are ad sensum exegetical glosses.

30:13 Num begins with ἐὰν δὲ περιελὼν περιέλῃ ὁ ἀνὴρ αὐτῆς "but if her husband should actually annul." The verb περιαιρέω means "to cancel, void," and adequately renders the Hebrew הפר יפר. As often in Num, the cognate free infinitive is rendered by a cognate participle, and serves the same function as in the Hebrew, viz. to place special emphasis on the verbal idea.[12] Num failed to render אתם, using περιέλῃ absolutely. Hex has duly added αυτα under the asterisk.

The verb ἀκούσῃ is modified by a πάντα ὅσα structure, i.e. "on the day that he would hear everything which came out of her lips, according to her vows and according to her self-imposed obligations (literally the obligations which were on herself)." The point being made once again is that the husband's cancelation takes place at the time of the wife's taking on vows and obligations, rather than later. This is a straightforward understanding of Num. Theoretically, since in the earlier cases ἀκούσῃ was used absolutely, the πάντα ὅσα structure could be taken to modify περιέλῃ, but this is incorrect, since the structure is again referred to by οὐ μενεῖ αὐτῇ "it shall not remain for her." The unstated subject is obviously the πάντα structure. MT has no equivalent for the ad sensum gloss αὐτῇ, and hex has placed it under the obelus.[13]

---

12. Theod renders the opening clause by καὶ ἐὰν διασκεδάζων διασκεδάσῃ αὐτὰ ὁ ἀνὴρ αὐτῆς. Aq has καὶ ἐὰν ἀκυρῶν ἀκυρώσῃ αὐτὰς ἀνὴρ αὐτῆς, while Sym reads ἐὰν δὲ διαλύσει διαλύσῃ αὐτὰς ὁ ἀνὴρ αὐτῆς.
13. Cod G mistakenly included οὐ μενεῖ as well; the obelus is in the wrong place.

For הפרם, Num simply has περιεῖλεν used absolutely as earlier in the verse. Again, hex has added αυτα under the asterisk to represent the suffix. For καθαριεῖ rendering יסלח, see comment at v.6. It might be noted that in the tradition the Hellenistic καθαρισει obtains in our oldest witnesses, B and 963, but this is nonetheless secondary; Num uses only the Attic future inflections throughout.[14]

30:14 Unusual is the description of the oath as אסר לענת נפש "obligation to afflict the person." Num usually rendered the noun אסר by ὁρισμός, but here Num uniquely uses δεσμοῦ "bond, tie," which in turn governs the infinitive κακῶσαι. The reference is to an oath binding one to maltreat oneself, i.e. a self-imposed asceticism. The entire structure up to this point is a pendant nominative, thus "As for every vow and every oath of binding to maltreat oneself." About the pendant, it is then said that "her husband may establish for her, and her husband may cancel." This is clearer in MT, where the pronominal verbal suffixes bring the pendant into the main sytactic structure. Obviously, the absolute use of the verbs must be understood to involve the pendant. In both cases, MT had suffixed the verbs, i.e. as יקימנו and יפרנו resp., though hex has restored neither one. It should be noted that Num has added a dative pronoun of advantage after στήσει, which has no equivalent in MT, but the change of this αὐτῇ modifying στῆσαι to αυτην by a popular F text actually equals MT, and may be a hex change. For the second verb, the *b* text adds αυτη, but this is a stylistic gloss.

30:15 "But if σιωπῶν παρασιωπήσῃ for her ἡμέραν ἐξ ἡμέρας" constitutes the protasis. MT adds אישה after "her," for which hex supplies a translation, ο ανηρ αυτης, under the asterisk. MT once again uses a cognate free infinitive plus inflected verb pattern, which Num translates by using the simplex cognate participle plus a compound verb, but the sense is clear: "he remains completely silent, and that for "day after a day," i.e. for more than a single day. I would understand the ἡμέραν as an accusative of extent of time, and the ἐξ ἡμέρας as "out of a day," i.e. a full day after the day of hearing the avowed promises. The Hebrew reads "from a day to a day," which is not as clear as it might be, but is probably correctly understood by Num; it seems to mean "from one to the next one."

---

14. See THGN 124.

The apodosis, introduced by an apodotic καί, and marked by the future tense, consists of two clauses in Num, plus a ὅτι clause. It reads "(then) he shall establish αὐτῇ all her vows, and the obligations which are on her, he shall establish αὐτῇ." The ὅτι clause then follows with "because he was silent for her in the day in which he heard." This differs considerably from the syntax of MT, which makes the first cut in the verse after "on her," with v.b reading "he established them because ...." Instead of "them," Num has another αὐτῇ following the pattern of στήσει αὐτῇ of the first clause. Hex typically does not correct this, since the slot is filled with an αὐτῇ. Hex correction should have been made to εστησεν αυτα! Furthermore, MT has no equivalent for the αὐτῇ in the first clause, which hex did place under the obelus. MT also has כל אסריה for "the obligations," and hex has added παντους under the asterisk before τοὺς ὁρισμούς, whereas the A Byz+ text has added an αυτης after the noun, which is probably also a recensional correction. It should be noted that ms 426 also has the αυτης, which enhances the possibility that the αυτης is recensional.

It might also be noted how different the Num translation patterns are from those of Deut. In Deut, case attraction of relative pronouns to that of their antecedent was common; here ἡμέρᾳ ᾗ is one of only two cases which I found in Num.[15]

30:16 Num begins with ἐὰν δὲ περιελὼν περιέλῃ αὐτῆς. For the verbal pattern used for rendering הפר יפר, see comment at v.13. The genitive αὐτῆς is unusual, but must here indicate advantage, i.e. "cancelled on her behalf, for her."[16] Actually, MT has אתם, though The Three all also added ὁ ἀνὴρ αὐτῆς after a plural pronoun, i.e. presupposing אתם אישה. In the tradition, an O t+ text read ο ανηρ αυτης instead of αὐτῆς, and one can speculate that either האיש or אתם אישה was an early reading, in which case the O reading, as representing hex, could have been due to homoiarchon. But there is no evidence for such in the Hebrew tradition, and it remains pure speculation.

In MT, the verbal complex is modified by אחרי שמעו "after his hearing (it)," which Num interprets correctly by "after τὴν ἡμεραν ἣν ἤκουσεν," which is what the abbreviated MT text must mean.

---

15. See THGN 99.
16. Theod has καὶ ἐὰν διασκεδάζων διασκεδάσῃ αὐτὰ ὁ ἀνὴρ αὐτῆς; Aq has καὶ ἐὰν ἀκυρῶν ἀκυρώσῃ αὐτὰς ὁ ἀνὴρ αὐτῆς, and Sym translates ἐὰν δὲ διαλύσει διαλύσῃ αὐτὰς ὁ ἀνὴρ αὐτῆς; the same readings obtain at v.13, which see.

The apodosis reads: "then he shall bear her guilt (את עונה)," but Num has καὶ λήμψεται τὴν ἁμαρτίαν αὐτοῦ, which follows the Sam text, עונו. In other words, the fault is his, and he must carry the responsibility; it was his mistake, his ἁμαρτίαν, not his wife's, as MT would have it. This is enhanced by the choice of ἁμαρτίαν to translate עון; it is not so much his iniquity or guilt, as his mistake, his failure. This interpretation of ἁμαρτίαν αὐτοῦ is consistent with Num's rendering of יסלח by καθαριεῖ in vv.6,9,13; see comment at v.6. I suspect that the adoption of αὐτοῦ rather than the feminine αυτης was intentional rather than textual in origin.

30:17 The subscription to the chapter: "These are the regulations (δικαιώματα), which the Lord commanded Moses between a man and his wife, καί between a father and daughter in (her) youth in the father's house." MT lacks the καί before the second בין, but Num followed the ובין of Sam; a conjunction is certainly expected. MT reads לבתו for "daughter," and hex added an αυτου under an asterisk to represent the suffix. Similarly, both "youth" and "father's" have third feminine suffixes, i.e. נעריה and אביה resp, and hex added an αυτης under the asterisk after νεότητι, and also added αυτης after πατρός.[17]

---

17. Though only Byz support for the second αυτης is certain; on the other hand, the combined support of ms 426 and Syh may well attest to the hex origin of the αυτης.

Chapter 31

31:2 For the cognate expression ἐκδίκει τὴν ἐκδίκησιν, see Note at Lev 26:25. Here it is modified by an ἐκ phrase, i.e. "exact vengeance from." V.b in MT begins with אחר "afterwards," but in Num it is preceded by καί as in Sam.[1] The adverb ἔσχατον really means "finally."[2] So finally, after retribution has been exacted from the Midianites, Moses will be added πρὸς τὸν λαόν σου, i.e. will die; cf Note at Gen 25:8. MT uses the plural noun עמיך; see 20:24.

31:3 MT has Moses say: "Let men from among you be equipped for the battle (לצבא for the army)." The verbal form according to the Masoretes is a Ni imperative. Num has made an active verb out of it, ἐξοπλίσατε, probably understanding the form as a Hi. The translator also took לצבא as a marked infinitive, i.e. "(equip men from among you) to draw up in battle array (παρατάξασθαι)." A majority A F M text has και παραταξασθε instead of the infinitive; this may represent an attempt at correcting the text more in line with the Hebrew.

MT makes the first cut at this point in the text, and proceeds with "and they shall be against Midian." Num apparently misread יהיו as יהוה; at least, it reads ἔναντι κυρίου; as to the conjunction of ויהיו becoming ἔναντι, that is more problematic. It does seem that some misreading did take place. The Hebrew ויהיו is in fact rather odd in the context, and may well be an early corruption of some kind.[3] Num is fully clear; the army is to arraign themselves for battle before the Lord against Madian. The purpose of this exercise is clear; it is ἀποδοῦναι ἐκδίκησιν παρὰ κυρίου τῇ Μαδιάν "to repay vengeance from the Lord to Madian." MT reads "the vengeance of Yahweh," which Num correctly understands as representing a subjective genitive, i.e. παρὰ κυρίου.[4] The dative is best understood as indicating an indirect object in modification of ἀποδοῦναι, though MT has במדין "against Midian." The infinitive is stronger than the Hebrew לתת

---

1. Kenn 181 also reads ואחר.
2. See Bauer sub ἔσχατον 2, where this meaning is attested for the third century BCE.
3. For לצבא ויהיו על מדין Theod and Aq read ἵνα δύνωνται καὶ ἔσονται ἐπὶ Μαδιάν; Sym simply disregards the difficult ויהיו, and has ἵνα δύνωνται ἐπὶ Μαδιάν.
4. Tar⁰ defines נקמת יהוה as פרענת דין עמא דיי, which Tarᴶ also attests, but without the word דין. It reads פורענות עמא דיי.

"to give, put, to exact (vengeance)"; the Greek reads "to pay back." In the tradition, the A B M majority text has articulated κυρίου, but Num never articulates the genitive of κύριος when it is used for יהוה,[5] and it must be secondary.

31:4 Num translates the distributive אלף למטה אלף למטה word for word, except for using ἐκ to render the preposition, i.e. "a thousand out of each tribe," and this must mean "an אלף from each tribe (out of all the tribes of Israel)." This modifies the verb ἀποστείλατε. The Hebrew לצבא "for the host, army" is again taken to represent a marked infinitive, purposive in nature, thus παρατάξασθαι "to arraign themselves in battle array."

In the tradition, the Byz s+ text has omitted the second χιλίους ἐκ φυλῆς, an obvious case of haplography. The majority A F M V text has coupled the two by a και, but the distributive pattern is not to be coordinated.

31:5 MT begins with וימסרו, which only occurs here and at v.16 where it is probably corrupt; it is thus practically a hapax legomenon for the Hebrew Bible. It is translated by καὶ ἐξηρίθμησαν, probably correctly in the sense of "to be counted, mustered," thus "selected."[6] The simplex verb ἀριθμέω was widely used in the variant A tradition as substitute for ἐπισκέπτομαι in the census report for the Hebrew פקד.[7] That the verb probably means "to muster, count" has been well argued by Milgrom.[8]

This mustering or counting concerns "a thousand per tribe from τῶν χιλιάδων of Israel." The term renders (אלפי ישראל). The term can, however, hardly mean "thousands," but as KB suggests, אלפים is a synonymn for משפחת. Since χιλιάς is a calque for אלף, the term should be translated by "clans, septs, divisions," i.e. a social unit larger than the extended family, but smaller than the "tribe"; see also 1:16; one might then render as "by tribal clans (or divisions)." The last structure is ἐνωπλισμένοι εἰς παράταξιν "armed in battle array." The masculine participle is nominalized, and is in apposition to χιλιάδες, which is feminine.

---

5. See THGN 104.
6. Tar[JO] have ואתבחרו "and they were chosen"; Pesh has a similar verb. Tar[N] has ואתחילו "and they were enlisted."
7. See especially U.Quast, MSU XX, 238—248, in which the ἀριθμέω/ἀριθμός tradition is carefully analyzed.
8. See Note on p.256.

31:6 Num has repeated χιλίους ἐκ φυλῆς as at v.4 against MT, and hex has placed the second one under the obelus. This is a case of haplography/dittography, but which is earlier cannot be determined. MT makes the first cut between צבא אתם "for the army; them and Phinees ...," while Num has σὺν δυνάμει αὐτῶν "with their army." I suspect that the translator was simply trying to make good sense. Hex fortunately made no attempt to render אתם, or did he possibly understand צבא אתם as an unusual bound phrase "the army of them," which would be rare indeed. More likely, Num understood אתם as the prepositional phrase meaning "with them," thus "their (army)."

καὶ Φινεές is coordinate with αὐτούς as the apposite υἱὸν Ἐλεαζάρ proves. In MT את פינחס is coordinate with אתם, i.e. "them and Phinehas," so Num has simply left out "them," but with Phinees coordinate with αὐτούς, Num managed somehow to keep close to MT. Num adds a further generation, υἱοῦ Ἀαρών, which hex quite rightly placed under the obelus, since it is not in MT. Whether τοῦ ἱερέως is intended to characterize Aaron or Eleazar is not certain, and is of no great importance, since both were priests.

With καὶ τὰ σκεύη a new clause begins, and it would be better to change the comma after ἱερέως to a colon. What is said is "both the holy vessels[9] and the trumpets of signals (i.e. for signalling) were in their hands." MT has בידו "in his hand," i.e. the hand of Phinehas, but this would be in conflict with 10:2 where "two silver trumpets" were to be made. Thus the αὐτῶν must refer to Phinees and Eleazar. By this change Num removes a possible contradiction from the text.

31:7 If the verb הרג is actually to be distinguished from הכה in that it means "killed after being captured" as opposed to "killed in battle,"[10] the distinction does not carry over into Greek; ἀποκτείνω simply means "kill, slay," though obviously in v.8 the slain kings of Madian had been captured. But here it is "every male" who is killed; these were killed in battle, not as captives.

31:8 The list of five Madianite kings is introduced by καί as well as connected individually by καί. MT begins the list without a conjunction. The first one, אוי, becomes Εὐίν. This at first blush might seem like a Hellenized ending, i.e. an

---
9. Rendering a bound phrase כלי הקדש by an adjectival one; see SS 65.
10. Attributed to Ehrlich by Milgrom, note 23.

accusative -ιν inflection, but this is unlikely for such an unknown name. An occasional better-known name is Hellenized by Num, but they are few and inevitably better known. It might also be noted that all other names in the list end with a closed syllable as well.[11] In the tradition, the O text, representing a hex correction, read ευει. Other witnesses confuse the nasal in ευ(ε)ιμ; dittography produced spellings with initial *nu* (τὸν) νευιν, νεβιν. Also found are ευηρε, ευηρι and ευρειν. The second name is רקם which becomes ʹΡόκομ in Num, but has been transposed to third position. In the tradition, the majority A F text has transposed it to second position. This is probably a recensional correction (hex?). Misspellings are mainly unique, at best limited to two witnesses; these include ροκεμ, ροκον, ροκαμ, ροκοβ, ροκοκ, κορομ and ροβοκ.

The third name צור, transcribed as Σούρ, is stable in the tradition, only σουι and συρ occurring as misspellings. The next name, Οὔρ represents חור. It too is stable, with only occasional misspellings: σουρ, ουρι, μουρ and νουν. The last of the five kings is problematic. The name רבע becomes ʹΡόβοκ, but an ʹ*ayin* does not transcribe as *kappa*. It can represent either a voiced pharyngeal fricative, which is transcribed either by zero or by vowel change, or a voiced velar fricative, the *ghain* of Arabic, which normally becomes *gamma*, whereas καππα represents *qoph*. Was *rbğ* actually devoiced in final position, or by attraction to the voiceless *pi* of πέντε with follows? I have no satisfactory explanation for this transcription,[12] but strongly suggest that a different parent text was read by Num. In the tradition, only the ροβο of ms 426 shows Hebrew (Aq?) influence. Other misspellings are simply transcription errors, such as ροβεκ, ροκομ, ροβοβ, ροβομ, βορακ and βωκ. These five kings were killed "together with (ἅμα) their wounded"; MT has על "besides."

"And Balaam, son of Beor, they killed with a sword σὺν τοῖς τραυματίαις αὐτῶν." The σύν phrase has no counterpart in MT, and hex has placed it under the obelus. Its source is clear; it is a variant of the ἅμα phrase applying to the five kings. It can only be called a careless case of harmonization with the earlier phrase as the αὐτῶν proves; its antecedent cannot be Βαλαάμ, but must be the "five kings of Madian."

---

11. The Others correct the transcription to Εὐεί.
12. Aq transcribed by ʹΡόβο, and Theod and Sym, by ʹΡόβαι. By the time of The Recensors the two phonemes had become one; the more common pharyngeal, either as voiced or voiceless, had won out over their velar counterparts.

31:9 MT distinguishes between the treatment of women and children as "taken captive," but of cattle, herds and goods (חיל) as "taken as booty." Num made no such distinction; everything was taken as prey, ἐπρονόμευσαν. For the opening clause, MT specified בני ישראל as subject of the verb, but Num does not, simply continuing with the subject of the previous verses, who are only named as being addressed in v.3 as τὸν λαόν; they are of course the υἱοὶ Ἰσραήλ. Hex added υιοι ισραηλ to equal the Hebrew. For ἀποσκευήν as a calque for טף, see Note at Gen 34:29.

V.b is chiastically arranged over against v.1, i.e. in an a:b::b´:a´ pattern. the a/a´ part is in both cases ἐπρονόμευσαν, whereas b/b´ consist of articulated modifiers, for b, "the women of Madian and their ἀποσκευήν, and for b´, "and their cattle and all their possessions and their δύναμιν," with only the middle one using "all." MT, on the other hand, has all three terms governed by כל. Hex has added πασαν under the asterisk before τὴν δύναμιν, but apparently not before τὰ κτήνη. The term חיל has a wide range of meaning; thus BDB lists "strength, efficiency, wealth and army," and KB lists 1. Vermögen, Kraft; 2. Vermögen, Habe; 3. Streitmacht, Heer, and 4. Oberschicht.[13] The term is usually rendered by δύναμις (169 times), and by δυνατός, 21 times. Other translations include ἰσχύς 30 times and πλοῦτος, 14. Another 33 cases of חיל are divided among 20 different Greek lexemes.[14] Here δύναμις is hardly the most appropriate rendering (πλοῦτος would have been better), and it constitutes a mechanical rendering, and must be taken in calque fashion as meaning חיל!

31:10 The preposed modifiers are two: "all their cities which are in their κατοικίαις, and their ἐπαύλεις." The B O+ text reads the simplex οικιαις, but this is certainly secondary; LXX never renders מושב by οἰκία, whereas κατοικία is regularly used thus.[15] The term κατοικίαις here must mean "dwelling places" rather than "dwellings," since the τὰς ἐν ταῖς κατοικίαις defines πολεῖς.[16]

The term ἐπαύλεις translates טירת "encampments." In MT it is modified by כל, and so hex has added πασας under the asterisk before ἐπαύλεις. The

---

13. No change was made in the latest (3rd) edition.
14. The statistics are those of Dos Santos.
15. See THGN 127.
16. A distinction which Dorival makes clear.

word occurs elsewhere in the Pentateuch for טירה only at Gen 25:16; see Note ad loc. The term occurs in ch.32 for גדרה at vv.16,24,36, but in v.41 (twice) for חוה. It is also used for חוץ in Num at 22:39, for which see comment ad loc, and for חצר at 34:4. The term contrasts with city or village dwelling, here probably referring to temporary dwelling, possibly defined by rows (טורים) of stones.

Of these it is said ἐνέπρησαν ἐν πυρί, "they burned with fire." The ἐν is a clear example of "means" or "instrument."[17]

31:11 The subject of ἔλαβον is not stated, but throughout remains the Israelites. They took "all the booty and all their spoils, from people up to cattle." Here προνομήν renders שלל, whereas σκῦλα is used for מלקוח "something taken." MT uses a nice word play, מלקוח ... יקחו, which is not reproduced in the Greek. The ἀπό ... ἕως pattern is a common merismus, i.e. it covers everything from "a" to "z," thus "from people to cattle."

31:12 The verse must be read with v.11. They took ... "and brought to Moses ... and to πάντας υἱοὺς Ἰσραήλ." This differs from MT which reads אל עדת בני ישראל, i.e. Num has "all" instead of "assembly." Sam reads כל before עדת,[18] but no other old witness lacks עדת. There seems to be no good reason for omitting עדת, although once a כל is part of the parent text, the עדת does become tautological. What they brought was "τὴν αἰχμαλωσίαν and the spoils and the booty." The αἰχμαλωσίαν renders השבי, i.e. the women and children. For σκῦλα translating מלקוח, see comment at v.11.[19] As in v.11, προνομήν renders שלל.[20] These were brought to the camp, which was εἰς Ἀραβὼθ Μωάβ. ערבת is not a place name, however, but means "steppes, or plains."[21] The copyists naturally took it to be a proper noun, as the occasional misspellings show: αραβαθ, σαραβωθ, παραβωθ and αραμωθ. The location of the camp on the Moabite plains as ἐπὶ τοῦ Ἰορδάνου κατὰ Ἰεριχώ often occurs in the book; see 26:3,63 33:48 36:13, but with παρὰ τόν instead of ἐπὶ τοῦ at 22:1 33:50 35:1.

---

17. See SS 117.
18. As do many Kenn mss, as well as Pesh and Vulg.
19. The Three translate the word etymologically by λῆψις (retroverted from Syh).
20. Theod, Aq and Sym all translate by (τὰ) λάφυρα.
21. Aq renders the phrase by πρὸς ὁμαλὰ Μωάβ, and Sym, by ἐπὶ τὴν πεδιάδα τῆς Μωάβ.

31:13 Num has the singular καὶ ἐξῆλθεν before a compound subject, and follows the usual practice of attraction to the first member which is here singular, but MT has the plural ויצאו.[22] On the other hand, Sam does have the singular.[23] For the rest, Num renders MT word for word.

31:14 Moses was angry with the ἐπισκόποις of the army, i.e. "the overseers," those in charge. Its Hebrew equivalent is פקודי "the appointed ones." It refers to the officers; in fact, the term is defined in terms of divisional leaders, i.e. χιλιάρχοις and ἑκατονάρχοις. They are described as "ἐρχομένοις from the battle line of the war," thus the so-called returning heroes.

31:15 Moses' anger is directed against the leaders because they had spared every female. Num has Moses ask "Why" have you kept every female alive, whereas MT simply makes an accusation. Num has followed the Sam text which introduces the clause with למה.[24] There is no evidence that hex placed ἵνα τί under the obelus.

31:16 The blame is put on Balaam's shoulders; this is clearer in Num, which makes the opening "these γάρ belonged to the Israelites according to Balaam's word." The antecedent of αὗται is πᾶν θῆλυ; the plural is ad sensum. MT has no correspondent for γάρ; in fact, it begins with הן which Num disregards. Since this is followed by הנה, it constitutes a case of haplography/dittography; which is original cannot be determined. MT reads בדבר בלעם "by the word of Balaam," which Num renders by a κατὰ phrase, i.e. "according to the word of Balaam,"[25] which is a good rendering.

In MT this is followed by a (purposive) infinitive plus modifier, למסר מעל ביהוה, which really makes little sense. The root מסר occurs elsewhere in the Hebrew Bible only at v.5, where it makes good sense, but here I can do nothing with it.[26] The translator also found it unintelligible, and paraphrased on the basis of the context. He explained the passage by τοῦ ἀποστῆσαι καὶ ὑπεριδεῖν τὸ ῥῆμα κυρίου. He is thus saying (in justification of the killing of Balaam by the sword)

---
22. But Kenn 84 reads ויצא.
23. See THGN 122.
24. So too Pesh and Vulg.
25. See SS 125.
26. The Tar render by שקר (Tar^N למשקרה/לשקרא).

that he had advised Israel that the Madianite women were legitimate prey, i.e. "they ἦσαν τοῖς υἱοῖς Ἰσραήλ ... in order to make (them) revolt against and disregard the word of the Lord." It is then according to Num, Balaam's fault that Israel apostatized; he had advised the Madianites on how to proceed, an advice completely at odds with the oracles of chh.23—24. The coordinate infinitives actually explicate the root מעל.

The reference to Φογώρ and the resultant plague is to 25:18, which see, but comp the preceding vv.6—17 as well.

31:17 The order to kill the Madianite captives, both "every male ἐν πάσῃ τῇ ἀπαρτίᾳ" and "every woman who has had carnal knowledge (literally, who has known coitus of a male)." The ἐν phrase has בטף as correspondent in MT; the πάσῃ has been placed under the obelus by hex since MT has no כל. The Hebrew term טף means "little children," and is commonly rendered by ἀποσκευή; see comment at v.9. A synonym of ἀποσκευή, which in non-translation Greek means "household goods, baggage," is ἀπαρτία, which is usually translated by "train," i.e. train of campfollowers of an army, but here it must take on the LXX usage of ἀποσκευή, i.e. as calque for טף.[27] It occurs for טף at v.18 as well, but nowhere else. The usual meaning of ἀπαρτία is hardly applicable here.[28] What is meant is "every male among all the little ones," in other words, the boys. This contrasts with v.18. The adult males had already been killed according to v.7. "(Every woman) ἥτις ἔγνωκεν κοίτην ἄρσενος" has as counterpart in MT ידעת איש למשכב זכר, but in v.18 the negative parallel reads אשר לא ידעו משכב זכר. It seems obvious that the translator harmonized with the text of the next verse. Hex has tried to "correct" the Num text by adding ανδρα εις under the asterisk after the verb to equal the איש ל of MT.

31:18 Num begins asyndetically over against MT, though whether this is original or not is not at all certain. One certainly would expect some kind of transfer signal, since v.18 contrasts with v.17. The hex text has added δε after the opening word, which is excellent Greek, and presupposes a syndetic parent text; the

---

27. Instead of ἐν πάσῃ τῇ ἀπαρτίᾳ, Theod has ἐν τῷ ὄχλῳ, but Aq and Sym render by ἐν τοῖς νηπίοις.
28. Dorival, however, renders the phrase by "en tout train," and in v.18, "tout le train des femmes."

majority A F M V text added καὶ at the beginning. The asyndetic clause is the more difficult reading, but it is supported by the oldest extant witness, cod B, and is almost certainly to be understood as original text.

Once again, טף is rendered by ἀπαρτίαν, for which see comment at v.7.²⁹ MT reads "and all the children בנשים," i.e. among the women, in other words, the girls. Num translates by the genitive τῶν γυναικῶν, which is legitimate, though not literal. Num makes it clear that "who has known" refers to ἀπαρτίαν; in MT the verb is plural, but common sense dictates that טף be understood as a collective. The actual directive is "keep αὐτάς alive," but MT has לכם, i.e. "for yourselves."

31:19 The verse begins with καὶ ὑμεῖς as a pendant nominative: "and as for you," which is then followed by an imperative "camp outside the camp ἑπτὰ ἡμέρας." The accusative is a classic example showing extent of time: "for seven days." The regulation is "every one who has killed and who touches a corpse (τετρωμένου, one who was killed) must be cleansed on the third day and on the seventh day." MT reads for the first subject כל הרג נפש "every one who kills a person." Hex is probably the source of the popular M gloss ψυχην after ἀνελών. In MT the second participle has a כל before it, and again hex has added πας before ὁ ἁπτόμενος to represent it.

The syntax of MT differs considerably from that of Num in that what is a compound subject with ἁγνισθήσεται as predicate has as counterpart in MT a pendant כל הרג נפש וכל נגע בחלל "as for anyone killing a person and anyone touching a corpse," which is then followed by a second person plural verb "you must cleanse yourself ...."

The verse then ends with an amplification of the initial ὑμεῖς by ὑμεῖς καὶ ἡ αἰχμαλωσία ὑμῶν "you and your captives"; the αἰχμαλωσία must be taken as a collective. This then is a further amplification of the pendant with which the verse begins, and is outside the clause, whereas in MT, אתם ושביכם further define the subject of תתחטאו.

---

29. Aq reads (πᾶν) νήπιον, and Theod, either νήπια or ὄχλον. Sym is also attested as reading ὄχλον. But in v.17 other attributions are made. There is something suspicious about these attributions. I suggest that the reading θ´ (νήπια) is a copyist error for σ´, and that the attribution σ´ θ´ is an error (possibly a dittograph in the uncial script of an original θ´) for θ´. It would be most unlikely that the recensors would be inconsistent with their renderings at v.17.

31:20 Why Num should have chosen περίβλημα to render בגד is puzzling. The rendering is not incorrect, but it is unique; normally LXX uses ἱμάτιον. One might render it by "habit" to distinguish it from the more usual "garment." Possibly the translator wanted to distinguish between the clothing of the Madianites and that of the Israelites. The word refers to that which one wraps around one, thus a wide outer garment. To be cleansed as well are "every leather article, and every ἐργασίαν αἰγείας and every wooden article." The term αἰγείας is a nominalized adjective from αἴγειος which means "of a goat," thus can apply to anything coming from or pertaining to a goat. Here it is a מעשה עזים, something made of goat hair. The term עזים can refer specifically to goat hair, for which see Note at Exod 25:4 where עזים is translated by τρίχας αἰγείας; comp also Exod 35:6,26. The verb in MT is a Hithp, which is odd. This made sense in v.19 where the reflexive is required, but here one expects a transitive verb, which is what Num has in ἀφαγνιεῖτε "you must cleanse." This does not mean that the parent text differed from MT; after all, the translator had to make sense. What the Hithp here might add is the notion of personal advantage, thus "you must cleanse for yourselves," i.e. before you can use a garment; this, however, Num does not convey.

31:21 It is now Eleazar the priest who speaks to "the soldiers (literally, men of the army), those coming out of the battle line of the war." This is not what MT says; it refers to the soldiers as הבאים למלחמה "the ones who had entered the war." Num is apparently a case of harmonization with v.14 based on a rationalizing change; i.e. how could Eleazar be speaking to soldiers who had entered the war; rather he spoke to the returnees to the camp which was where the priest was expected to be. The translator solved the dilemma by using the phrase of v.14 instead of following MT. Since τῆς παρατάξεως has no counterpart in MT, hex placed it under the obelus.

What he says to these returnees is "This is the regulation of the law which the Lord commanded Moses," thereby introducing vv.22—24.

31:22—23 Vv.22—24 detail the laws of purification for the warriors and their booty. V.22 lists the metals involved; these are listed coordinately throughout, whereas MT lists the first two and the last two in pairs, i.e. 1+2 3 4 5+6. Num follows the pattern of Sam by joining all the metals by καίs. Furthermore, the last pair in MT, את הבדיל ואת העפרת "the tin and the lead," is transposed in Num: καὶ μολίβου καὶ κασσιτέρου. In MT each of the six metals is articulated as well as governed by an את. In Num only the first two, "the gold and the silver" are articulated. Hex has articulated the last four as well as transposing the "lead" and the "tin," thereby equalling MT exactly.

The initial πλήν "except for, except that" is used to render אך, which is probably as good a rendering as any. אך is a restrictive particle which contrasts with what has preceded, and πλήν does likewise.

V.23 defines the metals of v.22 as πᾶν πρᾶγμα ὃ διελεύσεται ἐν πυρὶ καὶ καθαρισθήσεται "everything which shall pass through in fire and (so) shall be purified." That, however, is not sufficient; "but it must (also) be cleansed by the waters of cleansing." For this rite of the "waters of cleansing," see the discussion of ὕδωρ ῥαντισμοῦ ἅγνισμά ἐστιν at 19:9, and comp 8:7 where the waters of sprinkling are also mandatory for the cleansing of the Levites. MT again uses אך to indicate the contrast with the fire procedure, thus "except that it must be cleansed by the waters of נדה," for which see 19:9. Num does not use πλήν this time, but rather the adversative ἀλλ᾽ ἤ. The text of MT is more expansive with respect to the characterization of the metals. MT reads "everything which shall pass through in the fire תעבירו באש and it will be pure." Presumably, the translators overlooked the two words because of homoioteleuton, i.e. from באש 1° to באש 2°. Hex has added διαξετε εν πυρι under the asterisk after πυρί to make up for the omission.

V.b makes provision for "everything which could not pass through fire," i.e. booty which fire would consume. This constitutes the modifier of the verb תעבירו "you must cause to pass through." In Num, however, πάντα is nominative neuter plural, and the verbs are third singular, διαπορεύσεται and διελεύσεται. This accords with the Classical use of the neuter plural in agreement with a singular predicate. One might have expected תעבירו to have been rendered by a transitive second plural verb, but the translator used an intransitive third singular διελεύσεται "must go through (the water)." To the translator the subject was irrelevant; it was the process of passing through fire (and water) that was important. Actually, διαπορεύομαι is unique as a rendering of העביר. LXX used a large number of different verbs to this end, the most frequently used one being διάγω (10 times), followed in frequency by ἀφαιρέω and παράγω (each six times), and five each for διαβιβάζω and διέρχομαι. A large number of verbs are used four times or less. The Greek here voids the transitive notion, making it mean "(everything ...) must go through (water)."

31:24 The warriors must also undergo cleansing. According to v.19, the warriors, having killed off the Madianite males and the women who were no longer virgins, had to remain outside the camp for seven days. V.24 demands of the soldiers "πλυνεῖσθε the clothing on the seventh day, and you will be cleansed."[30] MT reads בגדיכם, i.e. with a second plural suffix. Num often omits a translation of such suffixes when a genitive pronoun would be superfluous,[31] thus τὰ ἱμάτια, to which hex has nonetheless added υμων under the asterisk to represent the suffix.

31:25 Instead of ויאמר, Num reads καὶ ἐλάλησεν, which presupposes a parent וידבר.[32]

31:26 The remainder of the chapter describes the distribution of the spoils. Moses is ordered to "take the sum total of the spoils of the captives from people to cattle." For the idiom λάβε τὸ κεφάλαιον, see comment at 4:2. For σκύλων, see comment at v.11. The σκύλων τῆς αἰχμαλωσίας is defined by the merismus ἀπὸ ἀνθρώπου ἕως κτήνους, which seems to interprets MT's באדם ובבהמה "among people and among cattle" adequately, since these constituted all the animate booty taken. Moses is, however, not alone; it is to involve "you and Eleazar the priest, and οἱ ἄρχοντες τῶν πατριῶν of the assembly," viz. "the chieftains of the paternal ancestral (houses);" cf comment at 1:16 and comp also at 1:2. These were the heads of the families of the people.

31:27 MT continues with orders to Moses, וחצית, but Num includes those who are to join in dividing the spoils by using the plural, καὶ διελεῖτε. The division was to be "between the πολεμιστῶν τῶν ἐκπεπορευμένων εἰς τὴν παράταξιν and the entire assembly." The term πολεμιστῶν "warriors" is neater than תפשי

---

30. Theod and Aq use the active form πλυνεῖτε, whereas Sym (mistakenly Aq in the codex) has an attributive participle πλυνάμενοι.
31. See SS 99.
32. See THGN 128.

המלחמה "those who grasped the battle," i.e. the combatants. In the tradition, the A B F V majority text had the present participle, ἐκπορευομένων rather than the perfect participle of Num. Num is consistent in the context. The division of spoils took place after, not during, the battle. The majority reading also is not attested by the oldest extant witness, 963, and is clearly secondary;[33] it would indeed be difficult to divide the spoils before battle's end. The εἰς phrase refers to active duty, i.e. "into the battle line," whereas MT has "those who went out to the army." Of course, both refer to participation in the war. Incidentally, כל העדה is rendered by Num without an article, as πάσης συναγωγῆς. The hex inserted an article before συναγωγῆς, which equals MT more precisely.

31:28 As in v.27, Num uses the plural second person verb rather than the singular of MT;[34] i.e. the order is directed not just to Moses, but to all those listed in v.26 as being in charge of the division of spoils. A τέλος is to be removed from the warriors' share of the booty. The term τέλος has a wide variety of meanings, but here represents מכס "a levy, tax," which τέλος can also mean.[35] The Hebrew lexeme occurs only in this chapter (five times in vv.37—41), and is always defined as ליהוה, except in v.41 as תרומת יהוה. It is then the Lord's portion of the spoils. For ἐκπεπορευμένων εἰς τὴν παράταξιν, see comment at v.27. The levy is to be one individual (ψυχήν) from 500, and is to be taken from people, κτηνῶν, βοῶν, προβάτων and ὄνων. MT has only three classes of animals, הבקר, החמרים and הצאן. There was a great deal of confusion in the tradition, beginning with a different parent text for Num. The O text, which usually represents hex, has omitted ὄνων, and transposed κτηνῶν and βοῶν. It does have three as in MT, but misread(?) החמרים in favor of הבהמה, which is far-fetched indeed, in other words, the text used by Origen must have been different as well. No Greek witness equals MT. Somewhat surprising is the substitution of αιγων for ὄνων by B V x+, but that would presuppose שעירים.[36] In any event, Num apparently has a doublet, reading both κτηνῶν and βοῶν for the first one of MT, and then transposing the last two. Incidentally, the verse has five cases of ἀπό which are all partitive.[37]

---

33. See THGN 125.
34. As does Pesh, both here and in v.27.
35. See LS sub voce I.8.
36. See THGN 130 for a fuller discussion.
37. See SS 168.

31:29 In contrast to MT, Num begins with a conjunction; in MT the first two words "from their half you shall take" is in the plural, תקחו, and refers to v.28. This is then followed by a singular verb, ונתתה, which must refer to Moses; the first verb is directed to those mentioned in v.26. The addition of an initial καί makes this less clear, but the change in number, i.e. λήμψεσθε to δώσεις, means that the change in addressee signifies the same change. To make this clearer, the punctuation in Num should be altered. The colon at the end of v.28 and the comma afer λήπψεσθε should be transposed.

What is to be given to Eleazar is תרומת יהוה "a dedicatory gift of Yahweh," which is translated by τὰς ἀπαρχὰς κυρίου. For the translation "first fruits," see discussion at 5:9. The plural is used presumably to indicate their source as plural, i.e. the list at the end of v.28.

31:30 "And from the Israelites' half you (singular i.e. Moses) must take one אחז (withdrawal) from fifty." Num reads "and from the half which (τοῦ) is of the Israelites, you must take one from fifty." Hex has omitted the τοῦ, thereby equaling MT. The peculiar אחז is also omitted by Num, possibly since אחז אחד looks in part like a dittograph. The word is vocalized as a passive participle, and hex has added τo κρατουμενον, after having changed ἕνα to εν, thus "one seized portion." Just what the masculine ἕνα refers to is not stated; one might have expected it to be ψυχήν as in v.28, but that is feminine.

The fifty as source for the portion differs somewhat from that of v.28. It reads "from people καί from herds καί from sheep and from asses καί from all cattle." MT lacks every καί,[38] and only has a conjunction for the fourth item, where, however, "asses" and "sheep" are transposed. Hex has transposed προβάτων and ὄνων, thereby equalling the order of MT.[39]

The final clause designates the Levites as the recipients of these portions. The Levites are characterized as "performing guard duties in the tent of the Lord." MT has the singular משמרת, which Num interpreted as plural τὰς φυλακάς; this the consonantal text would allow. In MT משמרת is bound to משכן, but Num does not interpret משכן by a genitive, but by an ἐν σκηνῇ. There is some confusion in Num about gender. Moses must take ἕνα from fifties, which is

---

38. But not so Sam, which Num follows.
39. 4QNum[b] supports the order of Num with its ה(צו)אן מן החמורים.

masculine accusative singular, but then he is to give αὐτά to the Levites; comp v.47 where the gender in a similar context is consistently neuter. One might consider ἕνα to be an error for εν, i.e. the result of dittography before ἀπό, but there is very little textual evidence for such in the tradition.

31:32 The subject of the clause is τὸ πλεόνασμα "the superabundance, surplus," but in MT it is המלקוח, which is followed by יתר (הבז). Num has disregarded המלקוח, making יתר the subject, but in the sense of "excess, abundance," which is not attested elsewhere in the Pentateuch, but does occur in the later parts of the Hebrew Bible.[40] Hex has supplied τα σκυλα under the asterisk to represent the absent המלקוח. Note that Num was able to preserve the use of the same root for the noun הבז and the verb בזזו in Greek by προνομῆς (ὅ) ἐπρονόμευσαν. The subject of the verb, however, differs; in MT it reads עם הצבא "the people of the army," but Num interprets this by identifying these people as οἱ ἄνδρες οἱ πολεμισταί. Just what οἱ ἄνδρες adds to this is unclear; of course, the warriors are men, so why "warrior men"? For πολεμισταί, see v.27.

Num has rendered צאן by a prepositional phrase, ἀπὸ τῶν προβάτων. That this was unnecessary is clear from vv.33—34 where simply καὶ βόες and καὶ ὄνοι obtain. I suspect that the parent text was מן הצאן; in fact, at v.37 MT does read מן הצאן, and then continues as here with ו(ה)בקר. The size of the booty from sheep was 675,000. In MT, this reads "six hundred thousand, and seventy אלף, and five thousand." Num, however, omits אלף, since it is quite unnecessary, but hex added χιλιαδες under the asterisk to equal the untranslated אלף.

31:33—34 Only B Byz+ support the nominative βόες and ὄνοι, whereas the majority text reads the genitive βοων and ονων resp. Either would be possible, though the genitive would be the easier text. The more difficult text of Num has no syntactic relation with v.32, which gives the theme for vv.32—34, viz. the abundance of the booty, and what it consisted of. Actually, the ἐγενήθη of v.32 is the zero element carried over into vv.33—34. Num for vv.33—35 has independent nominal clauses, thus "and (there were) cattle 72,000, and asses, 61,000." Both verses are introduced by καί, but B V+ omit the καί introducing v.34. The conjunction is, however, original for both verses and it equals MT.

---

40. See also Lee 99.

31:35 Num quite properly understood נפש אדם as a collective, and translated by ψυχαὶ ἀνθρώπων "human beings" (literally, "persons of human beings"); these are specifically identified as "ἀπὸ τῶν γυναικῶν who have not had carnal knowledge," for which see comment at v.17. Syntactically, all of v.a describes in summary fashion its apposite πᾶσαι ψυχαί "all persons" which serves as the actual subject of the nominal clause, "all persons (were) 32,000." MT reads כל נפש, for which see comment above. In the tradition, the popular A F M text reads the literalistic singular πασα ψυχη, but the plural is expected, and parallels the plural βόες (בקר) of v.33, i.e. both are understood as collectives.[41]

31:36—37 At v.32 it was suggested that ἀπὸ τῶν προβάτων might have presupposed a parent מן הצאן rather than the צאן of MT. But here the same pattern is followed in ἐκ τοῦ ἀριθμοῦ (τῶν προβάτων), whereas MT simply has מספר, but this noun is never governed by a מן in MT.

The subject of the clause, τὸ ἡμίσευμα, refers to the division ordered in v.27. This half of the booty is identified as "the portion τῶν ἐκπεπορευμένων to war." As at v.27 the majority A text reads the present participle εκπορευομενων, for which see comment at v.27.[42] This is modified by εἰς τὸν πόλεμον, which is a more exact rendering for בצבא than the εἰς τὴν παράταξιν of v.27 for לצבא. The number amounted to 330,000 and ἑπτακισχίλια καὶ πεντακόσια.[43] Hex has added χιλιαδες under the asterisk after τριακόσιαι to equal MT's אלף.

For the τέλος as rendering for מכס, see comment at v.28. It might be noted that the passive verb ἐγενήθη is used in v.36, but the middle ἐγένετο occurs in v.37. There is no semantic difference between the two whatsoever, but the middle is more popular in Num (30 instances) than the passive (with 10 cases).

31:38—39 V.38 begins with καὶ βόες which follows the ובקר of Sam rather than MT's והבקר. In both verses MT reads ומכסם ליהוה, and in both cases Num reads καὶ τὸ τέλος κυρίῳ. In v.38 hex has added αυτων under the asterisk after τέλος to represent the untranslated suffix, and added τω under the asterisk before κυριῳ to represent the preposition.

---

41. Sym adopts the collective rendering of Num, but Theod and Aq translate πᾶσα ψυχή.
42. See also THGN 125.
43. The Others preferred ἑπτακισχίλιαι καὶ πεντακόσιοι.

In v.39 hex may have done likewise, but no asterisks are attested in the tradition, nor are the αυτων and the τω glosses well-attested; in fact, only one hex ms, ms 376 from the O group, attests to them. In the tradition, an F V C⁾ s+ text has the feminine μια instead of εἷς, and it is unclear as to what this intends. Presumably, the μια understands ὄνοι as feminine, which is possible.

31:40 For the plural ψυχαὶ ἀνθρώπων as well as for the ψυχαί at the end of the verse translating the singular נפש אדם and נפש resp, see comment at v.35.

31:41 Num identifies τὸ τέλος by κυρίῳ, which harmonizes with other occurrences of τὸ τέλος, but MT simply has את מכס which, however, is bound to תרומת יהוה. Hex has dealt with this by omitting κυρίῳ to equal MT. Since Num had already designated the τέλος as being "for the Lord," the occurrence of תרומת יהוה was rendered by τὸ ἀφαίρεμα τοῦ θεοῦ, thereby avoiding a possible perception of a repeated יהוה for a parent text. The rendering of תרומה by ἀφαίρεμα "a dedicatory gift" also occurs at v.52. In fact, the usual rendering in Num of תרומה by ἀπαρχή would have been quite inappropriate here. For ἀφαίρεμα as an appropriate rendering for תרומה, see Note at Lev 7:4.

31:42 Vv.42—46 are parallel to vv.36—41; they concern the other half of the booty taken, i.e. "the half of the Israelites, which Moses had split from that of the warrior men," for which term, see v.32. The booty had been ordered split into two halves, i.e. διελεῖτε (v.27), but carried out by Moses (οὓς διεῖλεν Μωυσῆς). Here, however, the τέλος is not recorded for each class of booty, but is summarized in v.47.

MT introduced this section with a conjunction, but Num does not.⁴⁴

31:43 The מחצת העדה of MT is rendered literally by Num as τὸ ἡμίσευμα τῆς συναγωγῆς. In the tradition, the B F V 963 majority text has added an απο to govern τῆς συναγωγῆς. There is no basis for this in MT, and the genitive modifying ἡμίσευμα is reasonable; in both vv.42 and 47 τῶν υἱῶν Ἰσραήλ modifies this same word. It was probably a gloss derived from the many ἀπό phrases in the context (both in vv.42 and 43). An A M popular gloss has the article το

---

44. Pesh follows Num, but Vulg equals MT.

inserted between the two nominals, thus "the half that (τό) of the assembly." But MT has a simple bound phrase, and as in vv.42,47, no relative clause is attested.[45] For the number of sheep, see also v.37.

31:44—46 The size of the Israelites' half for βόες, ὄνοι and ψυχαὶ ἀνθρώπων is identical to that of the other half as given in vv.38—40. Num throughout follows MT exactly. In the tradition, the initial καί of v.45 is omitted by the A B F M V majority text, an omission which may well have been stylistically generated; the three verses all begin with καί, but in a list of three members, Greek often omits the καί before the second member, i.e. follows a pattern of a b+c. But the evidence of 963 which supports the καί of v.45 makes it likely that the translator rendered the verse exactly as the Hebrew with an introductory conjunction, i.e. as an a+b+c pattern.

Syntactically, the three verses are nominal clauses, but rhetorically the ἐγένετο is carried over to each verse. See also comment at vv.33—34 on v.32.

31:47 A summary statement on the tax as defined in v.30, i.e. "one out of fifty." At v.30 MT read אחד אחז, but here it reads את אחז אחד; in both verses Num read "one." and hex "corrected" the text by adding the participle κρατουμενον under the asterisk after τό to represent the untranslated את, or together with the article (after ἕνα in v.30); cf comment at v.30. Here, however, τὸ ἕν, i.e. a neuter obtains, not a masculine ἕνα as in v.30, which actually makes better sense than ἕνα; comp the discussion of the numeral at v.30. Thereafter "he gave αὐτά to the Levites τοῖς φυλάσσουσιν τὰς φυλακάς of the tent of the Lord."

31:48 Num has πάντες οἱ καθεσταμένοι εἰς τὰς χιλιαρχίας τῆς δυνάμεως "all those who had been established in the positions of commanders of the army." MT has no equivalent for πάντες, and hex has placed it under the obelus.[46]

The equivalent subject in MT is הפקדים אשר לאלפי הצבא "those appointed for the divisions of the army"; see comment at v.14 on τοῖς ἐπισκόποις τῆς δυνάμεως. For the ranks among the leaders of the army, χιλίαρχοι and ἑκατόναρχοι, see Notes at Exod 18:20.

---

45. See THGN 108.
46. But 4QNum[b] does read כול הפקודים. Obviously, the origin of πάντες was textual.

31:49 For the rendering εἰλήφασιν τὸ κεφάλαιον for MT's נשאו את ראש, see comments at v.26 and 4:2. The sum total of the warrior men τῶν παρ ἡμῶν had been taken. The adjectival phrase τῶν ἀνδρῶν τῶν πολεμιστῶν renders a bound phrase אנשי המלחמה "men of war."[47] The limiting modifier "those with us" renders the relative clause אשר בידנו "who are in our power," i.e. who are under our authority. What is meant is that the commanders had made a body count of their own men.

The result of the survey according to MT is that "not has been reviewed a man from us"; i.e. all are accounted for, none was missing. This is precisely how Num interpreted it by οὐ διαπεφώνηκεν ἀπ' αὐτῶν οὐδὲ εἷς. The only difference is in the pronoun in the prepositional phrase, where MT reads ממנו "from us" instead of "from them."[48] In MT, the commanders identify themselves with their troops, but Num thinks in terms of the troups as the ones reported on.

31:50 The opening clause reads "and we have brought the gift κυρίῳ," whereas in MT יהוה is the free element of the bound phrase את קרבן יהוה "Yahweh's gift." A few mss did change κυρίῳ to the genitive, which would equal MT more exactly, but the change is hardly recensional.

The clause is then explicated by ἀνὴρ ὃ εὗρεν "each what he found," exactly what MT says. This is then identified as "a golden article (σκεῦος χρυσοῦν), followed by a list specifying such golden articles. The list consists of five singular nouns identifying the particular item of jewelry intended. The conjunctival pattern followed in MT is 1+2 3 4+5, whereas Num has καί throughout.[49] The first one is χλιδῶνα, an ornament either an armlet or an anklet. The Hebrew is אצעדה "an ankle chain." This is followed by ψέλιον for צמיד "bracelet." The next one is δακτύλιον "ring" for טבעת "a signet ring." Then a περιδέξιον "armlet for the right arm" obtains for עגיל which is some kind of circular piece of jewelry, but precisely what it consisted of is uncertain. It only occurs twice in the Hebrew Bible (also at Ezek 16:12 where LXX makes it an ἐνώτιον for the nose). περιδέξιον may then be a correct rendering. The last piece

---
47. See SS 66.
48. The preposition is partitive according to SS 169.
49. The pattern in 4QNum[b] can only be seen for numbers four and five, which read ועגיל וכומז.

is ἐμπλόκιον "some article of braid," possibly "plaited clasp" for women's hair (?).⁵⁰ See Note at Exod 35:22 where ἐμπλόκια "plaited clasps" occurs. In both places, MT has כומז, the meaning of which is unknown. The point of bringing these gold ornaments was ἐξιλάσασθαι περὶ ἡμῶν ἔναντι κυρίου. For the meaning of the infinitive "to make atonement," see Note at Lev 1:4.

31:51 The singular of MT with coordinate subject is retained by Num. This is the usual pattern if the nearer noun is singular, provided that the subject follows the verb as here. The gold taken παρ' αὐτῶν is characterized as πᾶν σκεῦος εἰργασμένον "every wrought article."

31:52—53 MT speaks of all זהב התרומה "gold of the dedicatory gift," but Num seems to reflect הזהב התרומה by its (πᾶν) τὸ χρυσίον τὸ ἀφαίρεμα; i.e. "the dedicatory gift" is in apposition to "the gold." For ἀφαίρεμα, see comment at v.41. It is modified by a relative clause ὃ ἀφεῖλον κυρίῳ "which they dedicated to the Lord." The subject of ἀφεῖλον is the officer ranks of v.48. The cognate collocation of MT תרומה אשר הרימו is nicely retained in Num as ἀφαίρεμα ... ἀφεῖλον. The amount contributed by the officer ranks (the χιλιάρχων and the ἑκατοντάρχων) was enormous: 16,750 shekels. Num reads καί before "700," which follows Sam and 4QNumᵇ in reading ושבע. This would, computing the shekel as weighing 11.42 grams or 2/5 of an ounce, amount to cir 191 kg or 418.75 lbs.

By contrast, the ordinary soldiers in the ranks, οἱ ἄνδρες οἱ πολεμισταί for אנשי הצבא, "plundered each one for himself," i.e. retained whatever gold he had been able to gather.

31:54 V.a repeats most of v.51, but changes παρ' αὐτῶν to "from the chilarchs καὶ παρὰ τῶν ἑκατοντάρχων." MT simply reads והמאות, a compression of שרי המאות. The Hebrew represents a bound phrase in which שרי is the bound element, and the free element is the coordinate האלפים והמאות. Num correctly understood the structure.

V.b states that "εἰσήνεγκαν αὐτά into the tent of testimony." MT reads יבאו אתו, i.e. referring to "gold," whereas Num thinks in terms of all the golden

---

50. LS suggests a "hair clasp."

objects, and uses a plural pronoun. In the tradition, the A B F C′ s x+ text reads a singular εισηνεγκεν, which not only does not equal MT, it is also a most unlikely text by which Moses would be the sole bearer of the enormous amount of gold that had been contributed, into the sanctuary.[51] When a compound subject of two singular nouns follows the verb, the verb is in the singular, but when the verb follows, it must be plural. Obviously, the two men did the bringing in of the gold. This gold was brought into the sanctuary as a μνημόσυνον "a memorial offering," a זכרון of the Israelites before the Lord. MT reads "for the Israelites," לבני ישראל. In MT the זכרון is on behalf of the Israelites; in Num it is of the people. The b n+ text changed τῶν υἱῶν to τοις υιοις, which equals MT exactly. Its source was probably one of The Three.

---

51. See THGN 122.

Chapter 32

32:1 The adjective רב is rendered by the noun πλῆθος "multitude, abundance"; the adjective עצום is also translated by this noun, thus "the cattle was a multitude to the Roubenites and the Gadites, a great multitude." The datives are best rendered as indicating possession, thus "the Roubenites and Gadites had a multitude of cattle, a large multitude." For the peculiar variants to the name 'Ρουβήν, see Note at Gen 29:32. The rendering of עצום by πλῆθος is highly unusual; in fact, it is found elsewhere only in the textually questionable Deut 26:5; see Note ad loc. The translator clearly wanted to stress the fact that the livestock was very numerous, not that they were strong; the choice of πλῆθος is contextually driven. The structure πλῆθος σφόδρα is odd indeed, and the A F M majority text inserted πολυ to regularize the structure. The adverb σφόδρα is inappropriate as a noun modifier, but the Num translator was not a particularly good Greek grammarian, and the Num text is original.[1]

Note that the translator also makes his own interpretation of ארץ "land" in his τὴν χώραν of Yazer and τὴν χώραν of Galaad. This is not the land of promise, i.e. "the land," and by using the neutral term χώραν "area, region," the eventual settlement of these areas by Israelite tribes is clearly not to be identified as the redemption of God's promise to the patriarchs that he would give "this ארץ" to their seed. This is in a sense extraterritorial, and the translator is sensitive to this in the first mention of these areas as ארץ. ארץ is usually rendered by γῆ in LXX (2313 times); χώρα is the second most frequent rendering with 64 occurrences.[2] For Yazer, see comment at 21:24. Galaad is the area on both sides of the Jabbok, but here it deals mainly with the area between the Arnon and the Jabbok.

The last clause reads "and the district (τόπος) was a district for cattle," i.e. it was well-adapted for grazing livestock. MT introduces the clause with the clause modifier והנה, but Num simply has καί.

---

1. The Others also support the text of Num.
2. According to the count of Dos Santos.

32:2 Num subordinates the opening clause ויבאו to an attributive participle, thereby placing the stress sensibly on what the tribes said, not on the fact that they came. MT reversed the order of the tribes of v.1, reading "the Gadites and the Reubenites," but Num continues with the order of v.1. Hex has transposed 'Ρουβήν and Γάδ to conform to the consecution of MT. The majority text has the Classical second aorist ειπον instead of εἶπαν, but this is secondary. Num always uses the Hellenistic inflection for the verb εἴπω.[3]

32:3 Syntactically, the verse is the subject of γῆ κτηνοτρόφος ἐστίν of v.4, but see comment on τὴν γῆν at v.4. The nine cities are Transjordanian cities/towns, presumably part of already conquered territory; cf v.4. 'Αταρώθ is the transcription of עטרות, and was readily confused with the well-known name Astaroth, leading to the spellings ασταρωθ/ασταρωτ in V Byz+. Also popular was the -ρων ending of cod A, i.e. αταρων or ασταρων. Δαιβών also occurred at 21:30, which see. In the tradition, it is misspelled as δεβρων, αδαιβων, δασβων, δεβωρ and δεκων. 'Ιαζήρ is also mentioned as the χώραν seen by the tribes; see v.1. Ναμβρά is Num's transcription for נמרה.[4] The name also occurs at v.36.[5] It gave rise to a large number of misspellings including change of α 1° to ε, omission of μ or β or ν, change of nasals ν/μ or μ/ν, suffixing of a nasal -ν or -μ, change of βρ to ι, of β to η, and through the influence of better known names, to αμβραμ, αβραν, αβραμ and αμραμ. For the name 'Εσεβών for חשבון, see the comment at 21:25.

'Ελεαλή represents אלעלה, and is misspelled variously as ελεαη, ελιαλη, ελελλη, ελελαν, ελεαηλ, λεαλει, ελεαληλ and ελεαλοηθ. Largely influential for some of these errors is the similarity of the triangular uncials A and Λ which were easily confused by copyists. Σεβαμά represents the שבמה of Sam rather than the שבם of MT; comp also v.38. The name received rough treatment at the hands of copyists, but only one ms shows Hebrew influence; ms 426 has σεβαμ. Often the ε became α, and the first α became ε. The prefixing of ε is an auditory dittograph; the καί before it was pronounced /ke/. Other errors are εσσαβαμα, σεμαμα, σεμαβα, σεβανα, εσεβαμαν, εσβαιμα, σεραμα, βεσβαμα and βεβασμα.

---

3. See THGN 123.
4. The Others have Ναμρά.
5. For its transcription, see THGN 119.

Ναβαύ transcribes נבו. The confusion of consonantal υ and β, both realized in Hellenistic times as /v/, produced ναναυ, ναβαβ and νανα. Other errors include νααβαυ, ναβααυ, ναβου, ναβα, ναβατ, ναβαμ, ναβαν, βαναυ, ιαβα and ιεβα. The last name is Βαιάν for בעץ. Α/Λ confusion created βλιαν and βλια. Other misspellings are βαιν, βαιναν, βασαν, καιαν, βααν, μεαν and βαμα.

32:4 The verse begins with τὴν γῆν ἥν ..., which is surprising, since syntactically a nominative noun is expected, whereas the relative pronoun is correctly in the accusative as the direct object of παρέδωκεν (κύριος). This represents an unusual case of reverse assimilation in which the case of the antecedent is assimilated to the case of the relative pronoun. Though rare, this does occur; a good example obtains at Luke 1:73, where the case of ὅρκον (ὃν ὤμοσεν) ought to be genitive, since it modifies μνησθῆναι (διαθήκης ἁγίας αὐτοῦ); the usual genitive διαθήκης modifies the verbal form, and so one expects it to be followed by ορκου ὅν ....[6] Here too the case of the accusative is due to attraction to the relative pronoun ὅν.[7] Here then τὴν γῆν must be rendered as subject of γῆ κτηνοτρόφος ἐστίν.

According to MT, Yahweh smote (הכה) the land represented by the towns of v.3, before the assembly of Israel. Num did not translate הכה, probably because this was an overly graphic way of describing Yahweh's direction of Israel's affairs, and substituted παρέδωκεν, probably relying on 21:34,[8] where the Lord παρέδωκεν the Amorites to Israel. The Hi of נכה is never rendered in LXX by παραδίδωμι elsewhere, and here too the usual translations (especially πατάσσω - 343 times)[9] are avoided. Instead of עדת ישראל, Num has the more usual τῶν υἱῶν Ἰσραήλ.[10] In fact, Num never translated עדת ישראל by συναγωγὴ Ἰσραήλ. The name Ἰσραήλ occurs 208 times in Num, and only 39 times does it stand without a modifier (mainly in ch..22—24). It is modified by υἱοί 155 times. When a reference to συναγωγή does occur, as e.g. 13:26 14:5,7 15:26,36 19:9, it modifies υἱῶν Ἰσραήλ, never Ἰσραήλ. Other modifiers are insignificant, thus tribes and chieftains (four times each), elders (twice), and once each for army, leaders of thousands, firstborn, God, all, house, voice and thousands (or clans).

---

6. I am indebted to my colleague, Albert Pietersma, for this reference.
7. For a discussion of reverse attraction, see Bl-Debr 294.
8. As Dorival 71 suggests.
9. According to Dos Santos.
10. So too Pesh.

Clearly, "Israelites" are never called "assembly of Israel," but rather υἱοὶ Ἰσραήλ in Num.

The cities of v.3 are characterized as κτηνοτρόφος "pasture land," which is a fine rendering for MT's ארץ מקנה "cattle land." The point Num makes is that land is well-adapted to cattle grazing. Note that though the two tribes "said to Moses and to Eleazar ... and to the chieftains of the assembly" according to v.2, here and in v.5 they make their request only to Moses; their address is in second person singular.

32:5 Num's use of the imperfect ἔλεγον for יאמרו is probably impelled by the fact of the discourse beginning with the λέγοντες at the end of v.2, with two verses obtaining before the actual request is presented; the imperfect then shows that the discourse is continuing. The intervening argument had simply laid the basis for the plea of v.5.[11]

Num follows the Masoretic tradition of understanding יתן as a passive, thus δοθήτω "let (this land) be given τοῖς οἰκέταις σου. Only here is οἰκέτης used to render עבד in the book; in fact, in v.4 it was παισίν σου that occurred. παῖς also occurs at vv.25,27 as well as at 31:49, and it was also used of Caleb at 14:24. The word θεράπων is used when the עבד is of יהוה except at 32:31; see 11:11 12:7,8. The unique use of οἰκέταις here is undoubtedly intentional. Παῖς is the usual designation in polite or respectful speech, whereas θεράπων is usually used in Num of God's servant, but here where a special favor is sought, the submissive "household servant, slave" is used.

In MT the negative order אל תעברנו is asyndetic, but Num introduces the clause with καί, following the text of Sam.

32:6 Vv.6—15 constitute Moses' full reply to the request of the Gadites and the Roubenites to be permitted to settle in the conquered areas in Transjordan. MT begins with a question marker, whereas the question form can only be surmised in Num. What Moses says is "Your brothers πορεύσονται to war, and as for you, you would settle here"? In the tradition, a B V t+ text reads πορευονται. This is an error palaeographically inspired; it constitutes a haplograph based on the

---

11. Sym rendered ויאמרו by καὶ εἶπον.

uncial confusion of Σ/O, and it is a mistake. The two verbs in Moses' query are futures in both MT and Num.[12]

Much more difficult is the phrase εἰς πόλεμον. In MT למלחמה was vocalized by the Masoretes as a preposition, article plus noun. Of course, a consonantal text can be read with or without articulation, but support for the unarticulated noun is numerically weak, consisting of A B* plus nine cursive mss, all others witnessing to εις τον πολεμον. In such cases it nonetheless seemed prudent to follow the lead of the oldest witnesses, A and B. The majority reading is probably merely stylistic. The phrase also occurs at vv.20,27,29 and 21:33; only at v.27 is πόλεμον articulated.

32:7 MT asks "and why should you restrain the לב of the Israelites from crossing over"? The verb תניאון (the Qere reading) also occurred at 30:6 in the context of a father turning back, i.e. voiding the vow of a daughter, where the verb ἀνανεύω is used. Here it probably means to hold back an avowed intention to cross over (to the promised land). Num has made this even stronger by its διαστρέφετε τὰς διανοίας "are you perverting the minds." The use of διαστρέφω for נוא (or הניא) is unique; the Hebrew verb recurs at v.9 as (את לב) יניאו and is translated by ἀπέστησαν; cf comment ad loc. Num uses a present tense, probably since the request was not privately made to Moses and Eleazar, but also to the chieftains of the assembly, and so was public knowledge. The objection voices a present reality. Also to be noted is the use of the plural τὰς διανοίας to render את לב, which occurs as well at 15:39 in a similar context: διαστραφήσεσθε ὀπίσω τῶν διανοιῶν ὑμῶν. The plural individuates; after all, the Israelites had "hearts, minds." This contrasts, however, with the singular τὴν καρδίαν in v.9. διάνοια is not quite as frequent in the Pentateuch (28 times according to HR), as καρδία (35 times). In the tradition, a popular A M text reads τας καρδιας, and either could be used. The term לב or its variant לבב is rarely used in Num (only five times), and once (v.9) it is rendered by τὴν καρδίαν, and twice by the reflexive pronoun ἐμαυτοῦ (16:28 24:13).

The land to which the Israelites are to cross over is one "which κύριος δίδωσιν αὐτοῖς." In MT this reads נתן להם יהוה. The change of נתן "gave" to δίδωσιν is contextually driven. To Num the land of promise is one that the Lord

---

12. See THGN 125.

"is going to give" to them. The present tense is here intended as proleptic; what is meant is "which the Lord is on the point of giving to them." Hex has changed the word order by transposing κύριος to the end to conform to the order of MT. Actually, the translator may have taken נתן as a participle, which he usually renders by the present tense.

32:8 In contrast to MT, Num continues with a question by adding a negative at the beginning: "was it not thus that your fathers did," whereas MT reads "Thus did your fathers." The reference is to the occasion when Moses "sent αὐτούς from Kades Barne to see the land"; see ch.13 for the account of the sending out of the twelve spies at the Lord's behest. The temporal clause renders a prepositional structure with a bound infinitive plus suffix, בשלחי, correctly. The αὐτούς has no immediate reference, but must refer to the twelve representatives of the tribes mention in 13:2—16. Kades Barne occurs only here and at 34:4; usually it is simply called Kades; see Note at Gen 14:7. Num translated לראות well by κατανοῆσαι "to examine closely," which was what the spies were ordered to do. Actually, the verb used in ch.13 was κατασκέπτομαι; for κατανοέω in the sense used here, see Note at Gen 42:9, and comp Exod 2:11.

32:9 "And they (the spies) went up עד the Valley of the Grape Cluster and examined the land." Num did not translate עד, but simply used an accusative Φάραγγα βότρυος as modifier of ἀνέβησαν, thus "they went up the Valley ...." Whether the εἰς which is found in an M 58-426 (=hex?) *f n*+ text, or the οἱ εως reading were the result of Hebrew influence is not clear, since the critical text is a fully adequate interpretation of MT.

The idiom תניאון את לב of v.7 recurs here with a third person verb, which Num translates by ἀπέστησαν τὴν καρδίαν "turned aside the heart"; see comment at v.7. In v.7, for the relative clause אשר נתן להם יהוה, Num had used the present tense to render נתן, since the Lord was on the point of actualizing his intent to give the Israelites the land of promise. Here it becomes ἔδωκεν; the Lord had given it, but because of their rejection it was not to be given to them, but to the next generation. The difference in tense is intentional. The word order of Num differs from MT in its κύριος αὐτοῖς. The hex text is probably the source of the popular A F M transposition, which equals MT.

32:10 When Yahweh became angry, MT makes use of an unusual figure: ויחר אף
יהוה "and the nostril of Yahweh became hot." Num avoids what might be misunderstood as an anthropomorphic figure, and translates by a different syntagm καὶ ὠργίσθη θυμῷ κύριος. This Hebrew idiom occurs 24 times in the Pentateuch, ten of which are in this book, and is always rendered either by ἐθυμώθη alone, or by a verb of anger plus a dative noun meaning anger; in other words, the figure is always rejected in favor of its interpretation. "The Lord" is now the subject of "became angered with wrath." This idiom with variation occurs with some frequency; see Note at Exod 4:14, and in Num comp 11:10 12:9 22:22 25:3,4, as well as vv.13,14 below.

32:11 This is the oath that the Lord swore: "Not shall men οὗτοι who were coming up out of Egypt, from twenty years of age and upwards, see ... the land." The εἰ plus a future verb imitates the Hebrew oath אם יראו, a regular way of expressing a negative oath. It represents the kind of understood "I'll be damned if" type of swearing in English, or the Hebrew חלילה לי אם literally "profanation be to me if." What is taken for granted is a strong negative statement. MT has no equivalent for the demonstrative pronoun οὗτοι, and hex has placed a variant εκεινοι under the obelus, the O text reading εκεινοι.

After "from twenty years of age and upwards," Num has added οἱ ἐπιστάμενοι τὸ κακὸν καὶ τὸ ἀγαθόν "those who know evil and good," which has no basis in MT. That it is secondary as far as the Hebrew is concerned is clear from the obelus under which it was placed by hex. The parallel passsage in 14:23 is much more elaborate, and is its obvious source. There the Lord says to Moses: "not will they see the land which I swore to their fathers, but their children ... ὅσοι οὐκ οἴδασιν ἀγαθὸν οὐδὲ κακόν ... τούτοις δώσω τὴν γῆν, but all those who provoked me shall not see it." Num was obviously aware of the fuller statement here, and expanded the description of those who came out of Egypt as adults as contrasting with children. Children did not know good nor evil, but these did "know evil and good"; note that here "good" and "evil" are transposed; they know evil and good, i.e. evil precedes the good. The more usual order "good and evil" is read by the majority A F M text, but this is an ex par revision.

The Lord had sworn this oath to the patriarchs "to Abraam and Isaak and Jacob." MT does not have the conjunction repeated before "Isaak."

The verse ends with a γάρ clause giving the reason for the oath: "for not συνεπηκολούθησαν after me." The Hebrew verb is מלאו, i.e. "they were not fully after me." For this translation, see comment on ἐπηκολούθησέν μοι at 14:24. The double compound with συν- is used here because of the plural; at 14:24 only Caleb was involved, and the συν- element would have been inappropriate.

32:12 The two exceptions allowed in the divine oath were Caleb the son of Yephonne and Iesous son of Naue, "because they followed closely after the Lord." The latter idiom was also used, but negatively, in v.11, which see. In MT, Caleb is described as הקנזי "the Kenizzite," but the Kenizzites were an Edomite tribe, which eventually was assimilated into Judah; at 13:7 Caleb was representing the tribe of Judah in the spy account; see also 34:19. But that the loyal Caleb should have been a non-Israelite was an embarrassment, hence an old tradition that Caleb had "separated himself," is borrowed, and Num substitutes "ὁ διακεχωρισμένος for הקנזי.[13] Just what is meant by "the one who had separated himself" is not certain. Had he separated himself from his Edomite background, or from the combined report of the ten spies with their negative advice?[14] Probably it simply refers to his having separated himself from the majority spy report; see 14:6—9,[15] though this should have included Iesous as well.

The ὅτι clause represents the כי clause of MT, but unlike MT refers only to Ἰησούς, since the verb συνεπηκολούθησεν is singular, whereas MT has מלאו. The singular is an old reading supported by B V 963 and two cursives, all the other witnesses reading the plural. The latter, not only equals MT, but is obviously the easier reading. The much more difficult singular has been retained as Num, not only because of the support of the two oldest witnesses B 963, but also since a change to the singular which an original plural text would presuppose is very difficult to explain. Possibly the translator felt that Chaleb's being "the one who had

---

13. Theod and Sym read <ὁ> Ναζιραῖος, which also creates a problem. Possibly this is based on Num's notion that the Kenizzite is "one who has separated himself," which was also characteristic of the Nazirite, i.e. someone who vowed to keep himself from wine, etc., i.e. to practice asceticism. Admittedly, this is speculative on my part, and is not otherwise characteristic of the Recensors. Also possible (rather remotely) is a misreading of קנזי as נזיר.
14. Which H.J.Schoeps in Bibl 26(1945), 307—309 suggests. Schoeps also notes that the choice of Ναζιραῖος is not as far-fetched as it might seem at first sight. This could be based on 1 Par 4:11—12 in which the offspring of Χαλέβ were called the men of Ῥηχάβ. Since the Rechabites were usually identified as Nazirites whose ascetic way of life is described in Jer 35, this could explain the Recensors' identification of the Kenizzite as the Nazirite.
15. See Dorival 88, citing Z.Frankel, Vorstudien zu der Septuaginta (1841), 188.

separated himself" was meant to contrast with Yesous' following after the Lord. But the use of the συν- compound makes this even more difficult to understand. Or is the singular simply a mistake?

32:13 For ὠργίσθη θυμῷ κύριος, see comment at v.10. The Lord's anger resulted in ינעם "he made them wander back and forth," which Num rendered by the hapax legomenon κατερρέμβευσεν.[16] The simplex is, however, known; it occurs at Isa 23:16, and was also used by Aq at Jer 30:4 38:22. ρεμβεύω, according to LS, is the same as the better known ρέμβομαι "to roam, rove." In the tradition, cod B reads κατερρομβευσεν, which verb is not listed in LS, but again the word ρόμβος "something that whirls" is known; comp ρομβέω "cause to spin like a ρόμβος." The Num spelling is almost certainly correct.[17]

This wandering for forty years in the desert is to last, "ἕως ἐξανηλώθη all the generation which did evil things before the Lord."[18] The use of ἕως with the indicative is unusual, and only occurs once elsewhere in the book (12:15).[19] The normal use of ἕως is with ἄν and the subjunctive mood, and in the tradition, a popular A 963 text has changed ἐξανηλώθη to αν εξαναλωθη. Note that the singular ἡ γενεά has a plural modifier οἱ ποιοῦντες τὰ πονηρά, since γενεά by definition consists of people.

32:14 MT begins with a conjunction, but Num does not. The Byz+ text added a και before ἰδού, which equals MT, and could be understood as recensional. Moses' diatribe accuses the petitioners of standing "in the place of their fathers, a crowd of sinful men, to add again to the Lord's anger against Israel." The word σύστρεμμα "crowd, bunch, body" renders תרבות, which is a hapax legomenon. Its meaning is uncertain, though popularly it is translated as "brood" or "breed."[20] The infinitive προσθεῖναι is hardly purposive; the tribes did not make the request in order to anger the Lord; rather it shows the result. What is intended

---

16. Theod retained Num, but Aq translated the verb by ἐσάλευσεν, and Sym, by περιήγαγεν.
17. See THGN 130.
18. Instead of ἐξανηλώθη, Theod has ἐξέλιπεν; Aq reads τελειωθῇ, and Sym has ἐξαναλωθῇ.
19. See THGN 95.
20. Tar^JO translate by תלמידי "disciples of," but Tar^N has תרבו, i.e. takes over the MT reading into Aramaic.

is "thereby adding still more to the wrath of the anger of the Lord over against Israel." The infinitive renders לספות, but as לספת "to add," not לספות "to sweep away." The root must be יסף, not ספה;[21] in other words, the translator did not read the *plene* spelling of the marked infinitive. For τὸν θυμὸν τῆς ὀργῆς as rendering חרון אף, see comment on ויחר אף at 24:10.

32:15 In MT the opening כי is conditional, i.e. "if you should turn away from him (i.e. from Yahweh)," but Num renders this by ὅτι, which I would render "because you would turn away," since ὅτι is almost a calque for כי, but here it constitutes a prediction of what will happen if the tribes get their way.

The use of προσθεῖναι (ἔτι) plus an infinitive is commonly used to render the Hebrew ויסף עוד plus infinitive, which means "to repeat, to do again"; here, however, the clause has been reduced to an infinitival structure, probably under the influence of v.14 where προσθεῖναι ἔτι also occurred. On the other hand, here it occurs with an infinitive καταλιπεῖν αὐτόν (i.e. Israel), so it might be rendered "by again leaving him in the desert." The Hebrew has להניחו "to make him rest"; it is rendered only occasionally by καταλείπω; it only occurs elsewhere in the Pentateuch at Exod 16:23,24 and Lev 7:5(15), but here it is appropriate in the context.

The last clause is coordinate with the first, whereas in MT it is the apodosis. Num has it that not only will you, i.e. the two petitioning tribes, turn away from the Lord, but also (i.e. καί) "you will be acting lawlessly," or probably with εἰς, "inciting to lawlessness this entire assembly." That the verb is transitive is clearer in MT: ושחתם לכל העם הזה, where ל indicates the object of the verbal action. Highly unusual is the use of συναγωγήν to render עם; in fact, this occurs elsewhere in the Hebrew Bible only at Lev 10:3. It is possible that the translator distinguishes here between the assembly and Israel; after all, the Gadites and the Roubenites are part of Israel, but by their request to live outside the Promised Land are not part of the assembly, i.e. the term συναγωγή is used as the cultic assembly, and need not be identical with "Israel." In fact, Num avoids the notion of an "assembly of Israel"; see comment on עדת at v.4, and see also Note at Lev 10:3.

---

21. See GK 69h, note 1.

32:16 The collocation καὶ ἔλεγον for ויאמרו is put into the imperfect, not the aorist, by which it is clear that it is understood as a variant of לאמר and so indicates the onset of direct speech. What they say is in response to the rough reception and tongue lashing they received from Moses, and it continues through v.19. The verse outlines the two plans for the area they would occupy. First of all, "ἐπαύλεις for sheep we would build here for our cattle." The term ἐπαύλεις refers to walled-in areas, out in the open spaces, i.e. in the country as contrasted to πόλεις "cities"; in other words, "sheepfolds." Num has ὧδε immediately after the subjunctive verb, which is sensible, since it modifies the verb; in MT its counterpart פה follows למקננו "our cattle." Hex has transposed ὧδε after κτήνεσιν ἡμῶν to correspond to MT. Secondly, (we would build) "cities for our children" (ἀποσκευαῖς; for ἀποσκευή as rendering for טף, see comment at 16:27).

In the tradition, almost a third of the Greek witnesses read οἰκοδομησομεν, the future instead of Num's aorist subjunctive, οἰκοδομήσωμεν. This illustrates how copyists confused ο/ω, which were homophonous in Hellenistic and Byzantine Greek. Only the subjunctive case can have been intended by the translator. The future is simply a misspelling for the aorist subjunctive.

32:17 The καὶ ἡμεῖς for ואנחנו is a device used to contrast with v.16. Here our role in the conquest of the promised land is described. What MT says is נחלץ חשים before the Israelites, i.e. "we will arm ourselves hurrying before the Israelites." Num interprets this by a nominal clause, subordinating the Ni verb to a participle, ἐνοπλισαμένοι "having armed ourselves," and then making "προφυλακὴ πρότεροι the Israelites" the predicate. i.e. "(will be) a vanguard in front of the Israelites." In the tradition, an M ol z text has added παρελευσομεθα; this could be interpreted as influenced by the Ni verb נחלץ, thereby preserving the verbal clause of MT; on the other hand, it is probably simply an exegetical gloss on the part of a copyist who failed to understand the nominal clause. The Num text is a sensible though unique understanding. Those who hasten into the battle lines, the προφυλακὴ πρότεροι, are the vanguard; after all, they would be free of cattle and children, and able to concentrate on conquest. The bound phrase ערי המבצר is nicely interpreted by ἐν πόλεσιν τετειχισμέναις, an adjectival construction, in which the perfect passive participle correctly modifies πόλεσιν. The last clause is put into the future, κατοικήσει, i.e. it is not subject to the ἕως of the preceding clause, but is coordinate to all of v.a.

32:18 And we would remain to the end, i.e. "we would not return to our homes until the Israelites would have been given portions, i.e. each one (to) his inheritance." MT has a cognate structure for the "until" clause: התנחל בני ישראל איש נחלתו. The Hithp infinitive means "to possess for oneself," thus "until the Israelites possessed for themselves each his possession." Num uses a passive verb καταμερισθῶσιν, for which verb, see Note at Lev 25:46, where, however, an active inflection seems to render the Hithp verb.

32:19 Instead of כי לא, Num has a fine contextual καὶ οὐκέτι "and no longer." The verb is, however, then put into the aorist subjunctive, which is sensible, since only a potential is being expressed. MT, on the other hand, has a future "for we will not inherit." That inheritance is located ἀπὸ τοῦ πέραν τοῦ Ἰορδάνου καὶ ἐπέκεινα "beyond the Jordan yonder," i.e. from the perspective of Transjordan. The second כי clause gives the reason for this generosity: "because our inheritance has come to us across the Jordan eastward"; i.e. on the east side of the Jordan. Num has a different syntagm: "because we are receiving in full our portions (τοὺς κλήρους) in the east." The verb ἀπέχω means "to receive full payment,"[22] and is contextually what באה נחלתנו אלינו intends. The plural rendering of נחלתנו is ad sensum.

32:20 In Moses' reply (vv.20—24), he begins with the protasis: "if you should do according to this word ...." By "this word" is meant the undertaking which the two tribes had proposed in vv.16—19. MT has את governing the modifier in place of the κατά of Num, i.e "should do this matter."

This protasis is then defined more specifically as "if you should arm yourselves before the Lord[23] for war," which is what the tribes had promised to do.

32:21 Num begins the apodosis here, as the use of the future indicative verb shows.[24] This is not the usual understanding of MT, though it is a possible

---

22. See LS sub voce IV.1.
23. Milgrom makes the interesting suggestion that "before Yahweh" is to be taken literally as referring to the vanguard position which preceded the ark carried into battle.
24. SS 34 maintains that the indicative here is a mistake, showing "dass die Übersetzer sie (i.e. the moods) nicht immer beherrschen konnten." I would challenge this understanding.

interpretation. MT is usually understood with v.21 continuing the protasis, and the apodosis occurring in v.22, either at the beginning as "then when the land has been subdued ..., you will be innocent before Yahweh" (as NIV), or only beginning at "you shall be innocent ...." (as NJPS NRSV). But Num takes v.21 as part of the "then" clauses: "and (then) every hoplite (i.e. the armed soldier; see ἐξοπλίσησθε of v.20) shall cross the Jordan before the Lord." The word ὁπλίτης renders the passive participle חלוץ "one who is armed, equipped for battle." Admittedly, the Num rendering is somwhat clumsy, but the Hebrew certainly can be understood in this way.

The ἕως clause has ὁ ἐχθρὸς αὐτοῦ as subject and the passive verb ἐκτριβῇ as predicate, thus "until his enemy should be wiped out from before him." MT has an active statement "until he has dispossessed his enemies before him." For Num it is unclear what the antecedent of "his" and "him" is; it could be ὁ ὁπλίτης or κυρίου, but since the Canaanite who is to be wiped out is not a personal enemy of the soldier, but rather of Israel and its God, κυρίου is probably intended by the translator. MT is also vague, since the suffix of הורישו could similarly be taken to refer to חלוץ or to יהוה, though since איביו is plural, i.e. "his enemies," common sense would dictate that יהוה is the antecedent for the pronouns. Of course, the ἐχθρός of Num is to be understood as a collective, and is an adequate rendering of MT's plural. There is also a certain difference in what is to be done. In Num, the enemy is envisioned as exterminated, wiped out, whereas MT does not necessarily refer to their extinction, but rather to their dispossession; their land will be taken. The rendering of הוריש by ἐκτρίβω is unique, though the most common rendering, ἐξολεθρεύω, occurs 22 times, and also means "to destroy completely." Other frequent renderings are ἐξαίρω (17), κληρονομέω (13) and ἀπόλλυμι (8).[25]

32:22 Here the translator has clearly changed moods within the verse; the first clause has κατακυριευθῇ, an aorist passive subjunctive, but the next two clauses are future indicatives. What is intended is "and when the land should become lorded over before the Lord, then afterwards you may return ...." Note the neat word play in which the translator used the verb κατακυριεύω, reminiscent of Gen 1:28 κατακυριεύσατε αὐτῆς "have dominion over it" for כבשה "subdue it," and

---

25. The count is that of Dos Santos.

is then modified by ἔναντι κυρίου. MT is innocent of such a device, with its נכבשה modified by לפני יהוה. It is also possible to take the initial καί seriously, making the first clause coordinate with the ἕως clause ending v.21. But if that interpretation be favored, it would be preferable to end the clause with a colon rather than with a comma.

The return then means that ἔσεσθε ἀθῷοι ἔναντι κυρίου καὶ ἀπὸ Ἰσραήλ, whereas MT has "and you shall be נקיים מיהוה ומישראל "be freed (i.e. from further obligations) from Yahweh and from Israel." Num, however, distinguishes the relations of the tribes; they will be "innocent before the Lord," but "from Israel."[26] The distinction in prepositions makes for different relations. Being innocent from Israel does mean that their duties are over as far as their fellow-Israelites are concerned, but they are hardly innocent from their God; that relationship is not one of no further duties, but one of freedom from the specific duties involved in the Lord's fulfillment of his promise of the land of Canaan; only in that sense are they now innocent "before the Lord." This is realized by the final clause in which ἡ γῆ αὕτη, not the land of promise, "will become a κατασχέσει before the Lord." For the common use of κατάσχεσις to render אחזה, see Note at Gen 17:8.

32:23 The alternative: "but if you should not do thus." Note the fine use of the contrastive δέ. The apodosis is clear: "you will be sinning before the Lord." MT has הנה חטאתם "lo, you have sinned (over against Yahweh)." Num interprets by means of the future, whereas MT makes the failure to help their fellow-Israelites in the conquest a state of sin.

MT then issues a warning: "and know your sin which will find you out." Num expands on this by its interpretation: καὶ γνώσεσθε τὴν ἁμαρτίαν ὑμῶν ὅταν ὑμᾶς καταλάβῃ τὰ κακά. The imperative is changed to a prediction, i.e. a future tense, and the relative clause is expanded into a ὅταν clause "whenever evil overtakes you." MT does not define what תמצא involves; Num makes this clear with its τὰ κακά "evil, misfortune." In other words, Num defines the sin (which will find you out) as κακά. Hex has placed the nominal under the obelus, since it is merely implied, but not stated in MT, and hex has also transposed ὑμᾶς καταλάβῃ to equal the order of תמצא אתכם.

---

26. See THGN 95.

32:24 Num uses the future tense for the opening imperative as well as at the end of the verse where MT also has a future. בנו לכם is idiomatically rendered by καὶ οἰκοδομήσετε ὑμῖν αὐτοῖς "and you may build for yourselves." The καί has no equivalent in MT. Origen was apparently troubled by ὑμῖν αὐτοῖς for לכם; there was one word too many! And so ὑμῖν was placed under the obelus, thereby illustrating the purely quantitative approach used in the hexapla. What they may now build recalls their proposal in v.16, with two differences: the two items of v.16, the ἐπαύλεις and the πόλεις along with their dative complements are transposed, but the ἐπαύλεις are simply designated by τοῖς κτήνεσιν ὑμῶν, whereas at v.16 the ἐπαύλεις are also characterized as προβάτων. MT, however, has גדרת לצנאכם, i.e. "for your sheep," not "for your cattle." The influence of v.16 is evident.

A final reminder orders the tribes to keep their promise: "And what goes out of your mouth, you must do."

32:25 "The Roubenites and the Gadites" affirm their intention to do as Moses had ordered. MT has "Gadites and Reubenites," and hex has transposed the tribes to equal the order of MT.[27] Num "corrected" the number of the verb ויאמר by its εἶπαν, i.e. followed Sam's ויאמרו.[28]

Num also contextualized the אדני "my lord" by the plural pronoun, thus ὁ κύριος ἡμῶν. Incidentally, one might note the articulation of κύριος. This automatically means that the Hebrew read אדן, and not יהוה; it makes no difference whether אדני refers to God or to a human being; here it refers to Moses, and simply indicates a polite form of address, such as "Sir," "Monsieur," "Herr."

32:26 MT lists טפנו נשינו מקננו וכל בהמתנו "our children, our wives, our herds and all our livestock." Num lists only three, connecting them by conjunctions, i.e. in an a+b+c pattern. Num was faced with two terms מקנה and בהמה, which it usually did not distinguish, and solved this by omitting the third item, thus ἡ ἀποσκευὴ ἡμῶν καὶ αἱ γυναῖκες ἡμῶν καὶ πάντα τὰ κτήνη ἡμῶν, on the under-

---

27. But 4QNum[b] and Sam have (ב)ני ראובן ובני גד, and constitutes the parent text of Num.
28. As did many Kenn mss; in fact, of the ancient witnesses, only Tar[J] with its ואמר follows MT's obviously wrong reading.

standing that "all our κτήνη covered both items three and four. Hex, however, added και αι κτησεις ημων under the asterisk as a rendering for the third item.

Concerning these, MT said "they would be שם in the cities of Gilead." Num did not translate שם, simply reading ἔσονται ἐν ταῖς πόλεσιν Γαλαάδ. Hex added εκει after ἔσονται to represent the missing שם.[29]

32:27 Num begins with a contrastive δέ, thus "but your servants will cross over." These are characterized in MT as "כל חלוץ צבא before Yahweh for war." Since the referent is the plural עבדיך, Num changes the phrase to the plural. At 31:5 חלוצי צבא occurred, but was translated by ἐνωπλισμένοι εἰς παράταξιν "armed in battle array"; cf comment ad loc. But here Num has πάντες ἐνωπλισμένοι καὶ ἐκτεταγμένοι; this must have been triggered by צבא occurring as וצבא in the parent text, thus "armed and arranged in battle formation (before the Lord for war)." The כאשר clause is rendered as ὃν τρόπον ὁ κύριος λέγει, for MT's כאשר אדני דבר, i.e. a nominal clause structure. Num was aware of the tradition of reading דבר as a participle, since it uses the present tense, though not with its usual rendering λαλέω. Nor did Num render the suffix of אדני, and again hex supplied an equivalent with μου (or possibly ημων as some O witnesses read).[30]

32:28 MT begins with ויצו להם which one would normally render "and he ordered them." The trouble is that a further modifier follows, viz. three את phrases, which Num correctly translated by accusatives: "Eleazar the priest and Iesous ... and the chieftains ...." So here להם can hardly mean "to them," but probably means "concerning them (i.e. the two tribes)." Num circumvented the problem in double fashion, first by rendering להם by the dative αὐτοῖς, and then also by interpreting יצו by συνέστησεν "combine with," i.e. Moses brought together Eleazar ... and Iesous ... and the chieftains. In modern terms, he called a meeting of the executive committee, to make the situation clear to the main body of the Israelites the case of the two tribes, both in regard to their request and their promises. This verb also occurs for צוה at 27:23, but in quite a different context. In the tradition, the Byz+ text has reversed the case of the modifiers, i.e. it read "and Moses brought them (the two tribes in the accusative) together with Eleazar ... (in the dative)." This, however, is not what Num meant to say. It says that

---

29. The Others have also added ἐκεῖ.
30. See SS 99.

Moses called an executive meeting for the two tribes, i.e. to discuss their proposal.

The "executive" consisted not only of Eleazar and Iesous, but also of "the chieftains of the paternal clans τῶν φυλῶν Ἰσραήλ." MT had המטות לבני ישראל, i.e. Num has failed to render בני. Hex has added υιων before Ἰσραήλ to represent MT more precisely.[31] Another tradition, that of C' b+, substituted υιων for φυλῶν.

32:29 MT begins with "and said Moses to them," but Num placed the modifier before the subject, a word order preferred throughout the book. Hex has reordered πρὸς αὐτούς after Μωυσῆς to equal MT.

In the protasis, the subject of יעברו is "the Gadites and the Reubenites." As in v.25 Num has transposed the tribes, so that the Roubenites, representing the ancestral firstborn of Israel, precedes the Gadites. The pair generally follow a different order. The coordinate pair occurs seven times in the chapter; in MT "Reubenites and Gadites" occurs only in v.1, but as "Gadites and Reubenites" for the other six cases. In Num "Roubenites and Gadites" occurs in vv.1,2,25,29 and 31, and the reverse order only in vv.6 and 33. Num represents the more usual order; outside this chapter Deut 3:12 and in Ios 22:1,9,13,21,30,32,33 and 34 all used Rouben before Gad, and the reverse order obtains only in Ios 18:7 and 22:10,11 and 15, though MT has Reuben preceding Gad throughout Ios 22. After all, Reuben was the first born of the sons of Israel, and in the list of the tribes automatically comes first. Here in v.29, hex has transposed the two names to equal MT.

One might have expected the translator to adapt his rendering of כל חלוץ למלחמה to its plural context "the Reubenites and the Gadites," but he renders the singular exactly. The second clause governed by ἐάν reuses the ונכבשה הארץ of v.22, but Num adapts to a second person plural context, and translates by an active construction, καὶ κατακυριεύσητε τῆς γῆς. For the use of this verb as rendering for the root כבש, see comment at v.22.

The next clause is the apodosis, as the use of the future tense indicates. I would translate "then you must give them the land of Galaad for a possession. In imitation of MT, it is introduced by an apodotic καί. For ἐν κατασχέσει, see comment at v.22.

---

31. The Others also read τῶν φυλῶν υἱῶν Ἰσραήλ.

32:30 Num has considerably amplified this verse. MT has "and if they should not cross over armed with you, they shall receive a possession in your midst in the land of Canaan." Between "you" and "they" Num reads εἰς τὸν πόλεμον ἔναντι κυρίου, καὶ διαβιβάσετε τὴν ἀποσκευὴν αὐτῶν καὶ τὰς γυναῖκας αὐτῶν καὶ τὰ κτήνη αὐτῶν πρότερα ὑμῶν εἰς γῆν Χαναάν.[32] Hex has placed all of this text under the obelus. "To war before the Lord" modifies the verb διαβῶσιν, whereas the clause introduced by καὶ διαβιβάσετε introduces the apodosis. The clause explicates in greater detail what is to happen should the Roubenites and the Gadites not cross over armed for war before the Lord; then "you must bring over their children and their wives and their cattle in front of you into the land of Canaan." In other words, if the agreement is cancelled, the two tribes will do exactly what the other tribes do, viz. bring their camp with them, and thus "συγκατακληρονομηθήσονται with you in the land of Canaan." The verb is a hapax legomenon, but is readily understood: "they will coinherit (with their fellow-Israelites)." In view of the apparent witness of 4QNum[b] text as reconstructed in the above footnote, the longer text had a Hebrew basis; which Hebrew text is the earlier is difficult to determine. MT is almost cryptically concise, but could be understood as a summary statement mentioning only what was necessary: "If they should not come over with you, then they will coinherit." On the other hand, the longer text can easily be understood as the earlier text which is an exegetical expansion of an overly concise text, which the MT later condensed.

32:31 As in v.30, hex has transposed οἱ υἱοὶ 'Ρουβήν and οἱ υἱοὶ Γάδ to equal the order of MT; see discussion at v.30. The quoted speech of their statement of compliance reads in odd fashion: את אשר דבר יהוה אל עבדיך "what Yahweh spoke to your servants." One would expect either that the text would read a second person verb or that the addressee would read עבדיו. The translator smoothed out the text by substituting ὁ κύριος for יהוה, which can only refer to Moses, since יהוה is never rendered by an articulated κύριος, and ὁ κύριος presupposes אדני which can refer either to a human or a divine master or lord. Furthermore,

---

32. It would appear that 4QNum[b] had an equivalent text, though only)נשיה(is extant. There are approximately 51 spaces between)יעב of יעבורו and (ם)נשיה, which equals the equivalent of the lengthy plus of Num. This text as reconstructed would probably read something like [יעב]רו חלוצים אתכם למלחמה לפני יהוה והעברתם את טפם ואת] נשיה[ם.

the suffix of עבדיך has been rendered by αὐτοῦ, which hex has corrected to σου.³³ It was actually Moses who had given the orders; cf v.29, and ὁ κύριος must then refer to him; comp v.27's ὁ κύριος with the fuller ὁ κύριος ἡμῶν of v.25. What Num has done in articulating κύριος is to correct what is said to correspond with v.27. The use of λέγει for דבר is further testimony to Num's reliance on v.27 here, which the consonantal text does allow, i.e. reading דבר as a participle.

32:32 The ἡμεῖς does serve a contrastive purpose in Num, anticipating the reciprocal δώσετε of the next clause. In MT it serves no such purpose, since there is no second person verb. The double first person plural reference does give a sense of assurance, that "as for us, we will cross over armed before the Lord into the land of Canaan," which is exactly what MT also says. The Byz text has added τον ιορδανην as a modifier of διαβησόμεθα. The gloss is factually correct, but also unnecessary. The next clause is, however, quite different. Num makes a clear statement: "and you will give the possession to us in Transjordan." As stated above, MT has no second person verb, but it has אתנו "with us" as a predicate with the subject of the nominal clause אחזת נחלתנו, thus "and with us (will be) the possession of our inheritance (in Transjordan)." What the predicate means is "will remain with us." Num keeps the parcelling out of the inheritance in the proper hands, "you will give," presumably Moses and Eleazar, or possibly what I have called Israel's executive committee in v.28, will as the Lord's representatives grant the already-conquered area east of the Jordan to the two tribes. The notion that this is "with us," i.e. "we will have" is overly neutral as far as Num is concerned. Furthermore, Num has abbreviated אחזת נחלתנו to τὴν κατάσχεσιν ἡμῖν. Hex has intervened by adding της κληρονομιας under the asterisk after κατάσχεσιν to approximate MT. The Num text obviates what might seem tautological: "the possession of (our) inheritance." Since Num has changed the clause to a verbal one, the suffix of נחלתנו is rendered by the dative pronoun ἡμῖν as the indirect object of δώσετε.

32:33 It was specifically Moses, however, who made the assignment, i.e. "gave to them, to the Gadites and the Roubenites and to the half tribe of Manasse of the Josephites, the kingdom of Sion ... and the kingdom of Og ...." This represents

---

33. As did The Others.

in detail what MT says, except for "the Josephites," i.e υἱῶν Ἰωσήφ, for which MT reads בן יוסף. Apparently, the translator read בני instead of בן, a mistaken dittograph of the initial letter of יוסף, but comp 36:12 where υἱῶν Ἰωσήφ also occurs after Μανασσή. The question is What is meant by υἱῶν Ἰωσήφ. Possibly it would be better to translate by "of the sons of Joseph," since Manasse was one of two sons, i.e. Manasse and Ephraim. Or did the translator intend υἱῶν to refer to φυλῆς, i.e. "the tribe of Manasse, even Josephites?

What was assigned by Moses was "the land and the cities with its borders, cities of the land round about," i.e. of the surrounding land. The reference of αὐτῆς is to γῆν, i.e. "the borders of the land." MT's text is somewhat different, and quite obscure. It reads: "the land to its cities within (?) the borders of the cities of the land round about." Num is a bold attempt at making sense of MT. The αὐτῆς refers to γῆν. To the translator, "cities of the surrounding land" is explicative of "the cities with its (i.e. the city's) borders"; i.e. the two are in apposition to each other.

32:34 Vv.34—36 name the cities which the Gadites rebuilt. V.34 lists three cities, τὴν Δαιβών and τὴν Ἀταρώθ and τὴν Ἀροήρ. For Daibon and Ataroth, see comments at v.3. Ἀροήρ is variously spelled in the tradition as ταροηρ, αωηρ, αροηλ, αροην and αροηθ. All three names are articulated, the τήν in each case representing the preposition את in MT.

32:35 MT has a further three names: יגבהה and יעזר, עטרת שופן. The first two are each governed by את, but not the last one. Accordingly, the translator took only the first two as proper nouns. Num omitted עטרת entirely, and transcribed שופן as Σωφάρ, with hex prefixing the name αταρωθ under the asterisk. Possibly its omission was occasioned by the presence of עטרת in v.34, The name Σωφάρ was changed in the tradition to σωφαν, which is closer to MT, though its origin is uncertain; this was in turn corrupted to ωφαν, ζωφαν, σεφαν and σωφαμ. The second name became Ἰαζήρ, for which see comment at 21:24. The translator was misled by the third city, which was introduced only by a conjunction, i.e. as ויגבהה, easily taken as the verb גבה "to be high", or transitively as "to make high."[34] Num took the second *he* as a pronominal suffix, and translated καὶ

---

34. The Three according to the transcriptions in Syh, understood the third item as proper nouns, with Theod and Aq reading *lybgwh'*, and Sym, *lybqh'*. Obviously, the tradition has corrupted the letters from an original *lygbwh'*(?) and *lygbh'* readings.

ὕψωσαν αὐτάς "and they (the Gadites) raised (or erected) them (i.e. the listed cities).

32:36 Two more cities are listed as built up, i.e. as further modifiers of ᾠκοδόμησαν of v.34, Ναμβρά and Βαιθαράν. The first of these is בית נמרה in MT, though in v.3 it was simply called נמרה, which see. Hex has corrected the name as βηθναμρα. The name created havoc among copyists, and it was sometimes given a final closed syllable, either by a *mu* or *nu*.[35] For various ways in which the name was misspelled, see comment at v.3. The second city represents בית הרן. This also created confusion among copyists, and include βηθαρραν, βαιθαρρα, βαιθερραν, βαιθαραμ, βεθθαραν, βαιθραν, βαθαρ, βεθαραμ, βαιθωραν, βεθαρραν, βαιθωρ, βαθαρραν, κεθωραν and βαιραν. The cities are described as "fortified cities and walled enclosures for sheep." Presumably, this is intended to describe all the cities listed in vv.34—36.

32:37 As in the case of the cities rebuilt by the Gadites, those rebuilt by the Roubenites are also individually governed by an את. Num articulated only the first one, Ἐσεβών, and hex added την under the asterisk for both Ἐλεαλή and Καριαθάιμ to represent the preposition. For the first two cities, see comments at v.3.

Kariathaim is mentioned only here in the Pentateuch, though it also occurs in Ios 13:19. In the Moabite Stone (ll.9—10) it is mentioned as being built by Mesha the king in the time of Omri, king of Israel; see Bible Dictionaries for its probable location (and identification). In the tradition, the name was often written with a final *nu*. Other misspellings include καθαριαθεμ, καριαθειμ, καριαθαμ, καριαθιαρ, καριαθιαριμ and καριαθ.

32:38 Num begins with the second name, but it is doubtful that this is original text, and I would now take καὶ τὴν Ναβαύ, as original Greek. Since it was followed by καὶ τὴν Βεελμεών, its omission by B *b n z*+ was due to a visual error from καὶ τήν 1° to καὶ τήν 2°; see also the next paragraph. For the spelling of Ναβαύ, see v.3. In the tradition, it appears as ναβω, ναβωθ, ναβαω, ναβαβ,

---

35. See THGN 119, where the various misspellings are fully listed. It should be noted that the hex prefixing of βηθ, simply added to the confusion, leading e.g. to βηθαμραμ, βιθιαμραμ and βιθιαμαρμ.

ναβο, ναβδω, βαμω, αβω and αβωθ. The city Βεελμεών is modern Maʿin. It was also variously spelled as βελμεων, βαλαμεων, βεελβεων, βεελμων, βεελμεωθ and βεεαμεων.

This is followed in MT by מוסבת שם, which is obscure. It is usually interpreted as a Ho feminine plural participle of סבב, but referring to Nabo and Baalmeon, and meaning something like "have been turned about with respect to name." What is not explained is what names were changed to what names. Num clearly read מוסבת, but omitted שם, and interpreted as περικεκυκλωμένας "(they) being surrounded round about" (presumably by walls). Hex added ονοματι under the asterisk after the participle to account for the untranslated שם, though precisely what περικεκυκλωμέναι ονοματι was supposed to convey is obscure. Incidentally, the plural seems to presuppose the presence of an original καὶ τὴν Ναβαύ, though this is admittedly not ironclad, since the preceding verse named three other coordinate cities. The n text added an explanatory gloss και τετειχισμενας "and walled."[36] For Σεβαμά, see comment at v.3.

Num has interpreted the next clause in MT, "and they named בשמת the names of the cities which they rebuilt," by adding a genitive pronoun, i.e. κατὰ τὰ ὀνόματα αὐτῶν. What is meant is that they gave new names to the rebuilt cities, i.e. "according to *their* names." By adding αὐτῶν they understood "and they named with names" correctly as meaning "they renamed." There is certainly no need with BHS to emend בשמת to בשמתן.

32:39 MT speaks of בני מכיר, but Num has υἱὸς Μαχίρ. According to 26:33, Manasse had generated only one son, Μαχίρ, who in turn fathered Γαλαάδ, and apparently, Num "corrected" the text of MT by reading a singular καὶ ἐπορεύθη υἱὸς Μαχίρ, thereby making a consistent statement, which was then continued consistently throughout the verse. The Masoretes vocalized the next coordinate verb וילכדה as plural as well, "and they captured it," but the following one ויורש as singular. By its καὶ ἔλαβεν αὐτὴν καὶ ἀπώλεσεν Num made a consistent text. The Hi of ירש is usually understood to mean not only "to cause to inherit," but also more commonly in a negative sense "to disinherit, dispossess"; in LXX this is usually interpreted to mean "to destroy," "remove," or "kill," but in a positive sense "to inherit." See comment at v.21 for the translations of הוריש. Here

---

36. Sym read περιτετειχισμένας instead of the Num participle; comp Tar[N] which reads מקפן שורין רמין "surrounded by high walls."

Num is blunt: "and he killed the Amorite who was dwelling in it." MT simply has אשר בו, and hex has placed κατοικοῦντα under the obelus, since it had no equivalent in MT, though it certainly was what בו meant.

32:40 In Hebrew הגלעד is masculine, but in Num it is feminine in both vv.39—40, possibly since Galaad is not just a city, but an area, and thus a χώραν, which is feminine. In fact, the gender of Γαλαάδ is quite uncertain throughout LXX. Thus at 26:33 it is masculine. In the LXX as a whole it is modified by a masculine article 14 times, but by a feminine article 14 times as well, paritcularly in the historical books, though in Jdg it is always masculine, but in the Pentateuch the gender varies as it does in Jos.

As in the case of the two tribes, Machir received from Moses the right of possession. The Galaad referred to is northern Gilead, i.e. the area north of the Jabbok. It might be noted that here MT also has singular references; Moses gave Gilead, not to the Machirites, but "to Machir, the son of Manasseh, and he dwelt in it." Num translates the final prepositional phrase by ἐκεῖ.

32:41 That בן or ὁ τοῦ does not mean "son of," but "descendant of" is contextually obvious, since Machir was the sole son of Manasse. Yair was clearly a Machirite clan. For a discussion of the meaning of ἐπαύλεις, see comment at v.16 and at 22:39. Here it renders חות, the meaning of which is not fully clear, possibly "encampments," or "villages" in distinction from "cities." The Alexandrian thought these were ἐπαύλεις "walled encampments."[37]

32:42 The name נבח occurs twice, but Num transcribed it differently. The first time it occurs as Ναβαύ, the usual rendering for נבו, e.g. v.38. The second occurrence is transcribed Ναβώθ. There is no indication in the tradition of copyists' approximating the other transcription. Thus for Ναβαυ, the tradition offers ναβαν, ναναυ, ναβαβ, ναβα, ναβαω, ναββαω, νβαυ, ναβανθ, αναβαυ, ναυ and νααβ. On the other hand, Ναβώθ appears in the tradition as μαβωθ, ναβαιωθ, ναβαωθ, ναβουθ and ναβω, and two mss in the hex tradition read ναβαυ. How then can one understand what Num was doing? I suggest that another revision on the part of the Alexandrian gives us a clue. Num states that after

---

37. Milgrom suggests that חות were "fortified villages."

taking Κανάθ and its villages, "he renamed αὐτάς Naboth from his (own) name." MT, however, reads ויקרא לה, i.e. "and he renamed it," viz. קנת. But the -ωθ ending represents a feminine plural ending for nouns, and this ending is then further referred to by the plural pronoun αὐτάς. It is of course clear that Num did not read נבח, but rather נבו and as its plural נבות resp. What Num means is that Nabau renamed τὰς κώμας of Κανάθ by the plural name Ναβώθ. This is not what MT says; it says that Nobah captured Kenath, and renamed it with his own name, Nobah.

קנת is adequately transcribed by Κανάθ. A popular F M text spelled it κανααθ, which can not possibly represent קנת, but would presuppose some such parent as קנחת or קנעת, neither of which is attested anywhere, whereas קנת is also attested at 1 Chr 2:23.[38] Other misspellings include κααθ, καναηθ, κααναθ, καμαθα and κααδως.

---

38. See THGN 119.

Chapter 33

33:1 Num begins with καί over against MT. Since ch.33 has no organic connection with the preceding chapter, the conjunction is not overly appropriate.[1] The chapter deals with the itinerary of the Israelites throughout their desert wanderings, and the account is introduced by "οὖτοι σταθμοί of the Israelites," i.e. the stages or stations by which they progressed on their way to Canaan. This represents the מסעי of the Israelites, which stresses the Israelites' movements from their various encampments. The term σταθμοί is exactly what the chapter describes; they are the stopping places on their trek through the desert. The term is used in a military context; it represents the movement of the people σὺν δυνάμει αὐτῶν, i.e. with their army.

The בני ישראל is modified by a relative clause: "who went out from the land of Egypt," but Num interprets the אשר by ὡς, thus not by a relative clause, but a temporal one; "these are the stages of the Israelites as (or when) they went out," i.e. at the time of their exodus from Egypt. In Num, they left the land of Egypt σὺν δυνάμει αὐτῶν which renders MT's לצבאתם; this means "according to their hosts, i.e. in military order, host by host, and reflects the orderliness of chapter 2; see especially v.34. Num has failed to reflect this by using the singular; possibly in the light of Israel's extermination war with Midian (ch.31), the translator thought in terms of an Israelite army. Their departure from Egypt was ἐν χειρὶ Μωυσῆ καὶ Ἀαρών, by which is meant "under the direction of Moses and Aaron."

33:2 "Moses wrote down their ἀπάρσεις (departures)[2] and their σταθμοὺς διὰ ῥήματος of the Lord." MT has למסעיהם for the second member. Presumably, what MT meant was "their departures according to their stages," which the translator simplified by a coordinate structure, "their departures and their stopping places." That this is what is meant is clear from the pattern followed in the account. The pattern throughout is καὶ ἀπῆραν, referring to "their departures," and καὶ παρενέβαλον, referring to "their stopping places, their σταθμοί." What

---
1. Though it is also attested by Pesh, but not by Vulg.
2. Theod, Aq and Sym all rendered by τὰς ἐξόδους.

remains problematic, however, is the διά phrase. Does this refer to the starts and stops of their journey, or does it refer to the verb ἔγραψεν? Did Moses record the journey by divine orders, or were the various stages of the desert wanderings determined by the Lord's word? Either interpretation is possible, but I would suggest that the next clause, "and these are the stages of their πορείας (i.e. of their going, journey)" makes it likely that the latter interpretation was intended.

This nominal clause constitutes the second part of the verse. In it, Num has simplified MT's מסעיהם למוצאיהם. The term πορεία occurs only here in the Pentateuch, and never elsewhere for מוצא. Clearly, the translator wanted to avoid the ἀπάρσεις αὐτῶν of v.a by using an abstract general term for "journey"; it actually serves as a kind of superscription for what Moses wrote: "these are the stages of their journey." Hex, however, could hardly allow this to pass uncorrected, and added αυτων και under the asterisk after σταθμοί, thereby creating impossible Greek, but at least accounting for every untranslated morpheme of MT.

33:3 ויסעו "and they set out" is used throughout the chapter as signalling the departure, and is invariably rendered by ἀπῆραν "lift off," and so "depart, break camp." Their starting point in Egypt is given as from 'Ραμεσσή/רעמסס, for which see comments at Exod 1:11 12:37. In the tradition, the name is often spelled with a single *sigma* which is clearly a haplograph, since the Hebrew is spelled with a double *samekh*. An odd misspelling is that of B x+ in which the final η became -ων. Other misspellings include ραμμεση, ραμασση, ρεμεσση, ραμεσσης,[3] ραμεσης, κραμεσση, ραμεσσω and ραμεσων.

The date given is by a dative of time when: "τῷ μηνὶ τῷ πρώτῳ, on the fifteenth day of the first month." In MT, this is governed by the preposition ב, and the Byz text has supplied an εν, which may well be recensional.

A more exact delineation of the time of their departure is given in v.b, and is also in the dative: τῇ ἐπαύριον τοῦ πάσχα "on the morning of the pascha feast," but this modifies ἐξῆλθον which follows. Also modifying this verb is ἐν χειρὶ ὑψηλῇ "with a high hand," i.e. defiantly, for which see Note at Exod 14:8. The departure was done openly, "before all τῶν Αἰγυπτίων." MT had vocalized מצרים as "Egypt," but the plural gentilic seems more appropriate, a rendering which the consonantal text also permits.

---

3. The Others also spelled the name as 'Ραμεσσής.

33:4 This is particularly true of the opening of v.4 where ומצרים is rendered by καὶ οἱ Αἰγύπτιοι; technically, this ought to represent והמצרים, but an emendation is not justified. The predicate is plural ἔθαπτον, i.e. an imperfect verb, which renders the participial predicate מקברים of a nominal clause, i.e. "the Egyptians were burying ἐξ αὐτῶν τοὺς τεθνηκότας πάντας οὓς ἐπάταξεν κύριος," whereas MT has את אשר הכה יהוה בהם. Two remarks are here in order. a) Num lacks an equivalent for בהם after יהוה, and so hex provided for such by transposing ἐξ αὐτῶν—πάντας after κύριος 1°, thereby providing a rendering for the prepositional phrase, and b) τοὺς τεθνηκοτας πάντας has no equivalent in MT, and hex has placed these words under the obelus, thereby equalling MT. The Hebrew then defined "those whom the Lord smote" as כל בכור, to which Num added the gloss ἐν γῇ Αἰγύπτῳ, which hex also placed under the obelus.

The final clause reads "and on their gods executed τὴν ἐκδίκησιν κύριος"; i.e. the Lord executed judgment; comp Exod 12:12. MT is somewhat different with its שפטים יהוה. Hex has transposed these to equal MT. The plural שפטים is translated in the Hebrew Bible seven times by ἐκδίκησις, but only twice by the plural (Ezek 14:21, where the plural is required because it is identified as "four") and at 16:41; in all the other cases it is rendered by the singular (Exod 7:4 12:12 Ezek 25:11 30:14). Hex again intervened by transposing τὴν ἐκδίκησιν after κύριος, thereby equalling the word order of MT.

33:5 The first stage. Num subordinates the first clause to a participial one, thus: "and setting out ... they encamped in Σοκχώθ; see Note on Σοκχώθα at Exod 12:37. The variety of changes in spelling here are all found there as well. To be noted is the Hellenistic use of εἰς as indicating location, Classically shown by ἐν.

33:6 Stage number two. They set out from Sukkhoth, and encamped in βουθάν, which in MT is אתם or etham, and also found as such at Exod 13:20. Here it is governed by the preposition ב, hence the transcription with beta. The hex text changed the final nu to mu to correspond to the final mem of MT. Other spellings are βοθαν, μουθαν, βουθα, βιθαν, σουθαμ, and probably under hex influence οθομ, οθαμ and ουθαμ.[4] The place is said to be ὅ ἐστιν μέρος τι of the desert, i.e.

---

4. For a discussion of the name both here and in v.7, see THGN 117.

"which is a side (or an edge) of the desert."[5] This correctly represents MT's אשר בקצה המדבר. The place is unknown.

33:7 Though the departure for stage number three reads מאתם "from *Etham*," Num, having named the place βουθάν in v.6, uses it here as well; see comment and footnote at v.6. Num harmonized with the usual καὶ παρενέβαλον, though MT had changed to וישב "and they turned about," modified by על פי החירת, "towards *Pi-hahiroth*." The name also occurs at Exod 14:2,9, where it is rendered by τῆς ἐπαύλεως; see comments ad loc. The place is unknown, and Num translated the פי by στόμα, and transcribed החירת by Ἑιρώθ, disregarding the articulation entirely. Just what the translator meant by "the mouth of Eiroth" is not clear to me. Not surprisingly, the tradition reflects complete puzzlement, producing επι ειρωθ (Byz), i.e. reflecting both פי as στόμα and as a transcription: (ε)πι, επ(ε)ιρωθ, and without επι: αειρωθ, ιρωθ, εις ρωθ and ειρων. MT further pinpointed the location by two further geographic notes, אשר על פני בעל צפון and לפני מגדל, but neither of these is known. Num rendered the first of these adequately by ὅ ἐστιν ἀπέναντι Βεελσεπφών, for which see Note at Exod 14:2. The second one is rendered by ἀπέναντι Μαγδώλου, i.e. with a genitive inflectional ending. For Μαγδώλ(ου), also see Note at Exod 14:2. None of these designations has been identified, though many guesses have been made. All that is known with certainty is that they were near water; see v.8.

33:8 Stage four. MT recounts the Israelites' departure as מפני החירת, presumably originally מפי החירת, though the text of MT was parent for Num, which reads "and they set out ἀπέναντι Ἑιρώθ, i.e. ἀπέναντι represents מפני, not מפי; comp v.7. It was here that the Israelites διέβησαν μέσον τῆς θαλάσσης εἰς τὴν ἔρημον, for which event, see Exod 14:10—30. Thereafter "they travelled a three day road trip through the desert αὐτοί," which assures the Hebrew text במדבר אתם. Apparently, the Alexandrian could make no sense out of "in the desert of Etham," and understood אתם as the pronominal phrase meaning "them." In the context, the accusative αυτους would make little sense, and so he used the nominative, thereby recapitulating pronominally the subject of ἐπορεύθησαν. Note that ms 426 changed αὐτοί to ηθαμ, obviously through mediate Hebrew influence.

---

5. For a full discussion of μέρος in the sense of "side," see Lee 72—76.

The Israelites then encamped at מרה or *Mara*; at Exod 15:23 this was transcribed by (εἰς) Μέρραν, and commented on by "therefore the name of that place was named Πικρία." Here the translator also translated it by (ἐν) Πικρίαις.[6]

33:9 Stage five. The next place to which "they came" was Αἰλίμ, i.e. אילם or *Elim*. This verse is almost word for word the same as at Exod 15:27, which read ἐν Αἰλίμ instead of ἦσαν ἐκεῖ, used a δέ structure instead of καί for the last clause, and read τὰ ὕδατα instead of τὸ ὕδωρ at the end; see Notes ad loc. Num has in part harmonized with the Exodus account by adding παρὰ τὸ ὕδωρ, which has no counterpart in MT; hex has placed the παρά phrase under the obelus. The translator was obviously familiar with the Exodus account.

33:10 Stage six. The next encampment was ἐπὶ θάλασσαν ἐρυθράν. This renders על ים סוף. The term ים סוף "Sea of Reeds" is always rendered by "Red Sea" in LXX either with ἐρυθράν preceding "sea" as always in Exod, for which see Note at 10:19, or as here.

33:11 Stage seven brought the Israelites into the desert of Σίν for סין. For its location, see Note at Exod 16:1. This must not be confused with the desert of Σίν for צן at 13:22, for which see comment ad loc.

33:12 Stage eight. From the wilderness of Sin, they encamped in Ῥαφακά. MT reads דפקה. Neither *Dophkah* nor *Raphaka* is known, so whether the name began with ד or ר is unknown. The confusion of *daleth* and *resh* was common both in the old Phoenician script as well as in the later Aramaic alphabet. In the tradition, only one ms, 767, read δεφακα. Other spellings include ρεφακαι, ραφακαν, ραφακ, ραφα, ραφεκ, ρακαφα and ραφαειν (due to the better known name Raphaim).

33:13 Stage nine. The next encampment was at Αἰλούς, which transcribes אלוש or *Alush*. This place is completely unknown. In the tradition, the name has been spelled as ελως, αιλεις, αιλειμ, σελημ and αιλην. It should be mentioned once

---

6. Dorival points out that the plural is used in Greek for the names of cities such as Athens and Thebes, though Pikria was hardly a sufficiently important city to attract a plural form.

again, that I do not record variant spellings based on itacisms, or more accurately stated, I record only one spelling for an itacism. Instead of ἐν, the Byz+ text has εἰς, which it prefers throughout instead of ἐν in modification of παρενέβαλον in this chapter; see comment at v.16.

33:14 Stage ten. The next encampment was in Ῥαφιδίν, Raphidim. In MT the name is רפידם, and correction to a final *-mu* is recensional (in ms 426 and Byz). For the name, see Note at Exod 17:1. It is often thought to be located in the Wadi Refayid, cir 48 km or 30 mi. north of the tip of the Sinai peninsula, but this is by no means certain; see Bible Dictionaries. For the lack of drinking water here, see Exod 17:1. The text of Num reproduces MT accurately, except for the position of the adverb ἐκεῖ. In MT שם follows היה "and not was שם (there) water," but in Num ἐκεῖ occurs at the end of the clause, i.e. after πιεῖν. The adverb is reordered in a majority A F text to the Hebrew order, which is almost certainly hex in origin.

33:15 Stage 11. From Raphidin they set out for the desert of Σινά, which constitutes throughout LXX the transcription for סיני. A few mss, mainly *n*, read σιναι, obviously due to mediate Hebrew influence. The location of Sina(i) remains in dispute.

33:16 Stage 12. The next stage is בקברת התאוה Qibrroth haTa'wa, which is translated in Num as ἐν Μνήμασιν τῆν ἐπιθυμίας, for which see comment at 11:34, where a folk etymology explaining the name is given. The place remains unidentified. The Byz text changes ἐν Μνήμασιν to εἰς μνηματα, which is consistent with its preference suggested in a comment at v.13. An εἰς structure became the pattern in modification of παρενέβαλον from vv.21—35, 37—43, and again in v.45 in Num as well.

33:17 Stage 13. They moved on to Ἀσηρώθ. In the tradition, the place name Μνημάτων τῆς ἐπιθυμίας occurred without the article τῆς in B M V *O f x* text. The name obtained in v.16 with the article, and also occurs as such at 11:34,35. In all four cases, ἐπιθυμίας is articulated, which in view of the Hebrew התאוה is expected. The loss of the article is secondary, possibly influenced by the unarticulated Μνημάτων governing it,[7] which the Byz text has articulated as well. The name 'Ασηρώθ for חצרת is quite stable in the tradition, the only errors obtaining being ασσηρωθ by dittography, ασηδωθ by change of consonant, and σηρωθ by aphaeresis.

33:18 Stage 14. The next stage is 'Ραθαμά, which represents רתמה or *Rithma*. The name is related to רתם meaning "broom plant," which thrives only in desert areas. Its location is not known. In the tradition, it appears as ραθεμα, ραθμα, αραθαμα, ραμα, ραμαθα and θαραθαμα. The spelling ραθμα is *O*, and reflects the two syllable tradition of the Masoretic text.

33:19 Stage 15. The next place is called 'Ρεμμὼν Φάρες, which is also both unknown and occurs only in this list. The Hebrew equivalent is רמן פרץ or *Rimmon Pares*. The first word occurs in *C*' *d*+ as ρεμων. Other spellings include ραιμων, ρεμβων, ρεβων, ρεμω, ρεμμωθ and ρεμωθ. The second word is completely stable in the tradition for v.19, but one ms has φαρεθ in v.20.

33:20 Stage 16 is found at Λεβωνά for לבנה, for which the Masoretic tradition has a bisyllabic vocalization, *Libna*. The name is well-known as the name of a place in Judah, but not as a stage on the desert journey of the Israelites, though Λοβόν in Deut 1:1 might conceivably refer to the same place. The name was unknown to copyists as appears from the following spellings: λεβωμα, λωβενα, λαβωνα, λεβωνος, ρεβωνα, λεαβωνα, λεμβωνα, λεγωνα, λεμωνα (in B *x*+) and λεμωννα.[8]

33:21 Stage 17 took the Israelites to Δεσσά for רסה. As at vv.12—13 an ר and ד confusion has created two traditions as to the name of stage 17, either Dessa or *Rissa*. Here too the place has not been identified, is limited to two successive verses, and there is no way to ensure which spelling is original. In the tradition, however, a *rho* spelling did exist in an A F popular text. Since ρεσσα (plus subvariants) is fully supported *inter alia* by all the mss of *O*, this is certainly a hex correction. The *b* tradition actually combines the two in its δρεσσα, and cf θερσα. Also attested in the tradition are δεσα, δεσσαν and δασα.

---

7. See THGN 106.
8. See THGN 119.

33:22 Stage 18. From Δεσσά they proceeded to Μακελάθ, but MT reads קהלתה, vocalized as kᵃhelatha. Here too the place is unknown, and the name occurs only in the Hebrew Bible as stage 18. Obviously, the parent text must have read an initial *mim*, i.e. *מקהלתה. Possibly the parent text was influenced by the מקהלת of vv.25—26. The name is variously written in the mss, such as μακελεθ (C⁻' s+), μακελα, μακελα, μακελαθα, μακελαδ (b), μακαλαθ, μακωλαθ, μακεαθ, μακεδαδ as well as μακελλαθ (or -λλεθ), which is read by B M V Byz+. This could not be original, since the *he* in the name could hardly be represented by a *lambda*, but only by zero or by vowel change.⁹ The spelling is probably simply an error by dittography, though another possibility is that it reflects an original spelling *μακεαλαθ, i.e. that the *he* is represented by an *alpha*, which in an uncial text would read ΑΛ, easily becoming ΛΛ, and producing μακελλαθ. Though this does explain the old variant spelling, it is merely a possible reconstruction on my part, and it seems preferable to consider it simply a mistaken dittograph.

33:23 Stage 19 is another unknown place; in MT it is called הר שפר or Mount *Sapher*, but Num omitted הר and simply read Σάφαρ. There are two recensional corrections in the tradition. The obvious one is that of hex which has added ορος under the asterisk to represent the untranslated הר.¹⁰ A second tradition is the majority A F M text which read αρσαφαρ, i.e. transcribed the name fully. As might be expected, there are numerous variants of this second tradition, including σαραφαθ, ρασσαφαρ, σαρσαφαρ, σαρσαφα, ναρσαφαν, αρσαφαρθ, αρσαρφαρ, αρσαφαρεθ and αρσαφαρ. The original spelling Σάφαρ is quite straightforward, and produce few misspellings. Only αφαρ, σαφαρεθ and the Byz σασαφαρ (also as σεσαφαρ or ασσαφαρ) occur.

33:24 Stage 20 is at Χαραδάθ for חרדה or *Charada*, again an unknown place only attested in vv.24—25. For the textual history of Σάφαρ, see the discussion of the two recensions of the name at v.23, which also applies to this verse.¹¹

---

9. See THGN 119—120.
10. The Others read ὄρος Σάφαρ.
11. The Others also read ὄρος Σάφαρ here.

Instead of εἰς (Χαραδάθ), a majority A F text reads επι, but since MT uses the preposition ב, it is almost certainly secondary. The name is variously realized in the tradition: as χαραδα (possibly a hex correction?), χαρδαθ, χαραδαδ, χαραδαμ, χαραλαθ, χαρμαθ, χαραθ and χαραδ.

33:25 Stage 21 took the Israelites to another unidentified place, Μακηλώθ for the Hebrew מקהלת or *Makheloth*. It is unique in the Bible as stage 21. The place is easily confused with Μακελάθ of vv.22—23; in fact, the parent consonantal text of the two places may well have been identical, though the vocalization would have differed, particularly in the final syllable, the -ωθ ending constituting the usual feminine plural inflection of nouns, whereas -αθ can only be singular. In the tradition, the most prominent characteristic of variant spellings is the evidence of Λ—Δ confusion which goes back to an uncial parent, and the majority text actually reads μακηδωθ; in fact, cod A reads Μακηλώθ here, but μακηδωθ in v.26. Variant spellings all presuppose the *daleth*: μακηδωλ, μακηδω, μακηδωθ, μακεδωθ and μακεδωδ.

33:26 Stage 22. The name reads Κατάαθ, but MT has תחת or *tahat*. Once again, the name occurs only here and in v.27, and is completely unknown. Only the τάαθ equals תחת, and the Greek transcription presupposes קתחת.[12] Whether the actual name of the place was קתחת or תחת is impossible to determine. The copyists messed up the name considerably as the following variants show: καττααθ, κατθααθ, κατταθ, καταθ, κατθααθα, καγααθ, θααθ, καταθααθ, κατθααν, καθθαθι, κααθ, καθαδδι, τατααθ, καταν, καθθαακ and βατααθ.

33:27 Stage 23. They proceeded to Τάραθ, but in MT this read תרח i.e. *tarah*, also unknown and unidentified. The Greek transcription may have presupposed the Aramaic, rather than the old Canaanite, script, since the ה was mistakenly taken as a ת. But neither a תרת not a תרת is known. In the tradition, the spelling θαρα in ms 426 is probably a correction based on Hebrew mediation. Other spellings include the popular A M reading θαραθ, as well as θαραθα, θαρεθ,

---

12. Dorival is mistaken in his statement: "La LXX dépend sans doute d'un modèle qui inversait les deux premières consonnes de TM." The *ḥeth* is shown by the second, and unstressed, *alpha*, not by *kappa*.

θαραθαθ, θαραaθ τεραθ, ταρα, ραθαθ, ταραaθ, εκθαραθ, καθαραθ, σταραθ, εκαραθ and γαραραaθ.

33:28 Stage 24 was another unidentified and unique place name, Ματεκκά for מתקה. The Masoretes made of this a bisyllabic word *mitqa*. In the tradition, the majority A F M text read a *theta* instead of a *tau*. This was also the case with μαθεκκαθ, μαθεκα, μαθεκαν, μαθθεκα, μαθεκαθ, μαθεκακ, μακεθα and μαθεκκα. With *tau*, variants include ματεκκαν, ματεκα, ματτεκκα μετεκκα, μετεκα, ματτεκαν, ματτεκα and ματτικαα.

33:29 Stage 25. The next stop was at 'Ασελμωνά, but MT read חשמנה or *Hashmona*. In neither form are these names known outside of the name of this station, and it is also unidentified. The name is puzzling. Does the *lambda* represent some original חשלמנה*; this would presuppose an unusual quadraliteral root of which I can find no trace. But if MT's name is original, why would the Alexandrian insert a *lambda* without any basis? Probably the well-known root שלם interfered in the transcription? In the tradition, spellings without *lambda* depend on the hex correction to ασεμωνα, thus ασσεμωνα, σασεμωνα, ασσεμων. For the "l" tradition, there are ελμωνα, αλμωνα, λαμωνα, σαλμωνα and σελμωνα; the last-named is found in B V Byz *x*+, but it is secondary. Initial ח is never omitted, but is always shown by an initial vowel.[13]

33:30. Stage 26 introduces Μασουρούθ as the next station, while MT has מסרות or *Moseroth*. Elsewhere the name occurs in the Sam text for MT's Deut 10:6 for מוסרה, where the Greek reads Μισιδαί. It was the place where according to Deut Aaron died; cf Note ad loc. The location has not been identified. In the tradition, a few witnesses have a double *sigma* including cod B, which uniquely reads μασσουρωθ, but it is unusual for the translator of the book to have a double *sigma* in intervocalic position (the Δεσσά of vv.21,22 is unusual), and it is unlikely to be original. Its doubling is rather a case of dittography, since the *sigma* is followed by an *omicron*, both being very easily confused in the old uncial script.[14] Other misspellings includes μασουρουτ, μασουρωθ, μασερουθ, μασηρουθ and μαρσουρουθ.

---

13. See THGN 120.
14. See THGN 120.

33:31 Stage 27. They proceed to Βαναιακάν, which transcribes בני יעקן or bəne Ya'akan.[15] The name also occurs at Deut 10:6, where it appears as υἰῶν 'Ιακίμ. The place is completely unknown. For the treatment of the name in the Deut tradition, see Note at Deut 10:6. In the tradition, B V Byz x+ attest to a shorter form in both vv.31—32, in which the -καν ending is omitted. Since in both verses a καί follows the name, the short form is simple a case of parablepsis due to homoiarchon, the eye skipping from kappa 1° to kappa 2°.[16] The medieval (13th and 14th centuries ?) confusion between the cursive beta and mu led to spellings with initial mu in C'' f+. Other errors include βανιακαν, βενιακαν, βανικαν, βανακκαν, βανακκα and ζανιακαν.

33:32 Stage 28. From Banaiakan the Israelites went to the mountainous area (τὸ ὄρος) of Γαδγάδ for MT's חר הגדגד or Hor haGidgad, also mentioned at Deut 10:7, though without the חר; cf Note ad loc for numerous misreadings in the tradition. The word חר has been misread by Num in both verses as הר "mountain."[17] The area remains unidentified. Here the name yielded a varied lot of spellings in which the uncial confusion of the triangular ΑΔΛ graphemes created γαλδαδ, γαλγαλ, γαλααδ, as well as other misspellings including γαδδαδ, γαδιγαδ, γαγδαδ, χαλααδ, γαγδαγ, γαδαδ, γαδαθ, γαγαδ and even by haplography γαδ.

33:33 Stage 29. From there they went on to Ετεβάθα for the Hebrew יטבתה or Yotbatha. This unidentified place also occurs at Deut 10:7, which see.[18] In the tradition, hex has corrected to read an initial iota, i.e. as ιεταβαθα, which became popular, though mainly with a final nu, i.e. as ιεταβαθαν. Other errors include εταβαθα, ετεβαθ, τεβαθα, τεβαθ, τεβεθα, τεδαθα, βαθα, σετεβαθα, σεττεβαθα and σετεφαθα.

---

15. Sym has for בבני יעקן ἐν υἱοῖς 'Ιακάν.
16. See THGN 120.
17. Also read as הר in Kenn 109*; in the next verse מחר is read as מהר in Kenn 109* 260.
18. Milgrom notes that the name has been used for the Kibbutz Yotbatah, 40 km or 25 mi. north of Elath.

33:34 Stage 30. The next station to which the Israelites journeyed was Ἐβρωνά for the Hebrew עברנה or ʿAbrona, unique to this reference. The site is also unknown, though it has been identified as Tell el Kheleifah (i.e. at Elath).[19] The popular B M variant spelling with an initial *sigma*, σεβρωνα, is simply a case of dittography after εἰς, which is then carried over into the next verse (where, however, it follows ἐκ); also attested are σιεβρωνα, σεβρανα and σεβωνα. Other odd spellings are ευρωνα (since υ and β were both pronounced as /v/), αβρωνα, σεβρανα, σεβωνα, εσεβρωνα and ελμωνα.

33:35 Stage 31. The next station was Γεσιὼν Γάβερ, the transcription of עציון גבר or Eṣyon Gaber. The place was identified as Tell el Kheleifah by Nelson Glueck, but this identification has in recent years been severely challenged. What seems to be generally accepted is that it was located in the general area of Aqabah and/or Elath. the transcription Γασιών for עציון illustrates the fact that the two phonemes *ghayin* and ʿ*ayin* represented by the ע grapheme were still distinct. The root then must have been with an initial *ghayin*, not ʿ*ayin*. For the name see Note at Deut 2:8. In the tradition, Γασιών appears as γεσσιων, γασσιων, γεσιων, γεασιων, γεδσιων, γεθσιων, γεττζιων, γενεσιων and γεων. Γάβερ is stable, only two variants occurring γεβερ and γαδερ in v.35, but completely stable in v.36.

33:36 Stages 32–33. This verse records two journeys, first to the desert of Σίν for צן, and then to the desert of Φαράν, which is followed by αὕτη ἐστὶν Καδής. In MT this is only one stage, the second one, i.e. καὶ ἀπῆραν ἐκ τῆς ἐρήμῳ Σὶν καὶ παρενέβαλον εἰς τὴν ἔρημον Φαράν has no counterpart in MT, and has been placed under an obelus by hex. The addition in Num is to make the text a consistent account. At 13:27 the spies returned ... "to all the assembly of the Israelites εἰς τὴν ἔρημον Φαρὰν Καδής." The addition locates Kades, not in the wilderness of Sin as MT does, but rather in the wilderness of Pharan as 13:27(26) does. Num repairs the discrepancy by adding Stage 33.

As to the desert of Σίν, this one is mentioned at 13:22(21), and refers to the southern limits of the Negeb which the spies explored northward. This is not the same as the desert of Sin noted as stage seven in vv.11–12, which was located between the Red Sea and Raphaka (or Dophkah); see comment at v.11.

---

19. By B. Mazar, Eretz Israel 12, 46–48 cited by Milgrom (note 22).

In the tradition, two mss read σινα instead of Σίν, and Φαράν becomes φαρ in one ms (due to homoiarchon, the next word αὕτη beginning wtih *alpha*). The name Καδής was well-known, and the only significant variant supported by more than one ms is καδδης.

33:37 Stage 34. From Kades the Israelites journeyed "to Ὥρ the mountain near the land of Edom." The term "Hor the mountain" also occurred at 20:22—23; see the discussion at 20:22 on this interpretation of הר ההר. The same expression occurs in MT at 34:7—8 which is, however, quite different, referring to the northern borders of the Promised Land. Num is fully aware of this, and translates the expression by τὸ ὄρος τὸ ὄρος; see comment at 34:7. The location of Mt. Hor remains unclear, though much discussed. For a fair assessment, see Ashley at 20:22—23.

Its location is also more cautiously defined in Num. MT locates Mt. Hor בקצה ארץ אדום "on the edge of the land of Edom." This could be taken to mean that it was actually within Edom, right on its edge. Num avoids any such possible understanding by its πλησίον γῆς Ἐδώμ "near the land of Edom."

33:38—39 For a fuller account of Aaron's death, see 20:22—29. Here only a bare statement of his death is made, together with its date. MT states that Aaron the priest ascended אל הר ההר, a phrase which Num omitted, Admittedly, the phrase is not necessary, since Aaron ἀνέβη; furthermore, v.39 states that he died ἐν Ὥρ τῷ ὄρει. Hex, however, quite correctly added εις ωρ το ορος under the asterisk to represent the lacking phrase. The Byz text added επι το ορος, which, I suspect, is an ad sensum gloss rather than a recensional matter. Num also avoids a literal rendering of על פי יהוה by his διὰ προστάγματος κυρίου. Of course, that is what the anthropomorphic figure means; it is indeed "at the Lord's command"; Aaron was carrying out the Lord's marching orders.

The date is given based on the Exodus calendar. It took place "in the τεσσαρακοστῷ ἔτει of the exodus of the Israelites out of the land of Egypt in the fifth month on (day) one of the month." Ms 426 transposes "40th year" to equal the שנת הארבעים of MT

V.39 gives the age of Aaron when he died; he "ἦν three and twenty and a hundred years when he died." The omission of ἦν by 426 is also a revision based ultimately on MT, which has a nominal clause. The genitive is used to indicate time limits, and is here used to express the time within which Aaron died. This translates the Hebrew idiom expressing age by "son of xx years."

33:40 The full statement regarding the king of Arad and his fatal adventure with the Israelites was given in 21:1—3, which see. In fact, this verse reflects the introduction to the account in 21:1a. Syntactically, the verse is fragmentary; it reduces the opening clause of MT to a subordinate participial structure.[20] To show the fragmentary nature of the verse, one might translate it by "and on Chananis, king of Arad, hearing, while he was dwelling in the land of Canaan, when the Israelites were entering." This fails to render הנגב which precedes "in the land of Canaan," but for the rest translates the text of MT correctly, except for the reduction of the first clause to a participial structure. Hex has duly added εν τω νοτω under the asterisk to render the untranslated nominal.

The second clause in MT is a nominal one: .... והוא ישב, and Num uses the normal pattern of rendering such, viz. pronoun as subject, and a present or imperfect verb as predicate. Num reads καὶ οὗτος κατῴκει plus modifier. The ὅτε clause correctly renders the בבא בני ישראל structure.

In the tradition, the Byz text reads χαναναιος for Χανανίς, which reflects mediate (possible Theod?) Hebrew influence in rendering הכנעני as a gentilic noun.

33:41 Stage 35. From Mt.Hor the Israelites journeyed to Σελμωνά which occurs for the Hebrew צלמנה or *Salmona*. The place name occurs only in this context, and its location is unknown. In the tradition, the εἰς became εν in the A M O f+ text. Both prepositions are used with παρενέβαλον in this chapter, and the critical text throughout follows the oldest witness, cod B. The name Σελμωνά is relatively stable, though the following spellings do occur: σαλμωνα, ασελμωνα, σελμανα, σελμωναν and τελμωνα.

33:42 Stage 36 was Φινώ. It also occurs only in this context. In MT the name reads פונן or *Punan*, and it is usually identified with Khirbat Feinan, which lay on the east side of the Arabah. For its location, see Bible Dictionaries sub Punan. A popular A F M Text reads εν instead of εἰς; see comment at v.41. In the tradi-

---

20. Theod and Aq render וישמע הכנעני literally by καὶ ἤκουσεν ὁ Χαναναῖος (retroverted from Syh).

tion, the name has been revised by hex by adding a final *nu,* which resulted in a popular F text reading φινων (variant φιναν).

33:43 Stage 37 brought the community to 'Ωβώθ for MT's אבת or 'both. The place is unidentified, but it was also referred to in a similar context at 21:10—11, which see. In the tradition, the Byz text read ιωβωθ, whereas others, including B and V, read an initial *sigma* by dittography from the εἰς which preceded it, i.e. σωβωθ, as well as σαβωθ; cf also σοφωθ, σεβωθ and βωθ.

33:44 Stage 38. According to MT the next station was עיי העברים "the ruins of the area on the other side," of which Num made Γαὶ ἐν τῷ πέραν. At 21:11, Num read: And leaving from Oboth, they encamped ἐν 'Αχὲλ Γαὶ ἐκ τοῦ πέραν, where I suggested the possible understanding "in (the wadi) Gai on the other side," thus "on the opposite slope of the Gai valley"; see comment ad loc. Here, however, there is no 'Αχὲλ, but it does refer to the same region, thus "in Gai on the other side."[21] Γαί was also not familiar to copyists, who made of it γαιει (*b*), γαιν (*d*), γεειν, and even γαιδ.

33:45 Stage 39 brought the people to Δαιβὼν Γάδ. The name Δαιβών is well-known; it is the modern Dhiban, cir 6.4 km/4 miles north of the Wadi Arnon. According to 32:34 the Gadites rebuilt it, presumably giving rise to the name "Daibon of Gad." The name Δαιβών was relatively stable, only the following misspellings being witnessed in the mss: δεσβον, δεβωρ, δεβρω, δαιβωθ, δαιβω and γεδεβων.

33:46 Stage 40 is named Γελμὼν Δεβλαθάιμ for MT's עלמן דבלתימה, vocalized as ʿAlmon Diblathayəmah. It was probably referred to in the Moabite (or Mesha) Stone, line 30, where Mesha speaks of having "rebuilt [Meda]ba and Beth-diblathaim." It is now tentatively identified as Delailet eshSherqiya southeast of Amman (cir 48 km/30 miles). The name Γελμών for עלמן is unknown, and I have no satisfactory explanation for it. In the tradition, it is variously spelled: γελβων, γεδμων, γελμωλ, γελων, γεμων, γαλαμων, σελμων, σελαμαδ, γελμω, χελμων and δελμων. Δεβλαθάιμ is also chaotically dealt with as the following

---

21. Instead of ἐν Γαί, Sym has ἐν τοῖς ὑψηλοῖς.

demonstrate: δαιβααθαιμ, δαιθλαθαιμ, δαιβλαθεν, δεβαλθεν, δαιφλαθαιμ, διφθαθαιμ, δελβαθεν, δελαθαιμ, δεβλαθαιθ and δαιβλαθλαω. Also δεβλαθαμ, δεγλαθαιμ, δαιβλαθ and βλαθεν.

33:47 Stage 41 brought the people ἐπὶ τὰ ὄρη τὰ ᾽Αβαρίμ,[22] which is intended for הרי העברים "the mountains of Aberim"; this is distinct from עיי העברים; i.e. it contrasts with the "ruins (or possibly the valley, wadi; see at v.44) of Abarim." But here Num does not translate העברים, but transcribes it as a place name; comp הר העברים at 27:12, and comp Deut 32:49 and see Note ad loc. The major difference here is the plural τὰ ὄρη τά, whereas at 27:12 and Deut 32:49 τὸ ὄρος τό is read. The use of the plural makes it clear that it is not a single mountain that is intended, but a mountainous area, i.e. "the Abarim range." At 27:12 the structure is translated by τὸ ὄρος τὸ ἐν τῷ πέραν; see comment ad loc. That the area is ἀπέναντι Ναβαύ, i.e. in front of Nabau, is also clear from 27:12, where the collocation is identified as τοῦτο ὄρος Ναβαύ; in other words, the hilly area was actually called Ναβαύ.

33:48—49 Stage 42 is the final station before the crossing of the Jordan. V.48 is closely similar to 22:1, except that here they encamped ἐπὶ τοῦ ᾽Ιορδάνου, but 22:1 has παρὰ τὸν ᾽Ιορδάνην. For δυσμῶν as rendering for ערבת, see comment at 22:1. To speak of the "west" of Moab rather than "the plains" of Moab, though not in accordance with the vocalization of the Masoretes, does make sense geographically in the context. After all, the area of Moab is defined as "at the Jordan over against Jericho," both of which are on the western boundary of Moab.

V.49 defines the area where the Israelites encamped more precisely. It reads "and they encamped along the Jordan between Αισιμώθ up to Βελσαττίμ on the west of Moab." Instead of "between Haisimoth up to Belsattim," MT reads מבית הישמת עד אבל השטים. The place name בית הישמת or *Beth haYəshimoth* also occurs in Ios 13:20 where it reads Βαιθασιμώθ, and at 12:3 the name becomes κατὰ ᾽Ασιμώθ, and at Ezek 25:9, as οἶκον ᾽Ασιμούθ. Here the בית element was read as בין and translated by ἀνὰ μέσον. The name הישמת occurs only here.[23] It has now been identified as Tell el-ʿAzeimeh on the east of the Jordan just north of

---

22. For τὰ ᾽Αβαρίμ, Sym has παροδῶν (retroverted from Syh).
23. It was translated by Sym as τῆς ἀοικήτου.

the Dead Sea. It was misspelled as ασιμωθ, λισιμωθ, ασεμωθ, σιμωθ, νεσιμωθ, αισιμων and εσιμωσεα.

The name Βελσαττίμ presupposes that Num read בל or בעל rather than אבל. Furthermore, it also presupposes שטים of Sam rather than the השטים of MT. This is usually identified with the שטים of 25:1, though this could be distinct from אבל השטים or 'Abel haShittim ;see comment at 25:1. Or is אבל השטים simply the full name of השטים, which is also possible. In the tradition, the final *mu* is often changed to *nu*; the double *tau* often becomes a single one, and many witnesses through hex influence add *alpha* initially to equal MT. Other spellings include αβελσατμειμ, αβελσατθημ, αβελσαλτην, αβελσσαττειμ, αβερσαττειμ, βελεσαττιν, ωμελσαττειμ, γελσαττιμ, βελσατο and βιλσατο. For κατὰ δυσμὰς Μωάβ, see above at v.48.

33:50 For ἐπὶ δυσμῶν, see comment at v.48. For παρὰ τὸν Ἰορδάνην, cI' s+ read επι τον ιορδανην, but it becomes επι του ιορδανου in A and C under the influence of v.48.

33:51 Moses is directed to say to the Israelites: כי אתם עברים the Jordan into the land of Canaan. The כי clause is the temporal protasis for the following verses, which constitute instructions for action in the Promised Land. The כי introduces a typical nominal clause of pronoun as subject and a participle as predicate. Num as usual renders the nominal clause by a pronoun plus an inflected present tense, but failed to render the כי; hex has taken care of this by adding οτι under the asterisk. The failure is hardly a textual matter, however; it is probably merely a matter of interpretative elegance. It is hardly feasable to say "when you are crossing ... you must ...," or "because you are crossing ... you must." On the other hand, a present tense of incipient action without being bound by a ὅτι makes good sense. What Num is trying to say is "as for you, you are about to cross over the Jordan into the land of Canaan; and you must destroy ...."

33:52 The four clauses of MT form two pairs. For the first one, the verb precedes the modifiers, but for the second, the modifiers are preposed before the verb. Num does likewise. But in MT three verbs are used in an a:b::b´:c pattern, i.e. a equals the Hi of ירש; b twice equals the Pi of אבד, and c equals the Hi of שמד. Num uses only two verbs, i.e. in an a:b::a´:b´ pattern. For the rendering of the Hi of ירש in LXX, see comment at 32:21. The two pairs use the same verbs, ἀπόλλυμι and ἐξαίρω. Thus ἀπόλλυμι "to destroy" renders both the Hi of ירש "to dispossess," and the Pi of אבד "to do away with, make to vanish," and ἐξαίρω "lift up, remove" translates both the Pi of אבד and the Hi of שמד "to exterminate, annihilate." Both of these are unique readings in the Pentateuch; in fact, as a rendering for אבד it occurs only here in LXX, whereas for השמיד it occurs ten times outside the Pentateuch.[24] The different patterns of verbal choice do not distinguish the three notions of destruction in MT: dispossession, destruction and annihilation, but uses its own: "destroy" vs "remove." The change is obviously stylistically motivated.

The first clause orders the Israelites to destroy utterly "all the inhabitants of the land before your face," whereas MT has "from before," but מלפני is often rendered by a single preposition plus προσώπου.[25]

The second clause has a modifier את כל משכיתם "all their carved figures." Num has failed to note the כל, and hex has added πασας under the asterisk to represent it. More problematic is its rendering of the noun by τὰς σκοπιὰς αὐτῶν "their watchtower, place of viewing," which at first blush seems senseless. The equation is indeed unique. The word also occurs at 23:14 where שדה צפים is rendered by ἀγροῦ σκοπιάν "a watchtower of the field." The related word σκοπός is used once to render משכית describing an אבן at Lev 26:1; this becomes a λίθον σκοπόν as an object of worship; see Note ad loc. Dorival makes the interesting observation that "Les points d'observation sont les sommets où les Chananéens rendent leur culte à leurs dieux."[26] The term may then refer to high places.[27]

The third clause in MT reads "and all their molten images you must do away with," to which Num adds an otiose αὐτά, which hex correctly placed under the obelus. Syntactically, Num begins with an absolute accusative, "and as for all their molten idols," after which "you must destroy them" makes good sense. The omission by the $d+$ text of αὐτά is an easier reading, and is of course not original.

---

24. According to HR.
25. Only Syh has a double rendering for מלפני: mn qdm prṣwp' with mn under a sign which must have been intended as an asterisk.
26. P.554; the point is made in describing the place where Balak built seven altars.
27. Schl notes in commenting on this passage: "σκοπίας sunt loca excelsa, in quibus idola exposita erant."

The final clause, "and all their pillars (or stelae) you must remove" renders ואת כל במתם תשמידו "and all their high places you must annihilate." For στήλας as rendering for במות, see Note at Lev 26:30. It also occurs in Num at 21:28 22:41, but the term is never correctly rendered in the Pentateuch.

33:53 The first clause in MT reads והורשתם את הארץ "and you shall inherit the land." But in v.52 MT had read והורשתם את כל ישבי הארץ, and Num had translated the verb by ἀπολεῖτε. But it does not make much sense to say "and you shall destroy the land"; one can only destroy those who occupy it,—and Num reads "and you must destroy πάντας τοὺς κατοικοῦντας τὴν γῆν (and dwell in it)." This is not a case of harmonization with v.53, which reads "all those dwelling ἐν τῇ γῇ," and the translator in my opinion by using the accusative τὴν γῆν differentiates this verse from v.52. I would now also understand πάντας as an early intrusion into the text, regarding it as an intrusion from v.52. It is supported by the B M V Byz x+ text, whereas all others omit it. In fact, it seems clear that the πάντας was not present in Origen's text, since only τοὺς κατοικοῦντας is under the obelus. If the πάντας had been present, it too would have been included under it. I would now remove the πάντας from the critical text.

The reason for all these actions which must be done is given in a γάρ clause: ὑμῖν γὰρ δέδωκα τὴν γῆν αὐτῶν ἐν κλήρῳ. MT reads את הארץ לרשת אתה "the land to inherit it." Hex tried to make the text equal the Hebrew by transposing αὐτῶν and ἐν κλήρῳ, but that is atypical of LXX Greek; in fact, ἐν κλήρῳ occurs with a genitive pronoun elsewhere only at Iud 1:3, where Ioudas speaks to his brother Simeon "go up with me ἐν τῷ κλήρῳ μου ... and I will go with you ἐν τῷ κλήρῳ σου." But in the context of God's gift of land, the set idiom is simply ἐν κλήρῳ. That את הארץ should become τὴν γῆν αὐτῶν is hardly surprising. Since it is the inhabitants of the land whom you must destroy, what the Lord gives "to you" is "their land."

33:54 MT begins by "and you shall take possession for yourselves of the land by lot, according to your clans."[28] Num translates the Hithp verb by κατακληρονομήσετε, which also stresses the taking of possession, but the remainder of the

---

28. "lot," i.e. גורל, is rendered literally by κλῆρος. According to Dos Santos, this occurs 62 out of 69 times as its translation. The other seven cases are rendered by ὅριον (five times), and κληρονομία (twice).

clause differs somewhat from MT. First of all, "their land" in Num renders "land"; hex has placed the αὐτῶν under the obelus to show its lack of a correspondent in MT; and then, instead of למשפחתיכם, Num has κατὰ φυλὰς ὑμῶν, but the "tribe" was a larger social unit than the clan. Num presupposes only twelve lots, whereas in MT the lot was used to decide among the clans within the tribes. But whether and how these terms were intended to differentiate is not overly clear. Were the tribes first assigned a given territory, and then the clans within these tribal boundaries given their land by lot? That seems to be the intent of the last clause of the verse.

The principle that is to be followed for assignment of land is that of size. Thus "τοῖς πλείοσιν you must increase their holding, and τοῖς ἐλάττοσιν you must decrease their holding." MT has נחלתו "his share," since רב and מעט are both singular, but Num quite sensibly uses plurals "to those having more," and "to those having less," and so uses αὐτῶν. Oddly enough, MT changed to the singular midway. For "you must increase," the plural תרבו is retained, but for "you must decrease" the singular תמעיט obtains, for no obvious reason. Num has simplified this by making both plural. According to MT, Moses is the addressee for תמעיט, which is strange indeed, since Moses would not be allowed to enter the Promised Land. The Num text by using the plural is more rational. The Sam text has the singular for both verbs, i.e. Moses is ordered to make the assignment of the land.

Specifically for the individual, "εἰς ὃ ἄν whose name goes out there, his shall it be."[29] This constitutes an interpretation of MT's "to that which the lot goes out thither, his shall it be." Num seems to presuppose the kind of lot by which one's name is drawn, ἐξέλθῃ τὸ ὄνομα αὐτοῦ. Apparently, the translator translated שמה twice, first as τὸ ὄνομα αὐτοῦ, and then as ἐκεῖ. But all of this was confined למטות אבתיכם; in other words, the individual משפחה would receive its inheritance only within the tribal boundaries, i.e. "according to the tribes of your paternal ancestry." Note by the way that ההנחלו is now translated by the simplex κληρονομήσετε. In the tradition, an M Byz s^{ms}+ text has added an explanatory (ο) κλῆρος before the prepositional phrase. It is of course secondary, and has no equivalent in MT, which is made explicit by Syh which placed it under the obelus. The gloss must, however, have entered the text before the time of Origen's hex.

---

29. Theod has οὗ ἄν, whereas Sym has ὅταν ἄν.

33:55 "But should you not destroy those dwelling in the land"; Num renders the initial conjunction by a contrastive δέ. MT does not support the preposition ἐπί, and a number of witnesses, among then G-376, both O mss, read την γην instead of ἐπὶ τῆς γῆς; this could be a hex correction. The apodosis is introduced by καὶ ἔσται "then it will happen." What will happen is "whomever you might have left over of them (shall be) σκόλοπες in your eyes and βολίδες (i.e. spears) in your sides." A σκόλοψ is something pointed and sharp, and is intended to render שכים, a hapax legomenon possibly meaning "thorns," thus sharp objects in your eyes. The word βολίδες is used to render צנינם "darts, goads," a word which only occurs once elsewhere. Furthermore, "they will act in hostile fashion upon the land on which you will be dwelling." In MT, the verb (צררו) is modified by אתכם, and the majority A F M V text has added υμιν; this could be hex; it is certainly secondary.

33:56 The verse by its introductory καὶ ἔσται is coordinated to the καὶ ἔσται introducing the apodosis in v.55. Thus "if you do not destroy those dwelling in the land ..., and it will happen as I had intended to effect them, I will effect you," i.e. what I intended as their fate, will become yours. The use of an accusative modifier for ποιῆσαι and ποιήσω is unusual, and most witnesses have simplified this by changing αὐτούς to αυτοις, and ὑμᾶς to υμιν, but the more difficult accusative pronouns are to be preferred as original text; incidentally, the accusatives are supported by our oldest witnesses, B and 963. Hex has added the article του under the asterisk to render the infinitival marker ל of לעשות.

Chapter 34

34:2 Moses has been ordered: "command the Israelites, and say to them." In the tradition, the hex text has added λεγων under the obelus; in other words, Origen's Greek text must have had the gloss. As at 33:51, a כי clause introduces a nominal structure of pronoun plus participle, which Num translates without the כי, but renders the nominal clause in its usual way with a pronoun followed by a present tense verb. As expected, hex has added οτι under the asterisk to represent the כי. The context here is, however, rather different from that at 33:51, which the critical text makes clear by its punctuation. There the comma showed that the nominal is actually a temporal protasis; see comment ad loc. Here, however, Num has interpreted the Hebrew as a simple statement of fact as is clear from the colon: "You are on the point of entering the land of Canaan." It should be noted that in MT the text reads הארץ כנען, i.e. כנען is in apposition with הארץ; it means "the land, Canaan." But Num cannot differentiate between "land, Canaan" and "land of Canaan," since Χαναάν is never articulated in LXX.

V.b then states: "This will become for you the inheritance (or possession), the land of Canaan together with its borders." MT has a fuller statement reading "this הארץ אשר will fall to you as an inheritance ...." The words הארץ אשר have been omitted in Num, and hex has added η γη ητις under the asterisk to represent MT in full. Furthermore, the Hebrew תפל ל "shall fall to" is correctly understood as ἔσται plus a dative, since the reference is to ἐν κλήρῳ of 33:54. It is the lot that is referred to; "it will fall to you," which means "it will become yours." In the tradition, the majority A F M V text removes the article from τὴν κληρονομίαν, though both B and 963 support it. But the pattern in Num is to articulate κληρονομία throughout, except in such contexts where it is exegetically indefinite in intent.[1] The concluding prepositional phrase σὺν τοῖς ὁρίοις αὐτῆς "with its borders" is not quite what MT means by its לגבלתיה "according to its borders"; what is intended is "as defined by its borders." A κατά phrase would have been a better rendering.

---

1. See THGN 108.

34:3 "The side which is πρὸς λίβα shall be (i.e. will extend) for you from the desert of Σίν up to ἐχόμενον Edom."² The desert of Sin is צן in Hebrew, which is also mentioned at 13:22 and 33:36; see comment at 33:36. The name Σίν is ambiguous in Greek, since it can transcribe either צן or סין (as at 33:11—12). The combination ἕως ἐχόμενον is peculiar. It represents על ידי "besides, alongside of (Edom)."³ Presumably, what Num says is "up to besides," thus "up to the borders of."

V.b then explains "the borders to the south as being from the part of the Salt Sea which is on the east," i.e. the delineation of the southern boundary is to begin at its eastern edge at the Salt Sea. It might be noted that the translator follows the Classical rule for the neuter plural, ὅρια, as a collective noun; i.e. it is treated as a singular. The term μέρους renders קצה "edge." Since what is being described is the extent of the Promised Land, the term גבול "boundary" is throughout rendered by the plural (τὰ) ὅρια. Since MT reads גבול נגב, hex found τὰ ὅρια πρὸς λίβα not fully adequate, and articulated the prepositional phrase, i.e. added τα before πρός. Note that the bound phrase ים המלח is well-rendered by an adjectival phrase.

34:4 "(Then) the borders will curve around you southward to the Ascent of Ἀκραβίν." Since MT reads עקרבים, the correction to a final -mu is probably hex in origin. It was variously spelled including ακριβιν, ακραββειν, ακαβειν and κραρειν. The Ascent of Akrabin is not certainly known, but is often identified with Naqb asSafa cir 40 miles/65 km south of Hebron. Then the borders are to go through Σέννα, which Num took to be the name of some town.⁴ All that can be said of Σέννα is that it is a transcription of צנה, which probably refers to the wilderness of צן. In the tradition, it becomes σιννα, σειν, οσενακ, σεννακ, σενναχ, σεναχ, οεννακ, σεεναακ, σενααακ, σενακ, σεεννααακ, σεενεακ, σενδακ, σεεννακ, εννααακ, εναακ, εννακ, εννακχ, εναακ, εεννακ, εναχ and εννασή. Obviously, copyists had not the vaguest idea what or where Σέννα was.

---

2. Instead of λίβα, The Others read νότον.
3. In fact, Tar^JO render by על תחומי "along the borders of," and Tar^N translates similarly.
4. Dorival identifies it as the Σεννα of the Egyptian recension (Cod B+) at Ios 15:37, which, however, Margolis took to be a corruption of an original Senan, presumably by the transposition of -αν. This makes the identification highly dubious.

MT then states that תוצאתיו ("its limits") shall be to the south. Num renders this by ἡ διέξοδος αὐτοῦ "its outlet, passage." The term "its outlet" means that going southward the border ends here, south of Καδης τοῦ Βαρνή, usually identified with ʿain Qadesh.

Thereafter, it is to go out to the ἔπαυλιν Ἀράδ. For ἔπαυλις as a rendering for חצר, see Note at Lev 25:31. The term חצר refers to villages as over against fortified cities. The city of Arad is well-known, and lies cir. 25 km south of Hebron; see Bible Dictionaries. Thereafter the borders pass along Ἀσεμωνα for עצמנה; the place is unknown. It appears in the tradition as ασεβωνα, ασαμωνα, σεσεμονα, ασσαβωνα, αλσεμωνα, ασελμωνα, σελμωνα and σελμων.

34:5 "The borders from Asemona shall then go around the wadi of Egypt, and the outlet (or terminus) shall be the Sea." Num follows Sam's נחל "wadi," rather than the נחלה "property, possession" of MT, probably correctly. The reference is to the Wadi ʿArish. As at v.4, reference is made to תוצאתיו "its limits" (referring to the גבול), and is translated by ἡ διέξοδος.[5] Hex is followed by Byz in adding αυτου to represent the suffix. Thus "the outlet shall be The Sea." ἡ θάλασσα refers to the Mediterranean Sea. MT actually reads הימה, "seaward," but Sam has הים, which is a better candidate for parent text to Num.

34:6 The Sam text reads "And the border ימה (westward) shall be (יהיה) to you; the great sea shall act as border (יגבל); this shall be for you the border westward (ימה)." Note that MT has וגבול ים והיה לכם, i.e. והיה is a corruption of יהיה. Furthermore, it reads וגבול for Sam's יגבל. Beyond this, Sam distinguishes between ים "sea" and ימה "westward," which makes excellent sense; at the end of the verse Sam also uses ימה rather than ים. Num follows the clearer text of Sam throughout the verse. The translator was also bedeviled by the fact that ים not only means "sea," but The Sea being to the west of Canaan is also used to mean "west." Since Num refers to λίβα and βορρᾶν as well as to ἀνατολῶν, one must render τὰ ὅρια τῆς θαλάσσης by "the borders of the west." I would translate the verse in Num: "And the borders of the west shall be for you; the Great Sea shall act as boundary; this shall be for you the borders of the west." That τοῦτο has no obvious referent is hardly relevant; it simply refers to "the foregoing."

---

5. See SS 99.

34:7 "And this shall be for you גבול צפון," but Num calls this τὰ ὅρια ... πρὸς βορρᾶν. Possily its parent text was that of Sam, צפונה, though not necessarily, since the southern border in v.3 also read a prepositional phrase in τὰ ὅρια πρὸς λίβα. In fact, Sam refers to all the borders throughout with a directive *hē*: נגבה, ימה, צפונה and קדמה, whereas MT does not. For this border: "from the Great Sea you must measure out for yourselves along τὸ ὅρος τὸ ὅρος." In MT this is הר ההר which also occurred at 33:37, which see. This is, however, not the Mt. Hor where Aaron died, but is a mountainous area at the northern edge of Canaan. Num carefully distinguishes the two; at 33:37 it was called Ὤρ τὸ ὅρος, but here Num speaks of measuring out παρὰ τὸ ὅρος τὸ ὅρος "along the mountain range"; even the preposition is carefully chosen, and the measuring out is to take place along the mountains, i.e. along a string of mountains. The verb used in MT is slightly different; תתאו means "to mark out." In the tradition, πρὸς βορρᾶν is articulated, for which the comment at v.3 may also apply. The majority A F M V text's omission of τὸ ὅρος 2° is of course a case of haplography in view of MT's הר ההר.

34:8 Num begins with καί over against MT, following Sam's ומהר. From this verse it is clear that τὸ ὅρος is the designation for τοῦ ὅρους. What Num actually says grammatically is "from the mountainous region The Mountain Range," but what is meant is simply "the mountain range" as in v.7; cf comment ad loc. For καταμετρήσετε, also see comment at v.7. The αὐτοῖς has no counterpart in MT, and was apparently put under the obelus in hex. It means the same as ὑμῖν αὐτοῖς in v.7, thus "you shall measure out for yourselves at the entrance of Hamath," for which see comment at 13:22. The participle is a genitive of place at which: "at the entrances of Hamath." It constitutes a mistaken attempt at rendering לבוא, not recognizing it as a place name; in other words, MT intends "at Libweh of Hamath."

"And its outlet (ἡ διέξοδος) shall be the border of Σαραδά." This differs somewhat from MT, which reads והיו תוצאת הגבל צדדה. "and the extensions of the boundary shall go to Sadad."[6] תוצאת הגבל is a bound phrase, but Num has rewritten the clause completely, making τὰ ὅρια a predicate nominative modi-

---

6. The Others read Σαδαδά.

fying ἔσται; it has followed the pattern καὶ ἔσται ἡ διέξοδος αὐτοῦ as in v.4, and comp. also vv.6,9 and 12. Oddly enough, hex apparently did not place αὐτοῦ under the obelus, though it has no equivalent in MT. The *hē* directive was also misunderstood and made to be part of the name; furthermore, Σαραδά again illustrates the easy confusion of ר and ד. The place has been identified as Sedad on the edge of the desert, cir 55 km distant from Hamath. The name Σαραδά is dependent on the Sam reading צרדה. In the tradition, a popular B text read σαραδακ; the final *kappa* is a dittograph from the next letter, i.e. from καί. Also attested are σαρδακ, σαρδαχ, σαραδαδ, γαραδα, αραδακ, ασαραδδακ, as well as without *rho*: σαδαδα, σαδδακ, σαδακ, σασαδακ, σεδακ, ασαδακ and καδδακ.

34:9 "And the borders shall extend to Ζεφρώνα (for וזפרנה), and its outlet shall be at Ἀσερναίν." Neither place has been identified, but both were probably somewhere east of Sadad in the Syrian desert. In the tradition, the initial letter of Ζεφρώνα seemed to give trouble; note the spellings εφρωνα, εφρων, εφρωννα, εφωννα, εζεφρωνα, σεφρωνα, φρωνα and even δεφρωνα (but only in B);[7] one ms even had εξ εφρωνα; cf also ζεβρωνα.

The second name, Ἀσερναίν, represents MT's חצר עינן. The חצר equivalent, ασερ, also appears as αρσε, αρσερ, σερ, αρερ, ασε and ασαρ, but the second element, ναίν, suffered greatly as ναειμ, ναι, ενα, ηναν (in 426, obviously a correction based on the Hebrew), νασι, ναη, νααμ and αιν.

The description of the northern limits of the land ends with the subscription τοῦτο ἔσται ὑμῖν ὅρια ἀπὸ βορρᾶ. In MT this is a bound phrase גבול צפון, but Num interprets by an ἀπό phrase "borders from the north."[8]

34:10 The opening verb in MT differs from its parallels in vv.7–8 תתאו "to mark," which were translated by the verb καταμετρέω "measure out." Here, however, MT has התאויתם, but it is also rendered by the verb καταμετρέω. It seems clear that the root אוה is to be understood simply as a lexical variant of the root תאה, and not the well-known verb אוה "to desire," which would be rather senseless in this context. The לגבול קדמה is rendered by an accusative structure τὰ ὅρια ἀνατολῶν "the borders of the east," which disregards the preposition. The Byz text has added εἰς before τά, which is clearly a recensional correction,

---

7. See THGN 120.
8. See SS 69.

probably from one of The Three. These borders extend from Ἀσερναίν, for which see v.9, to Σεπφάμα, but the unstressed -α at the end represents a transcription of שפמה in which the final hē is directional, i.e. "to Shepham."⁹ This is fully clear from v.11 where the boundary reads משפם "from Shepham." That the translator misunderstood this is clear from the transcription Σεπφάμα here, but as Σεπφάμ at v.11. The place is unknown. In the tradition, it has been corrected by a prepositional gloss εως in 13 mss (mainly *ol z*), but this is ad sensum. The spelling varies considerably. Note the following: σεμφαμαρ, εμφαμαρ, σεπφαμαρ, σεφαμαρ, σεμφαμα, σεφαμα, σεπφαγμα, ασεφαμα, σεφαμαρ, σεμπφαμαρ and εφαμαρ.

34:11 Since none of the names in this verse, except for Χενέρεθ, is known, any reconstruction either of the Hebrew or the Greek must be in part conjectural. Roughly what Num seems to say is "and the borders shall go down from Sepham (to) Harbela eastward at (the) fountains, and the borders shall go down from Bela at the slope (literally the back) of the sea of Chenereth eastwards," i.e. the eastern slope of the Sea. The Hebrew is unfortunately not a bit clearer. It reads for "(to) Harbela" הרבלה "to Riblah," but this place is also unknown; it is certainly not the Riblah on the Orontes known from 2 Kgs 25:6. Riblah is said to be מקדם לעין "east of ʿAin," but that is no help, since that too is not known. Num translated the name by πηγάς "springs."

From there "the boundary shall go down and shall strike upon the eastern slope (shoulder) of the Sea of Kinnereth." Num obviously did not identify Bela as Arbela, as the context would seem to demand. The problem is that MT has no basis for mentioning either Bela or Arbela, since instead of a proper name it has ומחה "and shall strike." What is meant is that the boundary shall crash (i.e. land) on to the eastern slope of the Sea. Hex has made two changes: it has placed Βηλά under the obelus, and then added και συγκρουσει under the asterisk to represent the Hebrew ומחה.

In the tradition, Ἀρβελά appears as βηλα, αρβολα, αρβαλα, αρβηλ and αρναειν. The name Βηλά was misspelled as βηλ, αβηλ, αρβηλ, αρβηλα and even ισραηλ. The name Χενέρεθ was also misspelled as χεννερεθ, χερενεθ, χερεθ, χερερεθ, χενερ, χεναρ, χειναρ, χενερα, χεναρα, χεννερα, χενναρα, χενναερεθρα and χελαινερα.¹⁰

---

9. The Others read Σεφάμα.
10. See THGN 120.

34:12 The eastern border now becomes clear; from the Sea of Chenereth "the borders will descend down (ἐπί) the Jordan, and the outlet shall be the Salt Sea," for which see comment at v.3. MT has תוצאתיו, i.e. with a suffix, and hex has added αυτου after διέξοδος.[11]

V.b is a subscription to vv.1—11, the section tracing the outer boundaries, or borders of the Promised Land. "This shall be for you the land καὶ τὰ ὅρια αὐτῆς κύκλῳ." MT puts it a bit differently: "the land לגבלתיה round about," i.e. according to its boundaries.[12] It might appear that the change of καὶ τὰ (ὅρια) to κατα in cod G constituted a hex correction, but it is nothing of the sort; it is a common palaeographically inspired mistake.

34:13 Moses now addresses the Israelites about the division of the land. The land of Canaan is the land "which you will take it as an inheritance μετὰ κλήρου." The active verb renders a Hithp תתנחלו "you will take for yourselves as an inheritance." The μετά phrase renders בגורל, in which the ב is instrumental, thus "by lot."[13] The use of μετά with the genitive to express instrument is somewhat unusual, but it does occur in the sense of "in common with."[14] A convincing parallel obtains in Exod 3:19: μετὰ χειρὸς κραταιᾶς.

הארץ is modified by a second אשר clause in MT, "which Yahweh commanded to give (to the nine tribes and the half tribe)." Num made this a ὃν τρόπον clause, i.e. "as the Lord commanded." It is possible that the translator had כאשר, though this is by no means certain. Num also added αὐτήν after δοῦναι, and hex placed the pronoun under the obelus to show that it had no counterpart in MT, but this became necessary once the אשר was translated by ὃν τρόπον. In the tradition, the B Byz+ text added a dative τω μωυση after συνέταξεν κύριος. Since it is Moses speaking, putting himself as the indirect object of συνέταξεν by name as the indirect object is odd (though not impossible), but it is secondary; it has no basis in MT, nor is it expected; its source is ex par, since the statement "the Lord ordered (or addressed) Moses" appears with almost monotonous frequency through the last four books of the Pentateuch.[15]

---

11. The Others also read ἡ διέξοδος αὐτου.
12. And see THGN 130.
13. See SS 121, and comp p.119.
14. See LS sub voce A.II.
15. See THGN 135.

The datives modifying δοῦναι are quite in order; they are "to the nine and a half tribes," which half tribe is identified in Num as Μανασσή. Hex placed the name under the obelus, since MT does not have it, but it is based on v.14, and see also 32:33.

34:14 MT had a plural verb לקחו before the compound subjects "the tribe of the Reubenites and the tribes of the Gadites," but Num follows its usual practice with compound subjects following the verb, viz. attraction of number to the nearer subject, φυλή 1°, thus ἔλαβεν.[16] The Byz text, however, changed the verb to the plural, which could be a recensional change, though not necessarily. Unusual is the use of the gentilic to designate the Israelite tribes, i.e. as בני הראובני and בני הגדי. Normal usage would be בני ראובן and בני גד, in fact, when ראובני does occur in MT (see Deut 4:43 29:7) it becomes 'Ρουβήν in the Greek. The gentilic גדי which also occurs in Deuteronomy, at 4:43 29:8(7) becomes Γαδδί, though not at 3:12,16. In fact, the tribal designations "the sons of the Roubenites" and "the sons of the Gadites" occur only rarely, the former only here, and the latter elsewhere only at 2Sam 23:36.

Num has shortened the text of MT. In MT both "the Reubenite" and "the Gadite" are followed by לבית אבתם, but Num has κατ' οἴκους πατριῶν αὐτῶν only after Γάδ. Hex has also added the phrase under the asterisk after 'Ρουβήν.

The last clause reads "and the half tribe of Manasse ἀπέλαβον their τοὺς κλήρους." Note that here "tribe" is taken as a plural concept, since the verb is plural, as are the pronoun αὐτῶν and the noun κλήρους; thus "the half tribe of Manasse took their shares." The Masoretes, however, vocalized נחלתם as "their heritage," i.e. as a singular noun, but it was correctly understood as a collective noun, as the plural verb and pronominal suffix demand.

34:15 As in v.14, the singular noun נחלתם is rendered as a plural noun; in fact, its collective force is sensible; the suffix does refer to two and a half tribes. The force of ἔλαβον here is best rendered by a pluperfect; the action of taking their κλήρους was anterior to that of the nine and a half tribes.

The location of their heritages in Transjordan is viewed differently in Num. In MT, it is located ירחו קדמה מזרחה "at (i.e. opposite) Jericho eastward,

---

16. See THGN 122.

towards the sunrise." This probably struck the translator as tautologous, and he changed this to read (κατὰ 'Ιεριχὼ) ἀπὸ νότου κατ' ἀνατολάς, i.e. "from the south (side) towards the East." The notion of south-east with respect to Jericho is not entirely incorrect.[17]

34:17 Vv.17—29 give the names of the men who are responsible for dividing up the lands, but according to v.17 Eleazar and Yesous the son of Naue κληρονομήσουσιν ὑμῖν τὴν γῆν "inherit for you the land." This is exactly what MT says as well, with its ינחלו vocalized as a Qal. But the context requires a factitive sense, i.e. "make to inherit," and it is possible that the Qal should be understood in this way as well.[18] Num, however, has translated the Qal in its usual sense, and one must ask what the translator understood this to mean. It would seem that for Num Eleazar and Yesous were to serve as intermediaries; first, they, as the leaders of the people, receive the land of Canaan as the temporary, holding heirs of the land, and only thereafter tribal chieftains are to function as the assigners of land, i.e. vv.18—29. Comp also comment at 36:2.

34:18 "And you must take one chieftain out of a tribe to hand over to you the land as an inheritance."[19] Num does distinguish between the κληρονομήσουσιν of v.17, i.e. "shall inherit," and κατακληρονομῆσαι, which distinction is preserved by my rendering "to hand over as an inheritance." Clearly Num is trying to distinugish between the function of the verb of v.17 and that of v.18.

In MT נשיא אחד is repeated in the distributive sense, i.e. one chieftain for each tribe.[20] Hex has added a second αρχοντα ενα under the asterisk to represent the Hebrew text. Greek does not normally express the distributive in this fashion, and the repetition of "one chieftain" does not help a Greek reader's understanding; all it does is record the Hebrew idiom in Greek words, but then that is what

---

17. Dorival 155 states " ... par rapport à Jericho, le dévolu á Gad, Roubên et Manassê se situe moins á l'est qu'au sub-est."
18. In fact, most commentators emend the verb to the Pi; see e.g. BHS which orders: "read the Pi," here as well as for לנחל in v.18. Ashley (p.642 Note 1) points out that the meaning "to mark out for inheritance" is required by the context not only here but also in v.18 and at Ios 19:49. He says: "One wonders whether the better course is not to posit that the Qal may mean both 'to inherit' and 'to mark out for inheritance' rather than to emend three readings to fit another pattern." I suspect that he is right.
19. The ἐκ renders a partitive מן; see SS 168.
20. See GK 134q.

Origen sought to do in the Hexapla. A second difference between MT and Num is the addition of ὑμῖν in harmonization with v.17 where it occurs in exactly the same context. Hex has placed the ὑμῖν under the obelus to indicate that it had no basis in MT.

34:19 Throughout this chapter, Num uses the genitive to render the prepositional phrase למטה, thus τῆς φυλῆς. Presumably, in each case the person appointed was a member of the tribe, but that is not the point being made. The preposition would be better served by a dative of advantage, i.e. "for, on behalf of" the tribe; Num fails to make this point.

The man to κατακληρονομῆσαι for the tribe of Judah, presumably, the one to cast the κλῆρος, "the lot," was Χαλέβ the son of Ἰεφοννή. For the treatment of these names, see comment at 13:7(6).

34:20 Num is asyndetic over against MT, but Sam is also without an initial conjunction. MT refers to "the tribe of בני שמעון," but Num simply reads τὴν φυλῆς Συμεών. Hex has inserted υιων to represent the untranslated בני.[21] MT names the Simeonite chieftain as שמואל the son of עמיהוד. Num names him Σαλαμιήλ, which must have been due to the influence of the name of the tribal leader from the Simeonites assisting Moses and Aaron in conducting the first census in 1:6. The tribal representative was also named Σαλαμιήλ, but his parentage was different; he was the son of Σουρισαδαί; see also 2:12 7:36,41 and 10:19.[22] Num is of course in error.

In the tradition, the name appears as σαμαλιηλ, σαδαμιηλ, σαλαμηλ, σαμηλ, σαλαμινα, σαμρηλ and σαμουηλ (which is a marginal reading from one of The Three). The name Ἐμιούδ represents עמיהוד, and became αμιουδ,[23] as well as εμιουλ, ιεμιουδ, σεμιουδ, σεμεουδ and σεμιουλ in the tradition.

34:21 For the tribe of Benjamin Ἐλδάδ son of Χασλών did service. The name Ἐλδάδ also occurs as the name of a prophet at 11:26—27, but that one had nothing to do with this Benjaminite. In MT the name is אלידד, but Num follows the אלדד of Sam. The spelling was corrected through Hebrew influence in ms

---

21. The Others also add υἱῶν.
22. Aq and Sym both read Σαμουήλ.
23. The Others also read Ἀμιούδ.

426 to ελιδαδ. Other spellings include ελδααδ, ελααδ, ελεαδ, ελδαν, ελδας, αελδαν, ελαδ, ελεαδαδ, ιελιαδ, εαδαλ, ελιαβ and ελαβαν. Χασλών transcribes כסלון, and also received relatively harsh treatment at the hands of copyists. It was misspelled as χασδων, χασλωμ, χελων, σχαλων, χαιαλων, χεσαων, χασμων, χαλων, χασχων and χασελω. Incidentally, the Masoretic vocalization of the first syllable of כסלון with an "i" vowel is a regular development in an unstressed closed syllable from an earlier "a" vowel as represented in the Greek transcription.

34:22 The chieftain from the tribe of Dan was Βακχίρ the son of ’Εγλί. MT reads ומטה בני דן. Num follows Sam in its למטה.[24] Ms 426 and Byz correct Num by inserting υιων before Δάν, clearly a recensional reading.[25]

Βακχίρ has as counterpart in MT בקי. A *qoph* is otherwise transliterated simply by a *kappa*, and the -κχ- might seem problematic.[26] The Masoretic vocalization places a *daghesh* in the *qoph*, and the -κχ- may be an attempt to produce a heightened consonant in this fashion. There is, of course, the further problem of the final *rho*. It seems to me obvious that the parent text could not have been בקי, but must have been *בקיר. In the tradition, the misspellings may be divided into two groups, i.e. one group with, and the other one without, a *rho*. For the former, there are βακκειρ, βαχχιρ, βαχειρ, βοκκιρ, βαρχειρ, ακχειρ and μαχιρ. For the latter group, there are βακχι, βοκχι, μοκκι, βαχκι, μακχι, βακκε, βακκο, βοκκαι, βακειν, κοκκι, βαχχη, βοκι, βοκ, βοβκι and βοκκι. The father's name is ’Εγλί for the Hebrew יגלי. Other spellings include εκλι, εγλι, ελγει, εκχι, εκχειν, ιεγλι, ιογαι, ιοηλι, ιεκλι, ιοκλι, ιεκαι, σεκλι, συκλη, σιεκλι and σεκχι.

34:23 The verse begins with τῶν υἱῶν ’Ιωσήφ, which is meant to introduce both "the tribe of the Manassites" (v.23) and "the tribe of the Ephraimites" (v.24). For the Manassites the chieftain was ’Ανιήλ for חניאל; in the Byz text, this appears as αιηλ. The father's name, Οὐφίδ, was misspelled in various ways: as εφιδ, ουφει, and by dittography of the *sigma* of υιος: σουφιρ, σουφιλ, σουφιηλ, σουβηθ, σουφ(ε)ι (B M V 963 *b n+*), σεφι, σουφιδ. In spite of the impressive

---
24. Kenn 5,69,75,129,146 and 181 also read למטה.
25. The Others also add υἱῶν.
26. See THGN 118.

support for a final vowel spelling, this can only be secondary; MT has אפד, and only Οὐφίδ can be original.[27]

34:24 Over against MT Num begins asyndetically for vv.24—28. In v.24 this is particularly unfortunate, since a conjunction is expected to designate "the sons of Joseph" as "the tribe of the Manassites" *and* "the tribe of the Ephraimites." For the tribe of the Ephraimites, the chieftain was Καμουήλ the son of Σαβαθά. Καμουήλ, for קמואל, was very stable in the tradition, but Σαβαθά has as its MT counterpart שפטן. The name was misspelled in a variety of ways; cod A read σαβαθαν, and other spellings include σεβαθα, σαβαθαι, αβαθα, σαφατα, αμαθα, αβαθ, σεβαμα, αφαθα, σαφαταν, σαφταν (possibly hex), σατφαν, σαφαν, σαφτνα, σοφιταν, σαφσαν, σαφιταν, and even σαβαωδ.

34:25 MT reads בני זבולן, but Num has only Ζαβουλών, and hex corrects the text by adding υιων to represent the בני of MT. The name was a common one, though the tradition did confuse the name as ελισαφα, ελισαφαμ, ελισαφατ, ελισαφαθ, ελισαφαφ and ελισαφ. The chieftain's name was 'Ελισαφάν, not to be confused with the 'Ελισαφάν of 3:30, or of Exod 6:22 Lev 10:4. The father's name, however, set this 'Ελισαφάν apart. Φαρνάχ represents פרנך, and it is misspelled as φαναχ, φαραναχ, χαρναχ, φεναχ, φιναχ, φαρμαχ, εφαιναχ, φαρναχαν, φαρνααν, βανιναχ and ναχ.

34:26 The chieftain of the Issacharite tribe was Φαλτιήλ, representing פלטיאל. In the tradition, this appeared as φαλτινα, φαλτιην, φαντιηλ, φαλτηδ, φαατιηλ and φατιηλ. The father's name gave very little trouble. 'Οζά for עזן is unexpected, but corrections adding a final *nu* occur in only a few mss; all the uncials, all *O* mss, read 'Οζά, and οζαν is probably only a coincidence, not a recensional reading. It also occurred as ζα and αζευ. The parent text must have read something like עצה*.

34:27 For the tribe of the Asherites, the chieftain was 'Αχιωρ son of Σελεμί. MT has אחיהוד בן שלמי. The *daleth* was misread as *resh*, which is palaeographically explicable. The appearance of *rho* in the variants αρχιωρ and αριωχ is irrelevant;

---

27. See THGN 120.

the variants are due to common morphemes or names in Hebrew. Other variants are αχιηρ, αλιωρ, αχιωβ, αχιηλ and αχιω. For Σελεμί, wrong spellings include σεδεμι, σελαμι, ελεμι, συμελει, σεμιδι, σεμελι and σελεμ.

34:28 Instead of ולמטה בני נפתלי, Num reads an asyndetic τῆς φυλῆς Νεφθαλί, and without recognition of בני. Hex has duly noted the latter by adding υιων before Νεφθαλί to represent MT correctly. For the common spelling of Νεφθαλί with a final closed syllable, see Note at Gen 30:8, the first occurrence of the name. The chieftain's name was Φαδαήλ for פהדאל. In the tradition, this easily became φαδιηλ, as well as φαλαηλ, φαναηλ, φαλδαηλ, δαηλ, and even φαβιηλ and φαλανα. According to MT, he was בן עמיהוד "son of Amioud," but Num read בן twice, both as υἱός and as Βεν(αμιούδ). This developed into βενιαμιουδ, βενιαμεινιουδ, σελεμιουδ, σεμελιουδ, σελελιουλ and βενε. Possible revision towards MT might be seen in ιαμιουδ, εμιουδ, αβιουδ, ιαβιουδ, σαμιου and αμιουδ.

34:29 The subscription identifies the above list of chieftains as constituting "the ones οἷς the Lord gave command καταμερίσαι to the Israelites in the land of Canaan." Since ἐντέλλομαι is often modified by a dative of person, οἷς is not unexpected.[28] A popular variant text also reads ους. The verb καταμερίζω occurs only here for the Pi of נחל. It occurs once for the Hi at Deut 19:3 with κύριος as subject. Elsewhere it is attested only for the Hithp (in the passive at 32:18, which see, and as καταμεριεῖτε αὐτοὺς τοῖς τέκνοις ὑμῶν at Lev 25:46; see Note ad loc). Here the verb is most appropriate; it means "to divide up, distribute." The verb was, however, changed in the tradition to καταμετρησαι in A F oII f+; this could make sense, "to measure out," but it is rather far removed from the לנחל of MT. A popular variant read κατακληρονομησαι, which is a better known verb in LXX, but is here imported from v.18. The less frequently used verb is to be preferred here.

---

28. Both Theod and Aq adopt οἷς, but Sym has οὕς. Unfortunately, the verb which οὕς modified is not extant.

Chapter 35

35:1 This verse is an exact copy of 33:50; cf comments ad loc, including the variants on παρὰ τὸν Ἰορδάνην, which apply here as well.

35:2 The structure τῶν κλήρων κατασχέσεως αὐτῶν is unique, as is its Hebrew correspondent נחלת אחזתם. Though the two terms are related, they are not to be confused. A κατάσχεσις is simply a possession, whereas a κλῆρος is a "lot," and thus something assigned to one, a legacy, an inheritance. The same distinction is reflected by the Hebrew terms; comp also 36:3.

The syntax of the second clause is that of a coordinate clause: "and they must give," but this is in imitation of the Hebrew; in Greek one might have expected a ὅτι clause, showing what it was that the Israelites were commanded, viz. "that they should give, i.e. designate, for the Levites cities to inhabit from τῶν κλήρων κατασχέσεως αὐτῶν." This is clearly what is meant. The need for assigning cities for the Levites was obvious; they had been passed by in the tribal lottery of ch.33.

Furthermore, "they must also designate τὰ προάστια of the cities around them for the Levites." MT has תתנו "you must designate," but Num regularizes the person to agree with the δώσουσιν/ונתנו of the preceding clause, thereby giving a consistent picture. The change to second plural in MT is somewhat awkward, and Num has removed this by its change to third person.

The term προάστια means "suburbs," and occurs only here and at v.7, as an interpretation of מגרש, which refers to the grazing land surrounding a city, intended for cattle, not for human residence. For the meaning of the difficult term מגרש and its Greek renderings, see Note at Lev 25:34. The term also occurs at vv.3,4,5 and 7, but only at v.7 is it rendered by προάστια as here. For a more detailed statement, see comment at v.3. The majority text has προαστεια, which is the well-known adjectival form, but the noun is original, and the adjectival variant is only an itacistic spelling.[1] The pronoun αὐτῶν must refer to πόλεων, not to τὰ προάστια.

---

1. See Walters 48.

35:3 The cities and the מגרשיהם have different purposes; the cities are intended for the Levites to dwell in, but the open areas outside around the cities are meant for "their cattle and for all their quadrupeds." MT, however, has three items: לבהמתם ולרכשם ולכל חיתם. Hex has added as a middle item και τη υπαρχει αυτων under the asterisk. But as Dorival points out,[2] both בהמה and רכוש may be rendered by κτῆνος; at 16:32 τὰ κτήνη αὐτῶν (referring to all the men who were with Kore) has הרכוש as its correspondent in MT, whereas κτῆνος is commonly used to render בהמה. On the other hand, it should be mentioned that the rendering at 16:32 never occurs elsewhere in LXX, and the instinct of hex was quite correct. The omission was one of paraplepsis occasioned by homoiarchon. Note that ולרכשם and ולכל both begin with the same two letters. Hex was also active in changing the word order of αὐτοῖς αἱ πολεῖς to conform to the order of הערים להם in MT.

Here the term מגרשי is not translated by προάστια, but by τὰ ἀφορίσματα "the areas set apart."[3] Thus the translator begins (and ends at v.7) by using προάστια, and in the intervening verses defines more precisely what these "suburbs" are. First of all then, they are areas set apart for designated ends. In v.4 the מגרשי of the cities are interpreted by τὰ συγκυροῦντα; the participle refers to areas which happen to be near, or next to, the cities. The rendering occurs only here; similarly at v.5 a unique reading, τὰ ὅμορα, obtains. The adjective means "having the same borders," thus the areas contiguous to the cities' perimeters. The various attempts at defining מגרש are, except for αφορίσματα, at one in designating the immediate areas around the cities, as the areas where the cattle of the Levites may graze. For ἀφορίσματα interpreting מגרש, see Note at Lev 25:34. The verse in Num illustrates the Greek attraction of singular predicates to neuter plural subjects. V.a has the plural ἔσονται (οἱ πολεῖς), but v.b has ἔσται as predicate for the neuter plural τὰ ἀφορίσματα.

35:4 According to MT, "the open areas of the city which you must assign to the Levites from the wall of the city and outside is to be a thousand cubits round about." In the Greek, the מגרשי became τὰ συγκυροῦντα "the areas adjoining,"

---
2. Pp.564—565.
3. In Theod this becomes τὰ ἀποβλήματα "areas thrown away," probably intended as a synonym of τὰ ἀφορίσματα.

thus next to the outside of the wall; see comment at v.3. Num changed the dimensions to "δισχιλίους cubits round about" to harmonize with v.5. Various attempts have been made to explain how the extension from the wall to the outer limit could be a thousand cubits, but in v.5 each side is specified as being two thousand, but no satisfactory explanation which sounds convincing is known to me. Each explanation sounds forced, a kind of desperate attempt to explain what is a contradiction in terms. In any event, Num made no attempt to rationalize this; it simply changed אלף to δισχιλίους.[4] All the other ancient witnesses follow the contradictory measurements of MT. Note also that Num now follows the second person of MT with its δώσετε; see comment at v.2.

35:5 The order to measure individually the four sides of the city is in the singular; i.e. Moses is ordered to measure (μετρήσεις) outside the city (τῆς πόλεως).[5] I suspect that the change to the singular is deliberate. After all, it would be difficult for the people to go about the city with measuring tools; such a task is better carried out by an individual.

The first side to be measured, τὸ κλίτος τὸ πρὸς ἀνατολάς, renders the Hebrew את פאת קדמה adequately. The distance to be measured is δισχιλίους πήχεις. This pattern is then successively followed for the other sides, ... λίβα ... θάλασσαν and ... βορρᾶν. MT, however, does not repeat the three directions with a final unstressed ה, which Num rendered by πρός. Sam, however, used ימה נגבה, and צפונה resp., and such a text may have been parent text for Num, though this is by no means certain, since Num tends to regularize patterns.

MT concludes the verse with the statement: "And the city in the middle; this shall be for them (i.e. for the Levites) the open pasture lands of the cities." Num follows Sam in reading לכם instead of להם, and its text reads "and the city in the middle of this shall be for you, and the contiguous areas of the cities." Num, however, renders זה by the genitive τούτου. No grammatical antecedent for the pronoun is evident; it is contextually vague, and must refer to the arrangement of city and ὅμορα of the cities. The change in number in τῶν πόλεων is peculiar, but this merely follows MT. The conjunction καί connects ἡ πόλις and τὰ ὅμορα τῶν πόλεων; both shall be yours.

---

4. The Others read χιλίους (πήχεις).
5. Pesh follows Num in the use of both the singular verb and noun.

35:6 Vv.6—8 present a syntactic problem not immediately solvable. The verses present a series of accusatives as translations of את prepositional phrases, which seem to lack an antecedent verb to modify. This is true of both the Hebrew parent as well as of Num. There are two possible solutions that occur to me. It is possible to make the תן/δώσουσιν of v.8b do double duty; not only would it apply to the proportional scale of assignments which v.8 deals with, but also to the accusatives of vv.6 and 7. This is an awkward construction, and hardly evident on the face of it. Another possibility is to use δώσουσιν/ונתנו of v.2 in a double capacity. This too is a solution not immediately evident, but it is a possible understanding. This would mean that vv.3—5 are anacolouthic, an interruption in the narrative. I would then understand vv.6—8 to be explicative of πολεῖς κατοικεῖν καὶ τὰ προάστια τῶν πόλεων κύκλῳ αυτῶν of v.2. One might then translate the opening καί of v.6 by "even."

One solution which an early prehexaplaric omission in the tradition made was to omit the first ἅς, a shorter text supported by B V 963 b f x+. This would solve the syntactic problem; v.6 would then read "even the cities you must assign the Levites, the six cities ...." The same omission obtains in v.7, also supported by B V and x+. That the omission was prehexaplaric for v.6 is clear from the fact the ἅς appears under the asterisk; in other words, it was absent in Origen's LXX text. Nonetheless, the more difficult longer text is almost certainly original. It represents the text of MT, and its omission is explicable through homoioteleuton,[6] and the more difficult text is here to be preferred.[7]

The term מקלט occurs 11 times in the chapter, and the translator has created a new word, φυγαδευτήριον, to translate it. The term usually means "a place of banishment," though in LXX it means "a city of refuge," i.e. a place to which one can flee for safety. It occurs seven times in ch.35 (in vv.11,12,13,15,25, 32);[8] the term also occurs five times in Ios, and twice in 2 Par.

Not only are six cities thus designated as cities of refuge, but "πρὸς ταύταις 42 cities." Num failed to render the verb תתנו, and hex has added δωσετε under the asterisk to represent it. Presumably, the translator intended δώσετε 1° (or 2°) to carry over to the 42 extra cities.

---

6. See THGN 132.
7. Gray does say in his philological note on v.6a: "The cstr. is faulty but possibly original .... The meaning of the whole is clear."
8. According to Dos Santos, in 14 times out of a total of 19 occurrences of מקלט, φυγαδευτήριον is used to translate it.

35:7 This verse further defines τὰς πόλεις of v.6. For the omission of ἅς in the tradition, see comment at v.6. The total number of cities, i.e. πάσας τὰς πόλεις, comprise 48, i.e. the six plus the additional 42 of v.6, i.e. these and their suburbs. For προάστια, see comment at v.2.

35:8 The assignments from the Israelites' possession are to be proportional in number to the size of the tribe involved; thus "many from those τὰ πολλά, and less from the lesser ones." MT is syntactically easier in that with respect to the many תרבו, and for the small ones תמעיטו, but the intent of Num is the same. This was the principle enunciated at 26:54, which see; see comment ad loc. MT has exact parallels: מאת הרב תרבו and מאת המעט תמעיטו, but Num has different structures: ἀπὸ τῶν τὰ πολλὰ πολλά and ἀπὸ τῶν ἐλαττόνων ἐλάττω, though the meaning is clear: the wealthy are to give more, and the poor to give less.

The general principle to be followed is: "each one according to his inheritance, which they shall inherit, shall they assign (δώσουσιν) ἀπὸ τῶν πόλεων to the Levites." One might have expected a singular verb in the relative clause with its reference to ἕκαστος, but Num follows the MT pattern. MT, however, has a singular verb instead of δώσουσιν, presumably due to איש as subject, i.e. each one must assign some from his cities." The change in number is somewhat disconcerting: in MT "each" according to "his" inheritance, which "they" will inherit, יתן. Num agrees, but substitutes δώσουσιν for יתן. Note the use of a partitive ἀπό.[9] Num did not translate the suffix of מעריו, and hex has added αυτου under the asterisk after πόλεων to represent it, though in view of Num's use of δώσουσιν rather than a singular this creates a confusing text in hex: "they must give from his cities."

35:10 Over against MT Num simply makes a statement: ὑμεῖς διαβαίνετε τὸν Ἰορδάνην εἰς γῆν Χαναάν "you are about to cross the Jordan into the land of Canaan." MT introduces this with a temporal כי, thereby making v.10 the protasis for v.11; cf comments at 33:51 and 34:2. The nominal clause in which the predicate is a participle, is as usual rendered by a pronoun plus a present tense. Hex has "corrected" Num by adding οτι under the asterisk before ὑμεῖς to represent the כי.

---

9. See SS 162.

35:11 Num begins with "and you must set aside for yourselves cities." The verb διαστελεῖτε is contextually chosen, since the Hebrew has והקריתם, the Hi of קרה, which means "to meet, encounter, happen." But this seems quite inappropriate here; in fact, the Hi occurs elsewhere in LXX only in Gen 24:12 27:20, both times in the sense of "to make something happen successfully," which does not fit here at all. Num has simply made good sense in the context, "to designate, set aside," and this can hardly be faulted in view of the characterization of these cities as φυγαδευτήρια,[10] for which see comment at v.6. MT has ערי מקלט, and Num has no separate rendering for ערי. Hex has added πολεις under the asterisk, though failed to change φυγαδευτήρια to the genitive, a failure which betrays Origen's mechanical, quantitative approach to text criticism in his hexapla. Since φυγαδευτήρια is by definition "cities of refuge," the separate rendering of ערי is otiose as well as confusing.[11]

The subject of the infinitive φυγεῖν is τὸν φονευτήν, thus "for the slayer to flee there," thereby defining what the φυγαδευτήρια are to be to you. Note the rendering of תהיינה by the singular ἔσται, since its subject is a neuter plural. In MT, a separate clause states "and the killer may flee thither," which Num has interpreted by a purposive infinitival structure. The φονευτήν is then defined more particularly by a nominative expression limiting the slayer to "everyone who smites a person unintentionally."[12] The change to the nominative is a kind of "I mean anyone who ...." type of explanatory anacolouthon. MT has no equivalent for πᾶς, and hex has placed the word under the obelus.

35:12 MT defines "the cities" as למקלט, which Num simplifies by using the plural φυγαδευτήρια; the cities are (to be havens of escape) "from the ἀγχιστεύοντος τὸ αἷμα. This is a calque for the Hebrew גאל הדם, though here the full expression does not occur in MT, and the parent text probably read גאל הדם as in vv.19 and 25; see Note at Deut 19:6. Hex has quite correctly placed τὸ αἷμα under the obelus. Hex has also transposed αἱ πόλεις and ὑμῖν to equal MT's לכם,

---
10. It should be noted that the critical text has a misprint; ψυγαδευτήρια must be corrected to φυγαδευτήρια.
11. See SS 69.
12. See SS 127 for ἀκουσίως.

הערים. Actually, this is more often the order in Greek as well. When a verb is followed by both a subject and a pronominal modifier, the pronoun usually precedes the subject.

V.b explains the raison d'etre for the cities of refuge, and the conditions under which they operate. The "avenger of blood" does not reckon with intentionality; he demands an eye for an eye, a life for a life. A city of refuge protects the one who has killed by accident from revenge ἕως ἂν στῇ ἔναντι τῆς συναγωγῆς εἰς κρίσιν. The regulations concerning such cases obtain in vv.16—25 below.

35:13 MT reads "And the cities which you must designate shall be six cities of refuge for you." Num has made the first cut after "six cities," whereas MT has תתנו under the *ethnach*. Num has broken up the bound phrase ערי מקלט, assigning φυγαδευτήρια to the predicate, but πόλεις to a modifier of the subject. There is, however, an odd problem in Num. The relative clause ἃς δώσετε has the grammatically correct accusative ἅς as the modifier of δώσετε, but then τὰς ἓξ πόλεις is also in the accusative, apparently by attraction to the accusative ἅς. Normally, one would expect αι εξ πολεις, which common sense dictates as expected. The accusative nominal is a syntactic anacolouthon, and probably what is intended is something like "—I mean the six cities—."

35:14 The point of the anacolouthon in v.13 is now fully clear. The six cities of refuge referred to in v.6 are to be equally assigned to the Transjordan tribes and the land of Canaan, i.e. three such are to be designated for each side of the river. The perspective that the verse reflects with its ἐν τῷ πέραν τοῦ Ἰορδάνου is that of post-conquest times. Chapter 35 is still set both in MT and Num east of the Jordan, but the term "beyond the Jordan," as well as its MT counterpart מעבר לירדן, presuppose a geographic location within Canaan.

MT ends the verse with ערי מקלט תהיינה, but Num has placed this at the beginning of v.15, which after all, begins with prepositional phrases modifying the תהיינה of v.14.

35:15 Instead of the usual φυγαδευτήρια as a rendering for ערי מקלט, Num begins with φυγαδεῖον ἔσται "it will be a place of refuge." This seems to me an intentional deviation from the usual translation. The word derives from φυγαδεύω, and the majority A B F M V φυγαδιον is not a real word, but is simply an itacistic variant of φυγαδεῖον.¹³ The Hebrew has ערי מקלט, and hex has added πολεις under the asterisk at the beginnng to represent the ערי, and it also changed ἔσται to εσονται,¹⁴ but failed to change the case of φυλαδεῖον to the genitive!

The term παροίκῳ occurs only here in Num, but that is also true for its MT correspondent תושב. Num has simply taken over the equation πάροικος/תושב from Lev; on the difference between the προσήλυτος and the πάροικος, see Note at Lev 25:23. Num has ὑμῖν instead of בתוכם, possibly reading בתוככם by dittography. A third person referent is contextually more consistent, though either person is sensible.

Over against MT, the subject of the next clause, οἱ πόλεις αὗται, lacks the number "six," and hex has added εξ to represent the omitted שש of MT. Just where the new clause begins might seem problematic; I would suggest that the break should come before ἔσονται. I would accordingly suggest that a comma be placed between ὑμῖν and ἔσονται in the critical text. The second clause would then read: "these cities shall become a city of refuge for fleeing there for anyone smiting (i.e. fatally) a person unintentionally."

35:16 Vv.16—21 describe the kind of killing for which the cities of refuge are not a haven of escape from the blood avenger. V.16 begins with a δέ construction, as do all the instances which begin with ἐάν in the chapter. It is particularly appropriate here as a mark of contrast with what preceded v.16. "Should he (i.e. someone) smite him (i.e. someone else) ἐν σκεύει σιδήρου, and he (the second one) expire, he (the first one) is a murderer." The ἐν phrase is clearly instrumental;¹⁵ i.e. the object of iron is the means used to strike. The rendering of (כלי) ברזל by a genitive of material¹⁶ is an excellent rendering of the bound phrase.

The judgment follows: "let the murderer certainly be put to death." The free cognate infinitive מות serves to place added stress on the verbal notion of יומת. This is here represented by a cognate noun in the dative, as though "he must be put to death with death."

35:17 A second possibility is באבן יד "with a stone (in) hand," which Num interprets as ἐν λίθῳ ἐκ χειρός, i.e. "by a stone out of hand," thus a stone leaving the

---

13. See THGN 130 and Walters 43.
14. The Others also read the plural ἔσονται.
15. See SS 121.
16. See SS 63.

hand; this is further defined by ἐν ᾧ ἀποθανεῖται ἐν αὐτῷ "by which one might die." Note the otiose Hebraic ἐν αὐτῷ, which in better Greek would be omitted. The main verb of the protasis, however, is πατάξῃ (αὐτόν). The protasis as a whole may then be translated: "but if by means of a stone out of hand, by which one might die, he should smite him, and he (referring to αὐτόν) should die." For the apodosis, which is exactly the same as in v.16, see comment ad loc.

35:18 This verse parallels v.17, in MT differing only in the substitution of או בכלי עץ for ואם באבן; Num has ἐὰν δὲ ἐν σκεύει ξυλίνῳ, as well as ἐξ οὗ instead of ἐν ᾧ. Num was probably dependent on the reading of Sam, which had ואם instead of או.[17] The change of ἐν ᾧ to ἐξ οὗ represents an attempt to avoid the tautology inherent in ἐν ᾧ ... ἐν αὐτῷ. Both the relative pronoun and αὐτῷ refer to σκεύει ξυλίνῳ; in other words, the tautology is still present; if οὗ were feminine (i.e. ἧς), it would refer to χειρός. A majority A F M text made a stylistic improvement by omitting ἐν αὐτῷ. For the rest of the verse, see comments at vv.16,17.

35:19 Num translates MT word for word. It begins with a pendant nominative, ὁ ἀγχιστεύων τὸ αἷμα "as for the blood avenger." The actual clause has οὗτος ἀποκτενεῖ "this one (i.e. he) will kill (the murderer)." οὗτος refers to ὁ ἀγχιστεύων. The parallel second clause has a temporal protasis instead of a pendant nominative, viz. "whenever he should meet him." Num supports the ב phrase rather than the variant כ by its ὅταν. The apodosis repeats the first clause, but with a pronoun as modifier, οὗτος ἀποκτενεῖ αὐτόν.

35:20 The verse must be read together with v.21, since it presents only a first condition: "but if because of enmity he should push him and hurl any object (σκεῦος) on him from ambush, and he should die." This differs from MT in that the conjunction joining the first two verbs is correlative in MT, או; this is hardly an improvement, in that pushing someone or hurling something from ambush are difficult to harmonize as contiguous actions. Furthermore, the verbs change from the prefix inflection, יהדפנו "he should push him" to the suffix inflection, השליך "(or) did throw." This change may in fact have facilitated the change in conjunc-

---

17. Kenn 5ᵛⁱᵈ 589* also read ואם here. The reading is easily explicable as a secondary ex par variant.

tion. Num, as often, harmonizes by using a subjunctive form throughout; comp v.22. MT used the verb absolutely, but Num harmonized with v.22 by adding πᾶν σκεῦος. The nominal is omitted by mss G-426, which probably represents hex in the light of the shorter text of MT.

35:21 V.21 begins with an alternative protasis: "or because of anger he struck him with the hand." Note the use of an indicative rather than a subjunctive in rendering הכהו. Num makes a greater contrast between the ἔχθραν of v.20 and the μῆνιν of v.21 than does MT where שנאה and איבה are much closer in meaning, i.e. "hatred" vs "enmity," whereas Num contrasts "enmity" and "anger." MT also has a suffix in ידו, which is omitted by Num as otiose.[18] The attacker would hardly strike someone with someone else's hand!

The apodosis is verbose and repetitive. MT reads: "The attacker must surely be put to death—he is a murderer—the blood avenger shall kill the murderer when he meets him." Num has added a doublet (i.e. to the first clause) by inserting after φονευτής ἐστιν the words θανάτῳ θανατούσθω ὁ φονεύων. This repeats the first clause simply substituting ὁ φονεύων for ὁ πατάξας. The translator uses the participle rather than φονευτής, which he had already used to render רצח הוא. Surprisingly, the doublet had a textual basis, since 4QNum^b reads מות יומת הרוצח as well. In my opinion, this is an early doublet in Hebrew, which in turn was parent text for Num. It is of course true that throughout this section the one who must certainly die was a φονευτής; comp vv.16,17,18. Hex quite appropriately placed the doublet under the obelus.

35:22 Vv.22—25 deal with with accidental homicide. For such, the cities of refuge become a haven of safety for the killer. Vv.22—23 present the conditions, or protases; these are the reverse of the conditions of vv.16—21. The operative word is ἐξάπινα, the adverbial rendering for the phrase בפתע.[19] The word means "suddenly," i.e. without forethought, and might be rendered by "accidentally."[20] This is then further defined by οὐ δι ἔχθραν, for which see comment at v.21, where איבה was rendered by μῆνιν. The remainder of the verse is an exact copy of v.20, but with οὐκ before ἐξ ἐνέδρου; cf comments at v.20.

---

18. See SS 99.
19. See SS 127—128.
20. ἐξάπινα is retained by Theod and Aq, but Sym reads ἀνεπιτηδεύτως "unintentionally."

35:23 For ἐν ᾧ ἀποθανεῖται ἐν αὐτῷ, see comment at v.7. The instrumental dative παντὶ λίθῳ represents a ב phrase in MT, and hex has added εν before it.[21] The determinative element in the protasis is בלא ראות "without seeing," i.e. the stone was let fall (Hi of נפל), but the subject did not see the one struck. The translator, however, interpreted freely by οὐκ εἰδώς; in other words, not seeing the victim meant that the accident was unintended; it was not done knowingly.[22] Presumably, the translator did not vocalize ויפל as a Hi, but rather as a Qal. ἐπιπέσῃ is usually intransitive, but here I suspect that Num intended the verb to mean "let fall."

The syntax is somewhat peculiar, in that καί preceded the verb, and one must understand the opening structure as an incomplete fragment based on v.17, i.e. "or with any stone by which one might die" was taken over from v.17. What is meant is a case in which a stone was the unintended instrument of the chance killing. I would translate v.a by "or with any stone by which one might die— unwittingly has even let (it) fall on him, and he should die."

V.b further elaborates on this lack of intention, which is stressed by a contrastive δέ: "but he was not his enemy, nor was he seeking to do him harm." The Hebrew has "an enemy לו," which Num correctly understood as indicating possession. MT also has a particle, מבקש, which Num translates literally by a present participle, ζητῶν. The present tense is an excellent choice, since the "seeking" is an ongoing process.

35:24 The future tense κρινεῖ signals the onset of the apodosis. The verb is singular so as to agree with the subject ἡ συναγωγή, whereas MT has a plural verb, ושפטו, since the subject העדה is thought of as a collective. Either number is possible. The assembly is to decide the case between the killer and the blood avenger κατὰ τὰ κρίματα ταῦτα "according to these regulations." The demonstrative pronoun refers to the provisions of vv.16—23. What this means is that judgment is to be made on the point of intentionality, i.e. whether the issue was

---

21. The Others also read ἐν παντὶ λίθῳ.
22. Walters 201 states that "a glance at the Hebrew ... is proof that we must emend οὐκ ἰδών." This kind of automatic "tit for tat" process is not how the translators of the Pentateuch worked. The translator used his intelligence; if he did not see the victim, he did not kill knowingly. Incidentally, the proposed emendation is made up out of whole cloth; there is no variant text supporting it; in fact, all Greek witnesses support Num.

one of accidental or intentional homicide. What κρίματα really intends are "judicial criteria."

35:25 The verb ἐξελεῖται is commonly used as a rendering for הציל.[23] As in v.24, Num uses the singular verb with ἡ συναγωγή; see comment ad loc. Num states that "the assembly shall remove the killer from the blood avenger," which is what MT states more clearly by its "from the power (or authority) of the blood avenger." Num failed to render the יד in מיד גאל, and so hex has added χειρος under the asterisk before τοῦ ἀγχιστεύοντος.

In the second clause, ἡ συναγωγή is taken as a collective, and Num follows MT in using a plural verb, ἀποκαταστήσουσιν, which is odd in view of the ἐξελεῖται of the first clause which also has ἡ συναγωγή given as its subject. A popular A M text has changed the verb to the singular αποκαταστησει, which regularizes the usage of singular verbs with ἡ συναγωγή; the more difficult plural is clearly original. The verb implies that the judgment is to be rendered away from the city of refuge, and there is no scholarly consensus as to where this was to take place; it does say that "they will return him to the city of his refuge where he had taken refuge." The term φυγαδευτήριον means "city of refuge," and the structure πόλιν τοῦ φυγαδευτηρίου (αὐτοῦ) is a Hebraism. MT has the relative clause as אשר נס שמה, which Num renders adequately by οὗ κατέφυγεν, but hex has added εκει under the asterisk after κατέφυγεν to represent the שמה.

The killer must then remain there "until the great priest dies." The term ὁ ἱερεὺς ὁ μέγας is highly unusual for the Pentateuch, occurring elsewhere only at Lev 21:10, where, however, הגדול is followed by a comparative מן (ἀπὸ τῶν ἀδελφῶν αὐτοῦ); cf Note ad loc. The adjectival phrase is followed by a relative clause which is somewhat obscure. It reads ὃν ἔχρισαν αὐτὸν τῷ ἐλαίῳ τῷ ἁγίῳ "whom they had anointed with the holy oil." MT, however, reads אשר משח אתו בשמן הקדש, i.e. with a singular verb. Since the verb is transitive (note its modification by αὐτόν/אתו) the identity of the subject is unclear. I would take it to be indefinite; comp "on dit" with "they say," and so would render it by the passive "who had been anointed with the holy oil." The preposition governs a bound phrase in MT, but when the free element is הקדש, LXX often renders it by an adjectival phrase,[24] and simply as a dative of means, i.e. without a preposition.

---

23. According to Dos Santos, 81 times out of 199; it is exceeded only by ῥύομαι (from ἐρύω "protect") which occurs 84 times.
24. See SS 65.

25:26 This verse needs v.27 for completion; it is only a protasis, to which v.27a is coordinate, with v.b constituting the apodosis (but see below). The verbal figure in MT is a free infinitive plus a cognate verb, thus "(if) he should actually go out." The translator found no cognate noun for ἐξέλθῃ, and used a synonym which was a lexically related noun, ἐξόδῳ; Num thus reads "if by an exit he should leave."

What he should not leave (i.e. cross) are "the borders of the city," which in MT reads את גבול עיר מקלטו. Since עיר is further defined by the relative clause אשר ינוס שמה, the term מקלטו is technically unnecessary. Hex has, however, added του φυγαδευτηριου αυτου under the asterisk after "city" to represent MT's text more exactly. It should be noted that the relative clause is the same as in v.25, except for the change in verbal inflection, i.e. ינוס instead of נס. The translator made no such distinction, however, again using κατέφυγεν, but here did translate שמה by εκει, and rather than οὗ has εἰς ἥν, thereby creating a more literal rendering of the Hebrew.

35:27 The second condition is that "the blood avenger should find him outside the borders τῆς πόλεως καταφυγῆς αὐτοῦ." The phrase "the city of his καταφυγῆς is simply a variant for φυγαδευτηρίου, probably being used here and in v.28 as the more specific city of refuge in which the killer has found a safe haven from the vengeance of the blood avenger.

V.b is divided into two parts, a third condition, and the apodosis. The third protasis is "and should the blood avenger kill the slayer." Num has a subjunctive verb φονεύσῃ which is still governed by the ἐάν of v.26. MT, however, has מקלטו under the *ethnach*, which means that the Masoretes understood this to be part of the apodosis, i.e. "the blood avenger may kill the killer." MT continues with אין לו דם "he will have no bloodguilt," which Num understood correctly by its οὐκ ἔνοχός ἐστιν "he is not culpable." Either interpretation would be possible on the basis of a purely consonantal text.

35:28 MT uses the prefix tense form ישב "he must dwell," which Num neatly interprets by a third person imperative, κατοικείτω, "let him dwell." In any event, he may freely dwell without threat in the city τῆς καταφυγῆς, i.e. without the genitive pronoun αὐτοῦ which governed it in v.27; in the repeat occurrence of καταφυγῆς the pronoun is unnecessary.[25] The majority A F K M text does add αυτου, which is either recensional in origin, or added under the influence of the parallel in v.27.

The death of the great (or high) priest signals a release; afterwards, the blood avenger may no longer take vengeance. The one who killed "may return to the land of his possession." For κατασχέσεως, see comment at 13:3(2).

35:29 A subscription to vv.1—28. All the above, i.e. "ταῦτα shall become (ἔσται εἰς) δικαίωμα κρίματος." What is meant is that these (regulations) are to constitute "proper legal procedure." It renders לחקת משפט "ordinance of judgment," or as NJPS has it "law of procedure." Since these are to apply εἰς τὰς γενεὰς ὑμῶν ἐν πάσαις ταῖς κατοικίαις ὑμῶν, they are to be valid for all times and places.

35:30 The verse begins with a pendant nominative, πᾶς πατάξας ψυχήν, "anyone who smites (i.e. fatally) a person." The relevant statement then follows: διὰ μαρτύρων φονεύσεις τὸν φονεύσαντα "by witnesses," i.e. on the basis of witnesses, "you may kill the killer." MT has לפי עדים ירצח. Num has omitted פי, and hex has added στοματος under the asterisk before μαρτύρων to represent it. The change of the Hebrew third person verb to a second person "you may kill" would seem to solve the problem of the identity of the subject of ירצח. It could be the blood avenger, but there is no mention of the avenger in this section, vv.30—34. Or is it the tribunal, i.e. the העדה of vv.24,25 that is meant? But to whom is φονεύσεις addressed? The only second singular in the chapter refers to Moses, but that can hardly be intended in view of v.29. Or is the A M V majority third person reading φονευσει original? Unfortunately, I can see no good reason palaeographic or otherwise why an original φονευσει would have been changed to φονευσεις. Presumably, the translator meant the people, i.e. Israel as a community, but the text remains puzzling.

The second clause clarifies the significance of μαρτύρων in the first clause. "One witness," i.e. a single witness may not "serve as (sufficient) witness against a person to die." In other words, it takes more than one witness to justify killing a killer. The translation μαρτυρήσει might seem an odd rendering for MT's יענה

---

25. See SS 100.

"respond, answer," but it does reflect a well-established Hebrew understanding.[26] In other words, what "respond, answer" means according to Num is "serve as sufficient response as court witness."

35:31 The remainder of the chapter is obviously addressed to the assembly, as the repeated second person plural verbs make clear. It is forbidden to take a ransom for a person from one who has killed τοῦ ἐνόχου ὄντος ἀναιρεθῆναι, i.e. "one who is culpable of being killed." What is meant is one who is to incur capital punishment. This renders the Hebrew אשר הוא רשע למות "who is wicked (enough) to die," i.e. deserving to die. Here περὶ ψυχῆς "for a person" must mean "for a person's life." This is clear from what follows: one judicially found deserving of death. The רשע automatically excludes the subject of an accidental homicide.

35:32 MT begins with a conjunction, which Num omits. Hex has added an initial και under the asterisk to equal the Hebrew. The prohibition against taking a ransom also applies to the accidental homicide. In other words, one must flee to and remain in a city of refuge until the high priest dies; one can not buy one's way out of this. Num translates MT's עיר מקלטו rather oddly by πόλιν τῶν φυγαδευτηρίων "a city of refuge cities." I suspect that what Num means is "one of the cities of refuge." Hex has added αυτου to represent the suffix.

Num has correctly understood the idiom לשוב לשבת "to return to dwell" by its τοῦ πάλιν κατοικεῖν. Num has interpreted הכהן as being ὁ ἱερεὺς ὁ μέγας. Of course, it is the high priest who is meant, but MT has no equivalent for the adjective, and hex has rightly placed ὁ μέγας under the obelus. The Sam text does have הכהן הגדול, and was probably the parent reading for Num.[27]

35:33 Num twice interprets the Hi of חנף "pollute" by the verb φονοκτονέω literally "kill by murder" or simply "to murder." The verb also occurs at Ps 105:38, but the rendering there is probably dependent on the Num text. To Num pollution of the land means violently rendering the land lifeless, i.e. the land has been assassinated.[28] The pollution of the promised land is a deadly serious matter;

---

26. Both Tar^JO translate יענה by יסהד, and only Tar^N reads יענה.
27. Kenn 69 also reads הכהן הגדול.
28. Particularly instructive are the detailed comments by Dorival on this verb, both in his notes on the verse (p.574), as well as in his introduction (p.156).

it makes it incapable of producing life; in effect, "you may not murder the land εἰς ἥν you are dwelling." The preposition εἰς is obviously used here in a purely locative sense.²⁹ MT has אשר אתם בה, but Num harmonizes with such passages as v.34 and 33:55, both of which read אשר אתם ישבים בה; i.e. it reads εἰς ἥν ὑμεῖς κατοικεῖτε. Hex has added a translation of בה, which is completely unnecessary in Greek.

The basis for this command is given in a γάρ/כי clause: "For such (τοῦτο) blood will murder (i.e. pollute in MT) the land."

V.b has been simplified syntactically by changing לארץ to the nominative ἡ γῆ as subject of ἐξιλασθήσεται, i.e. "and the land cannot be expiated." Hex has rearranged the text by placing ἡ γῆ before οὐκ to approximate the order of MT. The verb is then modified by לדם, i.e. "expiation cannot be made for the land for the blood which was shed in it." Num has rendered this by ἀπὸ τοῦ αἵματος (which was shed on it), which is sensible. Expiation involves "purification from something," thus here the land is expiated from the blood.³⁰

Positively put, the expiation can and does occur ἐπὶ τοῦ αἵματος τοῦ ἐκχέοντος, i.e. expiation demands the death of the one who committed murder; bloodshed demands the shedding of blood. MT has an instrumental ב construction: בדם שפכו. Unusual is the use of ἐπί plus a genitive to show instrument.³¹ Num has left untranslated the pronominal suffix, and hex has added αυτο to represent it; the αυτο refers to αἵματος.

35:34 Num continues with the plural μιανεῖτε, whereas MT reads the singular תטמא, i.e. Num follows the text of Sam.³² Actually, the singular verb is difficult to defend in view of the relative clause which follows. "You must not pollute the land אשר אתם ישבים בה. Such a nominal structure is usually rendered in Num by a pronoun plus a present tense verb, but here Num fails to include an otiose pronoun, though hex does provide it by adding υμεις before the present tense verb κατοικεῖτε (ἐπ' αὐτῆς). This in turn is followed by another relative nominal clause, אשר אני שכן בתוכה "in the midst of which I am dwelling." Here Num uses another pattern of pronoun plus inflected future verb, ἐφ' ἧς ἐγὼ κατασκη-

---

29. See SS 132.
30. Sym in more idiomatic Greek has περί.
31. See SS 123.
32. As do Kenn 9,84, as well as the Tar and Pesh.

νώσω ἐν ὑμῖν. MT has Yahweh dwelling in the midst of the land, but Canaan is still only a promised land, and Num renders the participle by a future verb, and then personalizes it by ἐν ὑμῖν. This is probably done to be more consistent with the final clause: "because אני Yahweh שכן in the midst of the Israelites." Num has "ἐγὼ γάρ εἰμι κύριος κατασκηνῶν in the midst of the Israelites." The εἰμι has no counterpart in MT, and it does change the stress, though the *zaqqeph qaton* permits such an interpretation. Num is a matter of self-identification, i.e "for I am the Lord who dwells in the midst of the Israelites." Such a formula is a fitting conclusion to this section on regulations concerning accidental killing vs murder.

Chapter 36

36:1 In MT it was the chieftains of האבות למשפחת of the Galaadites who approached and spoke. Num, with its προσῆλθον οἱ ἄρχοντες φυλῆς υἱῶν Γαλααδ ..., omitted האבות, and rendered למשפחת by φυλῆς. Hex has added των πατριων after ἄρχοντες to correspond to the omitted האבות, and the rendering of משפחת "clan," a subunit of "tribe," by φυλῆς is not unusual.[1] It recurs later on in the identification of the chieftains as ממשפחת, which the Masoretes sensibly vocalized as plural with the preposition understood as a partitive,[2] while Num understood it as vocalized as a singular, thus ἐκ τῆς φυλῆς υἱῶν Ἰωσήφ (and hardly partitive!). Nor is that singular designation accurate, since the υἱῶν Ἰωσήφ were divided into two tribes, that of Manasse and of Ephraim. What must be intended is "from the tribe, (even one) of the sons of Joseph." In the tradition, some witnesses used γαδ instead of Γαλααδ, which is of course wrong, since the tribe of Γάδ was a separate tribe entirely; the variant is a classic case of parablepsis due to the recurrent *alpha*.

The second clause has the chieftains speaking before three parties, Moses, Eleazar the priest and the chieftains of the houses of the paternal lines of the Israelites, whereas MT has only two. The middle one, καὶ ἔναντι Ἐλεαζὰρ τοῦ ἱερέως, was ultimately taken from 27:2, where the daughters of Salpaad themselves appear before the three parties, though this plus was already in the parent Hebrew.[3] Hex has quite properly placed these words under the obelus. The third party created a problem for the translator in the consecution הנשאים ראשי, since Num usually translated both words by ἄρχοντες. He solved the difficulty by changing ראשי to οἴκων, i.e. "before τῶν ἀρχόντων οἴκων (πατριῶν υἱῶν Ἰσραήλ)." Note that the ראשי structure must be understood as an apposite of הנשאים; in other words, "the heads of the families of the Israelites" were "the chieftains". This was fully understood by Num; note the care taken to render only ἀρχόντων as articulated.

---

1. According to Dos Santos φυλή is used 42 times for משפחת, and the more accurate δῆμος, 112 times.
2. See SS 168.
3. 4QNum^b has ולפני אל[עזר הכוהן].

36:2 This verse illustrates the translation rule followed in the Pentateuch that יהוה is to be rendered by an unarticulated κύριος, but אדני, whether referring to a divine or a human master, is translated by an articulated ὁ κύριος. The singular suffix of את אדני, referring presumably to Moses, is rendered contextually, in view of the plural εἶπαν, by the plural pronoun (τῷ κυρίῳ) ἡμῶν, since a singular μου would sound peculiar to a Greek reader.

What they said is given in two clauses. In both clauses, the main verb is modified by לתת in MT, i.e. "(commanded) to give," but Num renders the first one by ἀποδοῦναι, and the second one by δοῦναι. So the first clause reads "to our lord the Lord commanded to return the land of inheritance by lot to the Israelites." What Num presupposes is a two-step process as at 34:17; cf comment on κληρονομήσουσιν ad loc. First, the inheritance is to "revert" to the Israelites as the temporary, holding heirs of the property in question.[4]

The second clause then proceeds to the second stage: "and to the lord the Lord ordered to assign (δοῦναι) the inheritance of Salpaad our brother to his daughters." MT has put this differently: "and אדני was ordered by Yahweh to give ...." MT has vocalized צוה as a Pu, and as in the first clause read אדני. Hex has added μου after τῷ κυρίῳ to represent the untranslated suffix, whereas Byz added ημων, consistent with the text of the first clause. One suspects that the Byz text is a secondary development of the hex text τω κυριω μου. The assignment of the κληρονομίας was to be ἐν κλήρῳ, i.e. "by lot." These represent the two stages noted above.

36:3 The case they present for adjudication to Moses is a possible scenario: "they may become wives to someone of the tribes of the Israelites"; what is meant is the tribes of the Israelites other than that of Manasse, to which Salpaad belonged. MT also had (שבטי) מבני for τῶν φυλῶν;[5] a translation for the בני would be otiose; no one could marry the tribe, and it is obvious that members from the tribes were meant. Hex, however, has duly added των υιων under the asterisk before τῶν φυλῶν to represent the otiose בני.

The next three clauses specify what would result from such a scenario, viz. possible infringement of tribal possessions; land allotted to the family of Salpaad

---

4. See the discussion at Dorival 155.
5. The τῶν φυλῶν is obviously partitive; see SS 108.

might in due course be transferred to another tribe. These concerns of the chieftains are described as a) "and their inheritance will be removed from the possession of our paternal lines." It should be noted that MT reads נחלתהן מנחלת, i.e. Num has rendered the first word by ὁ κλῆρος αὐτῶν, and the second one, by ἐκ τῆς κατασχέσεως. This is not incorrect, since the first נחלה is the process of inheriting, i.e. "the lot, the κλῆρος" and the second one is the general possession of land within the tribe. b) "and it will be added to the inheritance of the tribe to which they become wives." MT lacks the word "wives," the relative clause reading אשר תהיינה להם, but the Num text does interpret what was meant, i.e. Num has correctly understood that להם implied marriage. Note that here נחלה, the actual inheritance, is translated by a third lexeme, κληρονομίαν. It should be observed that a popular B V text omitted the article, but Num always articulates κληρονομία, except where exegetical reasons demand lack of articulation.[6] c) "and from the lot of our inheritance it will be removed." This is in essence a recapitulation of a).

36:4 The protasis states: "but should the release of the Israelites take place." The word ἄφεσις regularly renders י(ו)בל, i.e. the jubilee year, for which see Lev 25.[7]

It is the apodosis which disturbed the chieftains. In imitation of MT, this is introduced by an apodotic καί, thus "then their inheritance will be added to the inheritance of the tribe to which they would have become wives, and from the inheritance of the tribe of our paternal lines their inheritance will be removed." For the relative clause referring to γυναῖκες, see the discussion at v.3 where exactly the same clause obtains in both MT and Num.

In the tradition, the A F M V majority text has αφαιρεσις instead of ἄφεσις, but this must be a mistake, an addition of the syllable αιρ stimulated by the double occurrence of the verb ἀφαιρεθήσεται in the verse; i.e. this represents an early mistaken "improvement" of the text. Just what "the separation of the Israelites" was supposed to mean is not clear; the variant text simply does not make good sense, while ἄφεσις is the usual rendering for יבל. Nor does ἀφαίρεσις ever occur for יבל in the Greek Scriptures.

---

6. See THGN 108.
7. Theod retains ἡ ἄφεσις, but Aq translates ὁ παραφέρων, and Sym has ὁ Ἰωβήλ.

36:5 Moses responded by commanding the Israelites διὰ προστάγματος κυρίου. The term προστάγματος more commonly renders (ת)חק, but here it translates פי. Of course, "the mouth of Yahweh" means a spoken word by Yahweh, and is therefore an "ordinance, a command." Quite unusual is the use of the participle דברים in the context of "Thus ... are speaking," and Num substitutes the more usual λέγουσιν, i.e. presupposing אמרים. The present tense, however, is the usual rendering for a participial predicate. Note that its subject is the singular φυλή, thus "a tribe of the Josephites are saying." The word "tribe" is by definition composed of individuals, and the plural verb is justified.

36:6 The initial οὗ of the Lord's word refers to γυναῖκες, i.e. "let them be wives of whoever is pleasing before them." In other words, the daughters were free to marry. It should be noted that ἐναντίον αὐτῶν renders בעיניהם. This creates no problem for the Greek, since αὐτῶν has common gender, but the suffix הם- is masculine, though the reference must be to the daughters.[8] This is a case of masculine suffixes having feminine antecedents.[9] Num's text is a fine idiomatic rendering of the Hebrew "to the one who is good in their eyes they may become wives."

The freedom of choice is, however, limited by the πλήν structure: "only out of the clan of their father let them become wives." MT again has a masculine suffix, אביהם, whereas Sam has אביהן.[10] See the comment above on αὐτῶν 1°. MT also has a longer text, reading for "the clans," למשפחת מטה, and hex has "corrected" the text by adding της φυλης under the asterisk afer δήμου. Num seems to have difficulty in this chapter in differentiating between "clan" and "tribe"; note the comment at v.1 on φυλῆς for משפחת.

36:7 The general rule is that "an inheritance among Israelites may not circulate from tribe to tribe." This is the basis for the "word which the Lord commanded the daughters of Salpaad" in v.6. In the tradition, a popular F text articulated κληρονομία. Although it is true that Num usually articulates this word, here the word is indefinite; what is meant is that no inheritance may pass from one tribe to another, and the variant must be secondary.

---

8. Though Kenn 69ᶜ does read בעיניהן; the reading is a simplification, and probably secondary.
9. See GK 135o for a possible explanation.
10. As do Kenn 4,9,17,18,69,84,111,125,129,301.

The reason for the rule is given in a ὅτι clause: "because, the Israelites must cling each to the inheritance of his paternal tribe." MT has "of the tribe of his fathers." In such contexts Num often translates אבתיו by τῆς πατριᾶς αὐτοῦ, but here and in v.8 the adjectival πατρικῆς is used, hence the rendering "paternal tribe." In the tradition, the majority A B M text reads the more popular noun πατριᾶς instead of πατρικῆς, but in v.8 τὴν πατρικήν is assured, since it is universally attested except for του π̅ρ̅ς̅ of ms V.[11] Since Num tends to translate in consistent patterns, the adjectival phrase is probably original.

36:8 MT has as subject of the opening clause כל בת ירשת נחלה, which Num interprets by πᾶσα θυγάτηρ ἀγχιστεύουσα κληρονομίαν. To understand this rendering of ירשת by ἀγχιστεύουσα, one must recall 27:8 where the condition for the inheritance by a daughter is described. Should a man die without a son to inherit, "you must transfer his inheritance to his daughter." The following verses (9—11) describe further rules of succession: if there is no daughter, then his brother; if no brother, then a brother of his father, and if no uncle, then the household member nearest within his tribe. What is described is the nearest survivor; such a person is the ἀγχιστεύς, the nearest of kin. What ἀγχιστεύουσα κληρονομίαν means is "the next of kin legally entitled to the inheritance."[12] Though only in this verse does LXX render ירש by ἀγχιστεύω, it does represent accurately the juridical position of the heiress. The term is in turn modified by ἐκ τῶν φυλῶν τῶν υἱῶν Ἰσραήλ, which renders ממטות בני ישראל.[13]

The predicate of the clause is ἔσονται γυναῖκες, which is grammatically incorrect, since the subject is the singular πᾶσα θυγάτηρ. MT does have the singular תהיה לאשה. Obviously, the translator had the five daughters of Salpaad in mind. To justify such, one might take καὶ πᾶσα θυγάτηρ ... υἱῶν Ἰσραήλ as a pendant nominative, thus "and as for every daughter legally entitled to receive an inheritance (note the indefiniteness) out of the tribes of the Israelites." Then the main clause, ἔσονται γυναῖκες, refers to ταῖς θυγατράσιν Σαλπαάδ of v.6. This in turn is modified by a preposed dative ἐνὶ τῶν ἐκ τοῦ δήμου τοῦ πατρὸς αὐτῆς. In any event, Num reverts to the singular αὐτῆς. Num has failed to render מטה before אביה, and hex has added της φυλης under the asterisk after δήμου.

---

11. See THGN 130—131.
12. Se Dorival 167—168.
13. Theod retains the ἐκ, but Aq and Sym use ἀπό. Aq also attests to ῥάβδου instead of τῶν φυλῶν; this presupposes a singular of ממטות, i.e. ממטה.

The reason for this stricture is given in the ὅτι clause. Again the verb ἀγχιστεύσωσιν represents יירשו, for which see the discussion above. For τὴν πατρικήν, see comment at v.7.[14]

36:9 The rule stated in v.7 is here reaffirmed in different language; instead of κληρονομία the synonym κλῆρος is used to render נחלה, but this is merely for variety's sake. The rule is clear; an inheritance (κλῆρος) may not circulate from one tribe to another one.

Instead of the ὅτι clause of v.7, a shorter adversative ἀλλά clause obtains. Instead of "each in the inheritance τῆς φυλῆς τῆς πατρικῆς αὐτοῦ, v.9 simply has αὐτοῦ, i.e. "each in his inheritance." For προσκολληθήσονται οἱ υἱοὶ Ἰσραήλ modified by a ἕκαστος structure, see v.7.

36:10 Num renders MT word for word. For צוה Num used συνέταξεν,[15] which is less common than ἐντέλλομαι, though the two are synonyms.[16] See the discussion at 30:2 for the translations of צוה Piel.

36:11 The five daughters of Salpaad are listed syndetically, i.e. a+b+c+d+e, whereas MT follows the pattern: a b+c+d+e. Num follows the pattern of Sam.[17] Num also differs in the order of the names in that Μααλά appears in fifth position, but is listed first in MT. A popular A F text, probably hex in origin, has changed the order to correspond to the MT order. For variations in the spelling of the names of the daughters, comp the comments at 26:37(38); the list also recurs at 27:1. The order among the three lists varies; cf comments ad loc.

According to MT, they became לבני דדיהן לנשים "wives for their agnate cousins." Num simply has τοῖς ἀνεψιοῖς αὐτῶν "to their cousins." Greek does not distinguish between paternal and maternal cousins; the term simply means "cousins." Hex has added εἰς γυναῖκας under the asterisk at the end in order to represent the untranslated לנשים.[18] Why Num failed to render לנשים is puzzling,

---

14. For an adjectival phrase rendering for a bound structure, see SS 65—66, and comp also p.32.
15. The Others translate by ἐνετείλατο.
16. The Others read ἐνετείλατο rather than συνέταξεν.
17. It should be mentioned that Kenn 18,75,186ᶜ,196 and 198 also have ותרצה for the second daughter תרצה.
18. Theod, Aq and Sym also have εἰς γυναῖκας at the end.

though presumably, ἐγένοντο ... τοις ἀνεψιοῖς αὐτῶν could only be understood as referring to marriage.

36:12 Num has as its first clause ἐκ τοῦ δήμου τοῦ Μανασσῆ υἱῶν Ἰωσὴφ ἐγενήθησαν γυναῖκες, which may be translated "they became wives (to members) out of the clan of Manasse (one) of the sons of Joseph." The ἐκ renders a partitive מן.[19] MT is much clearer; it reads: "from the clans of the Manassites, son of Joseph, they became wives." The omission of בני before מנשה was unfortunate, and hex has added υιων before Μανασση.[20] Also peculiar is the plural υἱῶν for בן, which hex has corrected to υιου. Presumably, υἱῶν is to be understood as a partitive genitive, since Manasse was one of the two sons of Joseph. The plural is, however, original, and based on a reading בני, representing an error by dittography, since the *yodh* comes from the next word יוסף.

The second clause concludes the narrative: "καὶ ἐγένετο their inheritance ἐπί the tribe of the clan of their father." The verb plus ἐπί means that their inheritance remained within ("it became to") the original clan of Salpaad.[21]

36:13 The subscription to the book. Num says: "these are αἱ ἐντολαὶ καὶ τὰ δικαιώματα καὶ τὰ κρίματα," but MT has only two, המצות והמשפטים. Origen thought that the middle one, καὶ τὰ δικαιώματα, was the extra one, and marked it under the obelus, but whether or not that is correct is uncertain. Admittedly, κρίματα occurs only for משפטים, but there are only three cases in the book. On the other hand, δικαίωμα occurs for חק(ה) four times, but at 15:16 it renders משפט. The three occur in the same order at Deut 6:1, which may well be the source of the Num list. According to MT, these "the Lord commanded by the hand of Moses אל בני ישראל." Num omitted the prepositional phrase, but hex added προς τους υιους ισραηλ under the asterisk after Μωυσῆ. For the location ἐπὶ δυσμῶν Μωάβ ἐπὶ (or παρὰ) τοῦ Ἰορδάνου κατὰ Ἰεριχώ, see comment at 33:48—49, and for δυσμῶν Μωάβ, also at 22:1.

---

19. See SS 168.
20. Theod reads και ἐκ τῆς συγγενείας υἱῶν Μανασσή; Aq has εἰς συγγενείας υἱῶν Μανασσή, whereas Sym translated ἀπὸ δήμου υἱῶν Μανασσή.
21. Aq retained καὶ ἐγένετο, whereas Theod used the passive καὶ ἐγενήθη, and Sym translated by καὶ περιεγένετο.

APPENDIX A

Proposed changes in the critical text of Num

3:38	For ἀπ' ἀναατολῆς read ἀπὸ ἀνατολῶν
3:49	For πλεοναζόντων, read πλεοναζόντων
6:9	For αὐτῷ, παραχρῆμα read αὐτῳ παραχρῆμα,
6:21	For χεὶρ αὐτοῦ read χεὶρ αὐτοῦ,
9:1	For δευτέρῳ, read δευτέρῳ
9:21	For καὶ ἀπαροῦσιν read καὶ ἀπαροῦσιν·
9:21	For (νεφέλη) ἀπαροῦσιν read ἀπαροῦσιν·
9:22	For ἡμέρας 2° read ἢ ἡμέρας
11:27	For Μωυσῆ read τῷ Μωυσῆ
11:28	For Μωυσῆ read Μωυσῆ
11:33	For ἐλείπειν read ἐλίπειν
11:35	For ἐν 'Ασηρώθ. read ἐν 'Ασηρωθ,
13:1	For Φαράν read τοῦ Φαράν
13:29	For ἐπ' αὐτῆς read τὴν γῆν
18:3	Omit σου 2°
18:9	For καρπωμάτων, read καρπωμάτων·
21:3	For (ὑποχείριον) αὐτοῦ read αὐτῷ
21:11	For 'Αχελγαὶ read 'Αχὲλ Γαὶ
21:20	For λελαξευμένου read λελαξευμένου,
21:23	For 'Ιάσσα read 'Ιάσα
22:11	For κεκάλυφεν read ἐκάλυψεν
22:11	For αὐτόν, read αὐτόν·
23:3	For καὶ 2° read ἐγὼ δὲ
23:22	For Αἰγύπτου· read Αἰγύπτου
24:21	For Καιναῖον read Κεναῖον
27:12	For (τοῦτο ὄρος Ναβαύ) read —τοῦτο ὄρος Ναβαύ,
27:14	For ἔναντι read ἐναντίον
30:7	For οὓς read ὅσα

31:6   For ἱερέως, read ἱερέως·
31:28 For ὄνων· read ὄνων,
31:29 For λήμψεσθε, read λήμψεσθε·
32:38 For καὶ 1° read καὶ τὴν Ναβαύ, καὶ
33:53 Omit πάντας
35:11 For ψυγαδευτήρια read φυγαδευτήρια
35:15 For ὑμῖν read ὑμῖν,

Index of Greek Words and Phrases

A

'Αβιδάν, 7
'Αβιούδ, 32, 454
ἀγαθός, 532
ἄγγελος, 329
ἄγγελος κυρίου, 378
ἄγγελος τοῦ θεοῦ, 372
ἄγια, 63
ἁγιάζω, 8, 98, 267, 277, 327
ἅγιον τῶν ἁγίων, 56
ἅγιος, 96, 104, 256, 262, 292
ἅγιος τῶν ἁγίων, 299
ἁγνεία, 94
ἁγνίζω, 128, 170, 513
ἅγνισμα, 315, 515
ἁγνισμός, 120, 171, 319
ἀγνοέω, 189
ἀγχιστεύς, 605
ἀγχιστεύω, 589, 605
ἀγχιστεύων, 81
ἄγω, 85, 169
ἀδελφός, 5, 293
ἄζυμος, 103, 477
ἀθῷα, 88
ἀθῷος, 538
αἴγειος, 514
αἰγνιγματιστής, 355
αἷμα, 314
αἱρετίζω, 213
αἴρω, 17, 68, 166
Αἰσιμώθ, 565
αἰχμαλωσία, 338

αἰώνιος, 306, 426
ἀκολουθέω, 371
ἀκουζιάζω, 250
ἀκούσιος, 248
ἀκουσίως, 99, 247
ἀκούω, 217
ἀληθινός, 220
ἀληθινῶς, 2
ἀλήθω, 164
ἀλλ' ἤ, 515
ἀλλ' ἢ ὅτι, 204
ἀλλογενής, 18, 49, 295
ἀλλότριος, 277, 454
ἄλογος, 99
ἅλς, 304
ἅλων, 246, 307
'Αμαλήκ, 15, 205, 224, 233
ἁμαρτάνω, 343
ἁμάρτημα, 19
ἁμαρτία, 86, 138, 220, 503
'Αμμάν, 353
ἀμνός, 241
ἀμπελών, 374
'Αμράμ, 40
'Αμραμίς, 44
ἄμωμος, 100, 248, 311
ἀναβαίνω, 141, 207, 232
ἀναβιβάζω, 335, 392
ἀναζεύγνυμι, 28
ἀνάθεμα, 301

'Ανάθεμα, 340
ἀναθεματίζω, 301
ἀναίρεσις, 168
ἀναιρέω, 277, 513
ἀνακαλέω, 9
ἀναλαμβάνω, 210, 387
ἀναλίσκω, 290
ἀναμιμνήσκω, 150
ἀνάμνησις, 150
ἀνανεύω, 496
ἀνάπαυσις, 157
ἀναπαύω, 7
ἀναποιέω, 101
ἀνατέλλω, 13
ἀνατολάς, 147
ἀνατολή, 49, 388, 573
ἀναφέρω, 91, 303
ἀναφορά, 66
ἀναφορεύς, 58, 202
ἀναχωρέω, 270
ἀνδρὸς ἀνδρός, 83
ἀνεψιός, 606
ἀνήκοος, 289
ἀνήρ, 498
ἀνθίστημι, 149, 373
ἄνθρωπος, 6, 13, 21, 394
ἄνθρωπος ἄνθρωπος, 137
ἀνίστημι, 6, 7, 179, 258, 367, 372
ἀντί, 37
ἀντιπίπτω, 8
ἀξιόω, 368
ἄξων, 10
ἀπαίρω, 143, 360, 550
ἄπαρσις, 550
ἀπαρτία, 151, 512

ἀπαρχή, 82, 246, 297, 308, 518
ἀπειθέω, 172, 233
ἀπειλέω, 394
ἀπέναντι, 293, 325, 421
ἀπέρχομαι, 375
ἀπό, 231
ἀποδίδωμι, 81, 124, 299, 356, 505
ἀπόδομα, 125
ἀποθλίβω, 374
ἀποθνήσκω, 18, 291, 323, 342
ἀποκαθίστημι, 595
ἀποκαλύπτω, 87, 377
ἀποκριθείς, 177
ἀποκρίνομαι, 203
ἀποκτείνω, 168, 280, 323, 507, 592
ἀπολαμβάνω, 578
ἀπόλλυμι, 15, 216, 276, 356, 547, 566
ἀπολύω, 336
ἀποσκευή, 272, 509
ἀποστάτης, 214
ἀποστέλλω, 192, 198, 273, 380, 382
ἀποστρέφω, 1, 203, 393, 395
ἀποσχίζω, 269
ἀποτίθημι, 287, 288
ἀποτρέχω, 10
ἀποφέρω, 281
ἅπτομαι, 317, 320
ἁπτόμενος, 49
ἀρά, 89
'Αραβώθ, 432, 510
ἀράομαι, 388

ἀρέσκω, 379, 398
ἀρθήσεται, 26
ἀριθμέω, 39
'Αριθμοί, 1
ἀριθμός, 51, 490
ἀριστεράν, 375
'Αροήρ, 354
ἄρσεν, 512
ἀρσενικός, 299
ἀρτά, 70
ἄρτοι, 59, 245
ἀρχή, 67
ἀρχηγός, 147, 193, 212, 259, 421
ἄρχων, 4, 112, 147, 265, 286, 348, 370, 396, 601
ἀσθενής, 199
ἄσμα, 348
ἀστεῖος, 378
ἄστρον, 13
'Αταρώθ, 527
ἀτείχιστος, 199
αὖλαξ, 374
αὐλή, 43
αὐξάνω, 5
Αὐσή, 195
αὐτοί, 249
αὐτός, 100
αὐτοῦ, 364
ἀφαγνίζω, 94, 128, 317
ἀφαίρεμα, 104, 245, 304, 306, 307, 521, 524
ἀφαιρέω, 245, 304, 524
ἄφεσις, 603
ἀφίημι, 248, 367
ἀφίστημι, 228, 272, 511, 531

ἀφορίζω, 122
ἀφόρισμα, 245, 585
'Αχὲλ Γαί, 345
'Αχιέζερ, 7
'Αχιρέ, 8

Β

Βάαλ, 382
βαρυθυμέω, 266
βαρύς, 167, 332
βασιλεία, 5, 349
βασιλεύς, 349
βασιλικός, 330
βάσις, 48
βέβηλος, 495
βεβηλόω, 419
Βεελφεγώρ, 420
Βεώρ, 16
βιβλίον, 90, 346
βλαστάνω, 288
βλαστός, 288
βοάω, 190
βόλις, 570
βορέας, 573
βουλή, 259
βουνός, 389
βραχίων, 104, 303
βωμός, 36, 384

Γ

Γάδ, 527
Γαὶ ἐν τῷ πέραν, 564
Γαλαάδ, 442, 540, 547
Γαμαλιήλ, 6
γαμβρός, 154
γάρ, 379
Γεδσών, 39
γενεά, 155, 244, 306
γένεσις, 10, 32
γένημα, 309
γεννάω, 454
γένοιτο γένοιτο, 90
γένομαι, 242, 248
γέρας, 297
γερουσία, 360
Γεσιὼν Γάβερ, 561
γῆ, 86
γίγαρτον, 95
γίγας, 209
γιγνώσκω, 174, 273, 285, 512, 539
γογγύζω, 160, 226
γόγγυσις, 225
γογγυσμός, 286
γονορρυής, 79
Γουδιήλ, 197
γραμματεύς, 169
γράφω, 551
γυνή, 513, 603
Γώγ, 5

Δ

Δαιβών, 527
δάκνω, 344
δακτύλιος, 523
δάμαλις, 311
δέ, 16, 30, 88, 123, 212, 223, 249, 423, 435, 437, 539, 540, 569
δείκνυμι, 12, 274, 383
δέκατον δέκατον, 475
δεξίαν, 375
δέομαι, 189
δέρμα, 313
δεσμός, 319
δῆλος, 12
δῆμος, 2, 42, 44, 193, 293, 390, 432
ᾅδης, 274
διαβαίνω, 544, 588
διαβιάζω, 234
διαβιβαζω, 542
διαβολή, 377
διαγογγύζω, 210
διαθήκη, 157, 234, 304, 426
διαιρέω, 516, 521
διάκενος, 342
διαμαρτυρέω, 247
διάνοια, 256, 530
διανοίγω, 301
διὰ παντός, 59, 479
διαπορεύομαι, 163

διασκεδάζω, 251
διαστέλλω, 124, 589
διαστολή, 311, 497
διαστρέφω, 530
διασῴζω, 356
διατήρεσις, 297
διατηρέω, 296
διατήρησις, 289
διὰ τί, 165
διὰ τοῦτο, 327
διαφωνέω, 523
διαχορίζω, 533
δίδραχμον, 53
δίδωμι, 7, 285, 296, 325, 518, 530, 587
διεμβάλλω, 58
διέξοδος, 572
διέρχομαι, 330, 515
δικαίωμα, 6, 244, 597
διότι, 8
δισχίλιον, 586
δολιότης, 429
δόμα, 296, 471
δόμα δεδομένοι, 36
δόξα, 7, 11, 215, 269, 396
δρόσος, 164
δύναμαι, 167, 363
δύναμις, 3, 22, 105, 507
δυνατός, 207, 381
δυσμή, 360, 565
δῴη, 89
δῶρον, 85, 100, 108, 237, 298, 471, 480

E

ἑαυτοῖς, 262
Ἑβραῖος, 17
ἐγγίζω, 12
ἐγένετο, 520
ἐγενήθη, 520
ἐγίνετο, 140
ἐγκαθῆμαι, 362, 366
ἐγκαίνισις, 111, 117
ἐγκαινισμός, 111
ἐγκρίς, 164
ἐγκρυφίας, 164
ἐγὼ δέ, 385
ἐγὼ κύριος, 51
ἔδοξον, 395
ἐθέλω, 332
ἔθνος, 6, 428
εἰ, 168, 198, 211, 398, 532
εἰ ἄρα, 366
εἶδος, 120, 163, 187
εἶδος πυρός, 140
εἴδωλον, 420
εἰ καί, 266
εἶπον, 132
εἰρήνη, 107, 426
εἰρηνικός, 351
εἰσάγω, 9, 211, 328
εἰσακούω, 11, 222
εἰς ἅπαξ, 269
εἰσέρχομαι, 130, 424
εἰς ὁλοκαύτωμα, 98

εἰς τὸ πρωί, 138
εἰωθός, 1
ἕκαστος, 4, 268, 588
ἑκατόναρχος, 511
ἐκβάλλω, 358, 363, 499
ἐκδικέω, 505
ἐκδίκησις, 505, 552
ἐκδύω, 335
ἐκεῖ, 277
ἐκκεντέω, 376
ἐκκλησία, 326
ἐκκλησιάζω, 325
ἐκκλίνω, 373
ἐκλατομέω, 349
ἐκλέγω, 261, 286
ἐκλείπω, 180
ἐκλείχω, 361
ἐκλεκτός, 177
ἐκλιπεῖν, 180
ἐκλύτρωσις, 53
ἑκούσιος, 237
ἐκπεράω, 178
ἐκτάσσω, 540
ἐκτρίβω, 218, 252, 317, 537
ἔκτρωμα, 190
ἐκχέω, 320
ἐκχωρέω, 281
ἔλαιον, 300
ἐλατός, 146
ἐλαχύς, 451, 569
Ἐλεαλή, 527
ἐλεγμός, 87
ἐλεέω, 106
ἐλεημοσύνη, 107
ἔλεος, 168, 221

Ἐλιάβ, 6
Ἐλισαμά, 6
Ἐλισάφ, 8
Ἐλισούρ, 5
ἐμαυτοῦ, 273
ἐμβάλλω, 61, 87, 386
ἐμπαίζω, 375
ἐμπίπρημι, 510
ἐμπλόκιον, 523
ἐμπτύω, 191
Ἐμπυρισκός, 161
ἐν, 19, 88
ἔναντι, 2
ἐναντίοι, 19, 21
ἐναντίον, 9, 422
ἐναύσιος, 121
ἐνδελεχῶς, 472
ἐνδελιχισμός, 479
ἐνδιαβάλλω, 372
ἐνδύω, 335
ἐνεργέω, 130
ἐν κλήρῳ, 306, 568
ἐνοικέω, 322
ἐνοπλίζω, 506, 536
ἐνόρκιος, 89
ἔνοχος, 596
ἐν πολέμῳ, 211
ἐντέλλομαι, 494
ἐντέλλω, 11
ἐντίμως, 369
ἐντολή, 256
ἐντρέπω, 191
ἐξαγορεύω, 81

ἐξάγω, 9, 341
ἐξαιρέω, 595
ἐξαίρω, 18, 345
ἐξαίρω ἐν, 151
ἐξαλείφω, 3
ἐξαναλίσκω, 230, 269, 534
ἐξάπινα, 66, 593
ἐξαποστέλλω, 79
ἐξάπτω, 119
ἐξαριθμέω, 506
ἐξαρκέω, 174
ἔξαρσις, 148
ἐξάρχω, 348
ἐξεγείρω, 14, 158
ἐξεκκλησιάζω, 326
ἐξέρχομαι, 9, 178, 362
ἐξίλασις, 487
ἐξόδιον, 491
ἔξοδος, 596
ἐξολεθρεύω, 321
ἐξοπλίζω, 505
ἔξω, 254
ἑορτάζω, 487
ἑορτή, 150, 237, 471, 477
ἑορτὴ ἑβδομάδων, 481
ἐπακολουθέω, 224
ἐπαξονέω, 10
ἔπαυλις, 382, 509, 535
ἐπαύριον, 287, 551
ἐπέκεινα, 537
ἐπέρχομαι, 84
ἐπερωτάω, 392
ἐπεσκεμμένοι, 23
ἐπιβαίνω, 372
ἐπιβάλλω, 179, 281, 312

ἐπιβλέπω, 188, 344
ἐπιγράφω, 284
ἐπιδέκατον, 305
ἐπίθεμα, 103, 300
ἐπιθυμέω, 162
ἐπιθύμημα, 267
ἐπιθυμία, 162
ἐπικαλέω, 340
ἐπικαλύπτω, 61
ἐπικαταλαμβάνω, 174
ἐπικαταράομαι, 87
ἐπίκλητος, 8, 434, 478
ἐπίκλητος ἁγία, 483
ἐπίμυκτος, 161
ἐπιπίπτω, 594
ἐπισκέπτομαι, 2
ἐπισκέπτω, 9, 261
ἐπίσκεψις, 12, 29, 448
ἐπισκοπή, 65, 108, 273
ἐπισκοπός, 511
ἐπιστήμη, 11
ἐπίστημι, 17
ἐπιστρέφω, 158, 283, 358
ἐπισυνίστημι, 230
ἐπισυντρέφω, 280
ἐπισύστασις, 279
ἐπιτελέω, 397
ἐπιτίθημι, 102, 119, 262
ἐπιφαίνω, 106
ἐπονομάζω, 203
ἔργα, 56, 127
ἐργασία, 514
ἔργον, 478, 485

ἔργον λατρευτόν, 478
ἔργον τῶν ἔργων, 76
ἔρημος, 198, 337
ἐρυθρά, 554
ἔρχομαι, 176, 324
Ἐσεβών, 354
ἐσθίω, 309, 477
ἔσται, 127, 571
ἔσχατοι, 29, 148
ἔσχατον, 505
ἔσχατος τῶν ἡμερῶν, 11
ἔσω, 36
ἕτερος, 211
ἔτι, 391
ἕτοιμος, 267
εὐθύνω, 373
εὐθύς, 385
Εὐίν, 508
εὐλογέω, 106, 363, 390, 395, 398
εὔοδος, 232
εὑρίσκω, 329
εὐχή, 94, 97, 237, 495
εὔχομαι, 94, 161, 343, 494
ἐφέλκω, 142
ἐφίστημι, 11, 218
ἔχθρα, 593
ἐχθρός, 7, 537
ἐχόμενον, 572
ἐχόμενος, 21, 366
ἔχω, 10, 260, 376
ἕως εἰς τέλος, 291
ἕως τίνος, 225

Z

ζάω, 231, 275
ζῆλος, 425
ζηλοτυπία, 92
ζηλόω, 85, 178, 425
ζυγός, 312
ζῶ, 221
ζωγρία, 359
ζῶν, 86

H

ἡγεμονία, 26
ἤδη, 174, 282,376
ἡδονή, 164
ἥλιος, 421
ἦ μήν, 223, 226, 229
ἡμίσευμα, 520
ἡνίκα, 141
Ἠσαύ, 14
ηὐγμένος, 102

Θ

θάλασσα, 554, 573
θανατηφόρος, 305
θάνατος, 216, 435
θανατόω, 18, 342, 593
θάπτω, 552
θεός, 3, 251, 261, 264, 365, 367, 521
θεράπων, 165, 187

θῆλυ, 511
θνήσκω, 320, 552
θρασύς, 205
θραῦσις, 127, 283
θραύω, 282
θρίξ, 96
θυγατέρες Σαλπαάδ, 1
θυγάτηρ, 5, 605
θυμίαμα, 279
θυμός, 229, 295, 372
θυμόω, 8, 160, 181
θύραι, 272
θυσία, 101, 237, 238, 384, 419, 490
θυσία μνημοσύνου, 85
θυσίασμα, 299
θυσιαστήριον, 111

Ι

Ἰαβόκ, 353
ἰάομαι, 190
ἰδού, 37
ἱερατεία, 36, 292, 426
ἱερατεύω, 264
ἱερεύς, 278, 507
Ἰεριχώ, 360, 579
Ἰεφοννή, 194
Ἰησοῦς, 197, 456
ἱκανόω, 262
ἱλασμός, 82
ἵλεως, 221
ἱμάτιον, 315, 336
ἵν, 238
ἵνα τί, 165

ἵνα τί τοῦτο, 324
Ἰσαάρ, 40
Ἰσααρίς, 44
ἴσον, 190
Ἰσσαχάρ, 6
ἵστημι, 1, 86, 141, 374, 502
ἱστίον, 43
ἰσχυρός, 199, 207, 332
ἰσχύς, 219
ἰσχύω, 362
Ἰωχάβεδ, 453

Κ

Καάθ, 44
Καδής, 561
καθά, 129, 247, 289
καθάπερ, 13
καθαρίζω, 191, 220, 497
καθαρισμός, 220
καθαρός, 312, 316, 320
καθεσταμένος, 47
καθίστημι, 36, 347, 522
καθοράω, 1
καθ' ὥραν, 133
καί, 67, 293
καὶ ἐγώ, 296
καὶ ἡμεῖς, 536
καιρός, 133, 214, 361
καὶ σύ, 296
κακός, 532
κακόω, 17, 165, 485, 502
καλέω, 161, 390, 419

καλός, 10, 155, 171
κάλυμμα, 43, 60, 68
καλυπτήρ, 61
καλύπτω, 366
κάλως, 48
κάμινος, 424
καρδία, 530
κάρπωμα, 236, 249, 298, 471
κάρυον, 288
κασσίτερος, 515
κατά, 19, 82
κατὰ ἀριθμόν, 2
καταβαίνω, 164
καταγράφω, 176
καταδέω, 319
κατακαίω, 277, 313
κατακάλυμμα, 43
κατακαλύπτω, 362
κατὰ κεφαλήν, 3
κατακληρονομέω, 568
κατακλίνω, 7
κατακόπτω, 234
κατακυριεύω, 353
καταλαλέω, 341
καταλαμβάνω, 539
καταλείπω, 535
κατὰ λίβα, 48
κατάλοιπος, 44
καταλύω, 419
καταμένω, 322, 365
καταμερίζω, 536
καταμετρέω, 574
κατανίστημι, 260
κατανοέω, 531
κατάπαυσις, 158

καταπαύω, 425
καταπέτασμα, 36, 43
καταπίνω, 355
καταπρονομεύω, 338
κατάρα, 398
καταράομαι, 363
καταρρεμβεύω, 534
κατάρχω, 265
κατασιωπάω, 206
κατασκέπτομαι, 157
κατασκηνόω, 600
καταστρώννυμι, 219
κατάσχεσις, 192, 539, 544
καταφεύγω, 595
κατεῖπα, 231
κατέναντι, 285
κατεργάζομαι, 95
κατεσθίω, 160, 190, 355
κατηριθμημένος, 227
κατοικέω, 205, 322, 337, 563, 596
κατοίκησις, 236
Κεναῖος, 15
κεφάλαιον, 55, 516
κεφαλή, 98
κεφαλίς, 48
κιβωτόν, 58
κιβωτός, 157
κλαίω, 162, 172, 423
κληρονομέω, 228, 359
κληρονομία, 4, 571
κλῆρος, 451, 577, 584
κοίτη, 512
κοίτη σπέρματος, 84

κόκκινος, 60, 314
κόλπος, 166
κόμη, 96
κοπάζω, 283
κόπρος, 313
Κόρε, 258, 276
κόριον, 163
κόρος, 179
κορυφή, 392
κράζω, 160
κράσπεδον, 255
κρέας, 171, 303, 313
κρίμα, 594, 597
κρίνω, 594
κριός, 239
κρύπτω, 84
κρύσταλλος, 163
κτῆνος, 331, 539, 585
κτηνοτρόφος, 527
κύπτω, 377
κύριε, 177
κυριεύω, 6, 349
κύριος, 388, 602
κύριος, ὁ, 367, 543, 602
κῶλον, 226

Λ

λάβε ἀρχήν, 2
λαλέω, 183, 226, 253, 364
λαλέω κατά, 183
λαμβάνω, 33, 503, 518, 547
λαμβάνω ἐν γαστρί, 166
λαμπανικός, 109
λαμπηνή, 109

λανθάνω, 84
λαξεύω, 351, 392
λαός, 11, 198, 356
λατρεύω, 263
λέγοντες, 276
λέγω, 2, 166, 219
λειουργικός, 109
λειτουργέω, 17, 263
λειτουργέω πρός, 75
λειτούργημα, 110
λειτουργία, 129, 295
λεπράω, 188
λεπρόν, 79
Λευί, 288
λέων, 397
λίβα, 148
λιθοβολέω, 254
λίθος, 591
λίψ, 572
λόγιον, 3
λόγος, 351
λοιδορέω, 323
λοιδορία, 333
λύτρον, 37, 302
λυτρόω, 302
λυχνία, 119
λύχνος, 119

Μ

Μαδιάν, 361, 429
Μαδιανῖτις, 428
μακαρίζω, 12

μακράν, 137
μᾶλλον, 207
μᾶλλον ἤ, 216
μάννα, 163
μαντεία, 397
μαντεῖον, 364
Μαριάμ, 183
μαρτυρέω, 597
μαρτύριον, 140
μαρτύριος, 285
μάρτυς, 597
μάχαιρα, 353
Μαχίρ, 547
μεγαλύνω, 237
μεγάλως, 94
μέν ... δέ, 378
μένω, 496, 500
μέρος, 119, 160, 572
Μεσοποταμία, 387
μετά, 33
μετρέω, 586
μή, 166, 173, 183, 271, 326
μηθείς, 279
μήν, 476
μὴν ἡμερῶν, 172
μηνιαῖος, 302
μῆνις, 593
μητήρ, 190
μήτρα, 425
μιαίνω, 88, 92, 599
μιμνήσκω, 256
Μνήματα τῆς ἐπιθυμίας, 161, 181
Μνῆμα τῆς ἐπιθυμίας, 555
μνημόσυνον, 279, 525
μόλιβος, 515

μονόκερως, 7
μονοκέρως, 396
μόνος, 170, 184, 389
μόσχος, 241, 382
μόχθος, 329, 395
μοχλός, 48
μυκτήρ, 172
Μωυσῆς, 351

N

Ναασσών, 5
Ναβαύ, 6, 528
Ναβώθ, 548
Ναδάβ, 32
νάπη, 4
Ναυή, 177, 195
νεανίσκος, 176
νεκρός, 319
νέμω, 228
νέος, 480
νεότης, 376
νεφέλη, 140, 215
Νεφθαλί, 14
νεώτερος, 223
νόμιμος, 149, 306
νόμος, 93, 134, 244, 311, 318
νότος, 205, 579
νουμηνία, 475
νῦν, 330
νῦν οὖν, 9, 211

Ξ

ξύλα, 252
ξύλινος, 592
ξυρόν, 121

Ο

ὀβολός, 53
ὅδε, 387
ὁδηγέω, 6
ὁδόν, 337, 340, 358
οἶδα, 532
οἶδε, 232
οἰκεῖος, 422
οἰκέτης, 529
οἰκία, 318
οἰκοδομέω, 539
οἶκος, 3, 274, 320, 601
οἶνος, 95, 300
οἰφί, 85, 238, 473
οἰωνισμός, 397
οἰωνός, 1
ὀλεθρεύω, 65
ὀλιγοψυχέω, 341
ὁλκή, 112
ὁλοκαύτωμα, 101, 472
ὁλοκαύτωσις, 239
ὁλοπόρφυρος, 59
ὅλος, 120
'Ομμώθ, 428
ὄμνυμι, 495
ὁμοθυμαδόν, 18
ὅμορος, 586

'Ομουσί, 40
ὄνομα, 9, 218, 221, 451
ὄνος, 372, 517
ὃν τρόπον, 243
ὄξος, 95
ὀπίσω, 42
ὁπλίτης, 537
ὀπτάζομαι, 218
ὅρασις, 11
ὁράω, 288, 391
ὀργή, 160
ὀργὴ θυμοῦ, 188
ὀργίζω, 372, 531
ὀρθρίζω, 232
ὀρθῶς, 4
ὁρίζω, 495, 497
ὅριον, 330, 346, 571
ὁρισμός, 495, 497
ὁρκίζω, 88
ὅρκος, 88, 495, 528
ὁρμάω, 280
ὁρμή, 165, 170
ὄρος, 331, 388
ὄρος κυρίου, 157
ὀρτυγομήτρα, 178
ὅσα, 20, 271, 301
ὀσμὴ εὐωδίας, 239
ὀστέον, 319
ὅστις, 9
ὅταν, 236, 245, 309
ὅτι, 321, 327, 333, 455, 534
ὁ τοῦ, 212
οὐδέν, 163, 332

οὗ εἵνεκεν, 233
οὐκ, 398
οὐκέτι, 536
οὖν, 343
οὔτε, 352, 397
οὕτως, 209, 243, 265
οὐχί, 183, 391
οὐχὶ καί, 9
ὄφελον, 211, 323
ὀφθαλμός, 377
ὄφις, 343
ὄχλος, 332
ὀχυρός, 205
ὄψος, 173

Π

παιδίον, 228
παῖς, 224, 373
παρά, 27, 42, 268, 298, 505, 574
παραβαίνω, 8, 84, 232, 370
παραβολή, 387
παραγένομαι, 135
παραδειγματίζω, 421
παράδεισος, 4
παραδίδωμι, 338, 358, 528
παρὰ θάλασσαν, 48
παραιρέω, 175
παραλαμβάνω, 394, 398
παραναλίσκω, 290
παρασιωπάω, 498
παράταξις, 506, 517, 540
παρατάσσω, 352, 431, 505
παρατείνω, 399
παραχρῆμα, 185

πάρειμι, 371
παρεμβάλλω, 141, 550
παρεμβολή, 22, 80, 281
παρέρχομαι, 330
παρίημι, 199
παρίστημι, 5
παροικέω, 329, 591
παροξύνω, 215, 251, 334
παροράω, 80
πᾶς, 20
πάσσαλος, 48
πάσχα, 132, 551
πατάσσω, 181, 216, 359
πατήρ, 191, 496
πατριά, 9
πατρικός, 605
παύω, 275
πεδίον, 319, 351
πεδός, 173
πειράζω, 222
πενθέω, 231
περί, 137
περιαιρέω, 286, 501
περὶ ἁμαρτίας, 98
περίβλημα, 514
περιδέξιον, 523
περίθεμα, 277
περικυκλόω, 340, 546
περιρραίνω, 120
περιρραντίζω, 318
περισσός, 69
πέρος, 383
πηγή, 576

πήγνυμι, 4
Πικρία, 554
πίμπρημι, 89
πίπτω, 212, 226, 324
πιστεύω, 216, 327
πιστός, 187
πλάγια, 45
πλεονάζω, 52
πλεόνασμα, 519
πληγή, 425
πλῆθος, 526
πλημμέλεια, 80, 299
πλήν, 82, 456, 479, 515, 604
πληρόω τὰς χεῖρας, 117
πλησίον, 562
πλήσσω, 427
πλύνω, 315, 516
πνεῦμα, 2, 9, 170, 179, 224, 387
ποιέω, 217, 241, 472, 570
πολεμιστής, 516, 519
πόλεμος, 331, 520
πόλις, 535, 586
πολύς, 451, 569
πονηρός, 10, 165
πόνος, 353
πορεία, 551
πορεύομαι, 203, 352, 372, 547
πορνεία, 228
πορνεύω, 419
ποταμός, 4, 362
πρᾶγμα, 332
πραΰς, 184
πρέσβυς, 351, 361
πρεσβύτης, 156
προάστιον, 584

πρόβατον, 241, 382
πρόδρομος, 200
προκεῖμαι, 59
προνομεύω, 509
προνομή, 510, 519
προπορεύομαι, 157
πρός, 91, 169
προσάγω, 109, 122, 261, 472, 488
πρὸς βορρᾶν, 48
προσγένομαι, 242
προσεγγίζω, 128
προσεκκαίω, 357
προσέρχομαι, 147
πρὸς ἑσπέραν, 133
προσέχω, 267
προσήλυτος, 139
προσθλίβω, 374
προσκαρτερέω, 200
προσκεῖμαι, 244
προσκυνέω, 377
προσοχθίζω, 342
προσπορεύω, 18
πρόσταγμα, 141, 562, 604
προστάσσω, 79
προστίθημι, 175, 278, 534
προστρέχω, 176
πρόσφατος, 95
προσφέρω, 33, 85, 100, 103, 108, 240, 278, 472
προσχέω, 303
πρόσωπον, 377
προτεροί, 536
προφητεύω, 175

προφήτης, 178, 186
προφυλακή, 536
πρωί, 382
πρωτογένημα, 301
πρῶτοι, 22, 148, 151
πρωτότοκον, 303
πτερύγιον, 255
πῦρ, 454, 515
πυρεῖον, 277
πυρρός, 311

Ρ

ῥάβδος, 284, 286, 325
Ῥαγουήλ, 154
Ῥαμεσσή, 551
ῥαντισμός, 315, 318
Ῥαφιδίν, 555
ῥῆμα, 3, 231
ῥήματα, 364
Ῥόβοκ, 508
ῥόμβος, 534
ῥομφαία, 373
Ῥουβήν, 5, 527

Σ

σάββατα, 252, 474
Σαλπαάδ, 444
σάλπιγξ, 149
σαλπίζω, 146
Σαραδά, 574
σάρξ, 9, 190
Σαττίμ, 419
σέαυτον, 10

σεμίδαλις, 112
σημαίνω, 149
σημασία, 147, 483
σημεῖον, 222, 289, 343, 435
σήμερον, 376
σίδηρος, 591
σίκερα, 95
σίκλος, 53, 112, 302
σίκλος τῶν ἁγίων, 115
σίκυος, 162
Σίν, 200, 322, 561, 572
Σινά, 1, 132, 555
σιρομάστης, 423
σκεπάζω, 143
σκεῦος, 35, 63, 320, 507
σκηνή, 35, 43, 87, 263, 272, 274, 294
σκιάζω, 4, 159
σκληρός, 271
σκόλοψ, 570
σκοπία, 392, 567
σκόρδα, 162
σκῦλον, 510
σκύμνος, 397
Σοκχώθ, 552
Σουρισαδαί, 5
σπέρμα, 390
σποδιά, 319
σπονδή, 101, 482, 490
σταθμός, 550
σταφίς, 95
σταφυλή, 95
στέαρ, 303

στέμφυλον, 95
στερεός, 119
στήλη, 355, 382, 567
στῆτε αὐτοῦ, 136
στολή, 335
στρατιά, 154
στῦλος, 48
στῦλος πυρός, 218
συγγένεια, 2, 11
συγκαθίζω, 375
συγκαλύπτω, 63
συγκατακληρονομέω, 543
σύγκλητος, 259
συγκρίνω, 253
σύγκρισις, 134, 485, 490
συγκροτέω, 8
συγκυρόω, 354, 585
συγπορεύομαι, 379
συεπισκέπτω, 16
συλλογίζω, 389
συμπορεύομαι, 271
συνάγω, 122, 179, 333
συναγωγή, 8, 73, 212, 254, 270, 326, 521
συναθροίζω, 264
συνάντησις, 379
συναντιλαμβάνω, 170
συναπόλλυμι, 271
συνεπικολουθέω, 532
συνεπισκέπτω, 30
συνεπιτίθημι, 189
συνίστημι, 13, 260, 541
σύνταξις, 139
συντάσσω, 30, 247, 494
συντίμησις, 302

σύστρεμμα, 534
σφόδρα, 266, 526
σωτηρίον, 240

T

τάγμα, 21, 151
τάδε λέγει, 368
τὰς φυλακάς, 34
τειχήρης, 199
τειχίζω, 205, 536
τελειόω, 32
τελευτάω, 96
τελέω, 422
τέλος, 517, 520
τήνδε, 280
τὴν νύκτα, 364
τί, 365
τιμάω, 9
τίς, 162
τὶς δῴη, 178
τιτρώσκω, 513
τὸ ἐν τῷ πέραν, 6
τὸ ἑσπέρας, 140
τοῖχος, 374
τὸ ὄρος τὸ ὄρος, 574
τόπος, 526
τὸ πρωί, 472
τοῦ μαρτυρίου, 1
τράπεζα, 59
τραυματίας, 319

τρέπω, 234
τρίβω, 164
τρόπος, 296
τῶν, 5

Υ

ὑακίνθινον, 58
ὕδωρ, 318, 325
ὕδωρ ἁγνισμοῦ, 120
ὕδωρ ῥαντισμοῦ, 515
υἱοί, 41, 433
υἱός, 71
ὑπεναντίος, 149
ὑπερηφανία, 247
ὑπερμήκης, 208
ὑπέρογκος, 3
ὑπεροράω, 84, 376, 511
ὕπνος, 3
ὑπομένω, 371
ὑποχείριος, 338
ὑστερέω, 136
ὑφίστημι, 375
ὑψηλός, 551
ὑψόω, 5, 219, 545

Φ

Φαγαιήλ, 7
φαίνω, 385
Φάραγξ βότρυος, 202
Φαράν, 151, 192, 561
φάσμα, 274
φέρω, 109, 167, 170

φεύγω, 9, 589
φημί, 2
φιάλη, 62
Φινεές, 423
φλογίζω, 346
Φογόρ, 399
φονευτής, 589, 593
φονεύω, 597
φονοκτονέω, 598
φραγμός, 374
φρέαρ, 347, 348
φυγαδεῖον, 591
φυγαδευτήριον, 587
φύλαγμα, 71
φυλακή, 42, 131, 294
φυλάσσω, 34, 106, 380
φυλάσσω φυλακήν, 142
φυλή, 4, 65, 193, 285, 293, 451, 568, 601, 604
φυλὴ πατριᾶς, 16
φύραμα, 246
φωνή, 143, 193, 210

Χ

Χαλέβ, 194
Χάλεβ, 456, 580
χαλκοῦς, 344
Χαμώς, 356
Χαναάν, 571
Χανανίς, 337
Χασβί, 428
χεῖλος, 497

χειμάρρους, 347
Χενέρεθ, 576
χιλιάδας, 506
χιλιαρχία, 522
χιλίαρχοι, 9
χιλίαρχος, 511
χίμαρον ἐξ αἰγῶν, 476
χιών, 188
χλιδῶν, 523
χολέρα, 172
χρίω, 111, 595
χρυσίον, 524
χρυσοῦς, 523
χώρα, 526
χωρίς, 105

Ψ

ψέλιον, 523
ψυγμός, 180
ψυχή, 79, 96, 163, 277, 485, 495, 517
ψυχὴ ἀνθρώπου, 316

Ω

Ὠβάβ, 154
Ὤγ, 16
ὧδε, 399
ὤν, 391
Ὤρ, 332
ὥρα, 16
ὡσεί, 179, 190
ὥστε, 108, 123
ὦ ὤ, 17

Index of Hebrew Words and Phrases

א

אב..................496, 604	אך..................16, 515
אבד..................276, 290	אכל..................171
אביהוא..................32, 454	אל..................388
אבן..................591	אלה..................89
אגג..................5	אלף..................147, 506
אדן..................48, 540	אם..................173, 186, 223, 532
אדני..................177, 543, 602	אמור..................105
אדרעי..................358	אמות..................428
אהל..................3, 272, 294, 320	אם לא..................226
אהלים..................4	אמן אמן..................90
אהל מועד..................17	אמר..................215, 253
אוה..................162	אנחנו..................155
אוי..................17, 508	אסף..................15, 179
אולי..................378	אספסף..................161
אועד..................285	אסר..................495, 99
אורים..................468	אפים..................377
אות..................289	אף לו..................266
אזכרה..................85	אפס כי..................204
אזרח..................250	אצל..................175
אחז..................518, 522	ארגמן..................59
אחזה..................460, 539, 544	ארי..................397
אחים..................461	ארם..................387
אחרית..................15, 390	ארן העדה..................58
אחרית הימים..................11	ארץ..................526
איבה..................593	ארר..................363
איל..................239	אשה..................236, 249, 298, 471
איש..................394	אשם..................81, 299
איש איש..................4, 77, 83	אתו..................100
	אתון..................372
	אתם..................507

בקע	274	אתרים	337
בקר	261		
בקש	264	**ב**	
ברא	274		
ברגלי	332	באר	347
ברזל	591	בגד	335, 514
ברח	9	בד	58
בריאה	274	בדיל	515
בריח	48	בדלח	163
ברית	304, 426	בהמה	585
ברך	105, 391, 395	בו	466
בשר	171, 269, 465	בוא	130, 324, 371, 393, 514
בתוך	30	בז	519
		בזה	399
ג		בזז	519
		בחר	177, 261
גאואל	197	בי	189
גאל הדם	589	ביד רמה	247
גבול	330, 346, 573	בין הערבים	133
גבלת	571	בית אב	42
גבעה	389	בית אבות	285
גבר	2	בית אבתם	2
גדל	96, 219	בכה	162, 423
גדף	251	בכור	51, 301
גדרה	540	בכורי	200
גוז	178	בכורים	480
גוע	290, 323, 336	בכר	552
גור	242	בלול	238
גורל	577	בלולה	101
גלגלת	3	במות	355, 567
גלח	98	במות בעל	382
גר	242	בנה	539
		בני המרי	289
		בנת	354
		בפתע	593

ד

דבה	208
דבר	216, 219, 332, 365
דבר ב	183
דג	173
דגה	162
דגל	21, 26
דעת	11
דר	306
דרך	13, 375
דשן	61

ה

ה-	326
האהל	42
האזין	393
האיר	106
האמין	216, 327
האריך	142
הבדיל	124, 269
הביא	85
הביט	187, 395
הגיא	530
הגיד	385
הדף	592
הוד	467
הולך	281
הומת	253
הוסיף	333
הוציא	231, 341
הוקע	421
הורד	152
הוריש	216, 538, 547, 566
הושע	195
הזה	120
הזיר	96, 99
החניף	598
החרים	338
החריש	496
הטיב	155
היה	135, 267
היה ל	435
הכה	234, 359, 363, 427, 528
הכנעני	337
הכרית	65
הלא	380
הלאה	277
הלביש	335
הלוא	211
הלחם	366
הלילה	364
הלין	210
הלך	10, 203, 371
הם	249
המעיט	569, 588
הנה	37, 387
הנהר	362
הניא	496
הניח	285, 535
הניף	91, 103
הנקי	88
הסכין	376
העביר	121, 515
העלה	119, 270
הפיל	594

התעלל	375	הפסגה	392
התפלל	161	הפר	498, 251
התפקד	30	הפשיט	335
התקדש	170	הצה	434
		הציל	595
		הקדיש	327
ו		הקהיל	325, 122
		הקטיר	279, 91
ויהי	275	הקרה	589
ולמה	324	הקריב	488, 261, 240, 33
ומושי	40	הראה	385
ועד	55	הרבה	569
ועתה	9	הרג	507, 422, 168
		הרה	166
ז		הר ההר	574, 561, 332
		הר העברים	462
זבח	237	הרים	277
זג	95	הררי	388
זה	198	השיב	288
זהב	524	השיב דבר	203
זכרון	525, 150, 85	השליך	592, 314
זנה	256	השמיד	567, 566
זעם	388	השקה	91
זעק	160	השתחוה	420, 377
זקנים	360	השתרר	265
זר	295, 49, 18	התאבל	231
זרא	172	התאוה	575
זרה	277	התאנן	160
זרק	318	התודה	81
		התחזק	200
		התחטא	317, 128
		התיצב	372, 169
		התנבא	175
		התנחל	536
		התנחם	394

ח

חדש	475
חות	548
חזק	199, 332
חטא	138, 305, 314, 539
חטאת	100, 249, 315
חיל	509
חלב	303
חלוץ	537
חלות	101
חלל	495
חלץ	536
חלק	451
חמור	267
חמץ	95
חמר	517
חמשת חמשת	52
חן	168
חנה	23, 141, 345
חנכה	111
חנן	106
חסד	221
חפץ	213
חפר	349
חצה	516
חצרות	149
חצר	43, 573
חקה	244, 311, 462
חקק	349
חקת	134
חקת משפט	597
חרב	331, 373
חרה	181
חרה אף	160
חרם	301
חרמה	340
חרצנים	95
חשבון	354
חשים	536
חתן	154

ט

טהר	120, 128, 320
טובה	10
טירה	509
טמא	316, 599
טף	228, 272, 512

י

יד	123, 466
ידע	11, 156, 228
יהוה	261, 264, 505, 521, 543, 602
יובל	603
יוכבד	453
יחל	419
יכל	167, 207, 363
ילד	166
יליד	201
ים	573
ימה	27, 48, 573
ים המלח	572
ימים מספר	143
ים סוף	225, 340, 554
יסף	534

כפרים	82, 487	יצא	362
כרה	349	יצהר	40, 300
כרם	266	ירד	14
כרע	7	ירחו	360
כרת	180	ירט	378
כשית	183	ירק	191
כתב	284	ירש	353, 357, 605
כתף	110	יש	143
		ישב	205, 322, 329, 371, 596
ל		ישר	398
		ישראל	351
לאל	42	יששכר	6
לב	273, 530	יתר	519
לבב	256		
לבד	492	**כ**	
לבוא	574		
לביא	397	כאשר	289, 464, 469
לו	211, 323, 376	כבד	9, 167
לוי	293	כבלע	66
לולי	378	כבס	314
לון	230, 265, 293, 419	כבש	241
לחך	361	כה	392
לחם	214, 245, 471, 480	כה אמר	368
לחם התמיד	59	כהנה	37, 264, 427
לכד	547	כוכב	13
לכן	265, 426	כזבי	428
ללוים	128	כי	534
למה	165	כלה	275, 289
למה זה	172	כלי	62, 320
למשפחתם	2	כן	460
לעבד	109	כנען	192
לפני	458	כנף	255
		כסוי	58
		כסף	54
		כף	103

לקח..102, 169, 183, 258, 390, 394, 518	מי יתן 178
לקראת 352	מים 325
לרגע 269	מים קדשים 86
לשד 164	מים רבים 5
	מי נדה 316
מ	מכס 517, 520
	מכסה 43, 60, 68
מאד 369	מלא 532
מאן 332, 367	מלא ידם 32
מאס 228	מלאך 329, 351, 361
מארד 87	מלאכת העבדה 478
מבטא 497	מלח 304
מבצר 199, 536	מלחמה 149, 514
מגפה 431	מלך 5, 395
מגרש 584	מלכות 5
מדין 505	מלקוח 510
מוט 61, 202	ממחרת 287
מוסבת שם 546	מן 163
מועד 259, 471	מנגד 21
מועדים 492	מנה 389
מוצא 551	מנחה 113, 239, 299, 485
מושב 509	מנחת הבקר 474
מושבת 236	מסך 43, 68
מות 18, 317, 323, 342	מסלה 331
מזבח 37, 384	מסע 148, 550
מזרחה 22	מספר 50
מזרקת 62	מסר 506, 511
מחה 576	מעט 263, 451, 569
מחנה .... 26, , 296	מעל 80, 511
מחתת 277	מעשה 119
מטה 34, 193, 327, 541	מעשר 305
מי 162, 365	מצא 329, 539
מידד 176	מצה 103
מי חטאת 120	

נבל 429		מצרעת 188	
נגב 198, 205, 337, 572		מקדש 308	
נגד 421		מקל 374, 375	
נגף 127, 282, 295		מקלט 587	
נדבה 237, 492		מקנה 331, 529	
נדה 315, 515		מקרא 478	
נדיב 349		מקשה 119	
נדר 94, 95, 237, 492, 494		מראה 187	
נהר 4		מרד 214	
נולד 454		מרה 334, 464	
נון 177, 195		מריבה 464	
נוס 595		מרים 87, 183, 326	
נוע 533		משא 66, 70, 165	
נועד 147, 230		משח 595, 111	
נזיר 94		משכית 567	
נזכר 150		משכן 17, 35, 270, 272, 518	
נזר 95, 97		משכנות 3	
נחל 3, 347, 583		משלים 355	
נחל אשכל 202		משמרת 70, 131, 289	
נחלה 306, 450, 460, 544, 578		משעול 374	
נחשון 5		משענת 349	
נחשים 1		משפחה 462, 568	
נחש נחשת 344		משפחת 41, 448, 601	
נטה 347		משפט 244, 462, 485	
נטמא 84		משפטים 134	
נטע 4		מתיר 44	
נכבש 538		מתנה 349	
נכלם 191			
נכרת 252, 317, 321		**נ**	
נלחץ 374			
נס 343, 435		נא 368	
נסה 222		נאם 2	
נסך 485		נאסף 178, 333	
		נאץ 215	
		נביא 186	

ספק 8	נסע 141, 178, 345, 551
	נספה 271
ע	נסתר 84
	נעלה 141, 272
עבד 68, 84, 165, 187, 224, 263, 370, 529	נעלם 84
עבדה 127, 295	נער 176, 373
עבד עבדה 35	נעשה 248
עבר 232, 330, 370, 374, 542	נפילים 208
עגות 164	נפל 3, 99
עד 531	נפל ל 571
עד בקר 138	נפש 79, 163, 495
עדה 34, 73, 281	נפש אדם 316
עדים 597	נצב 272, 373
עדפים 52	נצמד 420
עולה 481	נקהל 280, 322
עולם 427	נקרה 385
עון 86, 220, 504	נשא 170, 221
עון המקדש 292	נשיא 9, 259, 287, 579
עז 204	נשיא נשיאים 46
עזים 514	נשים 513, 606
עינים 156	נשך 344
עלה 101, 237, 331, 335, 384	נשקף 351, 399
עלה תמיד 472	נתן 87, 262, 282, 320, 460, 506, 518, 530
עלי 348	נתנים 296
עליו 27	נתנים נתנים 125
על ירך 45	נתפש 84
על פני 33	
עם 11, 332, 535	**ס**
עמד 5, 218, 457, 468	
עמוד 48	סבב 340
עמון 353	סור 188, 214, 271
עמים 463	סין 200, 554
	סיני 1
	סלח 221, 497

פסח	132	עמלק	15
פעור	399	עמלקי	224
פעל	397	עמרמי	44
פקד	3	ענה	17, 177, 348, 485, 502, 598
פקדה	47, 64	ענו	184
פקדיום	53	עפל	234
פקדים	12, 448	עפר	86, 319
פקוד	29	עץ	199, 592
פרכת	57	עצום	362, 526
פרע	87, 96	עצים	252
פרש	61, 253	עצם	319
פתאם	185	עצרת	491
פתיל	255, 318	ערבות	360
		ערבת	432, 510, 565
צ		ערות	285
		ערכך	302
צאן	382	ערסת	247
צב	109	ערפת	515
צבא	16, 56, 130, 431, 506	עשה	241, 472
צבאת	550	עשרון	238
צבאתם	24	עתה	376
צבה	89		
צדד	574	**פ**	
צוה	335, 469, 541		
צור	389	פאתי	13
ציצת	255	פגר	226
צל	214	פדה	302, 311
צלח	232	פה	193, 468, 604
צן	200, 322, 572	פונן	563
צנין	570	פי	334
צפוי	277	פינחס	423
צפון	574	פלא	94, 237
צפים	392	פליט	356
		פן	271, 331
		פנה	188, 280, 358

639

קרית חצות 381	צפנה 48
קרקר 13	צרר 149, 429, 570
קרש 48	

ר

ק

ראה 174, 344, 395	קבב 369
ראם 7, 396	קבה 424
ראש 1, 4, 55, 81, 147, 212, 284	קברות התאוה 181
ראשים 421, 601	קבתה 425
ראשית 15, 246	קדם 388
ראשם נשא 17	קדמה 22
ראשנה 151	קדש 45, 64
רב 262, 451, 526, 569	קדש קדשים 299
רבה 588	קהל 148, 243, 260
רבע 390, 508	קול 210
רבץ 375	קום 367, 371, 496
רגל 357	קטרת 279, 281
רגם 253	קין 16
רגע 459	קיני 15
רוח 2, 170, 178	קיר 374
רום 245	קלעים 43
רזה 199	קלקל 342
רחם 106	קנא 178
רחץ 314	קנאה 425
ריב 323	קנזי 533
ריח 242	קסם 364
ריח ניחח 303, 471	קצה 160, 342, 383, 562, 572
רכב 372	קצף 19, 295
רכוש 585	קצר 174, 341
רמח 423	קרא 161, 186
רמם 281	קרב 18, 173, 290, 457
רע 160, 379	קרבן 85, 100, 298, 471
	קרה 174
	קרואי 259
	קרח 258

רעה	10	שית	1, 189
רעים	228	שכב	7
רעמסס	551	שכך	286
רפה	198, 190	שכם	232
רפידים	555	שכן	1, 141
רצח	593	שלוים	178
רק	332	שלום	107
רק אך	184	שלח	79, 193, 198, 382
רקע	278	שלל	510
רשע	271	שלמים	240
		שם	176, 222
		שמות	9
ש		שמנה	199
		שמע	218, 467
שאל	274, 468	שמר משמרת	34
שבט	1, 13, 65, 293, 602	שמש	421
שבטים	422	שנאה	593
שבי	338, 510	שני	121
שבעה	89, 500	שני תולעת	314
שבעתי	481	שפה	497
שבת	252, 474	שפטים	422, 552
שגג	250	שפי	385
שגגה	247	שקל	112
שדה	266, 319	שר	265, 348
שדי	3	שריד	14, 359
שה	241	שרף	313, 343
שוב	162, 230, 233	שרפה	277
שוק	104, 303	שרפים	342
שור	12, 241	שרת	18, 34, 131, 264
שחט	219	שתם	2
שחת	535		
שטה	84, 163		
שטח	180		
שטן	372, 377		
שטר	169		
שים	262, 281, 386		

ת

תאה 574
תודה 311
תולדת 2
תולעת שני 60
תועפת 7, 396
תוצאת 572
תור 200
תורה 244
תושב 591
תחש 58
תחת אישך 88
תימנה 48
תירוש 300
תכלת 59
תלאה 329
תלנות 226, 286
תמם 230
תמנה 187
תנואה 229
תנופה 91, 103, 245
תנופת 300
תעברה 161
תפש 517
תקע 146
תרבות 534
תרומה 82, 104, 245, 297, 304, 308, 521
תרועה 395, 483

Index of Grammatical and Textual Items

A

abbreviation of text.................. 15
acc. of duration of time............142
acc. of extent of time 99, 218, 228, 513
adjectival phrase 1, 80
adverbial 45
adverbial αὐτοῦ 136
adversative particle 273
adversative structure...............302
ambiguity 79, 83
anacoluthon............ 225, 455, 473
analogy..............................303
aorist cohortative 269
aorist optatives 106
aorist participle...................... 77
apodotic καί 138, 236, 307, 501
aposiopesis.......................... 88
articulated gentilics................. 44
attendant circumstance 423
augmented diphthong..............102
a μή question 263

B

bound phrase 80
burnt offering 248

C

calque..... ...67, 84, 216, 222, 227, 274, 281, 387, 420, 433, 477, 506, 509, 512
causal sense of ἐπί.................135
chiasm..............................306
Cod B, character of 76
cognate adverb 369
cognate free infinitive............207
cognate participles.................501
comparative מן 263
complementary infinitive . 108, 134, 215, 431
cognate structures.............45, 294
collectives..........................360
collective singulars 12
congruence of verbal number 15
congruence of verbs 324
congruence, rules of................ 39
contextual free infinitive..........495
contrary to fact condition ..266, 376
contrastive δέ. 16, 19, 88, 212, 223, 249, 435, 539

D

dat. of advantage...................172
dat. of means/instrument 327
dat. of possession 37, 41, 308
default aorist........................183
default future.......................... 3
demonstrative adjective 89

direct speech marker 292
discourse marker 37
disjunctive accents 217
distributives 229, 284, 475, 506
distributive locative 179
distributive sense 111, 579
dittography 41, 72, 76
dittography/haplography 83
double accusative 70
doublet 386, 517

E

elative degree 167
explicative infinitive .. .56, 165, 231

F

false gen. absolute 33
formulaic introduction 211
formulaic language 24
formulaic patterns 54
future passive, use of 191
future tense as potential 308
future tense, use of 294

G

gen. absolute 66, 96
gen. of instrument 577
gen. of material 591
gen. of time in which .. 1, 141, 371, 562
gen. pronouns, use of 68
gentilics 578

H

hapax legomenon 2, 9, 43, 53, 95, 109, 218, 234, 250, 342, 374, 424, 487, 506, 534, 570
Hebraism 224, 288, 368
Hebrew gentilics 42
Hebrew nominal clauses 245
Hellenistic forms 279
Hellenistic inflections 204, 367
hendiadys 178, 227
hex reordering of text 13
historical present 331, 368, 375
homoioteleuton 38, 63, 69, 91, 144, 209
homophony 426
hortatory subjunctives 212

I

idolatry 420
Iesous 533
imperative, use of 16
imperfect, use of ..... .10, 140, 162, 164, 210, 529
incongruence 75
indefinite plural verbs 312
indefinite rel. pronoun 80
indefinite singular as subject 77
isolate free infinitive 55, 429
itacism 207

K

Kethib/Qere 8

L

locatives 42, 254, 458
locative structure 135
locative with ἐπί 465
loose rhetoric 217

M

marked bound infinitive 56
marked infinitive 73
merismus 79, 510
metaphors 160, 214, 227, 355
metonymy 52, 59, 98, 170, 334, 468
modal distinctions 128

N

narrative imperfect 343
neologism 587
neuter plural, congruence of . 33, 51
nom. absolute 23
nominal clauses . 71, 330, 484, 500, 522
nominal clause, rendering of 566
nominalization of phrase 137
nom. pendant 52, 71, 292, 320, 360, 373, 478, 494, 502, 513, 592, 597
nom. absolute 23
nominal clauses . 71, 330, 484, 500, 522
nominal clause, rendering of 566
nominalization of phrase 137
nom. pendant 52, 71, 292, 320, 360, 373, 478, 494, 502, 513, 592, 597
northern border 574

O

objective gen. 92, 434
optative mood 361

P

palaeographic confusion ... 440, 556
parablepsis 144
parataxis 79
partitive 80
partitive ἀπό 231, 240, 298, 319, 517
partitive ἐκ 279
partitive gen. 86, 342, 422
partitive phrase 317
passive transform 10, 78, 278, 312, 395
pattern 23, 194, 432, 574
pendant construction 41, 213
pendant nom. 138
pendant structures 74
pendentive 228
perfect tense, use of 390
personal agent with ὑπό 72
phrases with κατά, use of 11
present of incipient action 12, 167, 571

present participle simplification of text 186
....23
present tense as durative...........142
present tense, use of... 46, 166, 265
progressive past figure 160
proleptic present 530
proleptic pronoun 273
purposive clause 34, 167
purposive infinitive.... 56, 263, 374

R

recapitulative phrase................173
reflexive, rendering of 18
rendering of nominal clauses.....211
result clause 269, 325, 421

S

second acc. 53
self-identification formula 256
simple condition 218
simplification of text 186
syntactic pattern......................76
subjective gen. 8, 11, 53, 434
synecdochy 52
syntactic anacoluthon..............590
syntactic calque 112, 178, 368
syntactic cut 30, 246

T

temporal clauses 108, 309
temporal expressions 244

tense contrasts.......................216
tense distinctions..............26, 184
tetragrammaton, articulation of..274
thematic verbs.......................331
theme 45
timer.... 1, 112, 126, 134, 210, 280
timer plus ויהי.......................287
translation Greek....................245
translation patterns.. ...12, 452, 489

V

V

verbal figure........................221
versification, change in 277

Z

zeugma 192, 224, 276

General Index*

*Items in **bold face** indicate the beginning of a new topic.

A

Aaronic benediction..............105
Aaronids 32
Aaronids, duties of 36, 49
Aaronids, status of.................. 36
Aaron's lineage 32
Aaron's rod 284
Aaron's vital statistics.............562
Abioud 32
abstinence, life of................... 95
accidental homicide................593
Achel Gai, meaning of............345
adminstrative account 108
adversative particle 273
adversative structure...............302
adytum 37
age for Levitical service 130
altar.................................384
Amalek........................15, 205
ambiguity 79, 83
Ammonites.........................353
Amorrites 346, 351
anacoluthon............ 225, 455, 473
analogy.............................303
Anathema 340
angel of God.......................372
Annual sacrifices 477

anthropomorphism... 160, 193, 334, 379, 531
anthropopathism 20
aposiopesis.......................... 88
ark of the covenant 157
Arnon...............................346
Aroer 380
arrogance...........................250
articulated gentilics................. 44
asseveration........................221
assignment of tribal lands 577
Athenian Senate...................259
atonement 82, 123
augury 397

B

Balaam as seer 3
Balaam's Oracles re Israel......384
Balaam's third oracle............... 1
Balak and Balaam................380
Balak sends for Balaam 360
Balak's sacrifice...................384
Bashan..............................358
Beelpeor...........................420
Beelphegor and the plague 419
blessing...................... 391, 395
booty...............................338
Boundaries of Canaan...........571
Bronze serpent 340

Burning.............................161
burnt offering 248

C

Caleb 533
calque... ......67, 84, 216, 222, 227,
    274, 281, 387, 420, 433,
    477, 506, 509, 512
cedars................................ 4
celebration of the festival..........132
census of Levites.................... 38
census review.......................108
Chaleb..............................580
Chamos.............................356
Chananis of Arad 337
Chenereth 576
cities assigned to Levites 584
Cities of Refuge....................588
city of refuge 587
clapping the hands.................. 8
club 375
Cod B, character of 76
collectives..........................360
collective singulars 12
commission of Yesous 467
common sense, use of.............. 17
complaints against Moses.........260
confession of sin 379
contextual rendering...............376
contrastive δέ......16, 19, 88, 212,
    223, 249, 435, 539
covenant of salt 304
cross ref. to Exod...................139
cultic uncleanness..................135

curse Israel.........................362

D

Daily sacrifices 472
date of the Exodus.................551
dating formula.....................132
daughters of Salpaad 444, 457
day of atonement...................485
day of the first fruits 480
Death of Aaron 332
death of Aaron 562
dedication offering.................116
dedicatory gift............... 304, 524
Defeat of Og 357
Defeat of Seon.....................351
deliberating council...............259
deliverance sacrifice...............101
Departure from Sina.............150
deposit offerings 300
desert 337
desert of Sin 572
diplomatic language 328
direct speech marker 292
discourse marker.................... 37
disobedient people 172
distribution of booty...............516
dittography................. 41, 72, 76
dittography/haplography........... 83
Diverse Oracles of Balaam 11
divination 397
divination, means of..............364
divine oath 532
dream revelation 3, 365

Duties of Levites 33

ecstatic prophecy 175
Edom 14
Edomite tribe 533
Eldad and Modad 176

elders 361
elders to Seon 351
Enakites 201
encampments 16, 382, 509
end of days 11
enemies 7
enrolment 10
ephah 238

eschatological hopes 5
execration 388
expiation 599

F

father's role 496
feast of tents 487
feast of the signal 483
female inheritance laws 460
festival closure 491
figure of Gog 5
first fruits 297, 300
First tribal census 1
folk etymology 161, 181
formulaic introduction 211
formulaic language 24
formulaic patterns 54
Fringes on garments 255
full month 172

G

Gadite cities 545
Gadites 526
Galaad 442, 540
Gedsonites and Merarites 67
gentilics 578
Gesion Gaber, location of 561
giants 209
glory of the Lord 269
Gog 5
gold 524
grain sacrifice 240
guard duties 34, 294
guardian angel 329

H

hapax legomenon 2, 9, 43, 53,
    95, 109, 218, 234, 250,
    342, 374, 424, 487, 506,
    534, 570
harmonization 21, 55, 71, 75,
    137, 247, 254, 301, 312,
    322, 334, 370, 390, 484,
    586
Hebraism 224, 288, 368
Hebron 201
-he directive, rendering of 352
Heirs of man without sons 457
Hellenistic kilns 424
Hewn Rock 392
high priest, responsibilities of 65
hin 238

Hobab and Moses.................154	Kore's group.......................434
homophony..........................426	
hoplite.................................537	**L**
πρὸς βορρᾶν.......................148	
husband's role.....................498	Lampstand and lamps...........119
idolatry...............................420	laws of purification...............514
Iesous.................................533	**legal appeal**........................601
implicit made explicit...............10	legal stipulation....................311
imprecation...........................89	leprosy of Mariam.................189
inauguration of altar..............112	Levi, sons of..........................39
incense altar..........................33	Levites, rank of.....................35
incomparability of God...........394	Levites, special duties of.........263
installation of Yesous.............467	Levites vs priests....................34
instructions to the spies...........198	**Levitical census**...................452
intestate...............................82	**Levitical cities**....................584
	Levitical duties.....................295
J	levy on booty.......................517
	lex talionis..........................590
Jaser..................................353	libation........................240, 241
jubilee year.........................603	Libweh of Hamath.................574
judicial decision....................604	limits on free choice..............604
judicial inquiry.....................458	lion...................................397
	loose rhetoric.......................217
	Lord vs the Lord..................602
K	
	M
Kaathites...........................55	
Kadesh...............................203	Madaba..............................357
Kadesh Barne......................531	Madian..............................361
Kenites................................15	Madianite captives................512
Kenizzite.............................533	magical potion......................87
king of Arad.................337, 562	mandatory retirement............130
king of Moab.......................360	manna................................163
Kittians................................17	Mariam and Aaron...............183
Kore, Dathan and Abiron......258	

Marriage of heiresses 601
married woman 497
meat to excess 172
men of renown 259
merismus 79, 510
Mesopotamia 387
metaphors 160, 214, 227, 355
metonymy 52, 59, 98, 170, 334, 468
Moab 346
Moabites 419
Moabite Stone 564
modal distinctions 128
Monthly sacrifices 475
Moses' apologia 165
Moses as prophet 187
Moses' intercession 217
Moses' intercession for Mariam .190
Moses' prayer 270
Moses' reaction 266
Most-High 11
mountain of the Lord 157
Mt. Hor 332, 562
MT inconsistency 55
murder 591

N

Naqb asSafa 572
Nazirites 94
neologism 587
new moons 150, 475
Nile 4
nom. absolute 23

nominal clauses 71, 330, 484, 500, 522
nominal clause, rendering of 566
nominalization of phrase 137
nom. pendant 52, 71, 292, 320, 360, 373, 478, 494, 502, 513, 592, 597
northern border 574

O

oath form 426
oath formula 223
Og 358
omens 1
On the way to Moab 345
oracle 387
ordeal 86
ordination of high priest 117
ordination rite 32
Oriental flattery 363
outlet 572

P

palaeographic confusion ... 440, 556
pascha festival 477
paternal houses 2
patriarchs 532
pattern 23, 194, 432, 574
penalty for violating the Sabbath 253
perpetual prescription 315
Pharan 151
Phinees 423
Phogor 399

pillar 383
plague 281, 425
plea for pardon 220
possession 539
priestly adjuration 88
Priestly benefits 297
priestly divination 468
priestly food 300
Priests and Levites 292
priests, duties of 295
procedent reference 453
promise of land 192
promises for the future.............. 6
protective coverings 57
purification rituals 191

Re Levites 120
report of tribal census 11
resident alien 242
Restitution for wrongdoing 80
restitution offering 123
risk of encroachment 127
rites of purification 120
role of Chaleb 206
Rosh ha-Shana 483
Roubenite cities 546
Roubenites 526
royal figure avoided 13
Rules for sacrifice 236
Rules re Cities of Refuge 589
ruling council......................361

Q

Quails 178

R

rationalization 20, 62, 103, 131, 270
rebellion of the asembly 341
Rebellion of the assembly 210
reconsecration 98
red 314
redemptive motif 257
Red Sea 340, 554
reflexive, rendering of 18
regiment............................ 26
region, area 350
register of Levites 50
rejoicing 150

S

Sabbath sacrifices 474
Sabbath, violation of 252
sacral state 97
sacred convocation 477
sacred shekel 112
Sacrificial calendar 471
sacrificial ram 82
Sam text............................ 63
sanctified offerings 83
sanctuary shekel.................... 52
sarcasm.............................381
sealing of vessels 318
second acc. 53
second delegation 368
second review of Levites 73
Second tribal census 431
Seir 14

self-identification formula 256
Sepulchre of Desire 181
seventy elders 176
seventy elders appointed 168
Sibling complaints against Moses....................183
signal 147
simple condition 218
Song of the Well...................348
southern boundary 572
spear...............................423
special status of Levites...........125
spirit 466
spirit of God.................... 2, 387
Spoils of war.......................516
syntactic pattern..................... 76
Stages in the desert...............550
standard 21
subjective gen. 8, 11, 53, 434
subscription 64, 104, 116, 197, 310, 462, 492, 583, 607
suburbs 586
Sukkhoth 552
summary 92
superscription 104, 432
Surrogates for Firstborn.......... 51
sympathetic magic.................. 90

T

tabu 301
Talking she-ass....................372
temporal expressions 244
tense contrasts......................216
tense distinctions..............26, 184

tent of testimony 42
Ten Words..........................289
tetragrammaton 106, 317, 343
tetragrammaton, articulation of..274
The Cloud and the Fire 139
the Herem ban......................339
thematic verbs......................331
theme 45
theophany 185
The Pascha festival...............132
The people's complaint..........160
The Presence 215
The Red Heifer 311
the River 362
The trumpets.....................146
The twelve spies..................192
tithes................................305
Tithes from tithes................301
total census count..................450
total destruction 359
Transjordanian tribes 526
translation patterns..... 12, 452, 489
trespass offering 99
tribal borders inviolable 606
tribal chieftains.....................147
Tribal encampment 21
Tribal gifts for altar dedication........................108
Tribal leaders 579
tribal possessions 602
Troubles with Edom 328
turtledoves 98

Unclean people 79
unicorn 7

V

verbal figure 221
versification, change in 277
Victory over Midianites 505
vow 161, 339
vows 494
Vows by females 494

W

Wadi-l-Hesa 4
Wadi-l-Mujib 4
Wadi of clusters 202
wadi Zared 345
war 338, 505
"War of the Lord" 346
watchtower 392
Water from the Rock 322
water of lustration 120
water of sprinkling 315
western border 573
Wife accused of adultery 83
wilderness of Sin 322, 554
Wilderness stages 550

Y

Yesous as Moses' successor 462
young doves 98

www.ingramcontent.com/pod-product-compliance
Lightning Source LLC
Chambersburg PA
CBHW031537300426
44111CB00006BA/89